EVERYMAN, I will go with thee,
and be thy guide,
In thy most need to go by thy side

The Everyman Companion to the Theatre

Peter Thomson
Professor of Drama, University of Exeter

Gāmini Salgādo
Formerly Professor of English, University of Exeter

J. M. Dent & Sons Ltd
London and Melbourne

First published 1985
© Peter Thomson and Gāmini Salgādo, 1985
New paperback edition, with revisions, 1987

Phototypeset by The Alden Press, Oxford
Printed and bound in Great Britain
by Cox and Wyman Ltd, Reading for
J. M. Dent & Sons Ltd
Aldine House, 33 Welbeck Street, London W1M 8LX

British Library Cataloguing in Publication Data

Thomson, Peter, 1938 —
    The Everyman companion to the theatre.——
    (Everyman reference)
    1. Theater — Dictionaries
    I. Title   II. Salgado, Gamini
    792′.03′21   PN2035

ISBN 0-460-12542-7

Contents

Gāmini Salgādo

Gāmini Salgādo died while this book was being prepared for publication. He was a unique and witty companion, who kept scholarship in touch with laughter and had no truck with clever solemnity. Gāmini was never a man for dull moments, and I hope his spirited approach to theatre can be seen to inform this book.

Peter Thomson   Exeter, July 1985

Preface

This book is designed as a companion to those who enjoy the theatre, and who would like their enjoyment to be better informed. Our decisions about what to put in and what to leave out have been guided by the intention to aid an English-speaking audience to see the English-speaking theatre in its context.

In the chronology, which opens the book, we have tried to set out certain significant events in the post-Renaissance theatre in such a way as to make possible a comparative assessment of developments in Britain, the United States and Europe.

The chronology is followed by three essays, dealing broadly and in turn with the evolution of theatres and performance spaces, the history of English drama and the history of American drama. In all of these essays, we have tried to hold in balance the written drama and its realization in performance. The alphabetical discussion of major theatre buildings and companies, dramatic movements and genres which follows, is best seen as complementary to the essays.

The next and most substantial section of the book consists of a series of brief entries, arranged alphabetically, about 'Theatre People' – playwrights, actors, directors, designers, critics. Our aim has been to make these lively where our knowledge and particular interests licensed such liveliness. It would be a pity if no one found cause to quarrel with our views. This is a companion, not a dictionary, and a good companion does not always acquiesce.

The final section is openly a miscellany, some of it light-hearted, all of it concerned to highlight the eccentricities which are so much a part of the theatre.

Within the alphabetical sections, cross-references to other entries are indicated by SMALL CAPITALS; the dates of plays refer, wherever possible, to the first stage production. The book is completed by three indexes, one for the three essays, one intended to help those readers who 'know the name of the play but can't remember who wrote it', and one simply to list all the alphabetical entries.

Exeter, January 1985

I   A Theatre Chronology

Dates in the Early History of Drama

3300– 2300 BC	Egyptian ritual dramas, two of which survive in records. No details of performance survive.
c. 700 BC	Earliest records of Chinese theatrical entertainment.
pre-600 BC	Choral performances (dithyrambs), evidently based on Homeric legend, performed in Greece by followers of Dionysus.
c. 534 BC	Peisistratus introduces competitive festival of tragedy in Athens. Thespis may have won the first.
c. 500 BC	Dionysian festival enlarged to include satyr play in addition to trilogy of tragedies.
c. 490 BC	Aeschylus competes for first time.
c. 486 BC	Contest in comedy inaugurated.
484 BC	Aeschylus' first victory at festival.
c. 472 BC	The *Persians* (generally considered the earliest extant play by Aeschylus) illustrates his use of second actor.
468 BC	Sophocles' first victory at festival. His use of a third actor affects the writing of tragedy in Greece.
458 BC	Aeschylus' latest surviving plays, the *Oresteia* trilogy, performed.
440– 400 BC	Old Comedy, best represented by Aristophanes' first nine plays, flourishes in Athens. In tragedy, the plays of Euripides imply a fall in the significance of the chorus.
392 BC	Aristophanes' last two extant plays, *Ecclesiazusae* and *Plutus*, prefigure transition to New Comedy, which, in its turn, provided a model for Roman Comedy.
364 BC	Performances involving clowns and flute players established at Circus Maximus in Rome.
c. 350– 290 BC	New Comedy develops and flourishes in Athens.
c. 340 BC	Theatre at Epidarus built.
c. 330 BC	Theatre of Dionysus in Athens built. This is the period during which Aristotle was working on the *Poetics*.
c. 240 BC	Literary plays (translations from the Greek) introduced to Rome. Plautus and Terence write in emulation.

c. 200 BC	Beginnings of Sanskrit drama in India, influenced by Greek New Comedy. (No plays earlier than first century AD have survived.)
c. 80 BC	First amphitheatre in Italy built at Pompeii.
55 BC	First stone theatre built in Italy at Pompeii.
c. 50 BC	Vitruvius' *De Architectura* includes plans for theatre building. Roman theatres on the Vitruvian model were established throughout the Roman Empire in the early Christian era. They alternately thrived and struggled until Justinian closed all theatres in the sixth century AD. In the West, for several centuries, formal theatrical performance was at an end. Itinerant mimes and acrobats continued to provide entertainment wherever they could, sometimes together with local folk-players, but more often alone.
7th C. AD	Chinese Emperor Ming Huang sets up theatrical academy in Pear Garden of Imperial Park.
8th C. AD	Emergence of masked dance drama in Japan.
970 AD	Earliest surviving example of Christian liturgical drama. Ethelwold, Bishop of Winchester, sets down instructions for performance of *Quem Quaeritis* trope.
10th C. AD	Hroswitha, Benedictine abbess from Gandersheim in Saxony, writes six Christian plays modelled on the Latin plays of Terence.
1170 AD	*Mystère d'Adam* performed in France.
13th C. AD	Rapid growth of drama in China follows Mongol abolition of Chinese Civil Service.
14th C. AD	Mystery and Miracle cycles flourish in England and in France, often around the Feast of Corpus Christi.
c. 1375 AD	Noh drama developed in Japan and its conventions codified.
1402 AD	Guild of amateur actors, the Confraternity of the Passion, formed in Paris.
1414 AD	Vitruvius' *De Architectura* discovered in manuscript in St Gallen.
c. 1425 AD	*The Castle of Perseverance*, a Morality play, performed in England, perhaps at Bury St Edmunds.
1470 AD	French farce, *Maître Pierre Pathelin*, performed by the *Enfants Sans Souci*.
1495 AD	Probable date of first English performance of the best-known of all Morality plays, *Everyman*. The play was first printed in Dutch in this year.

Theatre since 1500

A Comparative Chronology

	Great Britain	United States of America	Continental Europe
1513			Machiavelli, *La Mandragola*, written and performed in Florence.
1515	Skelton, *Magnyfycence*.		
1545			Publication in Paris of Serlio's *Second Book of Perspective*.
1548			Hôtel de Bourgogne opened in Paris.
1550			Hans Sachs stages plays in the Marthakirche, Nuremburg.
1571			Italian *commedia dell'arte* troupe, the Gelosi, visit France at the height of their fame.
1576	Opening of the Theatre.		
1579			Corral de la Cruz, first public theatre, opens in Madrid.
1585			Teatro Olimpico, designed by Palladio, opens in Vicenza.
1587	Marlowe, *Tamburlaine*.		

	Great Britain	United States of America	Continental Europe
1589	Children's companies involved in Marprelate controversy.		
1594	Formation of Lord Chamberlain's Men (Shakespeare a member).		
1598		Performance of a Spanish comedy near what is now El Paso.	
1599	Chamberlain's Men open the Globe.		
1605	Inigo Jones designs *The Masque of Blackness* for James I.		
1609	King's Men (Shakespeare's company) perform indoors at the Blackfriars.		Lope de Vega publishes *The New Art of Writing Plays*.
1611			Publication of Flaminio Scala's *Teatro*, a collection of *commedia* scenari from the Gelosi troupe.
1613	Burning of the Globe (rebuilt 1614: demolished 1644).		
1632	Prynne, *Histrio-Mastix* (a Puritan attack on theatre).		
1634			Théâtre du Marais opens in Paris.
1636			Corneille, *Le Cid.*

	Great Britain	United States of America	Continental Europe
1638	*Salmacida Spolia* (Jones/Davenant masque).		
1642	Act of Parliament closing all theatres.		
1644			Corneille, *Polyeucte*.
			Madrid theatres closed for six years.
1651			Calderon writes his first *auto sacramental*.
1656	Davenant stages *The Siege of Rhodes* at Rutland House.		Molière arrives in Paris.
1658			
1660	Dramatic performances restart: first professional actress appears as Desdemona.		
1661	Duke's Company opens theatre in Lincoln's Inn Fields.		Domenico Biancolelli plays Arlequino for Fiorelli troupe in Paris.
1662	Charles II issues Letters Patent to Killigrew and Davenant. Smock Alley Theatre, Dublin opens.		Molière, *L'École des femmes*.
1664		Three men tried in Virginia for having 'enacted a play'. Found 'not guilty of fault'.	
1665			Molière, *Tartuffe* (performed at Court and then banned).

	Great Britain	United States of America	Continental Europe
1667	Wren's Drury Lane opens.		Racine, *Andromaque*.
1674	Wycherley, *The Country Wife*.		
1675	Dryden, *All for Love*.		
1677	Tate's version of *King Lear*.		Racine, *Phèdre*.
1680			Official founding of Comédie-Française.
1682	Otway, *Venice Preserved*.		
1695	Congreve, *Love for Love*.		
1696	Lord Chamberlain requires that all plays be licensed before performance.		
1698	Publication of Collier's *Short View of the Immorality and Profaneness of the English Stage*.		
1700	Congreve, *The Way of the World*.		
1702			Paris establishes an office of censorship
1705	Playbills printed in *Daily Courant*.		
1706	Farquhar, *The Recruiting Officer*.		
1710	Colley Cibber joins management of Drury Lane.		

	Great Britain	United States of America	Continental Europe
1714	Quin acts at Drury Lane.	Robert Hunter, *Androboros*. (First play published in America.)	
1716		Theatre built in Williamsburg. (First known theatre in America.)	
1722			Danish National Theatre formed in Copenhagen. Holberg writes for it.
1728	Gay, *The Beggar's Opera*.		
1730	Fielding, *Tom Thumb the Great*.		Marivaux, *The Game of Love and Chance*.
1731	Lillo, *George Barnwell*.		
1737	Stage Licensing Act strengthens position of Lord Chamberlain.		
1741	Garrick's debut at Goodman's Fields.		
1746–7	Garrick begins management of Drury Lane.		
1749		Company of Lewis Hallam established in America.	Goldoni, *The Servant of Two Masters*.
1752			
1762			Goldoni driven out of Venice.
1766		Southwark Theatre, Philadelphia opens.	

	Great Britain	United States of America	Continental Europe
1767		Thomas Godfrey, *The Prince of Parthia*. (First professionally performed American play.)	Lessing, *Minna von Barnhelm*.
1768		John Street Theatre, New York opens.	
1769	Garrick in Stratford for Shakespeare Jubilee.		Publication of Lessing's *Hamburgische Dramaturgie*.
1771	De Loutherbourg at Drury Lane.		
1773	Goldsmith, *She Stoops to Conquer*.		Goethe, *Götz von Berlichingen*. (First *Sturm und Drang* play.)
1775	Unsuccessful London debut of Sarah Siddons.		
1777	Sheridan, *The School for Scandal*.		
1782	Astley's Amphitheatre in full operation for equestrian drama and displays.		Schiller, *The Robbers*.
1783	John Philip Kemble's London debut.		
1784			Beaumarchais, *The Marriage of Figaro*.
1787		Royall Tyler, *The Contrast*.	
1791			Talma joins Comédie-Française. Goethe becomes director of Weimar professional players.

	Great Britain	United States of America	Continental Europe
1794	Rebuilt Drury Lane seats 3,611.	Chestnut Street Theatre, Philadelphia opens.	
1798		Park Theatre, New York opens.	Pixérécourt, *Victor*.
1800	Morton, *Speed the Plough*. (Creator of Mrs Grundy.)		Schiller, *Mary Stuart*.
1802	Holcroft, *A Tale of Mystery*. (First English play to be billed as a melodrama.)		
1806			Kleist, *The Broken Jug*.
1809	Old Price riots at Covent Garden last sixty-seven nights.		
1810		George Frederick Cooke begins American tour in New York.	
1814	Edmund Kean's London debut.		
1815	Gas installed in Covent Garden.		
1816	Macready's London debut.		
1820			Russian serf Shchepkin freed by Prince Repnin to lead acting troupe.
1823	Antiquarian *King John* at Covent Garden.		
1830	Madame Vestris becomes manager of the Olympic Theatre.		Hugo's *Hernani* sparks off a riot in Paris.
1832		Dunlap's *History of the American Theatre* published.	

	Great Britain	United States of America	Continental Europe
1835			Büchner's *Danton's Death* published.
1836		Edwin Forrest performs in London. Charlotte Cushman plays Lady Macbeth in America for first time.	Gogol, *The Government Inspector*.
1843	Theatres Act rescinds the power of the Patent theatres.	Macready's first tour of America.	
1845		Anna Cora Mowatt, *Fashion*. Rachel tours American theatres.	
1846		Forrest hisses Macready's Hamlet in Edinburgh on his second British tour.	
1849		Macready's American tour ends with rioting in Astor Place – twenty dead.	Scribe, *Adrienne Lecouvreur*.
1851	Charles Kean begins management of Princess's Theatre.		Ibsen appointed to the Bergen Theatre.
1852			Labiche, *An Italian Straw Hat*. Dumas fils, *The Lady with the Camellias*.
1853		Boucicault arrives in New York.	
1856		Dramatic copyright law amended.	Salvini plays Othello for first time.

	Great Britain	United States of America	Continental Europe
1859		Boucicault, *The Octoroon.*	
1861		Adah Isaacs Menken makes her debut as Mazeppa.	
1865	T. W. Robertson, *Society.*	Assassination of President Lincoln in Ford's Theatre, Washington. Jefferson plays Rip Van Winkle for first time.	
1866			Chronegk joins the Meininger company as stage director.
1869		Daly begins thirty years of theatre management.	Sarah Bernhardt's first great success in *Le Passant.*
1871	Irving's Lyceum debut in *The Bells.*		
1873			Zola, *Thérèse Raquin.*
1878	Ellen Terry's Lyceum debut.		
1879			Ibsen, *A Doll's House.*
1881	Poel directs the bad quarto *Hamlet* on an Elizabethan stage.		Ibsen, *Ghosts.* Zola, *Le Naturalisme au théâtre.*
1882		David Belasco arrives in New York.	
1885			Ostrovsky appointed controller of Moscow's Imperial Theatres.
1887			Strindberg, *The Father.* Antoine opens Théâtre Libre in Paris.

	Great Britain	United States of America	Continental Europe
1888			Strindberg, *Miss Julie.*
1889	First English production of *A Doll's House.*	First American production of *A Doll's House.*	Otto Brahm founds Freie Bühne in Berlin.
1890			Ibsen, *Hedda Gabler.*
1891	J. T. Grein founds Independent Theatre Society. *Ghosts* is a controversial choice of play.		Wedekind, *Spring Awakening.*
1892	Shaw, *Mrs Warren's Profession.*		Hauptmann, *The Weavers* (at the Freie Bühne).
1893	Pinero, *The Second Mrs Tanqueray.*		
1894	Poel founds Elizabethan Stage Society.		
1895	Wilde, *The Importance of Being Earnest.* Irving's knighthood the first for an actor.		Publication of Appia's *La Mise-en-scène du drame wagnérien.*
1896		Formation of theatre managers' Syndicate.	Rioting at the Paris production of Jarry's *Ubu Roi.* Chekhov's *The Seagull* fails in St Petersburg.
1897	Forbes-Robertson's Hamlet.		
1898	Irish Literary Theatre formed.		Moscow Art Theatre founded.
1899		Gillette, *Sherlock Holmes.*	*The Seagull* is a triumph.

	Great Britain	United States of America	Continental Europe
1900	Craig's amateur production of *Dido and Aeneas*.		
1901		Seven Clyde Fitch plays on Broadway.	Strindberg, *A Dream Play*.
			Gorky, *The Lower Depths*.
			Chekhov, *The Cherry Orchard*.
1904	Royal Academy of Dramatic Art founded.		
	Abbey Theatre opens in Dublin.		
	First Barker/Vedrenne season at the Royal Court.		
1905	Shaw, *Man and Superman*.		Reinhardt appointed director of Deutsches Theater, Berlin.
			Meyerhold given charge of First Studio of Moscow Art Theatre.
1907	Riots at Abbey Theatre's opening of *The Playboy of the Western World*.		Strindberg and August Falck open the Intimate Theatre in Stockholm.
1908	First issue of Craig's journal, *The Mask*.		
	Four plays by Maugham in London's West End.		
1909		First year of George Pierce Baker's 47 Workshop at Harvard.	
1911	Publication of Craig's *On the Art of the Theatre*		

	Great Britain	United States of America	Continental Europe
1912	Lilian Baylis in sole charge of the Old Vic.		
1913	Barry Jackson founds Birmingham Repertory Theatre.		Copeau opens the Théâtre du Vieux Colombier in Paris.
1914			Taïrov becomes director of the Moscow Kamerny Theatre.
1915		Provincetown Players formed.	
1918		Theatre Guild founded.	First productions of the Habima Theatre in Moscow. Mayakovsky, *Mystery Bouffe* (directed by Meyerhold).
1920		O'Neill, *The Emperor Jones*.	First Salzburg Festival. Gémier founds the Théâtre National Populaire.
1921			Pirandello, *Six Characters in Search of an Author*.
1922		John Barrymore's Hamlet. Moscow Art Theatre in New York.	
1923	Shaw, *Saint Joan*. O'Casey, *The Shadow of a Gunman*.	Boleslavsky and Ouspenskaya found New York Laboratory Theatre.	
1924	O'Casey, *Juno and the Paycock*.		
1925			Pirandello opens Theatre of Art in Rome.

	Great Britain	United States of America	Continental Europe
1926	Terence Gray opens Cambridge Festival Theatre.		
1927			Artaud at the Théâtre Alfred Jarry.
1928	Abbey Theatre rejects O'Casey's *The Silver Tassie*.	Paul Robeson in Jerome Kern's *Show Boat*.	Brecht, *The Threepenny Opera*.
1929		Norman Bel Geddes directs *Hamlet*.	
1930	Gielgud's first Hamlet.		
1931		Group Theatre founded.	Habima moves from Moscow to Tel Aviv.
1932			Publication of Artaud's *First Manifesto of the Theatre of Cruelty*.
1933			Brecht and many others leave Germany.
1935	Olivier's Romeo and Mercutio, his first Shakespeare. Unity Theatre founded. T. S. Eliot, *Murder in the Cathedral*.	Odets, *Waiting for Lefty*. Federal Theatre Project inaugurated.	
1936		Living Newspaper, *Ethiopia*, banned.	
1938		Thornton Wilder, *Our Town*.	
1939		Federal Theatre Project stopped.	

	Great Britain	United States of America	Continental Europe
1943	Glasgow Citizens' Theatre founded.	*Oklahoma* begins its 2,248-night run.	Sartre, *The Flies.* Barrault directs Claudel's *The Satin Slipper.*
1946	Arts Council of Great Britain receives Royal Charter.		Formation of the Compagnie Madeleine Renaud-Jean Louis Barrault.
1947	First Edinburgh Festival sees quiet beginning of Fringe. Old Vic School established.	Williams, *A Streetcar Named Desire.* Actors' Studio founded. Julian Beck and Judith Malina form the Living Theatre. Brecht appears before the House UnAmerican Activities Committee. Brecht's *Galileo* opens with Laughton in the title role. Miller, *Death of a Salesman.*	Jean Vilar directs the first Avignon Festival. Piccolo Teatro, Milan opens.
1949			Brecht founds Berliner Ensemble.
1950			Ionesco, *The Bald Prima Donna.*
1951	Foundation stone of National Theatre laid.		Vilar appointed director of the Théâtre National Populaire.
1952		Williams, *Summer and Smoke* (Off-Broadway revival with Geraldine Page).	
1953	Joan Littlewood's Theatre Workshop moves to Stratford East.	Miller, *The Crucible.*	
1955			Beckett, *Waiting for Godot.*

	Great Britain	United States of America	Continental Europe
1956	English Stage Company at the Royal Court. Osborne, *Look Back in Anger*.	O'Neill, *Long Day's Journey into Night*.	Berliner Ensemble visits London.
1957		*West Side Story* opens.	Planchon appointed director of the Théâtre de la Cité in Villeurbanne.
1959		Joseph Papp directs his first Shakespeare in Central Park. Gelber, *The Connection*.	Barrault appointed director of Théâtre de France in Paris.
1960	Pinter, *The Caretaker*. Peter Hall becomes director of Royal Shakespeare Company.	Albee, *The Zoo Story*.	
1963	Olivier appointed director of National Theatre Company at the Old Vic. Peter Brook directs Theatre of Cruelty season.	Living Theatre leaves United States. Foundation of Open Theatre symbolizes the experimental theatre's loss of faith in Off-Broadway.	Hochhuth, *The Representative*.
1965	Bond's *Saved* banned by Lord Chamberlain.	Death of Malcolm X accelerates move towards separatism of black theatres. Leroi Jones becomes Amiri Baraka.	Grotowski's Theatre Laboratory established in Wroczlaw.
1967		Joseph Papp's 'naked' *Hamlet*. Sensational success of *Hair*.	

	Great Britain	United States of America	Continental Europe
1968	Abolition of stage-censorship powers of Lord Chamberlain. Jim Haynes opens Arts Lab in Drury Lane.		Barrault sacked by Minister of Culture after talking with students who had occupied his theatre.
1969		Bread and Puppet Theatre's *The Cry of the People for Meat*.	
1970	Brook's production of *A Midsummer Night's Dream*.		Brook's International Centre of Theatre Research opens in Paris. Peter Stein appointed director of Berlin Schaubühne.
1972			Planchon appointed director of the Théâtre National Populaire.
1973	Peter Hall replaces Olivier as director of the National Theatre.	Joseph Papp appointed director of the Lincoln Centre, New York.	
1976	National Theatre opens its new theatre.		
1978		Papp resigns from Lincoln Centre to concentrate on his Public Theatre.	
1980	Brenton's *The Romans in Britain* leads to private prosecution of the director.		
1982	Royal Shakespeare Company opens Barbican Centre.		

II Theatre, Theatres and Dramatic Genres

Theatre and Theatres

Theatre and Theatricality

There are some notions which are difficult to grasp clearly not because we are not sure what is covered by them, but because we cannot say with certainty what they do not cover. 'Theatre' and the terms associated with it form one such notion. Use it widely enough – and many of us do – and it seems to take in most aspects of life, public and private. Books with titles like *The Presentation of Self in Everyday Life* and *Theatricality: A Study of Convention in the Theatre and in Social Life* discuss the element of 'dramatization' in our daily life. Others, like *Revolution as Theatre*, see a series of socio-political events, such as the 'campus revolt' of the late 1960s, in terms of a theatrical performance. Religion, sport, politics, family life – 'theatre' seems to be an essential, if often elusive, aspect of all of these.

This connection between theatre and ordinary life has been felt from the time theatre began to exist as a separate and self-conscious activity (for theatre had to exist as a separate institution before ordinary life could be compared with it). One of the oldest metaphors in our culture is that which likens the world to a stage and human life to a play. Sometimes the stress has fallen on the helplessness of the individual as a puppet whose strings are moved by unseen forces, sometimes on human life as a performance to be applauded or condemned by a divine audience. Whatever emphasis it is given, the analogy itself goes back to Plato and probably beyond, and it has left its mark on the words all of us use in describing and judging our own and other people's behaviour. 'Don't make a scene', we might say, or 'he certainly knows how to hold the stage', or 'what a splendid entrance she made', or 'that was just an act he was putting on'. Indeed, the ambiguity that exists in many languages in words like 'act', 'acting' and 'actor' which can be used indifferently to describe events and people in real life or in a play, is at once both revealing and teasing. Clearly, it is not going to be possible to mention, let alone discuss, all the various uses of the idea of theatre. That would require an encyclopaedia and few people want an encyclopaedia for a companion. But, while the various forms of theatre in the narrower sense are the proper scope of this volume, it is just as well to begin by reminding ourselves that these forms are themselves rooted in features of our life which far antedate them, some of which may well be basic and irreducible.

When we think of theatre today, we think normally of a special kind of experience, closed at both ends, so to speak (though various attempts, which will be discussed elsewhere, have been made in the past few decades to challenge this 'closed-off' quality of theatre). Theatre usually 'means' a visit to a special kind of building to look at and listen to people speaking lines and performing actions which have been set down for them by others (author, director, choreographer, fight-arranger and so on) in a specially created setting, often in special clothes and accompanied by specially created effects of music or sound or both. If we try to decide which of these – building, text, gesture, costume – is absolutely basic to the idea of theatre itself, we may perhaps be asking a meaningless question or one to which there is no real answer, since there is no logical reason why any one feature of the developed theatre as we know it should be primary or basic. But once we ask the question 'What is theatre?' it will persist, especially if we are aware of the links between theatrical performance and social life. We seem to be left at last with the notion of *performance* which in this sense involves not only a performer but witnesses to the performance – in other words, an audience. That audience need not, of course, be passive – any more than a football crowd is – but some sense of separation between the performers and those who witness and assess the performance seems to be necessary before the idea of theatre can be present. Even in ordinary life we describe situations or people as 'theatrical' when we are slightly detached from them. (This is true even when we use the term to describe our own actions or situation, for at such moments we feel ourselves to be spectators of our own behaviour.) It is here that we come closest to the point where theatre as a separate activity and institution reveals itself as distinct from what was probably its historical ancestor, religion and religious practice.

From Ritual to the Theatre

Religion has already been mentioned as one area of life which is evidently theatrical and it is with religion – or rather some of those outward manifestations of religion loosely called ritual – that most historians of the theatre begin their story. This is convenient and helpful, for the aims and methods of both theatre and religious ritual often have a striking if sometimes superficial similarity. Both aim to communicate knowledge or doctrine, to impart a code of values, to glorify or condemn and in some degree to influence action in the outside world and both have an element of entertainment, however small. The means used by both are often identical – music and dance, costume and spectacle in a specially designated area before an audience. But when we talk of drama originating in religious ritual, we must bear in mind that 'religion' here stands for something vastly different from what the word usually signifies in the Western world. Furthermore, the origins of theatre as an institution cannot be incontrovertibly established, in spite of sociologists and theatre historians who often imply or even assert that they can. Indeed, it could hardly be so, since the questions involved take us far beyond anything that can properly be called historical or even archaeological record. The religious-ritual origin of theatre is one theory among others, an attractive, plausible and often illuminating theory, lighting up dark areas of human culture, flooding past and present with sweeps of dazzling conjecture. But it is a theory for all that, and there are others. Theatre may have originated in elaborations of tribal narrative or functional dance, for instance. Or religious ritual may have been a sacred and esoteric version of tribal lore while theatrical performance existed side by side with it as a more public expression of the same lore. We do not and cannot know for certain. We can only point to links where they seem to exist.

Though the ends and means of ritual and developed drama have been compared to each other, it is their differences that strike us when we consider the nature and function of ritual in the earliest human societies known to us. It is possible that some form of ritual existed among Ice Age men thirty millennia ago, but the earliest rituals of which we have historical record in some detail take us to the Near East between three and four thousand years before the birth of Christ. Egyptian hiero-glyphs of this period depict many rituals involving the struggles between various gods, though we cannot be certain that they were ever performed publicly. But from 2500 BC we hear of the so-called Memphite drama enacting the death and resurrection of Osiris and the crowning of his son Horus, who may have been impersonated by the Pharaoh. Even more important is the passion play enacted at the holy place of Abydos for nearly two thousand years from 2500 BC , surely the longest recorded tradition of performance in the world. In this, too, the myth of the god Osiris was dramatized. Osiris, born of Geb (earth) and Nut (sky), married his sister Isis, was slain and deposed by his jealous brother Seth, and his dismembered body buried all over Egypt to be gathered by Isis and made whole with the help of the god Anubis. Osiris then went as judge to the infernal regions while his son Horus recovered his lost kingdom of earth.

What we appear to have here is an outline of an elaborate and highly sophisticated ritual for which the term 'primitive' in its everyday sense is quite misleading. But it is in origin a ritual, not an independent piece of theatre. There is no evidence and little likelihood that a distinct theatre developed in Egypt in spite of the continuous tradition of performance we have noted. We seem able to perceive clearly in the Horus play the lineaments of a ritual of seasonal renewal, the death and rebirth of the year which is common to all primitive societies. For these societies, ritual was a way of making sense of the world about them, of coping with the troubled present and of constructing a desired future by re-presenting it.

Primitive man inhabited a world which was wholly dependent on the processes of nature – and yet one in which those processes could be disrupted by forces wholly unintelligible to him. Cushioned as we are from much of our environment by technology, we cannot easily imagine what it might have been like to have been 'unaccommodated man' in the dark and distant time. To those forces which he acknowledged but could not with certainty control, primitive man attributed human motives, though he did not always personify them. They had to be appeased and in some way subdued so that the order of the world – which was naturally felt in terms of seasonal change – could be restored. It was a task impossible for an individual, who could not even live by himself in such a world, let alone subdue it. So the vital, always-to-be-repeated task of wooing the life-giving forces and staving off those of death and destruction became the chief function of the community as a whole. Much ritual is the expression of that function.

This expression took the form of mimic representation and re-enactment of the struggle between life and death, destruction and renewal. Mimicry, the propensity to imitate, is fundamental to man. We can see it in young children and even among some animals. But this imitation was not undertaken only or chiefly to give pleasure, except perhaps to the unknown powers who were its intended and invisible audience. Those who took part in it – and in one way or another that included the entire community – came to it in a spirit of awed intensity, not so much supplicating the unseen forces as attempting to wrest some of their power by transporting the participants temporarily into something of that ecstatic frenzy through which the supernatural could be apprehended. The very word 'ecstasy' indicated the power to stand outside oneself, to put on the knowledge and the power of the Other. Music and dancing were some of the principal means by which this transformation could be affected. 'In song and dance man exhibits himself as a member of a higher community', wrote Nietzsche, 'he has forgotten how to speak and is on the point of taking a dancing flight into the air.' With our feet still on the ground we may note that verbal language may have been less developed than the arts of mimic gesture as a means of communicating with the unseen powers.

From this necessarily brief account of ritual we can see how it arose, what it was like and what it has in common with the developed drama. The universal form of primitive ritual includes some representation of the struggle between the old and new powers of the cosmos, the defeat of the old and the scattering of its strength throughout the earth, its regathering and the installation of a successor. The whole community participated in the ritual, which contained the elements of mimic portrayal, music and dance and which culminated in a state of ecstatic frenzy in which the participants aspired to go 'out of' themselves and unite with the unseen powers. The community did not passively wait to share these powers by divine grace but actively strove to partake of them by propitiation. The emphasis throughout was on physical existence, the life of the senses, rather than on spiritual exaltation, since the object was to render life on earth safer and more bearable. It is apparent that this is religious ritual in a sense which has to be sharply distinguished from the nature and purpose of ritual in the Christian church, at least in its central Catholic tradition. Here too the ritual is directed towards making something happen, but the emphasis is very much on God's grace and man's helplessness, and on the salvation of his soul, rather than the heightening of his bodily sensations. There is no attempt at identification between man and God in the sense of one partaking of the nature of the other. We shall have more to say about the relation between Christian ritual and drama when we reach that point in history where they confronted each other. For the moment, let us return to the very different religious practice of the near East and its connection with the earliest European drama.

The Cult of Dionysus and the Greek Theatre

In its earliest phase, primitive ritual had been rite rather than enactment of myth, the meticulous carrying-out of certain prescribed patterns without their being elaborated into dramatic narratives of gods, kings and heroes. Only with the emergence of myth, as in the Osiris story, does ritual come close to drama as we commonly understand it.

When the Greek historian Herodotus visited Egypt in the middle of the fifth century BC, he was struck by the resemblance between the portrayal of Osiris, the god of life and fertility, and the Greek god Dionysus in whose honour plays were presented at festivities in Athens and elsewhere. In fact, the cult of Dionysus, the god of fertility and wine (Romanized into Bacchus), was already old before the city of Athens incorporated plays at the festival in his honour. It had spread all over Greece from Thrace in the north and was well established by the time 'Homer' composed his epics of the Greek heroes, probably in the eighth century BC. The frenzied women, known as the Maenads, who participated in the cult held wild nocturnal orgies in the Thracian mountains. They wore long flowing garments made of animal skins, carried snakes sacred to the god and danced till they attained the ecstatic frenzy. The climax came when they fell upon the sacrificial beast – a goat or bull – who stood for the god, and devoured it raw in order to share in the god's power. The cult spread throughout Greece because it was open to all and needed no priests, only celebrants. It was in order to tame the wild and explosive energy of this cult that in the sixth century BC the Athenian civic authorities instituted festivals in honour of Dionysus, from the rites at which the first European drama was born. No doubt these later festivals were much tamer affairs than the original Thracian orgies. But, as late as 405 BC, a play such as Euripides' *Bacchae* still gives some sense of the elemental orgiastic fury and is clearly addressed to an audience that had not completely forgotten it.

The official connection between theatre and state began in *c.* 534 BC when Athens inaugurated a competition for the composer of the best tragedy presented at the City Dionysia, the most important of the four annual festivals in honour of the god. The literal sense of the word tragedy ('goat song') may hark back to a time when a goat was either a prize or a sacrificial victim. Its development into the marvellous flowering of Greek tragedy in the fifth century BC, when we meet the first dramatists to be known through complete extant plays – Aeschylus, Sophocles and Euripides – is, and will probably remain, swathed in mystery. By that time theatre, though still dedicated to the god, is a distinct and specialized activity which is not a religious ritual. Although we cannot know with certainty the stages by which the original orgiastic celebration became the orderly theatrical programme of the city festival, we can note some landmarks on the way.

The earliest account we have of the origins of Greek theatre is Aristotle's, and he lived long after the great age of Greek drama. Nevertheless, he was clearly acquainted with a great many Greek plays which have not survived, as well as with many official and other records. It is therefore unfortunate that the *Poetics* is vague and fragmentary, a happy and overcrowded hunting ground for scholarly theorists (the often unreadable in pursuit of the always unprovable). Aristotle tells us that tragedy, like comedy, began with improvisations, the former by the leader of the dithyramb, the latter by the leaders of phallic songs still prevalent in Aristotle's Greece. The dithyramb was originally a song in honour of Dionysus, though not necessarily always about him. (The word 'dithyramb' may signify 'twice born'; Dionysus was supposed to have been snatched unborn from the womb of his mother Semele, and then hidden in Zeus's thigh, whence he was 'born' a second time.) The story was probably improvised by the leader of the chorus while the chorus itself – several men dressed as satyrs in animal skin, horse's tail, phallus and mask – chanted and danced the traditional refrain. The fact that the story could be about events and personages unconnected with Dionysus evidently allowed for the introduction of the vast body of Homeric myth which is the substance of classical Greek drama. Arion of Methymna (*c.* 625–585 BC) is credited with being the first to compose literary dithyrambs, while to Thespis, an early leader of the chorus, said to be winner at the first dramatic festival of *c.* 534 BC, is attributed the idea of impersonation. He retained the satyr's mask but donned the garb of Hermes, messenger of the gods and god of eloquence, to set him apart from the chorus and perhaps to speak to them as well as to the audience. No plays by either Arion or Thespis survive, though the latter has bequeathed his name to the profession of which he was possibly the founder member.

The sixth-century reorganization of the City Dionysia had been carried out under the auspices of one of the great dynastic families of Greece, the Peisistratids. Twenty-four years later the ruling family was overthrown and a democracy established. The whole of Attica, of which Athens was the capital, was divided into ten geographical areas each occupied by a newly created tribe. The character of the festival was reorganized to suit the new political divisions. Each tribe was called upon to perform one dithyramb annually, in competition with the others. Satyr plays, which probably developed from the dithyramb concurrently with tragedy, appear to have been introduced to the festival in the late sixth century. These were boisterous burlesques featuring the misadventures of a mythic hero, often indecent and always associated with the partly animal satyrs or Sileni among whom the god Dionysus was said to have been reared. Each of the three competing dramatists at the festival had to present three tragedies and a satyr play. Thus, by the beginning of the fifth century BC, drama had come a long way from the improvised dithyramb of the chorus, to a civic theatre festival which was professional and secular, though still firmly connected with its religious roots. We can now look more closely at the organization of this festival, its physical setting and its relation to the community at large.

The City and the Theatre

Only the festivals of Dionysus had any connection with the Greek theatre, and of these the City Dionysia had the closest ties, though towards the end of the fifth century plays were performed at two of the other Dionysus festivals, the Lenaia and the Rural Dionysia. In early spring each year the City Dionysia commemorated the coming of the god in celebrations which lasted for several days. After a ceremony re-enacting the god's entry into the city came a triumphal procession which made its way through the principal streets, showing to Athens and the world the power of the god, his links with the city and the willingness and ability of the city to do him due honour. Though this procession obviously illustrated the intimate connection between religious ritual and the theatre, it also clearly indicated the distinct identity of each, both in the composition of the procession and in its conduct. It included the priests of Dionysus as well as the actors and musicians who were to perform in the plays. These were quite separate groups. The procession, which bore in triumph a statue of Dionysus, would perform various ritual dances in his honour at altars throughout the city, culminating in a sacrificial offering at the temple of Dionysus. But from here, after the announcement of the plays to be performed at the festival on the following days, the statue would be taken and set in a place of honour in the front row of the theatre which, though nearby, was a quite different structure from the temple. By the fifth century in Athens there was a clear distinction between ritual and drama, priests and actors, temple and theatre, participants and spectators. Without this distinction we would not have had the tragedies of Aeschylus, Sophocles and Euripides – to say nothing of the comedies of Aristophanes. The procession also included the chief magistrate of Athens who was in charge of all the festival arrangements, as well as the *choregoi*, wealthy citizens who had been appointed as sponsors to finance much of the costs of dramatic production. Each poet whose plays were chosen for performance had a *choregos*; doubtless the competing poets relied heavily on their sponsor's generosity and cooperation. As time went on, prizes at the festival were offered to sponsors and actors as well as to the dramatists themselves.

Later – as well as the three tragedies and the satyr play which were called for from each of the three dramatists whose works were to be performed – five comedies, each by a different playwright, were also presented. A whole day was taken up by the work of each tragic dramatist, with the tragedies performed continuously from sunrise to early evening, followed perhaps by an interval for refreshment, after which the satyr play took place. The comedies may have been presented together on a single day. How the competing dramatists were originally selected we do not know, but the names of those chosen for the next festival were announced at the end of the preceding one, allowing some eleven months for rehearsal and preparation, an enviable length of time in comparison with most modern theatrical conditions. It was considered a high honour to have one's work presented at the City Dionysia and most of the tragic dramatists directed their own work and, to begin with, acted in it as well. The acting profession too, in contrast to later periods, enjoyed a high social status. Actors were exempted from military service and had special permission to travel through foreign lands even in wartime. Two actors travelled from Athens to Macedonia at the time of the war against Philip of Macedon and actually helped with the peace negotiations. All those professionally concerned with the production of plays – actors, musicians, dancers, poets – were organized in a guild which must have been something nearer to a priestly caste than a trade union, though neither one nor the other.

'Drama' comes from a Greek word meaning 'the thing done' and 'theatre' from a word meaning 'viewing place' and related to the word for a spectator. These viewing places were associated with areas sacred to the gods but, as we have seen, by the time drama proper appears they are not temples. On the green slope of a hill overlooked by the Acropolis, in the sacred precinct of Dionysus Eleuthereus, some 15,000 spectators gathered. At first they sat on the bare hillside but later wooden benches and then stone and marble seats were provided. The best seats were naturally reserved for the high officials of the city and the competition judges, presided over by the god himself. Special areas were set aside for women and boys. The rows of seats followed the natural curve of the hillside in a horseshoe around the *orchestra* or dancing place, the earliest part of the theatre. Here the original chorus danced and sang. In the sixth century an altar was placed at the centre of the circle which formed the *orchestra*. For six hundred years or more this remained the essential shape of theatre all over the Western world.

By the time of Thespis a stone amphitheatre and a circular *orchestra* with an altar at its centre may have been a permanent part of the Greek theatre. Then came the *skene*, from which we derive our 'scene'. Originally this was a temporary booth or tent, probably used for storing properties and stage machines and as a dressing-room for the performers. The first extant work to make use of the *skene* as part of the theatrical setting was Aeschylus' *Oresteia*, but since most of Greek drama has perished, we cannot be certain that the credit for this imaginative innovation does not belong to some earlier and quite unknown dramatist.

We know very little for certain about how plays were performed in the Athenian theatre. Most extant Greek plays have only one locale, the precincts of a palace, temple or other building. Thus the *skene* would have served quite adequately as a scenic background. Where outdoor scenes were specifically indicated, the permanent *skene* could have been covered, or perhaps the audience, by an effort of imagination aided by a few relevant props and the dramatist's lines, could have ignored the *skene* and visualized the scene in the mind's eye.

How much attempt there was to represent an actual scene by painted scenery is another subject on which we have only the scantiest information. According to Aristotle (who, we must remember, was writing long after the age of the dramatists whose works have come down to us) Sophocles invented scene painting. Scholars disagree about just what sort of scene painting there was in the Greek theatre. There are references to flat painted panels called *pinakes*, much like the canvas 'flats' of the proscenium-arch theatre of later times, and to *periaktoi*, triangular columns with a picture on each surface that could be swivelled round to indicate change of scene. How realistically either of these kinds of scenery were painted or whether they were changed for each play or scene is a matter for scholarly argument. We may guess, given what we know about the Greek theatre, that no great attempt at surface realism was made; not many among the 15,000-odd spectators would have been able to see painted scenery in any sort of detail.

Two side doors and a larger double door at the centre served for entrances and exits on the later Greek stage. There were also probably steps leading up from the dancing place to the raised stage which had two levels, the upper one for gods or those supposed to be on a high vantage point, like the watchman at the opening of Aeschylus' *Agamemnon*. The stage seems to have been narrow (about eight feet wide) but long enough for chariots to go fairly slowly from one end to the other. The top of the stage building was as high as the last rows of seats and the back of the *skene* made an excellent sounding-board.

For tragedy not many properties were used, though a crane was occasionally called for, especially in the plays of Euripides, to bring down a god to the lower level. (It was Euripides' fondness for this device to provide a conclusion for his plays that gave us the term *deus ex machina* to describe any over-contrived ending in a fictional work.) Another notable feature of the staging was the use of the *ekkyklema*, a sort of large trolley which made possible the wheeling-on of tableaux. Since deeds of violence in Greek tragedy were always committed off-stage, these tableaux generally represented arrangements of dead bodies. The humorous possibilities of both these devices, and others, were exploited by the writers of comedy; for instance a character in

Aristophanes' *Peace* performs the *deus ex machina* journey in reverse, going up to Olympus on the back of a giant dung-beetle.

In an amphitheatre as vast as that of Athens, there was no real opportunity for the actors to achieve their effects by delicate nuances of facial expression, but it was not necessarily for that reason that masks were used. They may date back to a time when theatre had not separated itself from ritual, when the primitive celebrant wished to increase the efficacy of his portrayal of the unknown powers by altering his physical appearance. The masks of the Greek actors were originally made of stiffened linen but later of cork, which had better acoustic properties. They were slightly larger than life-size and entirely covered the head, with even the eye painted in and only a small hole left for the actor to see through. Reproductions of theatrical masks on Greek vases and statuettes do not suggest that realism was a desired end, at least in tragedy. The view that Greek performance was highly formalized is further borne out by the fact that the height of tragic actors was increased in later times by tall head-dresses and high boots, and that their costumes were heavily padded. The costumes themselves were neither contemporary nor historical but a dignified and colourful blend of both. The whole effect seems to have been designed to elevate characters in tragedy into a sphere far removed from the familiar everyday life of the spectators. That life was grotesquely mirrored in comedy. Only the comedies of Aristophanes have survived as complete plays, but their characters, plots, stage action and language are sufficient evidence of the truism that, from the earliest times, comedy has kept its feet firmly in the here and now, even in its wildest excursions into fantasy.

Thespis, as we have noted, is generally acknowledged to have become the first actor in the real sense when he distinguished himself from the chorus and adopted the guise of Hermes. Aeschylus, of whose eighty-odd plays only seven have survived, is credited with the introduction of a second actor, thereby giving more prominence to the dialogue in the total performance. With Sophocles, his younger rival (again, only seven plays survive out of a reputed total of a hundred), we meet the innovation of a third actor, which Aeschylus also adopted in his last plays. And throughout Greek drama, as far as we know, there were never more than three actors to take all the speaking parts. No doubt this was partly due to reasons of civic economy, for the actors' fees were paid by the city, not by the *choregos*. But the extant plays suggest that there were plenty of walk-on parts, attendants, slaves, spear-carriers and the like. The three actors, all male, had to impersonate a wide range of characters both male and female, and one effect of this must have been that even minor speaking parts were admirably portrayed. With the mask completely concealing the actor's face, an expressive voice with a wide tonal range would probably have been the actor's greatest asset.

Bread and Circuses: Theatre in the Roman Empire

By the end of the fourth century BC Athens was under Macedonian rule and the outspoken satirical comedies of Aristophanes had given way to the softer New Comedy principally associated with Menander (343–292 BC), who created a series of type figures – the wily slave, the parasite, the courtesan, and so on – who were to live for centuries on the European stage in various guises, being borrowed by the Latin comedy of Plautus and Terence and from them by the dramatists of the Renaissance and after. Similarly the tragedies of Euripides and Sophocles have had a continuing influence on the European stage, passing through Seneca (*c.* 5 BC–AD 65) to the Elizabethan dramatists and to Racine and Corneille in France in the seventeenth century. Seneca is the only Roman tragic dramatist whose plays have survived, Plautus and Terence the only comic ones.

As all this suggests, Roman theatre was largely derived from Greek origins, both in terms of the content of the drama and, with some alterations, the physical conditions of performance, although neighbouring Etruria also contributed to its development. In the third century BC Livius Andronicus, possibly a captive Greek slave, presented in Rome a tragedy in Latin adapted from a Greek original. He also translated Sophocles and Euripides into Latin, while the first native Roman playwright was Gnaeus Naevius (*c.* 270–*c.* 201 BC). But while the source material of drama was, to begin with, heavily indebted to the Greeks, the social function of theatre was rather different in Roman times. To the Romans the performance of the drama was not part of a religious festival – though loosely attached to the feast days of several gods – so much as a public holiday. By AD 354 more than a third of the year was given over to theatrical performances of one kind or another. The triumphal progress of a victorious general returning to the city could, for instance, culminate in the parade of his captives and booty in tableaux on specially erected stages (according to Cicero a boring substitute for drama). Theatres themselves were built on level ground, the raised stage having a sloping roof with elaborate façades of buildings at the rear, formalized by Serlio during the Renaissance as conventional settings for tragedy, comedy and satyr plays. The Roman theatre was probably the first to make use of a curtain to mask the stage from the audience, and the chorus of Greek drama was abolished in favour of lavish spectacle. Plays were performed throughout the year.

It is likely that masks were used from the earliest times in the Roman theatre, although the emphasis was on individual actors and their virtuosity. Roscius, the greatest of Roman actors and a specialist in comic roles, lent his name as a generic title for all actors of genius in later times. Paradoxically though, while acting skill was much admired, the social status of the actor in the Roman theatre was very low, especially if we compare him with his Greek counterpart. This was partly because it was easy for theatrical managers to form groups of slave actors and exploit them; all actors were indeed little better than slaves. With the decline of the status of actors, though not entirely because of it, there came also a decline in the quality of the plays themselves. Tragedy and comedy were increasingly ousted by farce, burlesque and pantomime. The emperor Nero favoured Roman audiences with tragic recitations, accompanying himself on the cither, and is said to have performed as Hercules, Orestes and Oedipus. Women appeared on stage chiefly as dancers, vocalists or instrumentalists.

In a very literal sense the Roman theatre was a theatre of cruelty. In addition to the regular gladiatorial contests and animal baiting that went on in the circuses, it was not uncommon for performers to be actually and deliberately killed during the course of the action. Thus Orpheus was literally torn to pieces and a robber was slowly crucified during a play. In later times Christian martyrs were forced into this role instead of convicted criminals. In the fifth century AD we hear of a Christian monk hurling himself into the arena in protest against the bloodthirsty theatrical practice of the time. He was stoned to death by the angry audience.

The Hellenic theatrical tradition, coarse but vigorous under the aegis of Rome, gradually disintegrated as the Empire itself did, though theatres of some kind flourished and remained a popular feature of Roman life. There were forty-eight under the emperor Augustus and more than a hundred during the reign of Constantine. It was, like the Elizabethan theatre, the only democratic institution in a highly undemocratic society. It was also a useful vehicle for propaganda, and the authorities therefore imposed many restrictions on actors and the theatre itself.

The polyglot audiences of the Roman Empire precluded much linguistic subtlety in dramatic dialogue and increasingly the emphasis came to fall on acrobatics, dancing and, above all, mime. At first these elements occurred at intervals during long literary tragedies and led to the creation of well observed contemporary types such as the city fool and the rustic fool. Dialogue was often improvised, a tradition subsequently preserved in the Italian *commedia dell'arte*. In later

Roman theatre women performed dramatic roles and may occasionally have appeared in the nude. The mime rapidly expanded to become the principle item of the performance, and actors (*histriones*) concentrated on miming the appropriate action while the story was sung or chanted. Eventually the *histriones* merged with the mimes.

The Christian Church and the Theatre

For fairly obvious reasons the early Christian church was vigorously opposed to the Roman theatre. In AD 4 the *Canons of Hippolytus* expressly prohibited members of the clergy from taking part in theatrical performances, an injunction which, presumably, circumstances made necessary. In order to become or marry a Christian a player was compelled to leave the acting profession. Theatrical performances were forbidden on Sundays and Church feast days, and St John Chrysostom and St Jerome issued edicts against the theatre for the Eastern and Western churches respectively. Theatres, however, continued stubbornly to flourish and in the last days of the empire the restrictions against them were fewer. (Justinian's Empress Theodora had been an actress.)

During the Gothic invasions of the fifth and sixth centuries theatre continued to have a vigorous if fitful existence but the death blow was probably delivered by the invasion of the Lombards from north Germany in AD 568. Actors now took to the roads and scraped what living they could by exhibiting their talents wherever they could find an audience. Theatrical displays became a feature of weddings, baptisms and similar occasions, though the Christian clergy usually left before the performance began. Many actors became either resident entertainers in a castle, if they were lucky, or, if they were not, wandering players, usually welcome in tavern or market-place as bringers of news. In 692 a council of the Church forbade all theatrical displays, and for the next four centuries the theatre led the shadowiest of half-lives, finally emerging into the clear light of history under the patronage of the very Christian church which had persecuted it for so long and so steadfastly.

Outdoor Staging in Europe

The preservation of the twelfth-century French play of *Adam* gives early indication of quite ambitious outdoor staging. The evolution of Christian drama in France is not, in outline, very different from its evolution in England. From the simple presentation of the liturgy in dialogue there developed, still inside the church buildings, a more elaborate presentation of the drama embedded in the liturgy. Platforms were erected at various locations, often around the stations of the Cross, for the better performance of tropes associated with the Church calendar. The likelihood is that the initial decisions to move the performances into the open air were taken sporadically, according to the climate, rather than dogmatically, according to the instructions of a priest or bishop. One date marks an important point in the evolution towards the open-air spectaculars, known variously in England as Mystery or Miracle cycles. That is 1264, the year in which Pope Urban IV instituted the Feast of Corpus Christi, to be celebrated throughout Europe on a date between 23 May and 24 June, a time when the weather was likely to be fair. The celebration of the sacrament of Christ's body involved contemplation of his crucifixion, which in turn could only be truly evaluated in relation to man's fall and his eventual redemption. Thus, the entire panorama of the Miracle cycles was latent in the papal instruction to celebrate the Feast of Corpus Christi.

It was not easy for the Church to cope with the physical requirements of celebration on a large scale. The English solution was similar to that of other European countries. That solution was, in brief, to hand over the responsibility for the staging of the processional and dramatic events to the trade guilds (or 'mysteries'). We have no adequate records of the growth of the Christian feast into the ambitious open-air festival of drama represented by the four surviving English mediaeval cycles and the equally complex Cornish one. (It has been estimated that there were a further 120 English cycles, whose texts have been lost.) Surviving records do, however, give us important clues about their staging. In France, the preference was for arranging platforms (as many as forty or as few as four) around an empty space. The audience would then promenade from platform to platform to watch the unfolding story of human history. Multiple staging was not unknown in England, where an alternative, mobile method was also developed. This involved the use of decorated wagons, each carrying actors and appropriate furnishings for the presentation of one of the episodes in the cycle. The pageant wagons were drawn through the streets for consecutive performance at fixed points in the city or town, or perhaps simply processed through for a single presentation in a favoured location. The expense and scale of these productions justify their description as quasi-professional, and there is, indeed, evidence that certain prominent players were paid to participate.

The English Reformation acted as a disincentive to the continuation of the Miracle cycles, which had passed their heyday by the end of the fifteenth century, but they did not disappear until much later. Archdeacon Rogers has left a description of a performance in Chester as late as 1594. By that time London had several open-air theatres whose staging techniques owed more to indoor than to outdoor performance traditions.

The last major European revival of the theatrical festivals of Corpus Christi belongs to Spain. There, in the seventeenth century, developed the form of the *auto sacramental*. What began as a simple scaffold performance had grown, by the second half of the century, when Calderon was writing his remarkable *autos sacramentales*, into a technically complex affair involving four carts carrying stage-machinery to serve actors on a fifth cart or scaffold. Elsewhere, the special status of open-air performance declined but never died. During the first decades of the twentieth century, many English towns celebrated their history in large-scale pageants. The French invention of the *son et lumière* has been widely imitated. Paul Green's outdoor pageant plays have dramatized locality throughout the American provinces. And, in France again, the annual Avignon drama festival has, since 1947, demonstrated the peculiar attractiveness of open-air performance.

On a smaller scale, in the London fairs and in the Italian tours of *commedia dell'arte* troupes, outdoor drama has been a major influence on indoor staging methods and acting styles. The booth stage – a simple arrangement of a raised scaffold backed by curtains – certainly affected Elizabethan architects and dramatists. Most of the great writers can be effectively performed on simple stages, and many of the major modern theatrical innovations have been based on a rediscovery of simplicity. Shut away behind its box office, a theatre deters the underprivileged and the culturally nervous, but a performance in a park by the San Francisco Mime Troupe, on a farm by El Teatro Campesino, at a factory gate in Lancashire by North West Spanner or in any street or open place by anyone who has the courage will still attract an audience.

Indoor Staging: The Beginnings

The large halls of the great European houses were naturally used for entertainment. Musicians would play during meals, minstrels would sing and jesters jest. Surviving Tudor halls are the best indication of the likely appearance of the upstage façade of the Elizabethan public theatres. A minstrels' gallery surmounts a dividing wall with a door at each end. Those serving the meal will use one door for entrances and the other for exits with dishes etc. On such a practical model, James Burbage probably constructed the players' portion of the Theatre in 1576. He would have been well aware, as a former member of Lord Leicester's acting troupe, of the possible uses of such a structure. It was in such halls, presumably to entertain diners at an appropriate point in a banquet, that the Interlude developed as a form. We know that Henry

VII employed four or five men to perform Interludes – short pieces, usually with a festive conclusion involving host and guests – and that they were sent to Scotland to entertain the company at the marriage of James IV to Henry's daughter. Their plays had to be easily adaptable to the different spaces in which they might be expected to perform them, so that there was no difficulty in shifting to more public venues, like guildhalls or even inns.

English actors depended on the patronage of a great lord, whose livery they wore. In France, the Confraternity of the Passion was more effectively organized. Formed in 1402 and constantly on the borders of professionalism, this group won a monopoly of all theatrical perfor-mances in Paris and maintained it until 1595. They seem to have preferred playing indoors from the start, not least because it facilitated the charging of entrance-fees. It was this privileged company that, in 1548, built the first permanent theatre in France. The Hôtel de Bourgogne was a long narrow room with a stage at one end and a tier of benches at the other. Between the two was an empty space which could have housed standing spectators. There were boxes down the two side walls, and stage and auditorium were lit from chandeliers. The shape was dictated by the fact that the building was constructed in the ruins of the palace of the Dukes of Burgundy. It relied, that is to say, on the given structure of a great hall.

The first purpose-built English theatre was quite different. Although Burbage was ready to copy the strengths of the Tudor halls, he had no reason to accept their weaknesses; and he hoped for a far larger audience than they could have accommodated. The Theatre was, almost certainly, a polygonal building with three galleries surrounding an empty space into which a raised platform jutted. As a businessman, Burbage would probably have wanted the stage to be removable to allow for in-the-round spectacles like bear-baiting and cock-fighting. He was a shrewd master-carpenter and would not, like a foolish grocer, put all his eggs in one basket. The success of the enterprise was sufficient to encourage competitors, and by the end of the sixteenth century London had four or five theatres more sophisticated than, but not radically different from, Burbage's original. In all of them the groundlings and most of the stage were in the open air. Spectators had to pay more for the privilege of protection from showers. The stage had the minstrels' gallery and the two doors of the Tudor great halls, augmented by machinery for raising and lowering a throne housed in a small shed over the stage. It was an inventive combination of outdoor and indoor features. It has, however, been too readily assumed that Elizabethan actors enjoyed working outdoors. There are indications to the contrary.

In 1576, the very year in which James Burbage opened the Theatre, a certain Richard Farrant, Master of the Children of Windsor Chapel, adapted a room in the old Blackfriars monastery for the performance of plays by his choirboys. Despite a brief, enforced interruption, caused by the involvement of the childrens' companies in the Marprelate controversy of 1589, the indoor plays of the Children of the Chapel (and those of a rival children's company at St Paul's) were popular for thirty years. That the adult companies were jealous of the facilities as well as the popularity of their young rivals is clear from the purchase by James Burbage, in 1597, of a lease on another hall in the Blackfriars. A petition by inhabitants of the Blackfriars precinct delayed their occupation, but in 1609 the King's Men, Shakespeare's company of players, staged their first plays in their own indoor theatre, though without relinquishing their interest in the open-air Globe. The necessary model, once again, was the Tudor great hall, but with staging facilities vastly improved. Whether or not the composition of the audience at the Blackfriars was greatly different from that at the Globe, the atmosphere certainly was. Artificial lighting transforms a performance space, as does the difference between a standing and a seated audience. But, in view of later developments, it should be stressed that the actors at the Blackfriars stood in the same room as the audience sat. There was no arch to separate the doer from the observer.

Indoor Staging: Perspective and Proscenium

The most significant developments in indoor staging during the Renaissance took place in Italy. The publication there of a new edition of the *De Architectura* of Vitruvius in 1486 created an extraordinary stir. Vitruvius had lived in the last century BC and the *De Architectura* included a handy guide to the building of a classical Roman theatre. Of the various theatres built in Italy under inspiration from Vitruvius, the finest was the Teatro Olimpico at Vicenza, designed by Palladio, opened in 1585 five years after Palladio's death and still standing. It is a splendid and totally impractical building, whose importance for the future of the theatre lies only in its invitation to make the stage look spectacular. Of more immediate effect was the perspective scenery of Sebastiano Serlio, whose three settings (Satyric, Comic and Tragic) were included in a book published in 1545. Serlio demonstrated how the building up of side-scenes towards a diminishing centre could give a stage setting the illusion of great depth. Italian architects took the new architectural ideas into the French and Dutch Theatre. Inigo Jones, after a visit to Italy, imported them to England himself. The elaborate Court Masques he devised for James I and Charles I introduced into England a recognition of the pictorial possibilities of perspective scenery set behind a proscenium that effectively divided the auditorium from the stage. The whole course of the European theatre was changed.

The outcome of Inigo Jones's innovations was delayed in England by the closing of the theatres during the Civil War. It was not until 1661, after the restoration of Charles II, that the London public could again go to the play. The first Restoration theatres were not particularly grand. The playhouse in Lincoln's Inn Fields, for example, though adapted by Davenant to accommodate a proscenium arch and changeable scenery, was no more than an altered tennis court, and the two theatres designed by Christopher Wren (Dorset Garden opened in 1671 and Drury Lane three years later) were not much bigger. The important difference was in the relationship of actor and audience. Although the actors would come downstage of the proscenium arch, on to the wide apron, to deliver their lines, their own space, territorially delineated by the wings and shutters of changeable scenery, was a separate room upstage of the proscenium. Two-dimensional scenery may look artificial to modern eyes, but there is no doubt that it was intended to look real to contemporary audiences. The theatre was becoming a picture-house with moving figures and recognizable locations that changed before your very eyes.

Theatres Large and Small
Throughout Europe during the seventeenth and eighteenth centuries the basic development of theatre building followed the logic of post-Renaissance pictorialism. Court theatres, like the one Goethe inherited in Weimar, were smaller and more elite than their public counterparts, but they were not, in architectural essentials, very different. In a lit auditorium, separated from similarly lit scenery, audiences sat to be entertained, to look and to be looked at. The theatre was a social meeting-place, a place of assignation and a well provided home for self-advertisement by audience as well as actors. The surviving Georgian Theatre in Richmond is small and exquisite, a miniature version of the increasingly vast patent houses of London. Backless benches in the pit were overlooked by galleries and surrounded by boxes. The story of Drury Lane and Covent Garden in the eighteenth century is one of frequent 'improvement', which generally took the form of enlargement and unnecessary decoration. By the end of the century, Drury Lane could seat 3,611 spectators, clearly not a place for subtle effects or quiet speaking. A difference of opinion, which would continue to be expressed for two centuries, was already apparent in some actors' preference for the Little Theatre in the Haymarket. But the drift

towards spectacle was unstemmable. De Loutherbourg's decade at Drury Lane (1771–81) introduced new refinements in stage-lighting, learned in the French theatre, and his extra-theatrical experiments with his Eidophusikon suggested mechanical progress of the kind that would soon declare itself in the Panorama and Diorama. Meanwhile Philip Astley was beginning to make his name as a horseman in the illegitimate theatres of London. From 1780 to 1860, Astley's Amphitheatre was a well loved home of equestrian spectaculars, pantomimes and melo-dramas. In the superbly equipped theatres of the nineteenth century, it was possible to stage everything from a shipwreck to a boat-race, and scene-builders and painters like Clarkson Stanfield and the Grieve family were as likely to draw audiences as the great actors like Kemble, Kean and Macready.

Even the legitimate theatre was caught up in the scramble for pictorial sensation. The Covent Garden *King John* of 1823 introduced to Shakespearean staging the idea of antiquarian accuracy, though not with the lavishness that was to characterize Charles Kean's productions at the Princess's in 1851–9. The demand for scenic Shakespeare was extravagant, but it was met by all the leading theatres. Serious actor though he was, Irving knew that he needed the assistance of top-class scene designers. His years at the Lyceum (1871–1905) brought the Victorian theatre to its fullest expression; flamboyance mingled with mystery, the exotic with the assertively respectable. When Irving toured, and he toured often, he took his scenery with him. The stage-effect was as important in Shakespeare as it was in melodrama. This was the background against which William Poel struggled to establish a return to Elizabethan bareness in the production of Shakespeare's plays. It was an important, but a losing, battle.

Two developments in the furnishing of the theatre helped towards a change in acting style. The first was lighting. The installation of gas at Covent Garden and the Olympic in 1815 vastly increased the flexibility of stage lighting. By 1829 the Haymarket was the only London theatre without it. The directional intensity of gas allowed actors to move upstage without forfeiting visibility so that, instead of acting *in front* of the scenery they could act *among* it. There were unforeseen social complications – gaslight was merciless to made-up faces in the auditor-ium as well as onstage – but they were far outweighed by the advan-tages. It was probably Irving who first hit on the idea of dowsing the lights in the auditorium to accentuate the pictorial separateness of the stage. His love of the shimmering secrecy of gaslight was well known and he refused, for as long as seemed tolerable, to change to electricity, despite the demonstrable reduction of fire-risk. The relationship of actors to an audience that could see them better than it could see its own knees was a totally new one. But there was a second equally significant development. It was not until the nineteenth century that the backless benches of the pit were replaced by individual stalls. Given their own seats in an unlit room, spectators are almost coerced into respectful silence. Instead of competing with a shifting, visible audience, Irving and actors like him could mesmerize an invisible, quiet and slightly fearful one.

The Twentieth Century

So many questions have been asked by twentieth-century theatre architects and designers and so many answers provided that it is impossible to take account of most of them. They inherited a set of assumptions from a profession that took it for granted that the task of everyone working on or behind the stage was to deceive the intelligent adults sitting in the auditorium into forgetting that they were in a theatre at all. The story of twentieth-century theatrical experiment is fundamentally one of attack on that sort of illusionism.

For those who associate Stanislavsky only with an acting style that eradicated the distinction between the impersonator and the imperso-nated, the Moscow Art Theatre will seem a strange place to start. But Stanislavsky was, in fact, well aware of the limitations of a naturalistic theatre of illusion. Not only the Studios of the Moscow Art Theatre, but also the main house, explored the aesthetics of symbolism, constructi-vism etc.; and it was under Stanislavsky's aegis that major innovators like Meyerhold and Vakhtangov studied their craft. Craig designed and directed *Hamlet* in Moscow in 1911–12, using his famous and infamous screens to capture the essence but certainly not the appearance of Elsinore. Aleksandra Exter's cubist designs for Taïrov at the Kamerny Theatre won her an invitation to the Second Studio of the Moscow Art Theatre in 1924. The preparedness to experiment in a theatre so well established gave an incentive to artists throughout Europe. One argument to which Stanislavsky was manifestly sympathetic was the old one in favour of smaller, intimate theatres. He had the example of Antoine's Théâtre Libre behind him and knew of Strindberg's involvement with the Intima Teatern in Stockholm, where, after 1907, the Swedish playwright staged his chamber plays. Max Reinhardt, famous for spectacular productions at Salzburg and for the conversion of theatres into Gothic cathedrals to house *The Miracle*, also built and worked in a Chamber Theatre in Berlin; and it has become almost axiomatic in Germany that all big civic theatres will have little theatres attached to them. In Britain and America, large new complexes like the

National Theatre, the Barbican and the Lincoln Centre have followed suit.

Much has been learnt from the achievements of more single-minded (and less wealthy) enthusiasts; from Appia's ideas of light and space, from Copeau's bare stage, from the antiquarian eccentricities of William Poel, from the all-out rejection of the proscenium arch by Norman Bel Geddes and Terence Gray. Tyrone Guthrie's demonstrations of the advantages of the thrust stage have led to the building of exciting theatres as far apart as Minneapolis, Chichester, and Stratford, Ontario. The recovery of what is probably the oldest of performance-shapes, theatre-in-the-round, was encouraged by Okhlopkov's work in the Moscow Realistic Theatre and championed in America by Margo Jones and in England by Stephen Joseph. In London's Puddle Dock, not far from the original site of the Blackfriars Theatre, Bernard Miles built the Mermaid in which audience and actors, like those in the Blackfriars, share the same room. The vogue for adaptable theatres has largely passed, because they have not often been adaptable enough, but it was an honest reflection of a new openness to variations on the actor-audience relationship.

It was in an attempt to rephrase that relationship that Meyerhold insisted on confronting his audiences with artifice that did not pretend to conceal art. In a variety of ways he used theatricality to intrude on the spectator's absorption in performance. For Brecht this was a matter of political urgency. How could an audience that was ready to convince itself that it wasn't where it was take seriously what happened while it was (or wasn't) there? The Berliner Ensemble displayed its lighting openly and its actors tried to remain separate enough from the characters they played to be able to share in the criticism of their behaviour. It is not an easy thing to do, and Brecht's ideas have been widely misinterpreted. Like Meyerhold, he did not want to perform before a passive audience but to share ideas with an active one. For Peter Brook, too, the participation of spectators is necessary to the total theatrical event – though the audience-participation is quite other than that invited by, for example, the Living Theatre. It is an issue which returns us to the ideas about theatricality with which this essay began. Every theatre architect or designer, like every actor or director, necessarily predicates the relationship between performer and spectator. If he or she wishes to emphasize, as in the twentieth century most do, that the theatre is not separate from ordinary life, it is necessary to define 'ordinary life' as well as 'theatre'. Even the most inspired analyses are bound to be partial. Only in a crude sense does Grotowski define his 'ordinary' audience by including it in his overall design. The techniques of performance art and environmental theatre are, however weird they may sometimes seem, aspects of a quest that many theatrical innovators would understand – to encourage us to recognize the strangeness of things we have taken for granted. For groups like the Bread and Puppet Theatre and Welfare State, the world is, after all, a stage.

English Drama and Performance

An Outline History

Somewhere around the year AD 900, an oddly significant development in church worship took place. Clerics, celebrating the Easter Mass, divided the chanted passage about Christ's resurrection into formalized dialogue. The division was simple. Instead of having one voice chant both the question, 'Whom do you seek in the sepulchre?', and the answer, 'Jesus of Nazareth', it was decided to give the question to one priest and the answer to another. It is often supposed that this *Quem Quaeritis* trope heralded the development of English drama. So, in a way, it did. By adopting a dramatic device, the Church brought the idea of 'performance' into the literate world, preparing the way for a sophisticated, literary form that would replace non-literary, 'primitive' performance. But it is a mistake to neglect the primitive, non-literary origins of drama. It is only superficially a paradox that the most progressive dramatic theorists of the nineteenth and twentieth centuries – Nietzsche, Artaud, Grotowski—have tended to hark back to the prehistory of drama, to the centuries before anything so complete and gift-wrapped as a play had been envisaged, in order to rediscover the vitality of an art-form that has spent the greater part of its life on what has looked to a lot of its adherents like its death-bed. Because the life of the drama is unavoidably public, the diagnosis of its health has been public too. When it has disappointed its public, or lost touch with it, it has been despaired of. When it has antagonized its public, it has often been at its liveliest. To some extent, the vivid history of the drama is a history of public shocks, and it is characteristic of many of these shocks that they confront the audience with the primitive.

All students of drama find themselves constantly referred back to the primitive power of the fears and passions which underpin its literary development. *Macbeth* reminds some critics of the scapegoat rituals, which required, at their most extreme, the sacrifice of a selected individual in order to ensure, in winter, the return of spring, and a prosperous future harvest for the community of killers. *A Midsummer Night's Dream* relies on the inherited memory of fertility rituals, which linked the making of human babies with the mysterious spread of spring and summer. Even so insistently verbal a play as Osborne's *Look Back in Anger* has evoked anthropological reminiscence of the role played in primitive societies by the official reviler of established order. The work of Harold Pinter is, for some of his admirers, a succession of veiled rituals. The common recognition is that primitive ritual, the doing of one thing simply in order to achieve another thing, was designed to be effective. Indeed, all human doing, whatever its outcome, is intended to be effective. It is not easy to determine exactly how much of the dwindling of drama is owed to its acceptance of the demand that it should 'entertain', but it is a general truth that 'great' plays retain a link, either consciously or unconsciously, with primitive ritual and the non-literary. The word 'drama' came into the English language from a Greek word meaning 'to do'. The watcher of the deed, who created 'theatre', came later. It is the attempt to return the effectiveness of drama to the theatre that has taken Nietzsche, Artaud, and Grotowski back into prehistory.

There were professional dramatic entertainers in England before the *Quem Quaeritis* so unexpectedly nudged drama into literature. Strolling minstrels, storytellers, acrobats visited towns and villages, or the homes of feudal lords, to provide a focus for celebration. An older 'effective' drama survives, in degenerate form, in Christmas mummings and in such startling relics as the Padstow 'oss. Unlike the *Quem Quaeritis* and the liturgical plays that followed tolerably soon, these folk-pieces would have been performed in the vernacular. The first major written drama in English combined formal, Latinate, liturgical elements with the disorderly, natural energies of folk-play. These were the Mystery plays, which were nourished inside the churches during the thirteenth century, outgrew the churches and the restrictions of ecclesiastical Latin, and burst on to the streets of towns and cities in England during the fourteenth and fifteenth centuries. The plays of the surviving Mystery cycles vary considerably in quality, but they all reveal, in a way that can still be godful in a godless age, the paradox that a theology as complex as Christianity's rests on simple faith and the innocence of story.

The impulse that translated the Latin of Christian worship into the English of the Mystery plays was, presumably, a missionary one – to help the common man perceive his holy heritage. Increasingly, the great civic festivals, for which the Mystery cycles provided a glittering centre, settled on to the Feast of Corpus Christi; and increasingly, the responsibility for staging the plays was transferred from the Church to the trade guilds. That was a stroke of casual genius. It provided England with its first evidence that great drama normally emerges during periods of adventurous and efficient theatre organization. We can assume that the Hatters' Guild competed with, say, the Chandlers' Guild for the plaudits of the town; but that competition is of less significance than is the corporate concern to learn and show, through spectacle and dialogue, that what happened centuries ago in the remote East (and we are talking of days when geography was as inaccurate and exotic as astrology) meant something *now* in Wakefield or Chester: that God *is* present, that Christ *is* being crucified now, that he *will* rise again. The present tense of the Mystery plays is irresistible.

Despite their exclusively religious provenance, the Mystery plays became the object of contention. This was partly a result of the spreading mood of solemn correctness that followed, not very appropriately, Henry VIII's raffish Reformation of the English Church. Not only were the Mystery plays a relic of Catholicism, but they also showed a greater concern for faith than for morality. They are not reliably instructive. Cain may be a black sheep, but he has wonderful spirit. The Serpent and Herod run off with the best lines. The emergence of the 'Morality' plays of the fifteenth century (*The Castle of Perseverance* dates from about 1405, *Everyman* from about 1497) reflects a growing ambition to tidy up the teaching of good behaviour through drama. The generalizations and the moral abstractions are less attractive than the startling insights and juxtapositions of the Mystery plays, but it was the Morality tradition, filtered through the Interludes played in the great houses of the Tudor nobility, that lingered into the great era of Elizabethan drama. Its presence in the extreme moral contrasts of *Doctor Faustus*, as well as in that play's consciousness of damnation, has been often commented on. Quite as significant is the effect of the Morality plays on the characters and dramaturgy of English comedy. This effect is less apparent in Shakespeare's comedies than it is in Ben Jonson's, but it was Jonson who provided the model for later English comedy. It is possible to see, in the rich history of English comedy, a varied peopling of the bare canvas of the Morality plays.

During the last decades of the sixteenth century, the strong Puritan minority objected to the Mystery plays because they were popular, often light-hearted, and fundamentally Catholic, and to Morality plays and Interludes because they had the taint of 'entertainment' on them. The 'shocking' theatre was well acknowledged by 1561, when Bishop Alley preached against players in St Paul's: and throughout the reign of Elizabeth I, the Puritan ginger-groups in the City of London were decrying the plays and actors, whilst the courtiers on the one hand, and the commoners on the other, were supporting them. This tug-of-war is a background to the greatest period in the whole history of English drama. It highlights the boldness and conviction that, in 1576, drove

James Burbage to build the first purpose-built 'theatre' in Britain, at least since Roman occupation.

Because of Burbage's enterprise, 1576 has been called 'the most significant date in the history of English drama'. The claim is worth making. Burbage was a businessman as well as an actor, and he calculated that the time was ripe for business and theatre to join hands. The building was called, simply, the Theatre. If the hunch had not paid off, Burbage would be forgotten, and Shakespeare possibly remembered as a poet rather than as a playwright. In fact, though, Burbage was responding sensitively to the spirit of his age. His was the first public playhouse, but in the same year Richard Farrant established the first 'private' playhouse in what had been the refectory of the Blackfriars before the dissolution of the monasteries. Farrant was Master of the Children of the Chapel Royal, and it was for his choirboys that he converted the refectory into an indoor theatre, where the boys played to a select audience of patrons, quite distinct from the boisterous groundlings of the public theatre. The split between a 'popular' audience and an educated 'minority' audience has, with varying degrees of harmfulness, continued to bedevil the British theatre ever since. So much so that, in the present-day theatre, a play that is, according to acceptable critical criteria, 'good', has at the same time to be recognized as 'unpopular'. It is rarely by staging a good play that a hard-pressed theatrical management will hope to recoup its losses.

There seems to have been no such distinction in the Elizabethan age. The taste for novelty did not frighten the playwrights. It challenged them. Between 1580 and 1630, you could hope to fill a theatre with a new play. It scarcely mattered who wrote it. But the lifetime of most plays was short – durability was generally a sign of quality. Shakespeare preferred to write alone (though his collaborative work on *Pericles, Henry VIII, The Two Noble Kinsmen* and *Sir Thomas More* is generally acknowledged), but his contemporaries often combined to expedite production. A theatre company could buy a five-act play for £6; and that money, as like as not, would be divided between three contributing dramatists. Thomas Dekker, let us say, might agree to write an Act One for Henslowe because all he was doing at the time was a final act for a boys' company and an alteration to an 'old' play, newly commanded at Court, for the Lord Chamberlain's Men.

It is impossible finally to explain why the forty years between 1576 and Shakespeare's death in 1616 should have produced so much superb drama. It is the only period in which great poets in plenty have proved also to be competent playmakers. Something is owed to a determination to resist with energy the Puritans' passionate repression. In 1597, a

Privy Council order that all playhouses in London be destroyed was circumvented. Forty-five years later, Charles I fled from London, and Puritan fervour succeeded in closing all theatres by an Act of Parliament. The great days were over by then. The theatre companies had, since early in the seventeenth century, recognized that the Court was a patron quite as important as the public – and an increasingly sophisticated and comparatively soft-bellied drama was competing for royal favour with the empty but spectacular Court Masques. The Jacobean and Caroline taste was more for Beaumont and Fletcher (who could take a strong theme and beautifully trivialize it) than for Shakespeare, Jonson and Webster. The major dramatic event of the years immediately following the closing of the theatres was the publication in 1647 of a Folio edition of the Comedies and Tragedies of Beaumont and Fletcher. The publication twenty-four years earlier of the Shakespeare Folio can be seen as a farewell to the old order; that of the Beaumont and Fletcher Folio as a promise that the theatre will not let itself be killed, but that it may settle for a lower life-style.

With the Restoration of Charles II in 1660, the hopes of the professional theatre revived. The King was not, however, in a position to take too many risks with a dangerously powerful public medium. The Letters Patent he issued in 1662 divided between two loyal servants of his exile (Thomas Killigrew and William Davenant) the control of all drama performed within the city of Westminster. The resultant monopoly by the Patent theatres of all legitimate (a difficult word to define – though it quickly came to mean 'non-musical') drama lasted until 1843; and the struggle between the two Patent theatres and the many minor theatres that sprang up, were harassed and suppressed, and were revived to fight on, is a major feature of 180 years of London's theatre history.

It is always interesting to see what survives after the forced interruption of historical evolution. The confusions and crises of the seventeenth century had destroyed the confidence in God's good order that is a bedrock of Elizabethan tragedy. George Steiner's view that tragedy cannot survive the disintegration of communal values has much to commend it. So does Wilson Knight's short view of comedy: 'The proper function of comedy is to assist the assimilation of instincts, especially sexual instincts.' Comedy survived the Civil War more easily than tragedy, but it carried the scars. At its best, in Wycherley and Congreve for example, Restoration comedy perceives and expresses acutely the motives and behaviour of people under emotional pressure. At its worst, it exploits sexual instincts. No theatre historian can neglect the impact on the written drama of the arrival of actresses on the public stage. Openly or covertly, the post-Restoration theatre has been preoccupied with sex. The emergence of the actress aided the significant downgrading of the dramatist. The Restoration theatre belongs as much to Betterton and Anne Oldfield as it does to Etherege and Vanbrugh. The quintessential figure is Colley Cibber, actor *and* dramatist, a gifted egotist with an eye for the main chance and a subtle knack of guiding any hand that offered to butter his bread.

In view of the emphatic sexuality of Restoration comedies, and the similar concerns of the heroic, wordy plays in rhymed couplets favoured by writers of tragedy, the widespread disapproval of the drama of the period is not surprising. Controversy raged, actors were assaulted, actresses made advantageous marriages, and an age with a taste for exhibitionism found itself reflected with canny accuracy in the theatre. The current tendency is to underrate Restoration comedy, perhaps because we are living at a time when sexual honesty is once again permissible, and virtually to ignore Restoration tragedy. That is all the more a pity because a study of the lacerating wit of the best Restoration writing, and of the peculiar relationship between satirical playwrights and an audience that almost liked to be offended, might still teach us something about ourselves. For the first time in the history of the English public theatre, the audience was a minority one – as it is now: and it was an audience that applauded the attacks on the rottenness of a society and a social system of which it was a beneficiary – as does the audience now.

Restoration comedy was offensive to the surviving Puritan spirit for venereal reasons. Its intricate plots accommodate adultery, and make a frolic out of lust. A reaction was inevitable. Theatre is invariably provoking. Jeremy Collier's *Short View of the Immorality and Profaneness of the English Stage* (1698) was the most effective of many attacks. Congreve allowed himself to be driven from the stage by the outcry, and a softer style of writing replaced his disconcerting acerbity. Restoration comedy owed much to Ben Jonson: its underlying toughness, its recognition that in a money-minded world a human being is a commodity, its delight in permitting the wit to expose the fool. The comedy of sentiment that ousted this comedy of manners in the early years of the eighteenth century was more benevolent and less accurate. The playwrights avoided any episode too strong to be forgotten in the euphoria of a happy ending. Any villain was likely to experience a change of heart in the fifth act after the frustrations of the first four. George Colman the Younger recalled a play sent to him at the Haymarket, whose final act included the marvellously inept stage direction, 'Here the Miser leans against the wall and grows generous.'

Although it has led to the unmerited neglect of such a skilful playwright as Arthur Murphy, the traditional verdict that the plays of Sheridan and Goldsmith's *She Stoops to Conquer* are outstanding amid eighteenth-century mediocrity is an understandable one. An occasional rediscovery, like the Royal Shakespeare Company's of John O'Keefe's *Wild Oats* (1791), cannot alter the significant fact that, after Congreve's angry rejection of the stage in 1700, the best writers fought shy of the theatre. With only a few notable exceptions, that holds true until 1956.

The increase of literacy in the eighteenth century encouraged the rise of the novel. If comedy felt the pinch, tragedy felt it more viciously. The graveyard of English drama is full of stillborn tragedies, ambitious responses to the assertion that English drama can be revived only through the birth of a new tragedy. Most of those who tried took Shakespeare as their model, peppering the lines with 'forsooth' and 'perchance', and hoping to make blank verse speak as directly to a later age as it had to the Elizabethans. The modest success of Lillo's *The London Merchant* (1731) was of a different kind. The play is written in pompous prose, and has not much more than its honesty to recommend it. Lillo wrote for a middle-class audience, and he preached the middle-class gospel of thrift with a cautionary tale about the corruption of a young apprentice by a scarlet woman. The place of bourgeois tragedy on the English stage was never central, but Lillo's example was followed by Edward Moore in *The Gamester* (1753), and had an acknowledged influence on the development of 'domestic' tragedy in France and Germany. It found a more natural home in nineteenth-century melodrama.

Neither comedy nor tragedy was sufficient to satisfy the audiences or the managers of the Patent theatres. The early years of the eighteenth century saw the legitimate drama looking increasingly for illegitimate aids to support it. None was more significant than pantomime. When John Rich, holder of the patent at the theatre in Lincoln's Inn Fields (Drury Lane was built in 1674, Covent Garden not until 1731), presented himself as a silent Harlequin in 1717, in a pantomime called *Harlequin Executed*, he set a fashion. When the manager of Drury Lane staged a rival pantomime, spectacle was in full competition with the legitimate drama for control of the public imagination. It is a mistake often made by those who write literary histories of the drama to suppose that a decline in the quality of its playwrights implies a decline in the fortunes of the theatre. On the contrary, the theatre has rarely, if ever, been as popular in England as it was during the eighteenth and nineteenth centuries, despite the fact that there were less fine plays written in those two hundred years than in the twenty years from 1588 to 1608, or in the twenty years from 1956 to 1976. During these two hundred years, theatre managers were less interested in staging good *new* plays than in staging good *old* plays, and spectacular new ones, however bad.

Two dates of major importance in the history of the English theatre need to be mentioned before we can leave the eighteenth century. The first is 1737, the year in which Walpole carried through parliament a system of theatrical censorship sufficiently rigorous more or less to prevent any playwright from saying anything serious about politics or religion. It was not until 1968 that these powers of the Lord Chamberlain's office were renounced. What had annoyed Walpole – it is an example of the 'shocking' power of the theatre – was the activity, at a minor, illegitimate theatre, of a man now much more famous as a novelist, Henry Fielding. What had annoyed Fielding was Walpole, and he made his annoyance felt in a series of witty political satires. The 1737 Licensing Act put a stop to that, and also, effectively, to Fielding's career as a dramatist. His plight is exemplary. What great writer will ever agree with all the established attitudes to politics and religion? And what art form can survive healthily the command to conform? The second date is 1741, the year in which, at a theatre in Goodman's Fields, David Garrick made his (strictly speaking illegal) professional debut as Richard III. Garrick was, without question, a great actor. What is almost equally significant, he was a man of culture and intelligence, acceptable to the society of the literary salons, friend of Samuel Johnson, and a force powerful enough to raise the status of the actor. His management of Drury Lane from 1746 to 1776 is one of the great events of English theatrical history. If the nineteenth century was the heyday of the star-actor and eventually of the actor-manager, Garrick led the way. After 1741, and certainly until Henry Irving's death in 1905, the history of the English drama is not separable from that of its leading actors and actresses.

In broad outline, the nineteenth century is not outstandingly different from the eighteenth. Most of the good plays performed were *old*. Most of the new plays written were suited to the average customer. The actor was king, and the designer and stage machinist his chief minister. The playwright was paid by the act, and according to the length of a play's run. He might have made his fortune by robbing a bank, but not until the copyright laws were established, and reinforced by a system that allowed the dramatist to share the profits of a successful run, did he have any chance of growing rich inside the theatre. Edward Fitzball records a melancholy occasion when the company forgot even to invite him to the celebration after the successful launching of one of his spectacular melodramas.

Melodrama is a word we have to pause on. The first play to be so styled on its English staging was Thomas Holcroft's *A Tale of Mystery*. That was in 1802, but there was nothing sudden or new about Holcroft's style. Disaster at your own hearthside had been dramatized by Lillo and his successors, and the Gothic novel (*The Castle of Otranto* dates from as early as 1764) heralded the taste that would appreciate exotic alternatives to domestic doom. Nor was the basic narrative device of melodrama – the trick of making tragedy unavoidable and then avoiding it – new: Shakespeare relies on it in *Measure for Measure* and there are innumerable other plays that do the same. Modern audiences find the exaggerated villainy and the overblown sentiment of nineteenth-century melodrama funny. The original audiences did not. Melodrama, unlike tragedy, plays on the nerves rather than the emotions, but you have to be afraid for the heroine, you have to accept that sex before marriage *is* a fate worse than death. There is something paradoxical in its popularity: for the respectable Victorian audience, melodrama was an acceptable form of entertainment, because right values won out in the end, but there is a pornographic, or at least a lubricious undercurrent which does quite as much to explain the success of the genre. Another vital factor was the spectacle. A scene-painter had to create a moonlit ruin or a dockland slum, and a machinist needed to be able to show a real train-crash, a fire at sea, or even the Boat Race. The cinema took over this aspect of melodrama, but not because the theatre's attempts were unimpressive. More recently, television has become the home of melodrama, newly dressed as a police or hospital series.

The nineteenth century saw an increase in the number of London's theatres to match the astonishing increase in the city's population. Some of them were huge. Drury Lane, rebuilt in 1794, could seat 3,600, Covent Garden a few hundred less. The rougher South Bank theatres, like the Surrey, may have accommodated even more. Such size affected playwrights as well as actors. Melodrama and farce rely on broad strokes and extremes of character. The most popular of Shakespeare's plays – *Othello, Macbeth, Richard III, Romeo and Juliet, The Merchant of Venice, Hamlet* – were those most easily adapted to the taste of the time, the most 'melodramatic'. The 'minor' theatres became bolder in their defiance of the Patent theatres' monopoly over the legitimate drama. The Theatres Act of 1843 abolished the monopoly, and the playwright and antiquarian Planché celebrated at the Olympic the fact that:

> Shakespeare now at Islington may shine,
> Marylebone echo Marlowe's mighty line.

It was Drury Lane and Covent Garden, the previously patented theatres, that felt the pinch. Too big for the newer, more naturalistic plays of the latter half of the nineteenth century, they soon abandoned drama in favour of spectacle and opera.

'Naturalistic' is a question-begging word. The simplest way of expressing the complex factors that prepared the way for the reception of Ibsen is historical. In 1867, a moderate but decidedly self-important actor called Squire Bancroft married a lady who had recently rejected a sensational career in burlesque at the Strand Theatre. (She gratified a forbidden Victorian delight in female legs by playing male leads in the burlesque travesties that attracted packed houses.) She was Marie Wilton, and had been, for two years, the manageress of the previously unfashionable Prince of Wales's Theatre. Mainly by luck, but partly by good judgment, she had decided to stage *Society*, a much-rejected play by a journeyman-dramatist called T.W. (Tom) Robertson. That was in 1865. It was followed the next year by another Robertson hit, *Ours*, and in 1867 by his masterpiece, *Caste*. Under the management of the Bancrofts, the day of the long run was established. So was Robertson, who died untimely in 1870. His plays are technically accomplished, and they had the priceless asset of novelty. Robertson domesticated melodrama, and turned it towards comedy. Where Boucicault might feature a sensational rescue or a fire at sea, Robertson featured the making of a roly-poly pudding (with real pastry!); and after Robertson, in what William Archer called 'the school of Robertsonian realism', came Henry Arthur Jones, Pinero, Galsworthy, Houghton, Brighouse, Noel Coward, Rattigan, Ayckbourn. The dialect changes, but the strategy remains the same. It risks the treatment of a serious social theme or moral issue, but goes no further than at least half of the audience would go.

Such caution is too readily derided. Oscar Wilde went no further in his plays than Pinero, though he allows his dandies some subversively witty lines. Only his best play, *The Importance of Being Earnest* (1895), resists the pull of Robertsonian realism by being consistently flippant. Its title is ironic, not only because it contradicts the play, but also because it cocks a snook at so much contemporary drama: for instance, at Henry James's *Guy Domville*, whose disastrous failure at the St James's forced George Alexander to stage Wilde's masterpiece earlier than he had intended. There, if you like, is an interesting illustration of the specialist art of the playwright. James was at the height of his literary career in 1895, perhaps planning *The Spoils of Poynton*, but he could not write a successful play.

The year 1895 is of interest for other reasons. It was the year in which

Wilde was first accused of the deed without a name (in response to the scandal, George Alexander closed the run of *The Importance of Being Earnest*). It was the year in which Henry Irving became the first actor ever to be knighted. And it was the year in which Irving's adversary, George Bernard Shaw, became drama critic of *The Saturday Review*. Martin Meisel has brilliantly shown how much Shaw depended, in his own plays, on the nineteenth-century modes he plundered, parodied, and exploited. Shaw was the first major writer since Sheridan to turn his attention fully to the theatre. He castigated Irving for his refusal to perform the new drama, and he wrote a spirited defence of Ibsen, which is also a puff for his own plays. Not all his plays are as effective as he was, but his verbal energy is unrivalled. He devoted his life to talking the hind legs off donkeys, and, in defiance of the censorship, he made the theatre his public forum. For all of forty years, his was the most adult and the most boyish voice in a theatre of arrested development.

The music halls had drained much of the popular interest from the theatre in the nineteenth century, and variety shows and working-men's clubs have continued to do so in the twentieth. Shaw's intention was to make the theatre worthier, more unrepentant, and no less popular, but the support for his Ibsenite theatre of social and moral challenge was dominantly highbrow. The effect has been to divide the serious playwright from his popular audience more completely than at any time since the Restoration. Provincial resistance to this division expressed itself in the Repertory Theatre movement. The performance of new and classical plays for short runs became a model, which has survived, with many variations, since Annie Horniman's patronage allowed the establishment of a Repertory Theatre in Manchester in 1908. Glasgow followed in 1909, Liverpool in 1911, and Birmingham in 1913. Miss Horniman's first venture into patronage had occurred in Dublin in 1903, when she provided vital finance for W. B. Yeats and the Abbey Theatre. The Irish Dramatic Movement impressed London, but it was not until O'Casey's quarrel with Yeats brought him to England that any of its major dramatists looked for initial performance to the English theatre. The astonishing work that grew in Dublin out of the Irish revival was never matched in the English Repertory Theatre, whose vital contribution has been to English acting more than to English writing, but the dignity of the provincial drama has been too often neglected.

Two events anticipated the recovery of English drama generally associated with the staging of Osborne's *Look Back in Anger* at the Royal Court in 1956. The first was the performance in London in 1955 of Beckett's *Waiting for Godot*, a play which rephrased the claims of drama as a philosophical form. The second was the visit to London in 1956 of the Berliner Ensemble to present a season of Brecht's plays. Brecht died two weeks before the visit, but his plays were a powerful statement of the potential of drama as a political form. George Devine, director of the English Stage Company at the Royal Court, was alert to the new possibilities, and an enlightened defender of the young playwrights whose work he presented. Osborne, Arden and Wesker were among those who benefited from his policies. They became leaders of a new drama more concerned to rock the boat than continue the cruise. The plays of Pinter reached the same audience, though at different theatres. Edward Bond has been the most prominent of a second generation of Royal Court apprentices.

The successes of British post-war drama could not have happened without subsidy from the Arts Council. The commercial theatre, undermined by increasing costs, has dwindled. The Repertory Theatre movement has had to take refuge in 'safe' programming underpinned by subsidy. The national companies, the Royal Shakespeare Company and the National Theatre, have struggled to make ends meet despite ample-sounding Arts Council support. The traditional Council policy of responsiveness tempered by occasional assassinations has always attracted hostility, but it remains difficult to foresee a future for the professional theatre without subsidy. During the ten years from 1968, the Arts Council was able to reward a vigorous crop of theatre groups, some, like 7:84 and Belt and Braces, politically radical, some, like the People Show and Pip Simmons, radically imaginative. They provided the stimulus for a new general of playwrights: Howard Brenton, David Hare, Caryl Churchill and David Edgar, for example, enhanced and benefited from this 'fringe' theatre. By 1980, the climate was less hospitable, and these same writers were finding more scope in the national companies.

The struggle for survival continues. It took a new turn in March 1984, when the Arts Council published a policy statement under the bucolic title *The Glory of the Garden*. The declared intention was to redistribute resources to the advantage of regional centres of excellence, but Government funding of the arts is insufficient to provide much benefit even to the favoured. Sir Peter Hall's view is widely shared in the gloom of 1985: 'Many theatres up and down the country are suffering a loss of nerve, because they feel that the Government and the Arts Council are no longer supporting them.' There is no doubt that the British theatre, its actors, playwrights and administrators, will continue to feel the pinch for the rest of the present century.

American Drama and Performance

An Outline History

It was not until quite late in the eighteenth century that serious attempts began to be made to establish for the American theatre an identity separate from England's. That is a familiar aspect of colonial history; the pioneer spirit does not extend to the arts at once. The territorial ambition of the seventeenth-century settlers left little time for the pursuit of cultural innovation. Add to that the strong Puritan element among English immigrants and the recipe for theatrical sterility is perfect. The first European play known to have been performed in the North American continent was in Spanish and it was the French, rather than the English, who made the early moves towards establishing dramatic performances. The native Indian tradition of dance and ritual, which is of considerable interest to modern anthropologists and historians of presentational art, was hidden from the invading pioneers.

The earliest 'English' theatre building of which there is any record was in Williamsburg, Virginia in 1716 and, before mid-century, there is evidence of dramatic activity in New York, Philadelphia and Charleston, South Carolina. The population was too small and too scattered to encourage anything more than sporadic performances. The first move towards a professional theatre was made by Walter Murray and Thomas Kean, who gathered a company in Philadelphia in 1749 and toured to New York and Williamsburg in 1750 and 1751. Better established and more influential was the English company of Lewis Hallam, which gave its first American performance in Williamsburg in 1752. It was this group, reorganized under Hallam's widow's second husband, David Douglass, that opened America's first 'permanent' theatre, the Southwark in Philadelphia, in 1766. The following year, Douglass staged the first play by an American, Thomas Godfrey's heroic tragedy, *The Prince of Parthia*, and in 1768 opened the John Street Theatre in New York.

It would be surprising if the War for Independence had had no impact on the growing American theatre. It is, perhaps, surprising that it had so little. The patriotic blank-verse squibs of Mercy Otis Warren, *The Adulateur* (1773) and *The Group* (1775), are intriguing documents but scarcely plays. They are among a handful of loyalist works in dramatic form, none of them staged. George Washington's interest in theatre (he held a box at the John Street Theatre during his first year as President) gave more of a fillip to native American talent than any written product of the conflict with England. It was in the regrouping of Douglass's company of actors under John Henry and Lewis Hallam Jr that the spirit of independence best declared itself. Boldly calling themselves the Old American Company, they toured America from Philadelphia to New York and on to Charleston. At the John Street Theatre in 1787 they presented the first notable American play, Royall Tyler's comedy *The Contrast*. The company was formed along familiar English lines, with stock types like 'gentleman comedian', 'low comedian', 'juvenile lead' and 'old gentleman', but it performed efficiently enough to increase the local demand for a theatre wherever it went. Quaker Philadelphia once again surrendered to public pressure and, in 1794, allowed the erection of the Chestnut Street Theatre. In the same year, the Federal Street Theatre opened in Boston. (At much the same time, the Franco-Spanish town of New Orleans was building its first theatres, to house drama in French. It was not until the arrival there in 1820 of James Caldwell that the English drama was established in New Orleans.)

The emergent American theatre at the turn of the century is well represented by William Dunlap (1766–1839), the country's first professional dramatist. Born in New Jersey, he was in England from 1784 to 1787, supposedly to study painting under Benjamin West, but increasingly lured into the London theatres. On his return to New York, he became immediately involved with the John Street Theatre, first as dramatist (*The Father*, 1789; *Leicester*, 1794, etc.) and then as joint manager from 1797 to 1798, during the building and opening of the Park Theatre. In trying to formulate a policy for the Park Theatre, Dunlap had little more than his own inventiveness to rely on. Between 1798 and 1800 he wrote and produced nineteen versions of plays by Kotzebue, as well as the best of his own plays, *André* (1798). The choice of Kotzebue was as effective in New York as it was, over exactly the same period, in London, but Dunlap's management was blighted by outbreaks of yellow fever and he was declared bankrupt in 1805. A year later, he was back in harness as assistant manager to the admired English actor, Thomas Abthorpe Cooper. It was also through Cooper that Dunlap became involved in the last, and in some ways the toughest, of his managerial enterprises. Cooper had engaged the English actor George Frederick Cooke to perform at the Park and subsequently to tour the American theatre circuit in 1812. It was a notable coup, for

Cooke was undoubtedly a fine actor, the greatest England had yet exported to America. Unfortunately, he was also a drunkard and it fell to the lot of the somewhat prim Dunlap to supervise the tour that, as it proved, occupied the last months of Cooke's life. If the experience of shepherding a dying and disorderly actor through a taxing tour caused Dunlap to abandon his active involvement in the theatre, it also initiated a new phase in his career. Within a year of Cooke's death, Dunlap had published a two-volume biography of the actor. He spent his remaining years painting and writing, his final significant contribution to the profession he had served so conscientiously being a *History of the American Theatre* (1832). Despite many inaccuracies, the book is a pointed identification of a national presence that Dunlap had helped to advance.

Cooke's engagement at the Park Theatre from 1810 and his tour of 1812 marked the beginning of the American theatre's dangerous commitment to a 'star system'. The old stock companies could not rival the attraction of a visit from a celebrity. The story of the American theatre between 1800 and the Civil War is primarily one of actors, not of dramatists. There was already some precedent in New York for the glorification of a single performer. In 1809, with the bravado that preserved him from slings and arrows in his own country as well as in England, John Howard Payne presented himself as an 'infant prodigy' at the Park Theatre in roles ranging from Romeo to Rolla in Sheridan's *Pizarro*. Payne was untutored, explosive and, at seventeen, a little too old to be called an infant. In the event, it was not his acting in America but his writing in England that did most for his country's theatrical reputation. His nineteen years in London (1813–32) were a mixed bag of triumph and disaster, but he returned home in 1832 as the author of a tragedy, *Brutus* (1818), in which Edmund Kean had starred at Drury Lane and which gave a mighty role, too, to the first American tragic star, Edwin Forrest.

Forrest was born in Philadelphia and made his debut at the Walnut Street Theatre there, but it was by touring in the South and by a rise to leading roles at the Charles Street Theatre in New Orleans that he prepared himself for his supremacy in the new capital of American drama, New York. Forrest's acting was a virile expression of the pioneering spirit of self-help and self-sufficiency. When the English actor, George Vandenhoff, saw him playing Metamora in 1842 he acknowledged that, 'for power of destructive energy, I never heard any thing on the stage so tremendous in its sustained crescendo swell, and crashing force of utterance'. That was thirteen years after Forrest had first caught the popular imagination of New York – he was always more admired by the mass than by the cultural European-minded elite – in the title role of John Augustus Stone's play. Fascinated by what he knew of the American Indians, Forrest had offered a prize 'for the best tragedy, in five acts, of which the hero shall be an aboriginal of this country', and Stone's *Metamora* had won it. It remained in Forrest's repertoire for forty years, alongside another American play, tailor-made for a display of muscular heroics, Robert Montgomery Bird's *The Gladiator* (1831). It was as Spartacus in Bird's play that Forrest opened his assault on English audiences at Drury Lane in 1836. That he was pugnaciously patriotic is certain. His challenge to English actors was as brash as that of a baseball batter taking on the English opening attack at Lord's. He was even prepared to risk himself in the favourite part of England's leading tragedian, Macready, that of Macbeth.

What followed is a fascinating story, illustrative not only of the difficult growth of the American theatre in the face of English snobbery, but also of the vehemence with which the nineteenth century fought its theatrical battles in both countries. We can trace it through Macready's *Diaries*. The two men first met on 14 October 1836. 'Liked him much,' noted Macready. 'A noble appearance, and a manly, mild, and interesting demeanour. . . . He mentioned to me his purpose of leaving the stage, and devoting himself to politics – if he should become President!' Ten days later, he recorded his reactions to reports of Forrest's Othello: 'It would be stupid and shallow hypocrisy to say that I was indifferent to the result – careless whether he is likely to be esteemed less or more than myself; it is of great importance to me to retain my superiority, and my wishes for his success follow the desire I have to be considered above him!' Throughout Forrest's London engagement, Macready followed his progress avidly, but he never went to watch him act. The opportunity to make good that omission came during Macready's American tour of 1843–4. Forrest welcomed him to New York on the day of his arrival there and Macready dined with him on 3 October 1843: 'I like all I see of Forrest very much. He appears a clear-headed, honest, kind man; what can be better?' But a note of caution, dangerously identified with national differences, entered into Macready's estimate of Forrest's acting of King Lear on 21 October: 'I could discern no imagination, no original thought, no poetry at all. . . . But the state of society here and the condition of the fine arts are in themselves evidences of the improbability of an artist being formed by them.' Needled by a newspaper comparison, Macready noted of Forrest on 28 October: 'Let him be an American actor – and a great American actor – but keep on this side of the Atlantic, and no one will gainsay his comparative excellence.'

Inevitably, Forrest got wind of Macready's criticisms and his response was characteristically combative. When Macready performed in Philadelphia, Forrest rallied his home-town support by acting at the Walnut Street Theatre the same parts Macready was playing at the Chestnut Street Theatre – and on the same nights. 'This is not the English generosity of rivalry,' Macready commented on 7 September 1844. It was an ominous background to Forrest's second English tour of 1846. Matters came to a head in Edinburgh on 2 March 1846, when Forrest was in the audience for Macready's Hamlet and hissed one of the English actor's favourite 'points'. There was uproar in the national press, culminating in Forrest's confessing to the hiss in a letter to *The Times*. 'I do not think that such an action has its parallel in all theatrical history!' wrote Macready. 'The low-minded ruffian! That man would commit a murder, *if he dare*.' From now on, for both men, the quarrel was not only personal but national. 'I feel I cannot *stomach* the United States as a nation,' noted Macready on 27 March 1846, and on 26 October, having read some favourable reviews of Forrest's acting in New York, admitted that they 'depressed me a little, in presenting America – or rather the United States – as a country for blackguards'.

Forrest has taken, and deserves, much blame for the tragic final episode of this discreditable saga, but Macready's sense of personal and national superiority was certainly provocative. When Macready set out for a further tour of America in September 1848, he had in mind the intention of putting an upstart theatre firmly in its place. Two days after his arrival, he was angrily complaining: 'The complacency, indeed the *approbation* with which a paper speaks of the "independence" of Mr Forrest (an ignorant, uneducated man, burning with envy and rancour at my success) hissing me in the Edinburgh Theatre, makes me feel that I seek in vain to accommodate myself to such utterly uncongenial natures.' The theatre of two nations was on trial, and Macready was as ready to judge as Forrest was to prosecute. 'Rehearsed with care,' reads the diary entry for 10 November 1848, 'but I have *brutes* to deal with – not intelligences – "*ignorance made drunk*" will well describe American actors from Mr Forrest downwards!' The whole of Macready's 1848–9 tour was a prolongation of his war with Forrest. The culmination came in New York in May 1849. With 'nativist' fervour at its height and with the urban proletariat rallying behind Forrest, Macready opened in *Macbeth* at the Astor Place Opera House on 7 May. The performance was made chaotic by interventions from the audience. A rotten egg was thrown, 'Down with the English hog!' was chanted and the management eventually brought down the curtain when chairs, hurled from the gallery, crashed on to the stage. Macready made a dignified escape through the back door of the theatre and determined to perform no more in New York. But prominent New Yorkers were determined to vindicate their city against the mob of 'Forresters' and prevailed upon their English visitor to play Macbeth again on 10 May. Trouble was inevitable and riot police were assembled around Astor Place. The night was an extraordinary one. Inside the theatre *Macbeth* was played through with only a few interruptions, but the catcalls of the mob outside were audible. With no hope of controlling them, the police withdrew to be replaced by the militia. By the time the sixty horsemen arrived, missiles of all kinds were being hurled at the theatre. The cavalrymen were routed and replaced by a troop of infantrymen with fixed bayonets. The Riot Act was read twice with no effect and eventually the order to fire was given. Some twenty Americans, most of them young labourers, were left dead in Astor Place when the rioters fled. At the nearby Broadway Theatre, Forrest completed his performance in *The Gladiator*. Macready mingled with the audience as it nervously left the Astor Place Opera House and escaped to Boston by way of New Rochelle.

The Forrest-Macready quarrel is an important background to the American theatre's quest for its own distinction. English stars continued to tour throughout the nineteenth century – Edmund Kean, Charles and Fanny Kemble, Henry Irving – often outshining native talent. Charlotte Cushman, who made her debut in New York in 1835, was not fully recognized in her own country until after she had triumphed in London. The staple fare of theatres from New England to Kentucky (a theatre was opened in Frankfort in 1815 – the first in the West) was not very different from that of the English provincial theatres. One original contribution was the 'Yankee', whose colourfully idiosyncratic way with words was first dramatized in the Jonathan of Royall Tyler's *The Contrast* as early as 1787. The specialist was George Handel Hill, but even he was impelled to test his authenticity in London in 1836. Nevertheless, the many Yankee plays written between 1830 and 1850, though they have little literary quality, were intrinsically celebrations of the American character. A more sophisticated and impressive vindication of the home-grown was Anna Cora Mowatt's comedy, *Fashion*, presented at New York's Park Theatre in 1845. Mrs Mowatt was a new phenomenon on the American stage. Not only was she a member of the best New York society when she decided to become an actress, but also she was accepted back into (Richmond) society when she made a second marriage to the Virginian journalist, William Ritchie. The significance of her brief theatrical career was not lost on such successors as Laura Keene, Mrs John Drew, Minnie Maddern Fiske and Ethel Barrymore.

The rich potential of the mid-century American theatre was both recognized and exploited by Dion Boucicault. The Irish actor-dramatist had left London as something of a black sheep, named by Charles Kean as the seducer of his ward, Agnes Robertson. Boucicault made reparation by marrying Agnes in New York in 1853, a month after his arrival in America, and immediately set about organizing for his wife an immensely successful tour of American theatres. He wrote with alacrity plays that together they performed with aplomb, and he was soon the major working dramatist in the country. A two-year tour from 1853 to 1855 included engagements in New York, Boston, Philadelphia, Mobile, New Orleans, Cincinnati and St Louis. At the end of it, Boucicault bought the lease of the Varieties Theatre in New Orleans, renamed it the Gaiety and began the first of his many short and uniformly disastrous periods in management. At various times over the next three decades he ran theatres in Washington, New York and San Francisco as well as in London. In addition, most of his major plays were written and first produced in America. *The Poor of New York* (1857) created a vogue for topical, localized drama. *Jessie Brown* (1858) took spectacular melodrama to new heights. *The Octoroon* (1859), however tentatively, introduced to New York a serious confrontation of the issues of slavery four days after the hanging of the abolitionist agitator John Brown. It was also in New York that Boucicault staged the first performances of his two finest plays, *The Colleen Bawn* (1860) and *The Shaughraun* (1874). But his impact on the American theatre was not confined to acting, writing and managing. It was his flair for public campaigning that added ginger to George Henry Boker's efforts to bring about a reform in the American copyright laws. By the amendment of 1856, playwrights were given, for the first time, 'the sole right to print and publish the said composition, the sole right also to act, perform, or represent the same, or cause it to be acted, performed, or represented, on any stage or public place'. In addition, Boucicault was unusually painstaking in the rehearsing and staging of his plays. To some extent he raised the standard and the expectations of actors, a contribution that was acknowledged in the last year of his life when he was invited to run a drama school attached to the Madison Square Theatre in New York. Prominent among actors who valued his advice was Joseph Jefferson III.

With a copyright law much more encouraging to native dramatists, and with a new generation of actors, among whom Jefferson and Lester Wallack had long careers ahead of them at mid-century and Laura

Keene and Matilda Heron briefer but vivid lives in melodrama, it seemed only a matter of time before the United States would produce a great playwright. There had been powerful achievements in the novel and in poetry: Melville's *Moby Dick* (1851), Hawthorne's *The Scarlet Letter* (1850), Poe's *Tales* (1845) and Whitman's *Leaves of Grass* (1855) were all published during a rich ten years: but drama, during the same ten years, had provided nothing more notable than Mrs Mowatt's *Fashion* (1845) and George Henry Boker's *Francesca da Rimini* (1855), unless one considers notable the many adaptations of *Uncle Tom's Cabin* that followed hotfoot on the novel's publication in 1852. It should be remembered that the story was much the same throughout Europe. For whatever reason, this most histrionic of centuries was undramatic.

The prevailing style of acting, and theatres designed so as to turn words into pictures, go some way towards explaining the lack of great plays. To be word-perfect in theatres that changed plays each day was impossible for most actors, and they had to substitute their personalities and their old tricks to cover for them. The techniques were unashamedly 'artful'. What was so remarkable about Jefferson's Rip Van Winkle (first played in 1865) and Matilda Heron's Camille (first played in 1855) was their apparent artlessness. American audiences were familiar with the naturalness of Yankee character-actors like Hill, or the Bowery Bhoy line in which Frank Chanfrau specialized, but not with performers in the legitimate drama who walked on to the stage as if into a real room rather than a framed and face-on one. The dramatists who took advantage of the new realism were not outstanding literary figures, but they were highly competent theatrically, and they had an advantage over those who had written for the pre-Civil War stage. The growth of the city population allowed the slow beginning of a long-run system in place of the nightly change of repertoire. Realistic plays needed realistic settings; special effects needed specially constructed scenery. Only if a play was likely to have several consecutive performances was it economically viable to provide it with genuinely appropriate, localizing sets. It was population growth that permitted the development of stage realism in America.

It is not easy to recognize the excitement of an audience when it first encounters doors that really open or log cabins made of logs, but if we are to understand the impact of realism in the final decades of the nineteenth century, we need to try. When, for example, Lester Wallack was presenting the plays of T. W. Robertson to the audiences of Wallack's Theatre in New York at much the same time as the Bancrofts were presenting them at the Prince of Wales's in London, he could rely, like them, on public pleasure in the contemplation of handles that turned and kettles that boiled. Young David Belasco, working in the Sacramento theatre in 1874, had the opportunity of watching one of the pioneers of sensational realism in action when Boucicault visited the town. Belasco was, briefly, Boucicault's secretary. He would remember the working camera of *The Octoroon* (1859), the ticking telegraph of *The Long Strike* (1866) and the last-second escape from the onrushing underground train in *After Dark* (1868).

There was one very influential figure in the American theatre who had probably also taken note of that scene in *After Dark*. That was Augustin Daly, from whose *Under the Gaslight* (1867) Boucicault had stolen it. Daly was working as a dramatic critic when he wrote his early plays, of which *The Flash of Lightning* (1868) was the most successful, but 1869 saw the beginning of thirty years of theatre management that provided Americans with a new model for commitment to theatre, not simply as a business, but also as an art. The majority of Daly's own plays are adaptations, cleverly 'americanized' versions of German or French originals or reshapings of English classics from Shakespeare to Sheridan, but they were skilfully suited to the company of actors gradually assembled at Daly's Theatre. By the time he undertook the first of several international tours, in 1884, Daly had brought together the first American ensemble. The actor-manager Henry Miller informatively recalls 'one of his remedies for a lack of action created by unbroken dialogue. Whenever we had a particularly long speech to read, Daly taught us to interpolate a stroll from one side of the stage to the other, under the pretence that some object at the further end of the room had caught our attention.' The 'Daly cross' was well known to his regular actors, of whom Ada Rehan and John Drew were outstanding. Not least, though not only, by impressing the London critics, Daly did as much as anyone to give the American theatre a confidence in its own identity.

Much louder, and more impressed with himself than with Daly, David Belasco took stagey realism into the realms of exhibitionism. His play *The Governor's Lady* (1912) required a restaurant interior, so he bought the fittings of a Child's restaurant, lock, stock and barrel, and put them on the stage intact. From Belasco's Broadway to Hollywood was a short step. He had travelled east from San Francisco in 1882 on tour with his own play, *La Belle Russe* (1881), and New York was his theatrical home for fifty years. During that time, above all in his own theatre, the Belasco, after 1907, his meticulous attention to stage detail and his fascination with effective lighting made his productions magically lifelike. The 'magic' was Belasco's signature. He was a 'show-biz' personality, born in the same year as Beerbohm Tree and combining, like Tree, enough artistry with his charlatanism to command attention even when he did not deserve it. His plays are blueprints for effective production, full of the panache that carried Broadway boldly into the new century. Inevitably, Belasco became the target of intelligent critics, who recognized his technique of dressing nineteenth-century plots in twentieth-century clothes. George Jean Nathan did his best to undermine Belasco's hold on the New York public and, as late as 1970, Brooks Atkinson seems still ashamed of the power he exerted. 'David Belasco,' he asserts in *Broadway*, 'was the master of mediocrity . . . a showman masquerading as an artist'; but even Atkinson applauds Belasco's resistance to the Syndicate.

The Syndicate was certainly detrimental to the advance of the American theatre, but it represents something so fundamental to its professional history that it requires some exploration. Abe Erlanger was the most dominant of the six businessmen who formed the Syndicate in 1896. To begin with, it promised a more efficient system for the booking of shows and, particularly, the planning of tours, but it quickly adopted the methods and morality that big business shares with gangsterism. An actor or producer who refused to sign a contract with the Syndicate found it 'strangely' hard to book a Broadway theatre. Critics who attacked Syndicate shows were 'inexplicably' dismissed by their newspapers. Actors, like Minnie Maddern Fiske or Richard Mansfield, who bypassed the Syndicate would 'surprisingly' fail to get favoured parts. Not all the members of the Syndicate were as crass as Erlanger. Charles Frohman, for example, loved the theatre and promoted the work of writers of quality. Bronson Howard's *Shenandoah* (1889) was his first production and *Peter Pan* (1905), with Maude Adams in the title role, his most famous. When he died in the *Lusitania* disaster of 1915, there was genuine regret on both sides of the Atlantic. By that time the monopoly of the Syndicate had been effectively challenged by the Shubert brothers, but more by imitation than by contradiction. By linking the Broadway stage to major theatres throughout the United States, the Syndicate, and the Shuberts after it, established a network of commercialism that effectively forced all theatrical adventurousness into the sidestreets. The successful American dramatists at the end of the nineteenth century and the beginning of the twentieth – Augustus Thomas, Bronson Howard, Clyde Fitch, William Gillette, Owen Davis – were conscientiously marketable even when they had something to say. Even its strongest advocates would admit that Broadway's values have not changed much.

The beginning of a new century has a powerful effect on the human imagination, and whilst many of the leaders of the American theatre continued to look back towards the pictorial glories of the nineteenth century, there were others determined to look around and ahead. James A. Herne's *Margaret Fleming* (1890) had shown a precocious alertness to the grimly deterministic school of European naturalism, but Herne's voice was muffled by outcries against Ibsen and Zola quite as booming as those in England. It was in the Little Theatre movement that America encountered the newest European ideas and discovered its own. Before World War I there was innovative work from the Chicago Little Theatre, the New York Stage Company, the Neighbourhood Playhouse and the Washington Square Players; and George Pierce Baker's astonishingly influential graduate course at Harvard on 'The Technique of the Drama' (English 47, and subsequently known as the '47 Workshop') began in 1909. It was, however, another group, whose articles of faith included a commitment to American dramatists, that proved the most significant of all the 'little' theatres.

The Provincetown Players was founded in 1915, under the politically inspired leadership of George Cram Cook and his wife, Susan Glaspell. Fresh from a spell in Baker's 47 Workshop, Eugene O'Neill wrote the best of his early plays for Cook's young company. With some marvellously resourceful designs by Robert Edmond Jones to help them on their way, these plays, which included *The Emperor Jones* (1920), *Anna Christie* (1921) and *The Hairy Ape* (1922), reached New York and ushered in the best and most mature twenty years of the Broadway theatre. O'Neill's sombre determinism sits oddly beside the communist idealism of Cook, so that there was no real likelihood that the Provincetown Players would have a long life. A brief brilliance was, however, sufficient to inaugurate a serious challenge to the Belasco tradition of fantastic fiction in 'real' settings. Most significant of all, it was this small and eccentric group that provided a context for the first great American dramatist. Between 1920 and 1934, New York saw a new O'Neill play almost every year. It is not easy to overstate their effect. Not only the range, from Expressionism to Freudian naturalism, but also the intensity of his output was unrivalled. In order to stage some of his work, the Provincetown Players, and Robert Edmond Jones in particular, had to initiate a scenic revolution. The quest was not for an accurate surface but for visual images that could express the mood of the piece. The new possibilities released into the American theatre by O'Neill's plays contributed to a new stagecraft, made visible not only in the designs of Jones, but also in those of Donald Oenslager, Jo Mielziner and Lee Simonson.

Even more radically critical of the old pictorial school was the maverick designer, Norman Bel Geddes. Architects in America, as elsewhere in the West, had assumed that the proscenium arch was as essential to the completeness of a theatre as a nose to the completeness of a face. Bel Geddes was one of the first to challenge this assumption. His grandest scheme, a production of Dante's *Divine Comedy* which he began planning in 1921, was never realized, but his designs for Max Reinhardt of *The Miracle* (1924), of his own production of *Hamlet* (1929) and for Sidney Kingsley's *Dead End* (1935) are among the finest twentieth-century examples of imaginative concept carried through in imaginative construction. He, if anyone, might have turned the grandiose visions of Steele MacKaye (1844–94), including the 'spectatorium' designed for the abortive Chicago World Fair of 1893, into reality. Later challenges to conventional theatre architecture have been more enduring. Margo Jones (1913–55) established the first professional theatre-in-the-round in Dallas in 1945, a forerunner of the Arena Theatre in Washington, DC and the Off-Broadway Circle-in-the-Square. The thrust stage of the Tyrone Guthrie Theatre in Minneapolis is a happy result of collaborations between an enlightened university and the professional theatre. But such later developments could not have been foreseen during the inter-war years.

Those inter-war years were a period of intense and innovative activity. Both directly and indirectly, the Theatre Guild was responsible for much of it. Formed in 1918–19 and intentionally recalling in its name the mediaeval trade guilds which had taken responsibility for the production of the English Miracle cycles, the Theatre Guild aimed to raise the artistic standards of the commercial theatre. It was not restrictive in its choice of plays – it was as likely to produce the work of George Bernard Shaw as that of O'Neill, a light-hearted revue as Copeau's adaptation (directed by Copeau himself) of *The Brothers Karamazov* – but it opposed the star system and hoped to build a company of actors. The spirit of the Guild was not unlike that of the founders of the English Repertory movement, in which, also, the unifying factor was a wish to find public support for plays of high quality but lacking obvious marketability. The Guild's first productions took place in the Garrick Theatre, where American experimental drama was given a notable boost by Elmer Rice's expressionistic piece, *The Adding Machine* (1923). The influence on this, as on John Howard Lawson's *Processional* (1925), was German, but the outcome critically American. Lawson's play was unabashed Marxist-socialist propaganda, a dramatization of class war during a coal strike in West Virginia; Rice's is brilliantly perceptive about the drift of technology towards automation and the resultant depersonalizing of the proletariat.

The Guild was not a political group, but it was responsive to the new alertness of a society that was wanting to take stock of itself. There was, inevitably, some reactionary suspicion: the American key-word 'freedom' has always had as many adherents in the Ku Klux Klan as in the Communist Party. In A. Mitchell Palmer, United States Attorney General in 1920, Senator Joseph McCarthy had a worthy predecessor. It was on his instructions that, on 1 May 1920, the entire New York police force was put on red alert to forestall a Communist takeover. That was the ludicrous extreme of a witch-hunt that saw thousands of Americans imprisoned without trial on mere suspicion of being Russian spies. Not surprisingly, the Theatre Guild was generally circumspect. It was, after all, heavily dependent on subscriptions. The support was sufficient to allow the building of the Guild Theatre in 1925. By the end of the decade, Lawrence Langner could boast also of its touring programme:

> The Theatre Guild, in the year 1929, is providing ten of the large cities in the United States with a program of from five to six artistic plays of the kind not ordinarily produced in the commercial theatre, acted by some of the best acting talent available in the country, and running for seasons of from five to fifteen weeks outside New York, to a full season of thirty weeks in New York itself.

If, after 1930, the Theatre Guild was no longer quite so obviously the leader of the nation's dramatic taste, that was because of other events and newer initiatives. It may be pertinent to consider these under two headings, the first of 'acting styles' and the second of 'social conditions'.

Although the Theatre Guild could, and did, call on the finest young actors in America – Helen Hayes, Katharine Cornell, Alfred Lunt and Lynn Fontanne, for example – it made no consistent attempts to develop an acting style that might be appropriate to the 'new' drama. There was not, after all, much precedent for trying. The Granville Barker season at Wallack's Theatre in 1915 had hinted at possibilities, but it was the 1923 visit of the Moscow Art Theatre that offered the clearest indication of the advantages of a disciplined ensemble. Richard Boleslavsky, a former member of the Stanislavsky company, accepted an invitation to lead a Laboratory Theatre in New York that was the direct outcome of the Moscow Art Theatre's success. Among the people who attended his acting classes were Harold Clurman and another member of the Theatre Guild, Lee Strasberg. Both were profoundly committed to theatre and Strasberg in particular was also attracted by the idea of discipline. Boleskavsky's classes inspired in them a wish not merely to emulate but also to outdo the Laboratory Theatre. Clurman's first attempt to establish an ensemble within the Guild failed, but three years later, in May 1931, the Group Theatre began its shoestring existence. The manner of its beginning is significant. Clurman had persuaded the Theatre Guild to release to him the rights on Paul Green's very southern play, *The House of Connelly*, but instead of going straight into rehearsal, Clurman, Strasberg and the third director, Cheryl Crawford, went with twenty-eight actors to a summer-camp in Connecticut, where they led acting classes and discussions and undertook a programme of physical training. What was different about the Group Theatre from the start was its intensity of aspiration, and that intensity had its roots in a belief, shared by Clurman and Strasberg, that 'true' acting was quite different from 'theatrical' acting. It was a belief that culminated in the founding of the Actors' Studio, of which Strasberg became director in 1951, and through which a controversially inward-looking style of performance known as the 'Method' proliferated throughout the American theatre.

If the founders of the Group Theatre would have been satisfied by the creation of an acting ensemble, social and economic forces worked against as well as with them. The Wall Street crash and its appalling aftermath in the Depression certainly intensified the American awareness of psychological need, and that awareness fed back into Strasberg's classes and rehearsals. Faced with constant evidence of the heartlessness of capitalism under economic pressure, the members of the Group asked more of their directors than evidence of artistry. The emergence of Clifford Odets from the status of minor actor to that of major dramatist of the Group has a retrospective inevitability that fails to comprehend what was, at the time, a startling reality. *Waiting for Lefty* (1935) remains one of the finest examples of socialist drama and *Awake and Sing!* (1935) one of the most compassionate. Even if the Group Theatre had achieved nothing more than the discovery of Clifford Odets, it would have a place in American theatre history. With the exception of Paul Green's *The House of Connelly* and *Johnny Johnson* (1936 – music by Kurt Weill), it produced no other major work, but its fervour (Clurman calls his account of the Group *The Fervent Years*) was stirring and exemplary.

Much more ambitious as a response to economic hardship was the Federal Theatre Project, initiated by Roosevelt's Works Progress Administration in 1935, protected by his personal assistant, Harry Hopkins, and led by a former student of George Pierce Baker, Hallie Flanagan. The Project ran for five years (1935–9) and was eventually closed, in the wake of unsubstantiated claims of communist infiltration, by the House of Representatives. Its various productions had, by then, been seen by over thirty million people, a remarkable testimonial to the government's bold initiative. The leading figures in the Federal Theatre Project shared a glowing social idealism which all too often seems naive at the shaky end of the twentieth century. It can be seen in the work of most of the leading dramatists, Odets, Elmer Rice, Sidney Howard, Lillian Hellman, Maxwell Anderson, Robert Sherwood and Sidney Kingsley among them, who supported the Project's aims. That these aims were on the grand scale can be easily demonstrated.

Organized on federal lines, with headquarters in New York and regional centres throughout the United States, the Federal Theatre Project was designed to reverse the slide of actors into unemployment, to aid the recovery of national morale and to bring high-class entertainment at low prices (or even, sometimes, free) to the underprivileged. There were five main divisions, or units: a try-out theatre which aimed to cooperate with commercial managements, an experimental theatre, a popular-price theatre for the presentation of new plays, a Negro Theatre and a Living Newspaper. On occasions the work was coordinated nationally, as on 27 October 1936, when Sinclair Lewis's *It Can't Happen Here* opened simultaneously in twenty-one theatres covering seventeen states. At other times, local initiatives received central or regional support. The most striking of the units was the Living Newspaper and the most portentous the Negro Theatre. Hallie Flanagan had already produced a Living Newspaper show at Vassar in 1931 as a direct result of her theatrical experience in Soviet Russia, but she entrusted the headship of the unit to Elmer Rice. Just how explosive a form it was became apparent at once when the first Living Newspaper, *Ethiopia*, was banned by the Works Progress Administration in January 1936 because it reflected unfavourably on a living head of state – Mussolini. Hallie Flanagan's increasingly impossible task was to reconcile the artistic and social shock-tactics of a Joseph Losey or an Orson Welles with the shoddy patriotism of the Dies Committee. Six Living Newspapers were produced before, to America's shame, the spirit of the Dies Committee overcame liberal resistance and the Federal Theatre Project was abandoned.

The legacy of the Negro Theatre Unit can be more clearly perceived than that of any other. Before 1935 black actors could be seen often enough shining stage shoes or singing and dancing in minstrel shows, but there were scarcely any opportunities for serious acting. Virtually the only chances came in plays by white dramatists, in Ridgely Torrence's *Three Plays for a Negro Theatre* which opened on Broadway in 1917, in the virtuoso solo role of O'Neill's *The Emperor Jones*, which turned first Charles Gilpin and then Paul Robeson into household names, in Paul Green's *In Abraham's Bosom* (1926) and in Marc Connelly's *The Green Pastures* (1930). But none of these plays avoids the depiction of the Negro as exotic or, in a special sense, 'folksy'. A note of racial protest was heard from a black dramatist on Broadway in Langston Hughes's *Mulatto* (1935), and more vividly in his poem, 'Notes on Commercial Theatre' (1940):

> You put me in Macbeth and Carmen Jones
> And all kinds of Swing Mikados
> And in everything but what's about me –
> But someday somebody'll
> Stand up and talk about me,
> And write about me –
> Black and beautiful.

Hughes here refers disparagingly to two of the great successes of the Federal Theatre Project's Negro Theatre division, Orson Welles's production of an all-black *Macbeth* (1936) and the Chicago *Swing Mikado* (1938). Much more uncompromising was Theodore Ward's *Big White Fog* (1938), another Chicago production; but the arrival of a more lucid black consciousness, the kind of which Langston Hughes was dreaming, was delayed by the constraints of the commercial theatre. James Baldwin spoke for it in *The Amen Corner* (1955) and *Blues for Mr Charlie* (1964), but Baldwin is not at his best in drama. A playwright who impressed white critics by speaking elegantly for black liberals was Lorraine Hansberry, who died young in 1965, having written two intelligent plays, *A Raisin in the Sun* (1959) and *The Sign in Sidney Brustein's Window* (1964). What can never be known is how far she would have been radicalized by the event that, above all others, stirred up the movement for black separatism. Hansberry died in January 1965; the following month Malcolm X was killed. Later that year his *Autobiography* was published and already *A Raisin in the Sun* looked strangely dated. 'I never knew I was black until I read Malcolm,' said an actress-member of the Free Southern Theatre, a group whose history is superbly documented in a book edited by Thomas Dent, Richard Schechner and Gilbert Moses. Founded as a mixed-race group in 1963, the Free Southern Theatre had to struggle, as all black theatre groups have struggled, against prejudice and poverty. From a centre in the black ghetto of Desire in New Orleans, it toured theatreless black communities in Texas, Louisiana, Mississippi, Tennessee, Alabama and Georgia:

Through theatre, we think to open a new area of protest. One that permits the development of playwrights and actors, one that permits the growth and self-knowledge of a Negro audience, one that supplements the present struggle for freedom.

That a group so idealistic should find itself forced to reject its white members and to shut itself off from white society says much about black consciousness in the sixties. The year 1965 was also that in which Leroi Jones changed his name to Amiri Baraka and fully espoused black militancy. His plays and those of Ed Bullins have become the central texts of black theatres in Harlem. Much more opaque, and perhaps because of that less militant, are the plays of Adrienne Kennedy. The black theatre of the United States struggles, like the white theatre, to reach a popular audience. In this struggle, and only in this struggle, it is recognizably in touch with the whole of Western drama.

In terms of marketability, something subtly different from popularity, the American musical stands alone. Since the phenomenal success of *Oklahoma* (2,248 nights on Broadway and a total American audience of eight million during the fifteen years that followed its opening in 1943), there have been many expensive flops, but the rewards of a hit can still carry backers beyond the milder dreams of avarice. If not an art form, the American musical is certainly a theatrical phenomenon. It must both look and be expensive, slick and efficiently put together. Since *Oklahoma*, it has also generally needed at least a specious fusion of story, song, dance and comedy. Oscar Hammerstein had long hoped to write the book for a musical that would aspire to the folk-opera status of *Porgy and Bess* (1935) when he tempted Richard Rodgers into a partnership that began with *Oklahoma* and continued with *Carousel* (1945), *South Pacific* (1949), *The King and I* (1951), *Flower Drum Song* (1958) and *The Sound of Music* (1959). For the last of these he wrote only the lyrics: the book was by another effective team, Howard Lindsay and Russel Crouse, whose success with Cole Porter's *Anything Goes* (1934) was eclipsed by their collaboration with Irving Berlin on *Call Me Madam* (1950).

Such businesslike combinations have been typical of musical drama since long before Gilbert and Sullivan. That of Alan Jay Lerner and Frederick Loewe has been one of the most consistent. The tendency of their work – *Brigadoon* (1947), *Paint Your Wagon* (1951), *My Fair Lady* (1956) and *Camelot* (1961), for example – has been romantic and fanciful, looking less towards folk-opera than towards the Ruritanian inventions of Sigmund Romberg, *The Student Prince* (1924) and *The Desert Song* (1926), or Rudolph Friml, *Rose Marie* (1924) and *The*

Vagabond King (1925), though with humour replacing sentiment at many of the joins. It is a more openly escapist approach than has been typical of post-war musicals, but it remains the general strategy of the genre to compensate in fiction for the shortcomings of fact. It is the implicit assumption of the musical that benevolence is the human norm, and that deviation from it is the temporary result of damage caused by twentieth-century living. After watching a musical, we are expected to love the human race from Paris, France to Tokyo and from Judd Fry to Officer Krupke. This is the case even in the finest of them all, *West Side Story* (1957), despite its rare preparedness to question the assumption that love will triumph in the end, provided enough people try to help it.

The spread of the spectacular musical from Broadway to Off-Broadway can be observed by anyone who wishes to check which shows are running in New York. Also observable in the 1980s is a disturbing return of the English play, performed by English companies. Since World War II only two major American playwrights, Arthur Miller and Tennessee Williams, have triumphed on Broadway. That would matter less or matter not at all if reputations were more easily passed across and around the United States. It is not necessary to deride the talent of Neil Simon in order to regret his representativeness. Broadway has witnessed the renaissance of Abe Erlanger, and American theatre is the poorer for it.

For a decade, between 1952 and 1963, Off-Broadway offered the promise of a real alternative. It is impossible to provide Off-Broadway with more than a negative definition. The term describes active theatres that are not in the Broadway area, as well as the ideals with which they hoped to counter Broadway's commercial incentives. Those ideals were not, of course, confined to New York City, which was neither more nor less than the best publicized beneficiary of a cultural explosion. San Francisco, Chicago, Washington, DC, Minneapolis and many other centres of population felt the impact of the mood that inspired Off-Broadway theatre. The first significant event, the production at the Circle-in-the-Square of Tennessee Williams's *Summer and Smoke*, was both 'the first' and 'significant' only because of theatre's dependence on the media of mass communication. It was a review by Brooks Atkinson in the *New York Times* that focused attention on *Summer and Smoke*, a play which had been greeted without much enthusiasm on Broadway in 1948. In the modest atmosphere of the Circle-in-the-Square, finely directed by Jose Quintero and with a superb performance from Geraldine Page, the play had a second life. With surprising speed, New York found itself with an acknowledged alternative kind of theatre, less lavishly produced than Broadway's, but with purer artistic ambitions.

It was Off-Broadway that the American theatre caught up with the European avant-garde and began to take stock of neglected native talent. Immensely disparate, it had peaks but never a level of achievement. The second of them, if *Summer and Smoke* was the first, was the Living Theatre's production of Jack Gelber's *The Connection* (1959). Audiences were astonished by the play's lack of moral charge. No American had ever thought of presenting a play on a subject like drug-addiction without first loading it. It seemed like the improper handling of a lethal weapon. In *The Connection* a group of drug-addicts, supposedly bribed by the producer and the playwright to turn up at the theatre for a free 'fix', wait for that fix throughout the first act. In the second, they receive and react to it. The structure of the play owes much to *Waiting for Godot* and the tricks are Pirandellian, but the subject belonged importantly to urban America. Gelber's junkies were not the reduced wrecks of the warning posters, but self-respecting members of the jazz scene. The ironic reference of the title is to E. M. Forster's 'only connect', a leading theme in much of the life-interpreting literature and criticism of the 1950s. Gelber's 'connection' is the bringer of drugs, a more effective way than Forster's for the junkies to put their world together.

The ability and the will to shock had deserted Broadway. Albee's *The Zoo Story* (1960) at the Provincetown Playhouse was a third Off-Broadway shocker. It gave notice of a new talent, soon pushed with dangerous alacrity into international repute. But by 1960 there were already signs of decline. Tempted by the comparative cheapness, Broadway producers were using Off-Broadway theatres for try-outs. Others began to house increasingly costly musicals. The last event in the Off-Broadway decade was the Living Theatre's production of Kenneth H. Brown's *The Brig* in 1963. The play-text is not much more than a libretto for a ballet of physical humiliation, set in a penal institution of the American Marines. It was the disturbing viciousness of the acting that affected audiences. Suddenly, in October 1963, the run of *The Brig* was interrupted by officers of the Internal Revenue Service, who seized the 14th Street Theatre, declaring it the property of the state to which the Living Theatre owed nearly thirty thousand dollars. The affair was clumsily conducted by the authorities, skilfully by Julian Beck and Judith Malina. Liberal opinion was jolted. The Living Theatre was socially provocative, certainly, but its gospel was of peace and love. What stuck in many throats was the possible connection between the Revenue Service's action and the fact that *The Brig* was overtly hostile to the great American Marines. It was not so long since the McCarthy witch-hunts. The Living Theatre was driven into

European exile, which may have been its gain, but was certainly Off-Broadway's loss. Radical experiment was driven further into ghettoes and garages as the mood of hope and anger built towards the events of 1967 and 1968. It was off-Off-Broadway that would carry the next attacks on the established theatre. Almost alone, Joseph Papp's Public Theatre has worked to maintain the original spirit of Off-Broadway, not without having to fend off a congressional committee's accusation that he was using Shakespeare's *Coriolanus* as communist propaganda. The gap between theatrical aspiration and ignorant authority has not narrowed since Hallie Flanagan was asked by a member of the House UnAmerican Activities Committee whether Christopher Marlowe was a communist.

The story of off-Off-Broadway is the story of the groups that have composed it, from the San Francisco Mime Troupe and El Teatro Campesino in the West to the Open Theatre and the Ontological-Hysteric Theatre in the East. In alternative theatre, the United States leads the world. It is perhaps the first time that has happened in the brief dramatic history of the country. Albee has a sentence in the introduction to his play *The American Dream* (1961) that, even taken out of context, is apposite to the off-Off-Broadway mood: 'It is a stand against the fiction that everything in this slipping land of ours is peachy-keen.'

Theatres, Companies and Dramatic Genres

Abbey Theatre. This Dublin theatre is both home and symbol of the Irish dramatic movement. By the time it opened in December 1904, the Irish Literary Theatre of Edward Martyn, George Moore, LADY GREGORY and W. B. YEATS and W. G. Fay's Irish National Dramatic Company had evolved into the Irish National Theatre Society, with Yeats as its President, and with the aim 'to create an Irish National Theatre, to act and produce plays in Irish or English, written by Irish writers, or on Irish subjects; and such dramatic works by foreign authors as would tend to educate and interest the public of this country in the higher aspects of dramatic art'. The money for the conversion and equipping of the Mechanics' Institute in Dublin's Abbey Street came from the English ANNIE HORNIMAN, but she was outmanoeuvred by Lady Gregory and J. M. SYNGE. By 1908, when the Fay brothers resigned, the control of the Abbey rested with the triumvirate of Yeats, Synge and Lady Gregory. They had ridden the storm over *The Playboy of the Western World* (1907), when riots broke out ostensibly because Irish morality was offended by mention of the word 'shift' (a woman's body-garment), and had built up a professional company competent enough to survive without the expertise of the Fays. The death of Synge in 1909 and Annie Horniman's removal of her financial support in 1910 were severe blows. The Abbey had to rely on tours of England and America to subsidize its Irish performances.

The year 1908 had seen the beginning of LENNOX ROBINSON's long association with the Abbey, when his play *The Clancy Name* was performed there. Robinson was one of the few professionals to hold his own with Yeats, whose autocracy was temperamental rather than malicious, but disagreements with Lady Gregory led to his resignation. By 1919, when Robinson reassumed his managerial role, the Abbey was on the verge of dissolution. There was nothing much wrong with the acting strength – Barry Fitzgerald, Arthur Shields, Maureen Delany, F. J. McCormick – but there was too little money, and morale was low. The first three plays of SEAN O'CASEY saved the theatre between 1923 and 1926, and a small subsidy from the new government of the Irish Free State in 1924 set a precedent in the English-speaking world. In 1928,

Yeats rejected O'Casey's THE SILVER TASSIE, thereby losing Dublin its greatest dramatist. For several years the theatre's popularity was sustained by the lesser, though certainly not inconsiderable, plays of GEORGE SHIELS, but by the time it was destroyed by fire in 1951, its reputation had fallen. It took until 1966 to complete the rebuilding, and a little longer to restore the Abbey to its position as the national theatre of Ireland.

Hugh Hunt, *The Abbey*, 1979.

Absurd, Theatre of the. The credit for inventing this effective description of a uniquely twentieth-century form of horrifying farce belongs to Martin Esslin, whose *The Theatre of the Absurd* was published in 1961. 'The Theatre of the Absurd,' he wrote, 'has renounced arguing *about* the absurdity of the human condition; it merely *presents* it in being – that is, in terms of concrete stage images of the absurdity of existence.' For Esslin, the chief practitioners were IONESCO, ADAMOV, BECKETT and GENET, but few of the major post-war dramatists escaped a mention, and precursors like JARRY, Kafka, Joyce, STRINDBERG and the Dadaists were alertly spotted. A description that can be applied so inclusively has obvious limitations. Since Esslin was concerned with dramatists who had ceased to argue about the human condition, he was less interested in CAMUS, for whom 'absurdity' was a term of crucial importance in his attempt to define the abiding responsibility of men in a world without God, and therefore without congruity. Esslin's emphasis, and it is perhaps the clearest available, is on plays in which the strength of the stage image itself is greater than can be explained by any determinate meaning. The later development of PERFORMANCE ART is one of its clearer outcomes. If Ionesco is to be taken as the leading exponent of the style, his delight in carrying logic *ad absurdum* and deploying it deliriously to confuse audiences has to be seen as one of the characteristics of a genre which defies easy definition. Among English and American writers who have sometimes been included with the absurdists are PINTER, N. F. Simpson, ALBEE and SHEPARD.

Ballad Opera. From 1711, when Handel's *Rinaldo* was performed in English at the Queen's Theatre, to 1728, the cult of the Italian opera dominated fashionable London. It was partly to satirize the excesses of that cult that John Gay wrote the songs of *The Beggar's Opera* (1728) to fit popular tunes. Ballad opera, then, began as a joke. Neither Gay nor RICH, the manager of the Lincoln's Inn Fields theatre where *The*

Beggar's Opera was staged, realized just how potent the joke might be. The Italian opera was not Gay's only target. The government in general and Robert Walpole in particular were vigorously lampooned in a style that was readily accessible. Over the next five years London audiences saw fifty ballad operas. FIELDING was among the dramatists who benefited from a craze which had passed its peak by 1740, but the technique of setting new words to well known tunes was effective in popularizing the religious fervour of the Methodist movement in the eighteenth century. A tune that had mocked Walpole could just as readily celebrate the efficacy of prayer.

E. M. Gagey, *Ballad Opera*, 1937.

Berliner Ensemble. When BRECHT escaped from the HOUSE UNAMERI-CAN ACTIVITIES COMMITTEE and returned to post-war Europe in 1947, he was still in search of a theatre. The invitation to present *Puntila* in Berlin became the pretext for the formation of a new company. The Berliner Ensemble opened officially in November 1949, and moved to a permanent home at the Theater am Schiffbauerdamm in 1954, remaining there until the opening of the new theatre in 1980. It was Brecht's intention to be a part of the company rather than its leader, but there is no doubt that his was the real influence. Two weeks after his death, in August 1956, the Ensemble paid an important visit to London. The style of playing had an immediate influence on the development of the English theatre. But in Berlin itself, HELENE WEIGEL, Brecht's widow, led the Ensemble into an alarmingly fallow period. It was not her fault that Brecht's plays, endlessly revived, came so soon to look like frozen classics. Some of the gifted young directors left to work elsewhere, and it was an important moment in the history of the Ensemble when MANFRED WEKWERTH returned in 1977. The detached but detailed acting of the company remains a feature of its productions. *Theaterarbeit* (Dresden, 1952 and Berlin, 1961) presents a valuable photographic record of the early years of the Berliner Ensemble.

Boulevard du Temple. When the French theatres, in the wake of the Revolution, were given their freedom in 1791, this street, already a popular place of resort, became a positive hotbed of theatrical develop-ment. The precise number of its theatres is not recorded, but twenty-five were closed by Imperial decree in 1807. Those that remained shared the territory with sideshows, waxworks and cafes. The popular plays of the Boulevard can be estimated by the calculation of the *Almanach des Spectacles* in 1823 that 151,702 crimes had been committed on its various stages in the twenty years since 1803. It was the happy hunting ground of PIXERÉCOURT, whose detractors were among those who proposed a change of name to the Boulevard du Crime. FRÉDÉRICK LEMAÎTRE and the mime DEBURAU made their reputations here, and DUMAS *père* wrote plays to the taste of the Boulevard audience. It was Boulevard drama that fed the Romantic movement in the French theatre, and housed its plays after 1830. However regrettable the demolition of the Boulevard du Temple, it is apt that its freebooting egalitarianism continues in the name of the Place de la République, built over the area where it used to stand.

Bread and Puppet Theatre. In the view of Peter Schumann, who founded the Bread and Puppet Theatre in 1961, theatre should be as basic to life as bread and as sacramental. It was his practice to share with his audiences the homemade bread on which his family relied. 'We would like to be able to feed people,' he has said. The work of the Bread and Puppet Theatre is closer to PERFORMANCE ART than to traditional drama. Much of it is designed for the open air, like the massive processional pageant in Davis, California, *A Monument for Ishi* (1975). The only British group working on so massive and imaginative a scale is Welfare State, founded in 1968 by John and Sue Fox under the influence of Peter Schumann. The style of Bread and Puppet Theatre is informal and untheatrical, but the visual preparation is elaborate. Huge puppets – twenty feet has been proved manageable – and banners contrast with tiny props in the simple telling of myths. It is not a political so much as an anti-materialist theatre, though Schumann's pacifism led him to make what amounted to political points during the Vietnam War with the sidewalk show, *A Man Says Goodbye to His Mother* (1968). *The Cry of the People for Meat* (1969) was an endearingly simple exposition of Christian ethics in humanist terms. *Ave Maris Stella* (1978) was conceived in the same spirit. Since 1974, when Schumann moved to a farm near Glover, Vermont, Bread and Puppet Theatre has come together only intermittently in order to prepare touring shows or for the annual *Domestic Resurrection Circus*, which celebrates and responds to the environment.

Broadway. Broadway runs for 146 miles from Bowling Green to Albany, but the theatrical area to which the term is applied is no more than a section of mid-town Manhattan. It is a district, according to the definition of Actors' Equity, 'bounded by Fifth Avenue and Ninth Avenue from 34th Street to 56th Street and Fifth Avenue and the Hudson River from 56th Street to 72nd Street'. What is more important than its geographical definition is its costliness. Since 1896, when Abe Erlanger took the lead in founding a Syndicate of theatre managers, Broadway has treated theatre as if it were commerce not necessarily embarrassed by much art. As a result it has always been vulnerable to shifts in financial confidence. The number of its theatres declines, and the cost of staging productions on Broadway is so deterringly high that few risks can be taken. The melancholy conclusion of Brooks Atkinson's book in 1970 was that 'Broadway is artistically and technically proficient, but no longer creative.' The position has not changed. Americans themselves are the most virulent critics of the whole system, in which they see a reflection of their country's conspicuous consumption of 'product' and eager dependence on 'product information'. The central figure on Broadway is the producer, whose only necessary qualification is the possession of or access to money. It is the producers who staff the show, gathering here a director, there a designer, somewhere else a star or two. They will, of course, take advice from the playwright or the director, but the real risk, being financial rather than artistic, is theirs. The Broadway producers aim not to create but to satisfy demand. At the end of their rainbow is a play possessing 'universal marketability'. Since the phenomenal success of *Oklahoma* (2,248 nights on Broadway and a total American audience of over eight million over the fifteen years that followed its opening in 1943) it has been the musical that has come closest to that dream. Robert Brustein, a brilliant and avowedly discontented critic of American theatre, once tried to imagine a composite Broadway hit: 'I instantly determined that the work would have to be a musical (Native American Art Form), with a Jewish flavour (Benefit Audience Appeal), and a "serious" theme (nod to the Cultural Explosion).' That was in 1962. Two years later *Fiddler on the Roof*, a musical with a Jewish flavour and a serious theme, was a Broadway hit. The complacent English theatregoer should note that it was a hit in London, too.

Brooks Atkinson, *Broadway*, 1970.

Cambridge Festival Theatre. During its seven-year life (1926–33), this converted Georgian playhouse became the centre of the new movement in theatre design in Britain. The conversion was planned by Terence Gray (b. 1895), who was also the mastermind behind most of the hundred or so productions that took place there. Gray removed the proscenium arch and built a thrust stage the whole width of the auditorium, with which it was linked by a fan-shaped flight of steps. A revolving stage accommodated architectural pieces such as ramps and flights of steps. Gray was influenced by JESSNER and MEYERHOLD in his quest for a theatrical theatre that would utterly reject 'the old game of illusion, glamour and all the rest of the nineteenth-century hocus pocus and bamboozli'. His 'hollow boxes' were an imaginative development from CRAIG's screens. These were twenty-four light-framework constructions – cubes, drums and cylinders of various sizes – which could be grouped into an infinite variety of shapes and transformed by lighting. Gray's lighting expert, Harold Ridge, a disciple of APPIA, installed in the theatre a lighting system that was in advance of almost any in the world. The experiment was short-lived, not least because Gray combined with the passion of a fanatic the habits of a dilettante. After his defection, the Festival Theatre was briefly run on commercial lines and then sold to the Cambridge Arts Theatre for use as a workshop and costume store.

Richard Cave, *Terence Gray and the Cambridge Festival Theatre*, 1980.

Children's Companies. The 'little eyases' abused by Hamlet were a popular feature of the English theatre during its Elizabethan and Jacobean heyday. The earliest recorded performance of the Children of the Chapel Royal was in 1516. This company, like its major rival the Children of St Paul's, was composed of choirboys whose choirmaster recognized their exploitability as clearly as Ralph Reader recognized the exploitability of twentieth-century Boy Scouts. So popular had children's performances become by 1576 that Richard Farrant, Master of the Children of the Chapel at Windsor, in that year leased a room in the Blackfriars and converted it to an indoor theatre. It was there that the Children of the Chapel Royal joined forces with the Children of Paul's in the early 1580s to present the first two plays of JOHN LYLY, who was holder of the lease when Sir William More decided that the time had come to foreclose. Much of the material of the Boys' Companies was controversial, and when the Children of Paul's became active in the Martin MARPRELATE disputes in 1588–9, measures were taken to suppress them. Recently discovered evidence has shown that the suppression was short-lived. By the early 1590s the Children of Paul's were active again, and in 1600 another room in the Blackfriars was leased by the sharp and unscrupulous Henry Evans for use by the reorganized Children of the Chapel Royal. In a lawsuit of 1601, Henry Clifton complained that his son had been kidnapped 'with great force and violence' while on his way to school, by one James Robinson, acting on orders from Evans. The traffic in boy actors was obviously profitable. It says something for their quality as entertainers that playwrights of the stature of JONSON, MARSTON and CHAPMAN wrote several plays for them. Under James I, despite that monarch's own proclivities, the popularity of the Boys' companies dwindled. The

Paul's Boys closed in 1607, and the Children of the Chapel were absorbed by an adult troupe in 1613.

M. Shapiro, *Children of the Revels*, 1977.

Closet Drama. It is perfectly reasonable to argue that this is a contradiction in terms – that, given the origins of the word, drama written to be read is not, properly speaking, 'drama' at all. On the other hand, some description has to be found for works written in dialogue form, however remote from the prospect of performance. The *Dialogues* of Plato are a kind of closet drama, as are the *Messingkauf Dialogues* BRECHT modelled on them. If a line is to be drawn, it would certainly exclude the conversational novels of Ivy Compton-Burnett or Virginia Woolf's *The Waves*, but mention of them indicates the dangerous vagueness of the notion of closet drama. It most aptly describes the response of writers who, whilst harbouring a distaste for the vulgarity of theatre, recognized the qualities of classical tragedy and coveted them. SENECA, even if those who claim that his plays were not performed are right, does not properly belong to this school, since he seems to have aimed at least at public recitation. Walter Savage Landor (1775–1864), in his tragedy *Count Julian* (1812) rather than in the more Platonic *Imaginary Conversations*, provides a good example, though even Landor, whose ignorance of the theatre was impenetrable, may have dreamt of performance. Shelley's *Prometheus Unbound*, perhaps Milton's *Samson Agonistes*, Arnold's *Merope* and *Empedocles on Etna*, Swinburne's *Locrine*, these are closet dramas. The plays of Byron, despite his protestations, are not. Nor, at least in intention, are the plays of Wordsworth, Coleridge, Keats, Browning and Tennyson. The point at which the name of 'closet drama' is given to plays which are not worth performing is the point where the term loses whatever usefulness it has.

Comédie-Française. Officially founded in 1680, the Comédie-Française is an astonishing example of theatrical conservation. The original company took its name to distinguish it from the Comédie-Italienne, which continued to play at the HÔTEL DE BOURGOGNE after MOLIÈRE's company had left that theatre to form part of the Comédie-Française. Popularly known as La Maison de Molière, the Comédie-Française continued its dominance of the Parisian theatre until the Revolution, when TALMA led a disaffected group of the more revolutionary actors to the Palais-Royal. It was not until 1803 that the breach was healed and the Comédie-Française fully restored. It has continued as the home of the classic French repertoire, alternately reviving and frustrating the talents of the leaders of French theatre. There is no end to the arguments pro and con such theatrical museums, in particular those that concern the art of the actor. The Comédie-Française is a cooperative society. An apprentice may become a *pensionnaire* if his work is considered to warrant it, and a *sociétaire* if the vote allows him to replace a former member. He is then entitled to a full share in the society and a pension on retirement.

Comedy. More, even, than TRAGEDY, comedy defies definition. ARISTOTLE's account has been lost, and the earliest surviving examples in the Western theatre are the plays of ARISTOPHANES. BEN JONSON wrote *Every Man out of His Humour* (1600) in conscious imitation of the apparently haphazard style of Aristophanes, in which the narrative is of less significance than the shortcomings of the characters, many of them well known to contemporary audiences. But most English comedy has followed the style of MENANDER's 'new' comedy (so-called to distinguish it from the 'old' comedy of Aristophanes) and of its Roman variations in the work of PLAUTUS and TERENCE. Terence in particular was seen as a model of carefully constructed 'intrigue' comedy. Most of Jonson's comedies take cognizance of Terence's example, and it was Jonson rather than SHAKESPEARE who established the English comic tradition, recognizable in the comedy of manners from ETHEREGE and the Restoration to OSCAR WILDE. The view that eighteenth-century comedy degenerated from correctness through respectability to gushy sentimentality has only the plays of MURPHY, GOLDSMITH and SHERIDAN to contradict it. The French theatre benefited from the moral strength of MOLIÈRE. Comedy is capable of great severity, and whilst a happy ending is a common feature of the genre, its greatest examples do not arrive at such an ending easily.

Comedy as a distinctive genre has not recognizably survived the increasing impurity of dramatic forms in the twentieth century. What may have originated as a ritual celebration of fertility and developed in its maturity into a considered and humane criticism of social morality has been rendered indistinct by the complexity of conflicting priorities. Three great dramatists, IBSEN, CHEKHOV and SHAW, each contributed in various ways to the confusion by writing plays that could not comfortably be called comedies nor confidently called anything else. The form of comedy, we might fairly conclude, is historical, its spirit timeless.

Commedia dell'Arte. This is the name given to a style of improvised comedy which flourished in Italy from the mid-sixteenth to the mid-eighteenth century, and whose influence was felt elsewhere in Europe, and still is. The origins of the *commedia* are obscure, and since it was essentially a responsive, popular form, it was always changing. However, certain features can be established. The performed pieces were based not on an established text, but on a rehearsed scenario, though set speeches were commonly learned by heart. Particular companies, of whom the Gelosi and the Fedeli were among the most successful, divided up the leading parts; these parts were distinguished by vivid masks; and the actors retained their own masks (almost *became* them) throughout their careers. A new actor could add a new mask, as Tiberio Fiorilli virtually invented Scaramuccia (Scaramouche) and another, unknown, Neapolitan invented Cetrulo, who became Pulcinella, reaching England as Punchinel in about 1650, and becoming Punch. A great actor would certainly modify the character of his or her mask, as Domenico Biancolelli (1640–88) modified Arlecchino during his years with the *Comédie-Italienne* in Paris. The English Harlequin became the lover of Columbine, whereas his Italian original was a witty servant. The adaptability is in the spirit of *commedia*. The degeneration into the mere mechanism of stereotypes may have encouraged the growth of the written drama that ousted it, but the potential richness of the masks is evident in their development in the work of MOLIÈRE, MARIVAUX and GOLDONI, to say nothing of twentieth-century theatrical experimenters like MEYERHOLD, COPEAU, JOUVET, DULLIN, SAINT-DENIS and BARRAULT. The glorious marriage of skills and intuition, which is one of the great hopes of theatrical art, is represented at its best by *commedia dell'arte*.

Allardyce Nicoll, *The World of Harlequin*, 1963.
P. L. Duchartre, *The Italian Comedy* (trans. R. T. Weaver), 1966.

Cruelty, Theatre of. This difficult concept derives from the work of ANTONIN ARTAUD, who published a *First Manifesto of the Theatre of Cruelty* in 1932, and a *Second Manifesto* the following year. Between the two he wrote to Jean Paulhan, 'There is no better *written* example of what can be understood by cruelty in the theatre than *all* the tragedies of SENECA, but above all than *Atraeus* and *Thyestes*. You know, it is still more visible in the mind. Those monsters are wicked as only blind forces can be and I believe the theatre only exists on a level which is not quite human.' The pursuit of theatre in its totality governed the last years of Artaud's tormented life. Outraged by the *rational* civilization of the West, he dreamt of an irrational (or super-rational) theatre of assault, which would make immense demands on actors and on audiences. It would be a theatre of explosive visual and tonal images reaching down to the central realities of human existence. The influence of these theories is immeasurable. Directors and actors like BARRAULT, BROOK, GROTOWSKI; playwrights like GENET, ARRABAL; theatre companies like the LIVING THEATRE, the OPEN THEATRE, the Pip Simmons Theatre Group; all these have been directly affected. But there are indirect effects to be considered, too. The potential of theatre has been redefined by Artaud. Brook wrote of his 1963 Theatre of Cruelty season that it consisted of 'shots at distant targets'. The recoil on British theatre has been considerable. A theatre more concerned to uproot than to entertain its audience has now to be taken account of.

Documentary Theatre. The impulse towards a theatre that documents history with apparent objectivity is as old as AESCHYLUS' *Persians*. But the modern impetus belongs to Germany in the sixties, and to HOCHHUTH's *The Representative* (1963) in particular. This play characteristically applies its research to the making of a political point. Its overtly unemotional presentation is designed to excite emotion in its audience. The same is certainly true of such successors as Kipphardt's *In the Matter of J. Robert Oppenheimer* (1964) and WEISS's *The Investigation* (1965). The style owes a lot to BRECHT. It has been so thoroughly assimilated into radio and television and into the political and social drama of the FRINGE theatre in Britain and America that it is scarcely ever recognized for what it is – a resourceful adaptation of the chronicle play. Some of the most endearing of British documentaries have come from the Victoria Theatre in Stoke-on-Trent, where Peter Cheeseman and his company are more concerned to explore local history than to make political points. The work of PAUL GREEN in America can be retrospectively seen in the context of Documentary theatre.

El Teatro Campesino. The name of this group reflects its origin (it means 'the farmworkers' theatre'). Luis Valdez, its founder, was a drama student at the University of California when, in 1965, he saw a performance by the SAN FRANCISCO MIME TROUPE. The direct style, colour and exuberance were reminiscent of his life among the Chicanos – an underprivileged North American racial group of Spanish and American-Indian ancestry. Returning to his birthplace, Delano, California, Valdez looked for ways of using theatre in support of a Chicano farmworkers' strike. He developed simple scenes, or *actos*, to spell out the issues behind the strike. El Teatro Campesino began as part of a trade union, and remained so until 1967. Its aims broadened between 1967 and 1969 and Valdez led his company into involvement with Chicano culture. *Vietnam Campesino* (1970) was the last political *acto* performed by the group. In 1971 they set up a permanent base in San Juan Bautista and developed a new form, the *mito* (myth), to embody their study of Mayan culture. *The Dance of the Giants* (1974), an attempt to recreate a ceremony of the Chorti Indians, was performed at a Chicano and Latin American Theatre Festival in Mexico, and created a storm of controversy. Valdez was accused of abandoning his political aims and selling out the Chicano theatre movement which he had originated. The accusation has some substance. A group that began as blatantly agitational had shifted towards a tangential exploration of anthropological harmony. But the progeny of El Teatro Campesino has been plentiful. By 1980 there were about eighty Chicano theatre companies.

Expressionism. An artistic movement whose centre was Germany, Expressionism found its energy around 1910 in opposition to the objectivity of NATURALISM and, more particularly, to the emphasis on external reality of the Impressionist painters. Expressionist artists asserted the validity of a personal vision, arguing that a work of art should be the expression, not of the external world, but of the painter himself. Among the playwrights who responded to the new fervour were KAISER, TOLLER and the youthful BRECHT. Some of the inspiration came from the tormented later work of STRINDBERG, whose *To Damascus* (1898–1904) seemed like a spiritual autobiography, and some from the explosive plays of WEDEKIND. Expressionist drama grew out of and fuelled social protest – against the repressiveness of prevailing morality, against the constraints of the family, against the ethics of capitalism. Plays like Toller's *The Machine Wreckers* (1921) and Kaiser's *Gas* trilogy (1917–20) are peppered with impassioned poetic outbursts, which allow the writer to voice his aspirations in the person of his hero. As in Brecht's *Baal* (1918), the enemy is grotesque materialism whose monumental smugness was seen as the enemy of progress. In place of well wrought plots, the Expressionist playwrights substituted short scenes, and in place of realistic scenery the jagged images of dreams. It was not long before the German cinema stole the Expressionist thunder from the German theatre, but the influence was felt in the U.S.A., above all by O'NEILL in *The Hairy Ape* (1922) and *The Great God Brown* (1926) and by ELMER RICE in *The Adding Machine* (1923), and reached London in the extraordinary second act of O'CASEY's *The Silver Tassie*, first staged in 1929.

John Willett, *Expressionism*, 1978.

Farce. It is no longer possible to dismiss farce as 'comedy with the meaning left out', as L. J. Potts did as recently as 1948. More recently, Eric Bentley has called attention to the violence and aggression that are features of farce, and that may suggest its relationship with mischief and the overthrow of order. The early history of farce is obscure. There is evidence of short village comedies in Dorian Greece, perhaps associated with Dionysiac festivities. Wine and fertility, associated with Dionysus, are no strangers to farce. The Atellan farces of Italian antiquity were rustic too, and it is possible to trace links with the English Mummers' plays, with their knockabout battles and magical resurrections. The Elizabethan jig, in the hands of RICHARD TARLTON and WILL KEMPE, was musical farce in all but name. A French/English Dictionary of 1611 translated the French word *farce* as 'a fond and dissolute Play, Comedy, or Interlude; also, the Jig at the end of the Interlude, wherein some pretty knavery is enacted'. Pretty knavery continued to characterize the farces which served as curtain-raisers or AFTERPIECES in the English theatre of the eighteenth and nineteenth centuries. The French took their farce more seriously, relishing the precision by which expanded logic could be made acceptable. FEYDEAU was the nineteenth-century master. The genre received new impetus in Britain after the success of Brandon Thomas's *Charley's Aunt* (1892) had crowned the achievements of PINERO in the previous decade. The Aldwych farces of BEN TRAVERS delighted London in the twenties, as, less subtly, Brian Rix delighted addicts at the Whitehall forty years later.

Eric Bentley, *The Life of the Drama*, 1964.
J. M. Davis, *Farce*, 1978.

Federal Theatre Project. An imaginative offshoot of the New Deal, the Federal Theatre Project was inaugurated in 1935, partly to give employment to theatre professionals, partly to extend the spread of entertainment in the dour years of the Depression. Its director, HALLIE FLANAGAN, was a university drama professor, with broad left-wing sympathies that need not have worried any non-criminal capitalist. At its height, the Project employed 10,000 people and operated in forty states. If it is particularly remembered for fostering the LIVING NEWSPAPER, its range was immensely wide. ELMER RICE recalls 'the Negro Youth Theatre, the One-Act-Play Unit, the German Unit, the Poetic Drama Unit, the Classical Repertory Unit . . . companies for the performance of SHAW, O'NEILL and Gilbert-and-Sullivan cycles; circus, marionette and dance units . . . a Children's Theatre . . . an Experimental Theatre for unconventional plays and new techniques of staging'.

There was also the Negro Theatre in Harlem, under the unorthodox direction of ORSON WELLES. But the all-too-familiar American backlash began even before the Project got under way. Elizabeth Dilling's discreditable *The Red Network* (1934) had already compiled a list of 'about 1,300 persons, who are or have been members of Communist, Anarchist, Socialist, I.W.W., or Pacifist-controlled organizations'. Some of the leaders of the Federal Theatre Project were on the list. In 1939, Hallie Flanagan herself was summoned before the HOUSE UNAMERICAN ACTIVITIES COMMITTEE, and in June of that year Congress terminated the Federal Theatre Project.

Hallie Flanagan, *Arena*, 1940.
Jane Mathews, *The Federal Theatre*, 1967.

Fringe Theatre. If it was ever clear precisely what was meant by 'fringe' theatre, it quickly became obscure. The British derivation can be traced to the Edinburgh Festival, where small theatre groups performed on the 'fringes' of the city. The oppositional movements of 1968 gave the fringe a political colouring, and a theatre of outrage and offence spread through the seventies. Resourcefully, the Arts Council of Great Britain rewarded enterprise with subsidy, and actors bent on revolution received their salaries more or less directly from the establishment they dreamt of overthrowing. An expatriate American, Jim Haynes, had been the prime mover in Edinburgh. In 1968 he opened (and closed) an Arts Lab in Drury Lane. Among a number of shorter-lived groups, the People Show and the Pip Simmons Theatre Group performed there. In 1971, the playwright JOHN MCGRATH founded 7:84 (q.v.) (7% of the population owns 84% of Britain's wealth), and led it in pursuit of effective revolutionary socialism. Belt and Braces, even more revolutionary, was an offshoot of 7:84, founded in 1974. The women's movement was championed by the Women's Theatre Group (1975) and Monstrous Regiment (1976), and gay liberation by Gay Sweatshop (1975). Most of these groups have to rely on income from touring, since they lack theatres of their own. Such activity is tough and costly, and less easily arranged than was the case with the old stock companies. Many groups have been worn down by the grind. The fervour was dying away by the mid-seventies, when Joint Stock Theatre Group was formed. This is a superior touring theatre (whatever 'superior' means), which employs established actors to work with playwrights in the devising of appropriate scripts. It can be taken, despite its left-wing sympathies, to represent a shift from political commitment to high-class performance. So can the decision of

Belt and Braces to take their production of DARIO FO's *Accidental Death of an Anarchist* into the West End in 1980. There is, though, a wealth of energy and concern that cannot be contained within the established theatre, and new groups spring up around Britain more often than old groups die. The sad economic fact is that these new groups immediately clamour for public subsidy, without which they cannot survive. It was the fringe theatre that stimulated the new playwrights of the seventies – John McGrath, DAVID EDGAR, HOWARD BARKER, Stephen Lowe, Snoo Wilson, HOWARD BRENTON, DAVID HARE and many others.

Peter Ansorge, *Disrupting the Spectacle*, 1975.
Sandy Craig (ed.), *Dreams and Deconstructions*, 1980.
Catherine Itzin, *Stages in the Revolution*, 1980.

Glasgow Citizens' Theatre. While the REPERTORY movement in almost every other British city dwindles, the Glasgow Citizens' thrives. It was founded in 1943 and, for the first eight years, was guided by JAMES BRIDIE. In 1952, the year after Bridie's death, his last play, *The Baikie Charivari*, was staged, and a revival of his *A Sleeping Clergyman*, was chosen to mark the theatre's twenty-first anniversary. It was the Citizens' policy to stage new plays, particularly Scottish ones, rather than classics, and that policy remained dominant until 1969, when Giles Havergal was appointed artistic director. Since then, the Citizens' has established a reputation for bold, even outrageous, revivals and reinterpretations of the classical repertoire. Havergal's is the guiding hand, but the theatre owes its international reputation as much to its extraordinary designer, Philip Prowse, as to Havergal. Together with the writer and translator, Robert David Macdonald, they have transformed a modest regional repertory theatre into an immodest international theatre, and they have done so without forfeiting local support. The Citizens' is located in the former slumland of the Gorbals and it has been its determined policy to keep the price of admission low. 'All seats 50p' was boldly painted across the front of the remodelled theatre in 1977. Two years later, the *Guardian* critic Cordelia Oliver reported that, 'Once the adjacent bingo hall queue used to block the Citizens' entrance; now there's no longer a bingo hall and the queue is for the Citizens'.'

Globe Theatre. The first Globe Theatre was built in 1599, partly out of the timbers salvaged by RICHARD BURBAGE and his brother Cuthbert from the demolition of the first purpose-built English playhouse, the Theatre. Very little is known about it, though much has been speculated on. It was almost certainly polygonal in structure – giving a general impression of roundness to which it might have owed its name – and three-storied. Its capacity has been variously estimated, but was probably over two thousand. It was the home, initially, of the Lord Chamberlain's Men, of which SHAKESPEARE was a leading member, and remained in the same hands when James I appointed them King's Men. It was on the wide, open stage of the Globe that Shakespeare's major plays were performed, and it was at a performance of *Henry VIII* that a discharged cannon caused the fire that destroyed the theatre in 1613. The second Globe, built on the same site, opened in 1614. This is the building mistitled 'Beere bayting' on Wenceslaus Hollar's magnificent panorama of London. Hollar completed this in Antwerp in 1647, not realizing that the Globe had been torn down three years before.

C. Walter Hodges, *The Globe Restored*, 1953.
Bernard Beckerman, *Shakespeare at the Globe*, 1962.
Peter Thomson, *Shakespeare's Theatre*, 1983.

Grand Guignol. By a transference which probably owes something to the casual violence of some puppet-shows, the name of Guignol, a French marionette invented in the early nineteenth century, has become attached to a form of theatre hardly related at all to the rural Guignol. In Grand Guignol, decadence tips over into perversion. Its themes are murder, rape, brutal violence as the climax of fierce threat, and horror of the kind much later featured in Hammer Films. Its theatrical centre was Montmartre, and its heyday the late nineteenth century. The London theatre watered it down for a famous SYBIL THORNDIKE season in 1920, and few dramatists have achieved much success with Grand Guignol in the English-speaking theatre. Patrick Hamilton's *Gaslight* (1938) was a late and comparatively subtle example, and Anthony Shaffer has reopened the vein with *Sleuth* (1976) and *Murder* (1979). Even those, though, are wholesome in comparison with French models and the modern theatre must look to the plays of ARRABAL to rival the unique nastinesss of nineteenth-century Grand Guignol.

Group Theatre. Founded in New York by HAROLD CLURMAN, LEE STRASBERG and Cheryl Crawford in 1931, the Group Theatre gathered together much of the best of youthful theatrical aspiration during the early years of the Depression. Gerald Weales has described it as 'the most successful failure in the history of American theatre', and it is certainly odd that a theatre company so riven by dissent, so dogged by financial panics, and so rarely meeting its own artistic standards in its productions should have merited and received so much attention. The Group owed much to the combative idealism of Harold Clurman and to Strasberg's fanatically blinkered application of Stanislavskian discipline in rehearsal. Outstanding among the twenty-three plays produced by the company before its dissolution in 1940 were PAUL GREEN'S *The House of Connelly* (1931) and *Johnny Johnson* (1936), JOHN HOWARD LAWSON's *Success Story* (1932), Robert Ardrey's *Thunder Rock* (1939), and above all a sequence of seven plays by CLIFFORD ODETS beginning with *Awake and Sing!* (1935) and ending with *Night Music* (1940). Odets had begun as a minor actor in a company that included, at various times, ELIA KAZAN, LEE J. COBB, MORRIS CARNOVSKY, Franchot Tone and Stella Adler, and the socialist fervour that he met in the Group Theatre stimulated him to write. It was a blow to the American theatre as a whole and to the Group Theatre in particular when Odets went to work and live in Hollywood, but the energetic hopefulness on which the Group had built its early successes was already threatened by the reaction against the Left in America. It is as a brave forerunner of the independently minded theatre companies of the sixties that the Group Theatre can be remembered.

Harold Clurman, *The Fervent Years*, 1945.

Habima. Founded in Moscow in 1917–18 in order to stage plays in Hebrew, the Habima (the word means 'stage') had the good fortune to enlist STANISLAVSKY's interest. Early productions, including *The Dybbuk* (1922), were directed by Stanislavsky's gifted pupil VAKHTANGOV, and the Habima became one of the studios of the MOSCOW ART THEATRE. A series of European and world tours culminated in a move to a permanent home in Tel Aviv in 1931. Since 1953, the Habima has been the official National Theatre of Israel.

Emanuel Levy, *The Habima – Israel's National Theatre*, 1979.

Happenings. The collision of art and life is forced by the Happening. It can be anarchic or highly organized. It can be loosed on the public or confined to the participants. The wheeling of a nude girl across the stage of a writers' forum at the Edinburgh Festival in 1963 was a Happening contrived to give the maximum offence with the minimum effort. The complex work of Allan Kaprow, Claes Oldenburg, or Ann Halprin is at an opposite extreme. Happenings of the kind they planned are often a joyful celebration of human activity in empty space. To that extent, they imitate drama.

Michael Kirby (ed.), *Happenings*, 1966.

Harlequinade. The evolution of the English pantomime is not easily traced, but the Harlequinade is inescapably part of it. When JOHN RICH took over the management of the theatre in Lincoln's Inn Fields on his father's death in 1714, he was already well known as a dancer and mime. His management coincided with a peak of popularity, within the English theatre, of adopted characters from the Italian COMMEDIA DELL'ARTE, and Rich was a specialist in the acrobatic (and usually silent) part of Harlequin. He delighted his public by interlarding plays like *The Rape of Proserpine* (1727) with scenes from the courtship of Harlequin and Columbine, so that whilst the story of Proserpine was allowed logically to continue, the audience had the regular *divertissement* of 'grotesque' scenes of dance and magic featuring the manager himself. Later the two strands were separated out, and it became the set pattern of pantomime to establish in the 'Opening' a simple story of young love frustrated by an unsympathetic parent and threatened by rival suitors, then to use the skill of the scenic artists to achieve a transformation and embark on the real business of the evening, the Harlequinade. The trick was to have the young lovers at the crisis of imminent separation transformed by magic into Harlequin and Columbine, their mundane world transformed into an enchanted land, and the unsympathetic characters from the Opening transformed into a fairy equivalent and eventually, after a complex pursuit, thwarted. Gradually, through the nineteenth century, the Opening was dropped and the Harlequinade became the pantomime. Equally gradually, the Harlequinade reintroduced the prosaic elements of the Opening, was absorbed by them, and became recognizable only in the transformation after the Grand Finale, an expensive feast of grand costumes and sudden scenery. Only rarely do the economics of the modern theatre permit even this vestige of the Harlequinade.

Maurice Sand, *The History of the Harlequinade*, 2 vols., 1915.

Hôtel de Bourgogne. When the Confraternity of the Passion, a group which had the legal monopoly of acting in Paris, were evicted from their premises, they set about building a theatre, the first in Paris, in the ruins of the palace of the Dukes of Burgundy. The theatre, known as the Hôtel de Bourgogne, was completed in 1548, but had its greatest years during the seventeenth-century pre-eminence of the King's Players.

That status was challenged by the arrival of MOLIÈRE in Paris in 1658. The King's Players were subsumed into the COMÉDIE-FRANÇAISE in 1673, and it was the Italian players, known as the Comédie-Italienne, who occupied the Hôtel de Bourgogne until its demise in 1783.

Indian Theatre. It is difficult for the historically trained occidental mind to appreciate the ancient art of Indian drama. Its divine origins are best accepted in the matter-of-fact language of the Hindu. When Brahma was asked by the god Indra to devise an art that would appeal to eye and ear, he turned to the sacred Vedas, choosing from each of the four one element: the spoken word, song, mime and emotion. These he combined into the *Natya Veda*, the Veda of drama and dance, and he entrusted the Indian sage Bharata to interpret the Veda for posterity. The *Natyashastra* was Bharata's response to Brahma's demand. It is an exhaustive manual of the mingled arts of classical Indian dance and drama, dealing not only with the aesthetics of performance but also with the practicalities of building theatres, composing plays, dances and music and making costumes. The fact that neither the *Natyashastra* nor its legendary author can be precisely dated (the earliest surviving copy probably dates from the eighth century AD, but dates up to 700 years earlier have been proposed) makes no difference to their importance in Indian tradition.

One crucial aspect of that tradition is its fusion of dance and drama. All Sanskrit drama involves dance, while the four major surviving dance-forms, Bharatanatyam, Manipuri, Kathak and Kathakali, have a strong dramatic and mimetic element, though only Kathakali recounts a connected narrative. It is easy to perceive the central source in regional variations of classical dance, like the Odissi form of Bharatanatyam, and even in the rougher rural forms, like the Bengali Chhau and the Punjabi Bhangra. The *Natyashastra* was evidently written at a time when the early forms of dance and mime were coming together in the fully fledged dramatic performance. In addition to the prescribed dance poses, the modes of walking and running on stage are carefully laid down, and the code of histrionic gestures is so intricate in its details that it makes European Renaissance manuals of rhetorical gesture seem crude and amateurish by comparison. The different gestures are codified according to the feelings they are intended to signify. There are 13 head-movements, 32 of the foot, 24 of each hand and separate movements of the neck, nose, cheek, eyes, torso and eyebrows. Together, these movements constitute an elaborate mimetic language, and it is clear that they embody a well understood communal convention rather than a single individual's arbitrary prescription.

The possible kinds of play are equally rigidly itemized, but very few classical texts have survived. *The Little Clay Cart*, conventionally attributed to 'King Shudraka', dates from the second century AD. Its untypically secular subject is the love of a merchant and a courtesan. Better known in the West is *Sakuntala*, one of three surviving plays by KALIDASA, a fifth-century dramatist of the Gupta court. It is a lyrical piece, dealing with the love of a king for a forest maiden, and its presiding mood (*rasa*) is the 'erotic', legitimized by Bharata. *Sakuntala* was first translated into English in 1789, when it created much interest but no discernible impact, although Germanists have detected an influence on GOETHE. For the most part, Western drama remains isolated from India. Even RABINDRANATH TAGORE, despite the adulation accorded to him by YEATS in the early years of the twentieth century, has proved untranslatable to the English-speaking theatre. Indian playwrights, on the other hand, have been manifestly affected by occidental drama. At their exciting best, as in the work of Girish Karnad in Kannada, they assimilate without being assimilated.

International Centre of Theatre Research. The Centre is a multifaceted reflection of the taste and temperament of its founding director, PETER BROOK. It began operations in 1970 at the Mobilier National in Paris. Brook's aim was to assemble actors from various countries and disparate cultures to participate in a quest for a universal language of theatre. Early workshops on HANDKE's *Kaspar*, based on the strange story of Kaspar Hauser, were an appropriate start to the quest whose first full performance outlet was *Orghast* (1971), staged outdoors as part of the Shiraz Festival in Persepolis. The text was in a language devised by Ted Hughes in association with Brook and the actors. In 1972–3, members of the Centre travelled through Africa, improvising in villages and developing a performance of *The Conference of the Birds*. They opened the Théâtre des Bouffes du Nord in 1975 with a first version of *The Ik*, a carefully formless dramatization of the effect of civilization on an African tribe, and followed it with a production of *Timon of Athens*. Performances and tours are only a part of the Centre's work. Like GROTOWSKI, Brook is tirelessly searching for new and better ways of illuminating the essence of theatre, and workshops and discussions are as vital to him as performance. Plays that have offered a way to discovery include CALDERON's *Life Is a Dream*, JARRY's *Ubu Roi*, CHEKHOV's *The Cherry Orchard* and a version of the *Mahabharata*.

A. C. H. Smith, *Orghast at Persepolis*, 1972.
John Heilpern, *The Conference of the Birds*, 1976.

Kabuki. Always more commercially inclined than NOH, Kabuki developed from the dance dramas performed by women in and around the major cities of seventeenth-century Japan. The brothel quarters became the accepted home of these dances, and the association of Kabuki and prostitution led to a ban on their performance by women in 1629 and subsequently (1652) on their performance by young male prostitutes. It was further demanded that the adult males who continued to perform Kabuki should increase its narrative content. Such legislation is, of course, unnecessary where there is no inclination to offend, and there is ample evidence that breaches of the law were frequent. In Japan's rigid hierarchical structure, actors and courtesans were lowly placed, and Samurai as well as others of the upper class were officially forbidden to frequent either brothels or theatres, but the ban was ineffective, not least because the performers of Kabuki were shrewd enough to make their art attractive. Eighteenth-century guide books often included appraisals of popular Kabuki players alongside their descriptions of celebrated courtesans. Such appraisals stress the stylized and skilful physical discipline of Kabuki, a theatre form which was initially developed by its performers almost without literary reference.

When the need for new stories became urgent, Kabuki actors turned to the plays written for the puppet-theatre, Ningyo-joruri (familiar in the West as Bunraku), which had reached a new level of sophistication during the seventeenth century. Takemoto Gidayu (1651–1714), a master-chanter of puppet-tales, had employed as a writer a man who had previously worked with a family of Kabuki actors. Chikamatsu (1653–1724), wrote for Takemoto from 1685 to 1688, returned to Kabuki from 1688 to 1703 and then devoted the rest of his writing life to Ningyo-joruri. Most of his masterpieces date from the final period, by which time it was customary for Kabuki actors to adapt puppet-plays. Chikamatsu's elaborate prose borders on poetry, and many of his plays remain in the Kabuki repertoire. They are mainly of two types, Jidaimono being historical dramas with Samurai heroes and Sewamono being domestic dramas set among the merchant classes. The conflict between duty and the heart is a dominant theme, and many of Chikamatsu's plays end with a double-suicide of lovers.

Kabuki actors were organized on a family basis from the early years of its institution. Training begins in childhood, and it is normal for the actors to specialize in either male or female roles. The stylized eroticism of the female performers (known as *oyama* or *onnagata*) is one of the many features that distinguishes Kabuki from Noh. Another is the greater preparedness of Kabuki to accommodate to changing tastes, although there has been no relaxation of the ban on female performers. During the Edo period (1615–1868), when Kabuki was at its height, performances were social events. They began in the morning and continued until dusk, and the audience was free to eat, drink and talk. It was the task of the actors to hold their attention by the display of elaborate costume, by feats of physical prowess and by the careful orchestration of the climactic poses (*mie*) of the players of male roles. In modern Japan, Kabuki has been monopolized by the Shochiku entertainment company. What began as a much more popular form of art than Noh has become almost equally a minority taste, though it remains a more robust form and more accessible to Western audiences.

Kyogen. A form of short, comic drama originally developed as an interlude in the stately NOH theatre of Japan. Kyogen can be roughly translated as 'mad words', and the translation aptly defines the topsy-turvy irreverence of many surviving examples, in which a quick-witted servant outsmarts his slow-thinking master. Kyogen was intelligently transposed to Lancashire in the Pongo Plays of the English playwright Henry Livings (b. 1929), in which Sam Pongo contrives to pull the wool over the eyes of the mill-owner master, 'a man of some substance and well thought of hereabouts'.

La MaMa Experimental Theatre Club. Begun as a coffee-house theatre group in New York in 1962, the La MaMa organization provided the first centre for off-Off-Broadway initiatives. The founder-patron was Ellen Stewart, and among the playwrights sponsored by the Club were Megan Terry, SAM SHEPARD, and Rochelle Owens. The inspiration was Artaudian, the pursuit a style of theatrical performance which would integrate music, word, and movement.

Lincoln Center. This New York Center for the Performing Arts was incorporated in 1956, but the first building, the Philharmonic Hall, was not completed until 1962. The Vivian Beaumont Theatre, designed by Eero Saarinen and stage-designer Jo Mielziner, opened in 1965, since when its impressive thrust stage has overwhelmed more actors than it has flattered. Robert Whitehead, who originated the plans for the theatrical component of this vast complex, hoped to provide New York with a permanent company of high standard and, perhaps, America with a national theatre. He chose ELIA KAZAN as his co-director, and Kazan looked to ARTHUR MILLER as a kind of resident dramatist. The Lincoln Center Repertory Theater was founded in 1964 and opened with a production, not yet in the Center itself, of Miller's *After the Fall*.

The play was controversial, and when it was followed by two failures the board of directors nervously replaced Whitehead and Kazan with Herbert Blau and Jules Irving. It was an ominous start to a difficult enterprise. The Lincoln Center is not, properly speaking, on BROADWAY, but its audiences have been slow to abandon the Broadway quest for hits. Blau resigned in 1967, and Irving soldiered on, under constant and often ungenerous pressure. In 1973 the directors turned to the impresario of the New York Shakespeare Festival, JOSEPH PAPP. Papp launched out on a policy of staging new American plays, not only in the three-hundred-seat Forum Theatre of the Center, but also in the Vivian Beaumont auditorium, which was too much for most of them. Papp was unlikely to be long confined in such a setting. By 1978 Richmond Crinkley was in office in his place, with Woody Allen as one of his fellow-directors. The search for the great American repertory theatre goes on.

Living Newspaper. The Living Newspaper Unit was established in New York in 1935 as part of the FEDERAL THEATRE PROJECT. Its intention was to present dramatizations of current issues in snappy, documentary style. The techniques of the Living Newspaper have a variety of sources, from BRECHT to the agit-prop of the post-revolutionary Blue Blouse movement in the Soviet Union. JOSEPH LOSEY, its most inventive American exponent, was certainly influenced by the free-flowing staging methods of Nikolai Okhlopkov, which he saw at the Realistic Theatre when he visited Moscow in 1935. In its turn, the work of the Unit has affected the development of politically motivated theatre in the West. Its own story is brief and full of vexation. The first show, *Ethiopia* (1936), was written (or compiled) under the aegis of ELMER RICE. At the last moment the State Department banned it. 'It was feared Il Duce might take offence!' says Rice. Rice resigned, and Losey was brought in to stage *Triple-A Plowed Under* (1936), which set the pattern for the subsequent shows by restricting itself to specifically American issues. The third piece, called simply *1935* and dealing in broad satirical terms with the events of that year, was hastily brought together to give time for the preparation of the more ambitious *Injunction Granted* (1936), in which the opposition of American labour and American capital was savagely highlighted. Losey's openly political commitment was too much for HALLIE FLANAGAN, who asked him to 'clean up the script and make it more objective'. Losey resigned, and the last two shows, *Power* (1937) and *One-Third of a Nation* (1938), showed a greater inclination to support New Deal policies. Even so, the Living Newspaper Unit was killed, along with the whole Federal Theatre Project, by a congressional order of 30 June 1939.

M. Y. Himelstein, *Drama Was a Weapon*, 1963.

Living Theatre. Since its foundation in 1947, the Living Theatre, led by Julian Beck (1925–85) and Judith Malina, has stalked through counter-culture like an avenging beast. The sub-title of Beck's *The Life of the Theatre* is a characteristic blend of fierce conviction and myopia: 'the relation of the artist to the struggle of the people'. The company began by presenting OFF-BROADWAY productions of plays that would have been anathema to the commercial theatre, making a famous splash with the drug-culture's masterpiece, Jack Gelber's *The Connection* (1959). The first of many world tours culminated with prize-winning performances at the Théâtre des Nations Festival in 1961. Increasingly affronted by the violence of the sixties and the pursuit of the war in Vietnam, the Living Theatre challenged and defied society. 'I demand everything,' Judith Malina declared from the stage of the Brooklyn Academy in 1968, 'total love, an end to all forms of violence and cruelty such as money, hunger, prisons, people doing work they hate', and she and Beck led the audience naked into the streets. Under banners like 'Fuck for Peace', the Living Theatre roamed the world, acting out in pieces like *Frankenstein* and *Paradise Now* the furies and fantasies of a tribe that resisted the values of an acquisitive world. 'The tribe has its own charisma,' Beck noted in Rio in 1970. 'The tribe is a group of people bound together by love. Therefore they find ways to survive, and therefore the tribe has a special fascination in a more or less loveless society.' And somehow or other, despite imprisonments, censorship, and exhaustion, the Living Theatre survived. The 1979 *Prometheus* was without the anger of earlier work. It was a confused and labyrinthine piece, with moments of beautiful, geometrical precision.

Pierre Biner, *The Living Theatre*, 1968.

Lyceum Theatre, London. Of the several theatres on the Wellington Street site, the one made famous by IRVING was opened in 1834. Early tenants included MADAME VESTRIS and CHARLES FECHTER. In 1871 the American 'Colonel' Bateman took possession of it with the firm intention of making famous as many of his four daughters as possible. With that in mind, it was probably a mistake to employ Irving, whose triumph in *The Bells* in the same year saved the theatre and threatened the Bateman girls with obscurity. Irving took over the Lyceum in 1878, and made it a temple for actors. 'There was a sacerdotal air about the entire building,' Herbert Swears recalled in 1938. 'The entrance hall was covered in sombre hangings. The lighting was dim. Small boys like acolytes distributed the programmes . . . . A high priest, in the shape of Mr Joseph Hurst, sat remotely in a box office. If he smiled when rendering your change, it was a thing to be remembered.' Irving retained sole control until 1898 when a series of problems, culminating in the burning of his scenery store, forced him into partnership. He made his last appearance there in 1902, and two years later the building was remodelled as a music hall. Under the Melville brothers from 1910 to 1939, it became familiar as a home for MELODRAMA. Scheduled for demolition in 1939, it housed farewell performances of GIELGUD's *Hamlet*, but the War brought a reprieve, and in 1945 the Lyceum was reopened—as a dance hall.

A. E. Wilson, *The Lyceum*, 1952.

Masque. At its height, in the court of James I, the English Masque combined the poetic genius of BEN JONSON with the scenic ingenuity of INIGO JONES. Probably originating in seasonal ritual, the Masque reached this level of sophistication gradually. In the great houses of Tudor England, the host would be 'surprised' by the sudden eruption of masked guests bearing gifts and inviting the host to join them in a ceremonial dance. As the interruptions became more elaborate, the dance was delayed, though not abandoned. The attention given to the royal Masques of Elizabeth I, James I and Charles I should not undermine our awareness of a custom that survived, with regional variants, throughout England until the Puritan revolution and the Civil War. The new theatre that developed after the restoration of Charles II assimilated much of the scenic splendour of the Masque and its submerged sexuality, too.

Meininger. This was the name under which the acting company of George II, Duke of Saxe-Meiningen (1826–1914) toured Europe, carrying the influence of its rationalizing reforms to England (where IRVING was impressed by the handling of crowd-scenes), to Brussels (where ANTOINE saw performances) and to Moscow (where STANIS-LAVSKY saw them in 1890). 'Their performance,' wrote Stanislavsky, 'showed Moscow for the first time productions that were historically true, with well directed mob scenes, fine outer form and amazing discipline.' He was particularly impressed by the 'restraint and cold-bloodedness' of the director, Ludwig Chronegk (1837–91). It is ironic that the problems of the 1890 visit to Moscow caused Chronegk's physical collapse and the dissolution of the Meininger players. Having been swept into power by Bismarck's determination to unite Germany, George II saw his tours as, above all, demonstrations of the greatness of the new country, but it is as an influence on the development of NATURALISM in the European theatre, particularly in the relationship of stage-design and drama, that the Meininger needs to be remembered.

Ann Marie Koller, *The Theatre Duke*, 1984.

Melodrama. It is possible to date with misleading precision the moment when 'mélodrame' moved from operatic into dramatic theatre. Although the Gothic taste that nurtured melodrama had flourished in Europe since 1750, it was in 1800 that PIXERÉCOURT's *Coelina* established a style that lasted for over a century in Europe and America. Two years later THOMAS HOLCROFT's *A Tale of Mystery* was the first English play (it was actually an adaptation of *Coelina*) to be billed as a melodrama. The idea of using music to give emotional support to elemental conflict was obviously operatic, and a musical definition of 'melodrama' will still refer to passages in which the spoken word is used against a musical background. As the nineteenth century progressed, musical support for melodrama became increasingly perfunctory. Threatening chords might announce the villain's approach, and 'hurry music' indicate a crisis in the action, but it was now sufficient justification for calling a play a melodrama if it opposed suffering virtue (particularly female virtue) to external threat. In the view of James L. Smith, 'it is this total dependence upon external adversaries which finally separates melodrama from all other serious dramatic forms'. It is a crucial part of that definition that melodrama, too, is seen as 'serious'. Smith goes on to assert that 'most of the serious plays ever written have been melodramas and not tragedies'. The modern habit of hissing the nineteenth-century villain accompanies an anachronistic preparedness to underrate his menace. In a prudish age, melodrama liberated sexual as well as patriotic fantasy. It played on the nerves with the assurance Hitchcock would later bring to the cinema. Above all, perhaps, melodrama commits itself to the values of *story*. In the television age, melodrama passes unnoticed because it is the basic mode.

R. B. Heilman, *Tragedy and Melodrama*, 1968.
James L. Smith, *Melodrama*, 1973.

Mermaid Theatre. At the Elizabethan Mermaid Tavern in Bread Street, the Friday Street Club, founded by Sir Walter Raleigh and attended by SHAKESPEARE, DONNE, BEAUMONT and FLETCHER, used to meet. 'What things have we seen done at the Mermaid!' wrote Beaumont in his lines 'To Ben Jonson'. It was the memory of that tavern that BERNARD MILES wished to recall when he named the little theatre in the grounds of his house in St John's Wood the Mermaid. That theatre had been designed along Elizabethan lines by Michael Stringer and C. Walter Hodges, and it opened in 1951 with performances of *Dido and Aeneas* and *The Tempest*. A second Mermaid, still under the guidance of Bernard Miles, was erected in the quadrangle of the Royal Exchange in 1953, in fulfilment of Miles's wish to see a theatre in the old City of London. That ambition was more fully met with the opening of the third Mermaid in Puddle Dock (not so far from Bread Street) in 1959. It was not an Elizabethan theatre, but because the stage was 'in the same room' as the audience, and because the auditorium was so simple and unfussy, it had echoes of the GLOBE. Refurbished and enlarged in 1981, the Mermaid continued to reflect the idiosyncratic tastes of its founder. The Mermaid is as famous for its annual productions of *Treasure Island*, with Miles as Long John Silver, as it is for its occasional rediscovery of the merits of minor Elizabethan plays. Its productions have rarely rivalled the success of *Lock Up Your Daughters*, a musical version of FIELDING's *Rape upon Rape*, with which the third Mermaid opened in 1959, and it has been constantly bedevilled by financial hardship, most recently in 1983 when, despite resistance from Miles, the trustees put it up for sale.

Method. Method acting is an American derivative of the MOSCOW ART THEATRE. Among the pupils of STANISLAVSKY was RICHARD BOLESLAVSKY, who emigrated to America and established a Laboratory Theatre in New York in the 1920s. One of his pupils there was LEE STRASBERG, who went on to teach the actors of the GROUP THEATRE his own intensely felt version of Stanislavsky. With the publication in America of *An Actor Prepares* in 1936, the 'inward' stress of Strasberg's Stanislavskian classes seemed to be confirmed. The result, at its worst, has been described by Robert Lewis: 'in attempting to agitate the emotional juices of the actor a sort of psychological constipation sets in, preventing the free flow of speech'. Method mumbling became notorious, and even the publication in 1949 of *Building a Character*, Stanislavsky's second and more insistently 'external' account of his system, failed to halt the limp of deeply moved but largely incomprehensible American actors. You can still find some of them, muttering passionately through auditions. An exasperated Peter Ustinov once shouted at one of them during a rehearsal, 'Don't just do something. Stand there!' Effectively taught, as they have been at the New York Actors' Studio since its foundation in 1947, Method actors have dominated Hollywood more than they have dominated Broadway. That is partly because, if you get the sound boom up really close on the set, you can hear what they say. It is also partly because some of them are superb actors.

Robert Lewis, *Method . . . or Madness?*, 1958.
Foster Hirsch, *A Method to Their Madness*, 1985.

Mickery Theatre. This small theatre in Amsterdam has, because of the extraordinary daring of its manager and director Ritsaert ten Cate, become the European centre of the alternative theatre since 1968.

Moscow Art Theatre. The night-long discussion between STANIS-LAVSKY and NEMIROVICH-DANCHENKO that led to the foundation of the Moscow Art Theatre in 1898 has been graphically described by both men. They shared a deep dissatisfaction with the artificial theatre of Imperial Russia, and determined to provide an alternative. Danchenko was a teacher of acting, and Stanislavsky a leader of a group of gifted amateurs. The first company combined students and amateurs. It was a risky adventure, and remained so until the triumphant staging of CHEKHOV's *The Seagull* in December 1898. In token of that triumph, a seagull became the emblem on the front curtain of the theatre. The NATURALISM that characterized the performance of Chekhov's play and the memorable 1905 production of GORKY's *The Lower Depths* was not the only style pursued by Stanislavsky. In the years before the Revolution, the Moscow Art Theatre was the home of experiment. Its reputation for classic preservation is post-revolutionary, the result of unexpected support from Lenin and his colleague Lunacharsky. The world tour of 1922–4 spread the international influence of the company, but there were problems of reassimilation on the return to the Soviet Union. The later history is not without its glories, but it is as Chekhov's theatre and Stanislavsky's temple of art that the Moscow Art Theatre will be best remembered.

National Theatre. The long history of the British pursuit of a National Theatre led eventually to the laying of a foundation stone on the South Bank of the Thames in 1951. There it stayed. In 1962, a National Theatre Board was appointed, and LAURENCE OLIVIER was made responsible for the creation and running of a National Theatre Company. An inaugural performance of *Hamlet* took place at the OLD VIC in October 1962, and in 1963 Denys Lasdun was chosen as the architect of the new theatrical complex. There are three auditoria. The Lyttelton opened in March 1976 with PEGGY ASHCROFT in BECKETT'S

Happy Days. It is an end-stage theatre with an adjustable proscenium. The Olivier, largest of the auditoria, has an open stage with the audience fanning out around it. It opened in October 1976 with PETER HALL's production of MARLOWE's *Tamburlaine*, starring ALBERT FINNEY. The Cottesloe is a smaller studio theatre, which opened in March 1977 with a production of a science-fiction extravaganza by Ken Campbell, *Illuminatus*. Before any of the theatres was complete, Olivier had been replaced as artistic director by PETER HALL. That was in 1973. Hall's energetic promotion of the National Theatre has not silenced all of its critics. Their complaints have quite as much to do with the cost of the enterprise as with its artistic achievements – and there remains a large question about what is meant by 'national', since the company is almost entirely London-orientated. (Tours, as Hall has often pointed out, will increase the costs and raise the demand for subsidy.) Lasdun intended the building as 'an extension of the lifeblood of the city . . . The decorations will be people, carpet, concrete and light, with views of the Thames and London beyond'. Subsidy is, by English standards, enormous, and provincial theatres have felt the pinch. This is the bare bones of an argument that is likely to continue. Meanwhile, the National Theatre maintains an extensive repertoire of plays, ranging from British and foreign classics to new writing.

Perhaps in anticipation of his own retirement in 1988, Hall has increasingly diversified the National's chain of command in the mid-80s, providing leadership opportunities to actors like IAN MCKELLEN and Edward Petherbridge, directors like John Dexter and Richard Eyre and writers like DAVID HARE and ALAN AYCKBOURN. He has also made increasingly vehement statements about the need for greater public subsidy. The future of the National Theatre under its designated directors, Richard Eyre and David Aukin, is not assured.

Naturalism. At an early performance of HAUPTMANN's *Before Sunrise* (1889), a disgusted doctor threw on to the stage a pair of forceps, shouting 'these may come in useful!' The incident is a useful reminder that, as a movement within the theatre at the end of the nineteenth century, Naturalism aimed at something much stronger than the approximation to reality (being 'lifelike', involving characters who are 'just like Auntie Ethel') that is meant by those who use the term loosely. The Naturalists of whom ZOLA is an outstanding example, took their lead from biology, and in particular from the post-Darwinian belief in the survival of the fittest. Zola, having read Claude Bernard's *Introduction to the Study of Experimental Medicine* (1865), recommended Bernard's system of observation and deduction to the literary practitioner, with the simple substitution of 'novelist' (or dramatist) for 'doctor'. It is biological and/or social conditioning (*tempérament*) that governs the action in his work rather than the individuating will (*caractère*). For the German dramatist and novelist Arno Holz (1863–1929), whose *Die Familie Selicke* (1890) was treated as a manifesto of the naturalistic drama, the process could be explained by the formula 'art = nature – x' where 'x' is the shortcomings of the writer. Zola's *Naturalism in the Theatre* (1881) is evidence of the controversial intentions of the movement, which antagonized respectable opinion by its authentic treatment of life in the lower depths of society, as well as by its preparedness to treat sex, in marriage or in adultery, as a physiological fact. As might be guessed from its title, GORKY's *The Lower Depths* (1902) is one of the classics of Naturalism, but it includes a concern for individual resistance to the tyranny of conditioning that gives the play a vital ambivalence. It is for Realists to take an unbiased and objective view. As pioneers of human ecology, Naturalists knew what they would find.

Noh. The Japanese classical drama customarily called Noh (or Nō) is the most carefully preserved of the world's ancient theatrical forms. It was created, almost artificially, in the fourteenth century as a synthesis of predominant entertainment styles, and the rapidity with which it established its own conventions owes much to the genius and industry of two men, Kanami Kiyotsugu (1333–84) and his son Zeami Motokiyo (1363–1443).

The Chinese character used to write the symbol Noh signifies 'to be able', hence 'accomplishment' or simply 'performance'. The principal performer is the *shite*, the doer, dancer or actor, assisted by the *waki* or explainer. Both may have subordinates (*tsure*). As their names imply, the *shite* dances or acts while the *waki* stands aside commenting and explaining. There is also a chanting chorus of ten or twelve men, while music is provided by a piercing flute, two hand-drums and occasionally a big stick-drum. Wooden masks are usually worn by the *shite* and those associated with him, never by the *waki* or his subordinates. In female roles or those of old men, the *shite* is always masked. To avoid too much realism, kings and emperors are played by child actors. Originally Noh performances took place in Shinto temples as part of the ceremonial rites. Sometimes the priests gave a performance in a specially constructed arena outside the temple and occasionally there were private performances in the houses of noblemen. But though the sponsorship of these plays came from the priestly or aristocratic class, the audience, at least during the early period, was by no means exclusively aristocratic. There are many anecdotes about the common man witnessing Noh drama and making naive comments about it. It was only when KABUKI and puppet theatre developed as the drama of the people that the audience for Noh drama became exclusive.

The modern Noh stage has a square acting area with a wooden floor, surrounded by the audience on two or three sides. Three sides of the stage are open, while a pine tree adorns the back wall. To the left of the audience, a passage runs at the back of the stage to the dressing-room, from which it is separated by a curtain. This is the *hashigakari* or gallery from which the actor makes his entrance. Three pine branches symbolizing earth, heaven and man, are tied to the railing of the gallery. At one of the far corners of the stage is the *kirido* ('hurry door' or 'stomach ache door') through which hasty exits may be made. At the other corner stands a stage-hand in ordinary clothes who fetches and carries as required. In a recess between them sit the musicians. The roof over the stage is modelled on that of a Shinto temple. The left-hand corner of the stage immediately in front of one end of the gallery is called 'the name-saying seat' and is occupied by the *shite*. Diagonally across from it the right-hand front corner is the *waki's* seat. Normally the *waki* looks towards a point midway along the left-hand edge of the stage. The chorus squats along the right-hand edge, in a line at right-angles to the line of musicians at the back. Properties used are in keeping with the bareness of the stage. A simple wooden frame serves as a boat or a chariot, four posts and a roof may signify a cottage or a palace and the actor's fan can become brush, knife or pen. Weapons are usually realistic. It was from the gorgeous and elaborately worked costumes that the Noh stage received its colour and spectacle. These, like all other aspects of Noh, are now traditional, but in its early days there appears to have been a good deal of experiment and variety in costume.

Much of what is known about Noh drama comes from the *Kadensho* or 'Book of the Handing on of the Flower' by Zeami Motokiyo, actor, playwright and theorist of Noh drama. Zeami's father, Kanami Kiyotsugu, was the priest of a temple near Nara. He and his son were both patronized by the great Shogun (military ruler) Yoshimitzu, and Zeami's treatise, an esoteric work kept for years within the family, contains valuable information about the philosophy, technique and disciplines of Noh drama. Zeami is also important as the author of some ninety surviving plays, many of them still in the modern repertoire. Deeply influenced by Zen doctrine, Zeami constantly uses the term *yugen*, derived from Zen, in discussing Noh drama. *Yugen* stands for the oblique, the subtle, the ambiguous, as opposed to the explicit, the obvious and over-emphatic. It is what YEATS probably had in mind when he called Noh drama 'distinguished, indirect, symbolic'. It may be applied equally to music and movement as well as to the writing of the drama. *Yugen* is symbolized by a bird bearing in its beak a white flower. *Hana*, the flower, is another symbol of crucial importance, signifying the achieved perfection of the art. The Noh actor began his training at seven, and till the age of twelve practised dancing and recitation. Training in impersonation followed and an actor was believed to have reached his peak at the age of forty-five according to the *Kadensho*. Thereafter, the wise Noh actor should play parts suited to his advancing age. A Noh play rarely has more than four or five roles though a very few have as many as nine. All actors are male.

The subject matter of Noh drama is largely derived from existing literary material, especially well known ballads and poems and familiar scriptures. Printed texts date from about the beginning of the seventeenth century when five official 'schools' of Noh, each with its variant texts, flourished in Japan. More than one play is usually presented at each performance and the plays themselves fall into five main groups: God plays, battle plays with a warrior-ghost, 'wig' plays where the principal character is a woman, demon plays, and plays dealing with magnanimity or political wisdom. Since the sixteenth century, a typical Noh programme would contain a play of each type. Congratulatory plays were also performed on special occasions. The texts do not give the words assigned to minor or 'everyday' characters such as boatmen or servants. Some eight hundred Noh texts survive, of which about two hundred and fifty are in the modern repertoire. Between individual Noh plays, it is customary to perform KYOGEN (wild or mad words), often parodies of the serious plays, bearing much the same relation to them as satyr plays perhaps have to tragedies in the performance of Greek drama. These Kyogen include a prayer to the Buddha to transform the actor's 'mad words' into an act of homage.

The language of Noh is composed of prose based on aristocratic speech of the fourteenth century, and verse with alternate lines of seven and five syllables, the normal metre of Japanese poetry. Like all great poetry it is ultimately untranslatable, but readers without Japanese can get some idea of its haunting resonance from Arthur Waley's justly famous versions. The syllables of the verse lines are fitted in recitation to the sixteen quarter-notes of a common-time musical bar. As noted above, the essence of Noh is *yugen*, that which is beneath the surface. It is a drama not of action in the present, but of action recollected in tranquillity or more often in inquietude, with ghosts and dreams passing shadowily before us, touching the passions of regret and nostalgia and awakening in the characters memories of old, unhappy far-off things and battles long ago. Its movement, though originally mimetic, is now highly stylized and an important part of it is the rhythmic tapping of the bare foot on the wooden stage floor to the accompaniment of the chanted words. Sounding jars are placed beneath the stage to enhance the effect. While Noh is a minority taste even among the Japanese, occasional performances in Europe have aroused enthusiastic applause among audiences who may have come simply to admire the exotic but often stay to be genuinely moved and thrilled. W. B. Yeats's *Purgatory* and other of his 'Plays for Dancers' has something of the spirit and structure of Noh. Noh still has the power it originally had to appeal to all kinds of audience. In the words of Zeami: 'The perfect actor is he who can win praise alike in palaces, temples or villages, or even at festivals held in the shrines of the remotest provinces.'

Kunio Komparu, *The Noh Theatre: Principles and Perspective*, 1984.

Off-Broadway. This is a term that is generally applied to plays and theatres in the city of New York that cost less than those on BROADWAY. It seems to have been first extensively used to describe the 1952 production at the Circle-in-the-Square of TENNESSEE WILLIAMS's *Summer and Smoke*. Until the mid-sixties, Off-Broadway promised to provide useful hospitality for young American dramatists, but commercial pressures tamed its experimental spirit. By 1970 it was not easy to distinguish its values from those of Broadway itself. It was used for Broadway 'tryouts' and production costs rocketed upwards. When the adventurous and rebellious members of the American avant-garde could no longer meet the financial conditions of the Off-Broadway theatres, they moved into basements, lofts, bars, any space they could find. The off-Off-Broadway movement preceded and reflected the revolutionary year of 1968. Its influence was felt in Europe and throughout the United States. It relates to the whole history of FRINGE theatre. As for Off-Broadway, its best hope lies now with the Public Theatre of JOSEPH PAPP's New York Shakespeare Festival, in which new American plays take precedence.

Old Vic Theatre. When it opened in 1818 this theatre, then known as the Coburg, was popular but unfashionable. Derided as the home of vulgar 'transpontine' MELODRAMA by theatregoers who preferred the more salubrious areas north of the river, it played to packed houses in days when the PATENT THEATRES were struggling to make ends meet. The name was changed to the Royal Victoria in 1833 and the affectionate 'Old Vic' came rapidly into parlance. The theatre fell on hard times in mid-century and was closed in 1880. It was then that an amazing lady called Emma Cons bought it and wedded it, as an amusement-hall, to the temperance movement. In 1898, Emma Cons was joined at the Old Vic by her equally amazing niece, LILIAN BAYLIS, who took over the management in 1912. By 1923 she had overseen performances of all the plays of SHAKESPEARE. Throughout the thirties the Old Vic remained a centre of excellence. It was bombed in 1941 and not fully repaired until 1950, but the damaged auditorium was the home of the influential Old Vic School, under MICHEL SAINT-DENIS, from 1947 to 1952. Between 1953 and 1958 Michael Benthall's five-year plan of presenting all the plays in the First Folio of Shakespeare's work was fulfilled. In 1963 the Old Vic became the first home of LAURENCE OLIVIER's National Theatre Company and remained so until 1976. Since then, the question of what to do with the Old Vic has preoccupied many committees, including the Arts Council. The wish of the touring Prospect company, which used it as its London base after 1976, to settle more permanently there was denied by the Arts Council which feared too much theatrical subsidy in London, and the Old Vic remained empty from 1981 to 1983, when it was bought by a Canadian businessman who, as 'Honest Ed', made his money selling cut-price clothes in Toronto.

Peter Roberts, *The Old Vic Story*, 1976.

Open Theatre. Perhaps the most impressive of the many American experimental theatre groups of the sixties, the Open Theatre was in operation from 1963 until 1973, when it disbanded for fear of becoming institutionalized. The founder and spokesman was Joseph Chaikin, who had worked with the LIVING THEATRE during its OFF-BROADWAY years, and who had sensed the problems of the naturalistic actor when asked to perform experimental drama. The Open Theatre was a theatre collective in which actors came increasingly to collaborate with writers in the creation of original works. Their most characteristic work was based on images developed from a central theme or idea. Chaikin's complex choreographic notions relied on a strict sound-and-movement training and on the actor's skill in swift transformations from one pattern of action to another. Jean-Claude van Itallie's *America Hurrah* (1965) was the Open Theatre's first international success. The same author's *The Serpent* (1968) was a fuller example of the company's wish to share in the evolution of a performance and led into the final three works, *Terminal* (1969), *The Mutation Show* (1971) and *Nightwalk* (1973), in which the uniqueness of the Open Theatre was best expressed. In the age of television, Chaikin was constantly searching for the special strength of the live theatre. What he saw as the basis of that strength is stated in the title of his provocative book, *The Presence of the Actor* (1972), and analysed by Eileen Blumenthal in *Joseph Chaikin* (1985).

Pantomime. See HARLEQUINADE.

Patent Theatres. The first purpose-built playhouse in Britain was the Theatre, erected in Shoreditch in 1576 by James Burbage. The authorities were immediately wary, and there was frequent legislation during the sixteenth and seventeenth centuries to control the public influence of the drama. Under Cromwell, the simpler measure of banning theatrical performances altogether was introduced, but the restoration of Charles II led quickly to the legalization of the performed drama. But Charles was a supporter of privilege and monopoly. Well pleased with THOMAS KILLIGREW and WILLIAM DAVENANT, he issued them with Letters Patent giving them the sole right to present plays in public within the City of Westminster. The subsequent history of these patents is very confused. They were divided, sold and quarrelled over. But the presence of two Patent Theatres persisted until 1843, and there is no doubt that this limitation restricted the free growth of drama in England at large and in London in particular. By the early eighteenth century the Letters Patent had settled on Drury Lane and Covent Garden. Only in these two theatres was it strictly legal to perform the 'LEGITIMATE' DRAMA. There was much dispute over the exact meaning of 'legitimate'. It was accepted that opera was not controlled by the monopoly, and the easy distinction between plays without music (legitimate) and plays with music (illegitimate) hardened into practice though never into law. Drury Lane and Covent Garden were vast theatres, each capable of seating over 3,000 at the end of the eighteenth century, and their costs were correspondingly vast. It must have been almost a relief to their hard-pressed managers when the Theatres Act of 1843 rescinded the power of the Patents. What it meant, of course, was that the authorities no longer considered the theatre powerful enough to be dangerous.

Peking Opera. This is the only form of Chinese theatre to have had a significant impact in the Western world. It is an amalgam of many ancient styles, includes dialogue, song, dance, music and acrobatics, and relies on the strict observance of conventions to carry its full significance to a knowing audience. The dominance of Peking Opera dates from the reign of the Emperor Ch'ien Lung (1736–95), who travelled the length and breadth of his vast country to find the best actors and singers. The form of theatre they evolved is highly disciplined and yet unusual among strict dramatic forms in accommodating, almost as a jazz-band accommodates its soloists, the instantaneous inspiration of its performers.

The plays of the Peking Opera are roughly divisible into two kinds, the military (*wu*) and the civil (*wen*), and the characters divisible into four types: male (*sheng*), female (*dan* or *tan*), the male with painted face, whose appearance defines his particular role (*ching* or *jing*) and the comic, generally low-life, male (*chou*). Each of these types can be further sub-divided, and the actor who trains to perform in Peking Opera must learn, over a period of years, to perform, not only the type, but also its various sub-types. Music is integral to the performance, and there is an intimate sign-relationship between actors and instrumentalists. The stories told in the plays will be familiar to a native audience – they may derive from history, legend or selected fiction – and there can be no unhappy endings, since the aim is to illustrate the indestructibility of the better by the worse. A table, a chair, painted cloths, a riding whip and a fly-whisk are traditional stage properties. It is the actor and the dramatic situation that determines whether the table is a hill, a cloud or – a table. By jumping on a chair, characters declare that they are invisible; by circling the stage they signify a long journey; by flourishing a whip they ride a horse and by taking up a fly-whisk they become supernatural. Stage-hands, in street clothes and in full view of the audience, bring on accessories as they are needed. But the Peking Opera is not frozen in its past: film and projections have been incorporated in recent years.

A form of theatre whose conventions of declamation, movement and significance are so precise puts enormous pressure on its actors. Training begins in childhood and must be maintained throughout the performer's active life. The objective is to bring individual force and distinction to the role without destroying the traditional structure or reducing its resonance.

Performance Art. An outgrowth of the FRINGE, closely related to HAPPENINGS, Performance Art is the meeting-point of theatre and three-dimensional art. It is an inclusive term, which may be used to describe the massive outdoor spectaculars of Welfare State in England and BREAD AND PUPPET THEATRE in the U.S.A., the more esoteric but still large-scale work of Snake Theatre in California, or the anarchic comedy of the People Show, as disruptive of conventional patterns of action as Richard Foreman's Ontological-Hysteric Theatre. The visual image is all-important, although many groups of performance artists are making increasing use of complex soundtracks as a complement or contrast to what is seen.

Jeff Nuttall, *Performance Art*, 1979.
Theodore Shank, *American Alternative Theatre*, 1982.

Piccolo Teatro, Milan. When it opened in 1947, the Piccolo was the first theatre in Italy to be supported by public funds and intended for the inhabitants of a single city. With Paolo Grassi as business manager and GIORGIO STREHLER as artistic director, it remained in virtual isolation for two decades, the only Italian theatre with an international reputation and sufficient seriousness of purpose to resist the incoherent pressures of the Italian tendency to identify great drama with grand opera. The opening production was GORKY's *The Lower Depths*, but the continuing reputation of the theatre owes more to Strehler's magnificent work on the plays of BRECHT. *The Threepenny Opera* of 1955 and *Galileo* of 1963 were high points in a series of productions that have made Strehler outstanding among Brechtian directors. It was typical of the enterprise of the Piccolo Teatro that it should respond to the explosive atmosphere of 1968 by taking its production of GOLDONI's *The Servant of Two Masters* into the industrial suburbs of Milan, but this was a troubled time for Strehler. Faced with a revolt from members of his company, he resigned. When he returned, in 1973, it was on the understanding that he would have complete artistic and administrative control (Grassi had meanwhile moved to La Scala). He has maintained the theatre's eclectic repertoire, and continued its regular foreign tours. The company has been seen in over thirty countries.

Provincetown Players. The most important of the many groups that contributed to the Little Theatre movement in America, the Provincetown Players opposed bourgeois materialism as well as the conventional realism of the contemporary theatre. The leading spirit in the formation of the group was the fiery visionary of a new society, George Cram Cook. 'I glow,' he said after reading a life of Nietzsche, 'with a white sense of the relation of a modern writer's social feeling to his art. It was, in the view of Cook and his wife SUSAN GLASPELL, no proper use of theatre to record in accurate detail the surface of men's lives when so much that was vital was necessarily hidden. The title of the first play performed by the Provincetown Players is indicative of the direction Cook hoped that a new movement in America would follow. *Suppressed Desires* was written jointly by Glaspell and Cook and was first performed in a friend's house in Provincetown, Massachusetts.

Encouraged by its reception, they repeated the play in a hastily adapted building on a Provincetown wharf. The year was 1915. The next year a full season was planned and a determination declared that the Provincetown Players would peform American plays only. The arrival of EUGENE O'NEILL in Provincetown was both fortuitous and fortunate, since Cook had no repertoire of available plays. It was the success of O'Neill's *Bound East for Cardiff* that consolidated the Provincetown Players. At the end of the summer season of 1916 they moved from the Wharf Theatre to a brownstone terrace house in Macdougal Street, New York, which they called the Playwrights' Theatre . It is above all for their nurturing of O'Neill's talent that the Provincetown Players are remembered, but the work of their leading designer ROBERT EDMOND JONES was equally innovative and Susan Glaspell's achievement was not negligible. Between 1915 and 1922 the Players produced work by forty-seven American playwrights. Partly disillusioned by the drift of the company towards BROADWAY, Cook and Glaspell left for Greece in 1922. They had seen the Players reach their peak with O'Neill's *The Emperor Jones* in 1920 and his *The Hairy Ape* had just completed its run when they left. There was a year's interim before the Provincetown Players regrouped under the management of O'Neill, Jones and Kenneth Macgowan, but the impetus was hard to sustain. O'Neill left the group in 1926 and its last production closed in 1929.

Repertory Theatre. A true 'repertory' system is one which rings regular changes on the 'repertoire' of plays ready for performance in any one theatre. The proper operation of such a system requires enormous resources (storage of scenery, a large company of actors and musicians, etc.). It was, nonetheless, the norm in the English theatre from the late sixteenth to the mid-nineteenth century. Its replacement by the long run was celebrated by many and resisted by some. One effect was to reduce the number of new plays performed. Another, more serious, was to select plays according to their long-term marketability. It was to provide performances for plays of likely minority appeal that the pioneers of the British Repertory movement worked. The early efforts were essentially amateur and opportunistic. The first full-scale repertory company, amateur in origin but professional through circumstance, was formed in the ABBEY THEATRE, Dublin, in 1904, but it was the Vedrenne-BARKER seasons at the ROYAL COURT in 1904–7 that brought the idea into prominence. The new Repertory Theatres were not based on the old 'repertoire' idea, but on the presentation of a series of worthwhile plays for short runs. As the movement spread – ANNIE HORNIMAN, having endowed the Abbey Theatre, endowed the Gaiety

Theatre in Manchester in 1908, Glasgow opened a theatre in 1909, Liverpool in 1911, Birmingham under BARRY JACKSON in 1913 – so the conditions varied. The OLD VIC under LILIAN BAYLIS, whilst part of the Repertory movement, had a policy quite unlike that of, for example, the Northampton Repertory Company (founded in 1927), nor were the impossible demands of weekly rep fully in the spirit of the movement's visionaries. With the creation of the Arts Council in 1946, the prospect of subsidy changed the policy of all British Repertory Theatres. Though the funds remained short, they were no longer embarrassingly so. Less beneficial was the tendency of subsidy to create league tables, with Bristol, Birmingham and Nottingham standing much higher than Dundee, Crewe and Chesterfield. Inflation and the ruinous Value Added Tax made further inroads on the adventurous spirit of all but the wealthiest Repertory Theatres, and by 1980 almost all were straining to remain solvent by providing a programme of plays that could not, at a glance, be distinguished from that of a commercial theatre or a reliable amateur company. As George Rowell and Anthony Jackson emphasize in *The Repertory Movement* (1984), a new spirit began in the provinces, and in many of them it is ending.

Royal Court Theatre. There have been two highly significant periods in this theatre's history, built in Sloane Square, London, in 1887–8 and originally called the Court. The first was in 1904–7, when three seasons under J. E. Vedrenne and GRANVILLE BARKER established SHAW in the British theatre as well as awakening a sluggish profession to the innovations of many European dramatists. The second followed the establishment of the English Stage Company under GEORGE DEVINE in 1956. It was at the Royal Court that OSBORNE's *Look Back in Anger* was staged in 1956 and the sweet breath of intelligent controversy was brought back into the British theatre. The contribution of the English Stage Company at the Royal Court to the revival of British drama has been lasting. Many of the best contemporary playwrights made their reputations in Sloane Square – Osborne, ARDEN, BOND, JELLICOE, BRENTON and HARE among them – and it remains one of the few theatres in which the dramatist's voice is prominent. Devine died in 1965. His was a hard act to follow, but subsequent artistic directors have maintained a policy geared to the presentation of new plays. The main auditorium of the Royal Court seats 400 in comfort but certainly not in splendour. All performances are accompanied by the regular sound of tube trains entering and leaving the neighbouring Sloane Square station. It is a building which offers theatre without frills, not only in the main theatre but also in the smaller studio Theatre Upstairs, which opened in 1969 and takes even more risks than George Devine did.

Desmond MacCarthy, *The Court Theatre; 1904–1907*, 1907.
Philip Roberts, *The Royal Court Theatre*, 1986.

Royal Shakespeare Company. The story of the evolution of the Shakespeare Memorial Festivals into a major theatre company has been excellently chronicled by Sally Beauman. The first initiative came in 1769, when DAVID GARRICK's three-day Jubilee in STRATFORD was nearly rained off. After that nothing happened for over a century, and when it did the originator was not a man of the theatre but a brewer. The fortunes of Shakespeare in Stratford were to remain closely linked with the Flower family for a further hundred years. Successively chairmen of the enterprise were Charles Flower (1874–92), his brother Edgar (1892–1903), Edgar's son Archibald (1903–44) and Archibald's son Fordham (1944–66). In their various ways the Flowers were as actively involved in the management of Stratford's theatres as LILIAN BAYLIS was in the management of the OLD VIC. It was Charles who saw to the building and opening of the Shakespeare Memorial Theatre in 1879 and who appointed F. R. BENSON as the director of the annual Shakespeare Festivals there. It was Archibald who replaced Benson with William Bridges-Adams, whose cultured concern for Shakespeare's text gave new impetus to the venture, and oversaw the building of the ambitious new theatre and its opening in 1932. Bridges-Adams (1919–34) was replaced, eccentrically, by Ben Iden Payne, again on Archibald Flower's initiative. In the war years, with Archibald's health failing, the Festivals made no headway. Payne resigned in 1942, to be followed briefly by Milton Rosmer and Robert Atkins, and it was Fordham Flower who persuaded Sir BARRY JACKSON to take over the directorship in 1945. Jackson's three seasons (1946–8) were notable for the work of PETER BROOK as director and PAUL SCOFIELD as actor, but it was not until ANTHONY QUAYLE's years as director (1949–57) that Stratford began to attract leading actors and leading critics to leave London.

PETER HALL was the inheritor of a promising but still unproved theatre when he opened his first season in 1960. Within a year he had leased a London theatre, the Aldwych, for the company, redesigned and enlarged the Stratford stage, for the first time persuaded actors to sign three-year contracts and changed the name of the Shakespeare Memorial Theatre to the Royal Shakespeare Theatre. It was during the Hall decade that the right was earned to claim for the Stratford actors an identity as the Royal Shakespeare Company. It was, above all, the achievement of the *Wars of the Roses* cycle (1963), in which Hall and his co-director John Barton edited and, for all the world like COLLEY CIBBER, rewrote Shakespeare's early history plays, that unified the company and began to establish a distinctive style, particularly in the speaking of the verse. The productions were not, of course, of a consistently high standard, but it became impossible to neglect them. It was under Hall's direction that Stratford first claimed subsidy from the Arts Council – its commercial independence had always been a source of pride – and rationalized a policy of performing in both Stratford and London. But Hall was disappointed at the delays over the opening of the new London Theatre in the Barbican and frustrated by the continuing problems of finance. He resigned in 1968 and was succeeded by TREVOR NUNN, under whose direction the Royal Shakespeare Company has established itself firmly as an international organization. Nunn and Terry Hands, who succeeded him in 1986, have been continually concerned to achieve adequate subsidy, often in competition with the NATIONAL THEATRE, but that has not prevented the significant development of small-scale work in Stratford (at The Other Place) and London (firstly at The Place, later at The Warehouse, and then at The Pit), nor the eventual opening of the theatre in the Barbican (1982).

Sally Beauman, *The Royal Shakespeare Company: A History of Ten Decades*, 1982.

San Fransisco Mime Troupe. R. G. Davis has given an account of the first ten years of the group which he founded in 1959 in *The San Francisco Mime Troupe* (1975). Its techniques were those of popular entertainers, juggling, busking, puppet shows, magic, music hall, etc., and the inspiration was a combination of mime and COMMEDIA DELL'ARTE. The increasing political commitment of the group brought opposition from the Californian authorities, particularly after 1962, when they began performing in the San Francisco parks and attracting audiences of mixed race and background. Davis was unabashed: 'We try in our own humble way to destroy the United States,' he asserted. The scripts they used were based on plays by MOLIÈRE, GOLDONI, JARRY, GHELDERODE, BRECHT and others, but the import was modern and openly subversive. *L'Amant Militaire* (1967), for example, though based on a play by Goldoni was a vigorous attack on the Vietnam War. The adaptation was by Joan Holden, who has been the group's leading writer since 1970, the year in which Davis and the more militantly Marxist members of the group severed their connections with it. Subsequent work has focused on socio-political issues, particularly on feminism and racism. An important issue has been the integration of non-white actors. The Troupe is still primarily concerned with the culturally disenfranchised. Joan Holden has explained that, 'The basic theme of all our plays is the same: there is a class system in this country that is not run in your interest. It is run in the interest of rich people and they fool you about your interest.'

7:84 Theatre Company. Founded in 1971 by the playwright JOHN MCGRATH, 7:84 takes its name from a statistical assessment that 7 per cent of the British population owned 84 per cent of the nation's wealth. McGrath's aim was to contribute to the creation of a counter-culture based on the working class. The company's first production, his own *Trees in the Wind*, was staged at the Edinburgh Festival in 1971. In 1972 they toured TREVOR GRIFFITHS' *Occupations*, and *The Ballygombeen Bequest*, a play by JOHN ARDEN and Margaretta D'Arcy about English and Anglo-Irish exploitation of Irish land. It caused one landlord enough concern to make him take out a court injunction and the tour had to end. In 1973, after some dissatisfaction about the effectiveness of its cooperative structure, 7:84 split into two groups, 7:84 England and 7:84 Scotland. With the Scottish section, McGrath staged the splendid political *ceilidh*, *The Cheviot, The Stag and the Black, Black Oil* (1973), *Boom* and *The Game's a Bogey* (1974) and *Little Red Hen* (1975). The company has reached working-class audiences in Scotland as effectively as any group on the political FRINGE. The English section has produced plays by DAVID EDGAR (*Wreckers*, 1977), Arden and D'Arcy (*Vandaleur's Folly*, 1978) and others. Increasingly reliant on Arts Council subsidy, 7:84, like all political theatre groups, struggles to sustain the hopeful idealism that led to its formation.

Catherine Itzin, *Stages in the Revolution*, 1980.

Shimpa. To purists, Shimpa is a degenerate form of KABUKI, based on sensational fiction and permitting the inclusion of female performers as well as, or even instead of, the *onnagata* of Kabuki. It developed in the late nineteenth century, and found its first expression in political plays, but its theatrical significance has less to do with its political origins – soon abandoned – than with its challenge to the monopoly of certain families over Kabuki-style performances. Even more than Kabuki, Shimpa is a commercially orientated form of dance-drama.

Stratford. Three notable theatres in three different countries celebrate in various ways the birth of SHAKESPEARE in the small market-town of Stratford-upon-Avon. The first Shakespeare Memorial Theatre in

England was opened in 1879. It was a Gothic extravaganza, destroyed by a benevolent fire in 1926. A second theatre on the same site was opened in 1932, not a great time for theatre building. Under William Bridges-Adams, Ben Iden Payne, Milton Rosmer, Robert Atkins, BARRY JACKSON (1946–8), ANTHONY QUAYLE (1949–57), and Glen Byam Shaw (1953–9), the theatre came gradually to prominence. Actors had been slow to accept engagements outside London. The appointment of PETER HALL as director of the newly named ROYAL SHAKESPEARE COMPANY in 1960 turned a provincial enterprise into a national theatre. The RSC found itself a London outlet at the Aldwych, and became a centre of the 'director's theatre'. Its policy of electing established or promising actors as Associate Artists gave hope of a developing ensemble. The momentum scarcely flagged when TREVOR NUNN took over from Peter Hall in 1970. The small Stratford Studio (The Other Place) continues to attract new plays and to refurbish old ones. The New Swan, opened in 1986, provides a third contrasting auditorium, a piece of dazzling architectural opportunism.

In Canada, at Stratford, Ontario, a theatre designed by Robert Fairfield along lines suggested by TYRONE GUTHRIE was opened in 1957. Its thrust stage and encircling auditorium provide a more Elizabethan flexibility than the English Stratford has. A quainter, half-timbered version of Elizabethan theatre informed the building of the theatre at Stratford, Connecticut in 1955. It is a cumbersome theatre in an attractive setting.

Sally Beauman, *The Royal Shakespeare Company: A History of Ten Decades*, 1982.

Sturm und Drang. The German movement gets its name (meaning Storm and Stress) from the title of a not very distinguished play by Klinger, written in 1775. By 1787, when SCHILLER completed *Don Carlos*, the movement's force was largely spent. It celebrated the rights of the individual, admired the 'formlessness' of SHAKESPEARE, and believed Rousseau's return to nature to be best identified in the actions of a rebellious hero, like GOETHE's Götz von Berlichingen. The movement is understandably, though not entirely accurately, associated with revolutionary ardour and the urge towards the unification of Germany. At its most indulgent, it takes a romantic view of crime and overrates ecstasy in caves. Its influence can be discerned in the nineteenth-century development of MELODRAMA.

Theatre, the. This was the plain name given to the first purpose-built public playhouse in England. The builder was James Burbage, a master-carpenter who had also been an actor with Lord Leicester's Men. The erection of the Theatre in 1576 was a commercial speculation, made possible by the preparedness of Burbage's brother-in-law John Brayne to shoulder the major part of the financial burden, £683. Very little is known directly about the Theatre, beyond the fact that it was built in Shoreditch, a little to the north of what is now Liverpool Street station, outside the walls of the City of London and therefore outside the jurisdiction of the Lord Mayor and his menacingly Puritan aldermen. From the stated fact that many of its timbers were later used in the construction of the GLOBE, it has been inferred that the Theatre was a polygonal structure with three galleries surrounding an open yard. The practical probability is that the raised stage was removable. Burbage was a business man, and, though plays may have been his main interest, he would not have wanted his new property to be suitable for nothing else – particularly in an age where public spectacles like fencing contests, bear-baiting and cock-fighting were of proven attractiveness. The lease on the Theatre's land ran out in 1597, and the building was dismantled in 1598. Some, at least, of its timbers were carried across London at dead of night on 28 December 1598 to assist in the erection of a new theatre on the south bank of the Thames. Among those who did the carrying was James Burbage's actor-son RICHARD, already well known for his performances in SHAKESPEARE's plays.

Theatre-in-the-Round. If you want a small audience to have clear sight of an event, you would probably advise them to stand in a circle. It is certainly an ideal shape for those audiences that have an eye to participation, and it remains the normal shape for sporting spectacles. But theatrical spectacle, as early as fifth-century Athens, developed a preference for particularity and detail. The 'actor' was placed in front of more and more of the audience, until, with the development of the proscenium arch, he was given a room of his own – albeit with one wall missing. So it was that Margo Jones in America and STEPHEN JOSEPH in England, found themselves having to present as 'new' what was anything but new. Margo Jones's work in Dallas opened enough eyes to encourage the building in Washington, DC in 1961 of an Arena theatre (the American use of 'arena' to describe in-the-round performances has been rendered ambiguous by the regrettable English use of the same word to describe thrust-staging). In England, Stephen Joseph established a summer theatre-in-the-round in the concert room of the Scarborough Library and the Victoria Theatre in Stoke-on-Trent in a converted cinema. More recently, the imaginative conversion of the Manchester Royal Exchange to a theatre-in-the-round has brought vigorous and enthusiastic responses. 'I act with my face,' Felix Aylmer protested at a public meeting in about 1965, not realizing that he was acting with his back, too!

Margo Jones, *Theatre-in-the-Round*, 1951.
Stephen Joseph, *Theatre-in-the-Round*, 1967.

Théâtre National Populaire. Every country has tried to establish a quality theatre for the people. The French attempt has been among the most successful, though not without vast tribulation. The TNP began in 1920, when Firmin Gémier (1865–1933) chose it as a name for his touring theatre. In 1937 the TNP was established in the impressive Palais de Chaillot, but it was not until JEAN VILAR was appointed director in 1951 that it achieved anything like success. A condition of state subsidy was that the prices should be kept down, and that 150 performances should be given in and around Paris each year. Vilar retired in 1963, and George Wilson took over until 1971. The events of 1968 demanded a reappraisal of the idea of a 'popular' theatre, and the appointment of ROGER PLANCHON as director in 1972 was timely. The new TNP includes Paris in its tours, but no longer specially favours it. Planchon, with the help of a second company under the direction of Patrice Chéreau, has tried to maintain the spirit of the promise he made in 1972: 'We will celebrate theatre for a month in every city!'

Tragedy. The first decisive attempt to define tragedy was ARISTOTLE's. Writing in the fourth century BC, he based his account on the plays of SOPHOCLES. It was certainly in Greece that the genre originated. Exactly how is a matter of dispute. In formal terms, a crucial development came when the leader of the dithyrambic chorus (a dithyramb was a choric hymn to the god Dionysus) adopted a solo role and could thus hold a sung or spoken dialogue with that chorus. But the more interesting speculations centre on the social and psychical origins of tragedy. Its association with Greek religion is manifest in the work of AESCHYLUS and Sophocles, and religious controversy is a vivid aspect of the plays of EURIPIDES. A marked shift of tone and intention is evident in the Roman tragedies of SENECA. The obvious inference is that tragedy is not a static form to be imitated, but a dynamic form that is redefined by each of its major exponents. It took the genius of CORNEILLE and, even more so, RACINE to transcend the sterile formalism of French neo-classical theorists. The freer climate of Elizabethan England had allowed the development of a blank-verse tragedy of great scope and flexibility. What seems common to all great tragedies is their exploration of the area of experience at which human potentiality encounters human limitation. Post-Jacobean attempts at writing great tragedy in English have suffered from a feckless imitativeness of Elizabethan achievement. An exception was the domestic style of GEORGE LILLO, later developed on a fuller scale in Germany by LESSING. The nineteenth century came to accommodate in MELODRAMA the middle-class moods of domestic tragedy. There is considerable substance in the argument of George Steiner (in *The Death of Tragedy*) that, since Shakespeare and Racine, 'the tragic voice in drama is blurred or still'. This is not to say that playwrights have abandoned the quest.

Unities. The unities of time, place and action became a matter of crucial importance to theorists of neo-classicism in the French seventeenth-century theatre. Deriving their authority from ARISTOTLE's *Poetics* and their urge to codify from their Gallic purism, they stated that a play should tell only one story, that its time-span should be at the most one day and that its events should all occur in one place. The classic statement of the necessity of preserving the unities is Jean Mairet's preface to his play, *Sylvanire* (1630). Mairet was twenty-six when he wrote it, and the success of the play reinforced the tenets of the preface. All the great writers of the seventeenth-century French theatre, CORNEILLE, RACINE and MOLIÈRE included, were expected to observe the unities. The quarrel over Corneille's alleged violation of them in *Le Cid* raged so fiercely that it was referred to Cardinal Richelieu for arbitration. Not surprisingly, the French theatre found it difficult to accommodate SHAKESPEARE, and it was not until the flamboyantly lavish plays of the romantics, HUGO and DUMAS *père* in particular, that the rigidity of the Unities was effectively challenged in France. The famous battle over Hugo's *Hernani* in 1830 was a last-ditch fight for the classicists. The constraints imposed by the Unities were not entirely detrimental since they aided the development of a drama as pure and potent as Racine's, but the snivellings of those who preferred a dying code to living practice are not edifying. The French theatre has not forgotten the Unities, and IONESCO's *Exit the King* (1963) is an amusingly allusive monument to their authority.

Unity Theatre. The first relatively stable labour movement theatre group in England was formed in 1935 by an alliance between the Rebel Players and Red Radio. An amateur group, it rented premises, seating one hundred, in Britannia Road, London. By 1939, membership stood at 7,000. Unity Theatre was effectively launched in 1935 with the production of a pirated version of ODETS' *Waiting for Lefty*. The following year, a play by two London taxi-drivers, *Where's That Bomb?*, demonstrated the group's concern to provide as much of its own material as possible. In 1937, conversion of a mission hall in Goldington Street, St Pancras was completed and Unity moved into its 320-seat theatre. The year 1938 saw a production of *Senora Carrar's Rifles*, the first BRECHT play to be performed in England, and two LIVING NEWSPAPERS based on the American originals, *Busmen* and *Crisis*. World War II forced a closure, though mobile units provided entertainment to people sheltering from the blitz in Underground stations. Unity's post-war policy was announced in a booklet called *To Build a People's Theatre* (1945). Rather than chase huge audiences, it preferred to establish regional branches, of which there were thirty-six by the end of 1946. Under Ted Willis's direction (in the years before *Dixon of Dock Green*), Unity stressed the responsibility of a left-wing theatre to its community, for example in the 1947 Living Newspaper, *Black Magic*, which aimed to recruit people to the pits. Equally characteristic were plays dramatizing working-class struggles, like Robert Mitchell's *The Matchgirls* (1947) and Burt Marnik's *Cyanamide* (1957). It also staged British premieres of plays by SARTRE and Brecht and a world premiere of ADAMOV's *Spring '71* (1962). Its own regular authors included Leonard Peck and Leonard Irwin. Despite its amateur status, Unity was not exempt from the problems confronting professional theatres in Britain, and its financial hopes were dashed in 1975, when its London premises were destroyed by fire.

Vaudeville. There are two theories about the origin of the word 'vaudeville'. According to the first it is a corruption of *voix de villes* (voice of the cities) and refers to street songs. According to the second, it derives from the Vau de Vire, a valley in Normandy, where Olivier Basselin, in the fifteenth century, sang satiric songs to popular tunes. Certainly the word came into French currency to describe topical songs set to familiar melodies. As a theatrical form, vaudeville was a response to legal constraints imposed in eighteenth-century France. The theatres of the fairs, banned from using dialogue, turned speech into song. The *comédie à vaudevilles*, popular by the end of the eighteenth century, was refined in the nineteenth, finding expression on the one hand in the farces of LABICHE and on the other in the *opéra comique* of Offenbach. The theatrical home of vaudeville was the Palais Royal, though other theatres, even at times the COMÉDIE-FRANÇAISE, exploited its popularity, and its spirit survived in the work of Sacha Guitry (1885–1957). Vaudeville has a much greater range than its English equivalent, burlesque. It encompasses BALLAD OPERA and the frothier work of NOEL

COWARD, along with *Charley's Aunt* and the Savoy Operas of GILBERT and Sullivan. CHEKHOV's first plays were vaudevilles. In America, vaudeville is more specifically allied to the English music hall. Its heyday began in about 1881, when Tony Pastor (1837–1908) opened a vaudeville theatre in 14th Street, New York and ended in about 1932, when the BROADWAY Palace Theatre was closed.

Verfremdung/Verfremdungseffekt. The word 'Verfremdung' was coined by BERTOLT BRECHT, and if its meaning is not crystal clear, the fault lies in part with those who have subsequently attempted to define it. For English readers, the problem begins with the translation of *Verfremdung* as 'alienation'. The kindred word *Entfremdung*, also translated as 'alienation', has a lively philosophical, economic and political history. Brecht would have known its important place in Hegel's work, and its application by Marx to the condition of the proletariat under capitalism. Many of Brecht's plays concern themselves with alienation in this sense. There is a danger of confusion here. If the alienation of the proletariat had been obvious, Marx would not have needed to expound it. It was not obvious because it was taken for granted, just as a Victorian industrialist took for granted that a woman's place was in the home, despite the fact that he employed women in his mill. If, like Marx or like Brecht, you do not believe that it is 'natural' that the majority of the world's population should labour mindlessly to fill the pockets of the minority, you will wish to establish, against the interests of that sophisticated minority, that it is not natural. You will want to have *recognized* as strange what you already believe *is* strange. That is to say that you will want to alienate alienation – to make strange the condition of estrangement. Brecht's *Verfremdungseffekte* were theatrical devices, some literary, some technical, some histrionic, deployed in order to bring audiences to recognize the strangeness of social conditions that they took for granted. The failure of *The Threepenny Opera* to do this at its Berlin premiere in 1928 deepened Brecht's thinking about effective theatre, but the word *Verfremdung* itself did not enter his vocabulary until after his visit to Moscow in 1935. He encountered there the phrase, used by the Russian critic Victor Shklovsky, 'priyom ostranyeniya' (a way of making strange). *Verfremdungseffekt* may be a translation of Shklovsky's Russian into Brecht's German. He used it almost at once in the title of an important essay on Chinese acting.

In most of the plays that annoyed him, Brecht watched actors striving to make events that are utterly extraordinary seem comparatively explicable. Brecht's anxiety was contrary, to make ordinary events *in*explicable. As he wrote in the *Short Organum*, perhaps the most useful single collection of his mature theatrical thoughts:

> Who mistrusts what he is used to? To transform himself from general passive acceptance to a corresponding state of suspicious inquiry a man would need to develop that detached eye with which the great Galileo observed a swinging chandelier. He was amazed by this pendulum motion, as if he had not expected it and could not understand its occurring, and this enabled him to come on the rules by which it was governed. Here is the outlook, disconcerting but fruitful, which the theatre must provoke with its representations of human social life. It must amaze its public, and this can be achieved by a technique of alienating the familiar.

Before familiarity can be excited into awareness, the familiar must be stripped of its inconspicuousness. The philosopher of the *Messingkauf Dialogues* states with surprising confidence that:

> Anyone who has observed with astonishment the eating habits, the judicial processes, the love life of savage peoples will also be able to observe our own eating customs, judicial processes and love life with astonishment.

But the confidence is an ironic masquerade. Brecht knew only too well the right hand's studied ignorance of the left hand's labour. 'True A-effects,' he wrote, 'are of a combative character'. Any *Verfremdungs-effekt* has the basic aim of drawing attention to events, ideas, principles, motives, or comparisons that would normally be ignored or, at least, skimpily observed, and drawing attention to them *so that they can be altered*.

III Theatre People

Theatre People

Abington, Frances (1737–1815). The first Lady Teazle in SHERIDAN's *The School for Scandal* (1777), also a success as the witless Miss Prue in CONGREVE's *Love for Love*. Reynolds painted her in this latter role. She started as a street singer and went on to become one of the most successful actresses of the time, though KITTY CLIVE and HANNAH PRITCHARD were more versatile rivals. She had the unusual distinction of being admired by Dr Johnson, who knew little of her adulteries and less of her addiction to gambling, but admired her wit and perhaps her clothes.

Achurch, Janet (1864–1916). English actress whose independence of mind was sufficient to enable her to defy decent opinion and stage the first professional production in London of IBSEN's *A Doll's House* (1889). SHAW called her 'the only tragic actress of genius we now possess'. *Mrs Warren's Profession* was written partly as a result of Achurch's prompting, and she was herself the author of a play on the same subject, *Mrs Daintree's Daughter*, which received a single performance in 1894. Achurch toured with F. R. BENSON and was a notable Cleopatra, but it is for the production of *A Doll's House* and for the later one of *Little Eyolf* (1896) that she is justly esteemed. She had the intelligence to perceive the importance of Ibsen and the courage to perform him.

Adamov, Arthur (1908–70). Adamov's wealthy father was forced to leave Russia in 1912. He took refuge in Germany, but Adamov himself, who had been taught after the fashionable Russian style to speak French as his first language, was more at home in Paris, where the family moved in 1924. In the shadow of new poverty, largely caused by his father's addicton to gambling, Adamov developed the obsessions (with suicide, poverty, impotence) that haunt his plays. He was involved with literary and political revolutionary groups, founded a surrealist review called *Discontinuité* whose single issue was published in 1928, became a friend of ARTAUD and, through him, an admirer of the work of STRINDBERG, and lived in constant penury. He wrote his first play in 1947, but later rejected all his dramatic work before *Professor Taranne*, an account of a dream he had had. Its production by ROGER PLANCHON in Lyon in 1953 marked the beginning of a fruitful collaboration between playwright and director. The Lyon production of *Paolo Paoli* in 1957 forced Adamov's name before the French public, which was never at ease with his bitter criticisms of decaying capitalist society. For a while it was possible to place Adamov among the apolitical leaders of the THEATRE OF THE ABSURD, but his reaction to the Algerian War was strident. Turning away from IONESCO and towards BRECHT, he wrote a play on the Paris Commune, *Spring '71* (1960). His brilliant attack on American society, *Off Limits* (1968), has the same sting. After his death (probably by suicide) Planchon staged at the THÉÂTRE NATIONAL POPULAIRE a remarkable collage of his work, *A.A. Theatres of Arthur Adamov* (1975), in which the dreams, neuroses, obsessions and engagement of this battered man are woven together.

Aeschylus (525–456 BC). The earliest of the three great tragic playwrights of ancient Greece, Aeschylus wrote upwards of ninety plays, of which seven have survived. They are, in possible chronological order, the *Persians* (472), the *Seven against Thebes* (469), a trilogy known collectively as the *Oresteia* and consisting of the *Agamemnon*, the *Libation Bearers* or *Choephori* and the *Eumenides* (458), the *Suppliant Women* and the *Prometheus Bound*. Recent scholarship has argued that the last two undated plays are late work, in which Aeschylus returns to earlier and less developed tragic models.

Aeschylus was born a decade after the foundation of the great festival of tragedy in Athens. His birthplace, Eleusis, was the home of the Eleusinian Mysteries, the best known of the many Greek initiation cults and ceremonies whose occultism is referred to by the later dramatist, EURIPIDES, in the *Bacchae*. Aeschylus is known to have been in the army that defeated the Persians at the Battle of Marathon in 490, and the Greek victory is the background to his earliest extant play. The scope of his humanity is startlingly expressed in his decision to present the tragedy from the point of view of the Persians. His sense of a universe presided over by gods does not imply a belief that men are mere puppets. As is clear from the *Oresteia* (the only complete trilogy to have survived from the great period of Greek tragedy), the gods can have their understanding sharpened by human endeavour. Aeschylus was above all a poet. The tragic form he inherited depended on a large chorus of singers and dancers (it has been suggested that Aeschylus himself reduced the number from fifty to fifteen or twelve), together with a single actor who might play two or three parts. By introducing a second actor, he opened up new possibilities for dialogue and extended conflict, but choral odes and lyrics retain a dominant role in his plays. The esteem in which he was held is vividly presented and fondly criticized in the *Frogs* of ARISTOPHANES.

H. D. F. Kitto, *Greek Tragedy*, 3rd ed., 1961.
George Thomson, *Aeschylus and Athens*, 1973.

Agate, James (1877–1947). Born in Manchester, this English critic wrote his earliest reviews for the *Manchester Guardian* and was dramatic critic for the *Sunday Times* from 1923 until his death. He became, perhaps, too much of a personality, but his determination that the critic should be, first and foremost, a writer is exemplary. In addition to several volumes of collected criticism, including *Brief Chronicles* (1943), *Red-Letter Nights* (1944) and *Immoment Toys* (1945), Agate published selections from his diary under the disarming title, *Ego*. There are nine volumes. They embody, wrote Ivor Brown in an obituary, 'the darting, eager, untiring spirit of one whom his friends, though often maddened by his caprice, will never be able to forget'. The verdict of another diarist, Arnold Bennett, was harsher. His Journal for 22 March 1920 reads: 'J. E. Agate came early for tea in order to get counsel. He is a man of forty or so, rather coarse-looking and therefore rather coarse in some things. Fattish. Has reputation for sexual perversity. Married a beautiful young French girl (twenty-three or so), who has now evidently left him . . . . Principal job; partner in some cotton trade concern. Has just sold out for (he says) £5000 and decided to come to London to make a living . . . . Writes with difficulty. Knows a deuce of a lot about French dramatic literature. Seems to understand acting. Has certain sensibilities. Yet his taste capricious and unreliable. Has various conventional prejudices against institutions. The man has points and refinements; but he is fundamentally unintelligent.' Agate learned to write with ease, but Bennett's strictures have some point.

James Harding, *Agate*, 1986.

Albee, Edward (1928–   ). *The Zoo Story* (1959) was an astonishingly accomplished first play. Of Albee's subsequent plays, only *Who's Afraid of Virginia Woolf?* (1962) matches it. It was probably no help to Albee to be so quickly hailed as the great new American dramatist. Some of his wayward poetic writing may have been the result of an attempt to justify his inflated literary reputation. His best work – *A Delicate Balance* (1966) can claim to be among it – provides a wide-awake answer to the American dream. In addition to writing plays, Albee has produced and directed in OFF-BROADWAY theatre, and laboured to provide performance outlets for new plays. Since he is the namesake and adopted grandson of one of the major figures in the development of the razzmatazz of American show-business, he may feel that he owes American theatre an alternative.

Anita M. Stenz, *Albee: The Poet of Loss*, 1978.

Aldridge, Ira (*c.* 1805–67). Probably born in Senegambia, a Christian member of the Fulah tribe. Aldridge had aspirations to become a missionary but he made his name as the first black Othello when he played the part at the Royalty Theatre, London in 1826. He had already acted in New York, but his reputation could not be made in his adopted home country, where negroes were neither a novelty nor a credible constituent of the new culture. It was in England, Germany and Russia that Aldridge was celebrated. An intelligent and sensitive man, he amassed a fair fortune, took a white wife, became a naturalized Englishman in 1863 and spent his last years in Germany. Othello was not his only part, though it was certainly his main one. His playing of King Lear in Russia won him the admiration and friendship of LEV TOLSTOY.

Herbert Marshall and Mildred Stock, *Ira Aldridge*, 1962.

Alleyn, Edward (1566–1626). Though he did not achieve his apparent ambition of being knighted, Alleyn did well enough as an actor to retire comparatively early (*c.* 1600) and found the College of God's Gift at Dulwich where his diary and papers still survive. He was the first great actor of the Elizabethan theatre about whom reliable details have come down to us, and made his name in a succession of Marlovian roles – Tamburlaine, Faustus and Barabbas. An attractive but unreliable tradition attributes his leaving the stage to the appearance, at a performance of *Faustus*, of the Devil in person. Alleyn joined Worcester's Men at the age of seventeen and the Admiral's Men shortly after. He was associated with the latter company and its impresario PHILIP HENSLOWE throughout most of his career and in 1592 married Henslowe's stepdaughter. His second wife, whom he married two years before his death, was the daughter of John Donne, then Dean of St Paul's. Many contemporaries, among them NASHE, JONSON and HEYWOOD refer to his acting prowess, while his diary and letters show him to be a shrewd businessman and a good husband and householder. He had a financial interest in the Fortune Theatre as well as in bear-baiting rings and brothels in the Bankside area, and was a churchwarden of St Saviour's, Southwark.

G. L. Hosking, *The Life and Times of Edward Alleyn*, 1952.

Anderson, Maxwell (1888–1959). American playwright, who wrote often in verse, and always with a sense of the seriousness of entertainment. This could lead him into bathos and bombast, but audiences of the thirties were somewhat earnest, and this teacher-turned-journalist became a BROADWAY favourite. *What Price Glory?* (1924), a war play, was his first success. Historical dramas like *Elizabeth the Queen* (1930), *Night over Taos* (1932), *Mary of Scotland* (1933) and *The Masque of Kings*(1937) inflated his reputation. Anderson is more fairly served if it is remembered that he collaborated with Kurt Weill on a good comic musical called *Knickerbocker Holiday* (1938) – the later collaboration on *Lost in the Stars* (1949) fell short of the Paton novel of South African injustice, *Cry, the Beloved Country*, from which it was bowdlerized – that he caused some unease by the wit of his political satire, *Both Your Houses* (1933), that he provided in *Key Largo* (1939) one of the better of the many inadequate plays on the aftermath of the Spanish Civil War, and that *Winterset* (1935) remains an honest and craftsmanlike investigation into the shame of America's treatment of Sacco and Vanzetti, executed as 'red' terrorists in 1927.

Alfred S. Shivers, *Maxwell Anderson*, 1976.

Anouilh, Jean (1910–   ). Born in Bordeaux, Anouilh came into his own a few years before the outbreak of World War II and was one of the most successful French dramatists during the immediate post-war period. After a brief career in advertising, he was secretary to LOUIS JOUVET and has said that it was seeing Jouvet's production of GIRAUDOUX's *Siegfried* in 1928 that turned him towards the theatre. His first play, *L'Hermine*, was produced by LUGNÉ-POË in 1932 and it was followed by a series of successes including *Traveller without Luggage* (1937), *Thieves' Carnival* (1938), *Eurydice* (1942) and *Antigone* (1944). The last of these was a notably subtle contribution to the boosting of French morale under German occupation. His plays were increasingly quickly translated into English and *Ring round the Moon*, CHRISTOPHER FRY's witty version of *L'Invitation au château* (1947), *The Waltz of the Toreadors* (1957), *The Lark* (1953), *Becket* (1959) and *Poor Bitos* (1963) have all been successful in Britain and America. Anouilh has divided his work into 'pièces roses', 'pièces noires', 'pièces brillantes' and 'pièces grinçantes', perhaps suggesting that the 'black' and 'grating' plays are more profound and truer to life than the 'pink' and 'shining'. Not everyone will agree. What is common to all of them is a fine sense of theatrical artifice, a romantic nostalgia for lost innocence in a world of squalid corruption and hard-nosed experience, and a sense of humour which makes the indulgent melancholy not only bearable but enjoyable.

H. G. McIntyre, *The Theatre of Jean Anouilh*, 1981.

Antoine, André (1858–1943). This French actor and director became the active champion of NATURALISM in 1887, when he founded the Théâtre Libre. He was working for the Paris Gas Company at the time, and his acting experience had all been amateur. He financed the venture with his savings, and, despite a *succès d'estime*, had to close his theatre in 1894. From 1897 to 1906, he ran the Théâtre Antoine, and was a director at the Odéon from 1906 until his virtual retirement in 1914. The essential feature of the style Antoine evolved at the Théâtre Libre was its commitment to the stage as an environment in which the actor/ characters lived their own lives behind a notional fourth wall. Antoine was not a great originator, nor even a great director, but he provided, in the small Théâtre Libre (the 343-seat capacity of the first hall was raised to 800 with an almost immediate shift to a second), a stage responsive to the new drama, and actors motivated to do it justice.

John A. Henderson, *The First Avant-Garde*, 1971.

Appia, Adolphe (1862–1928). Appia's characteristic stage designs are in black and white – colour is to be provided by the lighting – and they give room for the performer's movements in space to preserve a three-dimensional assertiveness. That is to say that this Swiss designer was a pioneer and a prodigy, surprisingly, though not sensationally, influential. He was born in Geneva, where his father was a surgeon. That father's stern Calvinism, and the sense of social mission that led him in 1863 to help found the Red Cross, had an adverse effect on his son, whose stutter, homosexuality, and strangely tormented life are susceptible to interpretation by Freudian cliché. Appia managed to live in reasonable comfort, despite a lack of income, and his father presumably made that possible. He also made possible the musical training that led Appia to appreciate Wagner, and to explore better ways of staging his work. His first book, *La Mise en scène du drame wagnérien* (1895), is the direct outcome of that early questioning. His second, *Music and the Art of the Theatre* (1899), was written in French, but first published in German as *Die Musik und die Inscenierung*. It is the best expression of his staging theories. The later *The Work of Living Art*, published in 1921 as *L'Oeuvre d'art vivant*, is a more general account of his aesthetic theories.

Walter R. Volbach, *Adolphe Appia*, 1968.

Arden, John (1930–   ). Arden trained as an architect, fights like a tiger, and has written more richly and variously than any other post-war British dramatist. Until 1970 his plays dealt starkly with social and political confrontations, but avoided partisanship. Since then he has become increasingly vehement in opposing establishment assumptions. With his wife, Margaretta D'Arcy, he has written about and worked in Ireland. *The Ballygombeen Bequest* (1972) excited a libel action from a landlord whose exploitation of the Irish poor it lampooned. *The Non-Stop Connolly Show* (1975) is a chronicle in six parts, combining doggerel, political caricature and socialist propaganda in a theatre-defying but profoundly serious exploration of one of Ireland's lost leaders. *Vandaleur's Folly* (1978) exposes English fear in the face of Irish social experiment. Such work has replaced the literary, ballad-based resonances of *Serjeant Musgrave's Dance* (1959) and *Armstrong's Last Goodnight* (1964), and the anarchic comedy of *The Happy Haven* (1960) and *The Workhouse Donkey* (1963) with a commitment to radical resistance. Anyone who saw and heard him protesting from the stage about the way the ROYAL SHAKESPEARE COMPANY had misdirected *The Island of the Mighty* (1972) will know that neither Arden nor Margaretta D'Arcy is afraid of the firing line. But the radio-play *Pearl* (1978) was a sudden reminder that Arden has not lost his love of venturesome words, nor his involvement in the history of the British theatre, whose tameness now he angrily resents.

Albert Hunt, *Arden: A Study of His Plays*, 1974.
Frances Gray, *John Arden*, 1982.

Aristophanes (*c*. 444–*c*. 380 BC). The only ancient Greek comic dramatist whose work survives in more than mere fragments, Aristophanes wrote forty comedies between 427 and 388 BC, of which eleven survive. Most of them display a relish for political and personal invective, bawdy innuendo and animal masquerade which hark back to the origins of COMEDY in phallic ritual and mime. Aristophanes' plays are generally regarded as representative of the so-called Old Comedy which flourished in Greece from the age of Pericles till the defeat of Athens in the Peloponnesian War (404 BC), a period of roughly eighty years; but as his are the only comedies which survive, it is difficult to say how representative they are. What they lack in plot, these comedies more than make up for in their ingenious, often fantastical development of an initial 'happy idea' such as the withholding of conjugal rights from husbands until they agree to their wives' demands to lay down arms (*Lysistrata*). Among the best known of Aristophanes' surviving comedies are the *Birds*, the *Acharnians*, the *Frogs*, the *Ecclesiazusae* (*The Ladies' Parliament* is an alternative title) and the *Clouds*, with its celebrated caricature of Socrates which, according to Plato, Socrates himself considered to have prejudiced the tribunal which eventually sentenced him to death.

K. J. Dover, *Aristophanic Comedy*, 1972.
Kenneth McLeish, *The Theatre of Aristophanes*, 1980.

Aristotle (384–322 BC). The *Poetics* is perhaps the most influential document on drama in the whole history of Western literature. It is a brilliant and exasperating analysis of the structure and function of TRAGEDY (a book on COMEDY has been lost), particularly of the tragedies of SOPHOCLES. Aristotle was a philosopher, whose intention it was to counter Plato's attack on drama and poetry for their failure to make men better. His argument includes the famous claim that, by exciting emotions of fear and pity, tragedy achieves a purging (*catharsis*) and strengthening of the audience. He proposed that tragedy should treat of the fall of great men through some flaw or error (*hamartia*), of which pride (*hubris*) was an example. Special attention was paid by neo-classical critics, particularly in France in the seventeenth and eighteenth centuries, to his observations on the UNITIES. It is true that Aristotle contrasted tragedy's unity of action with the diversity of epic, and that he advocated the restriction of the action to a single day, where that was possible. It is not true that he required a unity of place. He has been vastly misinterpreted, and the misinterpretations have been as influential as the accuracies. The history of tragedy would certainly not have been the same without him.

J. Jones, *On Aristotle and Greek Tragedy*, 1962.

Armin, Robert (1581–1615). The story that RICHARD TARLTON encouraged Armin as a clown bears witness more to the continuity of theatrical tradition than to anything else. Armin wrote several works, including plays, but it is as a clown, especially a Shakespearean clown that he earns his place here. He joined SHAKESPEARE's Company in about 1599 and probably played Dogberry in *Much Ado about Nothing*. But it is in the more inward-looking, almost melancholy kind of Shakespearean clown that Armin specialized, and the roles of Touchstone, Feste, Lavache and Lear's Fool were almost certainly specially written for him. Armin was apprenticed as a goldsmith in early youth and the name Touchstone (given to characters who follow this trade in several Elizabethan plays) may be an allusion to this.

C. S. Felver, *Robert Armin: Shakespeare's Fool*, 1961.
M. C. Bradbrook, *Shakespeare the Craftsman*, 1969.

Arrabal, Fernando (1932–   ). Born in what was then Spanish Morocco, Arrabal settled in France in 1954 and writes in French. His childhood memories are nightmarish, involving a mother who betrayed his father to the Fascists in the Spanish Civil War and was then made to witness, with her children, his torture. Whether this is truth or fantasy, it seems to have affected Arrabal's work, in which GRAND GUIGNOL is updated into surrealistic sadomasochism. *The Two Executioners* (1958) is a dramatization of his father's torture and the audience, as in far too much of Arrabal's work, is trapped into a voyeuristic role. The brilliantly precise and simple dialogue of *Orison* (1958) and *Fando and Lis* (1964) is a deception. It displays the charms of childishness, but the characters are childish only in the sense that Lizzie Borden was childish when she hit her mother forty whacks with an axe. Arrabal's themes are the themes of a pornographer – castration, necrophilia, coprolalia, orgasm – and his disturbing skill is to make laughter and original theatrical imagery out of them. His Theatre of Panic is a distorted reflection of ARTAUD's THEATRE OF CRUELTY.

Luis Arata, *The Festive Plays of Fernando Arrabal*, 1982.

Artaud, Antonin (1896–1948). French poet, actor and theorist whose idea of a visceral and unbridled theatre has had a seminal influence on later visionaries as disparate as BARRAULT, ARRABAL, GENET, PETER BROOK, Pip Simmons and Julian Beck – in fact on all those whose search is for a total theatre. Both physically and psychologically, Artaud's life was hellish. He contracted meningitis as a child, suffered continual fits of depression, was addicted to laudanum and underwent several detoxication treatments, and spent most of his last years in mental care. It is not easy to know whether Artaud was madder than the Western world that rejected him. Certainly he was driven by ideas that both grew from and increased his own suffering. His first work as an actor was with LUGNÉ-POË in 1921. Later that year he was with CHARLES DULLIN's company, and in 1923 with Pitoeff's. He joined the Surrealist movement in 1924, but was formally expelled from it in 1926. The dispute is interesting: to André Breton, Artaud seemed penned in the psyche; to Artaud, Breton was trapped in 'the realm of fact and matter'. By this time, as exemplified in the *Correspondence with Jacques Rivière* (1924), Artaud had discovered his true material in his own tortured self-absorption. At the Théâtre Alfred Jarry, from 1927 to 1929, he presented four productions, including STRINDBERG's *Dream Play* and culminating in Vitrac's anarchic *Victor*. The experience of Balinese dance at the 1931 Colonial Exhibition in the Bois de Vincennes contributed significantly to the *First Manifesto of the Theatre of Cruelty* (1932). Artaud was working in and with film at this time, and coming increasingly to reject the protected images of Western art. His aim was to release the repressed forces that govern man's innermost self. His own play/scenario, developed from Shelley's *The Cenci* (1935), took its place beside FORD's *'Tis Pity She's a Whore*, SENECA's *Thyestes* and BÜCHNER's *Woyzeck* in a notional repertoire of a new THEATRE OF CRUELTY. A visit to Mexico in 1936 was the climax of this most active phase of his life. *The Theatre and Its Double* (1938) was the literary outcome. The personal outcome was horrific. The intensity of these years broke him.

Bettina L. Knapp, *Antonin Artaud: Man of Vision*, 1969.
Martin Esslin, *Artaud*, 1976.
Ronald Hayman, *Artaud and After*, 1977.

Ashcroft, Peggy (1907–   ). English actress, born in Croydon, where a theatre named after her was opened in 1962. She made her debut in J. M. BARRIE's *Dear Brutus* at the Birmingham Repertory Theatre in 1926. Her promise was noted and she was recruited to the OLD VIC company under Harcourt Williams, but her first oustanding success was as Juliet in GIELGUD's production of *Romeo and Juliet* at the New Theatre in 1935. The gaiety and vulnerability of her performance was matched by the sensitivity of her verse-speaking. Her finest work is always in characters who hold out great hopes for life – Nina in CHEKHOV's *The Seagull* in 1936 was an early example and the same spirit was still informing her playing of Winnie in BECKETT's *Happy Days* at the inaugural performance of the new NATIONAL THEATRE in 1976. Her campaigning on behalf of artists suffering under totalitarian persecution is consistent with her magnificent portrayal of women who refuse to be cowed. Her Hedda Gabler in 1954 was such a woman as, very differently, is Shen-Te in BRECHT's *The Good Woman of Setzuan*, which she played at the Royal Court in 1956, the year in which she was created DBE. Peggy Ashcroft had played Juliet, Portia, Imogen, Perdita and Cleopatra at the Old Vic before she was thirty, and the lyricism of her style allowed her to play Viola, Rosalind and the Duchess of Malfi without impertinence when she was over forty. She became a director of the ROYAL SHAKESPEARE COMPANY in 1967 and was still capable of revealing new depths in a part—as she did with Margaret in the Wars of the Roses sequence at STRATFORD in 1963—when she played the Countess of Rousillon in *All's Well that Ends Well* in 1981.

Ayckbourn, Alan (1939–   ). The Ayckbourn phenomenon began in the English theatre with the London staging of *Relatively Speaking* in

1967 (it had been first staged, as *Meet My Father*, at Scarborough in 1965). It continued with *How the Other Half Loves* (1969), which has one of the wittiest sets in theatre history, and *Absurd Person Singular* (1972), which is a farce wrapped round neurosis. The startling second act, in which a desperate woman tries to kill herself among careless 'friends', ought to have alerted critics to the anxiety of Ayckbourn's vision. There remains, though, a tendency to think of him as the unique author of witty farces (in fact, his dialogue is not witty, though it is often superbly timed), a latter-day BEN TRAVERS. Such a tendency has been reinforced by the country-wide productions of the trio of plays composing *The Norman Conquests* (1973). For some reason, these sour comedies have been insistently presented as week-end romps for audiences who don't want to be made to think, but 'like a bit of entertainment'. If manic competitiveness among the alcoholic fringes of depressed consumerism is 'a bit of entertainment', *Bedroom Farce* (1975), *Just between Ourselves* (1976), *Joking Apart* (1978), *Sisterly Feelings* (1979), *Season's Greetings* (1980), *Way Upstream* (1982), *A Chorus of Disapproval* (1984) and *A Woman in Mind* (1985) can also take their place alongside the fallen trousers and fallen vicars of seaside sauciness. But this is not the appropriate context for Ayckbourn. He writes, without much affection – FARCE, you may say, is always cruel – about the victims of the rat-race as they thrash comically about in the rat-trap. Since 1970, when he left his job as a Radio Drama Producer in Leeds, Ayckbourn has been artistic director of a THEATRE-IN-THE-ROUND in Scarborough, appropriately named after STEPHEN JOSEPH, who gave Ayckbourn his first chances as a writer. The Stephen Joseph Theatre has an exemplary commitment to new plays, and an atmosphere as congenial as any in England.

Ian Watson, *Conversations with Ayckbourn*, 1981.
Michael Billington, *Alan Ayckbourn*, 1983.

Bancroft, Squire (1841–1926). English actor who had the timely advantage of looking more distinguished than he was. He made his debut in 1861, and his reputation in 1865, when he joined the company MARIE WILTON was establishing at the Prince of Wales's. He married into joint management in 1867, the year in which he created Hawtrey and she Polly in T. W. ROBERTSON's *Caste*. There is no doubt that they made important innovations, above all in raising the status and the standard of acting and actors. Bancroft was a gentleman from monocle to spat, and expected members of his company to behave as impeccably as he. In 1880, the Bancrofts took over the management of the more securely established Haymarket, and had earned enough to retire in

1885. He became the second theatrical knight (IRVING was the first) in 1897, and together with his wife wrote several books of reminiscence which are uncomfortably similar to each other.

Bannister, Jack (1760–1836). The son of an actor, Bannister was an art student before making his debut at the Haymarket in 1778. He remained a close friend and drinking companion of his fellow-student Thomas Rowlandson until Rowlandson's death in 1827. After a moderate success in tragedy at Drury Lane, he began a new career as a comedian when he created the part of Don Ferolo Whiskerandos in SHERIDAN's *The Critic* (1779). He became popular as a light comedian, with a tolerable singing voice and a genial temperament. At the Little Theatre in the Haymarket, he created several characters in the highly successful plays of GEORGE COLMAN the Younger, who returned the favour by helping Bannister compile one of the first authentic one-man shows under the title *Bannister's Budget*, which brought him substantial success in the latter half of his career. He retired in 1815.

John Adolphus, *Memoirs of John Bannister*, 2 vols., 1839.

Baraka, Amiri (1934–   ). There have been three distinct phases in the work of this richly talented black American playwright. In the first, as Leroi Jones, married to a white woman, he wrote for a mixed audience about the racial tensions of American society, and about the need to resolve them. *The Toilet* (1962), *Dutchman* (1964) and *The Slave* (1964) are strong and violent. In 1965 Jones was converted to the Kawaida sect of Islam, changed his name to Amiri Baraka, divorced his white wife, and moved to Newark's black ghetto. The black militant plays, like *A Black Mass* (1966), *Slave Ship* (1967) and *Madheart* (1967), were intended for blacks only, and played in segregated theatres. The third phase saw Baraka as a Maoist revolutionary, looking for class unity rather than racial separation. The plays from this phase include *S-1* (1976) and *The Motion of History* (1977). Baraka has written *The Autobiography of Leroi Jones* (1983), more an attack on racism in the USA than a conventional account of his early life.

Henry C. Lacey, *To Raise, Destroy and Create*, 1981.

Barker, Harley Granville (1877–1946). English actor, director, playwright and scholar. He started acting at the age of fourteen, was chosen by WILLIAM POEL as his Richard II in 1897, and by SHAW as Marchbanks for two performances of *Candida* in 1900. The contact with Shaw proved decisive when, from 1904 to 1907, Barker and J. E.

Vedrenne managed three remarkable seasons at the ROYAL COURT. It was London's first truly international repertory programme – it included work by IBSEN, SCHNITZLER, HAUPTMANN, MAETERLINCK and YEATS – but its chief achievement was to establish Shaw as a major force in the British theatre. Barker and his first wife, Lillah McCarthy, played many of the leading roles. His restrained style did not suit all the Shavian roles he tackled, but it was an excellent basis for his successful production of the subdued 'new' drama. Variable fortune rewarded Barker's work at the Haymarket, the Duke of York's, the Little, and the St James's, but the productions at the Savoy of *The Winter's Tale* and *Twelfth Night* (1912), and *A Midsummer Night's Dream* (1914) challenged and changed the whole tradition of laboriously spectacular Shakespearean production. Exquisitely designed by Albert Rutherston and Norman Wilkinson, the performances were light, speedy, and respectful. The famous *Prefaces to Shakespeare* (1927–47) had their origin at the Savoy. Barker's marriage to Lillah McCarthy ended in divorce in 1917, and the following year he married a wealthy American whose previous husband had founded a museum in Spain. It was symptomatic of the social pretensions of the new marriage that he began to hyphenate his surname. There was to be no more theatrical slumming, though he collaborated with his wife on a number of translations from the Spanish. The theatrical career of this opinionated but vastly talented man was over.

It is fitting that Barker's abilities as a playwright have been recognized by the NATIONAL THEATRE. As early as 1904 he joined with William Archer to present a *Scheme and Estimates for a National Theatre*. *The Marrying of Ann Leete* (1902), *The Voysey Inheritance* (1905), *Waste* (1907) and *The Madras House* (1910) are technically proficient plays, which both display and criticize the spirit of their age.

Eric Salmon, *Granville Barker: A Secret Life*, 1983.
Dennis Kennedy, *Granville Barker and the Dream of Theatre*, 1985.

Barker, Howard (1946–   ). The most consistently clear-thinking of contemporary political dramatists, Barker had his first plays, *Cheek* and *No One Was Saved,* produced upstairs at the ROYAL COURT in 1970. He has written prolifically since then, searching always for clear images of Britain's moral poverty and inviting recognition of the urgent need to change the social structures and priorities. *Claw* (1975), *Stripwell* (1975), *That Good between Us* (1977), *Fair Slaughter* (1977) *The Hang of the Gaol* (1978), *The Love of a Good Man* (1980), *The Loud Boy's Life* (1980), *No End of Blame* (1981), *Victory* (1982) and *A Passion in Six Days* (1983) are among his most successful pieces. When he was invited by ANN JELLICOE to write a community play for Bridport, he responded with the finely conceived *The Poor Man's Friend* (1981), an account of a hanging in a rope-making town, written for performance by a cast of nearly a hundred.

Barnes, Peter (1931–   ). English dramatist whose bizarrely iconoclastic comedy *The Ruling Class* (1968) demanded attention. It opened in Nottingham, where Barnes has done much of his subsequent work, some of it involving the adaptation of plays by writers as various as MARSTON, JONSON, WEDEKIND and FEYDEAU. Two short plays, *Leonardo's Last Supper* and *Noonday Demons* (1969), seek out comedy in unlikely places and carry it through frenzy into farce. *The Bewitched* (1973) is both brilliant and demented, a diseased epic. *Laughter* (1978) is a paradoxical Auschwitz 'comedy', like *Red Noses* (1985) the work of an idiosyncratic student of comedy.

Bernard Dukore, *The Theater of Peter Barnes*, 1981.

Barrault, Jean-Louis (1910–   ). French actor, director, theatre manager, mime, theoretician of total theatre, and playwright. His first chance was given to him by CHARLES DULLIN in 1931. Later influences included Decroux, who taught him mime, and ARTAUD. For the COMÉDIE–FRANÇAISE, of which he was a member from 1940 to 1946, he directed *Phèdre* (1942) and CLAUDEL's *Le Soulier de Satin* (1943). Together with his wife, he established at the Théâtre Marigny the Compagnie Madeleine Renaud – Jean-Louis Barrault in 1946. Among the many notable productions at the Marigny were Claudel's *Christophe Colomb* (1953) and the *Oresteia* (1955), in both of which he pursued his idea of a total theatre. In 1959, the company moved to the Odéon, at the instigation of the Minister of Culture, André Malraux. It was a triumphant recognition of the achievements of an independent repertory company, an enterprising rival to the monumental Comédie–Française. In 1968, after his theatre had been occupied by revolutionary students, Barrault was sacked by Malraux. Moving into a converted boxing stadium, Barrault and his company performed his own dramatic rhapsody, *Rabelais* (1968), as a total theatrical event. The world tour of this production in 1969 confirmed Barrault's international standing. It was followed by *Jarry sur la butte* (1970), a montage in the same style, presented in the Orsay theatre, within the disused railway station, the Gare d'Orsay. Also at the Orsay, between 1972 and 1980, Barrault presented large-scale montages around the work of La Fontaine, Nietzsche, Diderot and Voltaire. His Théâtre du Rond Point, constructed on the site of an ice-rink in the centre of Paris opened with a symposium of texts on love, *L'Amour de l'amour* (1981). Some of his essays have been translated as *The Theatre of Jean-Louis Barrault* (1961) and his autobiographical reflections are published as *Memories for Tomorrow* (1974).

Barrie, James Matthew (1860–1937). Scottish playwright, the interest in whose private life has tended recently to overshadow interest in his plays. The neglect is unfortunate. *Shall We Join the Ladies?* (1921), the first act of an uncompleted thriller, is wonderfully accomplished writing, and, whilst it is true that cloud-cuckooland was dangerously attractive to him, he took off for it from a world whose palpable reality reverberates through the fantasy. *The Admirable Crichton* (1902) is a Shavian morality *manqué*, and even *Quality Street* (1902) and *What Every Woman Knows* (1908) tread serious ground provocatively. It is the pre-eminence of *Peter Pan* (1904) that has tended to condition critical responses to the other plays, and this is neither fairer nor less fair than to read all of Dickens in the light of *A Christmas Carol*. Barrie was made a baronet in 1913.

Allen Wright, *Barrie*, 1976.

Barry, Elizabeth (1658–1713). The first notable English actress, Mrs Barry (the title was given to all actresses once they had reached maturity – Elizabeth Barry was not married) was not an immediate success. According to stage tradition, she was coached to glory by her lover, the poet and rake the Earl of Rochester, and became BETTERTON's leading lady from about 1673 until her retirement in 1710. The passionate rhetoric of NATHANIEL LEE's plays was written partly to suit her style of performance, and she was an outstanding interpreter of OTWAY's dramatic verse. She was the first player to be awarded a BENEFIT, probably in 1686, 'in consideration of the extraordinary applause that had followed her performance'.

Barry, Spranger (1719–77). Barry was a handsome Irishman, believed by many to be the finest romantic actor of the eighteenth century. He made his debut in Dublin in 1744 and joined GARRICK at Drury Lane two years later. For four seasons the two actors remained colleagues and rivals, but after 1750, when Barry joined the Covent Garden company, the competition between the two was open and regular. The most famous example was the *Romeo and Juliet* war of 1750, when Garrick staged the play as a conscious challenge to its simultaneous staging at Covent Garden. One witty lady observed that, had she been Juliet, she would have been pleased to have Garrick climb up on to her balcony but would have jumped down to Barry and there was a popular complaint:

> 'Well, what's to-night?' says Angry Ned,
> ~~As up from bed he rouses;~~
> 'Romeo again,' and shakes his head,
> 'Ah! pox on both your houses.'

Barry excelled in the tender passages of tragedy. However uneven, his Othello and Lear had fine moments.

Barrymore. Family of American actors, of whom the most prominent were:

(1) *Maurice Barrymore* (1847–1905). Born in India of one of those English families that are called 'well connected', he was intended for the Indian Civil Service. He was as lackadaisical an actor as he would have been a civil servant. Having drifted into an English debut in 1874, he drifted into an American one the following year. It was probably his marriage into the theatrically powerful DREW family in 1876 that confirmed his career. His wife was more serious about acting than he, and had it not been for the fact that she was also more serious about parenthood, she would probably have become a star in an era of stargazing. Barrymore had dashing good looks to thank for his successes. He looked particularly fine in military uniform. For the last four years of his life he was mentally deranged, and died in care. All his three children became famous.

(2) *Lionel Barrymore* (1878–1954). The oldest child would have preferred a career as an artist, or even as a composer. He made a minor reputation in both fields. His stage successes were in 'character' parts, and he was particularly fine at 'ageing' during the course of a play. As Milt Shanks in Augustus Thomas's *The Copperhead* (1918), he had an ideal opportunity to display his strengths. As Macbeth in 1921, in a production designed by ROBERT EDMOND JONES, he was lamentable. 'Macbeth seen dimly through a haze of art,' was one newspaper headline. The last thirty years of his career belonged to Hollywood and to American radio, where his annual readings of *A Christmas Carol* became a national institution. A serious hip injury in 1936 interrupted but did not end his work in films. The series of 'Dr Kildare' films, which

MGM began in 1938, gave him a famous wheel-chair part as the wise old Dr Gillespie.

(3) *Ethel Barrymore* (1879–1959). Ethel Barrymore made her reputation as the 'first lady' of the American stage in elegant, drawing-room plays. When PINERO wrote *Mid-Channel* for her, it was to give her a heavier part than her producer Charles Frohman normally dared risk her in. The opening was delayed until 1910 by the birth of the first of her three children. Her performance established for her some credibility as a serious actress, but of the classic roles she later attempted, only Lady Teazle in *The School for Scandal*, which she first played in 1923, was a notable achievement. The fact would seem to be that Ethel Barrymore of the elegant drawl represented, for her public in both America and England, the essence of gracious womanhood. As a young woman, she was a social success on both sides of the Atlantic. Winston Churchill was among the eligible bachelors with whom her name was linked. Her unsuccessful marriage to the son of an American millionaire was of a piece with her cocktails-and-furs image. It was her misfortune to be more conscientious as an actress than a socialite should be. Like all the Barrymores, she made and lost fortunes. It was as late as 1940, when she had already announced her retirement, that she found, in Emlyn Williams's *The Corn Is Green,* her finest part – as an eccentric Welsh schoolmistress. Other successes included roles in BARRIE's *Alice-Sit-by-the-Fire* and *The Twelve Pound Look.* She was clearly a great personality, but it seems unlikely that she was a great actress.

(4) *John Barrymore* (1882–1942). A genuinely versatile actor, whose life is a sad story of self-destruction. He had a gift for the grotesque and the bizarre, well realized in his 1920 performance as Richard III. He had also the wit and athleticism to play pratfalls in Hollywood silent comedies. And his 1922 Hamlet can claim to have been innovatory, though, given his temperament, his incestuous love for Gertrude might equally well have been the public image of his private infatuation for Blanche Yurka, who played her. John Barrymore made four marriages bad, and drank himself to death. From the beginning of his career, he changed his performance from night to night. After 1933, his lapses of memory and his improvisatory bad behaviour were more effective crowd-pullers than his acting: but in the twenties he was handsome, charismatic and memorable.

Hollis Alpert, *The Barrymores,* 1965.

Baylis, Lilian (1874–1937). English-born, and trained as a musician, Lilian Baylis spent many years in South Africa. She returned to

England to help her aunt run the Royal Victorian Coffee Music Hall (the name indicates that aunt's devotion to temperance as well as entertainment), and took over the management of what came to be known as the OLD VIC in 1912. From then until her death, it became the queen bee in her strange bonnet. She was cantankerous and usually tyrannical, fiercely religious and roguishly idiosyncratic, but she had the courage to provide her aunt's theatre with a policy – great works for the people. Between 1914 and 1923, all Shakespeare's plays were produced at the Old Vic. This is not made less remarkable by the fact that drama was not Lilian Baylis's real love. As TYRONE GUTHRIE reveals, 'God told Miss Baylis that the best in music was grand opera.' She found a home for it at Sadler's Wells in 1931.

Richard Findlater, *Lilian Baylis*, 1975.

Beaumarchais, Pierre Augustin Caron de (1732–99). Born in Paris, the son of a watchmaker, Beaumarchais was by turns a watchmaker himself, a musician, a financial speculator, a near-professional litigant, a spy, a supporter of the Americans in their war with England, an aspirant to nobility, an egalitarian and a playwright. He wrote five plays and an opera, but he is remembered vividly for only two of these. *The Barber of Seville* (written in 1772 but not performed until 1775) is squarely in a comic tradition that reaches back beyond the COMMEDIA DELL'ARTE to PLAUTUS and TERENCE, but it is a verbally adroit and dramatically acute reworking of an old tale, and it introduces, in the character of the Count's servant, Figaro, a servant who is so manifestly superior to his masters that he seems almost to propose the French Revolution. *The Marriage of Figaro* (written in 1778 and first staged in 1784) is an altogether more remarkable play, indeed one of the most original of all comedies. It is, perhaps, to Louis XVI's credit that he understood its implications well enough to consider them seditious. 'This man laughs at everything which ought to be respected in a government,' he is supposed to have said. Certainly he obstructed the play's performance, not least because of the sentiments expressed in the *tour de force* of Figaro's long soliloquy. The conventional characters of *The Barber of Seville* reappear, but their conventionality is challenged and finally reassessed in the course of a complex plot. When the Revolution came, nobody could be quite sure whose side Beaumarchais was on. Characteristically, though, he survived. Gun-runner to the King, he was also prepared to be a gun-runner to the King's executioners.

J. B. Ratermanis and W. R. Irwin, *The Comic Style of Beaumarchais*, 1961.

Beaumont, Francis (1584–1616). Beaumont is no more mentioned without FLETCHER than Fortnum without Mason or 'fro' without 'to'; yet the period of their collaboration lasted only half-a-dozen years (1608–13) and the only play by either which has been regularly played on the modern stage, *The Knight of the Burning Pestle* (1607), is Beaumont's unaided work. The younger son of a country gentleman, Beaumont began by studying law and gravitated to the theatre with *The Woman Hater* (1605), a prose comedy written for a children's company. But his enormous popularity dates from the period of his collaboration with John Fletcher. Beaumont only shared in the writing of a few plays but the pair became London's most celebrated theatrical partnership and their works were collected in a Folio volume, a distinction otherwise accorded only to SHAKESPEARE and BEN JONSON. Melodramatic tragi-comedy, where all is sacrificed to immediate theatrical effect, and spectacular scenes were the hallmark of the 'Beaumont and Fletcher plays'. *The Knight of the Burning Pestle,* on the other hand, is an uproarious comedy which sends up the theatrical taste of the citizenry but has a vigour and humour wholly independent of what it parodies. Beaumont retired from theatrical activity (except for occasional Court entertainments) when he married an heiress in 1613. Apart from plays he also produced some undistinguished verse including a surprisingly dull erotic poem, *Salmacis and Hermaphroditus* (1612).

L. B. Wallis, *Beaumont, Fletcher and Company: Entertainers to the Jacobean Gentry,* 1947.

E. Waith, *The Pattern of Tragicomedy in Beaumont and Fletcher,* 1952.

Beckett, Samuel (1906–   ). Irish playwright and novelist, long resident in Paris. In the post-war theatre, Beckett is the supreme creator of images in empty space and sounds among silences. *Waiting for Godot* (1955) was written and first performed in French. It revealed to the modern theatre a new philosophical dimension, grafting vaudeville double-acts on to nihilism, and finding in the idea of waiting a devastating expression of the human condition. 'Nothing happens – twice' was a perceptive critical comment. But subsequent plays are even sparer. In *Endgame* (1957) the symbiotic couplings remain, but hoping for an end rather than a new beginning. In *Krapp's Last Tape* (1958) an old poet has only the recorded voices of his dead selves as company in his pursuit of unnecessary exactitude. In *Happy Days* (1961) Winnie's monologue has an on-stage audience to parody the inattention of the theatrical audience. But her defiant cheerfulness is missing from *Not I* (1972), a shorter prose-poem for a female voice, in which the auditor is in shadow, and only the lips of the speaker are lit. In *Play* (1963) and *Come and Go* (1966) three characters recall an intertwining series of past relationships in patterns that could repeat themselves into eternity. In *Breath* (1970) there is only a heap of rubbish and a sound-track that begins with a birth cry followed by a single inhalation and exhalation and ends with a death rattle. 'They give birth astride of a grave, the light gleams an instant, then it's night once more.' Beginning, and especially ending, is something that all Beckett's characters must struggle with. He is a brilliant deviser of cul-de-sacs, and a man so learned that he can initiate any number of critical hunts for meaning. Better to follow the line of BRENDAN BEHAN, who compares reading Beckett to swimming in the sea: 'I don't know what it means, but I enjoy it.' The unusually rich radio play *All That Fall* (1957) shows clearly how musical Beckett's writing is. Alec Reid compares it to 'blues', and there is something in that. Beckett's own productions of his plays are direct and unpretentious, concerned with the accurate deployment of deliberately limited means. It has been his habit to obscure his biography. He told an English journalist in 1955 that he was unsure whether he was married (he had been since 1948), but that he was sure there were no children. There was the well known fact of his early association with James Joyce; his cricketing prowess at Trinity College, Dublin is recorded in *Wisden;* his stabbing by a Parisian *clochard* furnished Martin Esslin with an anecdotal illustration of the ABSURD; he was known to have been involved in the French Resistance to Nazism. His recent biographer took on a formidable job: naming the unnameable.

Alec Reid, *All I Can Manage, More Than I Could,* 1969.
Deirdre Bair, *Beckett: A Biography,* 1978.

Becque, Henri (1837–99). The best plays of this French dramatist are vivid examples of NATURALISM in the theatre. Bleak and squalid lives are displayed without moral comment, though with an irony that reflects Becque's own bitterness. He was at pains to dissociate himself from the group of French naturalists who followed ZOLA's lead, but he was certainly influenced by them. In their turn, his plays were influential in forming the taste of the writers who worked with ANTOINE in the Théâtre Libre. The sad fact is that his two major plays, *The Vultures* (1882) and *The Parisienne* (1885), failed in the theatre, and Becque abandoned the drama, observing with disillusion the growing admiration of the avant-garde in Paris for his *comédies rosses* (savage comedies).

Beerbohm, Max (1872–1956). It is not easy to separate Beerbohm's theatrical criticism, written for the *Saturday Review* from 1898 to 1910, from the elegant irony that characterized much of his other writing and his brilliant cartoons; but he was, in fact, a serious and sympathetic critic. Half-brother to HERBERT BEERBOHM TREE and the author of two excellent one-act plays (*The Happy Hypocrite* was produced in London in 1900 and *A Social Success* in 1913), Beerbohm enjoyed a wide range of theatre. His obituary essay on Dan Leno, for instance, is a lucid evocation of the craft of the music halls. After his marriage to the American actress Florence Kahn in 1910, Beerbohm left England for Rapallo and spent most of the rest of his life in Italy. He was knighted in 1939. His theatrical criticism has been collected in *Around Theatres* (1924), *More Theatres* (1969) and *Last Theatres* (1970).

Behan, Brendan (1923–64). Irish playwright, born in Dublin. Behan's involvement with the Irish Republican Army led to his being sent to a British borstal. His experiences there are the subject of a highly coloured and very lively autobiographical book, *Borstal Boy* (1958). In 1942 he was sentenced to fourteen years' imprisonment for the attempted murder of two detectives, released in a general amnesty in 1946, imprisoned again in 1947 and deported to Ireland in 1952. The posthumously published *Confessions of an Irish Rebel* (1965) contains fragmentary accounts of his life, spiced with humour and bitterness. Behan owed his theatrical reputation to the production by JOAN LITTLEWOOD and the Theatre Workshop Company of *The Quare Fellow* (1954) and *The Hostage* (1958). The first of these is set in an Irish prison on the eve of an execution. On the one hand is institutional violence, on the other an unsentimentalized flesh-and-blood warmth and humour. *The Hostage,* by contrast, is a pretext for anarchic performance, flawed by evasive over-simplifications. An English soldier is kidnapped and held in a Dublin brothel among a motley collection of misfits. The original London performances were famous for Behan's occasional unscripted curtain speeches. They are part of the alcoholic legend, supported by the fact that Behan drank himself to death. The unfinished *Richard's Cork Leg* (completed by Alan Simpson for production in 1972) and three short radio plays form the rest of his dramatic output.

Ulick O'Connor, *Behan,* 1970.

Behn, Aphra (*c.* 1640–1689). The exact date and circumstances in which England's first female playwright of any note was born are obscure. It is possible that she was the daughter of a Canterbury gentleman called Johnson. At the age of twenty-five she was married for a short time to a Dutchman who gave her the surname by which she is usually known. He may also have been responsible for the frequent occurrence in Aphra Behn's plays of the theme of forced marriage and marriage to old men. She was probably in the West Indies from 1658 to 1660 and certainly in the Low Countries a few years later, where she engaged in espionage. The reward promised for her services was not forthcoming and she came back to London in 1667, impoverished and in bad health. She lived for some time with a Gray's Inn lawyer, John Hoyle, who did not care much for her (or for women generally) and on whom she based some of the dissolute heroes of her plays. During the twenty years of her writing career, Aphra Behn produced sixteen plays as well as many novels, poems and translations. She is the first English woman author known to have made her living by her pen, though it was never a very handsome living. Her first play *The Forced Marriage* appeared in 1670 and brought her within the circle of Restoration wits and gallants. Disguise, mistaken identity and coincidence play an inordinate role in her plays, where elegant, cynical and incisive dialogue and occasional spectacle count for more than coherence or plausibility of plot. She died of rheumatic fever in 1689 and is buried in Westminster Abbey. Her plays, the best of which are probably *The Rover* (1677), *Sir Patient Fancy* (1678) and *The City Heiress* (1682), stand apart from the general ruck of Restoration comedy by virtue of their underlying melancholy and a genuine if often faint strain of poetic feeling.

Maureen Duffy, *The Passionate Shepherdess,* 1977.
Angeline Goreau, *Reconstructing Aphra,* 1981.

Belasco, David (1853–1931). Belasco was known as the 'Bishop of Broadway' because of his flamboyant taste fo. sacerdotal garments. He was an American, of Portuguese-Jewish descent, whose parents left England to join in the Gold Rush. Belasco's early theatrical experience was mostly in San Francisco, though he was briefly BOUCICAULT's secretary in Virginia City, Nevada in 1873. When his play *La Belle Russe* went to New York in 1882, Belasco went with it. He stayed, and directed or produced well over three hundred plays on BROADWAY during a career which established him as the leading American exponent of stage naturalism. The plays he wrote reflect his delight in the picturesque, the lyrical, and the theatrical, as well as in the fully realized physical environment. The same concern with atmosphere as well as accuracy, particularly in his work with light, characterized his directing. He is likely to be remembered for his Civil War drama *The Heart of Maryland* (1895), and for the two plays which furnished Puccini with operatic plots in the *verismo* style, *Madame Butterfly* (1900) and *The Girl of the Golden West* (1905), but he wrote also such costume pieces as *Du Barry* (1901) and *Sweet Kitty Bellairs* (1903), and the gently fanciful *The Return of Peter Grimm* (1911). When the reaction against naturalism established itself in America, Belasco became a chief target. His commitment to 'show-biz' made him vulnerable to the dismissive wit of such men as Stark Young and GEORGE JEAN NATHAN. Nathan, for instance, claimed to have seen on Belasco's inlaid onyx commode a signed photograph of Dante. But would that have been more remarkable than the drops-of-blood episode in *The Girl of the Golden West?*

Craig Timberlake, *The Life and Work of Belasco, The Bishop of Broadway*, 1954.
Lise-Lone Marker, *David Belasco*, 1975.

Bel Geddes, Norman (1893–1958). American designer who combined iconoclasm and whirlwind enthusiasm. He thrust himself into his first theatre work in 1916 when he wrote and designed a play about the Blackfeet Indians and persuaded a Los Angeles company to employ him on the strength of it. For the Chicago Opera in 1919 he designed an exuberantly original set for the ballet *Boudour*, but he was dreaming of bigger things. From as early as 1921 he began planning a vast production of Dante's *Divine Comedy*. The production never took place, but the 1924 publication of photographs of the model set, with all its changes of lighting and some of the 523 costume and mask designs, made it one of the most influential non-events in the history of stage design. Bel Geddes disliked the constraints of the proscenium arch. For the American staging of *The Miracle* (1924) he provided MAX REINHARDT with a Century Theatre transformed into a mediaeval cathedral. The visual environment was far finer than the play, and made Bel Geddes famous. Restlessly ambitious, he established in 1927 an office offering specialist advice on industrial building, and theatre had to share a place with other enterprises for the rest of his active life. His preference for directing the plays he designed led to a daring *Hamlet* in Skowhegan, Maine in 1929, on a unit set with angled steps leading to platforms on various levels. A further innovation was the use of recorded sound. When it reached New York in 1931, only slightly modified, it caused controversy and closed after two weeks, despite its success elsewhere. No one, though, could question its scenic virtuosity.

Bellamy, George Anne (1728–88). George Anne (so-called because of a clergyman's mishearing of 'Georgiana' at the font) was acknowledged and to some extent indulged by Lord Tyrawley whose natural child she was. But her decision to act was taken after she had displeased him by going to live with her mother, a minor actress. She made her debut in 1744 and was good and pretty enough to encourage GARRICK to make her his Juliet in the 1750 '*Romeo and Juliet* war' with SPRANGER BARRY. She was also a tolerable Desdemona and a Cordelia who made her audience cry. It was, however, high life rather than the theatre that most appealed to her, and she won access to some of the 'best' homes in London. Much scandal attached itself to her private life, though she did her best to turn her three liaisons into respectable marriages. Fellow actors were jealous of her social achievements, and as theatrical engagements became fewer, creditors multiplied. Hers is a cautionary tale of the problems of the actress who wanted to be virtuous but was not allowed to be. She retired from the stage in 1785, the year in which her six-volume *Apology* appeared. This is a fascinating book, full of references to members of contemporary 'society'. It belongs to the category of fictionalized biography, though George Anne Bellamy presented it as autobiographical fact.

C. H. Hartmann, *Enchanting Bellamy*, 1956.

Benson, Frank Robert (1858–1939). Benson was one of the last and one of the oddest of English actor-managers. His lifelong interest in sport and in theatre was already evident in 1881 when he produced in Greek the *Agamemnon* of AESCHYLUS and won the three-mile race for Oxford against Cambridge. His first professional engagement was with IRVING at the Lyceum in 1882. Advised to get more experience, he joined a touring Shakespearean company. When the manager absconded to avoid his creditors, Benson bought the remaining assets and was suddenly, at the age of twenty-five, manager of the F. R. Benson Company. Almost at once, and certainly before he was ready, he found himself engaged by Charles Flower to initiate the annual Shakespeare Festival at STRATFORD, and he remained associated with the Festival from 1886 to 1919. When he was not at Stratford, he was touring the British Isles. For many audiences, Shakespearean performance meant Benson. Over the years, he presented all but two of SHAKESPEARE's plays, making up in energy and splendid fights what he lacked in subtlety and vocal range. The mixture of athletics and aesthetics continued. MAX BEERBOHM, reviewing Benson's Henry V in a famously destructive article, noted that 'as a branch of university cricket, the whole performance was, indeed, beyond praise. But as a form of acting, it was less impressive.' The review is a little unfair, but Benson's work was erratic. Balliol Holloway, who acted with him for many years, confessed that 'he always gave his best performances on a Tuesday night, usually in somewhere like Peterborough'. Quite simply, he tried to do too much, and excelled, if at all, only in occasional performances as Richard II or Henry V. He was knighted in 1916 – in the Royal Box at Drury Lane – and deserves to be remembered because two generations of actors and playgoers received their basic training in Shakespeare from him.

J. C. Trewin, *Benson and the Bensonians*, 1960.

Bernhardt, Sarah (1844–1923). The illegitimate child of a Jewish cocotte, Bernhardt made an unmemorable debut at the COMÉDIE-FRANÇAISE in 1862. The breakthrough came in 1869, when she played (and sang) the part of a pure young man in Coppée's now forgotten play, *Le Passant*. A surviving photograph provides part of the explanation. Dark-eyed, and with her shapely legs elegantly displayed, she leans against a pillar looking straight at the camera as she must have looked at her audience. Even so young, Bernhardt revealed the genius for publicity that sustained her career. A sensational success as the Queen in HUGO's *Ruy Blas* in 1872 was the prelude to a return to the Comédie-Française. Watching her rehearse his play, *Le Sphinx*, Octave Feuillet found her 'the real actress of the novels, the courtesan-actress of the eighteenth century, elegant, painted, eccentric, an insolent tomboy'; but she was within her depth as RACINE's Phèdre, with which she opened a triumphant London tour in 1879. The following year, in New York, she played one of her most famous roles, Marguérite in *La Dame aux camélias*. In a film made three decades later (in 1911), she was still playing Marguérite. She was dangerously fond of young heroines and last acts; and though her Hamlet was esteemed by many discerning critics, she was probably better represented by romantic melodramas than by tragedy, more herself in the plays of Hugo, SARDOU and Rostand than in those of Racine and SHAKESPEARE. It was through survivors like Bernhardt that the nineteenth-century actor-manager tradition lived on. Although her leg was amputated in 1915, she continued to act right up until her death. 'I will die on stage,' she had told the Duchess of Teck, 'it is my battlefield.'

Cornelia Otis Skinner, *Madame Sarah*, 1967.

Betterton, Thomas (*c.* 1635–1710). The first star actor of the Restoration theatre, Betterton joined WILLIAM DAVENANT's Duke's Company in 1661 and appeared in a number of Shakespearean roles in the next two years. He and Henry Harris took over the management of the theatre on Davenant's death and during the following years there was much complicated manoeuvring with the rival theatre company, the King's Men. In 1705 Betterton established himself at a theatre in the Haymarket specially built for his company. He was unreservedly praised by many who saw him, including COLLEY CIBBER, Pepys and Alexander Pope. His Hamlet, Lear and Othello were among his outstanding portrayals and he also succeeded in making the pomposities of heroic drama bearable and even moving. Betterton married Mary Saunderson, one of the earliest English stage actresses, in 1662. At his death STEELE wrote a memorable obituary notice.

R. W. Lowe, *Thomas Betterton*, 1891.

Bickerstaffe, Isaac (1733–*c.* 1808). Born in Dublin, and destined for a career in the English army, Bickerstaffe can claim to have invented English comic opera. In collaboration with Thomas Arne, he wrote *Thomas and Sally* (1760), *Judith* (1761) and *Love in a Village* (1762). The last of these was a huge and lasting success. Bickerstaffe went on to work with Samuel Arnold on *The Maid of the Mill* (1765) and *The Royal Garland* (1768), and with Charles Dibdin on the splendid *Love in the City* (1767), *Lionel and Clarissa* (1768) and *The Padlock* (1768) among other more ephemeral pieces. There was some plagiarism in these works, but a genuine talent as a witty lyricist too. Unfortunately, Bickerstaffe was a homosexual in an unforgiving age. He fled to France in 1772 to avoid arrest, and lived in self-protective obscurity for the rest of his life. The *Biographia Dramatica* of 1782 records that 'he is said to be still living at some place abroad, to which *a deed without a name* has banished him, and where he exists poor and despised by all orders of people'.

Peter A. Tasch, *The Dramatic Cobbler*, 1971.

Bjørnson, Bjørnstjerne (1832–1910). A Norwegian contemporary of IBSEN, Bjørnson wrote plays which are, at their best, similarly concerned with contemporary themes, and with the 'realistic' relationship of character and environment. They include *The Newly Married* (1865), *A Bankruptcy* (1875) and *A Gauntlet* (1883), in which Bjørnson sets out to expose the acceptance in society of two laws, one for men and one for women. He has been overshadowed by Ibsen, but he wrote good plays, and should not be ignored.

Blin, Roger (1907–   ). French director and actor whose unusual (in the theatre) talent for self-effacement has obscured a remarkable contribution to the modern French theatre. Blin was a young disciple of ARTAUD and an actor with BARRAULT's company at the Marigny, but it was as a director of discernment that he staged the first performances of BECKETT's *Waiting for Godot* and *Endgame,* GENET's *The Blacks* and *The Screens,* and ADAMOV's first play, *The Parody.*

Boleslavsky, Richard (1889–1937). Born in Poland and educated in Russia, Boleslaw Srzednicki is known only by his stage name. He was accepted by the MOSCOW ART THEATRE as a trainee actor in 1906, and in 1909 played Belyayev in STANISLAVSKY's production of TURGENEV's *A Month in the Country*. He remained a member of the Moscow Art Theatre until 1920, increasingly ill-at-ease in post-revolutionary Russia. After making an escape from Russia, he directed plays at the Polski Theatre in Warsaw from 1920 to 1922. Late in 1922, Boleslavsky arrived in New York as director of an émigré Russian Revue. America became his home. Under the influence of the Moscow Art Theatre's 1923 visit to New York, American interest in Stanislavsky's techniques grew, and Boleslavsky agreed to lead a Laboratory Theatre in which Russian rehearsal methods would be explored. His teaching and directing at the Laboratory Theatre from 1923 to 1929 had a significant effect on American acting styles. Among his students there were two who would go on to found the GROUP THEATRE, HAROLD CLURMAN and LEE STRASBERG, carrying their interpretation of Boleslavsky's ideas into the mainstream of the American theatre. Boleslavsky himself left the Laboratory Theatre in 1929 and spent the remaining years of his life as a Hollywood director.

J. W. Roberts, *Richard Boleslavsky,* 1981.

Bond, Edward (1934-   ). English dramatist, perhaps the finest now writing, whose uniqueness was already evident in 1962, when *The Pope's Wedding* was given a Sunday night performance at the ROYAL COURT. Like *Saved* (1965), its brilliant successor, the play looks unusual even on the printed page. Writing about inarticulate people, Bond refuses to give them a false confidence with words. Page after page, tight against the left-hand margin, the dialogue shows the brief, stabbing attempts to communicate despite the lack of a vocabulary. *Saved* was banned by the Lord Chamberlain because of the scene in which a baby is stoned to death by bored youths protecting an image of their masculinity. How can such a crime compare, Bond asks in a published introduction, with the sanctioned horrors of a *blitzkrieg?* His real concern is characteristically ecological. Life has to be made better to correspond to the human urge that it should be good. Bond's passionate and rebellious humanity has not expressed itself in programmatic plays. On the contrary, the work is dense, and the values emerge through the complex schemes and counter-schemes with which his characters attempt to realize their representative motives. This is particularly the case in the large-scale 'historical' fantasies like *Early Morning* (1968), *Lear* (1971) and *The Woman* (1978). The introductions to the published texts and the separately available *Theatre Poems and Songs* (1978) are fine expressions of mature resistance to the misleaders of society. Bond takes seriously the responsibilities of the writer. In *Bingo* (1973) he makes SHAKESPEARE his leading character, the retired Shakespeare first committing and then reflecting on 'crimes' against the deprived. An artist should be unusually alert to social implications, even if, like John Clare's in *The Fool* (1976), his alertness is called madness. *Restoration* (1981) is a vivid dramatization of class conflicts. Bond's plays, from the earliest to *Human Cannon* (1984) and *The War Plays* (1985), are conceived at the highest level of theatre poetry, where the visual image is no longer distinguishable from its verbal accompaniment.

Malcolm Hay and Philip Roberts, *Bond: A Study of His Plays*, 1980.

Booth. Family of American actors, of whom the best known are:

(1) *Junius Brutus Booth* (1796-1852). Born in England into the family of a lawyer of republican convictions, Booth made his name in London as a rival to EDMUND KEAN. Like Kean, he was short and fiery; and he dared to challenge the great man in roles that Kean had laid claim to – Richard III, Sir Giles Overreach and Shylock. For the 1820 season he worked with Kean at Drury Lane, playing Iago to Kean's Othello and Edgar to his Lear, but in 1821 he abandoned his legal wife and son and sailed for America with his flower-seller mistress. Mary Anne Holmes bore him ten children, many of whom died in infancy. Booth drank too much and experienced periods of madness, and yet his reputation in America was high. To his son Edwin, he would sometimes express his sense of shame at the life of an actor. When people greeted him on the way to rehearsal, Edwin asked who they were: 'My child, I do not know these people! But everyone knows "Tom-fool"!' It was not until 1851 that his wife divorced him. He married Mary Anne at once. She remained on the Maryland farm that occupied Booth when he was not acting, while he went on what proved to be a final tour. On a Mississippi steamer, bound from New Orleans to Cincinnati, he died,

still massively talented and much loved, but mentally and physically wrecked.

(2) ***Edwin Booth*** (1833–93). Born in Bel Air, Maryland, Edwin was the child closest to Junius Brutus during the years of drink and madness. This, together with his brother's assassination of Lincoln, the early death of his first wife and the madness of his second, contributed to the melancholy temperament that made him a Hamlet almost by nature. 'Between ourselves,' said his brother John during the record-breaking run at the Winter Garden Theatre in 1864, 'he *is* Hamlet – melancholy and all.' For thirty years he was the leading romantic tragedian of the American theatre, an industrious actor with a fine, flexible voice and an expressive face. From 1863 to 1867 he managed the Winter Garden in New York. When that burned ('Not even a wig or a pair of tights left,' observed Booth, who had lost about 40,000 dollars by the fire), he built a new theatre of his own. Booth's Theatre opened in 1869 with *Romeo and Juliet*. By 1874, lavish productions and an economic slump had bankrupted him. A series of tours recouped his losses, but exhausted him. In England in 1880 and 1881, he had to cope with the jealous craziness of his sick wife. The famous alternation of Iago and Othello with HENRY IRVING had that as its background. Back in America, he toured with Lawrence Barrett and HELENA MODJESKA, continuing even after a stroke in 1889. He was chain-smoking cigars by now, so that it may not have been the stroke alone that clouded the once-magnificent voice.

Eleanor Ruggles, *Prince of Players*, 1953.

(3) ***John Wilkes Booth*** (1838–65). The most famous day in this man's life was 14 April 1865. It was Good Friday, and at 10.22 p.m. John Wilkes Booth shot Abraham Lincoln in Ford's Theatre, Washington. He was probably mad, but Lincoln had no shortage of Southern enemies. It is said that Booth half shouted 'Sic semper tyrannis' as he aimed his pocket derringer at Lincoln. Nearly two weeks later, he was hunted down in a tobacco barn near Port Royal, Virginia. Booth was a handsome man, a hard drinker, and a fine actor. There is something impressive about the family's attempts to cope with his notoriety, not least Edwin's four-year struggle for permission to bury his remains with those of his father and grandfather in Greenmount Cemetery, Baltimore. (See also MURDERED ACTORS.)

Stanley Kimmel, *The Mad Booths of Maryland*, 1940.
R. J. S. Gutman, *John Wilkes Booth Himself*, 1979.

Booth, Barton (1681–1733) After a short period in the Dublin theatre, Booth joined BETTERTON's company at Lincoln's Inn Fields in 1700 and quickly achieved a reputation as a tragic actor. The title role in Addison's *Cato* was one of his popular successes, and his distinctive style included the striking of 'attitudes', which he held on stage much to the admiration of his audience. He was for a time manager of Drury Lane theatre together with CIBBER and WILKS. Booth's acting was modelled on Betterton's as QUIN's came to be on Booth's. Not until GARRICK made his debut in 1741 was the 'school' of Betterton challenged.

Boucicault, Dionysius Lardner (1820–90). There is no denying this Dublin-born actor-dramatist's theatrical flair. His first success was with *London Assurance* at Covent Garden in 1841. MADAME VESTRIS staged this five-act comedy in a very early, arguably the first, version of a box set. Subsequent attempts at comedy failed firmly to establish his reputation or his earning capacity. London managers found it safer to commission adaptations of French plays. Always an opportunist, Boucicault went to Paris to trap French plots at source. *The Corsican Brothers* (1852) and *Louis XI* (1855) were fed to CHARLES KEAN along this familiar mid-century route, as were *The Vampire* (1852) and *Faust and Margaret* (1854). It was a decade in which MELODRAMA and FARCE overwhelmed comedy, and Boucicault went with the tide. His private life can seem as contrived as his plots. His first marriage, to a French woman older and richer than he, ended early; perhaps she died in a fall in the Swiss Alps. No one is certain. His relationship with Charles Kean culminated in a quarrel, and in Boucicault's eloping with Kean's ward. Thirty-two years later, in 1885, he eloped again for a bigamous last fling.

During fifty years as an active dramatist, Boucicault wrote, adapted, or concocted nearly two hundred stage-pieces, a number which includes farces, pantomimes, musical interludes and operettas, and not everyone would agree that melodrama was his most effective mode. He has an important place in the American theatre, since it was to New York that his 1853 elopement took him. Whilst acting there with his new young wife, Boucicault assessed the American audience's demand for 'the actual, the contemporaneous, the photographic', and gratified it in a series of fine melodramas, each distinguished by dialogue that can be spoken without shame and by the theatrical magic of a 'sensation scene'. The first is *The Poor of New York* (1857), later mutated for touring purposes into *The Poor of Liverpool*, *The Streets of London* and *The Streets of Dublin* (1864); the best, superbly resourceful, is *Jessie Brown;*

or The Relief of Lucknow (1858); the most obviously contemporaneous and photographic is *The Octoroon* (1859), whose subject is slavery in the American South and whose villain is unmasked by a camera. It was in New York that *The Colleen Bawn* (1860) was first staged. This play is noteworthy for two very different reasons. When Boucicault risked a profit-sharing agreement for its English production in place of the normal down-payment to authors, he paved the way to wealth for himself and for later dramatists. He also established himself as the leading Anglo-Irish dramatist of his age. In this play, together with *Arrah-na-Pogue* (1864) and *The Shaughraun* (1874), Boucicault provided himself with his best acting parts, comic Irishmen who combine an inventive indulgence in blarney with an instinctive heroism in the service of that great melodramatic virtue, loyalty. These are by no means his only Irish plays, but posterity's verdict that they are the best is probably a fair one.

Richard Fawkes, *Dion Boucicault*, 1979.

Bracegirdle, Anne (d. 1748). There is no agreement on the date of Anne Bracegirdle's birth. She is said to have been eight when she played the page to ELIZABETH BARRY's Monimia in OTWAY's *The Orphan* in 1680 and yet over eighty when she died in honourable retirement, having left the stage in 1707. The daughter of a Northamptonshire gentleman, Anne Bracegirdle turned to the stage when her father lost his money, and was fortunate to be guided by BETTERTON, whose company she joined. The notoriety that she gained when the murder of WILLIAM MOUNTFORT in 1692 was ascribed to rivalry over her did her career no harm, but the fact seems to be that she was outstandingly chaste among contemporary actresses. CONGREVE, who certainly desired her and wrote his most famous female roles for her, found his courtship teasing:

> Would I were free from this restraint
> Or else had hopes to win her;
> Would she could make of me a saint
> Or I of her a sinner.

As Congreve's Angelica in *Love for Love* (1695) and above all as Millamant in his *The Way of the World* (1700), she showed intelligence as well as charm.

Brahm, Otto (1856–1912). The first effective champion of NATURA-LISM in Germany, Brahm came from a Jewish merchant family in

Hamburg (he changed his name from Abrahamsohn to avoid the penalties of antisemitism). His study of theatre as a student informed his work as a theatre critic in Berlin, and it was as a critic that he began his advocacy of the new drama of IBSEN. The Freie Bühne, of which he was a founder-member and undisputed leader, was formed in 1889 and continued until 1909. It was influenced by, but not dependent on, ANTOINE's Théâtre Libre. Brahm was committed to ensemble playing (he allowed no curtain calls) and to the abandonment of theatricality in performance: 'the ideal actor is one who totally forgets that he is acting on the stage and who thinks he is surrounded by life when he is surrounded by the play,' he wrote. It was at a Freie Bühne performance of HAUPTMANN's *Before Sunrise* in 1889 that an outraged section of the audience rioted in protest at the squalor of such truth to contemporary life. Brahm was perceptive of talent in others, and ready to foster writers like Hauptmann or directors like MAX REINHARDT, to both of whom he gave room to develop.

Brando, Marlon (1924–   ). American actor, born in Nebraska. He was expelled for indiscipline by PISCATOR from his dramatic workshop in 1944, and made his BROADWAY debut in *I Remember Mama* the same year. ELIA KAZAN was impressed by his acting, and it was as Kowalski in Kazan's production of TENNESSEE WILLIAMS's *A Streetcar Named Desire* (1947) that he established himself as the 'new' leader of an inarticulate rebellion. Conservative critics relished his nickname, 'the slob', and the publicity photograph for the screen version of *Streetcar* – Brando in torn T-shirt kissing Blanche before he rapes her – seemed to validate it. After 1949, Brando acted almost exclusively in films. Detractors might call him a 'mannered mumbler', but there is no ignoring him. The combination of brutality and grace is unique. The internalized emotions of METHOD acting smoulder in Brando. Public outbursts, particularly in the stormy disputes with his first wife Anna Kashfi, did less harm to his ratings in the United States than his espousal of the cause of the Red Indians and his sympathy with black America. He remains a magnificently *dangerous* actor. He handled his film career carelessly, following his successes in the fifties (*A Streetcar Named Desire*, *Viva Zapata!*, *The Wild One*, *On the Waterfront*) with a succession of flops in the sixties. His triumph in *The Godfather* (1972), in a part that had previously been offered to LAURENCE OLIVIER, was a sensational comeback. He worked with JOHN GIELGUD in the 1953 film of *Julius Caesar*, but his magnificent boldness and his penchant for excess are of the Olivier kind, as was seen in such films as *Last Tango in Paris* (1972) and *Apocalypse Now* (1979).

Alan Frank, *Marlon Brando*, 1982.

Brecht, Bertold Eugen Friedrich (Bertolt) (1898–1956). By 1914, Brecht's father was managing director of the Augsburg paper mill in which he had worked since 1893. It was a secure middle-class environment, and Brecht was its sore thumb. He wrote surprisingly good poetry from an early age, whilst his engagement with the theatre began with his occasional employment as drama and opera critic for an Augsburg newspaper. The vehemence of his oppositional writing is immediately apparent. His doubts about German politics before and immediately after the war were dwarfed by his doubts about German culture, and his temperament permitted him to wreak havoc, not only in print but also in people's (particularly women's) lives. The iconoclasm in *Baal* (1918; revised and first performed, 1923) is fierce and precariously balanced, and its hero's prototypical revolt is rather too readily approved by Brecht. *Drums in the Night* (1918; revised and first performed, 1922) is more sceptical, more orthodox in construction, less exciting – and it was immediately successful. Brecht won the prestigious Kleist Prize, and became a controversial celebrity in a chaotic country.

The utopian pacifism of his early years remained with Brecht all his life, but his writing shows how hard he had to work to contain the anger and violence that invaded so many major artists in the inter-war years. *In the Jungle of Cities* (1921; revised and first performed, 1923) obscures the struggle in a metaphor. This play seems to describe the systematic reversal of a man's personality by another man who admits that he is motiveless. A similar theme is given vivid comic treatment in *Man Equals Man* (1926; revised 1931). A mild Indian porter here agrees to have himself transformed into a fighting-machine because he sees no point in making sacrifices to retain his 'true' personality. Brecht was, at the time, 'transforming' himself into a Marxist, but *Man Equals Man* is more importantly a comic/ironic prophecy of the process by which the German people would turn, unresistingly, to genocide. If this is to grant Brecht more foresight than he certainly had, it can nevertheless be seen that the plays of the twenties are all concerned to express his vision of the transformation of 'good' men by 'bad' values. The three operatic collaborations with Kurt Weill are variations on this theme, though such a grouping does no service to the distinctive brilliance of *The Threepenny Opera* (1928) and *The Rise and Fall of the City of Mahagonny* (written 1927–9; first performed 1930), and perhaps credits *Happy End* (1929) with a clearer purpose than it had. There followed a brief period of doctrinaire Marxist didacticism, in which Brecht risked teaching more than he had learned. *The Exception and the Rule* (1930), 'a short play for schools', is its most attractive outcome, and *St Joan of the Stockyards* (written 1929–31; first performed 1959), rich in promise, the most disappointing. This period reached its culmination in the 1932 production of *The Mother*, and in the making of the collaborative film *Kuhle Wampe*. It was brought to a sudden end by the Reichstag fire in 1933.

For the next fifteen years, Brecht was in exile – in France, Denmark, Sweden, Finland, America (1941–7) and Switzerland. He had been working spasmodically on an anti-Hitler version of Shakespeare's *Measure for Measure* since 1931. This untidy but potentially formidable *exposé* was retitled *The Round Heads and the Pointed Heads*. It is the first of a number of anti-Hitler pieces, which include the sequence of short sketches *Fear and Misery of the Third Reich* (1935–8), *Schweyk in the Second World War* (1941–3) and the brilliant gangster-pastiche *The Resistible Rise of Arturo Ui* (1941). Nothing is clearer from Brecht's voluminous critical writing about theatre than his hatred of false solemnity. It took wit and courage for a German exile to laugh at Hitler in 1941, and the play will always be underrated by humourless readers. It is among the great comic satires of dramatic history, and it was written during the richest years of Brecht's dramatic work, at a time – astonishingly – when his plays were virtually unperformed.

Brecht's greatest plays were written between 1937, when work on *Galileo* began, and 1945, when *The Caucasian Chalk Circle* was completed. They are witty, humane, and politically ambiguous. That is to say that a communist may have been proud to write them, but not *because* he was a communist. When, in 1947, Brecht was caught up in the American farce/tragedy of the anti-communist purges, he told the HOUSE UNAMERICAN ACTIVITIES COMMITTEE that he had never been a member of the Communist Party. We do not know whether he was telling the truth. What we do know is that, despite an undertaking to remain, he left America the following day, and was in East Berlin by the end of 1948. He spent his last years as a leader, but not *the* leader, of the Berliner Ensemble. Among the plays he worked on there were his own *Mother Courage and Her Children* (written 1938–9) and *Mr Puntila and His Hired Man Matti* (written 1940). In addition, there were various adaptations, but the only completely new work was *The Days of the Commune* (1948–9), which he never finished to his own satisfaction, and which was not performed in his lifetime.

Brecht has reached the dangerous stage of being a 'classic' dramatist, not only in East Germany but also throughout the Western world. That means that his plays are given boring performances at least as often as lively ones. It also means that he is influential even where he is misunderstood. Critical comment on his theories has often obscured them. His primary concern with the telling of stories found common cause with his desire to change the world for the better in his development of 'epic' drama, VERFREMDUNGSEFFEKTE, gestic acting, and almost all the other ideas which he explored over nearly forty years. His unwillingness to destroy anything he had written has not made life easier for his interpreters. The contradiction of other writers provided him with a major impetus for his own writing, and if sometimes he contradicted himself, that has to be preferred to his other fault of repeating himself. Too many of Brecht's antagonists, and almost all his admirers, have lacked his combative irony.

John Willett, *The Theatre of Bertolt Brecht*, 1959.
Klaus Völker, *Brecht: A Biography*, 1979.
Jan Needle and Peter Thomson, *Brecht*, 1981.
John Willett, *Brecht in Context*, 1983.

Brenton, Howard (1942–   ). British playwright whose first professional writing experience came with a Sunday-night performance of *It's My Criminal* at the ROYAL COURT in 1966. Brenton joined the Brighton Combination as an actor-writer in that year and *Gum and Goo* (1969), a disturbing exploration of children at play, was performed by the company. His interest in criminality as a reflection of capitalist society was apparent in two Royal Court plays of 1969, *Revenge* and *Christie in Love*. Brenton was a member of the adventurous Portable Theatre group from 1969 to 1972 and joined in two collaborative plays by various Portable writers, *Lay By* (1971) and *England's Ireland* (1972). The overt political commitment of the second of these was confirmed by the ambitious *Magnificence* (1973). Brenton has remained a leader of a generation of dramatists whose eagerness to affect rather than merely reflect the political balance in Britain may diminish but has not disappeared. His writing is sometimes careless but his sense of shape is subtle. *Epsom Downs* (1977) is a highly original piece. Brenton had been resident dramatist at the Royal Court in 1972–3 and his move on to the stages of the NATIONAL THEATRE – for example, with the controversial *The Romans in Britain* (1980) – has been seen as a betrayal by some and as a sell-out by others. Those who denigrate him, from the left as well as the right, may be wanting him to be less good than he is. He remains one of the most adventurous of Britain's political dramatists. The persistent influence of BRECHT was acknowledged, not only in his translation of *Galileo* for the National Theatre, but also in *The Genius*, a play that reviews Galileo's dilemma in the light of recent developments in the nuclear arms race. It was staged at the Royal Court in 1983. *Bloody Poetry* (1984) takes another historical conflict, that between Byron and

Shelley, as a context for an examination of radical theory and unruly practice. *Pravda* (1985), written with DAVID HARE, uses some of the techniques of FARCE to expose the chicanery of Fleet Street.

Bridie, James (1888–1951). 'Bridie' was the chosen pseudonym of Osborne Henry Mavor, a Scottish doctor whose best plays can fairly be compared with SHAW's, not only because of their competitive dialogue, but also because of their willingness to challenge moral strongholds. Bridie took some delight in feeding false clues to biographical detectives. The autobiographical *One Way of Living* (1939) is a splendid example of writing that tells you less than you think. Bridie did much for the theatre in Scotland – he was, for example, a founder of the GLASGOW CITIZENS' THEATRE in 1943 – but he is not, in a narrow sense, a Scottish dramatist. *The Anatomist* (1930) is a vivid portrait of the Dr Knox who let the palms of Burke and Hare be crossed. *Tobias and the Angel* (1930) and *Jonah and the Whale* (1932) are lively representations of biblical stories. *Mr Gillie* (1950) asks for more thought about the relationship between teacher and pupil. Many of Bridie's plays have sufficient energy and originality to deserve revival.

Helen L. Luybem, *Bridie: Clown and Philosopher*, 1965.

Brieux, Eugène (1858–1932). French dramatist, largely self-educated, who abandoned journalism for a career as a full-time playwright in 1892, partly out of enthusiasm for the work of ANTOINE at the Théâtre Libre. Brieux was a campaigner for reform, distinct from the gloomier NATURALISTS of the French avant-garde whom he was often taken to represent. In a famous preface to an English translation of three plays by Brieux, published in 1911, SHAW proclaimed him the most important European dramatist since IBSEN. He was exaggerating. Brieux is a clear-sighted but limited writer who had the courage to challenge the French establishment. The three plays Shaw prefaced are typical. *The Three Daughters of M. Dupont* (1897) attacks arranged marriages, *Damaged Goods* (1901) examines the social consequences of syphilis, and *Maternity* (1903) is a bold plea for birth control.

Brighouse, Harold (1882–1958). Born near and educated in Manchester, Brighouse was working in the cotton trade when the Gaiety Theatre opened in Manchester in 1908. Of the seventy plays he produced between 1909 and 1952, most take their inspiration from the Lancashire setting he knew. He is, with STANLEY HOUGHTON, the best known of the Manchester playwrights associated with the Gaiety, and if

Hobson's Choice (1915) is his monument, it is a pity that other accomplished plays like *Lonesome-Like* (1911), *The Odd Man Out* (1912) and *Zack* (1916) have been eclipsed by it. Brighouse was a masterly writer of one-act plays, and would be better known in a theatre that had more inclination to perform short pieces.

Brome, Richard (*c.* 1590–*c.* 1652). In the Induction to his *Bartholomew Fair,* BEN JONSON refers to himself in the third person as 'the poet' and to 'his man, Master Brome'. It is as Jonson's servant that we first hear of Brome and he remained a disciple of the older dramatist all his life. We know virtually nothing else about his personal life. The success of Brome's imitation or parody of heroic tragedy, *The Lovesick Court,* led Jonson to talk scornfully of 'Brome's sweepings', especially as it came soon after the failure of one of his own plays. Lacking both his master's verbal inventiveness and his flair for the grotesque, Brome nevertheless had a genuine comic gift, shown mainly in the management of plot and a vein of mild and amiable satire. His best plays are *The Northern Lass* (1629), *The Antipodes* (1636) and *The Jovial Crew* (1641), and the topical melodrama *The Late Lancashire Witches* (1634) written in collaboration with THOMAS HEYWOOD. In 1635 Brome signed a contract to write plays for the Salisbury Court Theatre, and although the original document is lost, it is from the record of a lawsuit in connection with it that we obtain much of our knowledge regarding dramatic authorship in the twilight years before the closing of the theatres in 1642.

R. J. Kaufmann, *Richard Brome: Caroline Playwright,* 1961.

Brook, Peter (1925–   ). English director who touches every play or opera on which he works with curiosity and promise. He was rushed into authority at Birmingham in 1945. PAUL SCOFIELD acted for him there, and again at STRATFORD the following year, when he played Don Armado in Brook's *Love's Labours Lost.* The alliance continued through *Ring round the Moon* (1950), *Venice Preserved* (1953), *Hamlet* (1955), *The Power and the Glory* and *The Family Reunion* (1956), and, most memorably, *King Lear* (1962). Increasingly concerned to present a theatre that affected people, Brook went to Paris to direct GENET's *The Balcony* in 1960, and in 1964 presented first the LAMDA Theatre of Cruelty season and then PETER WEISS's *Marat/Sade.* The same playwright's *The Investigation* was presented the following year, in a style of documentary plainness a world away from the flamboyance of the magnificent OLIVIER *Titus Andronicus* of exactly a decade earlier. Still trying to make theatre sting, Brook staged *US* in 1966 and SENECA's *Oedipus* in 1968. Then came the innovatory reassessment of the Shakespearean tradition in his joyous *A Midsummer Night's Dream* at Stratford (1970). That production was partly expressing its director's internationalism when it went on its world tour. Unable to find finance for an experimental base in England, Brook went to Paris in 1970 to found his INTERNATIONAL CENTRE OF THEATRE RESEARCH. The first outcome was *Orghast* (1971), an occult epic performed at the Shiraz Festival. A. C. H. Smith provides an account of it in *Orghast at Persepolis* (1972). The international group of actors is committed to works of adventure and discovery. The trip to Africa, recorded in John Heilpern's *Conference of the Birds* (1977), was a mission without a clear goal. Brook can give the impression that the search is more important than the discovery. His own book, *The Empty Space* (1968), is more interested in questions than in answers. Since returning from Africa, the Paris group has performed *Timon of Athens, Ubu Roi, Measure for Measure,* a play about an African tribe called *The Ik* and *The Cherry Orchard*. In 1985 the group staged an extraordinary nine-hour version of the *Mahabharata* at the Avignon Festival. Brook is a difficult man to judge on his *past* record.

J. C. Trewin, *Peter Brook*, 1971.

Büchner, Georg (1813–37). Two works by this short-lived German genius were published in his lifetime. The first was *Danton's Death* (1835); the second was an anatomical treatise on the barbel fish which won for him a post at the University of Zurich. The comedy *Leonce and Lena* and the brilliant *Woyzeck* appeared respectively in 1850 and 1879. Büchner's influence on modern German dramatists has been immense, but no one will ever rival *Woyzeck*. Vincent Price, Büchner's most successful translator, calls it 'a series of key dramatic moments, the stations of the cross on Woyzeck's way to catastrophe'. And he adds the caution that the play's Hessian dialect and its subtle dependence on the atmosphere of Hessian folk-songs make it untranslatable – except, perhaps, by Robert Burns.

Maurice Benn, *The Drama of Revolt*, 1976.
Julian Hilton, *Georg Büchner*, 1982.

Buckingham, George Villiers, Second Duke of (1628–87). The original of Zimri in DRYDEN's *Absalom and Achitophel*, Buckingham offered his portrayal of Dryden in the character of the dramatist Bayes in *The Rehearsal* (1671). This was Buckingham's only contribution to the theatre (apart from an adaptation of FLETCHER's comedy *The*

Chances) but it is enough to ensure him a place in English theatrical history. *The Rehearsal* is a brilliant parody of the conventions of seventeenth-century heroic tragedy and its success probably helped to kill off the genre. It certainly produced a whole spate of similar burlesques in the eighteenth century, of which only SHERIDAN's *The Critic: or, A Tragedy Rehearsed* (1779) rivals (and surpasses) the original.

H. W. Chapman, *Great Villiers,* 1949.
V. C. Clinton-Baddeley, *The Burlesque Tradition in the English Theatre after 1660,* 1952.

Bullins, Ed (1935–   ). Black American playwright whose early work was performed in the off-OFF-BROADWAY theatres of San Francisco. Bullins was brought up in a black ghetto and has said that all the men in his family belong to what the whites would call the criminal class. Living in San Francisco in the early sixties, Bullins became Minister of Culture for the Black Panthers. It was the high point of his political involvement. His move to Harlem and his subsequent association with the New Lafayette Theatre has been accompanied by a reduction in his political commitment. His writing is the undisputed centre of his life. Almost always, the setting of his plays is the urban black ghetto, and his characters speak with the authentic blazonry of the resistant downtrodden. *Clara's Ole Man* (1965) is an explosive charting of the territory. The *Four Dynamite Plays* of 1971 are violently anti-white, short and foul-mouthed. Bullins is the supreme poet of the urban black theatre. His ambitious cycle of plays designed to follow the Dawsons and their associated Afro-Americans from 1900 to 1999 includes *In New England Winter* (1967), *In the Wine Time* (1968) and *The Duplex* (1970). The plays in this cycle express the fragmentary lives of unsuccessful (in white terms) black Americans.

Bulwer, Edward (1803–73). English novelist, playwright and politician, who changed his name to Bulwer-Lytton on inheriting Knebworth House from his mother Elizabeth Lytton and was created Baron Lytton of Knebworth in 1866. Bulwer's jewelled life of leisure was interrupted by parental opposition to his disastrous marriage (Shattuck calls it 'a Strindbergian hell of incompatibility'), and he began an astonishingly productive literary career in order to earn money. Already famous as the author of *Eugene Aram* (1832), a crime novel, and *The Last Days of Pompeii* (1834) when he wrote his first plays, Bulwer was also a far-sighted agitator for theatrical reform. As a member of parliament, he had led a Select Committee of Enquiry into the legal foundations of the English stage in 1832. The three aims of the Committee were impeccable – to protect playwrights by establishing a copyright law, to destroy the monopoly of the PATENT THEATRES over legitimate drama and to abolish the Lord Chamberlain's prerogative of dramatic CENSORSHIP. (The first was a limited success, the second bore fruit eleven years later and the third faded into obscurity.) Bulwer's perceptive analysis of the theatre of his time is contained in Book IV of his remarkably acute social survey, *England and the English* (1833). The best of his plays were performed by MACREADY, with whom Bulwer maintained a correspondence that offers considerable insight into performance conditions. They are *The Duchess de la Vallière* (1837), *The Lady of Lyons* (1838), *Richelieu* (1839) and *Money* (1840), a particularly sharp commentary on contemporary values. Overrated in their time, Bulwer's plays still have considerable merit; *Money,* for example, was revived by the ROYAL SHAKESPEARE COMPANY in 1982.

Charles H. Shattuck, *Bulwer and Macready*, 1958.

Burbage, Richard (*c.* 1567–1619). SHAKESPEARE's first interpreter, the original creator on stage of Hamlet, Othello and Lear, was born into the theatre. His father James built the first public theatre in England, and Richard, in addition to being the most celebrated actor of his time, was also a competent painter and, with his brother Cuthbert, a theatre manager and owner. Indeed we first meet him involved in a theatre brawl, vigorously swinging a broomstick against some hapless individuals who had come to the Theatre to claim their share in the takings. Burbage's career with Shakespeare's company began in 1594 and ended only with his death over twenty-five years later. He was one of three fellow actors to whom Shakespeare in his will left money for a memorial ring. As innumerable contemporary allusions make plain, he was immensely popular and his fame has outlived him. A long elegy celebrates his many acting roles, while the shortest of English epitaphs, by the great antiquary William Camden, was also inspired by his death: 'Exit Burbage.'

C. C. Stopes, *Burbage and Shakespeare's Stage*, 1913.
M. Holmes, *Shakespeare and Burbage*, 1978.

Burgoyne, John (1722–92). Burgoyne is remembered for two things. He was the defeated general in 1777 at the decisive Battle of Saratoga during the American War for Independence and he wrote *The Heiress*, a comedy which was successfully staged at SHERIDAN's Drury Lane in

1786. The plot of the play is trivial but the dialogue is crisp and the social observation sharp. The witty and urbane Burgoyne, to whom SHAW devotes a memorable scene in *The Devil's Disciple*, was not a Shavian invention.

Paul Lewis, *The Man Who Lost America*, 1973.

Burton, Richard (1925–84). When Welsh rugby players turn professional they are greeted at home with a mixture of mourning and hatred. They are said to have 'gone north'. The public response when Richard Burton, Welsh-born and the possessor and inspirer of a peculiarly Welsh masculine sentimentality, went to Hollywood was similar. It had been fervently hoped, after he had shot to stardom in CHRISTOPHER FRY's *The Lady's Not for Burning* (1949), that Burton would become the great British actor to succeed OLIVIER and GIELGUD. He seemed to welcome stardom more than his near-contemporary PAUL SCOFIELD, though his playing of Henry V at Stratford was restrained and honest. He was a striking Hamlet at the OLD VIC in 1953, and his partnership at that theatre with John Neville (they alternated Othello and Iago in 1956) promised to be one of the British theatre's magical memories. But Burton was bought by Hollywood. The voice remains in the recording of Dylan Thomas's *Under Milk Wood* (1954), and public interest was sustained as much by his marriages with Elizabeth Taylor as by his performances in several films, not many of them worthy of his talent. Burton's genius as an actor, the resonant voice and the rock-like stillness that could suddenly be transformed into athletic movement, was largely wasted. He is the twentieth-century theatre's leading sacrifice to the technological revolution.

Paul Ferris, *Richard Burton*, 1981.

Bury, John (1925–   ). English stage-designer who, as head of the Design Department of the ROYAL SHAKESPEARE COMPANY (1964–71) and the NATIONAL THEATRE (since 1973), has spearheaded a move towards solid sets, responsive to the text rather than its decoration. Bury is notably concerned with the texture of walls and floors and with the effect that can be achieved by the play of strong light on roughened surfaces. His baptism to theatre was in JOAN LITTLEWOOD's Theatre Workshop, where he graduated from acting to the rough-and-ready style of design Littlewood favoured. 'I just used to put something together, usually from what was already around on the stage.' On the grander scale of STRATFORD-upon-Avon, Bury retained features of this practical, scenic opportunism, memorably in the Wars of the Roses sequence of 1963.

Byron, Henry James (1834-84). English playwright and punster, born in Manchester and apprenticed to a surgeon there. He abandoned medicine and joined a company of touring actors for whom he wrote the earliest of well over one hundred plays. His burlesque version of *Fra Diavolo* (1858) brought him his first success and he became the chief purveyor of the burlesque extravaganzas for which the Strand theatre was renowned. It was with MARIE WILTON, star of the Strand burlesques, that Byron undertook the management of the Prince of Wales's Theatre in 1865, but his rough-and-ready plays could not match the refinement of the regime established there by his partner and the actor she later married, SQUIRE BANCROFT. His nose put thoroughly out of joint by the success of ROBERTSON's plays at the Prince of Wales's, Byron entered into theatre management in Liverpool and, after 1874, at the Criterion in London. He was also, for various lengths of time, editor of *Fun, Comic Times* and *Mirth*, three of the many Victorian comic papers that encouraged a peculiarly punning and bathetic humour in rivalry to *Punch*. Byron's pantomime scripts are riotous with puns, and a love of verbal trickery did more to sustain even his more serious attempts at comedy, like *Cyril's Success* (1868) and *Our Boys* (1875), than the contrived plots on which he relied. Byron wasted a considerable talent, but is nonetheless an interestingly representative writer in a humorous mode that flourished mischievously underneath the skirts of Victorian severity.

Calderon de la Barca, Pedro (1600-81). Spanish playwright whose father was a Court official. Calderon was educated for the law, but his interest in writing declared itself early. His first play, *Love, Honour and Power*, was presented at Court in 1623. Its title indicates the themes that dominate the secular plays (he claimed to have written over one hundred) of the period from 1623 to 1650. Spanish *honor* is a concept as heroic and as demanding as the French *gloire* of which CORNEILLE wrote. Calderon's presentation of it, in such plays as *The Constant Prince, Secret Vengeance for Secret Insult, Devotion to the Cross* and *The Painter of His Own Dishonour*, is not uncritical. This is outstandingly the case in *The Mayor of Zalamea*, in which the rich peasant who has become mayor executes the nobleman who has raped his daughter and is rewarded rather than punished by the king. The successful Portuguese revolt against Spain in 1640 marked the beginning of a decline in Calderon's fortunes. With the closing of the theatres in Madrid and his own ill-health following service in the Spanish army, he sought security in religion, becoming a priest in 1651. Most of his later plays were *autos sacramentales* (lyrical dramatizations of Catholic theology). He claimed to have written seventy of these. That they were not a total departure from the secular plays is apparent in such work as *Life Is a Dream* and *The Great Theatre of the World*. It is not easy to date Calderon's plays accurately, nor to convey their peculiar verbal riches to an English audience. Calderon is one of the great poetic dramatists.

A. E. Sloman, *The Dramatic Craftsmanship of Calderon*, 1958.
John V. Bryans, *Calderon de la Barca*, 1977.

Campbell, Mrs Patrick (1865–1940). 'Mrs Campbell,' wrote SHAW about the performance of a forgotten play, 'is a charming Lady Hamilton. She even acts occasionally . . .' That was in 1897. Seventeen years later, when she was nearly fifty, the extraordinary Mrs Campbell created Eliza Doolittle in *Pygmalion*. She had taken London by storm in 1893 in *The Second Mrs Tanqueray*, and tempests continued to break out wherever she went. Unable to tolerate people who were frightened by her, she took a perverse delight in being frightening; but she was vastly appealing. The lines of her hair and body might have been drawn by Beardsley (as, inevitably, they were), and much of her daily dialogue written by WILDE. It is easy to forget, because she made a speciality of the 'lady-with-a-past', that she was an admired Juliet and a moving Ophelia to FORBES-ROBERTSON. *My Life and Some Letters* (1922) is an intermittently revealing autobiographical sketch. Mrs Campbell outlived her success and her money. After watching her attempted comeback in films, ALEXANDER WOOLLCOTT observed with ominous accuracy: 'She is like a sinking ship firing on its rescuers.'

Margot Peters, *The Life of Mrs Patrick Campbell*, 1984.

Camus, Albert (1913–60). French novelist, essayist and playwright, born in Algeria and brought up in great poverty there. He worked in the theatre in Algiers until the outbreak of World War II, playing Christy Mahon in *The Playboy of the Western World* in 1939 for a company of which he was the founder. Having been rejected for military service, he was active in the Resistance during the war. Confronted by crisis on such a scale, he developed the view of the absurdity of the human situation which formed the basis of his distinctly heroic brand of existentialism. Camus's hero is the rebel who knowingly performs actions representative of human possibilities, however callous they may seem and however doubtful their outcome. Of his plays, the most accomplished and original is *Caligula* (1945), in which the mad Emperor's frenzied abuse of power touches lyricism and grotesque humour. *The Just* (1949), based on the abortive 1905 uprising in Russia, explores the view that 'everything is permissible'. Camus worked with JEAN-LOUIS BARRAULT on *State of Siege* (1948), an allegory of totalitarian oppression for which an outbreak of the Plague serves as a symbol. As an approach to total theatre under the influence of ARTAUD, in the style of Barrault, it is only intermittently successful, but it was a prelude to Camus's return to active involvement in the theatre. In the years before his death in a car crash, he worked on experimental adaptations from CALDERON, LOPE DE VEGA and, in 1959, Dostoyevsky's *The Possessed*. Unlike SARTRE, with whom he found himself increasingly at odds, Camus accepted the award of the Nobel Prize in 1957.

Philip Thody, *Albert Camus*, 1957.

Čapek, Karel (1890–1938). Czech dramatist, who trained as a biologist, but recognized the philosophical implications of biology, and then the political parallels. He was a Czech nationalist in the years of independence following World War I, and he tried to excite resistance to Hitler's plans to pocket Czechoslovakia. A note of despair at a world with a will for self-destruction runs through much of his work. Čapek writes, in the *Letters from England* (1925), of his encounter with London traffic: 'I am of peasant blood and have been somewhat disturbed by what I have seen.' The disturbance is already apparent in *R.U.R.* (1920) and *The Insect Play* (1921), but is further developed in the lesser-known later plays like *The Makropoulos Affair* (1922), source of Janacek's opera, *Adam the Creator* (1927), and the politically based *Power and Glory* (1937) and *Mother* (1938).

Carnovsky, Morris (1897–   ). American actor, born in St Louis, Missouri. He made his professional debut in Boston, and his New York debut with the PROVINCETOWN PLAYERS in 1922. He was associated for the next decade with the Theatre Guild, and through the thirties with the GROUP THEATRE, of which he was an idealistic and hard-working senior member, and the creator of a number of roles in the plays of ODETS and others. When the Group Theatre broke up, Carnovsky continued acting, and in 1956 began a long association with the Shakespeare Festival in STRATFORD, Connecticut. His leading roles there have included Shylock, Lear and Prospero. 'My face, and I hereby give it credit, wore beards well,' he commented in 1974. He is one of the actors whose career survived the attempts of the HOUSE UNAMERICAN ACTIVITIES COMMITTEE to destroy it.

Centlivre, Susanna (*c.* 1670–1723). An English dramatist, celebrated in her time and for at least a century after it, she was one of the first to challenge, albeit somewhat nervously, sexual prejudice. Two plays of 1705, *The Gamester* and *The Basset Table*, were aimed to correct the reigning social vice of gambling, but Mrs Centlivre's best work is more spirited than these unctuous pieces. *The Busy Body* (1709) was notable for the creation of the prying Marplot, and *The Wonder: A Woman Keeps a Secret* (1714) provided in Don Felix one of GARRICK's favourite parts. Mrs Centlivre was a prominent Whig publicist and supporter of the Hanoverian succession. The FARCE *A Gotham Election* (1715) was an unusually overt political risk. Certainly she had guts, even to the point of tangling with Pope, and earning herself a contemptuous reference in the 1728 *Dunciad*. Her best play, *A Bold Stroke for a Wife* (1718), is an elaboration on the theme of amorous disguise.

J. W. Bowyer, *The Celebrated Mrs Centlivre*, 1952.

Chaikin, Joseph. See OPEN THEATRE.

Chapman, George (*c.* 1560–1634). Chapman's reputation as a dramatist is higher in the study than on the stage, where he is virtually unknown except for occasional university performances. Little of his early work has survived, but it brought him esteem and some popularity. Before committing himself to the perilous career of poet, Chapman had attended university (probably both Oxford and Cambridge) and served as a soldier on the Continent. On his return to England he became one of the group of playwrights employed by HENSLOWE to write for the Admiral's Men. To this period belong *The Blind Beggar of Alexandria* (1596) and *An Humorous Day's Mirth* (1597). After 1599 many of his plays were written for the fashionable CHILDREN'S COMPANIES. The titanic tragedies *Bussy D'Ambois* (1604) and *The Conspiracy and Tragedy of Charles Duke of Biron* (1608) were first performed by boys. The latter brought Chapman into conflict with the Court of James I only three years after he had served a term in prison for his part in the writing of the comedy *Eastward Ho*, which poked fun at the new King's Scottish courtiers. Chapman protested eloquently to the Master of the Revels against 'Illiterate Authority' that 'sets up his Bristles against Poverty'. The allusiveness and obscurity of much of his poetry may have been partly self-protective, though it reflected also his mystical-philosophical temperament.

Millar Maclure, *Chapman: A Critical Study*, 1966.

Charke, Charlotte. See CIBBER, CHARLOTTE.

Chekhov, Anton (1860–1904). Chekhov's origins were humble, and his early life a financial struggle. His first stories were published while he was a medical student at Moscow University, and the money he received for them helped to support his family. His early plays, in the popular 'vaudeville' style, were equally opportunistic, but Chekhov could follow no style without modifying it. *Ivanov* (1887), even though structurally a MELODRAMA, criticizes its own conventions. Actors, directors and theatregoers have been tempted to see in Chekhov's detailed characterizations an affection for the cultured but ineffective Russian liberals whose life-style dominates his great plays; but the affection is threatened, and perhaps deepened, by contempt. It is not accurate to read Chekhov's four great plays, *The Seagull* (1896), *Uncle Vanya* (1897), *The Three Sisters* (1901) and *The Cherry Orchard* (1904), as the prologue to revolution, but it is not impossible either. The sort of gentle sadness too often ascribed to him was alien to his temperament. We have to observe something much more mordant.

Chekhov's theatrical career was always uneasy. *The Seagull* flopped in St Petersburg in 1896, and its success at the MOSCOW ART THEATRE in 1898 is one of the most extraordinary events in the history of the theatre. STANISLAVSKY, who had shared its direction with NEMIROVICH-DAN-CHENKO, had little faith in, and not much feeling for, it. Yet he discovered in rehearsal the pressure, peculiar to Chekhov, of the unspoken on the spoken. With characteristic enthusiasm, he over-worked the discovery, and Chekhov was never entirely happy with Stanislavsky's direction. Nonetheless, it was the Moscow Art Theatre that established him as a playwright, and his last years were perplexed and enriched by his association with it. In 1901 he married OLGA KNIPPER, one of Stanislavsky's leading actresses, and he watched her play Ranevskaya on the opening night of *The Cherry Orchard*, when it was staged on what proved to be his last birthday. From 1897 onwards he had known he was dying of tuberculosis. The late stages of that illness provided the context in which he wrote his last, finest, and funniest play.

Maurice Valency, *The Breaking String*, 1966.
J. L. Styan, *Chekhov in Performance*, 1971.

Churchill, Caryl (1938–   ). English playwright whose work in collaboration with the Joint Stock Theatre Company has been a particularly notable example of the sharing of inspiration between writer and actors. The collaboration began with *Light Shining in Buckinghamshire* (1976), an unhysterical play about the millennial dreams of the Levellers. It marked Churchill's move away from expressions of private anxiety, as in *Owners* (1972), to thoughtful explorations of public and political issues. *Cloud Nine* (1978), whose use of transvestism was both witty and trenchant, was a study of imperialism in terms of sexual stereotypes. Like *Top Girls* (1982), *Fen* (1982) and *A Mouthful of Birds* (written with David Lan, 1986), it showed how hard-hitting a theatrical event can be if intelligent actors share in the act of creation with a resourceful playwright. Churchill is not a strident writer. She has described her commitment to socialism and to feminism as 'wary'. In the political theatre of the late twentieth century, hers is a mature voice.

Cibber. Several members of this family achieved prominence in the English theatre.

(1) **Colley Cibber** (1671–1757). The autobiographical *Apology for the Life of Mr Colley Cibber, Comedian* (1740) gives as vivid an account of the Restoration theatre from within as Pepys's *Diary* does from a spectator's standpoint. The son of an immigrant Dutch sculptor, Cibber braved family opposition to go on the stage and had a long and distinguished career as an actor, specializing in the portrayal of fatuous fops and sinister villains. He also managed Drury Lane Theatre, where he acted for most of his career, during a stormy period in that theatre's history. As Poet Laureate (1730) he was no worse than some of his predecessors (and successors) in spite of Pope's famous attack on him in *The Dunciad*. His plays include *Love's Last Shift* (1696) – whose hero's reformation inspired VANBRUGH to write a worldly-wise riposte in *The Relapse* – *The Careless Husband* (1704), and an adaptation of SHAKESPEARE's *Richard III* (1700) which displaced the original for two centuries and is the source of the much-quoted line: 'Off with his head! So much for Buckingham!' Cibber is historically important as a playwright who anticipated the drab decorum and insipid gentility of much eighteenth-century comedy while retaining occasional flashes of the earlier Restoration vivacity. He had ten children.

R. H. Barker, *Mr Cibber of Drury Lane*, 1939.
L. R. N. Ashley, *Cibber*, 1965.

(2) **Theophilus Cibber** (1703–58). This son of Colley Cibber merited the dislike of most of his contemporaries. His sole success as an actor, in a career which began at the age of sixteen, was as Ancient Pistol. His attempt at joint management of Drury Lane ended in disorder, and when his extravagance had led him so far into debt that he forced his second wife into a remunerative liaison, public outrage forced Theophi-

lus to take refuge in France. During a subsequent attempt to rehabilitate his career, he was drowned in the Irish Sea on the way to fulfil an engagement at Dublin's Smock Alley Theatre.

(3) *Charlotte Cibber* (1713–c. 1760). Better known under her married name of Charke, Charlotte was the most eccentric member of this eccentric family. After making a peculiar marriage, probably motivated by a wish to get away from home, she had an undistinguished career as an actress and an adventurous one as a puppet-master, conjuror's assistant and fairground performer. She was keeping a tavern in Drury Lane when she wrote her extraordinary autobiography, *Narrative of the Life of Mrs Charlotte Charke* (1755), a document in the history of sexual deviance. Charlotte favoured masculine attire both on stage and off it. The probability is that her sexual tastes were exclusively lesbian.

(4) *Susannah Cibber* (1714–66). Sister of the talented musician Thomas Arne, herself originally trained as a singer, Susannah was the unfortunate second wife of Theophilus Cibber. Her promising debut as an actress – she was versatile enough to play in comedy and tragedy – was profoundly damaged by her swaggering husband's attempt to steal, on her behalf, the part of Polly Peachum in *The Beggar's Opera* from KITTY CLIVE. Even worse was his forcing her into a liaison with a friend. There was some bravery in her comeback before the public scandal had died away. She was a fine leading lady at Drury Lane during the heyday of GARRICK's management. Garrick admired her peculiar strength in 'pathetic' roles. The reasons for this strength are the subject of mature and intelligent speculation in Mary Nash's fine biography.

Mary Nash, *The Provoked Wife*, 1977.

Claudel, Paul (1868–1955). Claudel's distinguished career as a French diplomat masked for a long time his daunting work as a dramatic poet. Even his detractors grant the monumental quality of his plays, but find turgid and overblown what his admirers find grandly lyrical. It was a production of *The Tidings Brought to Mary* (1909) in 1912 at the Théâtre de l'Oeuvre that introduced him to the Parisian public, and his work attracted the attention of innovators as various as ARTAUD in France and Edith Craig in England. It was in Edith Craig's production of *The Hostage* (1914) in 1919 that SYBIL THORNDIKE found one of her most rewarding roles. The later revival of interest in Claudel's work was largely owed to JEAN-LOUIS BARRAULT. It was his production of *The Satin Slipper* (1929) during the German occupation of Paris in 1943 that focused attention on Claudel's theatrical imagination. Like *Division of Noon* (1905) this is a play that explores, with Catholic intensity, the interaction of sin and grace. Barrault staged both with a boldness and lavishness that recalled Artaud's vision of a total theatre. His later production of *Head of Gold* (1889), Claudel's first play, confirmed the dramatist's place on Parnassus without greatly diminishing his unpopularity. It is not so much to audiences as to directors that Claudel appeals, and his particular contribution is to the literary tradition of the French theatre.

Joseph Chiari, *The Poetic Drama of Paul Claudel*, 1954.

Clive, Kitty (1711–85). Kitty Clive was a kind of female version of the clown who wants to play Hamlet. Though notably successful in FARCE and low comedy, she yearned to play tragic heroines. Her quarrels with GARRICK were partly due to his sensible efforts to prevent her playing parts in which she would make a fool of herself. Horace Walpole presented her with a house when she retired from the stage in 1769, Samuel Johnson enjoyed her conversation and Hogarth and many others painted her.

Percy Fitzgerald, *The Life of Mrs Catherine Clive*, 1888.

Clurman, Harold (1901–81). American director and critic who was the driving force behind the GROUP THEATRE of which he was co-founder. The triumphs and disasters of that passionate company are excitingly recorded in Clurman's book, *The Fervent Years* (1946). It is doubtful whether, without Clurman's encouragement, ODETS would have written the sequence of fine plays that are the Group Theatre's particular glory, and it is certain that Clurman's committed work on these socially questioning pieces helped them into popular acceptance. After the Group Theatre had finally folded, Clurman worked as a director on BROADWAY and in Hollywood. His book *On Directing* (1972) is one of the more intelligent handbooks on that elusive topic. Clurman was also a prominent dramatic critic, particularly during spells with *The New Republic* (1949–53) and the London *Observer* (1959–63). A collection of his reviews and essays was published under the title, *Lies Like Truth* (1958).

Cobb, Lee J. (1911–76). American actor, who made his professional debut in Pasadena in 1929. He was a stalwart member of the GROUP THEATRE in the late thirties, and had a notable career in films. His most famous stage role was as Willy Loman in ARTHUR MILLER's *Death of a*

Salesman in 1949. His performance of this average man at the moment of his breaking (the phrase is John Mason Brown's) was, for many who saw it, definitive. To Eric Bentley, he was an actor carrying a playwright's world on his shoulders. Cobb had the peculiarly American gift of overacting whilst seeming not to be acting at all. He occupied the stage like a dyspeptic truck-driver caught off duty, but thundered like Jove when the occasion allowed it. If his 1968 performance of King Lear was less successful, a cause can be found in a comment he made about his reasons for turning it down in 1950: 'I'd been playing Lear for two years – in *Death of a Salesman*.'

Colman, George, the Elder (1732–94). Colman's place in society was assured by his parentage. His father was a diplomat and his mother the Countess of Bath's sister. On inherited money, he purchased a share in Covent Garden Theatre in 1767, sold out in 1774 and bought outright the control of the Little Theatre in the Haymarket, together with its licence to perform the legitimate drama during the summer season when the PATENT THEATRES were closed. His aim in becoming a theatre manager was partly to stage his own plays, of which *Polly Honeycombe* (1760) was the first to succeed on stage. *The Jealous Wife* (1761) derived its plot from *Tom Jones* and its success from the acting of DAVID GARRICK. Colman and Garrick were friends, and their collaboration in writing *The Clandestine Marriage* (1766) produced one of the best comedies of the eighteenth century. Colman's dramatic work is all derivative, but he had the wit to choose good models. From 1789 until his death he was mentally deranged and 'committed to the care of a person at Paddington'.

Eugene R. Page, *Colman the Elder*, 1935.

Colman, George, the Younger (1762–1836). When his father went mad, young Colman took over the management of the Little Theatre. Despite the spectacular improvidence of his own life, he made a serious attempt at management, and developed a fondness for the playhouse whose dramatic repertoire he greatly strengthened. His first success was *Inkle and Yarico* (1787), a resourceful musical on the theme of slavery. He was the originator of a new kind of play (James Boaden bore witness to his contemporary fame when he called it 'a sort of Colman drama of three acts') in which Elizabethan blank verse and a solemn plot are interrupted by frequent songs and displaced comic characters. *The Iron Chest* (1796) is the best known, though not necessarily the best, of these. It is a mauled version of William Godwin's novel *Caleb Williams*. When he tried, which was rarely, Colman could write better. His comedy,

John Bull (1803), is his best work, though there are fine touches elsewhere. He knew the theatre so well that he could make almost any story work on the stage. For forty years at least, his plays were performed almost as often as SHAKESPEARE's, more often than anyone else's, in England and America, and actors like BANNISTER and the elder MATHEWS owed their reputations to him. It was a surprise to many when Colman was appointed Examiner of Plays in 1824. Not only was he a notorious *bon viveur* but the author as well of several *risqué* poems – and he had also spent several months in a debtors' prison. In the event, he used the blue pencil freely. No one was much impressed, and he outlived both his talent and his reputation.

J. F. Bagster-Collins, *George Colman the Younger*, 1946.

Condell, Henry. See HEMINGES, JOHN.

Congreve, William (1670–1729). Having been born a gentleman and educated as one, Congreve lived for a decade as a writer before 'retiring' at the age of thirty – about half-way through his life. He was supported by various government commissions, obtained for him by the Earl of Halifax – commissioner for licensing hackney coaches, commissioner of wine-licences, a place in the Pipe Office, another in the Customs and Excise Office, the secretaryship of Jamaica – and he spent his last years in moderate affluence, with one foot in the intellectual camp and the other among the nobility. When the Duchess of Marlborough paid for his monument in Westminster Abbey, there was no shortage of rumour and a modicum of first-hand knowledge. It was to her that Congreve had bequeathed a not inconsiderable legacy. The first thing Congreve wrote was a novel called *Incognita* (1692). 'I would rather praise it than read it,' wrote Dr Johnson in his censorious essay on Congreve. The year 1693 saw the performance of his first two plays, *The Old Bachelor* and *The Double Dealer*, but his reputation increased vastly when THOMAS BETTERTON decided to open his new theatre in Lincoln's Inn Fields with *Love for Love* (1695). The play's verbal energy overwhelmed its first audiences, and ought still to delight us. It was probably a mistake for Congreve to follow it with a tragedy. *The Mourning Bride* (1697), though successful in its time, reveals a lack of steady purpose. It was a controversial moment in theatrical history. JEREMY COLLIER was about to publish his *Short View of the Immorality and Profaneness of the English Stage* (1698), in which Congreve was singled out for attack. In retrospect, much of the behaviour of theatrical people of the period looks hysterical. Congreve, certainly, was stung.

After the comparative failure of his last and greatest play, *The Way of the World* (1700), he abandoned the way of the playwright.

John C. Hodges, *William Congreve, the Man*, 1941.
Brian Morris (ed.), *William Congreve*, 1972.
Harold Love, *Congreve*, 1974.

Connelly, Marc (1890–1980). American playwright, whose theatrical fame is so singly linked to the BROADWAY triumph of *The Green Pastures* (1930) that he might fairly be classed with ONE-PLAY AUTHORS. But Connelly's name was earlier connected with that of GEORGE S. KAUFMAN in a series of ten collaborations, including *Dulcy* (1921), *Merton of the Movies* (1922) and an EXPRESSIONIST experiment, *Beggar on Horseback* (1924). *The Green Pastures*, based on Roark Bradford's stories about Louisiana Negroes, gave black actors a rare chance to perform on Broadway. It is a humorous and often sentimental retelling of Old Testament stories, framed by scenes in a negro Sunday School.

Cooke, George Frederick (*c.* 1756–1812). Nothing is better known about Cooke than his drunkenness. He was the, probably illegitimate, son of a camp-following Scots girl, and was a provincial actor for over twenty years. Suddenly, in 1800, he hit the big time – Covent Garden – and held on as a leading actor until 1810. His great roles were Shylock, Richard III, Iago, Sir Giles Overreach, and Sir Archy MacSarcasm (in a play by CHARLES MACKLIN). His voice was powerful but harsh, and his movement comparatively ungainly. As a villain, he had obviously a chilling authority, that quality of 'danger' which would be usurped by EDMUND KEAN. Cooke's rival was the handsome gentleman-actor JOHN PHILIP KEMBLE, and honours were even when Cooke was persuaded to tour America, one of the first English actors to make the trip. His early performances there were triumphant, but he drank too hard, and the last eighteen months were unattractive. It is said that, when he lay dying of dropsy in New York, he called for a glass of water, confessing that on his death-bed a man should make friends with his enemies.

Arnold Hare, *George Frederick Cooke*, 1980.
D. B. Wilmeth, *George Frederick Cooke*, 1980.

Copeau, Jacques (1878–1949). French critic, actor, director, manager, theorist, perhaps above all, teacher and shy genius. Dissatisfied with both radical and traditional theatres in France, Copeau announced in 1913 the formation of a new Théâtre du Vieux-Colombier, whose aim would be, not revolution, but renovation. A young company, including

CHARLES DULLIN and LOUIS JOUVET, which had rehearsed through the summer of 1913 as an ensemble, and which accepted Copeau's 'naked stage' as the setting for skilful acting, performed fifteen plays from the classical repertoire before the outbreak of World War I interrupted the enterprise. During this period of enforced rest, Copeau met CRAIG, APPIA and Dalcroze, the originator of eurhythmics, and absorbed their influence in the school he established late in 1915. It was not the aim of this school to train stars, but to develop the resources of each individual through play, vocal and physical rhythm and improvisation. Subsequent drama training the world over has felt the influence of this brilliant educational experiment. Copeau himself sensed the possibilities of a 'renovation' of the improvisatory principles of the COMMEDIA DELL'ARTE, 'a brotherhood of jokers always acting together'. The plans were set aside from 1917 to 1919, when the Théâtre du Vieux-Colombier played its classical repertoire in New York, as part of French cultural propaganda. Returning to Paris in 1919, Copeau reopened his theatre after completing alterations that gave each new play a setting of unchangeable simplicity. The first production on the new stage was *The Winter's Tale* (1919). The following year, Copeau opened a second school, now developing the use of masks in order to achieve in the apprentice actors as neutral and at the same time dynamic a state as possible. The demands of his school and his theatre conflicted, and in 1924 Copeau shut both, and went with a select few to Burgundy, where, as Les Copiaus, the new company improvised scenarios or performed choric dramas on portable village stages. Les Copiaus broke up in 1929, though Copeau's nephew MICHEL SAINT-DENIS revived the spirit of the work almost at once, in La Compagnie des Quinze. Copeau himself spent more time writing after 1929, and his five years as a director with the COMÉDIE-FRANÇAISE (1936–41) were comparatively unmemorable.

John Rudlin, *Jacques Copeau*, 1986.

Corneille, Pierre (1606–84). French playwright, the only serious challenger to RACINE's status as France's greatest tragic poet. Born in Rouen and trained to the law, Corneille wrote his first play, a comedy, in 1629, and had written four more comedies and a tragicomedy before his first tragedy, *Médée* (1635). By that time he was in Cardinal Richelieu's employ, one of a group of writers whose task it was to turn the Cardinal's plots into plays. Temperamentally unsuited to the work, Corneille returned to Rouen, where he wrote *Le Cid* (1636–7) and thereby changed the course of French drama. *Le Cid* was based on a Spanish original whose six acts spanned several years, but Corneille compressed its action (including a war) into a single day, locating it also in a single town. Even so he was attacked for offending the UNITIES, and the subsequent controversy brought into focus dramatic principles that clarified, for Corneille, his own purposes. The tragedies that followed *Le Cid* – *Horace* (1640), *Cinna* (1641), *Polyeucte* (1642), *Rodogune* (1645), *Théodore* (1645), *Héraclitus* (1646) and *Nicomède* (1651) – continue to oppose love to honour and duty. The argument for love is conducted in fine dramatic poetry, but it is doomed to lose. Corneille's heroes have high and single minds, however they may be threatened by the softer passions. He continued to write until 1674, when his last play, *Suréna*, was performed at the HÔTEL DE BOURGOGNE. His fame had not dwindled since his election to the Academy in 1647, but neither had his wealth greatly increased. MOLIÈRE was a sturdy admirer, not least of his comedy, *Le Menteur* (1643), without which, Molière claimed, he would never have been able to write *The Misanthrope*. Corneille's tragedies were, and still are, revered, but critics have increasingly stressed the paradox that, whilst Corneille greatly reinforced neo-classical strictness, he was much less at ease with its constraints than Racine.

P. J. Yarrow, *Corneille*, 1963.

Cornell, Katharine (1893–1974). American actress who, after World War II, vied with HELEN HAYES for the title of 'first lady' of BROADWAY. Success did not come to her immediately. Her father was manager of a theatre in Buffalo, and she made her acting debut in New York in 1917. Her father had paid for her to be educated at a Westchester finishing school, and also financed a visit to London in 1919–20 during which she made a small stir by her playing of Jo in a dramatization of *Little Women*. It was playing on Broadway in Clemence Dane's *A Bill of Divorcement* in 1921 that lifted her towards stardom. Shortly before the opening she had married Guthrie McClintic, who was associated as director or manager with most of her subsequent successes. These included SHAW's Candida (1924), Elizabeth in *The Barretts of Wimpole Street* (1931), Juliet to Basil Rathbone's Romeo (1934) and Shaw's Saint Joan (1935). She looked as passionate and powerful as Emily Brontë, but she seemed to her detractors too ready to stand on her dignity. For Eric Bentley, 'Miss Cornell will never consent to be anything less than a princess in any role', and Brooks Atkinson, who admired her, recognized 'a core of decency that could not be eradicated or disguised'.

Tad Mosel, *Leading Lady*, 1978.

Coward, Noel (1899–1973). Coward made his London debut as an actor in 1911, playing, among other parts, Slightly in *Peter Pan*. His debut as a writer was almost equally precocious; *Ida Collaborates*, written with Esmé Wynne, was staged in 1917. His first major success was *The Vortex* (1924), in which he played the lead, 'all dope and crashing piano-chords', as J. C. Trewin remembers. *The Vortex* is a dated MELODRAMA, but Coward was soon to produce his finest plays, the drawing-room comedies *Fallen Angels* (1925), *Hay Fever* (1925) and *Private Lives* (1930), all elegant, witty, intelligent and finely finished. Together with the musical romance *Bitter Sweet* (1929), the more acerbic comedies *Design for Living* (1933) and *Present Laughter* (1942), and the farcical *Blithe Spirit* (1941), they form the basis of his abiding popularity. The pieces in which Coward spells out an almost maudlin patriotism, *Cavalcade* (1931), *This Happy Breed* (1942) and *Peace in Our Time* (1947), are, by contrast, heavy-handed. His admirers were relieved when he returned to comedy with *Relative Values* (1951) and *Quadrille* (1952), but the sparkle was missing, not least because times had changed. Coward's last work for the English stage was a triple bill under the title *Suite in Three Keys* (1966), of which the first 'key', *A Song at Twilight*, had an impressive autobiographical honesty in its portrait of an elderly writer coming to terms with his homosexual past.

When Coward was knighted in 1970, it was an acknowledgment, not only of his work as actor and playwright, but also as composer, lyricist and singer. Whoever first called him 'The Master' may have been half-jesting; but the description came to be used with deadly seriousness by the upholders of theatrical glamour. Coward's own sense of style was generally impeccable, but that of his camp-followers is not. The theatrical world that they inhabit, and into which they all too often force Coward, is too much like fairyland. Small wonder that the socially committed critic KENNETH TYNAN should have commented in 1951, not without some grudging admiration, 'Forty years ago he was Slightly in *Peter Pan*, and you might say he has been wholly in *Peter Pan* ever since.'

John Lahr, *Coward the Playwright*, 1982.

Cowley, Hannah (1743–1809). English playwright, born in Tiverton, Devon, who began writing for the stage eight years after marrying a captain in the East India Company. *The Runaway* (1776), her first play, may have been 'improved' by DAVID GARRICK, to whom it was dedicated. *Who's the Dupe?* (1779) was a popular AFTERPIECE and *The Belle's Stratagem* (1780) retained its place on the London stage, as a classic old comedy, until almost the end of the nineteenth century. Cowley's characters are stage-stereotypes, but her dialogue is deftly handled and her work is a sprightly contrast to much of the dreary sentimental comedy which dominated the London stage throughout her writing life.

Cox, Robert (1604–55). During the eighteen years (1642–60) when theatres in England were officially closed, short comic scenes derived from popular plays were performed, more or less surreptitiously. Cox was responsible for several of these, one of them being 'The Merry Conceits of Bottom the Weaver' taken from *A Midsummer Night's Dream*. He was also by all accounts a skilled performer. In 1653 he was arrested during a performance, having been betrayed to the army authorities by some fellow actors. He died in prison two years later.

Craig, Edward Gordon (1872–1966). One of the great theatrical mavericks, Craig was the illegitimate son of ELLEN TERRY and E. W. Godwin, the architect and stage designer. At first he followed his mother into acting, working for nine years at IRVING's Lyceum; but his real talent was closer to his father's. He was already establishing himself as an illustrator in 1900, when he designed and master-minded a highly original amateur production of *Dido and Aeneas*. Two years later he further tested his theories of lighting and design in a production of Handel's *Acis and Galatea*. He was precociously confident that the theatre of the future would depend on the unifying artistic vision of a single person – what the later cinema came to call an *auteur* – combining technical control with costume and stage design, and with a command of the actors now (but only rarely then) invested in the artistic director. Craig's subsequent professional productions included two with his mother in 1903, IBSEN's *The Vikings* [*of Helgeland*], and *Much Ado about Nothing*, and a few in which his professional services as a designer were used: *Venice Preserved* for OTTO BRAHM in Berlin in 1905, *Rosmersholm* with a puzzled ELEONORA DUSE in 1906, an ABBEY THEATRE production of YEATS's *The Hour Glass* in 1911, Hamlet at the MOSCOW ART THEATRE in 1911–12 and *The Pretenders* in Copenhagen in 1926. Brahm employed a second designer to modify Craig's designs, Duse finally refused to work with them, in the Abbey there was technical trouble with the famous Craig screens, and the traumas at the Moscow Art Theatre brought STANISLAVSKY into rare conflict with his designer, Sulerjitsky.

Not only, then, did Craig actually *do* very little, but also whatever he did raised problems. And yet his influence was enormous. Much of that influence is owed to the energy with which he edited and largely wrote the fifteen volumes of the magnificently illustrated periodical *The Mask* (1908–29), and to his books, *The Art of the Theatre* (1905) and the fuller *On the Art of the Theatre* (1911). After 1908, insufficiently honoured in his own country, Craig lived mostly in Italy. It was in the Arena Goldoni in Florence that he established his typically impractical school in 1912. It closed in 1914. Craig had always spent money, his own and other people's, easily, but after the death of his indulgent mother in 1928 he began to experience a rather shocking financial hardship. Certainly he was a difficult man, egotistical and always something of a spoiled child, with a philanderer's fondness for, and carelessness of, women. Even so, a country more artistically alert than England might have tried harder to accommodate his wayward genius.

Edward Craig, *Gordon Craig*, 1968.
Christopher Innes, *Edward Gordon Craig*, 1983.

Cumberland, Richard (1732–1811). Born and educated in Cambridge, and with a promising career in politics (he had been Lord Halifax's private secretary), Cumberland turned to writing plays in 1761, because he needed the money, and within a decade was established as the leading dramatist of the London stage. The taste of the period was for sentimental comedy in which fine sentiments eventually overcame the meanness of an acquisitive opposition, and Cumberland catered efficiently for that taste. He wrote over fifty plays, four of which continued to hold the stage well into the nineteenth century. *The Brothers* (1769) at Covent Garden was his first real success. *The West Indian* (1771), presented at Drury Lane by DAVID GARRICK, is a good example of the style of sentimental comedy, and its naive hero, Belcour, is the archetype of the naturally virtuous. *The Jew* (1794) is a worthy plea on behalf of a persecuted people. *The Wheel of Fortune* (1795) furnished JOHN PHILIP KEMBLE with a part in which he excelled, the grandly gloomy Penruddock. Notoriously sensitive to criticism, Cumberland received much, perhaps more than he deserved, particularly from SHERIDAN, who caricatured him for posterity as Sir Fretful Plagiary in *The Critic*. He is, in fact, the leading representative of a dramatic movement that believed in the popularity of virtue.

R. J. Dircks, *Cumberland*, 1976.

Cushman, Charlotte (1816–76). American actress, born in Boston where, after a career that made her a star in America and England, she died. Her initial intention was to sing in opera, but her voice broke under the strain. In 1836, she made her debut in the role that she made almost her own in the mid-nineteenth century, Lady Macbeth. Westland Marston considered that her 'unrelieved, level earnestness of manner' gave the part 'a sameness of gloom', and preferred her performance of Romeo. 'As a lover, the ardour of her devotion exceeded that of any male actor I have ever seen in the part.' Certainly, there was a masculine weightiness in Cushman's acting, and a force that could frighten audiences, as she did as Meg Merrilies in one of the many adaptations of Scott's *Guy Mannering*.

Joseph Leech, *Bright Particular Star*, 1970.

Daly, Augustin (1838–99). American playwright and theatre manager who was the first of his countrymen to seek complete artistic control of the productions that he staged. His own plays, written regularly in collaboration with his brother Joseph, include spectacular MELODRAMAS like *Under the Gaslight* (1867), *The Flash of Lightning* (1868) and *The Red Scarf* (1868), and social comedies like *Divorce* (1871), *Pique* (1875) and *Love on Crutches* (1884). He was also a tireless adapter of plays, not all of which would seem to modern taste to have needed adaptation. His Shakespeare versions, for instance, famous in their time because of the care he took over their staging, were a surrender rather than a challenge to contemporary sensibilities. It was Daly's habit to take plots from French or German playwrights and 'americanize' them to suit new characters. When he relied on his own invention, as in the frontier drama *Horizon* (1871), his episodes proliferated into confusion. He lacked, that is to say, a reliable sense of dramatic limit. His sense of theatre, on the other hand, was outstandingly reliable. Under his management and direction, particularly at Daly's Theatre in New York from 1879 until his death, American acting reached new heights, and his tours of London and Paris from 1884 to 1891 earned for the American theatre a new international respect. Daly was fanatically industrious. It was an industry that led to the first creation of an American ensemble.

Don Wilmeth and Rosemary Cullen, Introduction to *Selected Plays*, 1983.

Davenant, Sir William (1606–68). Though negligible as a dramatist, Davenant is a key figure in the history of English theatre. He came to the theatre with borrowed credentials, claiming to be SHAKESPEARE's natural son, on the strength of family acquaintance. His first play, *The Cruel Brother*, was performed at Blackfriars in 1627 and has all the outward sex and spectacle of Jacobean tragedy with none of its passion or spiritual intensity. Even during the period when the Puritans closed the theatres, Davenant contrived to circumvent the ban and produced theatrical entertainments whose quota of music enabled them to escape the prohibition. His *The Siege of Rhodes* (1656) may claim to be the first English opera. At the Restoration, Davenant, with THOMAS KILLIGREW, obtained a monopoly over the London theatre, not without a certain amount of sharp practice. His company included young THOMAS

BETTERTON, the greatest actor of the Restoration period. Davenant's most successful original play was a comedy, *The Wits* (1634), but fame and fortune came to him from the numerous adaptations of Shakespeare which he made, mostly in collaboration with DRYDEN. These showed a lively awareness of the possibilities of the post-Restoration playhouse, with its proscenium arch, perspective scenery and elaborate stage machines. Davenant may, as one critic alleged, have turned Shakespeare into pantomime but it was, by all accounts, gorgeous pantomime and Shakespeare did survive; Davenant it was that died.

A. Harbage, *Davenant: Poet, Venturer*, 1935.

Day, John (*c.* 1574–*c.* 1640). In T. S. ELIOT's *The Waste Land*, that vast echo-chamber of a poem, there is a reminiscence of some lines from John Day's *The Parliament of Bees*:

> When of the sudden, listening, you shall hear
> A noise of horns and hunting, which shall bring
> Actaeon to Diana in the spring.

This comes from a series of Vergilian pastoral dialogues. In his plays Day rarely rises to such heights. Perhaps he put less of himself into them, partly because they were mostly written to order for PHILIP HENSLOWE and partly because nearly all of them were written in collaboration. Born in Norfolk, Day was expelled from Cambridge University for stealing and joined Henslowe's stable of writers in 1598. The following year he killed a fellow dramatist, Henry Porter, in a duel. *The Isle of Gulls* (1600) is derived from Sidney's *Arcadia* and was written for the sophisticated audiences of the 'private' theatres, while *The Travels of the Three English Brothers* (1607) is in the more free-wheeling mode popularized by HEYWOOD. In the latter play Day collaborated with THOMAS DEKKER and George Wilkins; a more distinguished collaborator for Day, WILLIAM SHAKESPEARE, has been suggested in connection with *Pericles* (1608). Day has also been put forward, implausibly, as the author of the *Parnassus* plays. According to William Drummond, BEN JONSON held that Day, Dekker and others 'were all rogues'.

Deburau, Jean-Gaspard (1796–1846). Deburau was born in Bohemia, one of a touring family of acrobats, but his reputation and achievement are wholly French. He did not invent Pierrot, but his melancholy brilliance as the lovesick figure in loose white suit turned a minor Italian *commedia* mask into a major French comic role. Deburau's own life was desperately troubled. Having been taken on at the flea-pit theatre, the Funambules, on the notorious BOULEVARD DU TEMPLE, he worked as a stage-hand for several years. His debut as Pierrot may have come as late as 1825, though alternative romantic legends persist. He was by then a widower, his young wife having died in 1819, three months after their wedding. By a mistress who callously deceived him, he had four children. A daughter by his second wife died in infancy. It was while walking with this second wife in 1836 that Deburau killed an apprentice who was mocking them with shouts of 'Pierrot and his whore'. Dressed in black and weeping as the charge was read, Deburau was tried in Paris. He was found not guilty, and welcomed back to the Boulevard by cheering audiences; but he found it hard to reconcile his guilt and the innocence of Pierrot. Suffering severely from asthma, probably induced by his sensitive horror, Deburau continued to play Pierrot at the Funambules until his death. Few people ever knew that he had been taught as a child how to deliver a lethal blow with a stick.

De Filippo, Eduardo (1900–   ). Italian dramatist and actor-manager, whose plays are usually set in his native Naples. He writes consciously in an Italian tradition which includes both COMMEDIA DELL'ARTE and PIRANDELLO. He delights in surprising audiences and also in confirming their expectations. The compassionate magician who plays the central role in *Grand Magic* (1948) represents also De Filippo's understanding of the playwright's art. He is the compassionate magician of the Italian theatre. Not many of his plays have been translated into English. Among those that have, *Filumena Marturano* (1946) provided the basis for the successful film *Marriage Italian Style*, and *The Local Authority* (1960), if it did not inspire the film *The Godfather*, excels it. Mike Stott's decision to set *Ducking Out*, his 1982 adaption of *Christmas with the Cupiellos*, in the north of England was an honest response to the work of a dramatist who is insistently local. *Inner Voices*, a translation of *Le Voci di dentro* (1948) opened at the NATIONAL THEATRE, London, in 1983, with RALPH RICHARDSON, two years De Filippo's junior, in the part De Filippo played in Naples.

Dekker, Thomas (*c.* 1572–1632). Like several of his contemporaries, Dekker combined two careers, playwriting and pamphleteering, producing one outstanding work in each genre. His play *The Shoemaker's Holiday* (1599) is a romantic comedy full of dramatic life, in which Dekker's love of London is evident in his idealization of the citizenry. His prose pamphlet *The Gull's Horn-Book* (1609) gives a vivid and sharply satirical picture of a London gallant's day and is especially notable for its picture of the gallant in the playhouse. Dekker was plagued by debt all his life, and despite his prolific output of plays and pamphlets, spent six years in a debtors' prison. Of over forty plays in which he had a hand about a dozen survive; among these *The Witch of Edmonton* (1621), written in collaboration with JOHN FORD and WILLIAM ROWLEY, may be mentioned for its sympathetic portrayal of the old witch, and *The Honest Whore* (1604), in which THOMAS MIDDLETON also had a hand, for a similar view of the central figure. *The Belman of London* (1608) and *Lanthorn and Candlelight* (1608) are successful rogue pamphlets in the style made popular by ROBERT GREENE. *Old Fortunatus* (1600) is typical of the hodge-podge of dramatic forms which characterized the early Elizabethan theatre; it was already old-fashioned when Dekker wrote it.

K. L. Gregg, *Dekker: A Study in Economic and Social Backgrounds*, 1924.

Dench, Judi (1935–   ). English actress whose first job was with the OLD VIC company under Michael Benthall. She began her four seasons with the company playing Ophelia (1955–6) and ended them as a touching Juliet in Franco Zeffirelli's impressive interpretation of *Romeo and Juliet* (1959–60). As a member of the ROYAL SHAKESPEARE COMPANY she played a host of classic roles in the sixties and seventies, among the best being the Duchess of Malfi (1971) and Lady Macbeth in a fine studio production (1976). She is also an excellent comedienne, as she showed when she played Grace Harkaway in the 1970 revival of BOUCICAULT's *London Assurance* and a spinsterish Beatrice whose fun was always in touch with sadness in *Much Ado about Nothing* (1976). Dench's versatility was demonstrated in the first roles she played for the NATIONAL THEATRE company in 1982 – as Lady Bracknell in *The Importance of Being Earnest* ('needing only to remove her spectacles when she comes to the notorious hurdle of the handbag-line', wrote Richard Findlater) and then as Deborah in PINTER's *A Kind of Alaska*. She has always resisted the theatre's wish to trap her in the classics. Playing Sally Bowles in *Cabaret* in 1968 was one bold stroke, and her television work in John Hopkins's adventurous trilogy *Talking to a Stranger* (1966) another. More recently, she has had an immense success in a television comedy series, acting with her husband Michael Williams in *A Fine Romance*. Her comment to an interviewer illustrates the plight of the theatre in the age of television. 'You slog your guts out for twenty-four years, four hours a night, and then you do thirty-five minutes of telly and suddenly people start coming up to you in the street. I even had people asking me if *A Fine Romance* was the first thing I'd ever done!' It is a sobering thought that her performance as BRECHT's Mother Courage at the Barbican in London in 1984 will have been seen by a tiny fraction of her television audience.

Gerald Jacobs, *A Great Deal of Laughter*, 1985.

Dennis, John (1657–1734). Political pamphleteer, playwright and literary critic, it is probably for his achievement in the last category that Dennis is most significant. He was educated at Harrow and Cambridge and settled in London where the Duke of Marlborough was his patron. He wrote nine plays, none of which are familiar to anyone but scholars. Two of these were adaptations of SHAKESPEARE; *The Comical Gallant* (1702, from *The Merry Wives of Windsor*) and *The Invader of His Country* (1719, from *Coriolanus*). In adapting them, Dennis followed the logic of his classical aesthetic principles, believing that Shakespeare would have followed ARISTOTLE's rules if only he had known them. His classical tragedy *Iphigenia* involved a mighty storm which, when appropriated for another play, led Dennis to coin a phrase which has since passed into the language: 'They've stolen my thunder!' His essays on *The Grounds of Criticism in Poetry* (1704) and *The Genius and Writings of Shakespeare* (1712) are still worth reading; Dennis was a classicist, but not the unthinking dogmatic classicist Pope made him out to be.

H. G. Paul, *Dennis: His Life and Criticism*, 1911.

Devine, George (1910–66). English actor, director and teacher, Devine was the chief inspirer of the English theatre's new dignity after 1956. The year before, he had been surprised by his appointment as director of the English Stage Company at the ROYAL COURT. His record included the brilliant 'failures', in association with MICHEL SAINT-DENIS, of the London Theatre Studio and the Old Vic School and, independently, of the Young Vic Theatre Company. He had worked with GIELGUD during the important seasons of 1934 to 1938, but no one claimed he was a great actor. He was capable of great performances, for example as Tesman to PEGGY ASHCROFT's Hedda Gabler in 1954, but he was, above all, a fighter, with a marvellous faith in a theatre that constantly rebuffed him. 'For me,' he wrote, 'the theatre is a temple of ideas so well expressed it may be called art. So always look for the quality in the writing above what is being said.' Among the English dramatists who have reason to be grateful for his indomitable ambition at the Royal Court are OSBORNE, ARDEN, WESKER, BOND, PINTER, N.F. Simpson and Charles Wood.

Irving Wardle, *The Theatres of George Devine*, 1978.

Drew. American theatrical family of whom the most notable were:

(1) *Louisa Lane* (1820–97). London-born actress who was put on the stage as a child. Her widowed mother took her to New York in 1827 and almost at once set her acting again. She played Lady Macbeth at the age of sixteen and was admired by EDWIN FORREST. John Drew (1827–62), an Irish actor, was her third husband, and it was as Mrs John Drew that she continued to act after her marriage to him in 1850. From 1860 to 1892 she was a formidable manager of the Arch Street Theatre, Philadelphia. Until the collapse of her stock company in 1892, she continued also to act, most famously as Mrs Malaprop in a touring version of *The Rivals* which frequently co-starred JOSEPH JEFFERSON as Bob Acres. She was the grandmother of the three famous BARRYMORE children, whom she brought up when their parents were touring in plays.

(2) *John Drew* (1853–1927). In partnership with ADA REHAN under the management of AUGUSTIN DALY, Louisa Lane's son established himself as the leading gentlemanly comedian of the American stage. For Daly he played in modern comedies and in such classic revivals as *The Taming of the Shrew*, in which his Petruchio was admired, but after 1892, when Drew began his first engagement with Charles Frohman, he was very much a three-piece suit comedian, popular in London as well as in New York. *My Years on the Stage* (1922) is a stilted but interesting autobiography.

(3) *Georgiana Drew* (1856–93). The youngest child of Louisa Lane was already a member of her mother's stock company when she married Maurice Barrymore in 1876. Together they toured with HELENA MODJESKA. Georgiana's health was too fragile to cope with the combined careers of actress and mother and she died young, in the year in which her eldest child, Lionel, made his stage debut.

Dryden, John (1631–1700). By general consent Dryden was the most considerable literary figure of his age. His place in English drama depends less perhaps on his plays than on his *Essay of Dramatic Poesy* (1668) which influenced the course of dramatic criticism throughout the rest of the century and for most of the next. Here Dryden examines, in dialogue form, the relative claims of classical, Elizabethan and French plays as models for the English playwright. His commentary on

JONSON's *Epicoene* may claim to be the first piece of extended practical criticism in English, while his view of SHAKESPEARE as a towering genius hampered by living in a barbarous age was the ruling orthodoxy until the advent of Romanticism.

Dryden was born in Aldwinkle, Northamptonshire and educated at Westminster School and Trinity College, Cambridge. He came from a Puritan background but turned towards the Anglican and later towards the Roman Catholic church. Although best known today as a satiric poet, Dryden wrote a number of plays, some of which were notably successful in the theatre. These include a comedy of manners, *Marriage à la Mode* (1672), and heroic tragedies in blank verse such as the two parts of *The Conquest of Granada* (1670–71) and *Aureng-Zebe* (1675). His finest achievement in drama is *All for Love* (1677), a version of the Antony and Cleopatra story which, while it cannot bear comparison with Shakespeare, is a powerful and impressive play in its own right. It has tragic intensity within a strictly neo-classical framework. In comedy Dryden's best play is probably *Amphitryon* (1690), an updating of Zeus's scandalous conquest of Alkmene. In all Dryden wrote some thirty plays, including collaborative efforts. The most important of the latter were the adaptations of Shakespeare for which Dryden collaborated with WILLIAM DAVENANT. These were 'improvements' on Shakespeare not so much on the lines of neo-classical critical theories as in terms of what would work in the post-Restoration theatre of perspective scenery, lavish costume, dance and song and elaborate stage machinery. Among the most commercially successful was a *Tempest* in which Miranda has a brother who has never seen a woman and Caliban a sister. In spite of these monstrosities, Dryden had a real perception of the genius of Shakespeare, whom he referred to as 'the man who of all modern, and perhaps ancient poets, had the largest and most comprehensive soul'.

C. E. Ward, *Life of Dryden*, 1961.
B. King, *Dryden's Major Plays*, 1966.

Dullin, Charles (1885–1949). French actor and director, famous as Harpagon in MOLIÈRE's *L'Avare*. Dullin worked with COPEAU in the early years of the Vieux-Colombier, going on to establish his own Théâtre de l'Atelier in Paris, where JEAN VILAR was, for a while, his stage-manager. In the school-work associated with the theatre, Dullin taught improvisational disciplines in the style of Copeau. One of his pupils was JEAN-LOUIS BARRAULT. Dullin's physical deformity, a result of illness, limited his range as an actor. As a director, he combined a devotion to the classics with a willingness to experiment. He was, for instance, the man who brought PIRANDELLO to the French theatre.

Dumas, Alexandre, père (1803–70). The son of a mulatto general, Dumas was appointed secretary to the Duke of Orleans (later Louis-Philippe). He had an often naive appetite for the theatre and for French history. *Henri III and His Court* (1829) was the first play of the new 'romantic' drama in France. Dumas followed it with a number of other history plays and with dramatizations of his famous historical novels, becoming a popular writer on the BOULEVARD DU TEMPLE. Having made vast sums of money, he built and financed his own Théâtre Historique. The failure of this theatre in 1850 nearly ruined Dumas, who was profligate and gullible. It was in a dramatization of his novel *The Count of Monte Cristo* that the father of EUGENE O'NEILL made his American reputation, but Dumas's most remarkable play is *The Tower of Nesle* (1832) in which elements of GRAND GUIGNOL predominate.

F. H. Gribble, *Dumas, Father and Son*, 1930.
Edith Saunders, *The Prodigal Father*, 1951.

Dumas, Alexandre, fils (1824–95) The illegitimate son of DUMAS *père* rejected the bohemian life of his father whilst retaining a harassed affection for him. He cherished his status as a pillar of respectability, concealing the fact that he lived with Princess Naryschkine for many years before marrying her (secretly) in 1864. His dramatization of his own novel, *The Lady with the Camellias* (1852), became one of the most famous plays of the nineteenth century. Actresses as various as SARAH BERNHARDT and Greta Garbo have relished the central role of Marguérite Gautier. The play is not representative of the corrective morality of the later drama of Dumas *fils*. He was no rebel, and his developed attitude to the permissive world of his father is expressed in the distaste of *The Demi-Monde* (1855) and in a number of 'social problem' plays.

Dunlap, William (1766–1839). American dramatist, the first to whom the adjective 'professional' could be attached. Dunlap was born in New Jersey to Loyalist parents. Sent to London to study painting, he became fascinated by the theatre and wrote his first play in 1787, when he returned to New York. His comedy, *The Father*, produced at the John Street Theatre in 1789, established him as a writer and his tragedy, *Leicester* (1794), suggested that he was a versatile one. Dunlap was manager of the Park Theatre from 1798 to 1805, writing and producing there a long sequence of popular adaptations from KOTZEBUE, but epidemics of yellow fever and the high costs of maintaining a company bankrupted him in 1805. From 1806 to 1812 he was assistant-manager of the Park Theatre, ending his involvement in theatrical affairs as the organizer of a frantic tour of American theatres by the dying GEORGE FREDERICK COOKE, of whom he published a biography in 1813. Dunlap's plays, even the best of them, *André* (1798), are of small literary worth, though they show a sensitivity to contemporary stage conditions and taste. His most lasting contribution is the *History of the American Theatre* (1832).

Oral Coad, *William Dunlap*, 1917 (publication of the Dunlap Society, New York).

Dürrenmatt, Friedrich (1921–   ). Swiss playwright, novelist, and theoretician, whose *Theaterprobleme* ('Problems of the Theatre', 1954) is one of the most admired of recent essays on the state of the drama. Dürrenmatt is the son of a Protestant parson, and the grandson of a political diehard. Religion and a gloomy political vision both have a part in Dürrenmatt's comedy of the grotesque: 'I can only be understood . . . from the point of view of humour taken seriously,' he has written. His first play, *It Is Written* (1947), caused a scandal when it was staged in Zurich. In retrospect, that scandal can be seen as public resistance to a new, discomforting voice. In *Romulus the Great* (1949) and *The Marriage of Mr Mississippi* (1952), the extravagance that characterizes Dürrenmatt's best work embraces parody; but parody is too weak a word to describe the presentation of capitalist corruption in the brilliant *The Visit of the Old Lady* (1956), which is among the finest of all post-war plays in German. Subsequent plays have included *The Physicists* (1962), *The Meteor* (1966) and *Portrait of a Planet* (1970), as well as several adaptations from other dramatists, of which *Play Strindberg* (1969) has been particularly popular.

Kenneth S. Whitton, *The Theatre of Friedrich Dürrenmatt*, 1980.

Duse, Eleonora (1858–1924). In June 1895 the Italian Duse and the French SARAH BERNHARDT both played Magda in Sudermann's *Home* in London. The contest, so far as SHAW was concerned, was unequal: 'I doubt whether any of us realized, after Madame Bernhardt's very clever performance as Magda on Monday night, that there was room in the nature of things for its annihilation within forty-eight hours by so comparatively quiet a talent as Duse's.' He saw it as a classic confrontation of art and nature, and the natural Duse, who did not cover her facial lines with make-up, won hands down. CHEKHOV had seen her act in 1891 ('I have never seen anything like it before'), and the possibility that his style was affected by her performance has to be recognized. There are countless references to her enigmatic personality and to the expressiveness of her face and gestures. In the portrayal of tragic heroines, she called on her own pain. To Henri Lyonnet, she seemed 'toujours nerveuse, inquiète, malade, hystérique'. Her repertoire ranged from the romantic melodrama of SARDOU's *Tosca* to the new drama of IBSEN. She played Rebecca West in a 1906 production of *Rosmersholm*, with revolutionary stage designs by EDWARD GORDON CRAIG, as well as Hedda Gabler, Nora in *The Doll's House* and Ellida in *The Lady from the Sea*. More notorious at the time was her liaison with Gabriele D'Annunzio, a flamboyant amorist whose talent impressed his contemporaries more than it has impressed posterity. Her acting contributed to the overrating of his *La Citta Morta* (1898) and *La Gioconda* (1898). D'Annunzio's unscrupulous repayment was a sensational portrait of Duse in his novel *The Flame of Life* (1899).

Giovanni Pontiero (ed.), *Duse on Tour*, 1982.
William Weaver, *Duse*, 1984

Edgar, David (1948–   ). Edgar was a leading spokesman for the impressively conducted student revolution at Manchester University in 1968. He studied Drama there before becoming a journalist in Bradford, where he wrote his early plays, most of them exuberantly anti-establishment and custom-built for radical student actors and audiences. Having left journalism, though not forgetting the importance of selling a story, Edgar wrote for various touring groups on the political FRINGE, discovering a delicate skill in collaborative work with actors. *Dick Deterred* (1973) is among the liveliest plays of this period; it follows Richard Nixon's career from the 1968 election to his resignation ('A goat, a goat, my kingdom for a scapegoat!') at the same time as it follows the plot of *Richard III*. It was the production of *Destiny* by the ROYAL SHAKESPEARE COMPANY in 1976 that showed Edgar to be much more than a slick theatrical radical. The play is not only an exposure of British fascism but also an absorbing study of its origins and fertility in a class-based society. Humane socialism is the basis of two semi-documentary pieces, *Mary Barnes* (1977) and *The Jail Diary of Albie Sachs* (1978). That Edgar has retained an ability to work in collaboration with actors and directors was triumphantly proved by his adaptation of *Nicholas Nickleby* for and with the Royal Shakespeare Company (1981). *Maydays* (1983) asks questions of British socialism and finds it less robust now than in the early days to which Edgar gives panoramic consideration in his community play for Dorchester, *Entertaining Strangers* (1985).

Eliot, Thomas Stearns (1888–1965). American by birth, Eliot took British nationality in 1927. His place among poets is much securer than his place among dramatists. *Collected Poems 1909–1935* (1936) contains all his major poetry except *The Four Quartets*. It embodies his dominant influence during the inter-war years. For a brief period, it looked as if his verse plays might have a parallel authority in the development of a new drama. *Murder in the Cathedral*, produced in the Chapter House of Canterbury Cathedral in 1935, was a bold application of ancient forms to a timeless dilemma. It boosted the hopes for a renaissance of drama in verse. By contrast, *The Family Reunion* (1939) is programmatic, an uneasy displacement of AESCHYLUS. Whatever the incidental merits of the later plays, *The Cocktail Party* (1949), *The Confidential Clerk* (1953) and *The Elder Statesman* (1958), they exhibit too slight an interest in the telling of the tale. There is more life in the fragmentary *Sweeny Agonistes* (1932).

Carol H. Smith, *Eliot's Dramatic Theory and Practice*, 1963.

Elliston, Robert William (1774–1831). Elliston's father was a watchmaker and an alcoholic, but Elliston followed him only into alcoholism. He was a versatile actor, favouring tragedy but excellent in comedy, from his debut in 1791 until his death. He was also a theatre manager, commemorated by Charles Lamb as 'the Great Lessee'. Among the theatres he ran were the Surrey, the Olympic, the Theatres Royal of Manchester and Birmingham, theatres in Coventry, Croydon, King's Lynn, Leamington, Leicester, Northampton, Shrewsbury, Wells and Worcester, the Haymarket, and, from 1819 to 1827, Drury Lane. It was his task during the Drury Lane years to cope with the caprices of EDMUND KEAN. His favourite method was to join him in them.

Christopher Murray, *Robert William Elliston*, 1975.

Etherege, Sir George (*c.* 1635–1691). One of the 'mob of gentlemen who wrote with ease' at the Court of Charles II, Etherege came from an old Berkshire family and may have studied at Cambridge University. He read law at the Inns of Court and probably spent part of his youth abroad. He burst on the London theatrical scene with his first play, *The Comical Revenge, or Love in a Tub* (1664), which has a fair if not overwhelming claim to be regarded as the first Restoration comedy. Four years later came *She Would If She Could*, followed in 1676 by Etherege's last and most famous play and the only one to survive in the modern repertory, *The Man of Mode, or Sir Fopling Flutter*. Dorimant, the hero of this play, is the archetypal rake-gallant and is partly based on Etherege's friend John Wilmot, Earl of Rochester. From 1668 to 1670 Etherege was Secretary to the Ambassador at Istanbul and ten years later, having been knighted, he was able to marry a wealthy widow, whom he left in 1685 when he was himself appointed Ambassador in Ratisbon (Regensburg). His tenure of this office was distinguished by gambling, whoring and dancing attendance on a young actress from a travelling company, much to the disgust of the good burghers of Ratisbon. When James II was deposed in 1689, Etherege went to Paris to join him and died there two years later. In his own short life he amply displayed the aristocratic rake-hellism and cynical amorality which his finest comedy both celebrates and holds up to scrutiny.

Dale Underwood, *Etherege and the Seventeenth-Century Comedy of Manners*, 1957.

Euripides (484–406/7 BC). The youngest and the most controversial of the three Greek tragic poets. Little is known of his life, though his plays offer tempting clues towards a character study. Seventeen tragedies survive in full, together with the only extant satyr play, *Cyclops*. They display a quizzical intelligence at work on the great myths of Greece. Particularly in the plays whose subjects are shared with AESCHYLUS and SOPHOCLES, Euripides invites comparison by offering alternatives. *Electra* and *Orestes* contain uneasy studies of motive and manipulation. The emphasis is shifted from the community to the individual. The same shift is observable from Old to New Comedy, and it is possible to see Euripides' influence at work in the development of comedy as well as in the criticism of tragic conventions. The gods, in his plays, are wilful and self-assertive. This is supremely true of the magnificent *Bacchae*, one of the two extant plays posthumously staged at the Festival of Dionysus. Alone among extant Greek tragedy, this examines the authority of Dionysus himself, a dangerous god, who relishes and exploits turmoil. The importance of the tragic Chorus in the *Bacchae* is not typical of Euripides, whose work contributed to its eventual disappearance. His personality and style have been given an ambiguous immortality in the plays of ARISTOPHANES, whose parodies, particularly in the *Frogs*, are pointed, but not without affection.

T. B. L. Webster, *The Tragedies of Euripides*, 1967.

Evans, Edith (1888–1976). English actress, whose vocal vibrations could turn an incomprehensible archaism into a laugh-line. ('When I didn't understand it, I said it as if it was obscene,' she offered in explanation of her success in Restoration comedy.) She made her debut with WILLIAM POEL in 1912, and never forgot his concern for the voice above all else. As Millamant in *The Way of the World* at the Lyric,

Hammersmith in 1924, she gave what may well have been one of the supreme performances on the English stage. Later she played Mrs Sullen in *The Beaux' Stratagem* (the number of syllables she found in 'barbarity' delighted J. C. Trewin), Lady Fidget in *The Country Wife*, Laetitia in *The Old Bachelor*, and not Millamant but Lady Wishfort in the 1948 revival of *The Way of the World*. She has made it difficult for other actresses to play in Restoration comedy, but she was not confined to it. In 1926, she could be seen at the OLD VIC as Rosalind in *As You Like It* and as Juliet's Nurse. The latter was a role she repeated many times. As Lady Bracknell in *The Importance of Being Earnest* (1939 and subsequently), she invented a new way of saying 'hand-bag' and played cadenzas of patrician disgust. She was created DBE in 1946.

Bryan Forbes, *Ned's Girl*, 1977.

Farquhar, George (1678–1707). If he had lived longer Farquhar might have better confirmed his place as one of the most important dramatists of the post-Restoration period, for he had first-hand experience of the stage, a native wit and a genuine interest in character as expressed in situation. As it is he is the author of two distinguished comedies, *The Recruiting Officer* (1706) and *The Beaux' Stratagem* (1707), whose freshness and comparative realism set them apart and ensure their continuing vitality. Born in Dublin and educated at Trinity College, Farquhar began as an actor but left the stage after accidentally wounding a fellow-actor during a performance of DRYDEN's *The Indian Emperor*. His first play, *Love in a Bottle* (1698), was a success but it was with *The Constant Couple* (1699) that Farquhar achieved contemporary fame. The figure of Sir Harry Wildair became one of the most celebrated BREECHES PARTS (male roles played by actresses) of the age. Farquhar married a woman whom he mistakenly imagined to be an heiress and died in poverty at the age of twenty-nine. In addition to eight comedies he also wrote 'A Discourse upon Comedy in Reference to the English Stage'.

W. Connely, *Young George Farquhar*, 1949.
A. J. Farmer, *Farquhar*, 1966.

Fechter, Charles Albert (1824–79). Born in England of French parents, Fechter had separate and distinct careers in three countries. He made his name in Paris as a handsome, romantic hero, creating among other roles that of Armand Duval in DUMAS *fils*'s *The Lady with the Camellias* (1852). By 1860, when he moved to England, his reforming zeal was leading him towards staging innovations and a shift of acting style in tragedy towards something less majestic than the norm. His 1861 Hamlet, French accent notwithstanding, was triumphantly revolutionary. 'Fechter is lymphatic, delicate, handsome, and with his long flaxen curls, quivering sensitive nostrils, fine eye, and sympathetic voice, perfectly represents the graceful prince,' wrote GEORGE HENRY LEWES, who found the performance 'charming, because natural'. About Fechter's Othello, the same critic had contrary views: 'It had no one good quality. He attempted to make the character natural, and made it vulgar.' If not quite a fluke, the success of Fechter's Hamlet was not far short of it. He found in the play that vein of gentlemanly melodrama in which he excelled, and in which he specialized during his management of the Lyceum from 1863 to 1867. In 1869 he moved to America and established himself in a New York Theatre (the Globe) which he renamed Fechter's. He had a drink problem by now, and did nothing to improve his standing in the respectable new world by entering into a bigamous marriage in Philadelphia. He retired in 1876, and spent his last years ineffectively farming in Quakertown.

Feydeau, Georges (1862–1921). The last great exponent of French VAUDEVILLE died of syphilis in a lunatic asylum. The point is not just a cautionary one. Feydeau's plays are often brilliantly funny, but the characters who chase feverishly across the stage in flight from one woman and in pursuit of another end the play, as they began it, on the edge of nonentity. Feydeau was the product of a marriage between a minor writer and a lady of pleasure. His own theatrical career coincides with and criticizes *la belle époque*. The success of his first play, *Lady's Tailor* (1886), was premature. It was followed by a series of failures. Feydeau turned to the work of LABICHE for inspiration, and his subsequent FARCES can be read as an intelligent exploitation of two themes from Labiche, the chase (as, supremely, in *The Italian Straw Hat*) and the game of adultery (as in *The Happiest of the Three*). But Feydeau's is a different art from Labiche's. Courtship and marriage are more familiarly Labiche's themes. In Feydeau, the couples are already married and seeking for further amusement. 'To write a good vaudeville,' Feydeau explained, 'you take the most tragic situation possible and try to reveal its burlesque side.' It is a point of approach for his best work, *The Happy Hunter* (*Monsieur chasse*, 1892), *Champignol in Spite of Himself* (1892), *Hotel Paradiso* (1894), *A Flea in Her Ear* (1907) and *Look after Lulu* (*Occupe-toi d'Amélie*, 1908). Feydeau liked to direct his own plays, requiring of the actors that they performed without unnecessary exaggeration. The situation may be improbable, but the actors should not be. According to one of the leading performers of

Feydeau's chosen company, 'the essential thing is to remain true and approach life as closely as possible'.

Leonard C. Pronko, *Georges Feydeau*, 1975.

Field, Nathan (1587–1620). Field's father was a Puritan preacher vehemently opposed to the theatre. He died in 1588. Had he lived, the Jacobean theatre would have been deprived of one of its finest actors, for he would certainly have opposed his son's apprenticeship to the stage as a member of the CHILDREN'S COMPANY of the Chapel Royal. Field may have been taken into the company against his will, and there is some evidence that he was not satisfied with the career of an actor. Nevertheless, he made the most of it. From about 1600 to 1613 he remained a member of the Chapel Royal, graduating from female parts to, for example, Bussy d'Ambois in CHAPMAN's play. The prologue to the 1634 revival of that play regrets that 'Field is gone, whose action first did give it name'. BEN JONSON was prominent among Field's admirers during a distinguished stage career. After 1613, he was the leading actor of the Lady Elizabeth's Men and subsequently joined the King's Men shortly after that famous company had lost its leading playwright, SHAKESPEARE. A soulful portrait of him, now in Dulwich College, gives some support to the view that he excelled in the role of a young lover. In real life, contemporary scandal linked him with a child born to the wife of the Earl of Argyll. He was a good enough actor to be compared with ALLEYN and RICHARD BURBAGE. In addition, he wrote two competent comedies, *A Woman Is a Weathercock* (c. 1609) and *Amends for Ladies* (1611).

Fielding, Henry (1707–54). Though most people know Fielding only as the author of two fine comic novels, *Tom Jones* and *Joseph Andrews*, he began his career as a dramatist and turned to fiction only when political CENSORSHIP put an end to his activities as dramatist and theatre manager. His first plays were fairly mild literary and social satires, but *The Welsh Opera; or the Grey Mare the Better Horse* (1731) rather daringly brought the royal family on stage. For a time after this Fielding lay low, writing light comedies for the Drury Lane Theatre. But in *Don Quixote in England* (1734) he attacked Walpole's corrupt administration, following this with two more political satires, *Pasquin* (1736) and *The Historical Register for the Year 1736* (1737). These plays were staged at the Haymarket of which Fielding was now manager. Alarmed by their success, the Walpole government used the alleged scurrility of a play with which Fielding had nothing to do to pass the Licensing Act which restricted theatrical performances in London to Covent Garden and Drury Lane. The result was that the Haymarket was forced to go out of business, putting an end to Fielding's theatrical activity. Before this happened, however, he had produced some of the best burlesque theatrical writing in the language and one of his plays, *Rape upon Rape*, revised as *The Coffee-House Politician* (1730), has been successfully reincarnated as the musical *Lock Up Your Daughters*. In addition to being a man of letters, he was also a humane and conscientious magistrate. According to SHAW, Fielding was 'the greatest practising dramatist, with the single exception of Shakespeare, produced by England between the Middle Ages and the nineteenth century'.

John Loftis, *The Politics of Drama in Augustan England*, 1963.
Pat Rogers, *Henry Fielding: A Biography*, 1979.

Finney, Albert (1936–   ). British actor whose playing of Macbeth at the Birmingham Playhouse in 1958 was followed by a spell as LAURENCE OLIVIER's understudy as Coriolanus at STRATFORD in 1959. When Olivier fell ill, Finney stepped in to general admiration, but it was his playing of the eponymous hero of *Billy Liar* in London in 1960 that brought him to stardom. In 1961, he was in the title role of JOHN OSBORNE's *Luther*, and in 1965, as a member of the NATIONAL THEATRE company, he created the role of Armstrong in JOHN ARDEN's *Armstrong's Last Goodnight*. In all these parts, and also in his early films, *Saturday Night and Sunday Morning* (1960) and *Tom Jones* (1963), he seemed to represent the brawny stubbornness of proletarian revolt, but his delicate playing of FARCE in the National Theatre production of FEYDEAU's *A Flea in Her Ear* (1966) was evidence of an unexpected versatility. Finney's subsequent career displays his anxiety to put the money he has made to creative use. He has promoted plays in and out of London, directed and financed films, worked as an associate artistic director at the ROYAL COURT from 1972 to 1975, and formed and dissolved companies. There have not been many failures, though his Hamlet and Tamburlaine for the National Theatre in 1975 and 1976 were disappointingly small-scale performances, but neither has there been as much success as he might legitimately have hoped for. That he has maintained a titanic resolution is evident from his decision to direct and star in a revival of *Armstrong's Last Goodnight* at the OLD VIC in 1983.

Fiske, Minnie Maddern (1865–1932). American actress, daughter of a New Orleans theatrical agent. After early successes she retired from the stage in 1890 on marrying the editor of the *New York Dramatic Mirror*, Harrison Grey Fiske. In 1893 she made a comeback in a play by her husband, with whom she was determined to fight the monopoly of the best theatres by the Theatrical Syndicate of Managers. She was a sensational Tess of the D'Urbervilles in New York in 1897, and admired as Becky Sharp in an adaptation of *Vanity Fair*, but her championing of IBSEN on the New York stage and during her many tours is her outstanding achievement. She played Nora in *A Doll's House*, Hedda Gabler, and Rebecca West in *Rosmersholm*. Not everyone admired her acting, but no one could ignore her during the years from 1901 to 1907 when she acted and 'directed' in the Manhattan Theatre, and hers remained a powerful voice for twenty years after that. It was of that voice that Franklin Pierce Adams charmingly wrote:

> Somewords she runstogether,
> Some others are distinctly stated.
> Somecometoofast and
>   some too slow
> And some are $sy^{n}{}^{c}o_{p}a^{t}ed$
> And yet no voice – I am sincere –
> Exists that I prefer to hear.

Archie Binns, *Mrs Fiske and the American Theatre*, 1955.

Fitch, Clyde (1865–1909). American playwright who was a student journalist at Amherst College and then a full-time journalist in New York. His first play, *Beau Brummell* (1890), was written for, and partly by, RICHARD MANSFIELD. It was not long before Fitch became a phenomenon in his own right. He had seven plays produced in 1901, directing at least two of them himself, six in 1903 and four in 1905 and 1907. He was the first American to grow rich through writing plays and his exertions, more than anyone else's, established BROADWAY as a home for the native drama. There was, of course, a dangerous facility in his writing – one of his best plays, *The Truth* (1907), was said to have been written in a gondola on the Grand Canal – and a dangerous compulsiveness too. Fitch's strength lay in crafty plotting to expose the materialism and hypocrisy of high society in New York. *The Climbers* (1901) and *The Girl with Green Eyes* (1902) are among the best of his society melodramas. His last play, *The City* (1909), is a more sombre and angry attack on the moral standards of urban living. It was staged three months after Fitch had died of appendicitis in France.

Fitzmaurice, George (1877–1963). Irish playwright, born in County Kerry. His father was a Protestant clergyman and his mother a Catholic, and much of Fitzmaurice's sense of displacement was probably owed to this mixed marriage. His early writings, published in Irish newspapers, were stories about Kerry peasants. Fitzmaurice was working as a civil servant in Dublin when the ABBEY THEATRE opened, and his first play, *The Country Dressmaker*, was presented there in 1907. It is a comedy about Kerry peasants, like the vast majority of his work, already displaying the remarkable mixture of realism and fantasy that has earned for him an inevitable comparison with SYNGE. Two one-act tragicomedies, *The Pie-Dish* (1908) and *The Magic Glasses* (1913), were also produced at the Abbey, but what looked like a promising career as a house playwright was interrupted by World War I. Fitzmaurice's service with the British army cut him off from many former colleagues. Increasingly eccentric and reclusive, he actively discouraged performance of his plays, and only four others, including the tragedy *The Moonlighter* (c. 1914), were professionally produced in his lifetime. The posthumous publication, between 1967 and 1970, of his *Collected Plays* heralded a revival of interest in this extraordinary writer. Two of his greatest, *The Dandy Dolls* and *The Ointment Blue*, have now established themselves on the Dublin stage.

Howard K. Slaughter, *Fitzmaurice and His Enchanted Land*, 1972.

Flanagan, Hallie (1890–1969). Sometimes admired and sometimes unfairly blamed for her running of the immensely complex FEDERAL THEATRE PROJECT, Hallie Flanagan was a pioneering academic with an exemplary urge to raise the standards of American theatre. She owed her appointment as head of the Federal Theatre Project to her friendship with Harry Hopkins, who had been a fellow-student at Grinnell College, Iowa. Her Grinnell Experimental Theatre was a significant part of the American 'little theatre' movement. She toured European theatres in 1926 and 1927, being particularly impressed by some of the developments she saw in the Soviet Union. Her own verse plays, *Can You Hear Their Voices* (1931) and *We Demand* (1932), were produced at Vassar College, to which she was attached from 1925 to 1942. They show clearly her left-wing sympathies and her awareness of the Continental techniques which would later be displayed in the LIVING NEWSPAPER productions of the Federal Theatre Project. She was working with Michael Chekhov at Dartington Hall when Hopkins persuaded her to undertake the vast task of overseeing the Federal Theatre Project. Her struggles with the authorities and with some of her employees are recorded in her history of the Project, *Arena* (1940). After Congress had killed the whole magnificent experiment in 1939, Flanagan returned to Vassar. Something of the spirit of this remarkable lady can be perceived in her production at Smith College, of which she became Dean in 1942, of a LIVING NEWSPAPER on atomic power, $E = Mc^2$. She retired in 1946.

Fletcher, John (1579–1625). Though he is invariably linked with FRANCIS BEAUMONT, Fletcher wrote most of the numerous plays attributed to him either alone or in collaboration with other dramatists, including SHAKESPEARE and MASSINGER. He took over as leading dramatist for the King's Men when Shakespeare retired in about 1612, and three plays are generally believed to have been jointly written by Shakespeare and Fletcher – *The Two Noble Kinsmen*, *Cardenio* (now lost) and *Henry VIII*. Unlike Shakespeare but like Beaumont, Fletcher came from the ranks of the gentry. His father was vicar of Rye in Sussex when the dramatist was born, and later became bishop of Bristol, Worcester and London in turn. Fletcher studied at Cambridge University and spent most of his life in London writing for the stage. The dramatist's higher social standing reflected the growing elitism of theatre audiences in the seventeenth century. The poet Giles Fletcher the elder was his uncle, while the better-known poets Phineas Fletcher and the younger Giles were cousins. According to John Aubrey, Fletcher died of the plague in 1625.

Together with Shakespeare and JONSON, Fletcher was far and away the most popular English playwright of the time and his popularity continued after his death, until the end of the century. His comedy, *The Wild Goose Chase* (*c.* 1621), set the pattern for the later Restoration comedy of manners and was revised in 1702 by GEORGE FARQUHAR as *The Inconstant*. The five-year partnership with Beaumont produced three outstanding stage successes, *Philaster* (1610), *The Maid's Tragedy* (1611) and *A King and No King* (1611). All are marked by smoothly flowing and undemanding dialogue in both verse and prose, a penchant for intrigue plots which are set up as elegant problems for the sophisticated audiences to trifle with (much as the dramatists themselves do), and a cheerful readiness to sacrifice character, atmosphere, plausibility and anything else for the sake of the most theatrically effective dénouement within the individual scene or the play as a whole. The smart young law students and town gallants who made up most of the audiences at the indoor 'private' theatres where the plays were staged applauded them vigorously and clamoured for more, which Fletcher obligingly provided with a facility that never failed him. The two seventeenth-century Folio editions of the so-called 'Beaumont and Fletcher plays' contain fifty-two plays, in all of which Fletcher had a hand though Beaumont's collaboration was restricted to four or five plays. Fletcher has paid the price of too assiduously serving up what the limited public of his time wanted by suffering almost total neglect today. Yet, as a modern revival of *The Maid's Tragedy* proved, if theatrical effectiveness is the only criterion of excellence, Fletcher was an excellent playwright.

Clifford Leech, *The John Fletcher Plays*, 1962.

Fo, Dario (1926–   ). Italian dramatist, the thorn in the flesh of fascists and bureaucratic communists. He began as a scene designer and casual improviser of comic monologues for amateur groups in Milan, and in 1953 established Italy's first authentic, post-war cabaret. The political satire of such revues as *Il dito nell'occhio* and *Sani da legare* created a stir, and Fo had quickly an experience of the kind of censorship and danger that has continued. From 1959 to 1968, he and his wife (the actress Franca Rame) ran a theatre company within the terms of commercial theatre in Milan. Fo's own work was based on traditional comic forms, and was alert to the influences of popular culture. In 1968, having rejected the role of 'clown to the bourgeoisie', he committed himself to a more direct involvement in political agitation. *Accidental Death of an Anarchist* (1970) and its sequel, *Knock, Knock! Who's There? The Police* (1972) use the techniques of FARCE to expose police connivance in fascist atrocities. *We Can't Pay, We Won't Pay* (1974) celebrates the joyous anarchy of civil disobedience. Fo is one of the few political dramatists who has made laughter his stock-in-trade. It has not protected him from imprisonment (1973) and physical attack, nor saved his wife from abduction and assault. *Trumpets and Raspberries*, presented in London in 1984 to mixed reviews, requires the doubling of the roles of a communist and a leading capitalist. Its reception in England illustrates the difficulty of breaking convention by combining politics with farce.

Tony Mitchell, *Dario Fo*, 1984.

Fontanne, Lynn (1887–1983). English-born actress who made her London debut in 1905. Her partnership with her husband Alfred Lunt (1893–1977) was a famous one, especially in Lunt's home country, America, but also in England, where they often acted. Their involvement was vital to the Theatre Guild in the twenties. It was Lunt and Fontanne more than the play that made Molnar's *The Guardsman* a towering success in New York in 1924. Brooks Atkinson remembered the 'brio and counterpoint of two perfectly matched geniuses'. In 1925 they played together in *Arms and the Man* with the Theatre Guild and in 1926 in a version of *The Brothers Karamazov*. They were not inseparable – in late 1926, for example, Fontanne was a brilliant Eliza in *Pygmalion* and Lunt serious and dominant in SIDNEY HOWARD's *Ned McCobb's Daughter* – but they were at their best together. They left the Theatre Guild in 1929 to become their own promoters and scored a triumph in MAXWELL ANDERSON's *Elizabeth the Queen* (1930). They were mischievous in comedy, clever exploiters of overlapping dialogue and the sort of timing that turns a snigger into a laugh. Their gaiety invaded COWARD's *Design for Living* (1933), and *The Taming of the Shrew* (1935). But LAURENCE OLIVIER admits that he came to a new understanding of the seriousness of acting after meeting the Lunts in 1931. He was overwhelmed by their absorption in theatre. Whilst they were at ease in the comedies of S. N. Behrman, above all in his version of GIRAUDOUX's *Amphitryon 38* (1937), they performed ROBERT SHER-WOOD's *There Shall Be No Night* (1940) simply because they believed it had something important to say in New York and in London during the worst days of the war. Most remarkable of all was their capturing of the horrible humour of DÜRRENMATT's *The Visit*, which they opened in New York in 1958 and in London in 1960.

Foote, Samuel (1720–77). Foote was a Cornishman by birth, and could probably have been rich if he had been less extravagant. His contemporary fame owed as much to the power of his personality as it did to the variety of his theatrical undertakings. He went to Worcester College, Oxford, and then to the Temple, but completed no degree and gained no qualifications. In 1741 he married, in 1742 he was imprisoned for debt, and in 1744 he became an actor. His only remarkable talent was that of mimicry, and he exploited it in the plays he wrote as well as in the performances he gave. *The Englishman in Paris* (1753) was his first success, *The Minor* (1760) and *The Mayor of Garret* (1763) were highly esteemed, and *The Patron* (1764) and *The Commissary* (1765) are fair examples of his skill as a writer of dialogue. Even so, it was his resourcefulness in evading the licensing laws that made Foote particularly newsworthy. His 'lectures' and 'tea-parties', his 'auctions' and 'chocolate-shops', where the audience was charged for a commodity and given dramatic entertainments 'free' in buildings that had not been licensed for drama, were famous for their sometimes scurrilous portraits of prominent figures. Foote cited ARISTOPHANES as his forerunner, but will be lucky to last so long. In 1766, he lost a leg during some frolics involving the Duke of York's circle of friends, and, probably in royal compensation, was allowed a summer licence for the performance of plays in the Haymarket Theatre, of which he held the lease. He wrote plays with parts for his one-legged self, and continued to mock the famous and the fashionable, until the Duchess of Kingston took umbrage at his portrait of her in *A Trip to Calais* (1776). She had the play closed, and Foote scared out of the theatre with threats of a sodomy charge. A year later he was dead, just over a century too soon to play Long John Silver.

Simon Trefman, *Samuel Foote, Comedian*, 1971.

Forbes-Robertson, Johnston (1853–1937). In his theatrical reminiscences, *A Player under Three Reigns* (1925), this English actor confesses that, 'rarely, very rarely have I enjoyed myself in acting'. Those who saw his fastidious performances should not have been surprised. He was an intelligent (perhaps 'refined' is a more exact word) man, with a superbly melodious voice and a face that brought together aristocratic disdain and ascetic self-control. His Hamlet, which he first played at the Lyceum in 1897, was considered the greatest of its time. It survives on film, a little slow, but undeniably fine. 'We get,' wrote SHAW, 'light, freedom, naturalness, credibility, and Shakespeare.' Forbes-Robertson retired in 1913. He had had enough. His daughter Jean (1905–62) was a fine actress, whose eight consecutive years (1927–34) as Peter Pan should not be allowed to overshadow her Sonya in KOMISARJEVSKY'S 1925 *Uncle Vanya*, her Juliet (1926) and her Viola (1927). Johnston Forbes-Robertson was knighted in 1913. If people were surprised, it can only have been because they thought he was a knight already.

Ford, John (1586–1640). Like many dramatists of the time, Ford entered one of the Inns of Court after leaving Oxford University, but almost certainly never practised law. He was expelled from the Middle Temple for not paying his bills. Ford's dramatic career probably began with his collaboration with THOMAS DEKKER and WILLIAM ROWLEY on *The Witch of Edmonton* (*c.* 1621). This play is notable for its sympathetic portrayal of the central figure (based on real life) of an old woman accused of witchcraft and hounded by the community. Ford's share in the play was restricted to the sub-plot which deals with a young man's doom-laden progress towards murder.

Ford wrote eight plays apart from collaborative efforts. Most of these are concerned, in a somewhat intense and inward-looking way, with aristocratic dilemmas of love and honour which foreshadow the absurdities of later seventeenth-century heroic drama. But at least two of his plays, very different from each other, are among the finest things which Caroline drama has to offer. *Perkin Warbeck: A Strange Truth* (1622–32?) is a splendidly idiosyncratic example of the chronicle play in which the psychological complexities of role-playing are skilfully explored through the figure of the protagonist. *'Tis Pity She's a Whore* (1629–33?) is Ford's undoubted masterpiece and the finest tragedy in English since those of MIDDLETON. It handles the theme of incest, which many earlier dramatists had trifled with, with an unsparing honesty and compassion. Yet, though the dilemma of the lovers who are also brother and sister constitutes the core of the tragedy, Ford's real theme is not so much incest as the predicament of a young couple who find themselves torn between the imperative of an absolute commitment to each other and a society whose authority and traditions, secular and religious, are implacably opposed to them. The dramatic energy and truthfulness of Ford's presentation of this theme are still capable of moving audiences, as recent revivals and a brilliant Italian film version demonstrate. *'Tis Pity* is a precarious triumph, achieved in spite of, rather than because of, the generally narcissistic tastes of its elitist audience. Ford's other tragedies, among them *The Broken Heart* (1627–31?) and *Love's Sacrifice* (1632?) are more representative of that audience's interests and attitudes.

Clifford Leech, *Ford and the Drama of His Time*, 1957.

Forrest, Edwin (1806–72). The first American actor to challenge the supremacy of English actors in tragedy, Forrest was a fighter, in Alan Downer's description, 'the very apotheosis of the frontier "rip-tail-roarer"; with a body like an elephant'. The tendency to rant never deserted him, but his magnificent physique and the overwhelming urge to excel commanded respect, particularly in the beefy roles of Spartacus and Metamora, specially written for him. As Lear, Macbeth and Othello he had his admirers. A competitive quest underlay his season at Drury Lane in 1836–7, where there was an inherent challenge to the supremacy of MACREADY at Covent Garden. When Forrest paid a second visit in 1845, his reception was less enthusiastic. He blamed Macready and his cronies, and his retaliation, when Macready visited New York in 1849, was savage and discreditable. It culminated in the Astor Place riot, in which about twenty people died. Ostracized by many, Forrest retained a vociferously patriotic following. Some pathos attaches itself to the last, lonely years of this self-deluding giant.

Richard Moody, *Edwin Forrest*, 1960.

Friel, Brian (1929–   ). Irish playwright, whose first play, *This Doubtful Paradise* (1959), was staged in Belfast. The majority of his subsequent work has been first performed in Dublin. *Philadelphia Here I Come* (1964) brought him into prominence. It is an inventive and moving play on the familiar Irish theme of emigration. Friel's ability to find powerful stage metaphors for the Irish situation has been further exemplified in *Crystal and Fox* (1968), *The Freedom of the City* (1973), *Volunteers* (1975) and the brilliant *Translations* (1980). He is a writer of great talent and theatrical vision. The successive monologues of *Faith Healer* (1979), for example, constitute one of the most original of modern plays in English.

Frisch, Max (1911–   ). In his post-war Diary, this Swiss playwright and novelist recorded of his country, 'We heard the cries, but it was not ourselves that cried.' Frisch has done a lot of crying since then. *Now They Are Singing Again* (1945) was the first significant play written in German to make some attempt to come to terms with the war, and several subsequent plays, including *The Chinese Wall* (1946), *When the War Was Over* (1948), *The Fire Raisers* (1958) and *Andorra* (1961), are bitter reflections of the spiritual desecration of war. Frisch has no confidence in the ability of plays (or men, for that matter) to change the world. In this, he is consciously opposed to BRECHT, whom he admires, and from whom he borrowed his preference for theatrical parables. Frisch's establishment in 1943 of his own architectural firm gave him financial freedom to write without undue worry. The detached humanity of his plays and novels may owe something to that. He is certainly in no hurry to write, and neither *Biography* (1967) nor *Triptychon* (1980) has attracted as much attention as his earlier work.

U. Weisstein, *Frisch*, 1967.

Fry, Christopher (1907–   ). Fry's career reached a sudden peak with JOHN GIELGUD's 1948 production of *The Lady's Not for Burning*. The glittering language, with its delight in epigram and in the exploitation through metaphor of everyday experience, was an antidote to austerity in the drab, post-war world. Fry's was an individual voice in the brief revival of English verse drama. 'Poetry,' he wrote, 'is the language in which man explores his own amazement. It is the language in which he says heaven and earth in one word. It is the language in which he speaks of himself and his predicament as though for the first time.' The quotation goes some way to explaining why, alongside such comedies as *A Phoenix Too Frequent* (1946), and the seasonal quartet

The Lady's Not for Burning (Spring), 1948, *Venus Observed* (Autumn), 1950, *The Dark Is Light Enough* (Winter), 1954, and the delayed *A Yard of Sun* (Summer), 1970, Fry has written overtly religious plays like *Thor, with Angels* (1948) and *A Sleep of Prisoners* (1950). Fry's language can still surprise and excite, but playgoers have become critical of his preparedness to treat plots as pretexts for words.

Derek Stanford, *Fry*, 1954 (revised ed., 1962).

Fugard, Athol (1932–). South African playwright whose career in the theatre of his country has been a brave fight against reactionary repression. He was born in Cape Province to an English-speaking father and Afrikaner mother. His first theatre work was in Cape Town, where, in 1956, he founded an experimental theatre group, but his first play, *No-Good Friday* (1958), was set and performed in Johannesburg. Fugard himself played the role of the white missionary in a black community. In *The Blood Knot* (1961), he played the light-skinned brother who finds himself forced to play at being white, and he was also a leading actor in the first performances of *Hello and Goodbye* (1965) and *Boesman and Lena* (1969). These are good but fairly conventional plays. Fugard's more experimental work followed his engagement with the Serpent Players in Port Elizabeth and his reading of GROTOWSKI's *Towards a Poor Theatre*. With two magnificently contrasting black actors, John Kani and Winston Ntshona, he devised *Sizwe Bansi Is Dead* (1972) and *The Island* (1973). The verbal intricacies of these plays are a direct recording of the trapped African negro's flight into words. Fugard has continued to be responsive to the state of his nation. His continuing concern with the mythic parallels of racial tension is evident from the experimental *Orestes* (1971) to the confrontational *Master Harold and the Boys* (1982), and the more reflective *The Road to Mecca* (1985). Fugard's *Notebooks 1960–1977* (1984) are informative about the context of his theatre work in South Africa.

Dennis Walder, *Athol Fugard*, 1983.

Galsworthy, John (1867–1933). English novelist and playwright whose family background can be vividly adduced from the pages of *The Forsyte Saga*. His own desperately discreet liaison with his cousin's wife began in 1895, and did not subside into marriage until 1905, when Galsworthy's father was dead. His first play, *The Silver Box* (1906), was staged at the ROYAL COURT during the Vedrenne/BARKER seasons. It established Galsworthy as a craftsmanlike critic of social injustice, whose dialogue is well managed. *Strife* (1909) and *Justice* (1910) illustrate the same points better. There is, though, always a suspicion that Galsworthy is translating literary ideas into drama. Even so, the rehabilitation of his reputation, greatly advanced by the success of *The Forsyte Saga* when it was dramatized for television, is timely.

Catherine Dupré, *Galsworthy: A Biography*, 1976.

Garrick, David (1717–79). The major figure in the English theatre from 1747, when he began his joint management of Drury Lane, until 1776, when he retired, Garrick was a competent hack dramatist and an actor of genius. His was probably the smaller contribution to *The Clandestine Marriage* (1766), whose composition he shared with COLMAN the Elder, but his original work includes resourceful FARCES like *The Lying Valet* (1741), *The Irish Widow* (1772) and *Bon Ton* (1775), and the invention of the pageant and text of *The Jubilee* that accompanied the near-fiasco of his Shakespeare celebrations in STRATFORD in 1769. Garrick's background was middle class, and his education included a spell under Dr Johnson, whom he accompanied from Lichfield to London in the expectation of a new life. He worked in the wine trade, whilst engaging in the illicit pleasure of 'spouting' (i.e. amateur acting that veered towards recitation). His famous debut as Richard III in the unlicensed theatre in Goodman's Fields in 1741 was quickly the talk of the town. He was one of the shrewdest, most socially alert actors in the history of the theatre. He was also one of the most versatile. His Hamlet was famous, like his Richard III, but so was his comic Abel Drugger in *The Alchemist*. He raised the status of the theatre by almost everything he did. Not surprisingly in the Age of Scandal, he was much maligned, but he was also much loved. He was certainly volatile, and some thought him penny-pinching. Small and active (fidgety, according to George III), he had terrific power. 'His face,' said Charles Dibdin, 'was what he obliged you to fancy it.' It is the orthodox view that Garrick brought acting closer to nature. The same has been said of every major actor. Garrick was of his time in that he divided each role into a sequence of distinct passions, and linked them by striking transitions. The difference was that he did it supremely well.

K. A. Burnim, *David Garrick, Director*, 1961.
G. W. Stone Jr. and G. M. Kahrl, *David Garrick*, 1979.
Alan Kendall, *David Garrick*, 1985.

Genet, Jean (1910–86). Most of Genet's childhood, youth and early manhood was spent in prisons, reformatories and similar institutions and his plays display a strong sympathy for those who try to achieve personal fulfilment through a rebellion against bourgeois society and its mores. The characters in his plays are mostly derived from the underworld of contemporary society which Genet came to know at first hand – pimps, pandars and prostitutes, thieves and murderers and various kinds of sexual deviants. But through the evocative power of his language and the compelling artistry of his theatrical fables Genet is able to transmute personal obsession into shared insight and outrage. He uses to brilliant effect the contrast between the sordid and inchoate existence of his characters and the insistent impulse to ritual through which they attempt to give shape and definition to that existence. In *The Maids* (1947), first produced by JOUVET, the characters, by enacting their dream lives, expose the hollowness of the 'reality' in which they are trapped. In what is perhaps his most powerful play, *Le Balcon* (produced in London in 1957 as *The Balcony* three years before its French premiere), the brothel in which representative members of society's power groups act out their fantasies, calls into question the superior claims of the 'real' world. To Genet conventional 'evil' is a positive value if only because it is defined as the polar opposite of bourgeois notions of 'good'. Other notable plays include *Death Watch* (1947), *The Blacks* (1958) and the gargantuan *The Screens* (1966). Genet is also the author of some notable novels and an outstanding autobiography, *Journal du Voleur* (1948), which appeared in English as *The Thief's Journal* in 1964.

Jeanette L. Savona, *Jean Genet*, 1983.

George, Mlle (1787–1867). This was the stage name chosen by the French actress Marguerite-Josephine Weimer on the occasion of her debut as Clytemnestre in RACINE's *Iphigénie* at the COMÉDIE-FRANÇAISE. She was fifteen, the year was 1802, and there followed years of mingled scandal and triumph, which culminated in the 1817 demand from her fellow-actors that she resign from the Comédie-Française. Her subsequent acting career was uneven and finally disastrous. Her greatest social success was to be chosen as Napoleon's sleeping companion. As an actress, she relied on the fashion for Junoesque fleshiness more than she dared rely on talent. Her rivalry with Mlle Duchesnois was a sensation in its time; and though Duchesnois was the finer actress, she lacked Mlle George's off-stage appeal. It was rumoured that Talleyrand and Metternich succeeded Napoleon in her bed. It was her opulence that tempted men. Her acting in tragedy was archaic even in France by the time that she was forced by obesity into retirement. Jules Claretie remembered all his life the occasion in Limoges when the aging actress, having fallen to her knees in *Marie Tudor*, could not get up. While the audience howled with laughter, Mlle George wept. SARAH BERNHARDT was wont to claim that she once saw the old actress sitting on two chairs in the Tuileries.

Edith Saunders, *Napoleon and Mlle George*, 1958.

Ghelderode, Michel de (1898–1962). Belgian playwright, who wrote in French. His father was an archivist, and for a while Ghelderode was too, but after working with the Flemish Popular Theatre from 1927 to 1930 he withdrew into increasing solitude, peopling his plays with the distorted offspring of an often morbidly Gothic imagination. Ghelderode's mother claimed to have seen the Devil, and he was conscious of his own tendency to see things 'from beneath'. *Fastes d'enfer* (1929) caused a riot when it was produced in Paris in 1949. Ghelderode had, by then, been 'discovered' by BARRAULT, and there were post-war Parisian productions of the wonderfully demented short play *Escurial* (1927), *Mademoiselle Jaire* (1934) and *Hop! Signor* (1935). The bizarre and brilliant comedy of *Pantagleize* (1929), in which a Chaplinesque innocent is mistaken for a revolutionary leader, is some indication of the breadth of Ghelderode's artistry.

Gielgud, John (1904–   ). English actor and director who became a splendid 'front guy' for theatrical tradition without abandoning his interest in new developments. ELLEN TERRY was his great-aunt, and his upbringing was both genteel and theatrical. He made his first appearance at the OLD VIC in 1921, played Romeo in 1924, and took over NOEL COWARD's part in *The Vortex* in 1925. It was a promising beginning, but his miraculous decade began in 1929 when he returned to the Old Vic. It was there, in 1930, that he first played Hamlet – 'the prototype of all lost and lonely souls' was what Rosamond Gilder called him. As Richard II, and still more as Gordon Daviot's Richard of Bordeaux (1932), he was lyrical-romantic. Photographs show him relaxed, a little effete and already strong in the quality of repose. Even then, his voice was the special splendour. He directed *Romeo and Juliet* at the New Theatre in 1935, risking unfavourable comparisons with his athletic colleague by alternating Romeo and Mercutio with LAURENCE OLIVIER. Lacking Olivier's physical charisma, and perhaps a little jealous of it, Gielgud remained in uneasy rivalry with Olivier, whom he respected but considered too flashy. He was already openly ambitious, as he makes clear in the autobiographical *Early Stages* (1938), to lead the English theatre. The seasons at the Queen's (1937–8) and at the Haymarket

(1944–5) were essays towards a NATIONAL THEATRE. The Haymarket season followed his refusal of RALPH RICHARDSON's invitation to join him, Olivier and John Burrell in what would become a famous revival of the Old Vic's fortunes. 'It would be a disaster,' Gielgud remembers saying, 'you would have to spend all your time as referee between Larry and me.'

For a while after World War II, Gielgud's career continued to thrive. He was an eloquent Thomas Mendip in his own production of CHRISTOPHER FRY's *The Lady's Not for Burning* (1949), and a memorable STRATFORD season in 1950 saw him as Lear, Angelo, Cassius and Benedick. His playing of the latter was an important reminder of his comic skill. (He had played Benedick at the Old Vic in 1931, just after appearing as Jack Worthing in *The Importance of Being Earnest*.) The new mood of 1956 was inhospitable to Gielgud's style and it looked as if his career might sink. His Othello at Stratford in 1961 was a mistake; Gielgud's strength is his intelligence, and he is weak in predominantly physical parts. But he adapted to the theatre of the sixties and seventies superbly. His Prospero at the National Theatre in 1974 was authoritative and affecting. He was knighted in 1953, ungenerously late.

Ronald Hayman, *John Gielgud*, 1971.

Gilbert, William Schwenck (1836–1911). English playwright and librettist, who will inevitably remain paired in the public mind with Sullivan. Gilbert discovered his gifts as a player with words and follower of logic *ad absurdum* when he contributed hundreds of Bab Ballads to the comic paper *Fun* after 1861. His legal career was less successful. Gilbert's wit is remorselessly reductive, and it is only with difficulty that he can resist the urge to burlesque the work of other writers (or sometimes even his own). The advantage, of course, is that he has not much need to be original; the disadvantage is that prolonged acquaintance leads to utter predictability. It is pleasing to see Victorian double standards exposed, though Gilbert cheats a bit by moving his targets very close. It is less pleasing to find the same dislikes and even the same techniques repeated in genres as various as FARCE, MELODRAMA, and comic opera. Jane Stedman's collection of comic plays under the title *Gilbert before Sullivan* (1967) gives an indication of his early range, though the splendid fantasy *Pygmalion and Galatea* (1871) is missing. 1871 was also the year of *Thespis*, the first collaboration with Sullivan. *Trial by Jury* (1875), *H.M.S. Pinafore* (1878), *The Pirates of Penzance* (1879), *Patience* (1881), *Iolanthe* (1882), *Princess Ida* (1884), *The Mikado* (1885), *Ruddigore* (1887), *The Yeoman of the Guard* (1888), *The*

Gondoliers (1889), *Utopia (Limited)* (1893) and *The Grand Duke* (1896)
complete the Savoy Operas that were so long enshrined in the repertoire
of the perpetual-seeming D'Oyly Carte Company. They are as brilliant
as they are unnecessary, both speaking volumes for Victorian England
and studiously missing its point. That Gilbert might have done better is
evident from his comedy *Engaged* (1877), and fitfully in a number of
other plays. His concern for precision in staging suggests that he cared
more than he was prepared to admit. He was knighted in 1907.

Max Sutton, *Gilbert*, 1975.
William Cox-Ife, *Gilbert: Stage Director*, 1978.

Gillette, William Hooker (1855–1937). American actor and dramatist whose father had been a United States Senator and an abolitionist.
Gillette's ambition to become an actor was assisted by Mark Twain, a
family friend (the Gillettes were well known in Connecticut), who got
him a small part in *Colonel Sellers*, a dramatization of Twain's *The
Gilded Age*. His first plays, *The Professor* (1879) and *Esmeralda* (1881),
were moderately successful, but it was the Civil War drama *Held by the
Enemy* (1886), a stirring and highly improbable yarn about love, loyalty
and espionage, that made his name as both actor and playwright. *All the
Comforts of Home* (1890) is a resourceful farce, in which Gillette reveals
his sense of visual surprise. In *Secret Service* (1895), a much better Civil
War play, he rivals BELASCO in his flair for the stunning effect. Gillette
toured indefatigably in his own plays, bringing *Secret Service*, for
example, to London in 1897. It was during the run of this play at the
Adelphi that WILLIAM TERRISS was murdered at the stage door by a
disgruntled and demented actor – a murder that Gillette would have
staged much more effectively. The other greatly successful piece for
Gillette, as both actor and dramatist, was his compilation of three
stories from Conan Doyle, *Sherlock Holmes* (1899). Because he looked
like Doyle's character, and because he played him with such panache,
Gillette became identified with him. He played the role over 1,300 times
between 1899 and his retirement in 1935. By that time, Gillette was
living in the extraordinary house he had built in Hadlyme, Connecticut,
today known as Gillette Castle. The miniature railway he constructed
there now runs along the shores of Lake Compounce in an amusement
park in Southington, Connecticut.

Doris E. Cook, *Sherlock Holmes and Much More*, 1970.

Gilpin, Charles (1878–1930). Black American actor, who worked for
many years in minstrel shows and VAUDEVILLE. In 1916 Gilpin

undertook the management of the first all-black theatre company to be assembled in New York – at the Lafayette Theatre in Harlem. He played two roles on the 'white' stage, the first as a Negro clergyman in John Drinkwater's *Abraham Lincoln* (1919) and the second for the PROVINCETOWN PLAYERS in the title role of O'NEILL's *The Emperor Jones* (1921). 'They have acquired an actor,' wrote ALEXANDER WOOLCOTT, 'who has it in him to invoke the pity and the terror and the indescribable foreboding which are part of the secret of *The Emperor Jones*.' Gilpin retired in 1926, but continued to appear in occasional revivals of the play that had made him suddenly famous.

Giraudoux, Jean (1882–1944). French playwright, known to English audiences principally for his immensely enjoyable and witty reworking of the Amphitryon story, *Amphitryon 38* (1929), *The Trojan War Will Not Take Place* (1935, also known as *Tiger at the Gates*), *The Madwoman of Chaillot* (first performed in 1945) and *For Lucretia* (also known as *Duel of Angels* and first performed in 1953). Giraudoux was born in Bellac, entered the diplomatic service in 1910 and remained in it until the fall of France in 1940. He was a strong believer in the primacy of the word in the theatre and his plays are composed of lively debates, brilliantly inventive and studded with surprisingly surreal images. Their success in the theatre owed much to the scenic skill of LOUIS JOUVET, though it was JEAN VILAR's open-air production of *The Trojan War Will Not Take Place* at Avignon in 1962 that rescued Giraudoux from a temporary eclipse. He is admired by all those who wish to sustain the literary traditions of the French theatre.

Donald Inskip, *Jean Giraudoux: The Making of a Dramatist*, 1958.

Glaspell, Susan (1882–1948). The significant early dramatic work of this American playwright was done with the PROVINCETOWN PLAYERS. Glaspell was born and educated in Iowa. In 1907 she met George Cram Cook, an idealistic socialist, and her involvement in radical politics and social criticism owed much to his. Together they moved to Provincetown in Massachusetts, marrying in 1913 when Cook's divorce was finalized. It was with their collaborative play, *Suppressed Desires*, that the Provincetown Players announced themselves in 1915, and Cook and Glaspell played leading roles in the performance. Their involvement with the Provincetown Players continued until 1922. During that time, ten of Glaspell's plays were performed, ranging from the deft short piece *Trifles* (1916) to the formally ambitious *The Verge* (1921) in which the disintegration of a woman's mind is reflected in the changing style of the writing. Glaspell went with her husband to Greece in 1922 (his quixotic aim was nothing less than to re-establish the classic Greek theatre) and wrote only two plays after his death there in 1923. The first of these, *The Comic Artist* (1928), was written in collaboration with her second husband, Norman Matson. It asserts with characteristic fervour the survival of the conquering spirit of a dead man, a cartoonist, amid the deadening materialism of his widow's way of life. *Alison's House* (1930) is a vividly imagined reconstruction of events in the life (and death) of Emily Dickinson. Once again Glaspell proclaims a life-force that is greater than death. It was a confidence not easily sustained in the America of the Depression. Glaspell's second marriage ended in divorce in 1931, and though she wrote four moderate novels after that she never completed another play. The heady hopes of Provincetown are touchingly recorded in her biography of George Cram Cook, *The Road to the Temple* (1927).

Arthur E. Waterman, *Glaspell*, 1966.

Goethe, Johann Wolfgang von (1749–1832). Unquestionably the greatest name in German literature, Goethe wrote his first notable play under the influence of SHAKESPEARE. *Götz von Berlichingen* (1771; 2nd version, 1773) celebrates in heightened but very speakable prose the exploits of a sixteenth-century robber knight, whose energy and loyalty contrast with the effeteness of the politicians who oppose him. The sweep of the play and its admiration for heroic rebellion gave impetus to the movement that came to be known as STURM UND DRANG. *Clavigo* (1774) and *Stella* (1775), better constructed, are broadly similar in intention and technique. The epistolary novel of 1774, *The Sorrows of Young Werther*, had rushed Goethe into prominence. Having trained as a law student in Leipzig, whilst maintaining an interest in medicine and in alchemy, he now found himself courted by the culturally prominent. He responded by accepting the invitation of the young ruling Duke of Weimar to visit the small Duchy, and, quite against his plans, he remained in Weimar for most of the rest of his life. The hyperactivity of his youth steadied, but the intellectual diversity remained. By 1779 he was a Privy Councillor in Weimar, and in 1782 he became Finance Minister. There were other jobs, but the theatrically significant one was his responsibility for the direction of the professional actors in the Court Theatre from 1791 to 1817. His *Rules for Actors* (1803) was a product of this responsibility, and it was in Weimar that most of his later plays were first performed.

The first (prose) version of *Iphigenia in Tauris* (1779) marks the shift from the extravagant romanticism of *Sturm und Drang* towards the classicism, reinforced by a romantic idealism, which is the characteristic Weimar style. His visit to Italy in 1786 was a turning-point. *Egmont* (1788) had been begun in Frankfurt in 1775, and there are signs of this early provenance. The Italian experience is more vividly represented by the change to verse in the 1787 version of *Iphigenia* and in the complex *Torquato Tasso* (1789), where the pride and passion of the poet-hero reflect Goethe's self-image. His own love-affairs have been traced in almost prurient detail by scholarly biographers. Without them, certainly, the Gretchen romance of *Faust Part I* would have been different. *Faust* had occupied Goethe intermittently since 1774. Part I was finally published in 1808, and Part II completed in 1831, to be published posthumously the following year. It is a dramatic poem that can be effectively performed in the theatre only by a company prepared to match Goethe's vision. The shifts of style, from doggerel to lyrical eloquence, from knockabout FARCE to a tragic sense of loss, are extreme; and, if Part I is surprising enough, Part II is utterly astonishing.

Ronald Peacock, *Goethe's Major Plays*, 1959.
R. Friedenthal, *Goethe: His Life and Times*, 1965.

Gogol, Nikolai Vasilievich (1809–52). For students of abnormal psychology and religious mania, Gogol presents a case study. For students of drama, he is the author of a few short plays, which, like the longer farce *Marriage*, are a part of the Russian 'vaudeville' tradition on which CHEKHOV relied for his early one-act pieces, and of *The Government Inspector* (1836). In a letter of 1889, Chekhov called him 'the greatest Russian writer', and the claim is not negligible. Gogol's mind was crammed with fervent speculations on the meaning of life and the cut of a waistcoat. Mixed images of the cosmic and the trivial invade his art as they invade nightmares. When *The Government Inspector* was produced in the presence of Tsar Nicholas I, it was greeted as a realistic satire on provincial corruption. (Gogol was a Ukrainian, and could be supposed to know about such things.) It is that, and much more. The disgust and fear for the verminous human race take satire to the edge of damnation. The astonishing inventiveness that sustains for five acts a single case of mistaken identity is evidence of a superb comic gift, but the characters are as morally monstrous as any in *Tartuffe*, and there are no virtuous antagonists. Gogol, who could never be sure what he was writing about, was so distressed by the reactions to the play that he left Russia. He undertook, in his last phrenetic years, to write a work of prophecy that would stir the Russian people he had left. It was to be a

'Divine Comedy', and Gogol settled in Rome to write it. All that he completed was the first part, a scouringly funny novel called *Dead Souls* (1842). Obsessed by his personal quest for moral perfection, and unable to satisfy it, he prefigured TOLSTOY by renouncing art in favour of religion.

D. Magarshack, *Gogol: A Life*, 1957.
V. Nabokov, *Gogol*, 1959.

Goldoni, Carlo (1707–93). Italy's greatest playwright, whose serenity allowed him to ride several dangerous storms. Born in Venice, and trained as a lawyer (he qualified in 1732 and practised with some enterprise), he was stagestruck. The COMMEDIA DELL'ARTE troupes that had flourished in Italy for over a century were faltering. The inventive scenario was giving way to the protracted dirty joke. Initially by providing the popular masks – Pantalone, Brighella, Arlecchino, etc. – with a recognizable domestic setting and a completer text, Goldoni revitalized Venetian comedy. *The Venetian Twins* (1747) and *The Servant of Two Masters* (1749) are poised between the *commedia dell'arte* and the comedy of character that Goldoni was ready to write. He had great facility, could write a play in ten days, and in the 1750–51 season took on the challenge of writing sixteen plays for performance, and did it. He knew his actors (and his actresses even better), and was prepared to exhibit their foibles to the audience in the virtually plotless *The Comic Theatre* (1750). This play has a characteristic trick of charming its audience into its world. *The Mistress of the Inn* (*La Locandiera*, 1753) and *Campiello* (1756) record and rejoice in the spirit of Venetian carnival. In 1762, Goldoni signalled his farewell to Venice with a play entitled, a little sadly, *One of the Last Evenings of Carnival*. By then, he had been jostled into public disfavour by GOZZI and the defenders of the past. Always optimistic, Goldoni set out for Paris to write plays for the Comédie-Italienne. It was in Paris that he wrote *The Fan* (1763), one of his best-known plays; but the Comédie-Italienne was on its last legs. Goldoni left it in 1764, and scraped a living by royal patronage and his wits. In 1771 the COMÉDIE-FRANÇAISE staged his play, written in French, *Le Bourru bienfaisant*. It was also in French that he chose to write the three volumes of his *Memoirs*, less accurate than lively.

Timothy Holmes, *A Servant of Many Masters*, 1976.

Goldsmith, Oliver (1728–74). Born in Ireland and trained as a doctor (the chances are that he never qualified, whatever he may sometimes have claimed), Goldsmith made a precarious living out of writing after settling in London in 1756. Of his two familiar plays, *The Good-Natured Man* (1768) is a competent comedy with a nice touch of benevolent deception, and *She Stoops to Conquer* (1773) one of the few undoubted masterpieces of an unhappy period in the history of English drama. It is particularly in the figure of Tony Lumpkin, coarse despite his breeding, that Goldsmith reveals his independence of the class-ridden stereotypes who composed both the dramatis personae and the audience of most of the plays of the period.

John Ginger, *The Notable Man*, 1977.

Gorky, Maxim (1868–1936). Russian dramatist, born Alexey Peshkov, whose chosen pen-name means 'bitter'. From 1878 to 1884, Gorky was a nomad, and the figure of the dangerous, 'free' tramp who features in many of his early stories was born in these early days of his self-education. From 1897 onwards, he was under surveillance by the Tsarist secret police. His association with members of the MOSCOW ART THEATRE led to the writing of *The Philistines* (1901). It was refused a licence, presumably because the authorities could not stomach the bourgeois-bashing of the articulate proletarian Nils, but performed to subscribers after cuts had been made. *The Lower Depths* (1902) was received as a NATURALISTIC masterpiece. To an extent, it is, but Gorky had always a sense of the writer as a public figure, and *The Lower Depths* is also a symbolic social statement. *Summer Folk* (1904) deploys and exposes the 'superfluous' intelligentsia of the Tsarist twilight in over-conscious homage to CHEKHOV, and *Children of the Sun* (1905) struggles to reconcile eccentric comedy and social prophecy. This play was written during a period of imprisonment following the events of Bloody Sunday, in which Gorky was involved. After a disastrous fund-raising visit to America in 1906 (his virtuous host-country was shocked to discover that Mrs Gorky was not his wife), he settled in Capri, associating at various times with Lenin and Trotsky, but never joining the Party. *Enemies* (1906), on the specifically banned topic of industrial strife, could not be officially staged in Russia. It is one of Gorky's finest plays, a vivid representation of stasis. 'Always I can see this face,' says the disenchanted brother of the factory owner, 'this broad, unwashed face, staring at me with enormous eyes which ask . . . "well?" ' It was the question Gorky asked too, and he was so disillusioned with the answers provided under the post-revolutionary dispensation that Lenin persuaded him to leave Russia in 1921. Stalin, who persuaded him back in 1932, may well have had him killed in 1936 when his usefulness had ended.

Dan Levin, *Stormy Petrel*, 1965.

Gozzi, Carlo (1720–1806). Italian aristocrat, inspired to write plays by his contempt for GOLDONI. Gozzi claimed a preference for the improvised performances of the faltering COMMEDIA DELL'ARTE, but his own drama is extravagant. In defiance of Goldoni's realism, Gozzi turned to fable and fairy tale. *The Love of the Three Oranges* (1761) creates what Timothy Holmes has called 'an unreal, flashing, almost psychedelic world'. *The King Stag* (1762), *Turandot* and *The Beautiful Green Bird* (both 1764) have all been successfully revived in the modern theatre. Gozzi's bitter temperament is in constant tension with his fantastic fictions. His work invites extended dance-drama treatment.

Granville Barker, Harley. See BARKER, HARLEY GRANVILLE.

Green, Paul (1894–1981). This prolific American dramatist has been associated for much of his life with the southern state of North Carolina, where he was born and raised. But a career that has included baseball pitching, war service, cotton picking, screen writing, and teaching can hardly be called parochial. Green's early work was staged by the Carolina Playmakers. *White Dresses* (1923) is a compassionate and exquisite one-act play, less angry about the decadence of the South than *In Abraham's Bosom* (1926). It was an extended version of this latter play that began a new phase in Green's career, when the PROVINCETOWN PLAYERS staged it in New York in December 1926. *The Field God* (1927) failed on BROADWAY, but it was Green's impressively predatory *The House of Connelly* (1931) that began the lively decade of the GROUP THEATRE. This play is realistic enough to satisfy traditional tastes, but the two negro field women who bring it to its startling conclusion are vengeful furies from tragic ritual. *Tread the Green Grass* (1932) is one of several plays that develop further the style Green called 'symphonic drama'. *Hymn to the Rising Sun* (1936) is a savage 'penitentiary' play, whose open portrait of sadism is intentionally shocking. Nor does Green pull his punches in *Johnny Johnson* (1936), another Group Theatre piece for which Kurt Weill wrote strong music. Not easy to stage, and contentiously isolationist, this contains some of the most vivid anti-war writing of the thirties. With the open-air production of *The Last Colony* (1937), Green initiated a series of outdoor pageant plays on American history which lasted nearly four decades, and suited story to setting from Florida to Alaska; the last was *Louisiana Cavalier* (1976). Small wonder that Green is hard to categorize.

Vincent S. Kenny, *Paul Green*, 1971.

Greene, Robert (*c.* 1560–1592). Dramatist and pamphleteer, whose dissolute life would be less notorious were it not for his own obsession with it. *A Groatsworth of Wit Bought with a Million of Repentance* (1592) is a prose recantation, memorable in itself, but more often remembered for its allusion to SHAKESPEARE as 'An upstart crow beautified with our feathers . . .' Greene, we might suppose, was an intellectual snob, proud of his education (he was a student at both Oxford and Cambridge), and possessive of the benefits, but he seems also to have been a well intentioned, however wayward, man. Of the plays which can be fairly confidently ascribed to him, *James IV* is a chronicle history which bears comparison with early Shakespeare (Greene may well have contributed to the *Henry VI* plays), and *Friar Bacon and Friar Bungay* (*c.* 1589) is a charming and original comedy, good enough to suggest that Greene, had he lived, might have advanced the cause of English comedy along Shakespearean lines.

J. C. Jordan, *Robert Greene*, 1915.

Gregory, Lady (Isabella Augusta Perse) (1852–1932). By the time she met YEATS in 1896, this stately Irishwoman had been four years a widow. 'Not Yeats, nor Martyn, nor Miss Horniman,' wrote SEAN O'CASEY, 'gave the Abbey Theatre its enduring life, but this woman only, with the rugged cheeks, high upper lip, twinkling eyes, pricked with a dot of steel in their centres.' She was, in sober truth, co-founder with Yeats and Edward Martyn of the Irish Literary Theatre, which was almost at once associated with the ABBEY THEATRE, and she remained a director of that theatre until her death. *Our Irish Theatre* (1913) is an account of the first years of the Abbey. She was the author also of translations from the Irish, biographies and forty plays, many of them one-act comedies which combine folk traditions with Irish social and political history. Her dialogue exploits the comic potential of English spoken with Gaelic syntax. *Spreading the News* (1904) and *The Workhouse Ward* (1908) are outstanding examples. Hers is a patriotism that has to be reckoned with in such plays as *The White Cockade* (1905), *The Rising of the Moon* (1906), and the short peasant tragedy *The Gaol Gate* (1906). O'Casey was not the only one to recognize a great spirit in this grand lady.

Elizabeth Coxhead, *Lady Gregory: A Literary Portrait*, 1961.
Mary Lou Kohfeldt, *Lady Gregory: The Woman behind the Irish Renaissance*, 1985.

Grieve. A remarkable family of scene-painters. John Henderson

Grieve (1770–1845) was chief scene-painter at Covent Garden during the management of JOHN PHILIP KEMBLE. Together with his sons, Thomas (1799–1882) and William (1800–44), he inaugurated the vogue for picturesque Shakespeare productions, adding to the visual splendour sufficient touches of antiquarian accuracy to gratify the scholarly members of the audience. William was the only member of the family with aspirations to be more than a theatrical painter. He was briefly considered a rival to CLARKSON STANFIELD. Thomas survived to contribute to the lavish antiquarianism of CHARLES KEAN at the Princess's between 1853 and 1858. The surviving painting for the heath in Kean's 1858 *King Lear* is savage and desolate. The Grieves were not great innovators, though they were alert enough to the new demands of gas-lighting to develop a scenic glaze similar to that used in easel watercolours, and they accepted with enthusiasm the fascination of audiences with the moving PANORAMA.

Griffiths, Trevor (1935–   ). English playwright, born in Manchester, where his first play, *The Wages of Thin* (1969), was staged. Griffiths emerged from, and writes feelingly about, the urban proletariat. He is a Marxist, and it is his sense of the urgency of social change that has led him to write more for television than for theatre. Nevertheless, his contribution to the theatre has been notable. *Occupations* (1970) characteristically opposes the vigour of a left-wing idealist (the Italian Marxist, Gramsci) to the caution of a left-wing pragmatist. It was presented first at the short-lived Stables Theatre Club in Manchester, then by the ROYAL SHAKESPEARE COMPANY in London (1971), and then on tour by JOHN MCGRATH and the 7:84 THEATRE COMPANY (1973). Griffiths was one of the six writers who collaborated on the text of *Lay By* (1971), a disturbing exploration of violence and the law. *The Party* (1973), a savage debate play that was staged by the NATIONAL THEATRE, was moderately successful. Griffiths had left his job as Further Education Officer with the BBC in Leeds in 1972 to commit himself to writing. Increasingly, that involved him in writing for television, but he remained passionately concerned with education. His finest play, *Comedians* (1975), began with the image of a teacher and some people being taught, he told an interviewer. Ostensibly about a group of apprentice comedians, first learning and then testing their craft, it is a vividly angry attack on the priorities of capitalism. The anger remains in *Real Dreams* (1986), and so, to judge from critical responses, do the priorities.

Grotowski, Jerzy (1933–   ). Polish teacher, director, and theatrical experimenter. Grotowski trained at the Cracow Theatre School, and began his own investigations into the art of the actor in Opole in 1959. By the time he moved to Wroclaw in 1965, his Theatre Laboratory was fully established, and the Polish government subsidized it as an 'Institute for research into acting'. PETER BROOK sought assistance from him in his work on *US* (1965–6), and that was England's first experience of this secretive, obsessive prophet of a theatre of ultimate enactment. The training programme and some of Grotowski's *obiter dicta* are recorded in *Towards a Poor Theatre* (1969), together with photographs of some of the Theatre Laboratory's early productions, but we are allowed little more than glimpses into a guru's gnosis. His impact on European theatre at that time was amusingly satirized by ROGER PLANCHON in *The Tearing to Pieces of Le Cid*. Envisaging an appropriate death for this self-lacerating prophet of a total theatre, he proposed that, 'Mr Grotowski crucified himself, yes he did, Sir, swearing all the while that he was an atheist.' Grotowski has moved on since then, and very little of his newer activity has been reported in the West. Even so, he has powerfully influenced the teaching and performance of drama in Europe and the Americas.

Jennifer Kumiega, *The Theatre of Grotowski*, 1985.

Guinness, Alec (1914–   ). English actor who made his stage debut in 1934. He understudied OLIVIER's Hamlet at the OLD VIC in 1937 and was, as he later recalled, 'outraged at the gymnastic leaps and falls'. The comment says much about the fastidiousness and reticence of Guinness, whose habit of self-effacement is more commonly associated with character actors than with stars. TYRONE GUTHRIE, having directed the 1937 *Hamlet*, gave Guinness the part in his 1938 modern dress production at the Old Vic. The contrast with Olivier was extreme in Guinness's unemphatically sincere playing. Back with the Old Vic company after the war (1946–8), he played the Fool to Olivier's King Lear, a neurotically fascinating Dauphin in SHAW's *Saint Joan*, Abel Drugger in JONSON's *The Alchemist*, Khlestakov in GOGOL's *The Government Inspector*, and Richard II. These are all parts that invite the actor to share his histrionic temperament with the character he impersonates, and Guinness is a master of the style. His adaptations of *The Brothers Karamazov* and *Great Expectations* (1946) grew from his recognition of the self-dramatizing temperaments of Dostoyevsky and Dickens, and his idiosyncratic production of *Hamlet* (1951), in which he played the lead on the assumption that SHAKESPEARE had written himself as Hamlet, was in the same line. As Richard III at STRATFORD, Ontario (1953) and as T. E. Lawrence in TERENCE RATTIGAN's *Ross* (1960) he was again able to relish the quicksilver shifts of mood and emphasis that he captures so effortlessly. 'Alec Guinness, as Shaw once observed of Irving, has no face,' said KENNETH TYNAN. In calling his autobiography *Blessings in Disguise* (1985), Guinness alludes to his rare gift, shared with other protean actors from JACK BANNISTER and CHARLES MATHEWS to Peter Sellers, of donating his face to the character he plays. His knighthood in 1959 rewarded an achievement in cinema as well as theatre. Television audiences know him as John le Carré's George Smiley.

John Russell Taylor, *Alec Guinness*, 1984.

Guthrie, Tyrone (1900–71). 'A very Irish sort of Anglo-Scot', Guthrie was a great starter of things, magnificent at bringing people and ideas together. From 1926 to 1928 he was artistic producer of the Scottish National Players, committed to the touring of native plays. From 1929 to 1930 he was in charge of the CAMBRIDGE FESTIVAL THEATRE, where his production of *Iphigenia in Tauris* was the first of many notable achievements in Greek tragedy – a *leitmotif* in his career. From 1933 to 1939 he was largely involved with the OLD VIC. In the second Edinburgh Festival in 1948, he directed with startling effectiveness in the Assembly Hall the mediaeval Scottish play, *Ane Satire of the Three Estaits*. This was Guthrie at his best, finding the promised land where the maps had marked a desert, filling rehearsals with laughter, and every moment with business. The gifts of leadership and the accompanying flair (not reliable, but not infrequent either) had been spotted by a far-sighted group of Canadians associated with the small town of STRATFORD, Ontario. Guthrie's establishment, in a tent, of the Stratford Shakespeare Festivals was probably his greatest achievement. When he left in 1956 to begin a campaign for an American Repertory Theatre, the tent was being replaced by a permanent building with a stage that, in Guthrie's view, offered new scope to Shakespearean performances. And not only to Shakespearean performance. It was there that Guthrie directed a magnificent *Oedipus Rex*. 'For the first time in my life I've seen something which is as big as Picasso and Braque and the great sculptors,' wrote SYBIL THORNDIKE. The climax of his American campaign came with the opening of the Guthrie Theatre in Minneapolis, where his best work was in productions of CHEKHOV and a version of the *Oresteia* under the title of *The House of Atreus*. This theatre too has the aggressively jutting Guthrie stage. The force is often evident in Guthrie's opinionated and generous autobiography, *A Life in The Theatre* (1960). Guthrie was knighted in 1961.

James Forsyth, *Tyrone Guthrie*, 1976.

Gwyn, Nell (1650–87). Nell Gwyn is probably the best-known actress in the Restoration theatre, though not for her acting; she retired from the stage at the age of nineteen to pursue a more lucrative career among the upper echelons of her erstwhile audience. The fact that she was able to plead successfully before an angry crowd at Oxford that she should be unharmed because she was the *Protestant* whore gives some indication of her popularity and of the relationship between religion and morality in the period. She was admired more for panache than acting skill in comedy roles and made a hit in male dress as Florimel in DRYDEN's *Secret Love*. She was a mistress of Charles II, to name but one, and probably did begin her theatrical career selling oranges at Drury Lane. Pepys recalls a night at the theatre when 'to see Nell curse, for having so few people in the pit, was pretty'. She lives shadowily on in a number of plays based on her life, among them *Sweet Nell of Old Drury* by Paul Kester.

J. H. Wilson, *Nell Gwyn: Royal Mistress*, 1952.

Hall, Peter (1930–   ). Appointed director of the NATIONAL THEATRE in 1973, Hall is an effective organizer and a masterly marketer of the arts. He became a director in the professional theatre as soon as he graduated from Cambridge. His reputation was made during two impressive years at London's Arts Theatre, particularly with the production of *Waiting for Godot* that introduced BECKETT to English audiences. The choice of play was typical of Hall's extraordinary flair for taking risks on safe-ish bets – *Waiting for Godot*, though new to England, had a prior reputation in Europe. Hall's success at the Arts led to his appointment as artistic director of the STRATFORD Memorial Theatre in 1958 (his first season in office was delayed till 1960). With impressive speed he set about an expansionist programme, which included the renting of a London theatre, the Aldwych, the establishing of a nuclear group of actors under the new name of the ROYAL SHAKESPEARE COMPANY and a dream of turning that company into what he called 'the ICI of British theatre'. His best directorial work at Stratford includes *A Midsummer Night's Dream* (1959 and 1964) and, in tandem with John Barton, an innovative reworking of the *Henry VI* trilogy and *Richard III* under the composite title of *The Wars of the Roses* (1964). It was that production above all that established the company's style of verse-speaking, a blend of naturalism and rhetoric. In the following year, Hall directed a notable *Hamlet*, with David Warner as an alienated student-prince. It was during his years with the Royal Shakespeare Company (1958–68) that Hall proved his particular sensitivity to the plays of HAROLD PINTER as well as revealing his relaxed pleasure as a handler of the media. His enjoyment of artistic power is frank, as was illustrated by his preparedness, in 1983, to accept the appointment as artistic director of the Glyndebourne Festival whilst remaining director of the National Theatre, and as his disarmingly self-revealing *Diaries* (1983) underline. Hall was knighted in 1977.

Handke, Peter (1942–   ). Austrian dramatist, who trained as a lawyer, and knows how to split a hair better than most. Having condemned descriptive prose in a self-advertising outburst in the United States in 1966, Handke has tried to avoid using it. This has certainly made his plays 'different'. To audiences who miss whatever allusiveness is there, they are genuinely boring, though some of the titles are splendid: *Offending the Audience* (1966), *My Foot My Tutor* (1969), *The Ride over Lake Constance* (1971), *The Foolish Ones Die Out* (1974) and *A Sorrow beyond Dreams* (1977). It is not yet easy to ascertain whether Handke is a brilliant stylist or an accomplished charlatan. He has certainly read Wittgenstein, and *Kaspar* (1968) may well be an intelligent rhapsody on his themes.

Nicholas Hern, *Peter Handke*, 1971.

Hansberry, Lorraine (1930–65). American playwright, one of the few black writers to have aimed her plays at BROADWAY. Born in Chicago, she graduated at the University of Wisconsin. Only two of her plays were performed in her lifetime. The first, *A Raisin in the Sun* (1959), is a sympathetic but uncontroversial portrait of a crisis in the life of a black family, and the second, *The Sign in Sidney Brustein's Window* (1964), is set in a Jewish community in Greenwich Village. They show Hansberry to have been a skilful if conventional dramatist, set apart from black activists by her liberalism. Work unfinished at her death indicates a growing radicalism in response to the changing ethos of the sixties.

Hare, David (1947–   ). English playwright, who has been an articulate spokesman for the political theatre of the seventies. His best work is *Teeth 'n' Smiles* (1975), a vivid commentary on the pop scene. A talent for collaboration expressed itself with particular clarity in *Fanshen* (1975), which was developed alongside and performed by the Joint Stock Theatre Company. Hare was joint-founder, with Tony Bicat, of Portable Theatre (1968–72), which was the main centre of collaborative writing during the richest years of the British FRINGE. His recent work, like that of his former collaborator, HOWARD BRENTON, has been housed in the major subsidized theatres. *Plenty* (1978) and the

ambitious *Map of the World* (1983) both opened at the NATIONAL
THEATRE, the latter directed by Hare himself, and in 1984 his relation-
ship with the National was put on a more formal basis when he was
appointed an associate director. Since then he has collaborated with
Brenton on *Pravda* (1985) as well as writing and directing a film,
Wetherby (1985), and a double bill comprising *The Bay at Nice* and
Wrecked Eggs (1986).

Hauptmann, Gerhart (1862–1946). German dramatist, born in
Silesia, and much influenced by the social and linguistic peculiarities of
that region. Hauptmann wrote more bad plays than most comparably
important dramatists, but his early NATURALISTIC work is fine. *Before
Sunrise* (1889), *Lonely Lives* (1891), *The Weavers* (1892), *Drayman
Henschel* (1898) and *Rose Bernd* (1903) are accomplished tragedies with
strong, simple plots, in which fatality follows 'naturally' from hardship.
The Beaver Coat (1893) and *Schluck and Jau* (1900) are comedies, the
latter revealing the vein of fantasy that Hauptmann went on to develop
in *And Pippa Dances* (1906) and many of the later plays, in which he
turned to poetry to pursue a loftier vision. The fact is that his verse is too
turgid to sustain the plays he wrote after *The Rats* (1911), and that he
lacked the subtlety to be effective as a symbolist. Hitler took advantage
of his surprisingly simple mind, turning Hauptmann into a cultural
figurehead of the German Reich.

Margaret Sinden, *Gerhart Hauptmann: The Prose Plays*, 1975.

Hayes, Helen (1900–   ). American actress whose ambitious mother
jostled her into performing from early childhood. Her modesty has
contributed almost as much to her popularity in America as has her
talent. The critic Brooks Atkinson considered her perfectly cast in J. M.
BARRIE's *What Every Woman Knows* as 'a mousy, unassertive woman
who has a powerful influence on other people'. Franklin Adams
complained of her 'fallen archness' in a dire production of SHAW's
Caesar and Cleopatra in 1925, but she has subsequently proved 'good at
queens'. The part of Mary in MAXWELL ANDERSON's *Mary of Scotland*
(1933) brought her new critical acclaim for verse-speaking and for
'transcendence of spirit', and her playing in Laurence Housman's
Victoria Regina (1935) was outstanding. For over a decade from 1935
she shared with KATHARINE CORNELL the position of BROADWAY's first
lady, and her reputation was based almost as much on her diplomacy as
on her artistry. As Amanda in the London production of TENNESSEE
WILLIAMS's *The Glass Menagerie* (1948) and as Nora Melody in
O'NEILL's *A Touch of the Poet* (1958) she was considered competent

rather than outstanding. In 1955, in celebration of fifty years on the stage, a New York theatre (formerly the Fulton) was named after her, and in 1961 she was chosen to lead the international tour of the Theatre Guild American Repertory Company. *On Reflection* (1968) is an autobiography.

Kenneth Barrow, *Helen Hayes*, 1985.

Hazlitt, William (1778–1830). Hazlitt's five years as a dramatic critic (1813–18) form an integral part of his voluminous work. He took to the theatre the same intention that he took to his writing on metaphysics, poetry or art: 'I endeavour to recollect all I have ever observed or thought upon a subject, and to express it as nearly as I can.' His training as a painter had been based on the acuteness of his observation, and it is to that acuteness that we owe the memorable accounts of EDMUND KEAN, JOHN PHILIP KEMBLE and others. Hazlitt admired 'gusto', a divine energy shared by the heroes of the French Revolution (he remained a radical when Wordsworth and Coleridge, whom he recalled so finely in 'My First Acquaintance with Poets', were growing conservative) and by Kean. *A View of the English Stage* (1818) is a collection of his dramatic criticism. Most of the rest of Hazlitt's work belongs more properly to literature than to the theatre, though he was responsible for completing the unfinished *Memoirs of the Late Thomas Holcroft*, a rather grudging piece of hack-work, completed in 1810 but not published until 1816. What is unique about Hazlitt's essays on the theatre is their constant awareness of what he called in a later collection of literary portraits (1825) 'the spirit of the age'.

H. Baker, *William Hazlitt*, 1962.

Hellman, Lillian (1907–84). This American writer, born in New Orleans and inheriting a complex mixture of Jewish, German, and 'Southern' traits, has told much of her life in the impressionistic memoirs, *An Unfinished Woman* (1969), *Pentimento* (1973) and *Scoundrel Time* (1976). Her first play, *The Children's Hour* (1934), introduced the theme of blackmail and the excessive quest for power that continued to concern her through her two plays about the vicious Southern capitalism of an invented 'Hubbard' family, *The Little Foxes* (1939) and *Another Part of the Forest* (1946), and two more about the dangers of fascism, *Watch on the Rhine* (1941) and *The Searching Wind* (1944). An interest in CHEKHOV may have contributed to the lowering of the temperature in *The Autumn Garden* (1951) and *Toys in the Attic* (1960). Hellman's career was damaged by the discreditable activities of the HOUSE UNAMERICAN ACTIVITIES COMMITTEE, but it was not destroyed.

She retained the abrasive independence that was bound to worry people like McCarthy and Nixon in those crazy days.

Richard Moody, *Lillian Hellman: Playwright*, 1972.

Heminge(s), John (d. 1630). Best remembered today as first joint editor with Henry Condell of the plays of SHAKESPEARE (1623), Heminges was a leading actor, first with the Queen's and Lord Strange's Men and later with the Lord Chamberlain's Men, with whom he remained from about 1598 until he retired from acting some time after 1611 to devote himself exclusively to theatre administration. His business acumen is shown not only by the prosperity of his company but also by the choice of Heminges as their executor by many of his fellow-actors. He also appears to have been the representative of his own and sometimes of other acting companies in dealings with the government. A ballad about the burning of the Globe theatre in 1613 describes Heminges in the following couplet:

> Then with swol'n eyes, like drunken Flemings,
> Distressed stood old stuttering Heminges.

Charles Connell, *They Gave Us Shakespeare*, 1982.

Henslowe, Philip (d. 1616). Henslowe's Diary is the most important source of knowledge about Elizabethan and Jacobean theatre practice. Henslowe was apprenticed to a dyer, whose wealthy widow he married. Through agents, he carried on an active pawnbroking business as well as being what we would now call a property speculator. Among his properties, at various times, were the Rose, Fortune and Hope playhouses. Most significant of all, he was a moneylender, and it was in some part by usury that he maintained his hold over the actors in the Admiral's Men and in Worcester's Men, as well as over several playwrights, of whom Chettle and DEKKER were the most obvious 'victims'. Henslowe's daughter married the actor EDWARD ALLEYN, who deposited his father-in-law's papers in the school in Dulwich. There is no doubt that Henslowe's attitude to theatre was mercenary, but there is not sufficient evidence to confirm that it was more mercenary than that of, for example, James or even RICHARD BURBAGE. The method of finance was different, but the motive may well have been the same. Of course, Henslowe *could* have been a grasping philistine with no interest whatsoever in the art of the theatre. The speculation about this effective businessman will go on.

Bernard Beckerman, 'Philip Henslowe', in *The Theatrical Manager in England and America*, ed. Joseph Donohue, 1971.

Heron, Matilda (1830–77). Irish-born American actress, who made her debut in Philadelphia in 1851. Her considerable reputation was based almost entirely on her playing of the title role in her own version of the most famous play by DUMAS *fils*, which she called *Camille*. She first performed it at Wallack's Theatre, New York in 1855 and continued to play the part throughout the United States until the onset of insanity forced her to retire from the stage. Heron was, at some time, resident in Paris, and she brought to the American stage a style of acting that was impressively restrained and natural-seeming. 'The woman dared to come in upon that painted scene,' wrote Fitz-James O'Brien, 'as if it really was the home apartment it was represented to be.'

Heywood, John (*c.* 1497–1578). Poet, singer, musician and dramatist, John Heywood's claim to distinction in the last capacity rests mainly on the mildly witty Interludes he wrote for the Tudor courtly circle under Henry VIII. The best of these are *The Play of the Weather* (1533) and *The 4 P's* (*c.* 1543). Neither has any plot to speak of. The first consists of a series of appeals to Jupiter from various persons to change the weather to suit their particular vocation; Jupiter wisely does nothing and everyone applauds his inaction. *The 4 P's* takes the form of a lying contest between a Pardoner, a Palmer, a 'Pothecary and a Pedlar. Neither play is quite lively enough to hold an audience's attention today, though Heywood's homespun humour has an intermittent appeal. His best play is not an Interlude at all but a farce based on a French model, *Johan Johan, Tib and Sir John* (1533). Heywood died in Belgium, having been imprisoned and later pardoned for conspiring against Cranmer. He spent the last fourteen years of his life in exile.

R. C. Johnson, *John Heywood*, 1970.

Heywood, Thomas (1573–1641). Only about thirty of the 220 plays of which Heywood wrote parts or all have survived. His masterpiece – a considerable one – is the bourgeois tragedy, *A Woman Killed with Kindness* (1603), but the splendidly adventurous two-part romance, *The Fair Maid of the West* (1610 and 1631), invites admiration for its author's versatility and professionalism. Heywood was associated with PHILIP HENSLOWE, as actor, playwright, and possibly shareholder. His *An Apology for Actors* (1612) is a unique and literate statement from a man whose business was theatre. Heywood wrote, acted, translated, composed Lord Mayor's pageants and MASQUES, and prepared translations. He followed after money, and he did his honest best to earn it.

F. S. Boas, *Heywood*, 1950.

Hochhuth, Rolf (1931–   ). There is very little evidence of real talent in Hochhuth's plays. Given a taste for *réclame*, an idealistic moral fervour operating in the sphere of international policy, *and* the determination to write, almost anyone might have written a better play than *The Representative* (also translated as *The Deputy*), whose production in Berlin in 1963 caused an international furore. It accuses, ~~in five blank-verse acts, Pope Pius XII~~ of complicity through inaction in the Nazi persecution of the Jews. A second play, *Soldiers* (1967), centres on Churchill's decision to flatten Dresden. Its rejection by the board of governors of the English NATIONAL THEATRE caused an outcry and was a major factor in the abolition in Britain of the Lord Chamberlain's role as censor of plays; but the play itself is updated fustian. Hochhuth is not simply a German apologist, but he is not a good playwright.

Hofmannsthal, Hugo von (1874–1929). The neglect of this Austrian dramatist by the English-speaking theatre is surprising. His opera libretti, the offspring of an unlikely collaboration with the temperamentally divergent Richard Strauss, are better known. *Electra* (1903), though, was a play before it became a libretto in 1909, and the texts of *Der Rosenkavalier* (1911) and *Arabella* (1928) survive without their music as verse comedies in a tradition reaching back to MOLIÈRE. Hofmannsthal also wrote dance libretti, finding in the image of the dancer, as also in that of the actor, that suppression of the self which was at the centre of his artistic vision. His dramatic concern was not with individuals, but with what he called, in a lecture on SHAKESPEARE, 'the space between characters that is mystically alive'. Hofmannsthal was born in Vienna, and was already known as a symbolist poet when he went to the university there in 1892. By the end of the nineties he had also written several short dramatic poems, of which the best known is *Death and the Fool* (1893). It was not until 1899 that he began to write plays designed for the stage. MAX REINHARDT recognized the plastic possibilities of Hofmannsthal's work, and produced his version of *Oedipus Rex* (1909), the modern morality play *Everyman* (1911) and the fascinating comedy *The Difficult Man* (1918), in which his hero has to learn to live in a post-war Austria disturbed by Prussian assertiveness. Hofmannsthal was the guiding spirit behind the Salzburg Festival. The mystical leanings that made CALDERON his favourite study were expressed in *The Salzburg Great Theatre of the World* (1922) and in the cryptic prose tragedy *The Tower* (1925), which took Calderon's *Life Is a Dream* as its source. Until his sudden death, Hofmannsthal continued to serve the new Austrian republic and the idea of a new European community.

Brian Coghlan, *Hofmannsthal's Festival Dramas*, 1964.
Michael Hamburger, *Hofmannsthal: Three Essays*, 1972.

Holberg, Ludwig (1684–1754). Although born in Norway, Holberg has to be called, for both historical and linguistic reasons, a Danish dramatist: and a phenomenal one at that. When, in 1722, a Danish National Theatre was opened in Copenhagen, there was no native repertory. Holberg, who was by then a Professor of Philosophy (unwillingly) at the University of Copenhagen, but who had won a literary reputation with a long mock-heroic poem called *Peder Paars*, was invited to fill the void. He did so with a vengeance. Between 1722, when *The Political Tinker* was staged, and 1727, when the theatre was closed, he wrote twenty-seven plays. Production on that scale can only be achieved if there is a ready formula, and there is no doubt that Holberg relied on a gallery of types, somewhat after the model of the COMMEDIA DELL'ARTE scenarios he had read in Gherardi's *Le Théâtre Italien*. His situations vary, but the characters remain splendidly recognizable, none more so than the drunkard hero of *Jeppe on the Hill* (1722). Jeppe is slow-witted, henpecked, and deceitful, but, for reasons Falstaff might have understood, vastly endearing. He is what Christopher Sly might have become if SHAKESPEARE had given him a bigger part in *The Taming of the Shrew*. When the Danish Royal Theatre opened in 1748, Holberg provided six more plays. Some time, someone will give this extraordinary man his due. He is one of the great European writers of comedy.

O. J. Campbell, *The Comedies of Holberg*, 1914.

Holcroft, Thomas (1745–1809). The son of a shoemaker, Holcroft was (and needed to be) immensely industrious. He had the eager and sometimes dangerous energy of an autodidact. After a largely unsuccessful career as an actor, useful as a background to his first novel *Alwyn* (1780), he was persuaded by the success of his comedy *Duplicity* (1781) to earn his keep by writing. In 1784 he went to Paris in order to produce a pirated English version of BEAUMARCHAIS's *Le Mariage de Figaro* (produced at Covent Garden in December of that year under the title *The Follies of a Day*). Already radically inclined, he was excited by events in France. 'The French Revolution,' it is observed in his *Memoirs* (1816), 'was the only match that ever took place between philosophy and experience.' Two years after he had written his best comedy, *The Road to Ruin* (1792), Holcroft was indicted for High Treason. The arrest was an act of panic, and he was acquitted two months later, but his career as a dramatist was always controversial thereafter. Persecution (or a persecution complex) drove him into exile from 1799 to 1803. Two of the plays he 'borrowed' from France are of particular note. *Deaf and Dumb* (1801) advertised the taste for Gothic anguish, and *A Tale of Mystery* (1802), after PIXERÉCOURT, was the first 'English' play to be announced as a 'melodrama'. Holcroft earned too little from his plays and novels to be spared the chores of the unsuccessful writer. The outline of his life is a tale of woe – four times married, living on and sometimes below the breadline, the virtual witness of the suicide of his only son, who had robbed him – but the posthumously published *Memoirs* show the durability of this admirable man.

Horniman, Annie (Elizabeth Fredericka) (1860–1937). The daughter of a tea-merchant, Annie Horniman used her money (she was never vastly rich) to establish two notable theatrical ventures. Her first (and secret) promotion was of Florence Farr's 1894 season at London's Avenue Theatre. Through the performance of YEATS's *Land of Heart's Desire*, this led her to an interest in the Irish theatrical revival, and the building and equipping of the ABBEY THEATRE. Possibly, her real interest was in Yeats himself. They were both members of the Order of the Golden Dawn, and she had provided him with secretarial help (perhaps on the yellow paper SYNGE hated so much) when his eyes troubled him. Certainly she disliked the Abbey's nationalism during the years between its opening in 1904, and her final breaking off of relationships in 1910. In 1908 she bought and refurbished the Gaiety Theatre in Manchester, and oversaw productions there until 1917, establishing a repertory company committed to the painstaking performance of serious plays. British provincial theatre is deeply in her debt.

Rex Pogson, *Miss Horniman and the Gaiety Theatre, Manchester*, 1952. J. W. Flannery, *Miss Horniman and the Abbey Theatre*, 1971.

Houghton, Stanley (1881–1913). Already a book-reviewer and drama critic for the *Manchester Guardian* when he wrote his first play, *The Dear Departed* (1908), Houghton is associated with the group of Manchester playwrights who helped build up the repertoire and reputation of ANNIE HORNIMAN's Gaiety Theatre. His best-known play is *Hindle Wakes* (1912), an impressively feminist statement as well as a lively piece in its own right. Houghton's advanced views are also apparent in *The Younger Generation* (1910), in which the older generation is forced to ask itself some new questions.

Howard, Bronson (1842–1908). Howard worked as a journalist in his birthplace, Detroit, and in New York until the success of *Saratoga*

(1870) encouraged him to take the bold decision to earn his living as a playwright. The fact that he succeeded suggests that he was almost as good a businessman as those he wrote about so persistently. *Saratoga* was a FARCE set in a favourite American resort (Frank Marshall adapted it for the English stage under the title *Brighton*). Howard's more typical setting was the business world of America and its social context. *Young Mrs Winthrop* (1882), *The Henrietta* (1887) and *Aristocracy* (1892) are examples of his shallow but reliable craftsmanship. With *Shenandoah* (1888) he ventured interestingly into the more romantic realms of Civil War melodrama. Cleverly produced and promoted by Charles Frohman, it secured Howard a fortune. Despite his contemporary reputation as an innovator, Howard was a traditionalist whose aim it was to provide America with plays that encouraged virtue and castigated vice. Not too much could be expected from a man who proclaimed that 'the wife who has once taken the step from purity to impurity can never reinstate herself in the world of art on this side of the grave'.

Howard, Sidney (1891–1939). Born and educated in California, Howard graduated to playwriting by way of George Pierce Baker's famous Workshop 47 at Harvard. Until 1923 he earned his living as a journalist and was, for a year, Literary Editor of *Life* magazine. He was instrumental in the founding of the Theatre Guild in 1918–19 and one of the members of the short-lived Playwrights' Company from 1938. His death in a farming accident was a bitter blow to his colleagues in that influential group. He left unfinished a play about Benjamin Franklin. The American character was his favourite theme. *They Knew What They Wanted* (1924) is an American folk-play based on the story of Paolo and Francesca. It was produced by the Theatre Guild, as was *Lucky Sam McCarver* (1925), which caused something of a stir by its treatment of a sexual relationship between a society lady and a nightclub owner. The Freudianism of *The Silver Cord* (1926) was even more shocking. This is a highly emotional thesis play about a mother's pathological love for her sons. Howard was rarely experimental in his dramatic writing, relying rather on what Brooks Atkinson has called a 'special talent for endowing reality with glamour', but there is a move towards a more impersonal, abstract style in *Yellow Jack* (1934), which records the self-sacrificing research into the cause of yellow fever. Howard is a stalwart representative of the assertive American liberalism that hoped for so much after World War I. It is an irony that his securest hold on public attention is the screenplay of *Gone with the Wind* (1939).

Hugo, Victor-Marie (1802–85). Hugo's plays have lasted less vigorously than his poetry and his novels, but they are the central feature of the extraordinary decade (1827–37) which saw French Romantic drama shake the Parisian establishment by importing the full-bloodedness of Boulevard MELODRAMA onto the classical stage. The preface to the unperformable *Cromwell* (1827) was the manifesto of the new movement, but it was an enjambement in the opening couplet of *Hernani*, when it was performed at the Théâtre Français on 25 February 1830, that started the war of words. 'Brave times,' wrote Gautier, 'when the things of the mind and the intelligence could stir crowds to such excitement.' The political tensions that would lead France to revolution in 1848, and Hugo to exile from 1851 to 1870, were already in evidence. *Marion de Lorme*, suppressed in 1829, was staged in 1831, giving Marie Dorval a chance to shine in poetic tragedy as vividly as she already shone in Boulevard melodrama. *Le Roi s'amuse* (1832) opened on the evening of an assassination attempt on Louis-Philippe, and was immediately banned as an incitement to regicide. It provided the dramatic basis for Verdi's *Rigoletto*. The prose plays, *Lucrèce Borgia* and *Marie Tudor* (both 1833), are less assured than *Ruy Blas* (1838). They were written at the start of Hugo's long liaison with the actress Juliette Drouet. After the failure of *Les Burgraves* (1843), he abandoned the stage.

Linda Kelly, *The Young Romantics*, 1976.

Hunt, Leigh (1784–1859). Hunt's father was an immigrant to England from Barbados by way of the newly independent United States, where he had been a vigorous Royalist. Some of his fearless independence was inherited by two of his sons, John and Leigh. Leigh Hunt's first theatrical criticisms were written for the *News*, a paper of which John was editor, and he published a selection of them as *Critical Essays on the Performers of the London Theatres* (1808). That, in essence, is what they were. Hunt wrote about actors, and he wrote with seriousness and great facility. When his brother founded *The Examiner*, Hunt became its editor (1808), continuing his systematic visits to London theatres. The paper was prosecuted three times. On the first two occasions (they had exposed abuses in the British army) the Hunts were acquitted, but in 1813 they were imprisoned for two years following what was adjudged a libel on the Prince Regent. As a result, Hunt missed the London debut of EDMUND KEAN. On his release in early 1815, he was soon at Drury Lane to see Kean's *Richard III* and wrote one of his finest pieces of measured criticism to express his disappointment. Hunt was the father of a large and often hapless family and he undertook far too much work in order to repay debts. It probably mortified him that many of his friends – they included, at various times, Keats, Shelley, Byron, CHARLES LAMB, Carlyle, Browning, G. H. LEWES and Dickens – were better writers than he. Of the ten or so plays he wrote, or started to write, only two were staged in his lifetime, a verse tragedy called *A Legend of Florence* at Covent Garden in 1840 and a verse comedy called *Lovers' Amazements* at the Lyceum in 1858. To the end Hunt aspired to be more than he actually was, a superior journalist. His *Dramatic Criticism, 1808–31* can be read in an excellent selection by L. H. and C. W. Houtchens (1949).

Edmund Blunden, *Leigh Hunt*, 1930.

Ibsen, Henrik Johan (1828–1906). Norwegian dramatist whose work did more than anyone else's to raise the status of the drama in nineteenth-century Europe. Ibsen faced financial hardships in youth, was actively radical as a student, and never lost his admiration for the individual who resists the pressures of a nullifying society. From 1851 to 1864, he worked in the Norwegian theatre. His early plays met with no more than moderate success. The best of them, *Love's Comedy* (1862), a verse play with a contemporary setting and some social bite, had to wait eleven years for a production. From 1864 to 1891, he lived abroad, mostly in Italy and Germany. *Brand*, a verse drama whose uncompromising hero is confronted with a sequence of agonizing choices, was published in 1866, and the next year *Peer Gynt* confirmed his place as an original poetic dramatist. That, of course, says too little. *Peer Gynt* is a work of genius, which strangely embodies a vision of freedom and of social constraint in its miscreant hero. STRINDBERG detected in *Brand* 'the voice of a Savonarola in the middle of our aesthetic age'. In *Peer Gynt* there are many voices. In a poem written at about this time, Ibsen wrote that, 'Prose style is for ideas, verse for visions'. His next play, again with a contemporary Norwegian setting, was *The League of Youth* (1869), a comedy in prose. He was working now on the play in which he hoped to express his own spiritual discovery of the relationship between freedom and necessity. The play, in two five-act parts, was published in 1873 as *Emperor and Galilean*. It was written in prose, and its hero was the Roman Emperor Julian the Apostate. History's verdict is that Ibsen overrated it. But the rejection of verse in favour of 'the incomparably more difficult art of writing honest, straightforward, everyday language' is of crucial importance. At this mid-point in his career, Ibsen was about to embark on the most influential series of plays since those of MOLIÈRE. They are all in prose, though a prose never out of touch with poetry, and they all have a contemporary Norwegian setting.

This group of realistic modern dramas begins with *Pillars of Society* (1877) and ends with *Hedda Gabler* (1890). It includes *A Doll's House* (1879), *Ghosts* (1881), *An Enemy of the People* (1882), *The Wild Duck* (1884), *Rosmersholm* (1886) and *The Lady from the Sea* (1888). Edvard Beyer colourfully describes their interplay of past guilt and present aspiration as 'the voyage to new shores, but with a corpse – be it social or individual – in the cargo'. The shock-waves were felt throughout the Western world, where artists and critics had to declare themselves either a little Ibsenite or else a little conservative. When he returned to Norway in 1891, Ibsen met with a mixed reception. There was adulation on the one hand, and on the other, from the young novelist Knut Hamsun particularly, a vigorous rejection of this pillar of the older generation. The last plays reflect, in various ways, Ibsen's sense of his own artistic failure. They reflect also his responsiveness to the new interest in symbolism. *The Master Builder* (1892), *Little Eyolf* (1894), *John Gabriel Borkman* (1896) and *When We Dead Awaken* (1899) are fine works, enhanced by an elegiac wisdom that is without self-pity.

Michael Meyer, *Henrik Ibsen: A Biography*, 3 vols., 1967–70.
John Northam, *Ibsen: A Critical Study*, 1973.
Edvard Beyer, *Ibsen: The Man and His Work* (trans. Marie Wells), 1978.

Inchbald, Elizabeth (1753–1821). English playwright and novelist, who began her adult life as an actress. She met with limited success on the stage, but continued acting for a few years after the performance of her first plays, *A Mogul Tale* (1784), which exploited the contemporary interest in ballooning, *I'll Tell You What* (1785) and *The Widow's Vow* (1786). Her first notable success was *The Child of Nature* (1788), a drama from the French, though the comedy *Such Things Are* (1787) is a much more impressive play. *Animal Magnetism* (1788), which took its title from the pseudo-scientific experiments of the mysterious Dr Mesmer, relied on public interest in mesmerism to attract audiences to Covent Garden, where it was played. The best known of Inchbald's later work is her version of KOTZEBUE's *Lovers' Vows* (1798), generally supposed to be the script so shockingly rehearsed by Jane Austen's amateurs in *Mansfield Park*, though *Everyone Has His Fault* (1793), *Wives as They Were and Maids as They Are* (1797) and *To Marry, or Not to Marry* (1805) are livelier. Inchbald was a person of considerable independence, prepared to take issue with the formidable William Godwin, and to supervise the publication, under the familiar title of *Inchbald's British Theatre*, of a large collection of plays and FARCES. Her novels, *A Simple Story* (1791) and *Nature and Art* (1796), have aroused renewed critical interest in recent years.

S. R. Littlewood, *Elizabeth Inchbald and Her Circle*, 1921.

Ionesco, Eugène (1912–   ). French playwright born in Rumania. Ionesco's father was Rumanian and his mother French. He spent his early childhood in Paris, studied at the University of Bucharest, wrote poetry and criticism while teaching French in Rumania and returned to Paris in 1938 to write a thesis on sin and death in French poetry. An obsession with death became a feature of the plays he later wrote in French, but he began much more light-heartedly. Bored with his work as a proofreader in Paris, Ionesco decided to teach himself English, and it was his encounter with language text-books that gave him the idea for *The Bald Prima Donna* (1950). Performed in a small Parisian theatre, this play quickly gathered a cult following. It was followed by two other short plays, *The Lesson* (1951) and *The Chairs* (1952), in which, for the first time, Ionesco's fascinated following of linguistic logic *ad absurdum* collided with his brooding fantasies on mortality. More than any other writer, Ionesco set the pattern for what came to be known as the THEATRE OF THE ABSURD. Embroiled in a private nightmare, which is contingent on society but in no way conducive to its betterment, Ionesco has produced a series of profoundly disturbing FARCES whose hold on audiences throughout the world has passed its peak partly because his doom-laden dreams of mass-murder, materialistic surfeit and horror hidden behind decorous language have been taken over by the governments of the world. His full-length plays are less certain to last than his shorter pieces. Among the former are several involving, as the central character, a clown-like innocent, more acted upon than active, and given often the name of Bérenger, *The Killer* (1959), *Rhinoceros* (1960) and *Exit the King* (1962) being among the best.

Richard Coe, *Ionesco: A Study of His Plays*, 1961.

Irving, Henry (1838–1905). English actor, born in Somerset, and brought up by a Methodist aunt in Cornwall. He was intended for a respectable clerical career, but was stubbornly stagestruck. Changing his name from Brodribb, to protect his family, he joined a professional company in Sunderland in 1856. He played hundreds of parts in provincial theatres before settling in London in 1867, and had his first real success as Digby Grant in James Albery's *Two Roses* in 1870. He had, the previous year, contracted a marriage. His wife was the daughter of a Surgeon-General in the Indian Army, who had little time for actors. Like father, like daughter. Florence O'Callaghan gave her husband two sons, but little joy. The morbidly secretive sexuality that characterized Irving's acting owed something to this misalliance. He left his wife in 1871, when the runaway success of his Mathias in *The Bells* was turning a tolerable reputation into a sensational one, and he never spoke to her again, though she attended all his first nights, and relished the title of Lady Irving that her husband's knighthood (he was the first actor to be knighted) brought her in 1895.

The accolade was a reward for his years of management of the Lyceum, which began in 1878 and lasted almost until his death. During those years, the Lyceum was a National Theatre in all but name. Irving thought of it as a temple, and there are many witnesses to its quasi-religious atmosphere. That was partly the result of Irving's bold insistence on dousing the auditorium lights to give full play to the mysteries of gas lighting – augmented by LIMELIGHT, of course; but Irving would not install electricity. Then there was his delight in playing churchmen – Wolsey in *Henry VIII*, Cardinal Richelieu in BULWER-LYTTON's play of that name and Becket in Tennyson's among them. It was after giving a performance of Becket, against doctor's orders, that he died in the foyer of a Bradford hotel, to be mourned by thousands. And yet Irving did very little to advance the theatre. He hated IBSEN, rejected SHAW, restricted ELLEN TERRY to roles that suited his turn, presented pictorial SHAKESPEARE, and preferred costume drama because it allowed him to disguise his worst feature, his legs. He was a magnificent showman, at his best in the throes of secret guilt, conscious of the Lyceum's prime asset – himself – but skilful in the manipulation of other actors and of crowds to maximize that asset. His Hamlet (1874 and 1878) was admired, his Romeo (1882) mocked, but his best Shakespearean roles were Shylock, Iago and a surprisingly light Benedick (1882). Inside *his* theatre, this lonely man expressed hypnotically his secret self.

Edward Gordon Craig, *Henry Irving*, 1930.
Laurence Irving, *Henry Irving: The Actor and His World*, 1951.
Madeleine Bingham, *Henry Irving and the Victorian Theatre*, 1978.

Jackson, Barry (1879–1961). Theatrical promoter, designer, trained architect, director, whose money and enthusiasm founded the Birmingham Repertory Theatre in 1913, and who was knighted in 1925. His devotion to serious experiment is best exemplified by his modern-dress SHAKESPEARE productions and by the presentation in Birmingham in 1923 of all five parts of SHAW's *Back to Methuselah*. His concern for Shaw was furthered in the Malvern Festival, which he founded in 1929. Jackson also had an interest in a number of London theatres, and from 1945 to 1948 was Director of the Memorial Theatre at STRATFORD-upon-Avon. Shaw wrote of theatre's debt to such a patron in the Silver

Jubilee souvenir programme: '"How much a year are you out of pocket by this culture theatre of yours?" I said. He named an annual sum that would have sufficed to support fifty labourers and their families. I remarked that this was not more than it would cost him to keep a thousand-ton steam yacht. He said a theatre was more fun than a steam yacht, but said it in the tone of a man who could afford a steam yacht. That settled the matter. The impossible had become possible.'

J. C. Trewin, *The Birmingham Repertory Theatre*, 1963.

Jackson, Glenda (1938–   ). English actress whose power of personality and independence of outlook have worked against her long-term employment by any single major company. For the ROYAL SHAKESPEARE COMPANY at the Aldwych she was a riveting Charlotte Corday in PETER BROOK's production of WEISS's *Marat-Sade* (1964), the actress who made the issues of *US* (1967) most painful to the audience, and a disturbingly credible Hedda Gabler (1975). Brook turned to her again in 1978 to play Cleopatra at STRATFORD opposite Alan Howard's Antony. The event was less stunning than had been anticipated, not least because neither Brook nor Jackson is prepared to be dazzling to order. She is morally and temperamentally unhappy about 'stardom', preferring roles in which her own strength and abrasive intelligence are shared by the characters she impersonates. Ken Russell used her finely as Gudrun Brangwen in his film version of *Women in Love* (1970) precisely because he accepted and relished her combativeness. More recently, Glenda Jackson has loudly deplored the lack of parts for actresses between forty and sixty. Six West End productions, *Stevie* (1977), *Rose* (1980), *Summit Conference* (1982), the first English production of Botho Strauss's *Great and Small* (1983), O'NEILL's *Strange Interlude* (1984) and RACINE's *Phèdre* (1984) have confirmed her determination to confine her stage performances to plays, and more particularly to characters, that she can respect.

Ian Woodward, *Glenda Jackson*, 1986.

Jarry, Alfred (1873–1907). Jarry was fifteen, and living in Laval, when he wrote the first version of *Ubu Roi*. It was then a play for marionettes, built with schoolboy hyperbole on a monstrous caricature of a Laval schoolteacher. When a later version was staged at the Théâtre de l'Oeuvre in Paris in 1896, there was a scandalized riot. Nothing could have suited Jarry better. He had pictured the consuming bourgeois as King, and the consuming bourgeoisie obligingly revolted. It was a seminal event, and its imminent result was the birth of the dangerous modern theatre. Jarry's subsequent plays, also featuring the bloated Ubu, have not much importance. The influence of *Ubu Roi*, though, is discernible in the work of the surrealists and the absurdists, was paramount in Dada, and lingered into the pop-art movement and what PETER BROOK characterized as 'rough theatre'. Brook's revival of the play in 1978 is a further landmark in its extraordinary history. Jarry himself became a victim to his naive need to be unconventional, and died untimely, 'saturated with drink and ether'.

Roger Shattuck, *The Banquet Years*, 1959.

Jefferson, Joseph (1829–1905). Joseph Jefferson III was the most eminent of a theatrical family. At the age of four he was incorporated by the famous 'Jim Crow', Thomas D. Rice, in a black-faced double act in Washington and his education was scraped together during theatrical tours. Jefferson was already a moderately successful comedian when he became suddenly a star in the American premiere of TOM TAYLOR's *Our American Cousin* in 1858. BOUCICAULT immediately engaged him as a member of his company for the ambitious 1859 season at the Winter Garden Theatre in New York and persuaded him to risk the 'pathetic' part of Caleb Plummer in *Dot*, his version of Dickens's *The Cricket on the Hearth*. It was Jefferson's first straight role, and he was widely praised. The part of Caleb Plummer remained in his repertoire and he made his farewell appearance in it in 1904. In the same season of 1859 Jefferson created the role of Salem Scudder in Boucicault's *The Octoroon*. To Boucicault's alarm, Jefferson kept himself fit during the rehearsals for this play by sparring in his dressing room with an ex-professional boxer. After the death of his first wife in 1861, Jefferson went to Australia, acting there for four years before sailing to England in the hope of making a name for himself on the London stage. In search of an appropriate American part, he asked Boucicault to rework the unsatisfactory dramatization of *Rip Van Winkle* then current, and it was in Boucicault's version of the story by Washington Irving that he opened at the Adelphi in 1865. From then until his retirement, Jefferson need never have acted in anything else. 'The remarkable beauty of the performance,' wrote one critic, 'arises from nothing so much as its entire repose and equality.' By 1881 Jefferson had played Rip 'about twenty-five hundred times' according to his own calculations, and he continued to act it until his retirement. His splendid autobiography was originally called *Rip Van Winkle* (1890). Jefferson was a man of immense charm, in the view of the theatre historian Barnard Hewitt, 'probably the most lovable man, off the stage as well as on, our theatre has known'.

Jellicoe, Ann (1927–   ). English playwright and director who was associated with the ROYAL COURT in the early days of the English Stage Company. *The Sport of My Mad Mother* (1957), her first play, invests a squalid street scene with the primal urgency of ritual. It is a dazzlingly resourceful development of the improvisational work she explored as leader of the Writer's Group workshops at the Royal Court. *The Knack* (1961) is altogether quieter, but it too embroiders a familiar dramatic situation with improvisatory playfulness. Jellicoe is instinctively an organizer of the stage picture. Having left London to bring up her family in Lyme Regis, she founded the Colway Theatre Trust in 1979 and has written and directed for the Trust a number of large-scale community plays of which *The Tide* (1979) and *The Reckoning* (1980) were the first. Designed for a cast of one hundred or more, these plays require and secure the involvement of far more people than that, in small towns like Lyme Regis, Bridport, Sherborne and Crediton. Jellicoe has always been prepared to experiment on a grand scale. Her second play, written for the Girl Guides in 1960, had a cast of eight hundred girls and a hundred boys. Called *The Rising Generation*, it featured a conspiracy to eliminate men and cut them out of the history books. Discreet rather than valorous, the Girl Guides decided not to stage it.

Jessner, Leopold (1878–1945). German director whose important contribution was confined to the eleven years (1919–30) of his management of the Berlin Staatstheater. Jessner was a Jew (he was forced into exile in 1933) and an ardent Republican, and his unexpected appointment to the leading theatrical position in Germany reflected the early hopes of the Weimar Republic. His opening production in Berlin was an innovatory approach to a German classic, SCHILLER's *William Tell*. Instead of the traditional Alpine scenery, Jessner and his designer, Emil Pirchan, employed a permanent set of ramps, stairs and bridges. Except in Russia, the staging of a classic thus in 1919 was revolutionary. It was a declaration of Jessner's commitment to EXPRESSIONISM: 'Ideas demand the simplest, most immediately effective form of expression.' He used actors as part of the stage image, contributors to his 'transcendental sculpture'. A high point in his work was the 1920 production of *Richard III*. The simplicity of effect can be represented by a contrast of the opening and closing of the performance: Gloucester, dressed in black, begins the play by delivering his soliloquy before a black curtain, whilst Richmond ends it, dressed in white, by moving forward to allow the dropping of a white curtain behind him. But the overwhelming effect was the use of a massive staircase soaked in blood-red light. Jessner called it 'the abstract setting of mythical events'. 'Feudal history,' wrote Jan Kott in *Shakespeare Our Contemporary*, 'is like a great staircase on which there treads a constant procession of kings.' The metaphor was inspired by Jessner's production. The scenic simplicity was dangerously attractive. Asked what he had seen in the German theatres he had toured in 1925, Jessner replied, 'Nothing but steps'. It is a melancholy fact that Jessner is remembered for a staircase. He would be better served by the recognition that his appropriation of classic plays for the modern world was a significant influence on BRECHT.

Johnston, Denis (1901–84). Irish playwright, born in Dublin, where he was associated with both the ABBEY THEATRE and the Gate. His first play, *The Old Lady Says 'No!'* (1929), was rejected by the Abbey and staged at the Gate. Its theme is Irish patriotism, centred on the ambiguous figure of Robert Emmett, but its techniques are EXPRESSIONISTIC, even surrealistic. The Abbey was more at home with the realistic writing of *The Moon in the Yellow River* (1931), a subtle exploration of moral and political divisions in Ireland after the Civil War. But Johnston, like O'CASEY, was eager to stretch beyond realism, and perplexed many of his critics with plays too formally experimental for easy assimilation into the mainstream of Irish writing: *A Bride for the Unicorn* (1933), *Storm Song* (1934), *The Golden Cuckoo* (1938). His interest was caught by acts of eccentric self-assertion or curious episodes, like the wartime FARCE he wittily records in the one-act *A Fourth for Bridge* (written *c.* 1946). Johnston taught at American universities from 1950 to 1967, during which time he wrote *The Scythe and the Sunset* (1958), a play about the Easter Rising of 1916. As its title insists, this play takes account of O'Casey's *The Plough and the Stars*, whose pacifism it fondly criticizes. Of Johnston's remaining work, *The Dreaming Dust* (1940), a radio play about Jonathan Swift, is particularly interesting. Johnston's idiosyncratic views on the life of Swift were further developed in a critical biography, *In Search of Swift* (1959).

Gene A. Barnett, *Denis Johnston*, 1978.

Jones, Henry Arthur (1851–1929). Jones was an efficient professional with a sufficiently stubborn streak to achieve more by persistence than he could have hoped to by dexterity. *The Silver King* (1882) is an effective MELODRAMA, and the social comedies, like *The Liars* (1897) and *Whitewashing Julia* (1903), are sharpened by the withholding of approval from the characters he deploys. It was even rumoured at the time that OSCAR WILDE had written *The Liars*. Wilde's retort was: 'The first rule [for writing plays] is not to write like Henry Arthur Jones, the second and third rules are the same!' In his generally humourless attempts to re-establish drama as a branch of literature, Jones was not afraid to court controversy. *The Case of Rebellious Susan* (1894), *Michael and His Lost Angel* (1896) and *Mrs Dane's Defence* (1900) all touched on taboo subjects and understandably caused a stir, but the melancholy fact is that Jones, who had left school at twelve, worked as a draper's assistant for five years, as a commercial traveller for ten, and flirted with socialism as a young man, was converted by success into a diehard Tory. Perhaps much should be forgiven of the man about whom his daughter writes: 'During the last years of his life he was completely absorbed in political work, and on three occasions, when he stood still thinking in the middle of Finchley Road, he was knocked down by motor-cars.'

Doris Arthur Jones, *The Life and Letters of Henry Arthur Jones*, 1930.

Jones, Inigo (1573–1652). The first great stage designer of the English theatre was also, and primarily, an architect. His theatrical ideas were formed by a visit to the Teatro Olimpico in Vicenza, where he saw Scamozzi's perspective streets. His designs for the Court MASQUES of James I are based on Italian models. *The Masque of Blackness* (1605) was a first venture into the spectacular, with a sea that moved and a blue silk heaven set with silver stars. The development of a proscenium frame for the stage picture, of changeable scenery on shutters, of scenes in relief and of lighting effects with the aid of transparencies and coloured flame came later. Jones also designed the exquisite and lavish costumes which were a feature of the Court Masques under James I and Charles I. Partly through his association with DAVENANT, particularly on the staging of *Salmacida Spolia* (1638), and partly because of his own enduring genius, Jones's influence changed the course of the British theatre. His own fortunes slumped during the Civil War and he died in poverty.

Allardyce Nicoll, *Stuart Masques and the Renaissance Stage*, 1937.

Jones, Leroi. See BARAKA, AMIRI.

Jones, Robert Edmond (1887–1954). American designer and director whose ideas of theatre were transformed during a year in Europe (1913–1914). There he saw work by CRAIG, APPIA and COPEAU and was working on the design of REINHARDT's *The Merchant of Venice* when war broke out. Back in New York in 1915 he designed a posterlike set and extravagant costumes for a production by GRANVILLE BARKER of Anatole

France's *The Man Who Married a Dumb Wife*. It was the beginning of a new movement in American stage design. Jones's interest was not in the external details of 'reality' but in the whole mood of a play. For changes of mood, he preferred to rely on the subtleties of lighting. His association with the PROVINCETOWN PLAYERS increased his spiritual and imaginative absorption in the theatre, and the favourite saying, 'Keep in your soul some images of magnificence', became almost a design principle. His sets for O'NEILL's plays were more evocations than representations. For JOHN BARRYMORE and Arthur Hopkins, he designed *Richard III* in 1920 and *Hamlet* in 1922. On *Hamlet*'s London tour, JAMES AGATE found the scenery 'the most beautiful thing I have ever seen on any stage'. Other notable designs in a long and varied career include those for MARC CONNELLY's *The Green Pastures* (1930), Stravinsky's *Oedipus Rex* at the Metropolitan Opera House in 1931 and an *Othello* in 1937 which he also directed. Jones also wrote a remarkable book, *The Dramatic Imagination* (1941), in which his aspirations are finely expressed.

Ralph Pendleton (ed.), *The Theatre of Robert Edmond Jones*, 1958.

Jonson, Ben (1572–1637). Of all the dramatists of his time Jonson is most characteristically a Londoner. His best plays are redolent of the city, even when, as in *Volpone*, their ostensible setting is elsewhere. He was born in Westminster and for some years followed his stepfather's trade of bricklaying, a circumstance which his enemies in the literary and theatrical world delighted to recall. He went to Westminster School where the headmaster was the great antiquary and classical scholar William Camden. He served briefly as a soldier in the Netherlands and by 1597 was an actor with PHILIP HENSLOWE's company, the Admiral's Men. In 1598, he fought a duel with a fellow-actor, Gabriel Spencer, whom he killed, avoiding execution by pleading benefit of clergy. In the same year he scored a theatrical success with *Everyman in His Humour* in which SHAKESPEARE acted. Its sequel, *Everyman out of His Humour*, was less cordially received. Both plays are examples of the so-called 'comedy of humours' in which the centre of interest is the delineation of character in terms of a 'humour' or dominant trait. In the last years of the sixteenth century and the opening ones of the seventeenth, Jonson was involved in the 'War of the Theatres' in which most of the leading dramatists of the time took part. The 'war' was caused by a mixture of personal rivalry, opposed notions of theatrical art, and economic competition.

Jonson was the author of two tragedies based on classical heroes,

Sejanus (1603) and *Catiline* (1611), neither of which was successful on stage, though both contain some fine dramatic writing. His reputation as a playwright rests on four great comedies, *Volpone* (1605), *Epicoene or the Silent Woman* (1609), *The Alchemist* (1610) and *Bartholomew Fair* (1614). In these he contrived to combine his knowledge and love of London with his flair for the depiction of the grotesque, his feeling for the vigour and flamboyance of popular speech and the didactic impulse which he inherited from his acquaintance with classical literature. The classical and popular strains in his work are often at odds with each other, but the tension between them is precisely what energizes his finest plays. In addition to the plays he wrote for the public stage, Jonson became, in the first years of the seventeenth century, the writer of some splendid MASQUES presented at the Court of James I. By its nature the Masque is an ephemeral form of entertainment in which scenery, costume, dance and music inevitably play a more important role than dialogue. His increasing dissatisfaction with the subsidiary role accorded to the dramatist in Masque led to Jonson's break with INIGO JONES, the most celebrated theatrical designer of the period.

Commercial failure, failing health and fading artistic powers mark Jonson's final years; though even a late play like *The Staple of News* (1625) has flashes of the old inventiveness and humour. In addition to being a superb comic dramatist, Jonson was also the leading literary critic of his age and the author of some incomparable lyrics, among which 'Drink to Me Only with Thine Eyes' is probably familiar to many who have never heard of its author. He died in 1637, and a group of his admirers styling themselves The Sons of Ben produced a volume dedicated to his memory, *Jonsonus Virbius*. For all his pretensions to classical erudition and his avowed contempt for the populace, Jonson's best comedies survive on the modern stage by virtue of their brilliant employment of popular devices – colourful colloquialism, the break-neck energy of FARCE and an unfailing interest in the quirks and quiddities of human nature.

J. B. Bamborough, *Jonson*, 1970.
George Parfitt, *Ben Jonson: Public Poet and Private Man*, 1976.
Alexander Leggatt, *Ben Jonson: His Vision and His Art*, 1981.
Anne Barton, *Ben Jonson: Dramatist*, 1984.

Jordan, Dorothy (Dorothea) (1762–1816). The illegitimate daughter of an actress, Dorothy Jordan was herself the mother of no less than fifteen illegitimate children. Four of these were by a gentleman named

Richard Ford who, after the liaison had continued for years, could not bring himself to make an honest woman of her. Ten were by the Duke of Clarence, later William IV, who left her in 1811. The remaining child was fathered by the manager of the Dublin theatre where she appeared from 1780 to 1782. In spite of this incessant fertility and the consequent complications, Dorothy Jordan achieved solid success as an actress, specializing in playing SHAKESPEARE's comic heroines and in BREECHES PARTS such as that of Sir Harry Wildair in FARQUHAR's *The Constant Couple*. Most of the leading literary and artistic figures of the day praised her acting, among them Byron and Sir Joshua Reynolds. She was almost as securely the queen of comedy as SARAH SIDDONS was the queen of tragedy. Her charm was proverbial. 'She ran upon the stage as a playground,' said Reynolds, 'and laughed from sincere wildness of delight.'

Brian Fothergill, *Mrs Jordan*, 1965.

Joseph, (Michael) Stephen (1921–67). Stephen Joseph was the son of an unlikely marriage between the publisher Michael Joseph and the flamboyant actress Hermione Gingold. His influence as a teacher, both at Central School and in the Drama Department of Manchester University, has been considerable. He was the major advocate of THEATRE-IN-THE-ROUND in Britain, and the founder, at Scarborough and at Stoke, of the first two professional repertory theatres-in-the-round. His vivid awareness that in order to make a case heard you have often to overstate it misled many people into believing him a monomaniac. In fact, he was a man fascinated by theatre forms, and concerned primarily that the 'round' should join other forms, not that it should replace them. His ideas are set out in *Theatre in the Round* (1967), *New Theatre Forms* (1968) and *The Story of the Playhouse in England* (1968), the last of which is a delightfully simple account intended for children.

Jouvet, Louis (1887–1951). French actor and director who became the closest associate of COPEAU at the Vieux-Colombier between 1913 and 1922. He left to establish his own company in Paris. It was at the Comédie des Champs-Elysées in 1923 that he created one of his most famous roles as Jules Romains' Dr Knock. Jouvet's love of MOLIÈRE was reflected in his repertoire, though his most famous production – a *L'École des Femmes* in which he played Arnolphe – came as late as 1936, in which year he was appointed a director of the COMÉDIE-FRANÇAISE. By that time he had already begun his long creative collaboration with JEAN GIRAUDOUX. In a series of productions, beginning with *Siegfried* in

1927–8 and continuing after the playwright's death with *The Mad-woman of Chaillot* (1945), Jouvet established and celebrated Girau-doux's subtle stylishness. His own feeling for lighting and decor was a major factor in the success of these productions, in which he also played leading roles. His *Réflexions du comédien* (1939) show the seriousness of this sensitive man of the theatre.

Bettina Knapp, *Louis Jouvet: Man of the Theatre*, 1957.

Kaiser, Georg (1878–1945). German playwright, the author of over sixty plays, most of them forgotten. He was a leader of the anti-bourgeois EXPRESSIONIST movement in Germany, and most of his writing is overlaid with a visionary fervour that can slump sensationally into bitterness. *The Burghers of Calais*, staged in 1917, was a plea for pacifism written before the declaration of war. *From Morning to Midnight*, written in 1912 but not staged until 1917, is an anti-materialistic collage. The urgent need for spiritual renewal is an obsessive theme, at its most vivid in the trilogy of *The Coral* (1917), *Gas I* (1918) and *Gas II* (1920). Kaiser stayed in Hitler's Germany until 1938, his work outlawed but his moral fervour undiminished, and then emigrated to Switzerland.

B. J. Kenworthy, *Georg Kaiser*, 1957.

Kalidasa (*c.* 5th century AD). The only Sanskrit playwright to have established an independent identity in the West, Kalidasa is known by three surviving plays, *Malavikagnimitra*, *Vikramorvasiya* and *Sakun-tala*. The last of these, first translated into English in 1789, was incorporated by opportunistic Europeans in the struggle against neo-classicism. It is a finely crafted story about a king who falls in love with a hermit's foster-child. Nothing is known about Kalidasa, an ignorance which has allowed scholars to place him in any of the first five centuries after the birth of Christ.

Kaufman, George S. (1889–1961). American playwright and direc-tor, sometimes known as 'the Great Collaborator' because of his various co-authorships. The first of these was with MARC CONNELLY, a second with Edna Ferber (*The Royal Family*, a play about the DREWS and the BARRYMORES, in 1927, *Dinner at Eight* in 1932, *Stage Door* in 1936) and perhaps the most notable with Moss Hart. Their *You Can't Take It With You* (1936) won the Pulitzer Prize, and most contemporary critics thought that their *The Man Who Came to Dinner* (1939) would do the same.

Kazan, Elia (1909–   ). American director and actor, born in Turkey of Greek parents. He studied in the Yale School of Drama, and on graduation joined the GROUP THEATRE. Known as 'Gadget' (for unspecified reasons, according to HAROLD CLURMAN), he became a central member of the Group, playing leading parts in a number of plays (Clurman found him 'thunderously effective' in *Waiting for Lefty* and a reviewer of *Night Music* called him 'one of the most exciting actors of America') and eventually directing two plays by Robert Ardrey, *Casey Jones* (1938) and *Thunder Rock* (1939). It was his production of THORNTON WILDER's *The Skin of Our Teeth* (1942) on BROADWAY that established him as a director who thought both clearly and theatrically. Kazan had the necessary dash and vision to realize the delicacy as well as the brashness of *A Streetcar Named Desire* (1947). Despite growing commitments in Hollywood his mind was still on theatre rather than film at this time. In the *Streetcar* year of 1947 he founded, in association with Cheryl Crawford and Robert Lewis, the Actors' Studio, which LEE STRASBERG would later make famous as the home of METHOD acting. Kazan's claims to be the most effective interpreter on the American stage of both TENNESSEE WILLIAMS and ARTHUR MILLER are irresistible. The success of Miller's *Death of a Salesman* (1949) owed much to Kazan's direction and to his belief in the play. Later, as director of the repertory company of the LINCOLN CENTRE (1962–4), he worked on *After the Fall* and, with Clurman, *Incident at Vichy*. And for Williams, he added to the famous *Streetcar* production an equally perceptive *Cat on a Hot Tin Roof* and a simply magnificent *Sweet Bird of Youth* (1959). Eric Bentley, remembering Kazan's youthful communism and his later preparedness to name names to the HOUSE UNAMERICAN ACTIVITIES COMMITTEE, believes that the extra dimension in Kazan's directing is 'guilt'. It is not difficult to see how that would help with Miller and Williams.

Kean, Charles (1811–68). Son of EDMUND KEAN, but lamentably respectable by contrast, and an actor who seemed wooden to his most observant contemporaries. Surviving photographs tend to confirm this. Charles Kean had been sent to Eton by a father who was sufficiently paternal to hope his son would keep off the stage. There was a lingering effect, for Charles tried to be, not only a gentlemanly actor, but also a pedagogic manager. His tenure of the Princess's Theatre (1850–9) was notable for its combination of SHAKESPEARE and 'gentlemanly' MELODRAMA, for its attraction to a little-known theatre of a cultivated audience (Queen Victoria was a patroness), and for the carefully researched detail of its Shakespearean settings. Kean was a Fellow of the

Society of Antiquaries, and his designer, William Telbin, was able to realize the results of his research. The 'programmes' of the Princess's Shakespeare productions seem comically pedantic now, but they represent an earnest endeavour to raise the status of theatre. The Queen recognized Kean's services by appointing him to supervise several performances at Windsor Castle, and he made and husbanded a lot of money. It was a mixed blessing to be Edmund Kean's son, though, and it is not as an actor that Charles Kean deserves to be remembered. (Apart from physical and vocal limitations, he had also to contend with inadequately secured false teeth.) He is a central figure in the nineteenth century's pictorial staging of Shakespeare.

J. W. Cole, *Life and Theatrical Times of Charles Kean*, 2 vols., 1859.
J. M. D. Hardwick (ed.), *Emigrant in Motley*, 1954.

Kean, Edmund (1787–1833). 'To see him act,' said Coleridge, 'is like reading Shakespeare by flashes of lightning.' He then added, 'I do not think him thorough-bred gentleman enough to play Othello.' Both observations say a lot about Kean, though he was, in fact, one of the few actors to make a success as Othello. Kean was the illegitimate child of an actress. His childhood was a misery, his early career on the stage a struggle. He made an utterly astonishing debut at Drury Lane as Shylock in 1814, sustained his reputation for three or four years, drank and wenched to excess, became involved in a number of scandals, the worst of which had him hissed off the stage for a while, toured America to try to recoup his losses, made and lost several fortunes, and struggled on to a bitter end. Kean embodies histrionically the excesses of the Romantic period. He was admired by HAZLITT and LEIGH HUNT; Keats wrote *Otho the Great* in the hope that the great actor would 'smoke the hot-blood character of Ludolph'; Byron saw him at Drury Lane in February 1814, and noted in his Journal, 'Just returned from seeing Kean in Richard. By Jove, he is a soul! Life – nature – truth – without exaggeration or diminution.' Such adulation went to his head. The famous transitions, those sudden shifts from 'high' to 'low', became habitual rather than inspirational. He probably needed time to catch his breath, and had certainly to ration his dissipated energy. What Coleridge saw was a man who could only give of his best at selected moments. Unwittingly, Kean endorsed a style of acting SHAKESPEARE in which the making of 'points' superseded the creation of character and postponed ensemble playing. Nevertheless, in demonic or charismatic roles – Shylock, Richard III, Othello, Sir Giles Overreach – Kean was the most exciting actor England has known. GEORGE HENRY LEWES, who saw him only during the last seven years of his career, has left a powerful summary. 'It is his reading of the parts, his 'points', that we applaud. He was a real innovator. But the parts he could play were few. He had no gaiety; he could not laugh; he had no playfulness that was not as the playfulness of a panther showing her claws every moment . . . It was thoroughly feline – terrible yet beautiful.'

Barry Cornwall, *Life of Edmund Kean*, 2 vols., 1835.
F. W. Hawkins, *Life of Edmund Kean*, 2 vols., 1869
H. N. Hillebrand, *Edmund Kean*, 1933.
Raymond Fitzsimmons, *Edmund Kean: Fire from Heaven*, 1976.

Keene, Laura (*c.* 1830–1873). English-born actress whose career belongs to the United States. Having made her English debut in 1851, she settled in New York in 1855, and the following year was the first woman in America to become a theatre manager. Laura Keene's Theatre was what she called it, and it remained under her management until 1863. Its outstanding success was TOM TAYLOR's *Our American Cousin* (1858). Laura Keene was also instrumental in establishing DION BOUCICAULT's reputation in America. Her own acting was melodramatic and colourful.

Kemble. English theatrical family of whom the best known are:

(1) *Siddons, Sarah* (1755–1831). She was the oldest child of this extraordinary family whose father, a theatre manager, tried to keep his children off the stage. She became the leading tragic actress on the British stage from 1782 until her retirement in 1812. Success did not come easily to Sarah, whose first Drury Lane season in 1775–6 was unremarkable. She made her reputation in the provinces, above all in Bath, and returned to Drury Lane to play the title role in SOUTHERNE's *Isabella* in 1782. It gave scope for the magnificent suffering in which she excelled. (It is not for the reading of the letter, but for the sleep-walking that her Lady Macbeth is fabled.) In an age when audiences were prone to extravagant reactions, Mrs Siddons gave the pretext for weeping, for fainting, and for shrieking. Her own control was remarkable. It enabled her to eliminate the distinction between sentimental and emotional rhetoric, and thus to play with equal success in bad and good plays. It also gave her an undeserved reputation for personal coldness. According to contemporary gossip, 'Byron said he should as soon think of going to bed with the Archbishop of Canterbury as with Mrs Siddons.' The same could not have been said of most actresses (certainly not by Byron), and Mrs Siddons raised the dignity of her profession. She was a

dutiful wife to an uninspiring husband, gave him seven children, but was increasingly at odds with him. Scandal linked her name to that of the painter Sir Thomas Lawrence, whose relationship with two of her daughters reads like a melodramatic heightening of a novel by Jane Austen, but the probability is that this was an innocent friendship. It can remind us, though, that this redoubtable lady was much more vulnerable than her public was allowed to know.

Roger Manvell, *Sarah Siddons*, 1970.

(2) **Kemble, John Philip** (1757–1823). Eldest surviving son of the family, John was one of the many actors who laboured to raise the status of theatre. Having made his London debut in 1783, he remained at the head of his profession until 1816. A less unbending man might have had less trouble with the OLD PRICE RIOTS of 1809, when, as manager of the newly reopened Covent Garden Theatre, he tried to defend the increased cost of admission; but a less unbending man would have had less success as SHAKESPEARE's Roman heroes, Brutus and Coriolanus. Kemble was unrivalled in roles requiring stateliness and classic poise. His detractors, noting his habit of standing with one hand on his hip and the other outstretched, mocked him as the leader of 'the teapot school'. As an asthmatic, he had to take his time, and the Kemble pause was almost as famous as the MACREADY pause which replaced it. But he was an athletic actor when occasion demanded it. Lacking the charisma of EDMUND KEAN, Kemble had the good sense to retire soon after Kean's London debut. His career had seen him coping with the impossible SHERIDAN at Drury Lane from 1788 to 1802, and then as manager of Covent Garden from 1802 until his retirement in 1816. The austere and rather unattractive public image is only part of the truth. Kemble was a complex and passionate man who tried, and often failed, to hold his career at arm's length.

James Boaden, *Memoirs of the Life of John Philip Kemble*, 2 vols., 1825. Linda Kelly, *The Kemble Era*, 1980.

(3) **Kemble, Stephen** (1758–1822). Stephen was the fat brother, long celebrated for playing Falstaff without padding. His importance as a theatre manager in Newcastle and Edinburgh should not be neglected by students of the provincial theatre, but his acting was not universally admired. HAZLITT commented, after seeing him in *The Merry Wives of Windsor* at Drury Lane in 1816: 'We see no more reason why Mr Stephen Kemble should play Falstaff than why Louis XVIII is qualified to fill a throne, because he is fat, and belongs to a particular family.'

(4) *Kemble, Charles* (1775–1854). The eleventh child of the family, Charles made his London debut in 1794 as Malcolm to his brother John Philip's Macbeth. His sister Sarah was Lady Macbeth. He continued acting until 1836. He had the advantage of being tall, handsome and graceful – and well related. Less fortunately born, he might not have had the chance to play Hamlet, Benedick, Mercutio and Faulconbridge. He was, though, a well intentioned man. As actor-manager of Covent Garden from 1822 to 1832 he can claim the credit for the 1823 revival of *King John*, in which historically researched and carefully made costumes graced the Shakespearean stage for almost the first time, and for his perception of the attractiveness to audiences of Weber's *Der Freischütz*, staged at Covent Garden in 1824–5. From 1836 to 1840, he was a comparatively inoffensive Examiner of Plays for the Lord Chamberlain.

Jane Williamson, *Charles Kemble: Man of the Theatre*, 1970.

(5) *Kemble, Fanny* (1809–93). This indomitable Victorian lady was the daughter of Charles Kemble. She turned actress in 1829, when her father's management of Covent Garden hit financial crisis. After her debut as Juliet, she played a succession of roles which had been the property of her aunt Sarah. Touring America with her father, she fell in love with and married a rich young Philadelphian, not realizing that he was a slave-owner. This discovery, and her horror at the practices she witnessed, was a major factor in the breakdown of her marriage to Pierce Butler. She left him in 1845, and there was a divorce scandal. After a brief return to acting, Fanny Kemble began the famous series of Shakespeare readings which were her chief resource between 1848 and 1873. HENRY IRVING described his own experience of a Kemble reading to ELLEN TERRY a little uncharitably: 'After a portentous wait, on swept a lady with an extraordinarily flashing eye, a masculine and muscular outside. Pounding the book with terrific energy, as if she wished to knock the stuffing out of it, she announced in thrilling tones: HAM-A-LETTE. By Will-y-am Shak-es-peare.' Photographs and other accounts lend support to Irving's view. The taste of the age was for the grand effect, and Fanny Kemble had courage enough to carry her up to, and sometimes over, the top.

Constance Wright, *Fanny Kemble and the Lovely Land*, 1974.
Dorothy Marshall, *Fanny Kemble*, 1977.

Kempe, Will (*c.* 1550–*c.* 1607). Kempe was the best-loved clown in the London theatre after the death of RICHARD TARLTON. He specialized in broad comedy, relying on a rapport with his audience, and in the popular jigs (rhymed farces with song and dance) that followed the afternoon performance of plays in the open-air theatres. He was a leading member of SHAKESPEARE's company in the last decade of the sixteenth century and was certainly the original Dogberry in *Much Ado about Nothing*. His sudden departure when the company moved to the GLOBE in 1598–9 has given rise to speculation about Shakespeare's disapproval of his tendency to prefer his own words to the author's. He may also have been in dispute with his colleagues about the relative merits of plays and jigs. Whatever the reason, Kempe sold his share in the Globe and took his genius for self-advertisement elsewhere, most famously to Norwich on the nine-day morris dance from London in 1600, of which he published a pamphlet account under the title *Kemps Nine Daies Wonder*. This extravagant marathon was the result of a wager. It is the last we hear of Will Kempe. Even his death is obscure.

Chris Harris, *Will Kemp: Shakespeare's Forgotten Clown*, 1983.

Killigrew, Thomas (1612–83). Killigrew wrote several plays but his place in the history of drama does not depend on any of these, which is just as well. He was born in London, was a page to Charles I, was imprisoned during the Civil War and followed the future Charles II into exile in France. At the Restoration he obtained, with DAVENANT, a patent to produce plays in London. In 1663 he built the Theatre Royal in Drury Lane and was Master of the Revels from 1673. He had neither the inclination nor the aptitude to be a theatrical manager and resigned the job to his son Charles. Davenant's company soon outstripped Killigrew's in popularity.

A. Harbage, *Thomas Killigrew: Cavalier Dramatist*, 1930.

Kleist, Heinrich von (1777–1811). Born into a Prussian military family, and intended for the army, Kleist resigned his commission in 1799 to undertake a dangerously earnest moral education. His encounter with the philosophy of Kant destroyed his confidence in the possibility of purposeful living. The casual chaos, which he believed to be the alternative, tormented him for the rest of his life. He was contemplating suicide as early as 1803, and died finally in a carefully planned pact with the wife of a friend. Kleist's best-known play, *The Broken Jug* (1806), is a comedy which brilliantly rearranges the tragic ingredients of *Oedipus*. A corrupt village judge conducts a trial in which his whole endeavour is to protect the real culprit – himself. The Weimar production of 1807 was a failure, GOETHE having made the mistake of dividing the play's single act into three parts. *Das Kätchen von Heilbronn* (1810) was the only other play performed in Kleist's lifetime, but the German theatre has subsequently recovered *Amphitryon* (1805), *Penthesilea* (1807), and above all *Prinz Friedrich von Homburg* (1810).

W. Silz, *Heinrich von Kleist: Studies in His Work and Literary Character*, 1961.

Joachim Maass, *Kleist: A Biography*, 1984.

Knipper, Olga (1868–1959). One of the founder members of the MOSCOW ART THEATRE, for which she created her last role, as Lady Markby in OSCAR WILDE's *An Ideal Husband*, in 1946. She married the already ailing CHEKHOV in 1901, and it was in his plays, above all as Masha in *The Three Sisters*, that she excelled. Her decision to return to Moscow after the Revolution was not taken lightly. It would have been equally easy for her in 1922 to remain with what became known as the Prague Group of the Moscow Art Theatre. What cannot be said with confidence is that she never regretted the decision.

Harvey Pitcher, *Chekhov's Leading Lady*, 1979.

Knowles, James Sheridan (1784–1862). In a very fair dig at Knowles's inflated reputation, BULWER-LYTTON wrote to MACREADY in 1838, 'I say, when a door is to be shut, "Shut the door". Knowles would say, as I think he has said somewhere, "Let the room be airless".' The plain fact is that certain critics had hailed Knowles as the first great exponent of blank-verse tragedy since SHAKESPEARE. For that misjudgment, Macready was quite as responsible as Knowles. It was on Macready's recommendation that *Virginius* was staged at Covent Garden in 1820. His affecting performance in the title role confirmed his reputation and transformed Knowles's life. The story is the familiar one of Appius and Virginia, but the interest here is centred on Virginia's father. The formality of the verse cannot disguise the simple domesticity of paternal love – and that is precisely why the play worked. Fatherhood is as much a nineteenth-century theme as motherhood; stern morality and the bitten lip of overwhelming affection combine in it. Macready, in private life a passionate and suffering father, was its supreme theatrical portrayer. After *Virginius* Knowles wrote for him an undistinguished but tolerably successful play about another father, *William Tell* (1825), and the later paternal tragedy *John of Procida* (1840) was intended for, though rejected by, him. None of these plays deserves revival. If Knowles offers anything more than encouraging evidence that every age makes its mistakes, it may prove to be in his neglected comedies, *The Love-Chase* (1837) and *Old Maids* (1841), where there is much genuine sprightliness.

L. H. Meeks, *Knowles and the Theatre of His Time*, 1933.

Koltai, Ralph (1924–   ). Stage-designer, born in Berlin, but active primarily in the British theatre. Koltai's striking, textured sets for the ROYAL SHAKESPEARE COMPANY's productions of *The Jew of Malta* and *The Merchant of Venice* (1964–5) were a characteristically declamatory statement of his artistic talent. He is a stage-sculptor. *Brand* at the NATIONAL THEATRE (1978) had a set which combined the simplicity and the menace of a fairy tale by the brothers Grimm. Koltai relies on his own dominant impression of a play or opera, and there is always a risk that his set will do too much work.

Komisarjevsky, Theodore (1882–1954). Russian director, the son of an opera singer. He was active in the pre-Revolutionary Russian theatre and much influenced by STANISLAVSKY about whom he later wrote a book. He emigrated to England in 1919 and directed a series of Russian plays at an out-of-the-way theatre in Barnes. These attracted sufficient attention to give him wider access and the English theatre of the thirties was much enhanced by his high-spirited adventurousness. Komisarjevsky was almost as much concerned with design as with direction and the aluminium scenery of his STRATFORD *Macbeth* shocked the conservative audience of 1933. Later Stratford productions included a joyous *Merry Wives of Windsor* (1935) and a magnificent *King Lear* (1936). For the last eighteen years of his life, Komisarjevsky lived irrepressibly in America, directing plays and operas with flair and fun. His sister Vera Komisarjevskaya (1864–1910) was a leading actress in St Petersburg, where she ran her own theatre. Her experimental ardour led her, briefly, to employ MEYERHOLD as a director. In 1906 she played the lead in his productions of *Hedda Gabler* and MAETERLINCK's *Sister Beatrice*. By 1907, unwilling to serve as a puppet-actress, she was writing to Meyerhold a letter of dismissal: 'I have arrived at the firm conviction that you and I do not share the same views on the theatre.' Harassed by debts, she took her company on tour, first to the United States and then to Tashkent, where she contracted smallpox and died.

Kotzebue, August Friedrich Ferdinand von (1761–1819). The vogue for sensational passion, excited by SCHILLER's *Die Räuber*, was unerringly gratified by Kotzebue, who had the popular dramatist's ability to identify a taste and write down to it. Coleridge once called him 'the German Beaumont and Fletcher'. Several of his two hundred or so plays reached the English stage in variously mutilated versions, and were instrumental in establishing the mixed mode of MELODRAMA. At the end of the eighteenth century, patriotic dramatic critics were bemoaning the domination of the English stage by a German dramatist; a dramatist, to make matters worse, with a dangerously liberal attitude to sex. (During exactly the same years, WILLIAM DUNLAP was turning Kotzebue's plays into box-office salvation at the Park Theatre in New York.) *Menschenhass und Reue* (1789) was toned down by Benjamin Thompson for performance at Drury Lane as *The Stranger* in 1798. The same year had seen the presentation at Covent Garden of *Lovers' Vows*, MRS INCHBALD's version of *Das Kind der Liebe*. This is the play whose rehearsal precipitates and echoes some romantic excesses in Jane Austen's *Mansfield Park*. In 1799, SHERIDAN cashed in with *Pizarro*, a hastily written version of *Die Spanier in Peru*, which was a financial success at least. What is perhaps Kotzebue's best play, a comedy called *Die deutschen Kleinstädter* (1803), was much less influential. Any popular dramatist risks being remembered for inferior work. After a mixed career as civil servant, theatre manager and diplomat, Kotzebue was stabbed to death by a German university student, who was part of the Youth Movement that Kotzebue deplored.

L. F. Thompson, *Kotzebue*, 1928.

Kyd, Thomas (1558–94). One of the most popular and influential Elizabethan plays, *The Spanish Tragedy* (*c.* 1589), was written by Thomas Kyd, yet the first ten editions of the play (1592–1633) made no mention of his name, which goes to show how unimportant a figure an author was in the early days of English professional theatre. Kyd was born in London and educated at Merchant Taylor's School, and may have been a scrivener in his early youth. He shared rooms with CHRISTOPHER MARLOWE, whom he accused of heresy and blasphemy, probably under torture. He is very much a ONE-PLAY AUTHOR, his only other play being an adaptation of Robert Garnier's French tragedy *Cornelia*. *The Spanish Tragedy* was a sensational success and contemporary literature is full of allusions to and parodies of it. Fifteen years after it was first staged, PHILIP HENSLOWE, a hard-headed theatrical impresario, employed BEN JONSON, an established dramatist, to write some extra scenes for a revival. The play set the pattern for tragedies of revenge, based on SENECA's classical dramas of bloody familial intrigue. Its most distinguished English successor is *Hamlet*, itself possibly derived from an earlier play by Kyd. Though *The Spanish Tragedy* had long fallen out of favour, Kyd's sense of dramatic form and his handling of rhetorical figures have brought it some renewed success on the modern stage.

A. Freeman, *Kyd: Facts and Problems*, 1967.

Labiche, Eugène (1815–88). French playwright, born into the Parisian bourgeoisie of which he wrote so mercilessly and of which he remained contentedly a member. Instead of pursuing a legal career, he wrote reviews for the *Revue du théâtre* from 1835. Briefly affected by the tumultuous Romantic movement in the Parisian theatre, he nevertheless preferred to write his first play (1838) in the popular VAUDEVILLE style. His first real success was *A Young Man in a Hurry* (1848), a one-act play with songs staged at the Palais Royal, home of the vaudeville. This was one of only four plays (he is credited with 175) that Labiche wrote unaided by a collaborator. 'Vaudeville,' says one of the characters in the play, 'is the art of making the girl's father, who first said no, say yes'. That, with the inevitable aid of mistaken identity (FARCE relies on *quidproquo* even more than on doors), is what *A Young Man in a Hurry* does. It was *An Italian Straw Hat* (1851) that established Labiche as a leading dramatist. The play is a masterpiece of sustained confusion and the sheer rapidity of Labiche's invention is overwhelming. It made him rich and secure enough to buy a château in Sologne and combine the life of a gentleman farmer with that of a manufacturer of plays. *Monsieur Perrichon's Voyage* (1860) is a precise portrait of bourgeois values, warmer than Labiche's own favourite, *The Well-Liked Célimare* (1863). The 'cruel brand of realism camouflaged by whimsy' observed by Leonard Pronko is displayed in both these plays, as it is in *The Piggy Bank* (*La Cagnotte*, 1864). Labiche was flattered when the COMÉDIE-FRANÇAISE staged *Me* in 1864, but the Palais Royal was his natural home. When the public interest in vaudeville began to wane, he had the tact and the money to abandon writing plays. That was in 1877. The publication of his plays (fifty-seven of them selected by himself) in 1878 improved his standing and he was elected to the French Academy in 1880. Remembered as a superb farcemaker, he should also be recognized as a satirist. He wrote, in a literary retrospect: 'Among all the types possible, I chose the bourgeois. He is inexhaustible. He is a pearl of stupidity that can be strung a hundred different ways.'

Leonard C. Pronko, *Eugène Labiche and Georges Feydeau*, 1982.

Lamb, Charles (1775–1834). The contrasts in Lamb's life, on the one hand a humdrum job with the East India Company and on the other a self-sacrificing devotion to a sister so mentally unstable that she killed her mother in a fit of homicidal mania, are a drama in themselves. His own contributions to the theatre are of three distinct kinds. Firstly, he was a dramatist – of his four plays *John Woodvil* (1802) is a tragedy in which remorse dominates to the point of feebleness, *Mr H.* is a short FARCE which was hissed when performed at Drury Lane in 1806, and the other two are worse. Secondly, he was an essayist and occasional critic, best remembered for his endearing celebration of ELLISTON, whom he called 'the great lessee', and the comedian, Munden. Thirdly, he was a pioneering popularizer of the work of SHAKESPEARE and his contemporaries. His *Specimens of English Dramatic Poets who lived about the time of Shakespeare* (1808) was a landmark in the revival of interest in the great age of English drama and the *Tales from Shakespeare* (1807), which he wrote with his sister Mary, is a children's book of genius. In 1817, the timid Lamb fell in love with actress Fanny Kelly. His letter of proposal and her graceful rejection have survived and provide the outline of a touching episode (see Miscellany). Lamb seems to have made no other attempt at marriage. He remained with his sister until his death.

F. V. Morley, *Lamb before Elia*, 1932.

Lane, Louisa, See DREW.

Laughton, Charles (1899–1962). English actor, who became a Hollywood star, but was never at peace with himself, either despite or because of that. He was an outstanding Angelo in TYRONE GUTHRIE's *Measure for Measure* during the 1933–4 OLD VIC season, when he also played SHAKESPEARE's Henry VIII, whose 'private life' had been a famous film success for him. His remarkable collaboration with BRECHT on the American version of *Galileo* (1947) was celebrated by Brecht in essays, and in a poem on 'Laughton's Belly':

> All of them, the way they carry their bellies around
> You'd think it was swag with someone in pursuit of it
> But the great man Laughton performed his like a poem
> For his edification and nobody's discomfort.

It was the combination of hedonism and intellectual passion in Laughton's performance that made his Galileo so fine; for Laughton was always mentally as well as physically substantial. His last notable stage performances were as Bottom and King Lear at STRATFORD-upon-Avon in 1959. A sometimes tormented man, he was not easy to act with because he forgave himself no failure. When he was acting well, no one in the audience doubted that acting was important.

Charles Higham, *Charles Laughton*, 1976.

Lawson, John Howard (1894–1977). American writer of plays and films, whose career was cut short by the Hollywood probings of the HOUSE UNAMERICAN ACTIVITIES COMMITTEE. He had made his name with *Processional* (1925), an episodic marrying of VAUDEVILLE techniques and socialist optimism. Lawson's subsequent move towards communism did not lead to much improvement in his plays. *Success Story* (1932) and *Gentlewoman* (1934) were produced, without much success, by the GROUP THEATRE. Much of Lawson's intellectual energy after 1934 was consumed by his leadership of the communist 'factions' in Hollywood. In 1947, summoned before the House Committee, Lawson vehemently protested against the proceedings, and was dragged out. As one of the 'Hollywood Ten', he served a one-year sentence for contempt in 1950–1951. 'If I can be destroyed,' he said in the statement he was not allowed to read, 'no American is safe.' The disturbing truth is that he *was* virtually destroyed.

Lee, Nathaniel (*c.* 1653–1692). Almost completely forgotten today, Lee was one of the most popular tragic dramatists in an age when the idea of tragedy had shrunk to bombast and lurid spectacle. Lee's tragedies are certainly not lacking in these ingredients, but the best of them *The Rival Queens; or, The Death of Alexander the Great* (1677) has moments of genuine dramatic power and its language, while suffering from the metaphorical obsessiveness which characterized Lee's style, occasionally rises to an intensity which, if not truly tragic, comes acceptably close. Lee started life as an actor when he came up to London from Cambridge University, but soon turned to playwriting, confining himself almost entirely to tragedies on classical and Renaissance themes where he tried to apply neo-classic rules to what the age thought of as the Shakespearean manner. He also wrote a comedy, *The Princess of Cleve* (1681), adapted from Mme de la Fayette's novel, which contains a satirical portrait of his friend Rochester. Like many of the characters in his tragedies, Lee went mad and spent five years in Bedlam, dying shortly after his discharge.

Roswell G. Ham, *Otway and Lee*, 1931.

Leigh, Mike (1943–   ). Born and brought up in Salford and trained at the Royal Academy of Dramatic Art, Mike Leigh began working through improvisation towards a finished (or at least performable) play at the Midlands Arts Centre in Birmingham in 1965. Gradually he evolved a technique, as dependent on his own ability to withhold comment as it was on his equal ability to perceive possibilities, of beginning only with characters and arriving at an appropriate situation (or play) almost by stealth. *Bleak Moments* (1970) was the first piece to attract attention, particularly when its film version began to collect international prizes. It has been followed by *Hard Labour* (1973), devised for television, *Wholesome Glory* (1973), *Babies Grow Old* (1974), *Nuts in May* (1976), a television film, *Abigail's Party* (1977), which has its audience squirming with embarrassed self-recognition, *Ecstasy* (1979), *Goose-Pimples* (1981) and others. If, during rehearsal, Leigh and his actors get the characters right, the emerging play is certain to reflect, without any superimposed plan, the shopday crises, dreams and terrors of a society in a semi-recognized decline.

Paul Clements, *The Improvised Play: The Work of Mike Leigh*, 1983.

Leigh, Vivien (1913–67). English actress, born Vivian Hartley, whose delicate beauty won her the part of Scarlett O'Hara in the film of *Gone with the Wind* (1939) and whose incisive skill sustained it. She had achieved some success on the London stage, initially as a society prostitute in an unimpressive play called *The Mask of Virtue* (1935) and then with Ivor Novello in *The Happy Hypocrite* (1936). In 1937 she played Ophelia to LAURENCE OLIVIER's Hamlet on the OLD VIC tour to Denmark. Leigh and Olivier were married in 1940 and their Hollywood careers were interrupted by the events of World War II. The war years were not fruitful for Leigh, and the depressive illness that clouded her last years began to manifest itself. Playing Antigone at the Old Vic (1949) and, particularly, Blanche du Bois in TENNESSEE WILLIAMS's *A Streetcar Named Desire* (1949) exacerbated her condition, though her feverish honesty on stage remained impressive. It was as Blanche that she established herself as a major actress on the London stage. It was a triumph she never quite repeated.

Anne Edwards, *Vivien Leigh*, 1977.
John Russell Taylor, *Vivien Leigh*, 1984.

Lemaître, Frédérick (1800–76). French actor, whose brilliant career associates him with the excesses as well as the achievements of the French Romantic drama. He was a malevolent comedian, whose acting, according to HUGO, moved audiences to 'terror joined with laughter'. Lemaître was the brightest star of the Parisian alternative theatre in the

BOULEVARD DU TEMPLE. He made his debut as a lion in 1815, but it was in an undistinguished MELODRAMA called *L'Auberge des Adrets* (1823) that he made history. His playing of Robert Macaire turned this petty villain into a raffish symbol of the age's republican spirit. 'Types like Macaire are not created every day,' wrote Flaubert much later. 'Indeed, I cannot think of a greater one since Don Juan.' He was referring to Lemaître's own sequel, *Robert Macaire* (1834), a work which certainly contributed to the downfall of Louis-Philippe. Earlier successes included the frightening portrait of a rake's progress in *Trente ans* (1827), when he first teamed up with the actress Marie Dorval, the name part in *Richard Darlington* (1831), which a contemporary critic called 'not just a success, but a madness, a mania, a craving, a necessity', and Gennaro opposite MLLE GEORGE in HUGO's *Lucrèce Borgia* (1833). By then, Lemaître was living dangerously, drinking too much (even in old age, he consumed twenty-five bottles of bordeaux a week), and giving and taking offence. DUMAS called him the French KEAN, ' a man of a capricious nature, violent and passionate – and therefore very natural in passionate, violent and capricious parts'. In his own play, *Kean* (1836), Dumas provided Lemaître with a superb opportunity to merit the comparison, as Hugo did in *Ruy Blas* (1838). Lemaître's London performances earned him from the *Illustrated London News* in 1847 the title of 'the most extraordinary actor in the world'. Pierre Brasseur, playing Lemaître in the fascinating film *Les Enfants du paradis* (1944), sought ways of conveying the fierce charisma of this wayward star.

Robert Baldick, *The Life and Times of Frédérick Lemaître*, 1959.

Lessing, Gotthold Ephraim (1729–81). German dramatist and critic whose influence and example changed the course of the emergent German theatre. Lessing's was one of the great analytical intelligences – 'Making distinctions is his forte,' wrote GOETHE. His first plays were written while he was a student in Leipzig, and the drama remained his major, though not his exclusive, concern. *Laocoön* (1766), an aesthetic treatise establishing boundaries between poetry and the plastic arts, gave to German poets a liberating sense of new possibilities. In 1767, Lessing undertook the task of writing regular criticism for the new National Theatre in Hamburg. These essays, collected in the *Hamburgische Dramaturgie* (1769), combine criticism of performances with theoretical and historical reflections, all tending to further the cause of a German drama independent of the previously prevailing French models. Lessing preferred English models, including SHAKESPEARE, to whose subsequent influence in Germany he played herald. Of his own best-known plays, *Miss Sara Sampson* (1755) is a bourgeois tragedy influenced by Samuel Richardson's novels and LILLO's *George Barn-well*. With the best will in the world, it has to be called turgid. *Emilia Galotti* (1772) is a variation on the tragic story of Appius and Virginia. Despite Lessing's disclaimers, its middle-class protest against princely tyranny is unmistakable, but the play struggles to survive in an age less generous to emotion. The verse play *Nathan the Wise* (1779) is a wonderfully open-minded argument for religious tolerance, in which Lessing's fondness for the form of the fable finds extended expression. His finest play is the comedy *Minna von Barnhelm* (1767), which is built round carefully realized characters and given a contemporary setting. It can claim to be the first German comedy.

H. B. Garland, *Lessing: The Founder of Modern German Literature*, 1962.

F. J. Lamport, *Lessing and Drama*, 1982.

Lewes, George Henry (1817–78). The grandson of a notable actor, Charles Lee Lewes, George Henry Lewes was a man of many parts – philosopher, linguist, actor, dramatist, novelist, critic and dabbler in the law, business and medicine. Fourteen of his plays, most of them adaptations from the French, were performed during his lifetime, the most successful being *The Game of Speculation*, an adaptation of Balzac's *Le Faiseur*, which provided the younger CHARLES MATHEWS with one of his finest parts, that of Affable Hawk. Lewes's dramatic criticism has lasted better than his plays. The earliest examples were written for *The Leader* (1850–54), of which Lewes was joint-editor with LEIGH HUNT's son, Thornton. The longer essays he wrote for the *Pall Mall Gazette* in 1875 were published in book form under the title *On Actors and the Art of Acting*. They are among the best pieces ever written on the subject, eloquent and penetrating. Lewes was one of the distinguished amateurs who acted with Dickens, having earlier worked professionally for a brief spell in Manchester. It is a pity that his theatrical essays are less often remembered than his long liaison with George Eliot, which began in 1854 and lasted until his death.

Lillo, George (1693–1739). The popularity of *George Barnwell; or The London Merchant* (1731) lasted a century, and established the style of bourgeois tragedy which influenced LESSING and the German theatre. Little is known of Lillo, but the chances are that he was a complacent prig whose profession as a jeweller allowed him to strengthen the ties linking religion to the rise of capitalism. *The London Merchant*, like *The Christian Hero* (1734), *Fatal Curiosity* (1736) and *Arden of Faversham*

(1736?), is weighed down with moral exhortation, and tends to identify industry with virtue. It is like a series of Hogarth engravings with all the fine detail and humour removed. The eighteenth-century fashion of crying in the theatre suited Lillo, and audiences admired his ability 'to render the distresses of common and domestic life equally interesting to the audiences as those of kings and heroes'. For those delighted to see it done at all, it evidently mattered little that is was badly done.

Littlewood, Joan (1914–   ). London-born director and innovator. Having won a scholarship to the Royal Academy of Dramatic Art, she discovered a dislike of the theatre of privilege. She moved to Manchester, founding there with the folk-singer/dramatist Ewan MacColl the left-wing Theatre of Action. Still in Manchester after the war, she founded the Theatre Workshop which, after years of touring, settled in London's suburbs at the Theatre Royal, Stratford East in 1953. Major productions, characterized by a highly theatrical combustibility, included BEHAN's *The Quare Fellow* (1956) and *The Hostage* (1958), and Shelagh Delaney's *A Taste of Honey* (1958). Every success threatened the ensemble, either by turning the actors into stars or by pulling the company away from Stratford into the West End, and in 1961 Joan Littlewood decided to forsake the theatre for the 'fun palace'. The 'fun palace' scheme was a splendid one, a rough-and-tumble combination of art and self-expression for the people; but it proved financially over-challenging, and in 1963 Joan Littlewood was back in Stratford, devising with Charles Chilton and the company a documentary song-and-satire show which became famous as *Oh What a Lovely War*. Instinctively a Luddite, Joan Littlewood is a victim of the Arts Council's disarming preparedness to subsidize iconoclasm. Having celebrated and served what she has called 'the knockabout art of theatre', she seems to have been 'recognized' into comparative inno-cuousness. She will be remembered, though, for the marvellous damage she did to the dangerously decent English theatre.

Howard Goorney, *The Theatre Workshop Story*, 1981.

Lorca, Federico Garcia (1898–1936). Spanish poet and playwright, whose stated republican sympathies led to his 'execution' by right-wing rebels in the early days of the Civil War. He was born and killed in Granada, about which he wrote, when his historical play *Mariana Pineda* (1927) was performed, 'If by the grace of God I become famous, half of that fame will belong to Granada.' Much of Lorca's writing is intensely local, and all of it national. The peasant tragedies, *Blood Wedding* (1933), *Yerma* (1934) and *The House of Bernarda Alba* (1936), are his best-known plays; but the comic verve of *Don Perlimplin* (1931) and *The Shoemaker's Prodigious Wife* (1931), and the sombre tone of *Dona Rosita the Spinster* (1935) are impressive, too. With the advent of the Republic in 1931, Lorca was appointed director of La Barraca, a travelling theatre company with a social and educational mission. Amid the rumblings of reactionary hostility in 1936, he told an interviewer: 'At this dramatic point in time, the artist should laugh and cry with the people. We must put down the bunch of lilies and bury ourselves up to the waist in mud to help those who are *looking* for lilies.' Loathed for his homosexuality as well as for his republicanism by the violent factions of the right, Lorca was an early victim of the fascist terror in Granada.

Ian Gibson, *The Assassination of Lorca*, 1979.
Gwynne Edwards, *Lorca: The Theatre beneath the Sea*, 1980.

Losey, Joseph (1909–84). Better known as the director of such films as *The Servant* (1963), *Accident* (1967) and *The Go-Between* (1971), Losey was lost to the American theatre by the persecution of Senator Joseph McCarthy in 1951–2. He worked as a stage manager in New York in 1931–2, and retained an informed interest in the technicalities of staging plays. During a study visit to Russian theatres in 1935, Losey was excited by the adventurous direction of Nikolai Okhlopkov, and adapted Okhlopkov's methods of breaking out of the proscenium in the three pieces he directed for the LIVING NEWSPAPER in New York, particularly in *Injunction Granted* (1936). This production was too political even for HALLIE FLANAGAN, director of the FEDERAL THEATRE PROJECT, and Losey resigned from the Living Newspaper Unit. His use of film during these documentary pieces was already leading him towards the cinema, and he made his first film, a short called *Pete Roleum and His Cousins*, in 1939. After World War II, when he served in the American army, Losey's work in the theatre was limited, but it was his tact and forbearance as director of BRECHT's *Galileo* with CHARLES LAUGHTON in the title role that contrived to get the play staged, despite the awkward presence of both author and actor, in 1947. 'What's our motivation?' the American actors would ask, and Losey recalled how Brecht instructed him to answer, 'What's the motivation of a tightrope walker not to fall off the high wire?' As the director of *Galileo*, which he later made into a fine film, and of the Living Newspaper's most challenging work, Losey has a place in the modern American theatre.

Loutherbourg, Philip de (1740–1812). Born in Alsace, where he studied art, de Loutherbourg first worked in the theatre in Paris. He was a painter after the romantic style of Salvator Rosa, and he was interested in transferring the wild landscapes and dramatic lighting of his paintings on to the stage. His significant work in theatre design was done at Drury Lane between 1771 and 1782. There he challenged the rigid adherence to perspective scenery based on back flats and receding wings by introducing free-standing scenic pieces (there were forty-two of these in an ocean he designed for *Omai*). Equally important were his lighting innovations. By shining a light through revolving coloured silks at the side of the stage, he turned a forest in *A Christmas Tale* from green to sudden blood-red. The combination of romantic landscapes and changes of light was best displayed in the spectacular staging of *The Wonders of Derbyshire* (1779). De Loutherbourg had sketched landscapes in that county, and reproduced such eye-catching scenes as Matlock at sunset and Dovedale by moonlight. After leaving Drury Lane, he devoted much time to the exhibition of his Eidophusikon. This was a model theatre with a stage six feet wide and eight feet deep on which he produced atmospheric transformations by the play of light on transparencies. To enhance the popularity of the Eidophusikon, he added more and more sophisticated mechanical effects, including a wave machine turned on spindles and a display of clouds on rolling cylinders. His inventions were remembered by the builders of spectacular stage machinery in the nineteenth century.

Lowin, John (1576–1653). From his portrait in the Ashmolean Museum, Lowin appears to have been a big fat man, so it is no surprise to learn that, according to James Wright in *Historia Histrionica*, he played the role of Falstaff, among others. He is said to have instructed DAVENANT in the title role of SHAKESPEARE's *Henry VIII* and the latter to have instructed BETTERTON in the same part after the Restoration. If the tradition is true, Lowin represents one of the links between the pre- and post-Restoration theatre. His long acting career began with Worcester's Men in 1602 and according to Wright, Lowin was still acting in 1648, when troops raided the Cockpit Theatre. He seems to have died in poverty; but not before his memories of his years with the King's Men, recorded by later writers, had preserved some information about Shakespeare's company that would otherwise have been lost.

Lugné-Poë, Aurélien-Marie (1869–1940). French director and actor whose youthful enthusiasm for the avant-garde Symbolist movement in France led to his adding the name of Edgar Allan Poe to his own surname of Lugné. He was a founder-member of an adventurous amateur group, the Cercle des Escholiers, in 1886 and associated with

Paul Fort in the work of the Théâtre d'Art. He shared with Fort an eager delight in the indistinct symbolism of MAETERLINCK, playing a leading role in Fort's production of *The Intruder* in 1891. It was Lugné-Poë's determination to stage another Maeterlinck play, *Pelléas and Mélisande*, that led to his forming an independent company which became known as the Théâtre de l'Oeuvre. Lugné-Poë's interest in whatever was original or experimental was insufficiently discriminating, but his Theatre became the focus of all that was modern in French art. The painter Vuillard and the poet Mauclair were Lugné-Poë's associates in the foundation of the Théâtre de L'Oeuvre. He was self-consciously part of a vast movement whose aim was to extend the range of art, shocking the bourgeoisie on the way. Bold as Lugné-Poë was, JARRY was bolder, and the production of *Ubu Roi* at the Théâtre de L'Oeuvre was more the playwright's doing than Lugné-Poë's. The shock-waves did the cause more good than harm, but Lugné-Poë's theatrical style is better represented by the dimly lit symbolist productions of IBSEN's work – a *John Gabriel Borkman* with designs by Munch, in 1897 for example –than by the flamboyant crudity of *Ubu Roi*. Lugné-Poë brought to the attention of Parisian audiences many of the most prominent foreign dramatists, STRINDBERG and HAUPTMANN as well as Ibsen, and he remained in the forefront of theatrical experiment, even to the point of giving ARTAUD his first acting experience in 1921, long after most of his contemporaries had fallen silent.

Lunt, Alfred. See FONTANNE, LYNN.

Lyly, John (1553–1606). Lyly's career is almost a text-book example of the vicissitudes of professional life in Elizabeth I's Court. At Oxford University he had Elizabeth's chief minister Burleigh for a patron and later became secretary to Burleigh's son-in-law the Earl of Oxford, who supported a company of boy actors. Lyly was appointed assistant master of Paul's Boys (the company of child-actors and singers attached to the cathedral) after the phenomenal success of his pastoral prose romance *Euphues* (1578) and its sequel *Euphues and His England* (1580). Shortly after this he obtained a post in the Revels Office which supervised Court entertainment, and all his theatrical work was done for performance by Paul's Boys before Elizabeth and her Court. All his plays, most of them based on classical mythology, are frankly artificial in language, character and setting and are closer to Court MASQUE than to plays proper. Like the Masque they have courtly compliment and celebration rather than dramatic conflict as both theme and method. Many of them contain allegorical allusions to Court figures and situations, including that of the Queen herself, and some of them, such as *Endymion* (1588), deliberately dissolve the artificial play-world into the real world of Elizabeth and her Court at the close. In spite of a dramatic career devoted assiduously to Court flattery, Lyly was unsuccessful in his attempt to obtain the post of Master of the Revels and died an embittered man.

G. K. Hunter, *John Lyly: The Humanist as Courtier*, 1962.

Lytton, Lord. See BULWER, EDWARD.

Macklin, Charles (*c.* 1699–1797). Born in Ireland, and famous in England as an actor, a teacher of actors, and a litigant, Macklin was also the author of ten plays, four of which have serious claims on the attention of students of eighteenth-century theatre. *Covent Garden Theatre: or Pasquin Turned Drawcansir* (1752) is a characteristically cantankerous AFTERPIECE, which follows the example of FIELDING's *Pasquin* in attacking the vulgarity of contemporary theatrical and social values. *Love à-la-Mode* (1759) takes a Jonsonian delight in exposing the true colour of fools. It was immensely popular, and Macklin found a favourite part as the Scotsman, Sir Archy MacSarcasm. Like *The True-Born Irishman* (1762), also a two-act piece, it is not much more than a gallery of comic characters subjected to the scorn of their creator. *The Man of the World* (1764) is a five-act comedy with a voice of its own. Its performance in England was delayed for seventeen years by censorship. This was the period of the Scottish Lord Bute's unpopular supremacy at the Court of George III, and Macklin's hatred of the Scots, centred on the character of Sir Pertinax MacSycophant which he played himself, was too overt for the delicate defenders of Bute. Macklin's major acting role was Shylock, in which he made his debut in 1741. He revolutionized both the part and the play. His Shylock was still a villain, but no longer a pantaloon. His Macbeth, in tartan and Scottish accent, was more controversial. Controversy was never far from him. In 1735 he killed a fellow-actor in the Drury Lane GREEN ROOM. Eloquently conducting his own defence, he reduced the crime from murder to manslaughter. But the point was clear. Throughout his long life, Macklin was a dangerous man to tangle with.

W. W. Appleton, *Charles Macklin*, 1961.

Macready, William Charles (1793–1873). English tragic actor, who was sent to Rugby school by his theatrical father to prepare him for a better career. Alas for his hopes. Imprisoned for debt, Macready senior had to hand over his theatrical enterprises to his nervous son. Macready's intelligence was his main advantage as an actor. There were not too many others. Square-faced and as severe as a bank-manager, he was the least charismatic of the eminent nineteenth-century actors. 'He holds himself,' Stendhal complained, 'as if the pit were full of painters.' But, as his fascinating Diaries show, he worked hard in circumstances and with people he frequently found unattractive. He made his debut as Romeo in Birmingham in 1810. Six years later, with KEAN triumphant at Drury Lane, and anticipating the retirement of JOHN PHILIP KEMBLE, the manager of Covent Garden hired Macready. His first real success was in KNOWLES's *Virginius* in 1820. Suffering fatherhood looms large in Victorian art, and Macready, who would suffer much as a father, portrayed it finely. But the mutual support of Macready and Knowles has a further significance. Throughout his distinguished career, Macready sought to discover and encourage writers of poetic tragedy. Byron, BULWER-LYTTON and Browning were among his sputtering hopes. He was probably wrong to try to revive Elizabethan glories, but his concern was exemplary. It shines like a light against the philistinism of Macready's *bête noire*, Alfred Bunn, who was manager of Drury Lane in 1836, when Macready blacked his eye. As actor-manager, first of Covent Garden and then of Drury Lane, he established rehearsal disciplines and attacked abuses both on and off stage. Macbeth was his finest Shakespearan role, and the one he chose for his farewell performance in 1851. 'Thank God!' he concluded his Diary.

Alan S. Downer, *The Eminent Tragedian*, 1966.

Maeterlinck, Maurice (1862–1949). Belgian playwright whose moon-ily esoteric verse plays cast a spell over the European theatre at the turn of the century. The actor's task in a Maeterlinck play is to stand still, speak clearly the mannered language, and seem to be in touch with the mysterious centre of a world which can never be trivial to a Symbolist. Maeterlinck was educated at a Jesuit school, and practised law in Belgium, but he succumbed to the influence of the Parisian Symbolists, and made sufficient money from his plays to abandon the law, and live like a French aristocrat in what had once been an abbey. The muffling of the erotic in mysticism is common to *Pelléas and Mélisande* (1892), *Aglavaine and Selysette* (1896) and *Sister Beatrice* (1899). In *The Blind* (1890) and *The Interior* (1894), the oneiric stillness is sometimes impressive. *Monna Vanna* (1902) is a slightly hysterical MELODRAMA, which caused a scandal because its heroine was supposed to be naked under a cloak, a phrase which might well be applied to the whole of Maeterlinck's work, including the two fantasies *The Blue Bird* (1908) and *The Betrothal* (1918). In the years after 1918, Maeterlinck ceased to be a world figure.

Bettina Knapp, *Maurice Maeterlinck*, 1975.

Mansfield, Richard (1854–1907). American actor, the son of an English wine-merchant and a German prima donna. His earliest success was a moderate one – with touring companies playing GILBERT and Sullivan, and it was not until 1882, when he went to New York, that he began an extraordinary career as one of the last great stars. Part of this career was a fiction constructed by his own gigantic ego, but much of it was the result of hard work. His tour de force was in the dual role of a specially written version of *Dr Jekyll and Mr Hyde*, which he first played in Boston in 1887. His repertoire was a confusing mixture of the second-rate actor's vehicle and the admirably innovative. He was, for instance, the first to bring SHAW to America, with *Arms and the Man* in 1894 and *The Devil's Disciple* in 1897. The role of Dick Dudgeon in particular allowed him to exhibit his cutting wit alongside his romantic flair. He was also, despite his dislike of IBSEN's prose plays, broad-minded enough to admire *Peer Gynt*, of which, in Chicago in 1906, he gave the first performance in English. Mansfield lived royally on his immense American earnings, with a town house on Riverside Drive, a summer house near New London, Connecticut and a vast private yacht. Against the growing taste for social drama, Mansfield maintained and embodied the mystique of the magical theatre of HENRY IRVING – and he was good enough to make it work.

Paul Wilstach, *Richard Mansfield*, 1908.

Marivaux, Pierre Carlet de Chamblain de (1688–1763). French playwright associated primarily with the Comédie-Italienne. All his best comedies are about love, and there is nothing unusual about that. What is less common is Marivaux's preparedness to explore the subject through dialogue rather than through the complications of an intrigue plot. In such early plays as *Harlequin Polished by Love* (1720) and *The Double Inconstancy* (1723) true love is threatened by external forces, but Marivaux's mature work offers no threat to the lovers beyond their own uncertainties. What we watch and hear in *The Game of Love and Chance* (1730) and *The Test* (*L'Épreuve*, 1740), for instance, is the progress, by way of attraction, doubt, resistance and fear, to emotional awareness. Marivaux's dialogue is delicate and knowing. Those of his contemporaries who considered it too precious dismissed it contemptuously as *marivaudage*, a word which subsequent reassessment has turned into praise.

K. McKee, *The Theatre of Marivaux*, 1958.

Marlowe, Christopher (1564–93). During a lifetime of less than thirty years, Christopher Marlowe contrived to set the Elizabethan stage afire with his eloquence, become involved in espionage, acquire a reputation for atheism and homosexuality, kill a man in a street fight and be killed himself in a tavern brawl. His first play, *Tamburlaine* (1587), written shortly after his notorious years at Cambridge University, was such a spectacular success that echoes from it and allusions to it are found in writing for decades afterwards. A sequel was immediately called for. Together the plays chart the rise and fall of the protagonist from humble shepherd to conqueror of the known world. Moral judgment on Tamburlaine's callousness is passed by in favour of wide-eyed admiration for his heroic energy and single-minded pursuit of power. The 'mighty line' which Marlowe fashioned for him is the exact verbal equivalent of Tamburlaine's all-conquering sword, an equivalence which the Prologue spells out when it speaks of the hero

> Threatening the world with high astounding terms,
> And scourging kingdoms with his conquering sword.

The exact order in which Marlowe produced his plays is uncertain. What is certain is that *Doctor Faustus* (?1588) is one of the glories of the Elizabethan drama. Its text exists in two versions (1604 and 1616) neither of which is wholly reliable, though the later one is fuller than the earlier. Where Tamburlaine's progress to world domination is a continuously ascending curve terminated only by mortality, Faustus meets his doom because his thirst for power recognizes no limits until the very end, when the Devil to whom he has sold his soul compels him to acknowledge that he is only a man. Together these plays provide an enthralling metaphor for the perils and possibilities that lay before Renaissance man. In *The Jew of Malta* (?1589) Renaissance individualism is held up to an ironic scrutiny under which the hypocritical pretensions of the Christians come off worse than the larger-than-life villainy of the Jew. Barabbas is an intentionally comic version of the Machiavellian intriguer while the Guise in the badly garbled *The Massacre at Paris* (?1593) is perhaps an unintentionally comic one. Marlowe's most serious treatment of Renaissance individualism occurs in the figure of Mortimer in *Edward II*, a play in which the central figure comes to an end horrifying and obscene enough even for the twentieth century. *Dido, Queen of Carthage* (?1593), Marlowe's only other play, dramatized Book IV of Vergil's *Aeneid* and was originally written for the Children of the Chapel Royal; it makes good use of costume and stage effects. At his death Marlowe left an unfinished erotic poem, *Hero and Leander* (1598), which GEORGE CHAPMAN completed in a quite un-Marlovian fashion.

Harry Levin, *The Overreacher*, 1952.
Judith Weil, *Marlowe: Merlin's Prophet*, 1977.

Marston, John (1576–1634). Marston first caught the attention of Elizabethan London with his satirical verses *The Scourge of Villainy* (1598–9) which were burnt by the public hangman on the orders of the Archbishop of Canterbury. By the time he was thirty-two he had abandoned his legal studies and his literary career and, like a more famous contemporary satirist, John Donne, taken holy orders. In between he suffered a term of imprisonment, engaged in a famous theatrical quarrel with BEN JONSON, and wrote a number of satirical comedies and tragi-comedies for a CHILDREN'S COMPANY (Paul's Boys). It is especially difficult to discriminate in Marston's plays between the moral outrage of the satirist and the muck-raking of the sensation-monger. *The Malcontent* (1604) and *The Dutch Courtesan* (1603–4) show his dramatic talents at their best, while *Antonio and Mellida* (1599) and *Antonio's Revenge* (1599) are more extreme and perhaps more typical. No doubt the scabrous language of his plays had an added piquancy when spoken by young children, though SHAKESPEARE's company, the King's Men, thought well enough of *The Malcontent* to steal it.

P. J. Finkelpearl, *Marston of the Middle Temple*, 1969.
Michael Scott, *John Marston's Plays*, 1978.

Massinger, Philip (1583–1640). Massinger was born in Wiltshire and went to Oxford University under the auspices of the influential Herbert family. He left without taking a degree and may have started his theatrical career as an actor. As a playwright he collaborated with FIELD, Daborne, DEKKER and especially with JOHN FLETCHER, whom he succeeded as regular dramatist to the King's Men on Fletcher's death in 1625. Massinger was forthright in his handling of religious questions at a time when such forthrightness was hazardous, and in *The Renegado* (1624) made the most sympathetic figure a Jesuit priest. He wrote over thirty plays either alone or in collaboration. Of these, *The City Madam* (?1632) is noteworthy for its social satire, but it is through *A New Way to Pay Old Debts* (1621–2) that Massinger lives in the modern repertory. Larger-than-life actors from KEAN to WOLFIT have hurled themselves with gusto into the role of the demoniac extortioner Sir Giles Overreach, whose frenzied energy overwhelms the conservative moral straitjacket in which the dramatist attempts to constrain him.

T. A. Dunn, *Massinger: The Man and the Playwright*, 1957.

Mathews, Charles (1776–1835). A rubbery-featured comic actor, who came to specialize, in succession to JACK BANNISTER, in one-man shows of songs and sketches under the title of 'At Homes'. He had two prime assets as a performer – an amazing memory and a talent for mimicry. His popularity was already well established by 1808, when he embarked on his brilliantly successful 'At Homes'. During a long career, he created some four hundred roles at Drury Lane, Covent Garden and the Haymarket. He was one of the first English actors to tour America, but his visits there did nothing to alleviate the tendency to melancholy that coloured the last years of his life.

Mrs Mathews, *Memoirs of Charles Mathews*, 4 vols., 1839.

Mathews, Charles James (1803–78). Son of CHARLES MATHEWS, and an actor who made a notable contribution to the new, 'relaxed' acting of comedy in the second half of the nineteenth century. He was trained as an architect, but drifted from amateur acting into the professional theatre in 1835, making the fateful decision only after the death of his father. In 1838 he married MADAME VESTRIS, and together they managed Covent Garden and, later, the Lyceum. Neither venture was a financial success, and Mathews was left bankrupt on his wife's death. He was rescued by his own determination, and by the support of his American second wife . He made a number of overseas tours, and was the author of several pieces written to suit his own talents.

Charles Dickens (ed.), *The Life of Charles James Mathews*, 2 vols., 1879.

Maugham, (William) Somerset (1874–1965). Maugham had begun writing before he completed his training as a doctor in 1897. That was the year in which his first novel, *Liza of Lambeth*, was published. He was a splendid teller of stories, who managed to achieve popularity without ever trying to charm his public. His own colourful private life was sufficiently well concealed to make him an acceptable member of society, at least until his divorce in 1927. He will probably survive longer as a novelist and short-story writer than as a dramatist; but it is an important fact of dramatic history that he had four plays running simultaneously in London in 1908, the best of them being *Lady Frederick* (1907). Maugham writes sharp dialogue, and creates strong situations. *For Services Rendered* (1932), almost the last play he wrote, leaves a typically bitter taste in the mouth, and it shows its author's awareness of the hollow ring of dead values on the tongues of a dying generation. Other plays that have been successfully revived include

Home and Beauty (1919), *The Circle* (1921) and *The Constant Wife* (1926).

Frederic Raphael, *Maugham and His World*, 1976.
Ted Morgan, *Somerset Maugham*, 1980.

Mayakovsky, Vladimir Vladimirovich (1893–1930). Russian poet and dramatist whose fervent involvement with futurism and socialism led to imprisonment in Tsarist Russia. He was too egocentric and too excessive to be a reliable member of anything, but his efforts were heroic, and have been rewarded like a hero's in the Soviet Union. His dramatic work is not extensive, though much of his declamatory poetry is explosive dramatic monologue. He performed the principal part in his verse 'tragedy' *Vladimir Mayakovsky* at its presentation in St Petersburg in 1913, suffering as poet amid the pain and squalor of city life. His *Mystery-Bouffe*, staged by MEYERHOLD in 1918, is a guileless celebration of the Bolshevik Revolution, flamboyant and intentionally ephemeral. Two later plays, also staged by Meyerhold, *The Bed Bug* (1929) and *The Bath House* (1930), are fantastic FARCES, in which a primitively projected brave new world throws into unfavourable prominence the lingering bourgeois preoccupations of a society that was forgetting its Revolution. In April 1930, for reasons that can never be entirely clear, Mayakovsky shot himself. At the time, he was still a titanic figure in a shrinking society.

W. Woroszylski, *The Life of Mayakovsky* (trans. B. Taborski), 1972.
E. J. Brown, *Mayakovsky: A Poet in the Revolution*, 1973.

McGrath, John (1935–   ). McGrath is the finest representative of the political FRINGE movement of the seventies in British theatre. He wrote plays as a student at Oxford, joined the BBC as a television director, wrote early scripts for the pioneeringly 'realistic' police series *Z Cars* and completed a play, *Events While Guarding the Bofors Gun* (1966), which was an unusually vigorous and skilful attack on British cold war militarism, but which was recognizably within a tradition that could also accommodate WESKER's *Chips with Everything*. The political tumult of 1968 affected McGrath profoundly, leading him to an articulate rejection of bourgeois cultural values. Like many other young writers, he had hopes that Britain in 1970 was in a pre-revolutionary condition. In that year he began working with the Everyman Theatre in Liverpool and wrote two plays with a specific design on working-class audiences, *Fish in the Sea* and *Soft or a Girl?* In 1971 he founded 7: 84 THEATRE COMPANY (a current statistic suggested that 7 per cent of the population of Britain owned 84 per cent of its wealth), which staged his

Trees in the Wind at the Edinburgh Festival. When 7:84 divided into two geographically separated units in 1973, McGrath went with the Scottish group for which he wrote an outstandingly and genuinely 'popular' political entertainment, *The Cheviot, The Stag and the Black, Black Oil* (1973), confronting Scottish working communities with the parallels between the Highland clearances and the social effects of North Sea oil. The form is intentionally mixed, sing-song alternating with diatribe, knockabout with naturalism, because McGrath believes that such variety is a forgotten element of the true folk-play. Subsequent plays for 7:84 Scotland, *The Game's a Bogey* (1974), *Little Red Hen* (1975) and *The Imperial Policeman* (1984), for example, have been equally various. Asked in 1975 whether he would write a play for the NATIONAL THEATRE, McGrath replied, 'I'd rather have a bad night in Bootle'. His three-part television play *Blood Red Roses* (1986) is as trenchantly provocative as the essays collected in *A Good Night Out* (1981).

McKellen, Ian (1939–   ). British actor whose intelligent radicalism has supported many of the more thoughtful reforms in the organization of the theatre. His double performance of MARLOWE's Edward II and SHAKESPEARE's Richard II at the Edinburgh Festival in 1969 brought him what amounted to a cult following which seriously misjudged his egalitarian temperament. His concern for the actor in a theatre dominated by directors expressed itself in his helping to form the Actors' Company in 1972. He is not at ease in rhetorical performance of the classics in large theatres and his best work with the ROYAL SHAKESPEARE COMPANY was his Macbeth in The Other Place at STRATFORD in 1976. This outstanding production, in which he shared the honours with JUDI DENCH and director TREVOR NUNN, allowed him to exploit his own intensity, as did the playing of Max in Martin Sherman's *Bent* (1979). McKellen's mannerisms are prominent in his best as well as his worst work. They have earned him admiration and some mockery in recent NATIONAL THEATRE performances as CHEKHOV's Platonov (1984), WEBSTER's Bosola (1985) and Shakespeare's Coriolanus (1985). He has some of the boldness of the old actor-managers. Interestingly, he is also one of the British actors most qualified for managerial roles. Having led an RSC tour in 1978, he was an associate director of the National Theatre from 1984 to 1986. It is unlikely to be long before he returns to management.

Joy Leslie Gibson, *Ian McKellen*, 1986.

Medwall, Henry (*fl.* 1500). Medwall lived in the latter part of the fifteenth century and was chaplain to John Morton, Archbishop of

Canterbury, at whose household entertainments we are told young Thomas More improvised on at least one occasion. Medwall can claim to be the earliest English dramatist known by name, but even without this accidental distinction his interlude *Fulgens and Lucrece* (1497) entitles him to serious attention as a dramatist. Its theme, birth versus merit, is conventional enough, but Medwall's handling of it shows a fine sense of the resources of the Tudor banqueting hall in which it was staged, its audience and the convivial occasion. While unsuitable for performance in a large public theatre, *Fulgens and Lucrece* still shows its dramatic vitality in more intimate productions. Medwall's other known play, *Nature*, is a morality drama with a clumsy plot but some lively dialogue.

T. W. Craik, *The Tudor Interlude*, 1958.

Mei Lanfang (1894–1961). Chinese actor whose performances abroad between 1919 and 1935 introduced the Western world to the disciplines of the PEKING OPERA. Mei Lanfang made his first public appearance at the age of fourteen, after at least five years' training. His brilliance in female roles shifted the emphasis of the Peking Opera from the *laosheng* (elderly male) to the *dan* (female), and his performances caught the attention of the two major theorists of Western acting, STANISLAVSKY and BRECHT. 'The Chinese performer,' wrote Brecht, 'is in no trance. He can be interrupted at any moment . . . . He does not mind if the setting is changed around him as he plays.' The experience of watching Mei Lanfang in Moscow in 1935 advanced Brecht's thinking about the VERFREMDUNGSEFFEKT.

A. C. Scott, *Mei Lan-Fang*, 1959.

Menander (c. 342–292 BC). The discovery, in 1957, of a papyrus codex, dating probably from the third century AD, gave us the fullest text of a Menander play, the *Dyskolos*. Another papyrus, discovered in 1905, had provided sizable fragments of four plays. It is possible now to understand the contemporary reputation and subsequent influence of this Athenian poet and dramatist. His plays are carefully plotted intrigue dramas, containing various of the types familiar from Roman and later comedy – the interfering slave, the angry old man, the abused maid – and enlivened by wittily sententious dialogue. Menander was an imitable model in a way that ARISTOPHANES was not. His plays describe the mishaps and resourcefulness of individuals, and the Aristophanic chorus has been replaced by *entr'acte* singers and dancers. In calling TERENCE a 'half-Menander', Caesar was attesting to both the skill and the reputation of this supreme author of New Comedy.

T. B. L. Webster *An Introduction to Menander*, 1974.
S. M. Goldberg, *The Making of Menander's Comedy*, 1980.

Mercer, David (1928–80). English playwright, much of whose work deploys all or any of three themes – the struggle to retain a faith in socialism; the alienation of a working-class northerner who has been educated into the middle class; and the splendid anomy of roguish insanity. All these themes have autobiographical reference. The second dominates in such television plays as *The Generations* trilogy (1964), and was still dominant in the amusing *A Rod of Iron* (1980), where it is the father rather than the sons who receives the real attention. The television trilogy, *On the Eve of Publication* (1970), traces the career and contacts of the hard-drinking, cantankerous writer Robert Kelvin in the light of his socialism. *Cousin Vladimir* (1978) is a later example of Mercer's determination to lacerate himself for political bad faith. (He seems torn between blaming the mirror for the cracks in his face, and blaming his face for cracking the mirror.) In *A Suitable Case for Treatment* (1962), he celebrates and mourns the raucously insane individualism of Morgan. Mental health is treated with more gravity in *In Two Minds* (1967), and lawless individualism with less reserve in *Flint* (1970). The self-destructive energy in this tormented writer contributed to his untimely death. Of his stage plays, the best are probably *Flint* and two performed by the ROYAL SHAKESPEARE COMPANY, *Belcher's Luck* (1966) and *After Haggerty* (1970).

Meyerhold, Vsevolod Emilievich (1874–1940). Russian director, who was trained as an actor by NEMIROVICH-DANCHENKO. In 1898, he played Treplev in the MOSCOW ART THEATRE's famous production of CHEKHOV's *The Seagull*, but he was temperamentally unsuited to playing second fiddle. Recognizing this, STANISLAVSKY made him director of the New Theatre-Studio in 1905, and then – not without cause – got cold feet. Meyerhold's interest, even at this time, was in a theatre that declared its artifice, Stanislavsky's in a theatre that concealed its art. A Soviet critic later compared Stanislavsky 'the novelist-director' with Meyerhold 'the poet-director'. Some such contrast is unavoidable. While Stanislavsky was giving traditional acting a new language, Meyerhold was a true modernist. His 1906 production of Blok's *The Fairground Booth* sharpened his interest in COMMEDIA DELL'ARTE techniques. Meyerhold himself played Pierrot, a part he later danced in a Fokine ballet one extraordinary night in 1910, in the company of Nijinsky and Karsavina. A concern for popular theatre, and for the vital role of the audience in the theatrical event, remained with him. His productions of classic plays exemplified his view that 'a play is simply the excuse for the revelation of its theme on the level at which that revelation may appear vital today'. Famous examples were Lermontov's *Masquerade* (1917), Verhaeren's *The Dawn* (1920), OSTROVSKY's *The Forest* (1924) and, supremely, GOGOL's *The Government Inspector* (1926).

For a while after the Revolution, Meyerhold was the party's blue-eyed boy. He produced two versions of MAYAⷆOVSKY's celebratory *Mystery-Bouffe* (in 1918 and 1921), but the authorities were less certain about the same author's *The Bed Bug* in 1929, and positively critical of *The Bath House* in 1930. Meyerhold was too uncompromising. In 1938 his theatre was liquidated, and the ailing Stanislavsky made the wonderful gesture of offering him an assistantship at the Opera Theatre. In 1939, though, Meyerhold was arrested, and on 2 February 1940, he was shot in a Moscow prison.

Edward Braun, *The Theatre of Meyerhold*, 1979.

Middleton, Thomas (1580–1627). It is reasonable to claim for Middleton the distinction of having written the best Jacobean satirical comedy outside JONSON, *A Chaste Maid in Cheapside* (1611), and the best Jacobean tragedy outside SHAKESPEARE, *The Changeling* (with WILLIAM ROWLEY, 1622). Middleton went to Oxford University and then (probably) to the Middle Temple and began his career, like many dramatists of the time, working for PHILIP HENSLOWE. In the course of a long career he wrote for both adult and child companies and was City Chronologer of London from 1620 to 1627, in which capacity he devised several MASQUES and pageants now lost. He wrote some forty plays, many in collaboration, but three of the best, aside from those already mentioned, are his own work. These are the comedies, *A Mad World, My Masters* (1604–6) and *A Trick to Catch the Old One* (1604–1606), and the tragedy *Women Beware Women* (1625–7). In both comedies and tragedies Middleton shows a Jonsonian awareness of the grotesque aspects of human behaviour and a moral sensibility which is detached yet humane. He also shows a sympathetic understanding of the predicament of women in a male-dominated acquisitive society, which is quite un-Jonsonian. Middleton made theatrical history with a fiercely anti-Spanish topical satire against the projected marriage of Prince Charles to the Spanish Infanta, *A Game at Chess* (1624). The play somehow evaded the censor and had a record-breaking run of nine days before the Spanish Ambassador's protests led to its suppression.

D. M. Holmes, *The Art of Middleton: A Critical Study*, 1970.

Miles, Bernard (1907–   ). English actor whose major contribution to the theatre has been his idiosyncratic and passionate handling of the

MERMAID THEATRE in Puddle Dock, London. Despite his knighthood in 1969 and his later elevation to the peerage, Miles has remained emphatically proletarian. His early work in theatre included stage management, carpentry and props-making, and he was not much noticed by critics before his Iago for the OLD VIC in 1941. At the Mermaid he has been a famous and frequent Long John Silver, and also Falstaff and BRECHT's Galileo.

Miller, Arthur (1915–). American playwright, brought up in Brooklyn amid the injured pride of a Depression-damaged Jewish family. His version of IBSEN's *An Enemy of the People* (1950) signals his admiration for the Norwegian writer's carefully plotted plays in which family and social pressures are related and the interaction of past and present exposed. The first notable example in Miller's own work is *All My Sons* (1947), in which Joe Keller is forced to the guilty realization that other men have sons too, but the best is *Death of a Salesman* (1949), one of the finest of all bourgeois tragedies. In this play, Miller takes as his representative hero a small man with great dreams. It is much more than a cautionary tale about the dangers of the American need to succeed. Miller's concern is with personal integrity and common guilt. In *The Crucible* (1953) the distribution of blame for the witchcraft persecutions in Salem is subtle and compelling, whereas it is too blatant in *A View from the Bridge* (1955).

For nearly a decade after this, Miller produced no new plays, but 1956 was a significant year for him. He divorced his first wife, made his improbable marriage with Marilyn Monroe and was summoned before the HOUSE UNAMERICAN ACTIVITIES COMMITTEE to explain his attitude to the Communist Party. All these events figure prominently in *After the Fall* (1964), which New York audiences considered profoundly tasteless (Marilyn Monroe had committed suicide in 1962, a year after her divorce from Miller). Miller's dignified refusal to name names at the House Committee had made him something of a hero, but *After the Fall*, a much better play than its hysterical reception allowed, blemished his reputation. *Incident at Vichy*, also performed at the newly opened LINCOLN CENTRE in 1964, was not a strong enough play to re-establish him. The theme is that of Nazi persecution of the Jews, but the mechanism is too melodramatic and the blame too easily laid. *The Price* (1968) returns to themes of family guilt, more laboured now, though enlivened with humour, but the humour of Miller's next play, *The Creation of the World and Other Business* (1972), was too clumsy. Understandably nervous of his New York audience, Miller chose to present *The Archbishop's Ceiling* (1977) and *The American Clock* (1979) elsewhere. Like the short pieces, *Elegy for a Lady* (1982) and *Some Kind of a Love Story* (1982), they explore the difficulty of establishing a basis for human trust. For this bruised American playwright, the experience of directing *Death of a Salesman* in China in 1983 was more invigorating than any of his recent contact with the American theatre. He records it shrewdly in *Salesman in Beijing* (1984).

Dennis Welland, *Miller: A Study of His Plays*, 1979.

Modjeska, Helena (1840–1909). Polish actress, who made a second career for herself in America after emigrating in 1876 with her second husband. He had been involved in anti-Tsarist plotting, and it was to a communistic Polish community in California that he took his wife. Personal freedom (Modjeska was 'associated' with Sienkiewicz, the Polish author of *Quo Vadis*) in the land of the free brought cash problems, and, despite her limited knowledge of English, Modjeska made her debut in San Francisco in 1877 in the barnstorming part of Adrienne Lecouvreur in the play by SCRIBE and Legouvé. It was a role in the BERNHARDT line, and Modjeska had a similar beauty of face and eyes together with the captivating combination of fragility and passion. Juliet was her first Shakespearean part in America, but Lady Macbeth became her greatest. She toured England from 1880 to 1882 and again in 1890. SHAW remembered hers as 'the best manufactured acting I ever saw'. She played opposite EDWIN BOOTH – her cigarettes competing with his cigars in a backstage inferno – and MAURICE BARRYMORE, and starred in the first American performance of IBSEN's *A Doll's House*. She was a personality actress with a style of her own, well in accordance with the beguiling assumption that Continental ladies are superb lovers.

A. Gronowicz, *Modjeska: Her Life and Loves*, 1956.

Molière (1622–73). Born Jean-Baptiste Poquelin, the man who became the finest writer of comedies in the history of Western theatre adopted a pseudonym to save his worthy bourgeois father from humiliation. He had been intended for a career at Court, and to that end his father had sent him to the famous Jesuit college of Clermont before financing his legal studies. The knowledge of French law then acquired proved useful to Molière both in his plays and in his theatrical management. His sudden conversion to the stage was largely brought about under the influence of the Béjarts, a cheerful group fecklessly treading the shadowy ground between theatre and vagabondage. Royal, or at least noble, patronage was essential to any theatre-group in seventeenth-century France, and when Molière joined with the Béjarts in 1644 to form a troupe called the Illustre-Théâtre, he led the quest for a patron. Early failures culminated in his imprisonment for debt, and when the troupe started again it was in Narbonne and under the patronage of the Duc d'Épernon. For thirteen years they toured the provinces, increasingly accomplished and increasingly admired. It was not until 1658 that they arrived in Paris to perform before the young Louis XIV, whose brother became their official patron. Their playing of CORNEILLE's *Nicomède* was not much admired by the distinguished audience, and it was a lost afterpiece, *Le Docteur amoureux*, by Molière himself that made the day auspicious. Molière had provided the company with a number of short FARCES based on characters and situations from the COMMEDIA DELL'ARTE, and this was presumably one of them. It was with *Les Précieuses ridicules* (1658), a comedy of manners satirizing the affectations of the upper-class habitués of the Parisian salons, that Molière first found his own distinctive voice. 'The correction of social absurdity,' he wrote in the published version, 'must at all times be the matter of true comedy.' In keeping with this classical precept he wrote, and performed in, a succession of comic masterpieces, including *L'École des maris* (1661) and its companion-piece *L'École des femmes* (1662), *Tartuffe* (1664), a supreme study of pious hypocrisy, *Le Misanthrope* (1666) and *L'Avare* (1668). His one unqualified disaster was his single heroic tragedy, *Don Garcie* (1661).

Opposition to Molière, which began after the success of *L'École des maris*, increased as triumph followed comic triumph. It was joined by the gentry whom he had offended, jealous minor writers and the discomforted actors of the previously unrivalled HÔTEL DE BOURGOGNE. Some of it was scurrilously personal. Molière had certainly loved Madeleine Béjart, but it was her younger sister Armande that he married in 1662. Noting that Armande was twenty years younger than Madeleine, his enemies claimed that Molière had married his own illegitimate daughter. A 'Comic War' was conducted in pamphlets and the accusation was taken to Louis XIV. The King's sympathies were with Molière, whose own brilliant responses to the 'Comic War' included *La Critique de l'école des femmes* (1663) and *L'Impromptu de Versailles*, but trouble flared up again in 1664 when religious diehards worked to suppress public performance of *Tartuffe*. Louis XIV went so far as to arrange for a private performance of Molière's masterpiece before a papal legate, but he dared not sanction its public presentation, and its sensational success in Paris was delayed until 1669. Meanwhile Molière continued to provide entertainments for Louis XIV's Court. *Georges Dandin* (1668) and *Le Bourgeois gentilhomme* (1670) were Court plays, first presented at Versailles.

Molière is a key figure in French theatre. He was an actor of skill and enormous magnetism, a producer-director equally at home on the small scale of Italianate farce, the comedy of manners and the elaborate Court spectacular, and a dramatist of genius. The sheer verbal exuberance of his writing challenges translators and much is inevitably lost in the English versions of his plays. He died, as he had lived for thirty years, embroiled in theatre. On 17 February 1673, whilst playing the lead in *Le Malade imaginaire*, his last play, he was taken ill. He died that night, before a priest could be found to give him the last rites.

J. D. Hubert, *Molière and the Comedy of Intellect*, 1962.
L. Gossman, *Men and Masks: A Study of Molière*, 1963.

Moody, William Vaughn (1869–1910). American playwright and poet, born and brought up in Indiana and educated at Harvard. From 1894 to 1907 he taught English at Harvard, Ratcliffe and the University of Chicago, publishing a number of scholarly editions of prose and poetry as well as *A History of English Literature* (with Robert Morss Lovett, 1902). *Selected Poems* (1931) is a representative collection of his own poetry, serious, derivative and often eschatological. It was in the same spirit that he undertook to write a trilogy of verse plays, *The Masque of Judgment* (1900), *The Fire-Bringer* (1904) and *The Death of Eve*, of which only one act was ever completed. Much more important to the development of the American theatre was the prose play, *The Great Divide* (first produced in Chicago as *A Sabine Woman*, 1906). It is a carefully crafted treatment of cultural conflict in the United States, describing the abduction of a woman from Massachusetts by an unsophisticated man from Arizona and the processes that lead to their eventual marriage. Its realism and its steady interest in its theme challenged the melodramatic conventions of the contemporary American stage. A second prose play, *The Faith Healer* (1909), less firmly grounded in realism, was the last work Moody completed before his early death.

Morton, Thomas (1764–1838). English dramatist who succeeded in maintaining a privacy remarkable in an age when the theatrical press was notoriously gossip-hungry. It is known that he studied law, but not whether he practised it. Certainly he was a keen cricketer on the famous ground newly acquired by Thomas Lord. For some years after 1816 he seems to have lived in France, from the theatres of which country he continued to filch most of his plays, and between 1828 and 1833 he was successively reader of plays for Covent Garden and for Drury Lane.

The best known of his own plays was and remains *Speed the Plough* (1800), famous above all for its invention of MRS GRUNDY, a threateningly disapproving lady who never appears on stage but is frequently referred to. The play is a characteristic mixture of pathos and broad comedy. It is one of nine five-act COMEDIES written by Morton, all of them demonstrating the close links between the traditional intrigue comedy and the newer fashion for Gothic MELODRAMA. *The School for Reform* (1805) is another striking example.

Mowatt, Anna Cora (1819–70). American dramatist and actress, the daughter of a wealthy and highly respected New York family. Her marriage to James Mowatt, a lawyer much older than herself, maintained her place in society until he lost both his money and his health. She wrote her social comedy, *Fashion* (1845), in order to make money. Not only was it one of the first and certainly one of the best American comedies, but also Mrs Mowatt was the first to challenge social prejudice against the theatre from members of her own circle by writing for professional performance. She went further. From 1845 to 1854 she worked as an actress, including an English tour (1848–50) in a busy itinerary, before marrying a second husband and returning to social eminence in Richmond, Virginia and in London.

Eric Wollencott Barnes, *The Lady of Fashion*, 1954.

Mrozek, Slawomir (1930–   ). Polish playwright, whose *Tango* (1964) was one of the first plays to cross the Iron Curtain. He himself settled in the West after the Russians invaded Czechoslovakia in 1968. Mrozek is a cartoonist as well as a writer, and the grotesque images and macabre humour that put his plays in touch with the THEATRE OF THE ABSURD have a graphic quality. They include *The Turkey Cock* (1961), *The Enchanted Night* (1963) and *The Hunchback* (1976).

Munday, Anthony (1560–1633). In *Palladis Tamia* (1598) Francis Meres described Munday as 'our best plotter', drawing attention to a skill in dividing stories into dramatic episodes that brought him regular commissions. During his relatively long life Munday was printer's apprentice, spy, translator, ballad- and pamphlet-writer, actor, deviser of pageants, playwright, and possibly draper, in more or less that order. Many of his plays are lost; among those surviving, two of the best are *The Downfall of Robert, Earl of Huntingdon* and *The Death of Robert, Earl of Huntingdon* (both 1598). When Macbeth says that

> this my hand will rather
> The multitudinous seas incarnadine,
> Making the green one red,

he echoes lines from both plays. Another link between Munday and SHAKESPEARE is that both appear to have had a hand in the play *Sir Thomas More* (1594–5).

Celeste Turner, *Munday: An Elizabethan Man of Letters*, 1928.

Murphy, Arthur (1727–1805). This Irish-born dramatist has been consistently underrated because he is virtually unread. It can fairly be argued that his *The Way to Keep Him* (1760, revised in 1761) revived the flagging fortunes of native comedy years before GOLDSMITH or SHERIDAN. It is not falsely sentimental, nor, for the most part, are *All in the Wrong* (1761) and *Know Your Own Mind* (1777). His attempts at tragedy, like *The Orphan of China* (1759) and *The Grecian Daughter* (1772), were flattered into some success by contemporary actors and audiences. As COLLEY CIBBER observed of slightly earlier attempts at the genre, tragedy, is 'allowed to say many fine things that nature never spoke . . .' Having made the mistake of providing journalistic support for Lord Bute against John Wilkes, Murphy had a struggle to establish himself in the theatre. What he wrote supremely well was the two-act AFTERPIECE, and any of *The Apprentice* (1756), *The Upholsterer* (1758), *The Citizen* (1761) and *What We Must All Come To* (1764 – but existing also in altered versions as *Marriage à la Mode* and *Three Weeks after Marriage*) could stand revival.

H. H. Dunbar, *The Dramatic Career of Arthur Murphy*, 1946.

Nashe, Thomas (1567–1601). English pamphleteer whose combative involvement, on the anti-Puritan side, in the MARPRELATE CONTROVERSY of 1589 had got him into serious trouble with the authorities when he was very young. His next major scrape came with the performance by Pembroke's Men, playing at the Swan, of *The Isle of Dogs*. Its criticism of the government, either of the City of London or of the country at large, caused the Privy Council to instruct the Middlesex justices to investigate 'a lewd play that was played in one of the playhouses on the Bankside, containing very seditious and slanderous matter'. BEN JONSON, who was Nashe's collaborator in the play, was imprisoned, but Nashe seems to have escaped, perhaps to a refuge in France. The text is lost. The only dramatic work of Nashe's to survive – it is not quite a play nor quite a MASQUE – is *Summer's Last Will and Testament*, whose punning title related both to the season and to Henry VIII's jester, Will Summers. Nashe is better represented by his prose works than by his drama.

G. R. Hibbard, *Thomas Nashe*, 1962.

Nathan, George Jean (1882–1958). American drama critic whose crusade against the crassness of BROADWAY before World War I was a negative aspect of his fight for an American drama of worth. Nathan joined the *New York Herald* in 1905 and continued to write about drama for over fifty years. He was a showman, famous for his tailored suits with a breast pocket idiosyncratically on the right and a variety of modish overcoats. His abusiveness was legendary, as were his attacks on BELASCO, whom he called 'the Broadway Rasputin'. But his advocacy of O'NEILL was crucial to the playwright himself and his later support of O'CASEY gave the Irish playwright a New York audience when he had lost his own in Dublin. As joint-editor with H. L. Mencken of the *Smart Set*, Nathan introduced writers as various as Joyce, BRIEUX and WEDEKIND to American readers.

Neher, Caspar (1897–1962). German designer, born in Augsburg where he was a close schoolfriend of BERTOLT BRECHT. Neher's study of art in Munich was interrupted by military service from 1915. After World War I he renewed his association with Brecht, advising him on the writing of *Baal* and *Drums in the Night* and designing the productions of *In the Jungle of Cities* and *Edward II*. From then until he left Germany in 1933, Brecht always relied on Neher's collaboration. 'He is a great painter,' Brecht wrote, 'but above all he is an ingenious storyteller. He knows better than anyone that whatever does not further the narrative harms it.' It became customary for Neher to make sketches of the scenes in Brecht's plays, proposing indicative stage-groupings and highlighting central incidents in terms of the stage picture. Neher remained in Germany during the Hitler years, though his preference for subdued colour and a well worn, tactile appearance found little favour. After World War II, he became leading designer for Oskar Schuh in West Berlin, as well as renewing his collaboration with Brecht. Having designed *What Price Glory?* for PISCATOR in 1929, Neher provided an inventive set for the same director's Berlin production of *Danton's Death* in 1956. But the Brecht connection meant much more to him. He was co-director with Brecht in Switzerland of *Antigone* (1948) and Lenz's *The Tutor* (1950) and helped in the writing of *The Days of the Commune*. Had it not been for the Nazi interruption, the partnership of Brecht and Neher would have been one of the most remarkable in the whole history of theatre. They were two men who used their different arts to tell stories.

John Willett, *Caspar Neher – Brecht's Designer*, 1986.

Nemirovich-Danchenko, Vladimir (1859–1943). Although his plays and novels are forgotten, Nemirovich-Danchenko is remembered as co-founder with STANISLAVSKY of the MOSCOW ART THEATRE. It was his admiration for CHEKHOV that overcame Stanislavsky's doubts and led to the crucial staging of *The Seagull* in 1898, and it was the actors he had trained at the Moscow Philharmonic School who formed the nucleus, with Stanislavsky's amateurs, of the theatre company. He also directed the lion's share of *The Seagull*, but Stanislavsky stole the notices. That, in many ways, was the story of Danchenko's life, though he tells it a little differently in his informative autobiography, *My Life in the Russian Theatre* (1937).

Nestroy, Johann (1801–62). Austrian playwright, actor and singer who abandoned a legal training at the University of Vienna to take up a career on the stage. Chronically shy in private life, he was a confident and fluent actor. His first play, written in 1823, was an imitative tragedy, but the remaining seventy-seven of his extant plays are comedies. His acting partnership with Wenzel Scholz was based on a classic physical contrast – the tall, angular Nestroy and the short, fat Scholz. His plays, on the other hand, brought to the Viennese popular theatre a new spirit of social criticism. Nestroy was a supreme parodist whose irreverence towards the literary establishment endeared him to popular audiences. It is ironic that his own management of the Carl Theater, from 1854 to 1860, saw a decline in the appeal of Viennese comedy. He had, after all, been uniquely responsible for its popularity. Nestroy's plays have not been widely known in England and America, though THORNTON WILDER derived *The Matchmaker* (later to be turned into the musical *Hello Dolly!*) from his *Einen Jux will es sich machen* (1842) as, very differently, did TOM STOPPARD his *On the Razzle*.

W. E. Yates, *Nestroy*, 1972.

Norton, Thomas. See SACKVILLE, THOMAS.

Nunn, Trevor (1940-   ). English director, who went straight from Cambridge University to the Belgrade Theatre, Coventry and then to the ROYAL SHAKESPEARE COMPANY as associate director in 1965. It was his production of *The Revenger's Tragedy* (1966) that established him. Its theatricality was a magnificently imaginative exploitation of the play's grotesque flights of bizarre horror. Nunn's work at STRATFORD has shown his skill in the orchestration of big scenes as well as in the highlighting of small psychological shifts of purpose, together with a sometimes ham-fisted insistence on spelling out the significance of images that might better be inferred. What became clear during his years as artistic director of the Royal Shakespeare Company (1968–86) was his managerial skill and endurance. His finest directorial work has included a *King Lear* (1976) in the main theatre at Stratford and a *Macbeth* at the small Other Place in the same season and the brilliantly inventive story-telling of DAVID EDGAR's *Nicholas Nickleby* (1980). Unique among Stratford directors, he has gone on getting better despite the burdens of the job, and his production of *All's Well that Ends Well* (1981) was both sensitive and innovatory. After so many years with Shakespeare, Nunn figured in 1986 as director of three musicals running in London's West End, *Starlight Express*, *Cats* and *Chess*. What began in 1984 as a year's break may have become a habit.

O'Casey, Sean (1880–1964). O'Casey has told most of his own life story in six extraordinary volumes of autobiography (1939–54). Not that the detail can be relied on, since it is invaded by torrents of language, and since, as with his plays, he loves the dizzying leap from experience into imagination. He was the fifth surviving child of a struggling Protestant family in Dublin. Poor health, and trachoma that permanently damaged his eyes, spoiled his early years and education. He began work at thirteen, and the most influential of his youthful heroes was the Irish labour leader Jim Larkin. Proletarian sympathies mingled with, but took precedence over, nationalism. When he resigned from the Irish Citizen Army in 1914, it was in protest against the admission of anti-Union feeling in this proletarian body. After rejecting several of his plays, the ABBEY THEATRE staged *The Shadow of a Gunman* (1922) in 1923, and followed it with *Juno and the Paycock* (1924) and *The Plough and the Stars* (1926). These tragi-comedies, with their blathering, feckless men and indomitable women, are set among the Dublin tenements against a background of rebellion and Civil War. They are socially accurate enough to have misled admirers into supposing that NATURALISM was O'Casey's aim. YEATS was among the misled. When O'Casey sent THE SILVER TASSIE (1928) to the Abbey, Yeats rejected it. It was a confrontation as dramatic as any in fiction. Ireland's most popular playwright spurned by the Irish poet-statesman. Why? Because *The Silver Tassie* has the World War as its context, and Yeats thought O'Casey knew nothing outside Ireland; and because the second act is an isolated and astonishing pacifist poem, set among three acts written in the vivid prose of O'Casey's earlier successes. To Yeats it seemed a breach of decorum. To O'Casey it was an insult. Newly married, and settled temporarily in London, he decided never to return to Ireland. His remaining plays, never as popular as the three Abbey successes, continue to experiment with

EXPRESSIONISM, symbolism and theatrical fantasy. Some, like *The Star Turns Red* (1940) and *Red Roses for Me* (1942), carry communist symbols. Others, like *Purple Dust* (1943), the splendid *Cock-a-Doodle Dandy* (1949) and *The Bishop's Bonfire* (1955), set out to counter the grey repression of priest-bound Ireland with colour and sexual mischief. A stubborn and startling people's poet almost to the end of his long life, O'Casey has still to be fully relished in the professional theatre.

David Krause, *Sean O'Casey: The Man and His Work*, 1960.

Odets, Clifford (1906–63). There is some truth in the stock image of Odets as the radical American dramatist of the depressed thirties, who sold out to Hollywood, and even named names to the HOUSE UNAMERI- CAN ACTIVITIES COMMITTEE in 1952, but it takes small account of the inherent suffering. Odets was a member, and to some extent the creation, of the GROUP THEATRE, which staged all his early plays. *Waiting for Lefty* (1935) is a one-act battle-cry for the workers of America. It was met with fervour and with fear. Odets' more typical work is conventio- nally realistic, and less overtly political. *Awake and Sing!* (1935) challenges the gloom of a Jewish family in the Depression with a communist call to action, but the strengths of the play are the accuracy of its family portrait, and the strenuousness of its language. *Golden Boy* (1937) sustains the energetic criticism of American values despite the vulnerability of a story that imposes on its Italian-American hero a choice between becoming a boxer or a violinist. Odets' first Hollywood writing was for Gary Cooper and Madeleine Carroll in *The General Died at Dawn*, as early as 1936. ('Odets, where is thy sting?' asked Frank Nugent.) There is too much self-pity in the play in which he defines the destructive impact of Hollywood, *The Big Knife* (1949), and more than a trace of it in *The Country Girl* (1950). Odets never found anything as satisfying as his early communist convictions.

Edward Murray, *Clifford Odets: The Thirties and After*, 1968.
Gerald Weales, *Odets, the Playwright*, 1985.

O'Keefe, John (1747–1833). Had it not been for the weakness of his eyes, O'Keefe would probably have become a fifth-rate painter instead of a fourth-rate dramatist. He was a charming, industrious Dubliner whose blindness earned him a benefit at Covent Garden in 1800 and a state pension in 1826, but whose life was otherwise a constant struggle for money and survival. Of the sixty-eight dramatic pieces he acknow- ledges in his *Recollections* (1826), over twenty are called 'operas' – which is no more than a way of assuring contemporary audiences that the dialogue will be fairly frequently interrupted by songs. It is a single play, *Wild Oats* (1791), that has preserved O'Keefe's reputation as a writer of true (i.e. 'unsentimental' so far as contemporaries were concerned) comedy. The play depends on an alias, a mistaken identity, a sequence of coincidences, and a lost baby miraculously rediscovered in the person of the leading character, a strolling player provisionally named Rover. If compared with other comedies of the period, it is not especially innovatory – except perhaps in its veiled egalitarianism and the hostility it expresses towards Quaker values.

Oldfield, Anne (1683–1730). English actress, daughter of a London innkeeper. She was, for a while, the mistress of GEORGE FARQUHAR, but it was Sir JOHN VANBRUGH whose interest won her a place in the Drury Lane company in 1699. Her progress was halted by company rivalries and it was not until 1704, when she played Lady Betty Modish in COLLEY CIBBER's *The Careless Husband*, that she reached stardom. Her relationship with Arthur Maynwaring, by introducing her into leading Whig circles, increased her hold on London society. She had two children by this witty journalist who, according to Pope, was the leading conversationalist of the Kit-cat Club. Oldfield remained faithful to him until his early death in 1712, subsequently becoming the mistress of a nephew of the great Duke of Marlborough, by whom she had a further child. From 1705 almost until her death she was the leading actress of the London stage, playing in both comedy (she succeeded ANNE BRACEGIRDLE as Millamant in CONGREVE's *The Way of the World* and created the roles of Silvia in Farquhar's *The Recruiting Officer* and Violante in SUSANNAH CENTLIVRE's *The Wonder*) and tragedy. The contemporary fame of NICHOLAS ROWE's rhetorical tragedies owed much to her strength of voice. On her death, leading Whigs arranged for her burial in Westminster Abbey, though they could not persuade the Dean to allow so irregular a life the extra dignity of a monument.

R. Gore-Browne, *Gay Was the Pit*, 1957.

Olivier, Laurence (1907–). English actor and director who became stagestruck at school in London. SYBIL THORNDIKE saw him playing Kate in *The Taming of the Shrew*, and remembered him as 'the best Kate I ever saw. Some people are born with technical ability. And Larry was. He didn't have to work hard enough at technical things because he knew it all from the start, instinctively.' The point is a challenging one, concealing an implicit contrast with Olivier's great contemporary, JOHN GIELGUD. Despite the honours that have come his way (he was knighted in 1947 and, in 1970, became the first actor ever to be granted a life peerage), Olivier is in the rogue tradition. He is a hogger of the limelight, who combines with a concern for the character he impersonates a relish of his own individuality. His finest performances have been based on decisive and sometimes quirky details, both vocal and physical. After early experience with the Birmingham Repertory Theatre, he created the part of Stanhope in R. C. Sherriff's *Journey's End* in 1928, but declined to stay with the production when it moved to London's West End because he preferred the matinee-idol prospects of playing Beau Geste in a cobbled version of P. C. Wren's novel. It was the 1930 production of NOEL COWARD's *Private Lives* that first brought him critical attention. The production also took him to New York, and from there to some disappointing failures in Hollywood as a contract artist with RKO. There was still no suggestion that he was a classical actor, and it was Gielgud's production of *Romeo and Juliet* (1935), in which he and Olivier alternated Romeo and Mercutio, that caused the decisive shift in Olivier's career. TYRONE GUTHRIE, who directed him as Hamlet at the OLD VIC in 1937, feared that he had 'too strong an instinct for the sort of theatrical effect which is striking and memorable'. Certainly, the homosexual Iago opposite RALPH RICHARDSON's bemused Othello at the Old Vic in 1938 was an excess, rapidly atoned for by a splendid Coriolanus in the same year of 1938.

Olivier was briefly in the Fleet Air Arm during World War II, and his patriotism played a significant part in his film version of *Henry V* (1943–1944) and in his decision to join Richardson in reviving the fortunes of the bomb-damaged Old Vic in 1944. Like Gielgud elsewhere, they were hoping to lay the foundation of a British NATIONAL THEATRE during the Old Vic years of 1944–9, and the decision of the theatre's governors not to renew their contracts was a bitter blow. Olivier gave some of his finest performances in those seasons – Richard III (1944), a doubling of Hotspur and Justice Shallow (1945), Oedipus and Puff in a peculiar double-bill combining SOPHOCLES and SHERIDAN (1945), Lear (1946). The pairings in particular displayed his delight in the wizardry of his own versatility. Much of 1947 was occupied with the making of the film of *Hamlet*, and there followed some troubled years as his marriage to VIVIEN LEIGH tottered. They acted together at the St James's in 1951 in the Cleopatra plays of SHAKESPEARE and SHAW and again in 1953 in TERENCE RATTIGAN's *The Sleeping Prince*, and they were the joint stars of the STRATFORD season of 1955, when Olivier stole the honours in PETER BROOK's brilliant production of *Titus Andronicus*. Associating himself importantly with the new movement in the English theatre, Olivier played Archie Rice in JOHN OSBORNE's *The Entertainer* at the ROYAL COURT in 1957. His appointment as director of the first Chichester

Festival in 1962 was a popular one. It led, naturally as it seemed, to his becoming the first artistic director of the National Theatre in 1963. His support of EDWARD BOND's *Saved* against the Lord Chamberlain was characteristically bold. So was his 'African' Othello in 1964 and his playing in *The Dance of Death* three years later. It may have been ill health that deprived Olivier of the deserved honour of leading the National Theatre company into its own new home in 1976. His *Confessions of an Actor* (1982) is a highly readable autobiography.

Thomas Kiernan, *Olivier*, 1981.
Robert Tanitch, *Olivier*, 1985.

O'Neill, Eugene (1888–1953). American playwright whose reputation seems to defy his country's tendency to destroy its own culture-heroes. Productions of his plays reveal new subtleties without muffling the sound of the 'force behind'. O'Neill's father was an actor whose runaway success as the Count of Monte Cristo trapped him into soul-destroying repetition. James O'Neill and the miserly father of his son's tragic masterpiece, *Long Day's Journey into Night* (written 1939–41, but discovered and first produced after the author's death), are not necessarily the same person, but they had, obviously, a terrible similarity for the son. His alcoholic elder brother reappears in an emotionally ambitious tragi-comedy, *A Moon for the Misbegotten* (1943). The man-on-the-run is an ominous familiar in O'Neill's plays, from *Anna Christie* (1920) and *The Emperor Jones* (1920), through *The Hairy Ape* (1922) and *The Great God Brown* (1926), to *The Iceman Cometh* (written 1939, produced 1946). The fugitive escapes, if he escapes at all, into Nirvana, by way of alcohol or opium. It is not without significance that O'Neill called the California home where he wrote his last plays, and where the progressive degeneration of slow paralysis set in, Tao House.

O'Neill's achievement is uneven. There are as many flaws in a single play as in the whole output of lesser writers. But his work can overpower a receptive audience. He has no reticence, was admittedly self-obsessed and dangerously self-lacerating, but his quest for objectivity is admirable. Many critics thought, wrongly, that he had found it in his new England trilogy (after the *Oresteia* of AESCHYLUS) *Mourning Becomes Electra* (1931). It was works of this magnitude – from *Strange Interlude* (1928) he was occupied with large-scale projects until illness beat him – that won him the Nobel Prize in 1936, and a place in Humbert Wolfe's *ABC of the Theatre*:

> O is O'Neill. The theatre was packed,
> Though a few may have died in the 49th Act.

Even in success, as with *Desire under the Elms* (1924), O'Neill remained a stricken son, reaching out for a past that nearly was.

T. M. Bogard, *Contour in Time*, 1972.
Louis Sheaffer, *O'Neill: Son and Playwright*, 1968 and
  O'Neill: Son and Artist, 1973.

Orton, Joe (1933–67). Having trained as an actor, and served a brief term in prison, Orton found a way of making hatred funny. His first two plays, *The Ruffian on the Stair* (1964) and *Entertaining Mr Sloane* (1964), have the setting, familiar from PINTER, of a room and an alien visitor. But the artfulness of the language is not Pinter's. A 'combination of elegance and crudity', which Orton observed in GENET, and noted in his diary as 'irresistibly funny', became the distinguishing characteristic of his style. His malice – towards the Church, the police, intellectuals, supporters of routine – displays itself in polished jokes and monstrous innuendoes. In *Loot* (1966) a mother's corpse becomes a comic property. In *The Erpingham Camp* (1966) religion is valued along with clean chalets, and defiled along with them in a violently anarchic climax. *What the Butler Saw* (1969), a FARCE which had ceased to shock a decade later, was not performed until after Orton had been murdered in a sensationally bloody way by his male lover, who subsequently killed himself. *The Orton Diaries* (1986) blithely cover the eight preceding months.

John Lahr, *Prick Up Your Ears*, 1978.
C. W. E. Bigsby, *Joe Orton*, 1982.

Osborne, John (1929–   ). English playwright, whose *Look Back in Anger* (1956) at the ROYAL COURT heralded the revival of the 'relevant' theatre. Its hero, Jimmy Porter, is a misplaced person who looses his tongue on the British establishment. Osborne, at this time, was an actor, but he quickly became a writer, then a company director, and with ironic haste a member of the establishment. Of his later plays, *The Entertainer* (1957) and *Inadmissible Evidence* (1964) are the ones most assured of a place in the national repertoire. *Luther* (1961) and *A Patriot for Me* (1966) promise more than they achieve – partly because Osborne loses confidence in his own narrative techniques. He has retained his skill in the composition of rhetorical set pieces, but he has done very little to keep him apart from the efficient, run-of-the-mill dramatists whose financial home is television.

Martin Banham, *Osborne*, 1969.
Simon Trussler, *The Plays of Osborne*, 1969.

Ostrovsky, Alexander Nikolayevich (1823–86). It is extraordinary that this man, who almost single-handed gave to the Russian theatre a substantial repertoire, should have been so neglected in the English-speaking world. His father was a successful civil servant in the vilely repressive Russia of Nicholas I, and Ostrovsky was a disappointment to him. His first play, originally called *The Bankrupt*, was banned by the censor in 1849 because it was considered 'an insult to the Russian merchant-class'. Like many of its successors (Ostrovsky was sole author of forty-seven plays), it is certainly vigorously critical of corruption and licensed family bullying. The tragic outcome of such licence is exposed in *The Storm* (1859), but most of Ostrovsky's plays are critical comedies, robustly written, and requiring robust acting. *Poverty Is No Crime* (1853), *Even a Wise Man Stumbles* (1868, translated by Eugene Bristow as *The Scoundrel*) and *Wolves and Sheep* (1875) are among those to have appeared in English translation. Ostrovsky's lifelong commitment to improving the Russian theatre was rewarded by his appointment in 1885 to the supervisory control of the Moscow Imperial Theatres. His attempt to do a good job damaged his health, but his admiration for the theatre and his love of actors is recorded in two of his finest plays, *The Forest* (1871) and *Artistes and Admirers* (1881).

Margaret Wettlin, Introduction to *Plays*, Moscow, 1974.

Otway, Thomas (1652–85). In a short life, Otway traced the classic path from a clergyman's home to a destitute death in a pub. 'Some have said,' reports *Biographia Dramatica*, 'that downright hunger compelling him to fall too eagerly upon a piece of bread, of which he had been some time in want, the first mouthful choked him, and instantly put a period to his days.' Before that end, he had been an actor, a soldier, a poet, the (? unrequited) lover of MRS BARRY, and the author of a tragedy in heroic couplets, *Don Carlos* (1676), and of two of the few post-Jacobean tragedies in blank verse to have challenged critical attention, *The Orphan* (1680) and *Venice Preserved* (1682). Like RACINE, whom he translated (*Titus and Berenice*, 1677), he was known as the tragedian of 'Love', and there has been historical neglect of his comedies, *The Soldier's Fortune* (1680) and *The Atheist* (1683). Otway's rhetoric is not mere bombast. He was a poet of distinction.

A. Taylor, *Next to Shakespeare*, 1950.

Page, Geraldine (1924–   ). American actress whom it is reasonable to associate with the presentation of neurotic heroines in the work of TENNESSEE WILLIAMS. It was playing Alma in his *Summer and Smoke*

OFF-BROADWAY in 1952 that brought her to critical attention. 'I worked with a psychoanalyst on that,' she told an interviewer. That would have been approved by her mentor, LEE STRASBERG. As the Princess in *Sweet Bird of Youth* (1959) she was stunning. The mannerisms – 'syncopated and fluttery', Eric Bentley has called them – may result from a conflict between the studied naturalness of the METHOD school of acting and a wider, more histrionic instinct. As Nina Leeds in O'NEILL's mammoth *Strange Interlude* (1963) and as successively Masha and Olga in CHEKHOV's *The Three Sisters* (1964) she gave evidence of her extraordinary stamina and variety. Her gift for comedy was tested in a New York production of AYCKBOURN's *Absurd Person Singular* (1974), and in 1980, back on more familiar ground, she created the part of Zelda Fitzgerald in TENNESSEE WILLIAMS's *Clothes for a Summer Hotel*.

Papp, Joseph (1922–   ). American director, who has been called a cultural politician even by his friends. After early post-war experience with the Actors' Lab, and a brief association with CBS, terminated when Papp was sacked after his appearance before the HOUSE UNAMERICAN ACTIVITIES COMMITTEE, he put all his formidable energies into theatrical production. His first Central Park open-air production with the New York Shakespeare Festival was in 1957. Ten years later came the controversial 'naked' *Hamlet*, performed with music in the rock tradition which had been recently popularized by *Hair* (1967). Papp's belief in growth – escalation or extinction was an opposition he quickly recognized – involved him in failures, like the all-black *Cherry Orchard* (1972), and constant quests for money. Even so, it was he who was called in to 'save' the theatres of the LINCOLN CENTRE in 1973. For some young dramatists, the appointment of Papp to so influential a post offered new possibilities, and Papp's policy of presenting their work in the OFF-BROADWAY Public Theatre remains exemplary, long after his 1978 resignation from the Lincoln Centre. Few theatrical businessmen have so persistently ridden with the avant-garde.

Stuart W. Little, *Enter Joseph Papp*, 1974.

Payne, John Howard (1791–1852). American playwright and actor. Payne was born into poverty and fought his own way into the emergent American theatre. In 1809 he played a season at the Park Theatre, New York as an 'infant prodigy', though he was too old to merit the title. He carried a strong sense of his own underrated worth to England in 1813. There he acted, with moderate success, and wrote plays. A visit to Paris, where he became a friend and admirer of TALMA, introduced him to the work of PIXERÉCOURT, which he translated and adapted for the English stage. These and other adaptations were staged at Drury Lane, where his tragedy *Brutus* (1818) provided EDMUND KEAN with one of his most effective roles. Encouraged by the play's success, Payne took on the management of Sadler's Wells, where he lost so much money that he had to spend a year in a debtors' prison. He wrote his way out with *Thérèse* (1821) and took refuge in Paris, but made an effective return to London with the libretto for *Clari* (1823), notable for the song 'Home Sweet Home', and a comedy called *Charles the Second* (1824). He returned to New York as a celebrity in 1832, but became increasingly bitter about the lack of opportunities in the American theatre. His plans for an original work, based on voluminous notes about the Cherokee Indians, came to nothing, and he accepted an appointment as American consul in Tunis in 1842. He spent the rest of his life there, planning literary work but writing very little. Payne did more for the reputation of American drama than any of his contemporaries, though his own work is decidedly derivative.

Peele, George (1558–96). George Peele was one of the group of 'university wits' (others included MARLOWE and GREENE) who gave the English secular theatre its first great period in the last quarter of the sixteenth century. His first extant play, *The Arraignment of Paris* (?1584), is an elaborate flattery of Elizabeth I with classical trappings; it depended for its full effect on the actual presence of the Queen in the audience. Among Peele's other plays, all written for the public theatre, *The Battle of Alcazar* (?1589) is an unsuccessful attempt to cash in on the appeal of *Tamburlaine* and revenge tragedy, *Edward I* (?1593) is a hotch-potch of comedy and romance with only the most tenuous links with history, and *David and Bethsabe* (?1594) one of the few Elizabethan plays on a biblical theme. But Peele's finest dramatic achievement is *The Old Wives' Tale* (?1591–4), a charming piece in which romantic adventure, classical legend, folklore and homespun humour are combined within the framework of a play within a play. It is frequently revived, though professional productions are rare.

G. K. Hunter, *Lyly and Peele*, 1968.

Phelps, Samuel (1804–78). English actor, whose great achievement was to present almost all the plays of SHAKESPEARE at Sadler's Wells in the years following the abolition of the patent monopoly in 1843. Phelps was a disciplined, hard-working actor, lacking the charisma of his younger contemporary IRVING, whose reign at the Lyceum began in the year of Phelps's death. 'To excite his full passion,' wrote Westland Marston, 'he needed the kindling power of indignation.' That he had considerable range is suggested by his success as King Lear and as Falstaff. He lived in Islington, close to the theatre where he worked, the supreme nineteenth-century theatrical artisan.

Shirley Allen, *Samuel Phelps and the Sadler's Wells Theatre*, 1971.

Pinero, Arthur Wing (1855–1934). It may have been Pinero's experience as an actor that taught him how close to the wind it was safe to sail in the Victorian theatre. In two distinct styles, he was the most effective English dramatist of his day. As a writer of FARCES – *The Magistrate* (1885), *The Schoolmistress* (1886), *Dandy Dick* (1887) – he has dexterity without more or less than a hint of offensiveness. As a writer of emotional and social 'problem' plays, he earned a formidable contemporary reputation. *The Profligate* (1889) was admired in its time, though it reads now as a posturing moral tale of seduction and eventual suicide (for which a softer ending had to be provided in the first production). It opened Pinero's eyes to the advantages of controversy, and to the extraordinarily low level of public honesty about sexual relations. When *The Second Mrs Tanqueray* (1893) opened at the fashionable St James's Theatre, most people heard in it a master's voice. What irritated SHAW, and will probably irritate a modern audience too, is Pinero's assumption that Paula Tanqueray must aspire to the respectability she has forfeited before the play begins. Her suicide is a tame surrender to the Victorian moral code. *The Notorious Mrs Ebbsmith* (1895) makes a similar compromise, and deserves less attention than *The Benefit of the Doubt* (1895) and *His House in Order* (1906). Pinero may have challenged society's unforgiving attitude to fallen women, but the challenge was delivered *sotto voce*. It would be foolish to expect more. Pinero was a liberal conformist with a craftsman's skill in playmaking. As morals became freer, he looked increasingly old-fashioned. His theatrical values are lovingly enshrined in *Trelawny of the 'Wells'* (1898), perhaps his best play, sentimental but never silly. Whatever claims may be made for the innovations of *Playgoers* (1913), *Monica's Blue Boy* (1918), *The Freaks* (1918) and *Dr Harmer's Holidays* (1924), we should not look to Pinero for modernism. He was knighted in 1909.

Walter Lazenby, *Pinero*, 1972.

Pinter, Harold (1930–   ). There are few proletarian dramatists. At the beginning of his career, Pinter was one. The images in the early plays – *The Room* (1957), *The Birthday Party* (1956–8), *The Dumb Waiter* (1960), *The Caretaker* (1960) – are proletarian. In uncomfortable rooms, people who ought to know each other (but don't) sit, read tabloid newspapers, talk in spurts, and exhibit a nervous awareness that they do not possess what may be necessary information. The audience may know that these characters would not know what to do with the information if they had it, but if the characters know that too, the knowledge is part of the general uneasiness. 'Comedy of menace' was a term usefully applied to these early plays. They were funny, mostly because they brilliantly exploited the repetitions and aggressions of trivial conversation, elucidating its hidden rhythms. The whole acting style of the English theatre was affected. University students, trainee actors, the writers of television commercials, all of them developed the trick of investing with immense significance words that were meaningless, or whose meaning escaped them. By refusing to 'explain' his plays, Pinter added fuel to the fire. They read and perform now as brilliantly persuasive accounts of twentieth-century alienation.

The critical rush to turn Pinter into a philosopher may have had its adverse effect on him. Having shown an interest in the games people play in their social and sexual lives – *A Slight Ache* (1961), *The Collection* (1962), *The Lover* (1963) – Pinter gave the idea extended treatment in *The Homecoming* (1965), in which a family of men manoeuvres around a single woman. He has written nothing as absorbing since then. The drift has been towards an increasingly reflexive interest in poetry, in the unverifiability of memory, and in the vagaries of time. *Landscape* and *Silence* (1968 and 1969) are sporadically engaging exercises for actors. *Old Times* (1971) is a musical elaboration on the theme of memory. As with *No Man's Land* (1975) and *Betrayal* (1978), the skill remains, but Pinter has much less to write about, though a NATIONAL THEATRE triple bill including *A Kind of Alaska* (1982) gave new heart to his admirers.

Martin Esslin, *Pinter: A Study of His Plays*, 1973.

Pirandello, Luigi (1867–1936). Italian playwright, novelist, and prolific writer of short stories. He was born in Sicily, where his father was a wealthy owner of sulphur mines. Pirandello was sent to the University of Rome, and in 1894 made an arranged marriage to the daughter of his father's partner. Two years later the mines failed, and Pirandello became a teacher in Rome. His wife's madness expressed itself as hysterical jealousy. Until her death in 1918, Pirandello had no escape from her. His plays' concern with insanity is not surprising. He touched on themes that were not yet important in the theatre, and he touched on them so effectively as to make them important – the nature of identity superbly in *Henry IV* (1922), the uncertain distinction between the real and the fictional in such experimental pieces as *Each in His Own Way* (1924), and the impossibility of communication in, for example, *Right You Are, If You Think So* (1916). All these themes are brought together in his masterpiece, one of the greatest of all theatre games, *Six Characters in Search of an Author* (1921; revised 1925).

Anne Paolucci, *Pirandello's Theatre*, 1974.
Susan Basnett-McGuire, *Luigi Pirandello*, 1983.

Piscator, Erwin (1893–1966). German director whose influence BRECHT readily acknowledged. Piscator joined the German Communist Party on the last day of 1918, and his theatre work in Germany from then until 1931 was overtly political. An adventurous updating of SCHILLER's *The Robbers* in 1926 won him financial backing for the establishment of his own company in Berlin. His imaginative use of stage technology was more remarkable than anything else – certainly more remarkable than the plays he selected and his handling of authors and actors. The treadmill stage of *The Adventures of the Good Soldier Schweyk* (1927) was a major factor in the success of that mediocre script, and the use of film, photo-montage, revolves, and massively constructed sets became a keynote in Piscator's work. He was the first to make use of the term 'Epic Theatre' to describe his preference for plays constructed of short scenes and big ambitions, and his proselytizing collage of photographs and explosive text, *The Political Theatre* (1929), was a bold showing of his hand. After being arrested in 1931 for failure to pay entertainment tax, Piscator went to the Soviet Union, and remained there till 1936, respected but underemployed. When the mass murders of Stalin began, Piscator prudently withdrew, finally sailing for New York at the end of 1938. He was employed in the New School, where his work involved both teaching and directing, but the American years were compromised and generally unremarkable. There is evidence of the compromise in his decision in 1951 to settle in West Germany – though he did occasional work in East Germany. These post-war years were a struggle for him, and he may have been lucky to get the appointment in 1962 as artistic director of the West Berlin Volksbühne. It was there that he produced his sequence of German 'confessional' plays, which included HOCHHUTH's *The Representative* (1963) and WEISS's *The Investigation* (1965). Piscator was prominent among the Germans who refused to forget about Hitler.

C. D. Innes, *Erwin Piscator's Political Theatre*, 1972.
John Willett, *The Theatre of Erwin Piscator*, 1978.

Pixérécourt, Guilbert de (1773–1844). It was the boast of this busy French dramatist that, 'I write for those who cannot read.' Certainly he was, between 1797 and 1835, the leading light of the popular Parisian theatres. About half of his hundred plays were *melodrames*. He was the first writer to use the word as it is now understood. *Victor* (1798) and *Coelina* (1800), the second of which provided the plot for HOLCROFT's *A Tale of Mystery*, brought him sudden and extraordinary fame. Jules Janin recorded that 'men, women, children, young girls, the aged, followed him at a distance . . . when he deigned to promenade on the BOULEVARD DU TEMPLE, enveloped in his velvet cloak, decorated with the Cross of the Legion of Honour'. His earlier life was a struggle. Having fled to Coblenz on the outbreak of the Revolution, he returned to serve in the revolutionary army, offended Robespierre, and had to scrape a living by painting fans. He admired, translated, and sometimes plundered the plays of KOTZEBUE, for example in *La Femme à deux maris* (1802). His own favourite play, *Tékéli* (1803), is an example of the historical MELODRAMA as distinct from the domestic melodrama of Kotzebue, and Pixérécourt also contributed to the fashion for melodramas of contemporary crime, as in *Le Suicide* (1816) and *La Chapelle des bois* (1818). He took his work and his responsibilities with immense seriousness, tormenting himself over failures, and taking great pains over staging the sensation scenes he favoured.

Alexander Lacy, *Pixérécourt and the French Romantic Drama*, 1928.
Frank Rahill, *The World of Melodrama*, 1967.

Planché, James Robinson (1796–1880). This prolific English dramatist and librettist is primarily notable for his work at the Olympic Theatre with MADAME VESTRIS, for whom he wrote charmingly whimsical extravaganzas from 1831 to 1838. The importance of these in the history of English pantomime is acknowledged, though Planché was less concerned to invent the principal boy than to provide pretexts for Madame Vestris to show her legs. His puns are less outrageous than those of his successors, and his doggerel more delicately flavoured, and without the bite of GILBERT. Increasingly, and somewhat to his annoyance, Planché found himself shouldered into the background by scenic display. But he has to take some of the blame for that. He was one of the great theatrical costumiers, whose taste for historical accuracy was expressed by his Fellowship of the Society of Antiquaries and by his eventual appointment as a Somerset Herald. The learned and serious side of his theatrical involvement is amply exhibited in the autobiographical *Recollections and Reflections* (1872), but so is the preparedness to turn his hand to anything. He is an exemplary figure in the nineteenth-century British theatre – a man of high standards, who was quite prepared to lower them.

Donald Roy, Introduction to *Selected Plays*, 1985.

Planchon, Roger (1931–   ). French actor, director and playwright whose work in Villeurbanne has earned him an international reputation. Villeurbanne is near Lyon. Planchon has called it 'a small town, made up of workers, somewhat *embourgeoisés*'. It is as provincial as North-ampton, and yet, in 1972, it was chosen to replace Paris as the home base of the THÉÂTRE NATIONAL POPULAIRE. The decision rewarded Planchon's leadership of the popular theatre movement in France.

Planchon was born in the Ardèche and grew up in Lyon where he conducted his early theatrical experiments, already influenced by BRECHT and by the techniques of cinema. In 1957 he became director of the Théâtre de la Cité in Villeurbanne and went in search of an elusive 'popular' audience – 'an immense body of human beings made up of all those who still have no access and no possibility of access to cultural reality in the forms which it persists in taking', as the Villeurbanne declaration of May 1968 expressed it. The revolutionary events of 1968 and their comparative lack of discernible aftermath disturbed Planchon as they disturbed everyone involved in 'popular' theatre. Before then he had established himself as a director with a strong sense of story and a concern with characters in their social context. He had produced plays by Brecht and drawn attention to the work of ADAMOV. With the French classics, like *Tartuffe* and RACINE's *Bérénice*, he had been iconoclastic, believing that a classic must yield itself afresh to the scrutiny of posterity. The attitude was vividly expressed in *The Tearing to Pieces of Le Cid* (1969), a collage created by Planchon and his company, eclectic and irreverent about theatrical fashion. It has been Planchon's aim, since his appointment to the TNP, to visit French cities at regular intervals rather than giving special treatment to Paris. His own plays include extravagant romps like *Bourgeois Follies* (1975), memory plays like *The Return* (1962) and ambitious studies of the common people under the stress of great events like *Blues, Whites and Reds* (1967) and *The Black Pig* (1973). In his own words, 'You could say that all the plays I've written have been a long meditation on Brecht's work.'

Yvette Daoust, *Roger Planchon: Director and Playwright*, 1981.

Plautus, Titus Macc(i)us (*c.* 254–*c.* 184 BC). Roman playwright, probably born a slave, who must have worked in the theatre as an actor or manager of plays. Twenty plays attributed to him survive, among the best known being *Menaechmi*, which provided SHAKESPEARE with the plot for *A Comedy of Errors, Amphitruo, Mostellaria* and *Rudens*. These are, almost certainly, loose translations from Greek New Comedy, to which Plautus brings wit, high spirits and a charming vulgarity. He was not a careful craftsman, but he had an eye for comic tricks, and it is no extravagant step from his work to the triumphs of the COMMEDIA DELL'ARTE. He was a great theatrical entertainer.

E. Segal, *Roman Laughter*, 1968.
W. G. Arnott, *Menander, Plautus, Terence*, 1975.

Poel, William (1852–1934). In 1875 William Pole abandoned his job with Lucas Bros just as that building firm was completing Liverpool Street Station, went to Bristol to join the acting company of his idol, CHARLES JAMES MATHEWS, and became William Poel. The change of name may have been the result of a printing error on the playbill or it may have been the intentional outcome of a wish to spare his respectable father any embarrassment. It was the beginning of a strange and obsessive stage career. For a while he was employed by Emma Cons as manager of what became the OLD VIC and then for the first six months of 1884 he was F. R. BENSON's stage manager. Before either of these brief encounters, Poel had staged, in St George's Hall in London, his first tentative attempt to recapture SHAKESPEARE on a platform approximate to that of the original GLOBE. The year was 1881 and the play was the bad quarto of *Hamlet*, with Poel playing the lead. It was an isolated and probably excruciating event, but it heralded a lifetime's commitment to the urge to replace the spectacular pictorial Shakespeare of the Victorian and Edwardian theatre with a Shakespeare truer to his own time. Poel might have been more successful had he been less quirky. An 1893 production of *Measure for Measure* was genuinely plain and impressive, and the series of productions undertaken with the Elizabethan Stage Society between 1895 and 1905 constitute a substantial body of pioneering work which would have an immediate and important influence on HARLEY GRANVILLE BARKER and a delayed but measurable one on the development of Shakespearean performances in the twentieth century. But Poel's obsession with austerity was matched by his fanatical views on voice production. The result was too often risible. Increasingly he barricaded himself behind his ideas. His voluminous writing is fairly represented by the selection in *Shakespeare in the Theatre* (1913) and his startling bloody-mindedness admirably captured in his decision to reject the knighthood proffered to him in 1929 because 'it was inconceivable to me that my name could be added to the long list of theatrical Knights not one of whom was in sympathy with an Elizabethan method of presentation'.

Robert Speaight, *William Poel and the Elizabethan Revival*, 1954.

Priestley, John Boynton (1894–1984). To those who listened to 'Postcripts' during World War II, Priestley sounded like one of the voices of England – gruff, healthy and as durable as Sheffield steel. The impression is not worthless. This Bradford-born novelist, playwright, essayist, biographer and social historian has always been worth heeding. As well as writing comfortably wrapped plays like *Laburnum Grove* (1933), *Eden End* (1934) and *The Linden Tree* (1947), a commercially immoral FARCE like *When We Are Married* (1938), a commercially moral MELODRAMA like *An Inspector Calls* (1945), he also experimented with space and time in *Johnson over Jordan* (1939), *Time and the Conways* (1937), *I Have Been Here Before* (1937) and the artfully dated television play *Anyone for Tennis?* (1968). Priestley's autobiography, *Instead of the Trees* (1977), shows just how good a writer he remained into old age.

G. L. Evans, *Priestley the Dramatist*, 1964.

Pritchard, Hannah (1711–68). English actress, the daughter of a London staymaker. She was married and a mother before she made her debut at Drury Lane in 1732. An industrious and reliable actress, she remained a medium-rank player until 1740, when her performance as Rosalind in *As You Like It* (KITTY CLIVE was Celia and JAMES QUIN was Jacques) charmed a critical audience. DAVID GARRICK was keen to engage her when he became manager of Drury Lane in 1747, at which time her husband, William Pritchard, became Treasurer of the theatre. The birth of three daughters had done nothing to combat a natural tendency to stoutness, and it was as a burly Lady Macbeth to Garrick's slighter Macbeth (the contrast is apparent in Zoffany's famous portrait) that she achieved her greatest success. A poignant contemporary note records that, 'Mrs Pritchard for a long time lived upon vegetables to prevent obesity, though without effect.' Nevertheless, she continued to play in comedy and tragedy for a further twenty years, playing Lady Macbeth at her farewell performance six months before her death. It was evidence of her prudence that she joined with her husband in a dressmaking business in Covent Garden from about 1750, and was so highly rated that she was appointed dresser to Queen Charlotte for George III's coronation in 1761. Her voice was universally admired, and there were many who preferred her playing of Lady Macbeth to that of SARAH SIDDONS. It says much for her equable temperament that she remained a close friend of the excitable Kitty Clive for nearly forty years. Unusual among eighteenth-century actresses, 'she went to the grave with an irreproachable, unblemished character'.

Anthony Vaughan, *Born to Please*, 1979.

Quayle, Anthony (1913–   ). English actor and director who made his stage debut in 1931 and who was a reliable member of the OLD VIC company, mainly in supporting roles, from 1932. Quayle left the Royal Artillery in 1945 with a considerable respect for military discipline and a renewed ambition to make a mark in the theatre. When he succeeded Sir BARRY JACKSON as director of the Shakespeare Memorial Theatre at STRATFORD in 1949, he made it an article of faith to attract to that theatre the major stars of the London stage. It was a policy that made the Stratford theatre a national cynosure without ever quite confirming Quayle's own greatness either as actor or director. His best work was as Falstaff (1951), Mosca in *Volpone* (1952) and a powerful Aaron in PETER BROOK's production of *Titus Andronicus* (1955). After leaving Stratford in 1957, Quayle has worked predominantly in films, though he was an effective James Tyrone in O'NEILL's *A Long Day's Journey into Night* (1958), and an admired Galileo in a New York production of BRECHT's play in 1967. In 1978 he directed *The Rivals* and played King Lear at the Old Vic.

Quin, James (1693–1766). Walpole was in a distinct minority in preferring Quin's acting to that of his younger rival, DAVID GARRICK. 'If the young fellow is right,' said Quin of Garrick, 'I and the rest of the players have been all wrong.' The young fellow was right, as far as the town's (and posterity's) judgment was concerned, and Quin retired in 1751, after years of fruitless rivalry with Garrick. Before that, however, he had had a distinguished acting career in Dublin and London, playing, among other parts, those of Othello, Lear and Falstaff. In tragedy he inherited the mantle of THOMAS BETTERTON and BARTON BOOTH. The legs were firmly planted and arms and hands signalled emotional shifts while the voice half-spoke and half-chanted the verse. In 1718, evidence of his skill as a duellist as well as of his short temper, Quin was tried for the murder of a fellow-actor and found guilty of manslaughter. On at least two other occasions he was involved in dangerous quarrels in which he wounded his adversaries. And yet he had also a deserved reputation as a wit, capable of winning his battles without recourse to his sword.

Rachel (1821–48). This is the name by which the French Jewish actress, Elizabeth Félix, became famous. Her family was poor, but industrious, and it owed something to Rachel's hard work that she was admitted to the Conservatoire of the COMÉDIE-FRANÇAISE in 1836. She made her debut there two years later, as Camille in CORNEILLE's *Horace*. In that and other classical roles, culminating in Phèdre in 1843, she revived the fortunes of the Comédie-Française; but she was the first of the international stars, and not all her French admirers approved her absences. Janin, the critic whose influence had done most to establish her reputation, began to turn against her: 'She did not love Paris as it should be loved, with that violent, exalted and exclusive love, a love which knows no other.' By 1845, when she risked an American tour, her Parisian rating was unsteady. The transatlantic reception was not the disaster it has sometimes been painted. There were those who discerned the passion behind the finely spoken French and the lack of action. There were others who excused Rachel a sinful past, of which two bastards bore witness. But there were enough assaults on both her talent and her morals to accelerate the breakdown in her health. By the time she returned to France, Rachel was in the late stages of consumption. Her rise from rags to riches, her unfashionable slimness, her voice, her liaisons and the theatrical qualities which made GEORGE HENRY LEWES call her a panther and Charlotte Brontë confess that 'her acting thrilled me with horror' have combined to give the story of Rachel a romantic excitement. It should not be forgotten that she rejected a play because 'the part is full of rapid and violent movements': as an actress, she was controlled and forceful; and much stiller than she was allowed often to be in a life that ended far too early.

Joanna Richardson, *Rachel*, 1956.

Racine, Jean (1639–99). It is said that CORNEILLE, after hearing Racine read his second performed tragedy, *Alexandra* (1665), told him he was unfitted for drama. There will always be some to agree. Where the landscape is vast and Shakespearean, Racine's small formal garden can look prissily artificial. But the comparison is best avoided. You cannot get much out of a sonnet by asking it to be an epic, and if the rooms in which Racine's plays unfold seem to exclude whole realms of experience, that exclusiveness intensifies the experience they contain.

As a boy, Racine felt but did not absorb the austerity of Jansenism. The writing of plays was an act of defiance. Between 1664, when *La Thébaïde* was performed by MOLIÈRE's company, and 1677, when he became reconciled with the Jansenists of Port-Royal, married, was appointed historiographer royal, and abandoned the theatre, he wrote eight further tragedies, and one comedy, *Les Plaideurs* (1668). His affairs with the actresses Duparc and Champmeslé were not conducted secretly. He gave (to Molière among many others) and took offence too readily. The discipline of his verse is in constant tension with the violence of the passions his characters conceal or reveal. It is doubtful whether any poet has ever subjected love to more pressure. The 'tragedy' of *Bérénice* (1670) is in the parting of lovers, and the play is tragic only if it persuades us of the fatality of separation. The subject, like that of *Britannicus* (1669), *Bajazet* (1672) and *Mithridate* (1673), is, however idiosyncratically, historical. For *Andromaque* (1667), *Iphigénie* (1674) and *Phèdre* (1677), Racine turned to EURIPIDES, and for his last plays, *Esther* (1689) and *Athalie* (1691), to the Bible, but the essential intention to create 'a simple action, sustained by the violence of the passions, the beauty of the sentiments, and the elegance of the expression' (preface to *Britannicus*) remains. Racine is a precision artist. Word-counts have shown how small his vocabulary is, and yet the words are all the action in his plays. If you were to have entered the HÔTEL DE BOURGOGNE at a characteristic moment during the performance of a play by Racine, you would have seen, on an uncluttered stage, two actors classically draped and statuesque, several feet apart and facing forward, and you would have heard declamation bordering on chant for minute after minute – and if you had half an ear for love poetry, you would have been moved.

G. Brereton, *Jean Racine*, 2nd ed., 1973.
P. J. Yarrow, *Racine*, 1978.

Rastell, John (*c.* 1475–1536). Printer, member of parliament for a Cornish constituency and brother-in-law of Sir Thomas More, Rastell translated one of TERENCE's comedies into English and wrote three extant plays of his own, as well as polemical works on behalf of Protestantism to which he was a convert. Rastell is a key figure in the history of English dramatic writing. We can see in his plays the old religious morality being secularized. Thus in *The Nature of the Four Elements* (?1517–27), the hero, Humanity, is introduced to Renaissance humanist education, aided by Studious Desire and Experience, and temporarily distracted by Ignorance and Sensual Appetite. If this summary makes Rastell's work sound more like a tract than a play, the impression is not misleading. *Gentleness and Nobility* (?1527) presents a debate on the familiar theme of noble birth versus noble behaviour; it compares unfavourably with the 'discussion drama' written by Rastell's son-in-law, JOHN HEYWOOD, which is a fairly damning criticism. Even in *Calisto and Melibea* (?1527), a play with real characters based on a Spanish romance, Rastell's didactic drive gets in the way of the dramatic development. His importance is therefore almost entirely historical.

Rattigan, Terence (1911–77). English playwright whose reputation is being made again after two decades in which it was fashionable to decry him. His carefully constructed plays 'have retained a hold on the unacknowledged audiences of amateur theatres, schools, and some provincial repertory companies. It was the frothy *French without Tears* (1936) that brought him his first astonishing (and scarcely deserved) success. *Flare Path* (1942) is a play about the war, written during Rattigan's own war service in Coastal Command. *The Winslow Boy* (1946) was the first of a number of plays to dramatize historical characters and actual incidents. *Adventure Story* (1949), *Ross* (1960), *A Bequest to the Nation* (1970) and *Cause Célèbre* (1977) are others – though it would be too easy to think of them as all of one kind. A deeper concern can be traced through *The Browning Version* (1948), *The Deep Blue Sea* (1952) and *Separate Tables* (1954) to *Man and Boy* (1963) and *In Praise of Love* (1973). It is a compassion for the lonely people whose confidence in themselves is threatened by sexual failure or by disallowed sexual success. Rattigan's best plays are about shame.

Michael Darlow and Gillian Hodson, *Rattigan: The Man and His Work*, 1978.

Ravenscroft, Edward (*c.* 1650–*c.* 1697). Almost nothing is known about Ravenscroft's life except that, like many dramatists of the time, he was a member of one of the Inns of Court. As DRYDEN scornfully remarked, Ravenscroft was a crowd-pleaser who provoked critical disapproval. Apart from writing several original plays, he produced a version of SHAKESPEARE's *Titus Andronicus* (or, *The Rape of Lavinia*) in which the physical horrors of the original are not so much diluted as redistributed. Ravenscroft's most popular play, *The London Cuckolds* (1681), adapted and amplifed from MOLIÈRE, held the stage for over a century while *The Anatomist* (1696) was one of GARRICK's favourite pieces.

Redgrave. British theatrical family of whom the most prominent are:

(1) *Redgrave, Michael* (1908–85). Son and grandson of actors, he abandoned a career as a schoolmaster to join the Liverpool Repertory Theatre in 1934. He was part of TYRONE GUTHRIE's strong company at

the OLD VIC in 1937, when he made the most of Orlando in *As You Like It* and Laertes in *Hamlet*. Tall, handsome and gentle-voiced, he was popular – for example in Hitchcock's fine film *The Lady Vanishes* – before he was critically acclaimed. It is perhaps a pity that his undoubted aptitude for playing the part of a tormented and highly educated gentleman who rides the storms of life with great charm has denied him opportunities to develop the talent for comedy he exhibited in WYCHERLEY's Horner (1936) and in Sir Andrew Aguecheek (1938). The more familiar role of the victim of *Weltschmerz* brought him deserved success as Crocker-Harris in RATTIGAN's *The Browning Version* (1948), Rakitin in TURGENEV's *A Month in the Country* (1949) with the Old Vic company and the title role in *Uncle Vanya* at Chichester in 1962. His great years began with his Macbeth at the Aldwych in 1947, included a fine Berowne in the Old Vic *Love's Labour's Lost* (1949) and an extraordinary run at STRATFORD between 1951 and 1953 of Richard II, Hotspur, Prospero, Shylock, Lear and Antony, and perhaps ended with his faltering attempt to play Hamlet at the age of fifty. Much as he achieved, Redgrave could probably have achieved more. The sensitivity and intelligence displayed in his essays in *The Actor's Ways and Means* (1955) and *Mask or Face* (1958) promised something better than a knighthood (1959) and a season as director of the Yvonne Arnaud Theatre in Guildford (1965). His autobiography *In My Mind's Eye* (1983) is a wry retrospect on his theatrical career.

(2) **Redgrave, Vanessa** (1937–   ). Eldest child of Michael Redgrave and his actress-wife Rachel Kempson, and an actress of outstanding individuality. Tall and commanding, she was a thrilling Rosalind in Michael Elliott's 1961 production of *As You Like It* at Stratford. In continuing partnership with Elliott, mostly in Manchester, she played a number of IBSEN's heroines, culminating in a repeat performance as Ellida in *The Lady from the Sea* in 1982, a role she had also played in 1976 and 1979. Vanessa Redgrave's political activities on behalf of the Worker's Revolutionary Party and her outspoken condemnation of much that an entrenched capitalist society prefers not to notice has made her a controversial figure. Her quality as an actress, whatever the circumstances, cannot be questioned. Most recently it has been in evidence as Arkadina in CHEKHOV's *The Seagull* (1985), as Shakespeare's Cleopatra and shrewish Kate (1986) and as a commanding Mrs Alving in Ibsen's *Ghosts* (1986). There is an astonishing clarity in Vanessa Redgrave's acting, the product of a rare collaboration between anger and intelligence. She operates supremely in the common ground between personal and public politics.

Rehan, Ada (1860–1916). American actress who came to prominence as a member of AUGUSTIN DALY's company after 1879. She was an exquisitely arch partner to JOHN DREW in Shakespearean and modern comedy, but SHAW, who admired her sometimes to the point of idolatry, was not alone in complaining about Daly's unwillingness to risk her outside the charming, light roles in which she excelled: 'Ada Rehan has as yet created nothing but Ada Rehan. She will probably never excel that masterpiece; but why should she not superimpose a character study or two on it!' One effect of Daly's policy was to leave Rehan high and dry when he died in 1899. Despite his reservations, Shaw, who saw her in *Two Gentlemen of Verona*, *A Midsummer Night's Dream*, *As You Like It* and *Twelfth Night*, tended to use her as a model for the playing of Shakespearean comedy.

Reinhardt, Max (1873–1943). Born Max Goldmann, near Vienna, Reinhardt acted for ten years (1890–1900) and directed plays for over forty. He was the first truly international director – and there have been few since, only PETER BROOK of rival stature. His engagement as an actor with OTTO BRAHM in 1894 gave him early experience of the detailed NATURALISM of the Freie Bühne. It was a style that he absorbed but declined to be absorbed by. The astonishing feature of his career as a director is its eclecticism. He opened a cabaret theatre in Berlin in 1901, changing its name to the Kleines Theater in 1902. In this small house he staged naturalistic plays like GORKY's *The Lower Depths* and BECQUE's *The Crows* (1903) and early examples of EXPRESSIONISM like WEDEKIND's *Earth Spirit* (1902). Already he was showing an ability to search out the appropriate style for each play. At the larger Deutsches Theater, of which he became director in 1905 and which he bought outright in 1906, he established his own school of acting. He remained its director until 1933, when the Nazis demanded that he give all his theatres to the German people. It became a home for large-scale productions of the German classics and of SHAKESPEARE. In 1913–14, for example, he produced ten Shakespeare plays in a four-month festival. (The Festival idea, whether indoor or open-air, was largely his brain-child, the Salzburg Festival, which he founded in 1920, being its grandest expression.) But though Reinhardt was happy to undertake spectacular productions, he liked also to operate on a smaller scale. The chamber theatre (Kammerspiele) next door to the Deutsches Theater was the setting for a profoundly influential production of Wedekind's *Spring Awakening* in 1906. It was his arena production of *Oedipus Rex*, which played in ten European capitals (1910–12), that made him widely known. He followed it with spectacular stagings of HOFMANNSTHAL's

Everyman and Volmoeller's *The Miracle*. These baroque spectacles have misleadingly conditioned the popular image of Reinhardt. He should rather be remembered as a man for all seasons.

Oliver Sayler, *Max Reinhardt and His Theatre*, 1924.
J. L. Styan, *Max Reinhardt*, 1982.

Rice, Elmer (1892–1967). American playwright, who left school early, worked at night school to qualify for the New York Bar, was admitted to it in 1913, and promptly abandoned the law for the theatre. The success of *On Trial* (1914) bought him time to write. It is a clever thriller. Nothing more. Throughout his career, Rice retained an ability and a preparedness to write pot-boilers. More surprisingly, he also retained principles. *The Adding Machine* (1923) was a pioneering EXPRESSIONIST play in the American theatre, with a vividly displayed message about the annihilation of the individual in a mechanized society. *Street Scene* (1929) is a typically large-cast slice of New York life, and was a huge success on BROADWAY. Rice had directed it. His involvement in theatre was total. From 1934 to 1937, he owned and wrote for the Belasco Theatre. *Judgment Day* (1934), his indictment of fascism, was staged there, as was the social discussion-play, *Between Two Worlds* (1934). At the same time, Rice was active in the planning of the FEDERAL THEATRE PROJECT, which was launched in 1935. It was he who directed and largely created *Ethiopia*, which would have been the first LIVING NEWSPAPER performance in America had it not been banned after dress rehearsal. Rice resigned from the Project, and shortly afterwards withdrew from rehearsal at the Belasco his angry pastiche of attitudes to drama, *Not for Children*. His later work, even that for the Playwright's Company from 1938 to 1940, is slighter, but the combative, resilient man who emerges from the long autobiography, *Minority Report* (1963), should not be neglected.

Robert Hogan, *The Independence of Rice*, 1965.

Rich, Christopher (d. 1714). In the annals of theatre management Rich's name stands high on the list of all-time despots, Scrooges and assorted villains. In 1689 he bought the share of the Drury Lane patent inherited by DAVENANT's son, and for the next few years the history of that unfortunate theatre was one of exploitation, penny-pinching and tortuous litigation. When they had had enough, several actors, led by BETTERTON, left to form their own company. Rich carried on with the mediocre remnant, but was eventually forced out, through the wiles of COLLEY CIBBER, in 1710. It was then that he took up again his obsession with building, and set about constructing a new theatre in Lincoln's Inn Fields. He died before the theatre was complete, leaving it in the hands of his young son, JOHN RICH.

Rich, John (*c.* 1692–1761). John was altogether different from his father. CHRISTOPHER RICH had been a lawyer, but John was an actor, gifted in all but his voice. 'Every motion of his hand or head, or of any part of his body, was a kind of dumb eloquence that was readily understood by the audience,' wrote a contemporary critic. Rich was shrewd enough to know his limitations. Calling himself John Lun, he became a specialist in the speechless part of Harlequin. First at Lincoln's Inn Fields, and then, after the success of *The Beggar's Opera* (1728) had made him wealthy, in the grander new building at Covent Garden, he made the annual pantomime with its spectacular HARLEQUI-NADE a feature. He remained in control of the fortunes of Covent Garden until his death.

Paul Sawyer, 'John Rich's Contribution', in *The Eighteenth Century English Stage*, ed. Kenneth Richards and Peter Thomson, 1972.

Richardson, Ralph (1902–83). British actor who made his early reputation at the Birmingham Repertory Theatre. He joined the OLD VIC company in 1930, and his association with that theatre was to be of great significance. He was a notably unselfish actor, deliberate where OLIVIER was dynamic, rough where GIELGUD was smooth. His career brought him often into the company of those two great contemporaries, and he generally found Gielgud easier to act with, for example in DAVID STOREY's *Home* (1970) and PINTER's *No Man's Land* (1975). His friendship with Olivier had to survive a number of less happy experiences, the Old Vic *Othello* of 1938 for example, when Olivier's prancing Iago kept Richardson's Othello on the retreat. Nonetheless, when Richardson was asked, in 1944, to revive the fortunes of the bomb-damaged Old Vic, he asked both Gielgud (who declined) and Olivier to join him. He and Olivier could clearly see the Old Vic seasons of 1944–9 as the basis for an English NATIONAL THEATRE. Richardson, during these Old Vic seasons, excelled as Peer Gynt and Cyrano de Bergerac. His Falstaff was much praised, though he again encountered some difficulty with the magnetic Olivier as Hotspur and Justice Shallow. Richardson was knighted in 1947, six months before Olivier, and he could have been forgiven for supposing that his Old Vic policies had the seal of approval. To most people's surprise, he and Olivier were informed in 1948 that their five-year contracts would not be renewed. It was not until 1956, when he played the title role in *Timon of Athens*, that Richardson returned to the Old Vic. Although not at all a spectacular actor, Richardson made the stage real when he was on it. He had doubts and hesitancies that his audiences could recognize. This studied ordinariness helped him to make memorable several plays by J. B. PRIESTLEY, particularly *Johnson over Jordan* (1939), and Robert Bolt's *Flowering Cherry* (1957).

Garry O'Connor, *Ralph Richardson*, 1982.

Ristori, Adelaide (1822–1906). Italian actress, who made her debut at the age of twelve, and had already played one of her greatest parts, that of SCHILLER's Mary Stuart, by the time she was eighteen. She was an indefatigable tourer and one of the great international stars. Her Lady Macbeth (in Italian) at Covent Garden in 1857 was admired, but not, on the whole, ecstatically. She was an excellent ambassador for Italy, but GEORGE HENRY LEWES was probably right to call her a 'conventional' actress. 'All is artificial, but then all is congruous. A noble unity of impression is produced.' Ristori retired in 1885, and her *Studies and Memoirs* were published in English three years later. Her life in the theatre was either unusually pure (she was certainly not a particularly sexual actress), or uniquely discreet. Delacroix, who met her in Paris in 1855, noted in his diary: 'Ristori is a large woman with a cold expression. Her little husband looks as if he were her oldest son. He is a marquis or a Roman prince.' He was, in fact, the Marchese Giuliano del Grillo, to whom Ristori was married from 1847 until he died in 1881.

Henry Knepler, *The Gilded Stage*, 1968.

Robertson, Thomas William (1829–71). It is, by any reckoning, extraordinary that a dramatist as conventional and intellectually drab as Robertson should have had so radical an influence on the English theatre. He was the eldest child of a vast theatrical family, destined for the stage as part of the family business. He proved a weak actor, and was scraping a living as a journalist and hack dramatist when he had a lucky break. The actor Edward Askew Sothern had made all the money he could out of the part of Lord Dundreary (of the whiskers) in TOM TAYLOR's *Our American Cousin*, and was looking around for a new hit. He lighted on Robertson's *David Garrick*, an adaptation from the French of the kind almost any other hack might have made, and realized its susceptibility to his style of personality acting. That was in 1864, and it gave Robertson the confidence to write out of his conviction that the stage could accommodate more realism. When MARIE WILTON leased the little Prince of Wales's Theatre the next year, she took a risk with Robertson's *Society*. It was a fashionable success, to be followed at annual intervals by *Ours* (1866), *Caste* (1867), *Play* (1868), *School* (1869) and the play that was in rehearsal as its author lay dying, *M.P.* (1870). They are not great plays, but they take the stage seriously, and invite from actors the kind of ensemble performance that Marie Wilton and SQUIRE BANCROFT asked from their company. By a very slight redeployment of the theatrical stereotypes he had described in the *Illustrated Times* a few years before, Robertson raised the status of the English drama. PINERO rewards him, in *Trelawny of the 'Wells'*, with an over-sentimental appearance as Tom Wrench, but there is some truth in that fictional playwright's preference for real doors with real handles. It was the confirmed opinion of William Archer (who was no fool) at the beginning of the next century that 'Robertsonian realism' had established itself as the one true style for ever.

M. Savin, *Robertson: His Plays and Stagecraft*, 1950.

Robeson, Paul (1898–1976). American singer and actor, born in Princeton, New Jersey where his father, once a runaway slave, was a presbyterian minister. At Rutgers College he excelled as a footballer and was selected by Walter Camp for his All-American team in 1918. During his law training in Columbia he was intermittently a professional footballer. He made his acting debut in 1920 in Ridgeley Torrence's *Simon the Cyrenean* and, while still a law student, toured the provincial theatres of England in a production of Mary Wiborg's *Voodoo* as co-star to MRS PATRICK CAMPBELL. Back in New York, he began singing in Harlem's Cotton Club, making his first record of Negro spirituals in 1925. He was, by then, well known for his performances in O'NEILL's *All God's Chillun Got Wings* (1924) and *The Emperor Jones* (1925), and his twin careers as actor and singer were combined in Jerome Kern's *Show Boat* (1928), in which his singing of 'Ol' Man River' made him an international star. He played Othello at London's Savoy Theatre in 1930 and O'Neill's *The Hairy Ape* at the Ambassador's in 1931.

It was his encounter with England in the Depression that raised his political awareness: 'I came here unshaped. Great parts of my working-class roots are here,' he said in 1960. He made the first of many trips to Moscow in 1934, and sent his son to school there in 1936 'so the boy need not contend with discrimination because of colour'. He was associated with the UNITY THEATRE in London, appearing in *Plant in the Sun* (1938), a play about American trades unions. Intransigently vocal about segregation in the United States and increasingly frank about his communism (a mountain in the Soviet Union was named after him in 1949 and he won the Stalin Peace Prize in 1952), he was much reviled in his own country, had his passport withheld from 1950 to 1958 and was called before the HOUSE UNAMERICAN ACTIVITIES COMMITTEE in 1956. 'You are the UnAmericans,' he told the committee. His involvement in politics and in films reduced his theatre work after the thirties, but he played his first American Othello, directed by Margaret Webster, in 1942, and his last English one at STRATFORD in 1959. His autobiography, *Here I Stand* (1958), makes clear his right to a proud place in the American Civil Rights movement.

Edwin Hoyt, *Paul Robeson: The American Othello*, 1967.

Robinson, Lennox (1886–1958). Irish playwright, actor, director and dramatic critic, associated with the ABBEY THEATRE from 1908, when his first play *The Clancy Name* was staged there, until his death. Robinson's best-known play is a comedy, *The White-Headed Boy* (1916), a tightly crafted story of a charming Irish scapegrace who comes good. *The Far-Off Hills* (1928) and *Church Street* (1934) are also gently ironic manners comedies. But Robinson wrote also of Irish politics in *Patriots* (1912), *The Dreamers* (1913) and *The Big House* (1926). His awareness of comic contradictions at the heart of the Irish tragedy is evident in *The Lost Leader* (1918), which tantalizingly refuses to reveal whether or not the old innkeeper is, in fact, the lost leader, Parnell, in hiding. Perhaps most impressive of all, certainly as evidence of Robinson's profound involvement in the Irish theatre, is *Drama at Inish* (1933), which records the impact on a small Irish seaside town of a visit from a group of ambitious actors. The play was successfully revived in the Peacock Theatre, Dublin in 1983. Robinson is the author of *Curtain Up* (1941) and *A History of the Abbey Theatre* (1951) and editor of collected lectures under the title *The Irish Theatre* (1939).

Michael J. O'Neill, *Lennox Robinson*, 1964.

Robson, Flora (1902–84). English actress, whose fascinating, brooding face seemed always to be concealing more than it revealed. After scarcely two years on the stage, she abandoned acting in 1924, and it took the persuasion of her friend TYRONE GUTHRIE to recall her in 1928 to play the stepdaughter in his production of PIRANDELLO's *Six Characters in Search of an Author* at the CAMBRIDGE FESTIVAL THEATRE. Three years later he cast her as a prostitute in his London production of BRIDIE's *The Anatomist*. She had only a single scene, but her playing of it was powerful enough to win her a cherished part in J. B. PRIESTLEY's

Dangerous Corner in 1932. She was a leading member of the OLD VIC company in 1933, as successful in high comedy (as Gwendolen in *The Importance of Being Earnest*, for example) as in the neurotic roles for which her superb portrayal of controlled tension seemed best to suit her. Although she twice played Lady Macbeth (1933 and 1948), her best-known Shakespearean performance was in the comparatively minor role of Paulina in JOHN GIELGUD's 1951 production of *The Winter's Tale*. She is one of the very few actors ever to have achieved greatness in a stage-career predominantly restricted to supporting roles. Having been created DBE in 1960, Flora Robson made her last London appearance in 1969.

Janet Dunbar, *Flora Robson*, 1960.
Kenneth Barrow, *Flora*, 1981.

Robson, Frederick (1821–64). Robson was, briefly, a phenomenon. No actor has so consistently impressed critics with the suddenness of his shifts from hilarity to horror. IRVING said that 'he was great enough to know he could only be great for three minutes'. Those three minutes, though, were magical. From 1853, until stage fright and dutch courage overcame him in 1863, he was the star of the Olympic Theatre, a tiny man who could make his audience's hair stand on end in the middle of a burlesque. As the popularizer of the song 'Vilikens and his Dinah', which he sang as Jem Bags in *The Wandering Minstrel*, he has also a place in the history of music hall. He was the Dickensian actor *par excellence*, quirky, exaggerated and yet oddly familiar.

Mollie Sands, *Robson of the Olympic*, 1979.

Roscius, Quintus (d. 62 BC). Pliny reports that this famous comic actor received enough from his performances to make him massively wealthy. We know too little about other Roman actors to make useful comparisons. It would seem that Rosicus was a careful actor, whose preparations were as detailed as an orator's.

Rotrou, Jean de (1609–50). French playwright, very popular in his day, and notable still as the best exponent of the fashionable tragi-comedies that provoked the opposition of French literary purists and inspired their rigid insistence on adherence to the UNITIES of time, place and action. Rotrou was also responsible for introducing the first Spanish play (a comedy by LOPE DE VEGA) to the French theatre. He wrote for the actors of the HÔTEL DE BOURGOGNE and was prolific enough to have four plays staged there in 1636, famous as the year of

CORNEILLE's *Le Cid*. His best plays include a tragedy, *Venceslas* (1647), a comedy on the Amphitryon story, *The Lookalikes* (*Les Sosies*) and *The Veritable Martyr*, which tells the story of Saint Genesius, converted to Christianity whilst acting the role of a martyr. Rotrou died of the plague, having refused to leave his native town, Dreux, where he was civil lieutenant.

Rowe, Nicholas (1674–1718). Rowe's most distinguished contribution to English drama was undoubtedly the six-volume edition of the *Works of Shakespeare* which appeared in 1709. He was the first editor of SHAKESPEARE in the modern sense of the term. He began as a lawyer but gave this up for playwriting when he came into the family property in 1692. His tragedies were among the most popular stage successes of the first half of the eighteenth century and continued to be played throughout the nineteenth. He specialized in sentimental melodrama with a strong infusion of pathos, and in plays such as *The Fair Penitent* (1703), *Lady Jane Grey* (1715) and *Jane Shore* (1715) provided female roles which tragediennes such as OLDFIELD, PRITCHARD and SIDDONS seized with both hands. Dr Johnson was a judicious admirer of Rowe's tragedies.

L. C. Burns, *Pity and Tears: The Tragedies of Rowe*, 1974.

Rowley, William (*c*. 1585–1626). Beginning his theatrical career as an actor with the Duke of York's (later Prince Charles') Company, Rowley eventually joined the King's Men, the most distinguished acting company of the day, and achieved some reputation as a comic actor before becoming one of the most prolific dramatic collaborators of the early seventeenth century; fifty plays or more may have some portion for which he was responsible. He collaborated with some of the best dramatists of the period, including MIDDLETON, WEBSTER and FLETCHER. It was with the first of these that he produced his finest work, the sub-plot of *The Changeling*, where the bizarre madhouse comedy meshes with ironic aptness into the tragic main plot. His experience of playing clowns also doubtless helped Rowley to create such satisfactory comic figures as Cuddy Banks in *The Witch of Edmonton* (1621, with DEKKER and FORD). On his own, Rowley wrote two citizen comedies of uncertain date, *A Woman Never Vexed* and *A Match at Midnight*, and a convoluted tragedy, *All's Lost by Lust* (?1619–20).

Sackville, Thomas (1536–1608). Sackville was the 1st Earl of Dorset and one of Elizabeth's Privy Councillors. Together with Thomas Norton, a member of the Inner Temple, he wrote *The Tragedy of*

Gorboduc (1561), the first English tragedy. Though lacking the 'classical UNITIES' of time and place, it has many features of classical tragedy, such as choruses, and action which is reported rather than shown. It also has DUMB SHOWS which prefigure the action, a non-classical feature. The theme, the ruin which befalls a divided kingdom, had obvious political relevance to an age which anxiously waited for the Virgin Queen to name a successor or bear one. Sackville also wrote the 'complaint' of the Duke of Buckingham for the 1563 edition of *The Mirror for Magistrates* as well as a long 'induction' to the work, which deals with the fall of great men from prosperity to adversity.

Normand Berlin, *Thomas Sackville*, 1974.

Saint-Denis, Michel (1897–1971). In his fine book *Theatre: The Rediscovery of Style* (1960), Saint-Denis describes his forty years as actor, director and innovative teacher as 'an experiment directed towards the discovery of all the means by which reality can be given to fiction on the stage'. Born and brought up in France, where he was much influenced by his uncle JACQUES COPEAU, Saint-Denis founded the Compagnie des Quinze in 1931. The company worked to revive French classical traditions with a livelier popular style. The plays of André Obey, who wrote for it, give some indication of the taste and mood. In 1936 Saint-Denis was persuaded to establish the London Theatre Studio, precursor of the more famous Old Vic School where he taught from 1946 to 1952. English dramatic poetry became and remained an inspiration to him. Among his productions in England were *Macbeth* with LAURENCE OLIVIER in 1937, *The Three Sisters* in 1938 with JOHN GIELGUD, *Oedipus Rex* in 1945 again with Olivier, *The Cherry Orchard* in 1962 and BRECHT's *Puntila* in 1965. The last two were staged by the ROYAL SHAKESPEARE COMPANY, of which he became a director in 1962. The intangible but abiding influence of Saint-Denis is that of his teaching. His aim was to instil into his students the skills and the passion of an omnicompetent theatrical ensemble; and his methods employed both his charm and his autocratic idealism. Stories of his terrifying classes abound. According to Yvonne Mitchell, 'Michel did not admit pain.'

Salvini, Tommaso (1829–1915). Italian actor, whose worldwide fame rested largely on his playing, in Italian, SHAKESPEARE's Othello. STANISLAVSKY thought it the finest acting in the nineteenth-century theatre: 'The Othello of Salvini is a bronze monument, a law unto eternity which can never change.' ELLEN TERRY, less solemnly, noted that, 'Salvini's Hamlet made me scream with mirth, but his Othello was the grandest, biggest, most glorious thing.' It was based on a superb voice, sensitive to rhythm and tempo, and it won him audiences all over Europe and America. Salvini's parents were actors. He made his professional debut in Padua at the age of fourteen, and had his first great success with ADELAIDE RISTORI's company in 1848. The following year he enlisted in the army that fought for Italian independence. He was back with Ristori in Rome in 1851, and played Othello for the first time in 1856. He retired in 1890. *Leaves from the Autobiography* (1893) is moderately interesting. More so, perhaps, is the influence Salvini had, through his admirer WILIAM POEL, on the development in England of a less spectacular, more textual approach to the production of Shakespeare's plays.

Marvin Carlson, *The Italian Shakespearians*, 1985.

Sardou, Victorien (1831–1908). The unrivalled popularity of this French playwright disgusted GEORGE BERNARD SHAW, who coined the word 'Sardoodledom' to describe the well made drama of the lowest common denominator by which Sardou guaranteed his success. It was Sardou's habit to take passionate activity to the brink of significance, and then to withdraw tactfully into insignificance. He does it in *Dora* (1877), *Divorçons* (1880), *Fédora* (1882) and *La Tosca* (1887). It was in the year of *La Tosca* that Sardou was elected to the French Academy. It might have been fairer to elect SARAH BERNHARDT, whose acting deceived Sardou's public into reverence for his plays. 'Who but he,' asked Blanche Roosevelt in a deplorable study, 'can find those ingenious situations, those startling attitudes and audacious chimeras which abound in his works?' Who indeed, and who cares? And yet, the fading of Sardou's name would have astonished the audiences of *Madame Sans-Gêne* (1893), in France, England or America. The once-reliable machinery of his plays is obsolete, and the catastrophic contrivances excite scorn now. You can perceive the general problem from this observation of Shaw's: 'Sardou's plan of playwriting is first to invent the action of his piece, and then to carefully keep it off the stage and have it announced merely by letters and telegrams.'

Saroyan, William (1908–81). American playwright and novelist, born in California of Armenian parents. Saroyan's work is not easy to classify. His detractors find him coy and suspect him of insincerity; his admirers cherish his lack of sophistication and the buoyancy of his fictions. His first play, a long one-act rhapsody on poetic integrity called *My Heart's in the Highlands* (1939), was produced by the GROUP THEATRE. His second, *The Time of Your Life* (1939), was awarded the

Pulitzer Prize which Saroyan, signalling his contempt for commercial patronage, rejected. *The Beautiful People* (1941) carries the whimsical optimism of *The Time of Your Life* to extremes, and the sentimentality is hard to accept, as it is also in *Across the Board on Tomorrow Morning* (1941). The one-act *Hello, Out There* (1942) is much better, as is *The Cave Dwellers* (1957), a rambling play set on the stage of an empty theatre to which a group of big-hearted misfits have fled for comfort and safety. JOAN LITTLEWOOD's improvisation on a script by Saroyan, *Sam, the Highest Jumper of Them All* (1960) was an unexpected homage to an off-beat people's writer, but it was not one of the Theatre Workshop's successes, and Saroyan wrote little for the stage between its production and his death.

Howard R. Floan, *Saroyan*, 1966.

Sartre, Jean-Paul (1905–80). French philosopher, novelist and playwright who was the leading proponent and publicist of existentialism. This philosophy, with its stress on personal responsibility for decisions taken, had an immense appeal to the post-war generation. His major philosophical work, *Being and Nothingness* (1943), was published in the same year as his first play, *The Flies*. This was an anti-Vichy assertion of the possibility of individual rebellion, and its staging was only permitted because it confused the French and German authorities by taking as its overt theme the killing of Clytemnestra by Orestes. Sartre preached the need for writers to be engaged in the social and political life of their day, and his decision to write plays was of immense importance in re-establishing the drama as a vehicle for serious political and philosophical reflection. *Huis-Clos* (variously translated as *In Camera*, *Vicious Circle* and *No Exit*), staged in Paris in 1944, is a relentless short play which places three people in the Hell of each other's eternal company. It was an acknowledged influence on the early writing of HAROLD PINTER. Subsequent plays, like *Men without Shadows* (1946), *Dirty Hands* (1948), *Altona* (1959) and the cartoon-like satire *Nekrassov* (1956), took Sartre further into the politics of resistance. His refusal of the proffered Nobel Prize in 1964 was an act of personal resistance to Western values.

Philip Thody, *Sartre*, 1971.
J. H. MacMahon, *Humans Being*, 1972.

Schiller, Johann Christoph Friedrich von (1759–1805). The aspirations towards nationhood and reasoned liberty that flowered in Germany under the Napoleonic threat were expressed with particular eloquence by Schiller. He was the son of an army surgeon, and was himself serving as a military doctor when his first play *The Robbers*, cautiously adapted to suit the theatre's manager, was staged in Mannheim in 1782. Despite the caution, the play 'turned the theatre into a madhouse'. Its revolutionary egalitarianism and its advocacy of individual rights appealed to idealistic German youth. It is not hard to see why. Stories (cf. the Gloucester sub-plot in *King Lear*) about the bad brother who is really the good brother, have a romantic charm. And Schiller, who had already a taste for complex motivation, does not sentimentalize in order to make his moral point. This play, together with *The Conspiracy of Fiesco at Genoa* (1782) and *Intrigue and Love* (1784), is a landmark in the high-spirited STURM UND DRANG movement. *Don Carlos* (1787), whilst still responsive to SHAKESPEARE, takes a cooler look at the influence of Rousseau. It was Schiller's first verse play, and the creative aspect of the historical activity that led to the publication in 1788 of the first part of his long *History of the Revolt of the Netherlands against Spain*. Having been appointed Professor of History at the University of Jena, he wrote next a *History of the Thirty Years War* (1792). The creative aspect of this was the monumental *Wallenstein* trilogy (1797–9), of which the final part, *The Death of Wallenstein*, is often separately performed. The trilogy was first staged at Weimar, where GOETHE supervised its performance, as he did later performances of *Mary Stuart* (1800), considered by many to be Schiller's greatest play, *The Maid of Orleans* (1801), *The Bride of Messina* (1803) and *William Tell* (1804). Schiller died of consumption, leaving an incomplete play called *Demetrius*. He was a fine poet, who composed plays and speeches within plays on the scale of grand opera. Much taken by the multiplicity of Shakespeare, he never rivalled Shakespeare's compression. That is one of many reasons for the English-speaking theatre's nervousness of him.

H. B. Garland, *Schiller the Dramatic Writer*, 1969.
Ilse Graham, *Schiller: A Master of the Tragic Form*, 1975.

Schnitzler, Arthur (1862–1931). Austrian playwright and novelist, the son of a wealthy Jewish doctor, Schnitzler had already flirted with literature before he qualified as a doctor. He enjoyed, too, the dissipations of life in Vienna. The figure of the *süsses Mädel* – the 'sweet girl' whose sweetness includes a readiness to give in before the man has really started trying – was not confined to his fiction. His first performed play, *Farewell Supper* (1893), was also the first of the *Anatol* cycle that made him famous. The hero is a sophisticated man-about-

Vienna whose sequence of sexual conquests is repeated from scene to scene until its lightness becomes indistinguishable from sterility. The similarity of theme to *Reigen* (better known as *La Ronde*), which was written by 1900, first performed in Hungary in 1912, and first performed in German in Berlin in 1920, is unmistakable. *Reigen* is a ten-scene sequence of interlinked dialogues occurring just before and just after sexual intercourse. Both in Berlin and in Vienna in 1921, its performance caused public outcry and legal action. That Schnitzler was aware of the dangers of Viennese permissiveness is clear from *Liebelei* (1895) – adapted as *Dalliance* by TOM STOPPARD for London's NATIONAL THEATRE in 1986 – to *Professor Bernhardi* (1912). His characters often behave badly, but are rarely 'bad'. Their complexity is owed partly to Schnitzler's up-to-date interest in psychoanalysis and partly to his taste for the bizarre. *Der einsame Weg* (1904), presented at London's OLD VIC as *The Lonely Road* (1985), and *Das weite Land* (1911), adapted by Stoppard for the National as *Undiscovered Country* (1979), characteristically mingle melodrama and manners comedy, exploiting the plunge from climax to bathos. The shared shortcomings of Schnitzler and his city, implicit in many of his plays, are made explicit in the autobiographical *My Youth in Vienna* (published 1968).

Martin Swales, *Arthur Schnitzler*, 1971.

Scofield, Paul (1922–   ). English actor, considered by many to be the finest of his generation, and certainly one of the most versatile. After early successes in Birmingham, where PETER BROOK directed him as the Bastard in *King John* in 1945, he was a leading member of BARRY JACKSON's new STRATFORD company in 1946 and 1947. It was at Stratford that he played his first Hamlet in 1948. The second, directed by Peter Brook, was the major theatrical event of 1955, and created history by visiting the MOSCOW ART THEATRE, the first time an English company had visited the Soviet Union since the Bolshevik Revolution of 1917. Scofield was well established by then, having had an outstanding success in the testing but attractive double-role of the twins in ANOUILH's *Ring round the Moon* (1950). As Hamlet and as the dissimilar twins, Scofield was able to combine lyricism and irony and to exploit the remarkable flexibility of his voice. Other major roles have included Sir Thomas More in Robert Bolt's *A Man for All Seasons* (1960), King Lear (1962), Timon (1965), the title role in CHEKHOV's *Uncle Vanya* (1970), Prospero (1974), JONSON's Volpone (1977) and Salieri in PETER SHAFFER's *Amadeus* (1979). As a leading member of the NATIONAL THEATRE company, he has proved himself an actor with the range of OLIVIER and something of the same magnetism.

Scott, Clement (1841–1904). English dramatic critic who became the leader of the resistance to the new drama at the end of the nineteenth century. Scott was the reviewer of plays for the *Daily Telegraph*, 1872–97, and editor of a monthly magazine, *The Theatre*, 1877–97. He was a pugnacious man and a tolerable writer, but he lost his bearings. Self-satisfied as the acknowledged leader of his profession, he made the mistake of identifying all that was good in theatre with HENRY IRVING and all that was bad with IBSEN. His own dramatic preference was for SARDOU, many of whose plays he adapted for the English stage under the laboured pseudonym of 'Saville Rowe'. His reviews of first nights at Irving's Lyceum were collected in book form as *From 'The Bells' to 'King Arthur'* (1895). They are an invaluable record of majority taste. Scott's own career came to a melancholy end when he gave an interview to the magazine *Great Thoughts* in 1897. 'There is no school on earth so bad for the formation of character, or that so readily, so quickly draws out all that is bad in man and woman as the stage,' he said, partly, perhaps, because his wife was, at the time, trying to become an actress. An outraged theatrical profession, led by the comparatively moderate Irving, drummed him out of his job and he retired to the Continent. The publication of *The Drama of Yesterday and Today* (1899) was a doomed attempt to rehabilitate himself.

Scribe, (Augustin) Eugène (1791–1861). The only play by this prolific French dramatist that can be said to have lasted is *Adrienne Lecouvreur* (1849); and the endurance of that piece is a result of the actresses who have exploited the pathos of the title role – BERNHARDT, RACHEL, RISTORI, MODJESKA. Singly, or in collaboration (*Adrienne Lecouvreur* was shared with Ernest Legouvé), Scribe wrote upwards of five hundred plays between 1815 and 1861. To him is owed the famous formula of the *pièce bien faite*, a formula that guaranteed to keep the audience on tenterhooks from scene to scene and act to act. It is the drama of consumerism; Scribe would have known how to exploit television.

Seneca, Lucius Annaeus (*c.* 4 BC–AD 65). Roman statesman, philosopher and dramatist, who was Nero's tutor. The nine verse tragedies which survive had an ambiguous effect on the writers of tragedy in England at the end of the sixteenth century. Bloody revenge, as in *Titus Andronicus*, is a direct descendant of Seneca's *Thyestes*, but the dignity and Stoic endurance of some of those who suffer, and the delight in verbal ingenuity, are no less characteristic. There is some debate over whether or not Seneca expected his plays to be staged. Majority opinion proposes that they were written for public recitation rather than public performance, but a weakness of this majority is its failure to conceive of alternative performance possibilities of the kind charted by PETER BROOK in his 1966 production of *Oedipus*. The plays of Seneca can be sung and danced. It may be that they were so presented at Nero's court. The prospect of so much violence would have tempted the prurient Emperor, on whose order Seneca committed suicide.

A. L. Motto, *Seneca*, 1973.

Settle, Elkanah (1648–1724). During his long literary and dramatic career, Settle became involved in a feud with DRYDEN who immortalized him as Og in *Absalom and Achitophel*. Settle achieved immortality of a more reputable if rather oblique kind by writing the libretto which Purcell set to music for *The Fairy Queen* (1692). He had immediate success with his first play *Cambyses* (?1667), the second bombastic drama of that title in English. *The Empress of Morocco* (?1667) was an outstanding success and is a prime example of the inflated heroic tragedy, with its impossible heroes impaled on implacable absolutes, which the later seventeenth century took briefly to its heart if not to its head; the genre is magnificently parodied in *The Rehearsal* by BUCK-INGHAM and others.

Frank C. Brown, *Settle: His Life and Works*, 1910.

Shadwell, Thomas (1641–92). Shadwell came from an old Norfolk family and studied at Caius College, Cambridge and the Inner Temple. He is perhaps best remembered as the chief target of DRYDEN's satire in *MacFlecknoe* and as an object of scorn in the second part of *Absalom and Achitophel*; it is fair to recall that Shadwell provoked Dryden by making a personal attack on him in *The Medal of John Bayes*. The quarrel between the two went on for several years, with Dryden making up in force of impact what he conceded to Shadwell in sheer volume. As a playwright, Shadwell was not as dull as Dryden made him out to be, but he was dull enough. He wrote eighteen plays, the first of which, *The Sullen Lovers* (1668), is a wooden imitation of the Jonsonian comedy of humours. His best satirical comedies, *Epsom Wells* (1672), *The Virtuoso* (1676) and *The Squire of Alsatia* (1688), do have flashes of Jonsonian comic inventiveness, though these are few and far between. Unlike many other Restoration dramatists, Shadwell was essentially middle class in his outlook, and his Whig politics kept him away from the circle of Court wits. The heroes of his plays undergo a change from Restoration gallants to worthy Christian gentlemen who might be fair company for Addison's Sir Roger de Coverley. As a professional dramatist Shadwell was compelled to cater to the vagaries of changing public taste which he did successfully for nearly a quarter of a century.

Don R. Kunz, *The Drama of Thomas Shadwell*, 1972.

Shaffer, Peter (1926–). English playwright, who was a coal-mining 'Bevin boy' before going to Cambridge University, then a librarian and assistant to a music publisher. During these years, he was writing novels with his twin brother, Anthony. *Five Finger Exercise* (1958), his first performed play, is an intense example of 'the psychological play'. The investigation of motive remains the concern of the highly praised (and certainly theatrically effective) *Equus* (1973) and *Amadeus* (1979), as, despite its epic dressing, it was of *The Royal Hunt of the Sun* (1964). The slighter short comedies, *The Private Ear*, *The Public Eye* (1962) and *Black Comedy* (1965), might in the end prove more durable. Shaffer caters for the theatre-going public with intelligent popular plays as RATTIGAN did for an earlier audience.

Dennis A. Klein, *Peter Shaffer*, 1979.

Shakespeare, William (1564–1616). We know a good deal more about Shakespeare than we do about many other dramatists of the period. STRATFORD-upon-Avon, where he was born, has virtually made its living off him ever since GARRICK's Shakespeare Jubilee in 1769. The exact date of Shakespeare's birth is unknown, but he was baptized at Holy Trinity Church, Stratford on 26 April 1564, and it is reasonable to assume, as is usually done, that he was born on St George's Day, 23 April. His father was John Shakespeare, glover and whittawer (dresser of white leather) who became mayor of Stratford in 1568. Our evidence as to the house in Henley Street where he was born dates from the eighteenth century, though it is not unlikely that this was indeed his birthplace as it was one of two properties owned by his father at the time. Shakespeare's mother, Mary Arden, belonged to an old Warwickshire family. The records of Stratford grammar school are lost, but Shakespeare was almost certainly a pupil there from about the age of six. His education would have been based on Latin literature and Roman history. Here he would have made his first acquaintance with the comedies of PLAUTUS, which served as a model for what was probably his first play, *The Comedy of Errors*. Here too he would have come across the poetry of Ovid, the single most important classical influence on his work. He was eighteen when he married Anne Hathaway, who was eight years older. Anne was pregnant at the time and their first child Susanna was born in May 1583. Two years later the twins Hamnet and Judith were born. Hamnet died in 1596.

We have no firm evidence as to what Shakespeare did, or where, between the years 1585 and 1592. He may have joined a troupe of actors or he may have been a country schoolmaster, as John Aubrey records on the basis of information given by an actor, William Beeston. The first extant reference to Shakespeare is in 1592 when ROBERT GREENE, dramatist, pamphleteer and starving bohemian, wrote his deathbed confession, *Greene's Groatsworth of Wit, Bought with a Million of Repentance*, in which he speaks of 'an upstart crow, beautified with our feathers, that with his tiger's heart wrapped in a player's hide supposes he is as well able to bombast out a blank verse as the best of you; and, being an absolute Johannes Factotum, is in his own conceit the only Shake-scene in the country'. The play on Shakespeare's name and the paraphrase of a line from one of his early plays, *Henry VI* Part 3, make the reference unmistakable. It seems to show that by 1592 Shakespeare had achieved sufficient reputation in the professional theatre to arouse the envy of a Cambridge man like Greene, who resented the fact that a provincial non-university intruder had done so well in the fiercely competitive world of the London stage. In 1596 Shakespeare successfully applied to the College of Heralds for a coat-of-arms (which his father had vainly attempted to obtain twenty years earlier). His motto 'Non sans droit' (Not without right) was held up to ridicule by BEN JONSON in one of his plays as 'Not without mustard'.

Shakespeare was not only a playwright but a professional actor of some repute, a member of the most distinguished theatrical company of his day, the Lord Chamberlain's Men (later, in the reign of James I, the King's Men). We know for certain that he acted in two of Jonson's plays, and tradition also casts him as the original ghost in *Hamlet* and old Adam in *As You Like It*. In terms of financial success, his being a 'sharer' (shareholder) in a successful acting company was far more significant than the fact that his plays were popular in their printed form. His share as an actor enabled him eventually to retire to Stratford and purchase New Place, the second largest house in the town (the largest was not for sale at the time), while there is nothing to suggest that Shakespeare was particularly interested in the printing and publication of his plays (in this he differed notably from his contemporary and rival Ben Jonson). Only half of the thirty-six plays collected in the posthumous First Folio (1623) were published in Shakespeare's lifetime.

For a whole year, from December 1592, London was ravaged by the plague and the theatres were closed by law. During this period

Shakespeare wrote two long narrative poems, *Venus and Adonis* and *The Rape of Lucrece*, erotic poems exploiting the fashion set by MARLOWE's *Hero and Leander*. Both poems were dedicated to Henry Wriothesley, 3rd Earl of Southampton, who is also a favourite candidate for the 'Mr. W.H.' to whom the publisher of Shakespeare's Sonnets (1609) dedicated them. By 1594 he was a leading member of the Chamberlain's Men and had written his first group of English history plays, the three parts of *Henry VI* and *Richard III*, as well as *The Comedy of Errors*, *Love's Labour's Lost* and *Titus Andronicus*, a gory Senecan tragedy in the manner of KYD's *The Spanish Tragedy*.

The first public theatre building in England opened for business in 1576 and was called, simply, the THEATRE. It was occupied by the company to which Shakespeare belonged. When the lease ran out at the end of 1598, the owner of the land proposed to dismantle the building. But the company dismantled it themselves and took the timber south of the Thames to Bankside, where they used it to build a new theatre, the GLOBE, probably the most famous theatre in the English-speaking world. Here, for the next fourteen years, Shakespeare's plays and others were performed for the delight of London audiences who crossed the river in their thousands to see RICHARD BURBAGE, the most famous tragedian of his day, and clowns like WILL KEMPE and ROBERT ARMIN bring to life some of the great Shakespearean characters. It was at a performance of Shakespeare's last play, *Henry VIII*, written in collaboration with JOHN FLETCHER, that the shooting of a cannon accidentally set fire to the thatched roof of the playhouse destroying it entirely. When the theatre was rebuilt the following year the roof was tiled.

Shakespeare's career as a playwright spans not only the years during which the professional secular theatre emerged as a national institution appealing to all classes, but also the period during which the English language developed prodigiously in range and flexibility, accelerated by the spate of translations from Latin, Italian and French in the generation immediately preceding Shakespeare's. Add to this the fact that Elizabethans were accustomed to assimilate a good deal more through listening than through reading (the flowering of music as a national pastime is noteworthy here) and the brilliant growth of the drama finds a context in which it becomes more intelligible. Nothing can 'explain' Shakespeare, but the circumstances in which he lived and wrote at least help us to understand why so much of the finest talent of the age flowed into the drama.

The exact order in which the plays were written is not known, but there is fairly general agreement about a broad pattern of development.

After *Titus Andronicus, Henry VI, Richard III* and *The Comedy of Errors,* we have two comedies with Italian settings, the farcical *The Taming of the Shrew* and the romantic *Two Gentlemen of Verona.* To this period, too, belongs *Love's Labour's Lost,* Shakespeare's imitation of and improvement on the sophisticated artificial comedy of verbal exuberance made popular by the plays and romances of JOHN LYLY. These were followed by *Romeo and Juliet, Richard II, A Midsummer Night's Dream* and *King John,* all written within about three years from early 1594 to 1596. It will be apparent that there is no particular logic of theme, subject or structure in Shakespeare's dramatic development. He appears to have turned his hand to whatever kind of play was popular at the time and set the unmistakable stamp of genius upon it. *Richard II,* though complete in itself, is also the first play in Shakespeare's second historical cycle which contains in addition the two parts of *Henry IV,* and *Henry V.* Here Shakespeare traces the image of kingship from the last legitimate monarch of the Plantagenet line, deposed by his more powerful and practical cousin Bolingbroke with dire consequences for the country as a whole. With Bolingbroke's son Henry V and his conquest of France, the 'sin' of usurpation is at last extirpated. This at least is what a superficial viewing of the cycle suggests. But attentive reading or sensitive performance reveals obliquities and ironies which totally belie such simple and platitudinous generalities.

At about the same time as the second historical tetralogy, Shakespeare wrote two comedies very different from each other, *The Merchant of Venice* and *Much Ado about Nothing.* The turn of the century saw *Julius Caesar,* often regarded as 'the gateway to the tragedies', as well as two of the most popular comedies, *As You Like It* and *Twelfth Night.* The great tragedies begin with *Hamlet,* written in about 1601 and based on an older treatment of the same story, possibly by Thomas Kyd. This was followed between 1603 and 1608 by *Othello, King Lear, Macbeth, Antony and Cleopatra, Coriolanus* and *Timon of Athens.* While all these plays in their different ways embody a vision of the heroic possibilities of human nature battling against itself, Shakespeare also wrote at this time a series of plays in which a much darker picture of man is painted. These, sometimes called 'the problem plays' or 'the dark comedies', include *Troilus and Cressida, All's Well That Ends Well* and *Measure for Measure.* In them we see the 'Jacobean Shakespeare' in whom doubt, cynicism and something very like despair are much more evident than the humanism of the earlier plays. But this too, like almost every judgment on Shakespeare, is an oversimplification.

The last phase of Shakespeare's dramatic career covers the years 1607 to 1612, and is mainly taken up with a group of plays variously called the

Late Plays or the Romances. The best known of these is *The Tempest* and the others are *Pericles*, *Cymbeline* and *The Winter's Tale*. To this last period also belongs *Henry VIII*, a nostalgic pageant of English history, probably written in collaboration with John Fletcher. In the Romances Shakespeare forsook history for myth, and attempted to reconcile the sombre vision of tragedy with the faith in the creativity of life on which comedy is founded. More specifically he tried, often with spectacular success, to fashion his plays out of song, dance, MASQUE and pageant, which were increasingly popular in the early seventeenth century, particularly in the so-called 'private' theatres (indoor structures catering for smaller, more sophisticated audiences than those of the larger public playhouses). Shakespeare's company had acquired such a theatre, the Blackfriars, in 1608.

In about 1612 Shakespeare retired from the theatre and went back to his native Stratford. In so doing he was following a pattern common among men of his class and time who made their fortune in London but went back to the place of their birth in their last years. He died four years later, on his fifty-second birthday, and was buried in the chancel of Holy Trinity Church. The monument bust over the tomb may be one of the two authentic likenesses of Shakespeare (the other being the engraved portrait which forms the frontispiece to the First Folio). The inscription on the tomb reads:

> Good friend, for Jesus' sake forbear
> To dig the dust enclosèd here.
> Blest be the man that spares these stones
> And curst be he that moves my bones.

K. Muir and S. Schoenbaum (eds.), *A New Companion to Shakespeare Studies*, 1971.
S. Schoenbaum, *William Shakespeare: A Documentary Life*, 1975.
Gareth and Barbara Lloyd Evans, *Everyman's Companion to Shakespeare*, 1978.

Shaw, George Bernard (1856–1950). Irish-born playwright, whose career in journalism began in 1879, who became a socialist in 1882 and began a second career in polemics, who was first a music critic and then a drama critic before he began writing for the stage, and who was a member of the Fabian Society from 1884 and joint-founder with the Webbs of the *New Statesman*. Shaw was witty, formidably intelligent, and devoted to controversy. What critics found, and still find, difficult to cope with is the presence of this inspired jester among the mysteries of religious faith – *Androcles and the Lion* (1913), *Back to Methuselah* (1921), *Saint Joan* (1923); the solemnities of political ideology – *John Bull's Other Island* (1904), *The Apple Cart* (1929); the moral shibboleths of a stable society – *Mrs Warren's Profession* (1892), *Major Barbara* (1905), *The Doctor's Dilemma* (1906). These were areas into which the Edwardian Englishman entered po-faced. Shaw strode in grinning, and turned on its head everything from a dramatic convention to a sacred cow. He is the greatest saboteur in the English-speaking theatre.

Shaw's first dramatic cause was IBSEN (*The Quintessence of Ibsenism*, 1891), whom he saw as a social reformer and the necessary leader of any attempt to restore drama to its high status among the literary arts. He was sternly opposed by leading critics like CLEMENT SCOTT, leading actors like IRVING, leading dramatists like the already-forgotten Sydney Grundy, and by all the sanctimonious busybodies who wanted nothing to do with socialism. It was in the ROYAL COURT seasons of GRANVILLE BARKER and Vedrenne in 1904–6 that Shaw's reputation as a playwright was confirmed, above all with *Man and Superman* (1905). *Pygmalion* (1913), performed by HERBERT BEERBOHM TREE and MRS CAMPBELL, was the next sensation, and then the uncharacteristically elegiac *Heartbreak House* (1920) and the sparkling *Saint Joan*. Shaw's gift for the musical phrasing of dramatic dialogue is too often missed by readers and actors who have ears only for the debates his dialogue houses. Sometimes, it is true, his characters talk too much, particularly in the plays of his old age, from *The Apple Cart* (1929) to *Geneva* (1938) and *In Good King Charles's Golden Days* (1939).

Eric Bentley, *Shaw: A Reconsideration*, revised ed., 1957.
Martin Meisel, *Shaw and the Nineteenth-Century Theatre*, 1963.
Margery Morgan, *The Shavian Playground*, 1972.

Shchepkin, Mikhail (1788–1863). Shchepkin was born a serf, but freed in 1820 because the self-interested Prince Repnin admired his acting. That made him a symbol of the liberalizing potential of the theatre in a repressive country. He repaid his patrons with twenty years of meticulous comic acting, raising the level of Russian performance by example, and by the autobiographical notebooks he published after his retirement. His correspondence with GOGOL provides evidence of a pioneering intelligence. To STANISLAVSKY he was 'the great artist and lawgiver of the Russian stage', and 'the first to introduce simplicity and lifelikeness into the Russian theatre'.

Laurence Senelick, *Serf Actor*, 1984.

Shepard, Sam (1943–   ). American playwright and actor, who spoke vividly for the sixties, and has continued to experiment. Of the many jobs he had during his early years, the most significant was as a musician with the Holy Modal Rounders. It is the kind of band that could easily find room in his plays – bizarre, but fashionably so, and blasphemous, but only in the pursuit of an alternative religion. Shepard's plays are musical, somewhat in the style of a 'jam' session in jazz, and hallucinatory. Jack Gelber has called them 'trips', and there is no doubt that drug culture mixes in with the older traditions of quest literature, and with visions as picturesque as the mediaeval *Dream of the Rood*. His first plays were produced in 1964, and he remains prolific. Among the particularly effective works are *Icarus' Mother* (1965), *La Turista* (1966), *Melodrama Play* (1967), *Operation Sidewinder* (1970), *Mad Dog Blues* (1971), *The Tooth of Crime* (1972), *Geography of a Horse Dreamer* (1974) and *Angel City* (1976). He is not easy to read, since his plays depend so wholly on sound and image. They have a kind of anarchic vitality that signals a profuse imagination, and a determination to involve popular culture in enduring American myths. The three plays that constitute what Shepard has called his 'family trilogy', *Curse of the Starving Class* (1976), *Buried Child* (1978) and *True West* (1980) are more traditional in form, but still characterized by stunning images and monologues. *Fool for Love* (1983) is even better, a melodrama and a memory-play set at the remotest edge of 'God's own country'.

Bonnie Marranca (ed.), *American Dreams: The Imagination of Sam Shepard*, 1982.

Sheridan, Richard Brinsley (1751–1816). Sheridan's career has three distinct aspects. As a playwright, he wrote two of the best five-act comedies in English, *The Rivals* (1775) and *The School for Scandal* (1777), and one of the finest of all burlesques, *The Critic* (1779). He also wrote a negligible comic opera, very popular in its time, *The Duenna* (1775), a short FARCE, *St Patrick's Day* (1775), and, with his tongue lamentably absent from his cheek, a turgid version of a play by KOTZEBUE, *Pizarro* (1799), which was an enormous success and is now well buried. As a theatre manager, he had the nerve to buy (or borrow) himself into Drury Lane on GARRICK's retirement in 1776, and held on there through thick and thin (there was always a lot of 'thin' at Drury Lane) until the fire of 1809 bankrupted him, and Samuel Whitbread edged him out. As a politician, he held a seat in the House of Commons from 1780 to 1812 and various offices during that time, was famous as an orator (predominantly on the side of the angels), and was in the running for high office during the Regency Crisis of 1788. Had greatness been thrust upon him, he would probably have squandered it. From his impassioned marriage to Elizabeth Linley in 1773 to his arrest for debt in 1813, he was given to repenting at leisure what he had undertaken with rashness. But he was a great playwright, in a mode that is temporarily out of fashion, and a humane and witty man.

John Loftis, *Sheridan and the Drama of Georgian England*, 1976.

Sherwood, Robert Emmet (1896–1955). American playwright whose plays embody the generous liberalism that found expression in the New Deal. It is appropriate that Sherwood should have been a speechwriter for Roosevelt just before and during World War II. His war experience with the Canadian Black Watch in World War I followed fast on his graduation from Harvard, and contributed to a pacifism that was reluctantly but poignantly abandoned in 1940. The abandonment is recorded in his last major play, *There Shall Be No Night* (1940). Sherwood wrote his first plays, slightly prankish and too easily iconoclastic, for the BROADWAY audiences of the twenties. *The Road to Rome* (1926) conceals its plea for peace behind a joky approach to Hannibal and Rome, and *The Queen's Husband* (1928) is not much more than a royal romp. Sherwood's work as film critic for *Life* magazine was, at this time, more distinguished than his plays. *Reunion in Vienna* (1931), given an impressive performance by LYNNE FONTANNE and ALFRED LUNT, was an attempt to divert Americans from Marxism by a mocking display of the dullness of totalitarianism. Sherwood's best work began with *The Petrified Forest* (1935), a well made melodrama which warned of the dangers of ineffectual intelligence in a context of violence. *Idiot's Delight* (1936) has a startling last act, in which Sherwood's hatred of war is strongly conveyed, and *Abe Lincoln in Illinois* (1938) is an impressive document in the literature of idealistic democracy. It was one of the finest plays to be produced by the short-lived Playwrights' Company, of which Sherwood became a founder-member in 1937. His recognition that a democracy must defend itself found full expression in his work at the Office of War Information.

John Mason Brown, *The Worlds of Sherwood*, 1965.

Shiels, George (1886–1949). The continuing neglect of this admirable Irish dramatist is surprising. It was his work more than any other that sustained the ABBEY THEATRE in the lean years following O'CASEY's departure for England. An adventurous youth was interrupted by an accident when he was working on railway construction in America.

Permanently disabled, Shiels returned to Ireland to make his living by writing. He lived in the border country of Northern Ireland and Eire, and his plays reflect and assimilate the incongruous tensions that followed partition. They are tragicomic in mood, ironic and beautifully observed. Among the best are *Paul Twyning* (1922), *Cartney and Kevney* (1927), *The New Gossoon* (1930), *The Passing Day* (1936), *The Rugged Path* (1940) and *The Caretakers* (1948), the last play to be performed in his lifetime. Shiels was an acceptable playwright in both Belfast and Dublin, a fact which says something about the subtlety of his irony.

Shirley, James (1596–1666). Shirley was the last dramatist of any importance before the closing of the theatres in 1642. He attended both ancient universities and was a parish priest in St Albans until 1625, when he resigned on being converted to Roman Catholicism. He was a favourite dramatist of the Caroline Court and when the London theatres were closed because of the plague from 1636 to 1640 Shirley wrote for Ogilvy's theatre in Dublin. He was a great admirer of BEAUMONT and FLETCHER and wrote many tragi-comedies in the Fletcherian manner. But his best plays are probably the comedies *Hyde Park* (1632) and *The Lady of Pleasure* (1635), which provide a link between Jonsonian comedy and the later comedy of manners, and the tragedies *The Traitor* (1631) and *The Cardinal* (1641), which have a brooding intensity faintly reminiscent of WEBSTER. Shirley is said to have died as a result of injuries sustained in the Great Fire of London in 1666.

A. H. Nason, *Shirley: A Biographical and Critical Study*, 1915.

Siddons, Sarah. See KEMBLE.

Simon, Neil (1927–   ). Popular American playwright whose witty portraits of the emotionally stricken have brought him huge successes on BROADWAY and in Hollywood. His first play, *Come Blow Your Horn* (1961), came after several years as a writer of revue sketches, and the influence is recognizable in the delight he takes in sharp exchanges and sudden turns of fortune. *Barefoot in the Park* (1963), *The Odd Couple* (1965) and the three one-act plays that compose *Plaza Suite* (1968) were unpatronizingly fashioned for theatrical success, as were his 'books' for the musicals *Sweet Charity* (1966) and *Promises, Promises* (1968). Each of these musicals is based on a film, the latter recording a debt to the splendid scripts of Billy Wilder. After *The Last of the Red Hot Lovers*

(1969), Simon's popularity faltered a little, not least because he tried to test his adoring public with plays of more social substance, like *The Gingerbread Lady* (1970) and *Prisoner of Second Avenue* (1971), but *California Suite* (1976) returned to the formula of *Plaza Suite* and was a popular hit on Broadway. Later work includes *Chapter Two* (1977), *I Ought to Be in Pictures* (1980) and *Biloxi Blues* (1984).

Sinden, Donald (1923–   ). English actor who was an effective and consistent player of secondary roles in STRATFORD in 1945. He was a member of the Bristol Old Vic company during the second half of that decade and earned himself an eight-year contract with J. Arthur Rank Films in 1952. In the films of the fifties he tended to be asked to represent the British navy (commissioned officer class) and his rare gift for comedy went largely unnoticed. Sinden has been a regular member of the ROYAL SHAKESPEARE COMPANY since 1963. His Lord Foppington in VANBRUGH's *The Relapse* (1967) was a revelation for those who still associated him with gallantry at sea and his Sir Harcourt Courtly was a major contribution to the surprise success of BOUCICAULT's *London Assurance* (1971). Sinden is a student of theatre history and his comic style accommodates stage tradition within modernity. He is not afraid of the broad comic effect, a boldness which, for a while, threatened to typecast him again in roles involving lechery and fraught *noblesse oblige*. In 1976, in brilliant defiance of such typecasting, he played Benedick and King Lear at Stratford and was estimable in both. His Othello (1979), by contrast, added his name to a distinguished list of actors who have lost out to their Iagos (Bob Peck was Sinden's accidental adversary). Sinden has been prepared to try anything, including situation comedy on television, and opera. Of his major-domo (pained butlers are easily within his range) in Strauss's *Ariadne on Naxos* at the Colosseum (1983) the *Guardian* music critic commented, 'I can recall no spoken role in opera so upstaging the music.' That is an achievement that the modest Sinden would certainly not have intended, but he is an actor who finds it difficult to contain himself in comedy. Of two autobiographical volumes, *A Touch of the Memoirs* (1983) outreaches *Laughter in the Second Act* (1985).

Smithson, Harriet (1800–54). The Irish-born daughter of an English theatre-manager, this actress took Paris by storm when she played Juliet and Ophelia there in 1827. Admired by HUGO, DUMAS *père*, Gautier, Sainte-Beuve and ecstatically by Berlioz, she played some part in arousing the enthusiasm that led to the Romantic revolution in French drama. She had made her English debut at Drury Lane in 1818, but even after her Parisian success she failed greatly to excite English audiences. After a lengthy and extravagant courtship, Berlioz persuaded her to marry him in 1833. By 1844 the marriage was in shreds. Isolated in France, Harriet turned to brandy as a comforter. When she died, Liszt thought it sufficient to write to Berlioz: 'She inspired you, you loved her and sang of her; her task was done.'

Peter Raby, *Fair Ophelia*, 1982.

Sophocles (496–406 BC). Greek dramatist, born at Colonus, the setting for his last play *Oedipus at Colonus*, written at the very end of his long life and produced posthumously. Certain details of Sophocles' life are known; that he was celebrated for his beauty, that he won eighteen victories in the dramatic competition at the Festival of Dionysus in Athens, that he held high public office, and that he was greatly admired by contemporaries for the serenity and dignity of his demeanour. The surviving plays, of which there are seven, give the lie to any resultant supposition that he was priggish or pompous. *Ajax* (*c.* 442), *Antigone* (*c.* 441), the *Trachiniae* (date unknown), *Oedipus the King* (*c.* 429), *Electra* (date unknown), *Philoctetes* (*c.* 409) and *Oedipus at Colonus* summarize a vast achievement. The poetry is supple and the stagecraft assured. Sophocles, whilst clearly involved in the great moral debates of a critical century in the history of Athens, was also deeply engaged in the practice of theatre. He is often credited with the introduction of a third actor to extend the range of dramatic conflict, with the increasing of the Chorus from twelve to fifteen and with the scenic innovation of the revolving screens or *periaktoi* to enhance the sense of place during performances of his work. It was on his plays that ARISTOTLE based his important analysis of TRAGEDY in the *Poetics*, which has meant, in effect, that a Sophoclean ideal has determined the development of Western tragedy.

C. H. Whitman, *Sophocles: A Study of Heroic Humanism*, 1951.
R. P. Winnington-Ingram, *Sophocles: An Interpretation*, 1980.

Southerne, Thomas (1660–1746). Southerne was born near Dublin and after attending Trinity College, Dublin and the Middle Temple, served as a soldier until 1685. For the next forty years he was active as a dramatist, his best work being done in the last years of the seventeenth century. His pathetic tragedies such as *The Fatal Marriage* (1694) caught the popular taste, but his best play, *The Wives' Excuse* (1691), was a failure when it was first produced. It is a fine satire on London fashion which recalls an earlier comic masterpiece, WYCHERLEY's *The Country Wife*.

J. W. Dobbs, *Thomas Southerne: Dramatist*, 1933.

Soyinka, Wole (1934–   ). Nigerian playwright whose six years in England – at the University of Leeds and as play-reader at the ROYAL COURT – have helped him to establish subtle inter-relationships between African and European culture. *The Swamp Dwellers* (1958) and *The Lion and the Jewel* (1959) treat African village life. *A Dance of the Forests* (1963) is much more complex. The reinterpretation of myth and ritual that informs his adaptation of the *Bacchae* (1973), and that provides the plot as well as the purpose of *The Strong Breed* (1966) is obscure in the earlier play. Having founded a theatre company in Nigeria in 1960, Soyinka has taught successively at the Universities of Ibadan, Ife, Lagos, and again Ife. From 1967 to 1969 he was imprisoned, largely in solitary confinement, for alleged Biafran sympathies. The experience was recorded in a bitter autobiographical outburst, *The Man Died* (1973), and underlies the adventurous play, *Madmen and Specialists* (1971). In *Death and the King's Horseman* (1975) African values overwhelm the attempts of a 'decent' English couple to save a life. That Europe looks to him is demonstrated by the awarding of the 1986 Nobel Prize for Literature.

Oyin Ogunba, *The Movement of Transition*, 1975.

Stanfield, Clarkson (1793–1867). English painter and scene-designer, named after a leading abolitionist by his sailor-turned-actor father. After a brief apprenticeship to an heraldic painter, Stanfield was at sea from 1808 to 1815. In the latter year he was appointed scene-painter at the East London Theatre. After a spell at the Coburg, he was engaged as one of a team of scene-painters and designers at ELLISTON's Drury Lane in 1823 with the object of challenging the scenic supremacy of Covent Garden under the GRIEVE family. He remained at Drury Lane until 1834, when he resigned after a quarrel with the unbearable Alfred Bunn. Throughout his busy theatre years, Stanfield had continued easel painting, and built for himself a deserved reputation as a marine and landscape artist. He was elected a member of the Royal Academy in 1835 and contemporaries paid him the compliment of comparing him with Turner, who was a friend. MACREADY persuaded him to resume his theatrical career in 1839 and Stanfield painted several scenes for the great actor during his management of Covent Garden. Particularly famous was the 1839 DIORAMA for *Henry V*. It was probably Macready who introduced Stanfield to Dickens; painter and novelist remained close friends until Stanfield's death, and Dickens took advantage of his friend's expertise to enhance the scenic effect of his famous readings. Stanfield owed his pre-eminence among scene-painters to his extraordinary dioramas, which allowed him scope to express his love of the subtle colourings of water. Pieter van der Merwe has calculated that he was responsible for over 550 scenes. No painter of equal quality has done more theatre work.

The Spectacular Career of Clarkson Stanfield, 1979. (Exhibition Catalogue, Tyne and Wear County Council Museums.)

Stanislavsky, Constantin Sergeivich (1863–1938). Born into a wealthy Moscow family, Stanislavsky was one of those awkward children who take family theatricals seriously. His parents indulged him, and he received lessons in ballet and singing. Whilst working in his father's trading company, eventually as director and chairman, right through to the 1917 Revolution, he involved himself tirelessly in amateur opera and drama. The habit of self-criticism, fostered by his reading of SHCHEPKIN, entered his soul (Stanislavsky was always soulful), and his foundation in 1888 of a Society of Literature and Art in Moscow was the beginning of a lifelong quest for theatrical perfection. The quest is recorded in a series of so far haphazardly translated books, of which the autobiographical *My Life in Art* (1924) was the first. Of the three 'text-books', only *An Actor Prepares* (1926) appeared in his lifetime. An edited translation into English was published in 1936, to be followed by *Building a Character* (1949) and *Creating a Role* (1961).

It is too often assumed, particularly by adherents of the American METHOD, that Stanislavsky's whole interest was in natural acting and naturalistic drama. To be sure, when he and NEMIROVICH-DANCHENKO founded the MOSCOW ART THEATRE in 1898, they were motivated by a dislike of the stilted style of the Imperial Theatres, and the first real triumph came with the performance of CHEKHOV's *The Seagull* through which Stanislavsky discovered what he later called 'the line of the intuition of feelings'. He remained faithful to the conviction that an actor's creativeness must come from within, and it is reasonable to see his subsequent explorations as an attempt to find a reliable way of translating into theatrical expression the perceptions of the psyche. But he was not slavishly committed to the discovery of subtext where there is none, and his repertoire was not restricted to plays that demanded no reappraisal. The road of the actor, he wrote, is 'the road of images', and as actor, director and teacher he led the search for a reliable system for the actor's conscious exploitation of inspiration.

David Magarshack, *Stanislavsky on the Art of the Stage*, 1950.

Steele, Sir Richard (1672–1729). Among his many claims to a place in theatrical history, the intrinsic merit of Steele's plays is by no means the strongest. In 1720 he founded *The Theatre*, the first English magazine devoted to the drama. Earlier he had been involved in theatrical journalism through a number of periodicals of which he was either founder or co-founder, the most celebrated being *The Tatler* and *The Spectator* in both of which Addison was his collaborator. In 1715, Steele obtained a life patent of the Drury Lane theatre. Steele was very conscious of JEREMY COLLIER's attacks on the stage and made a deliberate effort to write morally exemplary plays which would satisfy the conscience of the aspiring new middle class. The result was not uniformly disastrous. *The Funeral* (1701) has a briskly moving plot and some lively female characters. *The Lying Lover* (1703) was, in Steele's own words, 'damn'd for its piety' and *The Tender Husband* (1703) has two characters who foreshadow SHERIDAN's Lydia Languish and GOLDSMITH's Tony Lumpkin. Steele's last and best-known play, *The Conscious Lovers*, did not appear until 1722. It was a comedy designed to produce tears rather than laughter, which it did in ample measure not only in England but on the Continent where it was a major influence on the French *comédie larmoyante*.

John Loftis, *Steele at Drury Lane*, 1952.

Stein, Peter (1937–   ). German director who came to immediate prominence with his first professional production, EDWARD BOND's *Saved* at the Munich Kammerspiele in 1967. Many of his trademarks were already in evidence: long and intensive rehearsal involving discussion with the actors, the radical questioning of any gesture or intonation that seemed hackneyed, a quest for clarity, an emphasis on the word and (in this case in obedience to the text) a long episode of silent action. Stein became a hero of the left when his fourth production, WEISS's *Vietnam Discourse*, caused a political scandal in Munich and Berlin in 1968–9. His own sympathies remained Marxist, but he has disappointed extremists by his retrospective acceptance of a statement made at the time by the directors of the Berlin Schaubühne: 'In the present social situation theatre can fulfil merely the function of enlightenment but not of revolution.'

It is remarkable, in view of the trouble caused by *Vietnam Discourse*, that Stein was appointed director of the Berlin Schaubühne in 1970 and that he was allowed to reorganize the theatre on socialist lines. He has remained with the Schaubühne since then, supervising the 1982–3 move into the converted Mendelssohn building in the Kurfürsten-damm, a move that can be read as a final submission to the hegemony of bourgeois capitalism or as a socialist theatre's preparedness to exploit the benefits of wealth. Stein is no longer a fiery radical. His productions are massively methodical, so much so that PETER ZADEK has compared his actors to vegetables cooked for so long as to lose their flavour. A Stein production will begin with detailed research, sometimes over a period of years, undergo a 'doubting process' when director and actors explore the text, be broken down and then painstakingly assembled in such a way as to lay bare the socio-historical context after the style of BRECHT, and only then be slotted into the repertoire. Major work at the Schaubühne has included *Peer Gynt* (1971), KLEIST's *Prince Friedrich von Homburg* (1972), GORKY's *Summerfolk* (1974), *As You Like It* (1977) and the *Oresteia* of AESCHYLUS (1980). It is Stein's advantage to work in a theatre so well subsidized that he needs to stage no more than four productions each year.

Michael Patterson, *Peter Stein*, 1981.

Sternheim, Carl (1878–1943). Flaying the bourgeoisie was the particular talent of this idiosyncratic German dramatist. He was a banker's son, and knew the world he hated. Literary terrorism at this level deploys parody, FARCE and obsequious hypocrisy. Sternheim is a brilliant stylist, and his best plays are uncomfortably funny. These include *Bürger Schippel* (1912) and a group concentrating on the monstrous Maske family, *Die Hose* (1911, variously translated as *The Bloomers*, *The Knickers* and *The Underpants*), *Der Snob* (1913), *1913* (1915) and *Das Fossil* (1923).

Stoppard, Tom (1937–   ). English dramatist, born in Czechoslovakia. He was a journalist from 1954 to 1963, when his first play, *A Walk on the Water* (revised as *Enter a Free Man*), was televised. It was with the production of *Rosencrantz and Guildenstern Are Dead* (1966) that Stoppard achieved prominence. The prosaic speculations of the two philosophical friends mock the pretensions of Hamlet's language. The witty and ingenious meditation on once-modish ideas or conventions is a feature also of *The Real Inspector Hound* (1968), *Jumpers* (1972) and *Travesties* (1974). Stoppard had found the secret of making people laugh at jokes they did not quite understand but which they knew were at somebody else's expense. The writing is too good-humoured to hurt much, but the effect is reductive. Stoppard's more recent plays have shown a greater concern for the defence of threatened freedoms than hostile critics could have expected. The television play *Professional Foul* (1977) involves a football-crazy academic in iron-curtain skulduggery. The humour is sustained, but not at the cost of the seriousness. The play for actors and orchestra, *Every Good Boy Deserves Favour* (1977), also looks askance at the attacks on freedom under tyrannical communism, as does the television play *Squaring the Circle* (1984), whilst *Night and Day* (1978) maintains the theme, but shifts the setting to Africa. That Stoppard still relishes something close to 'pure' craftmanship was demonstrated by his *On the Razzle* (1981), a version of a play by NESTROY. Another adaptation, written, like *On the Razzle*, for the NATIONAL THEATRE, was *Undiscovered Country* (1979), from a play by ARTHUR SCHNITZLER, but although the skilful shaping and sudden shocks remain, there is also an emotional depth that continues into Stoppard's more recent exploration of adultery, *The Real Thing* (1982).

C. W. E. Bigsby, *Tom Stoppard*, 1976.
Jim Hunter, *Tom Stoppard's Plays*, 1982.

Storey, David (1933–   ). English playwright and novelist. Storey was at art school from 1951 to 1956, for the last four years of which he was also a professional rugby league player. Much of his work deals with square pegs in self-destructive searches for round holes. It relates clearly to the experience of incongruity – but it is not glumly accepting. There is a sense of fiery resistance in Storey's best work. His natural style is fairly traditional, and *The Restoration of Arnold Middleton* (1966) and *In Celebration* (1969) have a novelist's feeling for narrative sequence. It is with the plays of physical process that Storey has made his most original contribution – the marquee erecting of *The Contractor* (1969), the rugby league setting of *The Changing Room* (1971), the artistic activity of *Life Class* (1974) – and although the reticence of *Home* (1970) is notably compassionate, neither that play, nor *Mother's Day* (1976), *Sisters* (1978) and *Early Days* (1980) have established new ground.

Strasberg, Lee (1901–82). American director, actor, and teacher, who was working with the Theatre Guild when HAROLD CLURMAN persuaded him to become a founder-director of the GROUP THEATRE. Strasberg directed most of the early productions for the Group, and also began the teaching sessions that distinguished it. He relied on notes from RICHARD BOLESLAVSKY's classes at the American Laboratory Theatre, as Boleslavsky in turn relied on STANISLAVSKY. Strasberg resigned from the Group Theatre in 1936, directed on and around BROADWAY for several years, and in 1951 became director of the Actors' Studio in New York. His influence on three decades of American acting has been immense. He was the leading exponent of the METHOD (from Stanislavsky via

Boleslavsky, with many misconceptions on the way), which he expounds rather turgidly in *Strasberg at the Studio*. Harold Clurman tells of an occasion, early in the history of the Group Theatre, when he questioned Strasberg's view that the actors' private lives were the directors' business. 'Everything is our business,' was Strasberg's vivid response.

Strehler, Giorgio (1921–   ). Italian director whose association with the PICCOLO TEATRO in Milan, of which he was co-founder with Paolo Grassi, began in 1947 and has continued, with a break of four years from 1968 to 1972, into the eighties. Among Strehler's outstanding productions have been many of the plays by BRECHT, a remarkable interpretation of *The Tempest* and two productions of GOLDONI's *The Servant of Two Masters*. Strehler has learned some of his scenic craft from the great directors of the Italian cinema, but his rationality is Brechtian.

Strindberg, August (1849–1912). Swedish dramatist and strangely driven polymath, whose prodigious achievement defies definition. He wrote his first (lost) play in 1869, but it was the production in 1881 of *Master Olof* (1872), an iconoclastic history play, that established him in the Swedish theatre. *Sir Bengt's Wife* (1883), which starred his first wife Siri von Essen, is embroiled already in the ferocious battle of the sexes that distinguishes his NATURALISTIC masterpieces, *The Father* (1887), *Miss Julie* (1888) and *Creditors* (1888). 'An uglier, more revolting scene has probably never been presented in a Danish theatre,' wrote one reviewer of the Copenhagen premiere of *The Father*, and he was probably right. A Strindberg play can scar you, perhaps because its distortions are perilously close to truths. The weight of implication, and the malicious collaboration of fretful antagonists with the mechanisms that will destroy them, have hidden from many audiences the humour of some Strindbergian arguments. *The Bond* (1892) and *Playing with Fire* (1892) are not funny plays, but like the other predominantly naturalistic plays, they have moments of devilish, and often self-lacerating, wit.

Strindberg's first marriage ended in 1891, and his second, to Frida Uhl, began in 1893. It was a travesty, and it contributed to and was made nightmarish by what has come to be known as the Inferno crisis, after the autobiographical novel *Inferno* (1897). The crisis silenced Strindberg, and the majority of the plays that he wrote immediately after it had passed were attempts, through history, to keep autobiography at bay. They included *Erik XIV* (1899), *Gustavus Vasa* (1899) and *Gustavus Adolphus* (1899). The interest in Swedish history lingered into

Charles XII (1901) and *Kristina* (1903) among others. Historical drama is a significant part of Strindberg's output, but its impact has not been great outside Sweden. He was looking for new positives, and the EXPRESSIONIST dramas of pilgrimage, of which the *To Damascus* trilogy (1898 and 1904) and *A Dream Play* (1901) are outstanding examples, provide bold images of the quest.

In 1901 Strindberg married again, this time to the twenty-two-year-old actress, Harriet Bosse. The failure of this marriage is the saddest of all, because they both tried hard to make it work. The marital horrors of the two-part *Dance of Death* (1901) look ominous in retrospect. Written so soon after the redemptive *Easter* (1900), this play may fairly illustrate the unstable temperament of its author. But he never stopped trying. In 1907 he and a young actor called August Falck began three seasons of work in the 161-seat Intimate Theatre in Stockholm. It was in connection with this that Strindberg wrote his *Open Letters to the Intimate Theatre* (1908), and the Chamber plays that crown his dramatic career. *The Storm, The Pelican, The Ghost Sonata* and *The Burnt House* were written in 1907, and staged at the Intimate Theatre. But Strindberg quarrelled with Falck, as he quarrelled with everyone. After 1908 he lived a largely solitary life in Stockholm, producing books on philology and articles for the radical press. His *Collected Works* fill fifty-five volumes.

Evert Sprinchorn, *Strindberg as Dramatist*, 1982.
Michael Meyer, *Strindberg*, 1985.

Svoboda, Josef (1920–   ). Czech stage-designer whose work has become internationally known since his appointment as chief designer at the National Theatre in Prague in 1948. In London he designed for the NATIONAL THEATRE a moody, abstract set for OSTROVSKY's *The Storm* (1966) and an astonishing construction of silver hanging cords for *The Three Sisters* (1967). His interest in kinetic projections led to his invention of the simultaneous Polyecran System, to which he gave early prominence in a Covent Garden production of *Die Frau ohne Schatten* and which he now pursues with the Laterna Magika group (founded 1973).

Jarka Burian, *The Scenography of Josef Svoboda*, 1971.

Synge, (Edmund) John Millington (1871–1909). Born into an evangelical protestant Dublin family, and educated privately because of his delicate health, Synge was his decent mother's favourite and her despair. He was a solitary, and could conform neither to the religious fervour of his family, nor to the patriotic fervour of Maud Gonne and YEATS, with whom he was associated in the early years of the ABBEY THEATRE. It is dangerously easy to hear the effect of his musical training in his dramatic dialogue. What is certain is that he embroidered brilliantly what he acutely heard in Wicklow and, in the years from 1898 to 1902, on the Aran Islands. Yeats's advice that he seek his subject matter among the Aran islanders is famous; but Synge went there already as temperamentally alert as Gauguin to Tahiti. A draft of his book *The Aran Islands* (1907) was complete in 1902. He had found, in 'these few acres at the extreme border of Europe, where it is only in wild jests and laughter that they can express their loneliness and desolation', an openness to fairy fable, a dappling of pagan and Christian folklore, and an adherence to the mysterious power of words that was only fully there because he took part of it with him. His first plays, *In the Shadow of the Glen* (1902) and *The Tinker's Wedding* (not considered safe for production until 1909), are realistic comedies, which shocked the publicly holy Irish middle classes with their preference for the shamelessly vagrant over the respectably sedentary. The tone of comedy is threatened in the darker *The Well of the Saints* (1905) and in the challenges laid down by *The Playboy of the Western World* (1907), whose Dublin production was greeted with a week of riots. *Riders to the Sea* (1904), the only play actually set in the Aran Islands, is short, harsh, and durable. For his last play, 'an interesting experiment, full of new difficulties' as he noted, Synge demythologized and enriched *Deirdre of the Sorrows*. It was staged in 1910, after its author had died of Hodgkin's disease.

David H. Green and Edward Stephens, *Synge*, 1959.
Weldon Thornton, *J. M. Synge and the Western Mind*, 1979.

Tagore, Rabindranath (1861–1941). Indian playwright, poet and teacher, whose international reputation won him the Nobel Prize for Literature in 1913. Tagore's plays, most of which he himself translated from Bengali into English, authenticated the dreaminess of YEATS and MAETERLINCK, partly because they were misunderstood in their Western context. *Sacrifice* (1890), *The King of the Dark Chamber* (1910), *The Post Office* (1913), *Chitra* (1914) and *Red Oleanders* (1924), for example, are much more robust than can ever be perceived through Western eyes. They tackle questions of attitude, and are misunderstood when they are perceived as behavioural. Tagore's surviving monument is the university he founded on his estate in Santiniketan. It requires a strenuous effort on the part of an English-speaking reader to penetrate the poetic mists in order to reach Tagore's mature morality.

Taïrov, Alexander Yakovlevich (1885–1950). The name of this Russian director is associated with the Moscow Kamerny ('Chamber') Theatre, which he formed in 1914 and continued to run until it was liquidated in the year of his death. In talking of his theatre as 'synthetic', Taïrov was referring to his attempts to combine the arts of ballet, opera, circus and music hall with those of the dramatic actor, but it is tempting to see his vision as a synthesis of STANISLAVSKY's emotional truth and MEYERHOLD's theatrical artifice. Theirs were the leading contrary influences in the Moscow theatre, and Taïrov was certainly conscious of both. Like Meyerhold, he wanted a theatrical theatre, but he also believed, like Stanislavsky, in the need for 'emotional saturation' from the actor. Whilst he welcomed the Revolution, Taïrov was ill at ease in the utilitarian theatre. His single Soviet success was with Vishnevsky's *Optimistic Tragedy* in 1933, though the pioneering productions of O'NEILL's work in the twenties were an acceptable compromise. His *Notes of a Director* give an account of the first seven years at the Kamerny.

Talma, François-Joseph (1763–1826). French actor, son of a dentist with a fashionable London practice. Talma made his debut at the COMÉDIE-FRANÇAISE in 1787, and was dangerously confident enough to challenge his seniors, scarcely a year later, by playing a small part in Voltaire's *Brutus* in Roman rather than contemporary French dress. It was an important step in the reform of costuming on the French stage, and, as so often in Talma's career, it had much to do with the influence of a notable friend, in this case the painter David. Unlike many of the senior actors in Paris, Talma was revolutionary in his sympathies. It was in Chénier's radical *Charles IX* that he came to real prominence in November 1789. With a good voice and a strong face, Talma combined the ability to grip and to terrify his audiences. To contemporary English taste, he seemed old-fashioned ('Talma was constantly etruscanizing himself,' wrote a friend of JOHN PHILIP KEMBLE in 1803), but he brought to the classical French repertoire a new commitment to real feeling. Few actors could rival his social eminence – the comparison with GARRICK in England is irresistible. His first wife, Julie Careau, continued to run a select salon after their marriage. Both she and his second wife, the actress Caroline Vanhove, divorced him when his philandering exceeded acceptable bounds – whatever they were in the loose-loined days of the Napoleonic Empire. It was the friendship with Napoleon himself that was the crucial measure of, and sometimes a contributing factor to, Talma's success. Briefly in 1812, he was the lover of Napoleon's sister, the Princesse Borghese. Madame de Staël, who records her impressions of Talma in Chapter 27 of *De l'Allemagne*, tried to succumb to him in 1809. It is not known whether she succeeded.

Herbert F. Collins, *Talma*, 1964.

Tarlton, Richard (d. 1588). When Tarlton died during Armada year, his fame was so great that a spate of pamphlets purporting to give authentic information about his life and career poured from the presses, including a ballad, 'Tarlton's Farewell'. Most of these contain information which is traditional or apocryphal. Among the few known facts about Tarlton are that he joined the Queen's Men when they were formed in 1583, was the author of several jigs (rhymed farces sung and danced to traditional airs) in which he appeared, and was Queen Elizabeth's favourite clown. He was a well known ad-libber and the posthumous collection, *Tarlton's Jests* (c. 1599), probably contains a good many jokes which he originated. Some scholars believe he was the model for Yorick in *Hamlet*.

Tate, Nahum (1652–1715). Tate's place in the history of English drama is assured. He it was who rewrote *King Lear* with no Fool and a happy ending in which Lear leaves his restored kingdom to the young lovers, Cordelia and Edgar. It is easy to mock Tate's emasculation of a tragic masterpiece; it is more pertinent to ponder the theatrical taste which acclaimed the displacement of SHAKESPEARE's play by the 'improved' version for 150 years. Tate also adapted Shakespeare's *Richard II* and *Coriolanus* as well as plays by WEBSTER and JONSON, and wrote the words for Purcell's *Dido and Aeneas* (1689).

Christopher Spencer, *Nahum Tate*, 1972.

Taylor, Laurette (1884–1946). Actress, born in New York, but always ready to boast of her Irish descent. She made her New York debut in 1903, and had a major success as Peg in *Peg o' My Heart* (1914), one of several plays written for her by her second husband, J. Hartley Manners. She played with simplicity and a powerful imagination. When Manners died in 1928, she went, as she told an interviewer, on 'the longest wake in history'. Her terrible struggle with drink, her fluffed comebacks and her eventual triumph as Amanda in TENNESSEE WILLIAMS's *The Glass Menagerie* (1945) made of her life a sob-story. She was playing Amanda when she died.

Marguerite Courtney, *Laurette*, 1955.

Taylor, Tom˙(1817–1880). For the last six years of his immensely busy life, Taylor was editor of *Punch*, but it is as a busy and intermittently admirable dramatist that he is most to be remembered. *Our American Cousin* (1858) was his most successful play (it was the one Mrs Lincoln might have enjoyed if it had not been for the assassination of her husband by JOHN WILKES BOOTH), but that success was largely owing to the actor, Edward Sothern. His best plays include mature comedies (*To Oblige Benson*, 1854 and *Still Waters Run Deep*, 1855) and the effective MELODRAMA 'from the French', *The Ticket-of-Leave Man* (1863). As impressive as any is the neglected 'shipwreck' play, *The Overland Route* (1860).

Winton Tolles, *Tom Taylor and the Victorian Drama*, 1940.

Terence (*c.* 190–159 BC). It is generally supposed that Publius Terentius Afer was born a slave in Carthage. That he was well educated is certain. His plays are carefully constructed versions of Greek originals, whose attention to plausibility distinguishes them from the buffoonery of PLAUTUS. Six of them survive, all of them produced between 166 and 160 BC. His influence is traceable in English comedy from the fifteenth century until well into the eighteenth. Since his plays were regularly studied in schools, there is nothing surprising about this. His polish was proverbial. *Adelphi*, *Andria* and *Eunuchus* all show his willingness to add subleties to his Greek originals, and it is, perhaps, unfortunate that his dramaturgical innovations have received so much more attention than his comic flair.

G. E. Duckworth, *The Nature of Roman Comedy*, 1952.
W. G. Arnott, *Menander, Plautus, Terence*, 1975.

Terriss, William (1847–1897). Breezy Bill Terriss was born too early for the swashbuckling Hollywood success that would best have represented him. He played 'butch' roles for IRVING at the Lyceum before setting up under his own management at the Adelphi in 1885. The Adelphi was a home for muscular MELODRAMA while Terriss was there, and it was at the stage door that he was murdered by a jealous madman. The sum of £40,000 was collected for a memorial, and the money was spent on building a lifeboat house in Eastbourne. It was an appropriate monument for a man who had earned a medal from the Royal Humane Society in 1885 for saving a boy from drowning off the South Foreland. Terriss's daughter Ellaline (1871–1971) was an actress and a famous beauty. She married the actor-dramatist Seymour Hicks (1871–1949).

A. J. Smythe, *The Life of William Terris*, 1898.

Terry, Ellen (1847–1928). The outstanding member of an astonishing theatrical family. Her parents were actors, though not very good ones. Her sisters, Kate, Marion and Florence, were all capable actresses. Her brother Fred (1864–1932), though he eventually settled for flummery like *The Scarlet Pimpernel*, had the life and talent to play Benedick. Her own debut was in 1856, when she played Mamillius to CHARLES KEAN's Leontes in *The Winter's Tale*. There can be no certainty that she was ever a great actress, nor any doubt that she had phenomenal charm, both on stage and off it. Her 1864 marriage to the painter, G. F. Watts, was a sad mismatch. It did not last long, but it gave Watts the chance to exploit in paint her unusual combination of opulence and innocence. The protracted affair with Edward Godwin was much more serious, not least because he was the father of her two extraordinary children, Edith Craig and EDWARD GORDON CRAIG. Had the relationship prospered, Ellen might never have returned to the stage. It was the novelist and playwright Charles Reade who managed her comeback, and her performance of Portia in an 1875 *Merchant of Venice* (brilliantly designed by Godwin and expertly staged by BANCROFT) gave her for the first time 'the feeling of the conqueror'.

In 1878 IRVING invited her to the Lyceum as his leading lady. Ophelia was her first part there. Later she played Portia (1879), Desdemona (1881), Juliet (1882), Beatrice (1882), Viola (1884), Lady Macbeth (1888), Queen Katherine (1892), Cordelia (1892), Imogen (1896) and Volumnia (1901). She was the extrovert of the partnership, Irving the introverted egocentric. She was, as SHAW complained, second fiddle. Shaw claimed that Irving wasted Ellen Terry's genius, contrasting them: 'She, all brains and sympathy, scattering them everywhere and on everybody: he, all self, concentrating that self on his stage as on a pedestal.' When Irving died, she was nearly sixty, a public figure dominated in private by the two children she loved and ruined. (To a measurable financial extent, they returned the compliment by ruining her.) The emotional generosity remained. Her short-lived second marriage of 1877 (to Charles Kelly) was followed by a third in 1907, also short lived, to a man not much more than half her age. She was, by this time, decidedly ample, as is clear in surviving photographs of her Lady Cecily Waynflete in Shaw's *Captain Brassbound's Conversion* (1906), but the charm and grace remained. Friends and relatives quarrelled over her, and her acceptance of the status of a 'valuable property' ran alongside her continuing defiance of Victorian hypocrisy. She was always immensely easy to forgive.

Roger Manvell, *Ellen Terry*, 1968.

Thespis. We know nothing about Thespis that could be relied on. He is believed to have won the prize at the first tragic contest in Athens in about 534 BC, and is further credited with the decision to separate the first actor from the tragic chorus. If he did, he can certainly claim to have invented acting as a profession. Whether he did or not, the traditional description of actors as 'Thespians' will not be affected. The historical Thespis would have thought of himself as a poet.

Thomas, Augustus (1857–1934). American dramatist, particularly interesting for his regional work. Thomas had no social or educational advantages. He began writing plays while working in the freight department of a St Louis railway company, and had his first real success with *Arizona* (1899), though earlier regional plays, like *Alabama* (1891) and *In Mizzoura* (1893), demonstrated his ability to rest melodramatic plots on topics of current social concern. *The Witching Hour* (1907) is an effective drama about a man who has killed under hypnosis and *The Copperhead* (1918) was, for its time, an acceptably realistic play about the life of a midwestern town during the Civil War. After 1888, when he moved to New York, Thomas was active in the professional theatre.

Thorndike, Sybil (1882–1976). English actress, whose enthusiasm and generosity remained with her into old age. She could gush like a sycophant, but the difference was that she meant it. She had an enviable habit of enriching life. Her early training as a pianist was abandoned when a weakness of the wrists manifested itself. In 1908 she joined the Gaiety Theatre in Manchester, and began her extraordinary marriage to the actor-director Lewis Casson (1875–1969). They remained provocatively engaged with each other and with the theatre for sixty years. Her finest stage performance was as SHAW's Saint Joan in 1924. It was generally in roles combining spirituality and lyricism that she excelled, as she did in the Gilbert Murray versions of EURIPIDES (*The Trojan Women* and *Medea*, 1920), in T. S. ELIOT's *The Family Reunion* (1956 revival) and in the sometimes shrill plays of Clemence Dane. Her association with the OLD VIC under LILIAN BAYLIS began in 1914. She was created DBE in 1931, and a Companion of Honour in 1970.

Sheridan Morley, *Sybil Thorndike*, 1977.

Toller, Ernst (1893–1939). German playwright, born in Prussia of Jewish parentage. He was invalided out of the German army in 1916, and his pacifist feelings are expressed in his first play, *Transfiguration* (*Die Wandlung,* 1918). He was arrested for his part in the Bavarian

Soviet Republic, and wrote his early plays, including *Masses and Man* (*Masse-Mensch*, 1920) and *The Machine-Wreckers* (1921), during his five-year imprisonment. Toller's heart was always in the right place, but his language was less reliable. PISCATOR tried to play down the poetic excess of *Hoppla! We're Alive* (1927) when he directed the play. But he admired Toller's recognition of the realities of the industrial proletariat. Moral fervour bordering on hysteria is easy to understand in the threatened Germany of the Weimar Republic. Toller's was the first name on the Nazi list of undesirable writers. He had left Germany before the Reichstag Fire, but his exile was distressing to him. That he suffered in an extreme form the sense of fruitless displacement so common in political refugees could have been predicted by readers of his autobiographical *I Was a German* (1933), and was horribly proved by his suicide in New York.

W. A. Willibrand, *Ernst Toller and His Ideology*, 1945.
M. Ossar, *Anarchism in the Dramas of Ernst Toller*, 1980.

Tolstoy, Lev Nikolayevich (1828–1910). Tolstoy's plays are minor only in comparison with his novels. Some short pieces preceded completion of *War and Peace* (1869) and *Anna Karenina* (1877), but the four major plays were written during the years when Tolstoy struggled to reconcile his art with a bewildering variety of missions in life. *The Power of Darkness* (1886) is a peasant tragedy that still seems startlingly outspoken. It was in rehearsal in St Petersburg when the censors took fright and banned it. Under the new Tsar Nicholas II, it was accepted for performance in Moscow in 1895, and its success encouraged Tolstoy to begin a fascinating autobiographical fantasy, *The Light Shines in Darkness*. Work on this was interrupted, and despite a resumption in 1902 the play's final act was never completed. Together with *The Live Corpse* (1902), it reveals the weird mixture in Tolstoy of aggressive self-justification and histrionic self-abasement. These two plays lack the theatrical assurance of the satirical comedy *The Fruits of Enlightenment* (1889), but they have the restless excitement that made Tolstoy what he was – a jagged combination of Rasputin and Mahatma Gandhi.

Henri Troyat, *Tolstoy* (trans. Nancy Amphoux), 1967.

Tourneur, Cyril (*c.* 1575–1626). Very little is known about Tourneur except that he was in the service of the Vere and Cecil families and died when he was put ashore in Ireland on Cecil's expedition to Cadiz. Of the two plays attributed to him, by far the greater, *The Revenger's Tragedy* (1606–7), may not be by him at all. The other, *The Atheist's Tragedy*

(1607–11), is surely one of the most hilarious tragedies ever written and has a deathless stage-direction which calls for the destruction of the hero-villain even as he attempts to chop his enemy's head off: *As he raises up the axe [he] strikes out his own brains.* By contrast, *The Revenger's Tragedy* has a tragic intensity which is heightened rather than diminished by its occasional flashes of black humour. Its vision of the self-destructive momentum of lust, of corruption in high places and of the self-love which leads the revenger to overreach himself makes it one of the great Jacobean tragedies.

Peter B. Murray, *A Study of Tourneur*, 1964.

Travers, Ben (1886–1980). In a Travers FARCE, elaborate attempts are made to preserve threatened proprieties, and in the end even Aunt Edna has nothing to worry about. Between 1922 and 1933, Travers wrote a series of plays to suit the talented Aldwych company. The best of these, *A Cuckoo in the Nest* (1925), *Rookery Nook* (1926), *Thark* (1927) and *Plunder* (1928), have an assured place in the repertoire of amateur and professional theatre companies, whatever may be said by sound critics about the respectability of blowing up a wind in order to sail close to it. Travers worked in his father's firm until World War I, when he had a distinguished career with the Royal Naval Air Service. It was not until 1922 that he first wrote for his boyhood love, the theatre. His best plays were composed under the scrutiny of Tom Walls, leading actor and manager of the Aldwych Theatre, who knew what he wanted and made sure that Travers provided it. Away from the Aldwych after 1933, Travers was less successful, though *The Bed before Yesterday* (1975) is a poignant retrospect on his earlier work. *Vale of Laughter* (1957) and *A-Sitting on a Gate* (1978) are sketchily written autobiographies.

Tree, Herbert Beerbohm (1853–1917). A flamboyant and splendidly improvident man, Tree is best known for the sumptuous (often risibly so) stagings of SHAKESPEARE that made Her Majesty's Theatre famous under his management. He was not a great Shakespearean actor, though his Falstaff was admired and his Richard II in advance of its time. His real excellence was in 'character', particularly where artistic make-up was needed. As Svengali in *Trilby* (1895) he was a sensation, and not much less so as Fagin in the Comyns Carr adaptation of *Oliver Twist* (1905). As a pioneer supporter of actor-training, Tree can claim the credit for founding the Royal Academy of Dramatic Art in 1904 and even housing it at his own expense. Since, in sober truth, he did not much believe in the training of actors he was presumably trying to fool someone. Posterity? He would certainly have been amused by the solemnity of subsequent practitioners of the art he handled so lightly. Tree was an Edwardian even before the death of Queen Victoria. His wife Maud gave him three daughters. A mysterious May Pinney, with whom he lived a simultaneous family life, gave him five sons and another daughter (one of the sons was the distinguished film director Carol Reed), and at the age of sixty-four he had his last child by a minor actress called Muriel Ridley. And he worked himself to death trying to support them all.

Madeleine Bingham, *The Great Lover*, 1978.

Turgenev, Ivan Sergeyevich (1818–83). Novelist and dramatist, his best-known play, *A Month in the Country* (1850), is a subtle reflection of his own life. Having lived on a large provincial estate, he spent much of his life in voluntary exile from Russia, constantly willing to accept a role like that of Rakitin in the play – *cavalier servente* to the famous singer Pauline Viardot and friend to her husband, in whose household he was a semi-permanent resident. Turgenev identified himself with the liberal noblemen who advocated and welcomed the liberation of the serfs in 1861. His hatred of the reactionary bullies of Tsarist Russia informs his plays and his novels. The authorities were nervous of him, and banned both *A Month in the Country* (not performed until 1872) and an excellent two-act play, variously known in English as *The Poor Gentleman*, *The Boarder* and *Alien Bread* (written in 1851, but banned even from publication until 1857). Three one-act plays, two dramatic sketches, and a three-act comedy called *The Bachelor* (written and performed in 1849) complete Turgenev's dramatic output. He underrated his own merits as a playwright. He is more than merely a precursor of CHEKHOV, though the Chekhovian promise of *A Month in the Country* is unmistakable.

Leonard Schapiro, *Turgenev: His Life and Times*, 1978.

Tynan, Kenneth (1927–80). English drama critic whose delight in controversy was the mischievous aspect of a passionate determination to emphasize the importance of the theatre to a society that needed it. Tynan became director of the Lichfield Repertory Company immediately after graduating from Oxford in 1949, and a brief theatrical career included his playing of the First Player in a *Hamlet* with ALEC GUINNESS in the lead (1951). His first spell as drama critic of the *Observer* (1954–8) coincided with a vital period in English drama. Tynan invited the new generation of dramatists to take account of BRECHT, but it was the wit of his literary manner as much as the forcefulness of the matter that made him a leader of the assault on the establishment rather than just its commentator. Between 1958 and 1960 he took his trenchant insights to the American theatre as critic for the *New Yorker* and then returned to the *Observer* (1960–63). From 1963 to 1969 he was Literary Manager of the NATIONAL THEATRE under LAURENCE OLIVIER. During that time he spearheaded the assault on theatrical CENSORSHIP in Britain, celebrating the abolition of the Lord Chamberlain's authority over the theatre by staging his 'erotic revue', *Oh! Calcutta!* (1968). *Curtains* (1961) contains many of his most pertinent reviews, *Bull Fever* (1955) records his enthusiasm for bull-fighting, and favourite actors Alec Guinness and Laurence Olivier are the subject of extended studies.

Udall, Nicholas (*c.* 1505–1556). Although a contemporary, John Bale, refers to 'several comedies' by Udall and he is known to have written plays acted before Mary Tudor and Elizabeth I, only one play is known for certain to be by him. This is *Ralph Roister Doister*, one of the most charming of early English comedies. Though it is based on the five-act structure of Latin comedy and the classical UNITIES, the play is as English as Hampstead Heath, as names like Dobinet Doughty, Tib Talkapace and Madge Mumblecrust indicate (although there is a servant with a Latin name, Harpax). The earliest extant English secular comedy, it introduces classical stereotypes such as the braggart soldier and the parasite who were to be completely naturalized in the Elizabethan theatre. Udall taught at both Eton and Westminster (he confessed to sodomy with his students) and probably wrote *Ralph Roister Doister* during his Westminster period.

Vakhtangov, Evgeny (1883–1922). Russian director and actor, who became first a disciple, then a friend and finally, without losing his friendship, a critic of STANISLAVSKY. After directing and acting in several plays as a student at Moscow University, Vakhtangov joined the MOSCOW ART THEATRE in 1911. His gifts as a teacher were quickly noticed, and he was put in charge of a group of young actors. For the First Studio of the Art Theatre he directed HAUPTMANN's *Holiday of Peace* in 1913 and became increasingly recognized as Stanislavsky's heir. At the opening production of the HABIMA in 1918, he directed three Jewish one-act plays. He was, at that time, committed to naturalistic production, but by 1920, when he directed CHEKHOV's FARCE *A Wedding* in his own Studio, he had developed a distinctive interest in grotesque invention. His finest work, in greatly contrasting styles, was presented in the year of his death, *The Dybbuk* at the Habima and GOZZI's *Princess Turandot* at the Third Studio of the Moscow Art Theatre. Vakhtangov was much loved by colleagues, and a dangerous gushiness obscures most of the available commentaries on his work. There is some truth in the view that he combined the strengths of Stanislavsky and MEYERHOLD in the directorial style which he sometimes called 'fantastic realism'.

Ruben Simonov, *Stanislavsky's Protégé*, 1969.

Vanbrugh, Sir John (1664-1736). Vanbrugh is equally well known as an architect and as a playwright. In the former capacity he was responsible for, among other buildings, Blenheim Palace and (with Nicholas Hawksmoor) Castle Howard. He also had two supplementary careers, first as a soldier, and, in later life, as Clarenceaux King of Arms in the College of Heralds. He was born in Chester, one of the nineteen children of a Flemish baker. He became a captain under Marlborough (for whom he later built Blenheim), was arrested as a spy in France and imprisoned in the Bastille in 1691-2, the rigours of incarceration being somewhat alleviated by the privilege of a bottle of Burgundy at lunch and two at dinner. While in prison Vanbrugh wrote the first draft of *The Provoked Wife*, his second original play. His first, a sequel to and satirical criticism of CIBBER's sentimental success *Love's Last Shift*, was *The Relapse: or Virtue in Danger* (1696). It is noteworthy, like all Vanbrugh's plays, for its comic gusto and its realistic and sympathetic account of the predicament of marriage as seen from a woman's viewpoint. It contains the most memorable versions of two Restoration stereotypes, the foppish beau Lord Foppington (transformed beyond recognition from Sir Novelty Fashion in Cibber's play) and the outlandish country knight Sir Tunbelly Clumsy. *The Provoked Wife* is remarkable, among much else, for the scene in which Sir John Brute goes on the rampage disguised as a clergyman. This scene so provoked the indignation of the worthy clergyman and theatre-hater JEREMY COLLIER that Vanbrugh altered it, this time disguising Sir John as Lady Brute. Vanbrugh gave Collier much better than he got in his *Short Vindication* (1698) where he assumes throughout that Collier's mind has been corrupted by reading too many bawdy plays. Apart from *A Journey to London*, left unfinished at his death and sentimentalized by Cibber into *The Provoked Husband* (1728), Vanbrugh was responsible for several lively adaptations from the French, one of which, *The Confederacy* (1705), is still occasionally revived.

Lawrence Whistler, *Vanbrugh: Architect and Dramatist*, 1938.
Bernard Harris, *Vanbrugh*, 1967.

Vega Carpio, Lope de (1562-1635). Perhaps the most prolific dramatist in history, Lope de Vega claimed to have written 1500 plays, and even scrupulous modern research is prepared to grant him about 400. The astonishing fact is that many of those that survive are good. He was a child prodigy and an established poet in Madrid by the time he was twenty. It was some libellous verses on an actress who abandoned him that caused his eight-year exile from that city. As secretary to the Duke of Sessa he composed plays as well as amorous verses, and was acknowledged as a leading writer of comedies by the time he returned to the capital. His plays cannot be accurately dated, nor, often, can they be neatly divided into genres. There is a mingling of tragedy and comedy in such pieces as *Frederick's Falcon* (based on a story in the *Decameron* which Tennyson also dramatized), the superb *Fuenteovejuna*, in which a spirited egalitarianism enriches the acceptance of social hierarchies, *The Prudent Man's Justice* and *The Kitchen Maid*. Lope de Vega's plays are not bound by the strict code of honour that dehumanizes much contemporary Spanish writing, and, although he accepts the necessity for social divisions, he does so only because order produces harmony. The heroine of *The Gardener's Dog* suffers because she damages her society by demeaning herself in love. *Justice without Revenge* and *Peribanez* are harsher but not merciless, and in the delightful *The Stupid Lady* there is a fine character study of a witless woman enlightened by love. Lope de Vega's craftsmanship in the creation of character and the shaping of a plot, however various its complications, is given ironical critical support in his *The New Art of Writing Plays* (1609). His influence in France was much greater than in England where his work has been disappointingly neglected.

F. C. Hayes, *Lope de Vega*, 1967.
M. Wilson, *The Spanish Drama of the Golden Age*, 1969.

Vestris, Madame (Lucy Elizabeth) (1797–1856). Madame Vestris was dark, bright-eyed, beautiful, and not quite as free with her favours as contemporary English gossip used to claim. Her first marriage, in 1813, was to the dancer Armand Vestris. Two years later, she made her debut as a singer at the King's Theatre in the Haymarket. Her breakthrough came in 1820 with her performance at Drury Lane in *Don Giovanni in London*. It gave her a BREECHES PART, and established the importance of her legs to her career. That she could sing as well was established by her success with 'Cherry Ripe' in *Paul Pry* (1828). She was not satisfied, however, by success achieved so easily, and challenged social prejudice by becoming, in late 1830, manager of the Olympic Theatre. A hundred and fifty years later, that would still not seem commonplace boldness. The Olympic seasons, which lasted until 1839, were notable for PLANCHÉ's extravaganzas, for the care with which the plays were staged, and for her collaboration with CHARLES JAMES MATHEWS, whom she married in 1838. Together they took over Covent Garden in 1839, failing financially by 1842 but succeeding as well as anyone else in maintaining a high artistic standard in the patented grave of English dramatic hopes. *London Assurance* (1841) there made BOUCICAULT's reputation, and began the development of the box set. Mathews had a precociously relaxed style of acting, and Madame Vestris an advanced taste in scenic precision. Their theatres were in the vanguard of reform. 'She cultivated,' Westland Marston recorded, 'a personal understanding with her audience.'

Clifford John Williams, *Madame Vestris*, 1973.
W. W. Appleton, *Madame Vestris and the London Stage*, 1974.

Vilar, Jean (1912–71). French actor and director whose first theatrical employment was as CHARLES DULLIN's stage manager. During World War II he toured the French provinces with a small company and with a growing commitment to the idea of a popular theatre. That idea was significantly tested in 1945 when he played Becket in his own production of ELIOT's *Murder in the Cathedral* in an outdoor setting. Partly on the strength of that he was appointed first director of the summer festival at Avignon in 1947. Performing in the open air, virtually without scenery, Vilar learned to rely on the human voice (his own was deep and resonant) and on careful lighting and costume. When in 1951, he was appointed director of France's first subsidized people's theatre, the THÉÂTRE NATIONAL POPULAIRE, he combined performances at the Palais de Chaillot in Paris with yearly visits to Avignon and irregular visits to other major cities. Productions of BRECHT, BÜCHNER (Vilar played Robespierre in *Danton's Death*) and, at a sensitive moment during the Algerian war, the *Peace* of ARISTOPHANES, were genuine contributions to political debate in France. Disappointed at the lack of adequate finance for growth, Vilar resigned from the TNP in 1962–3, but continued at Avignon until the tumultuous summer of 1968. Then, in dignified response to the attack on him as a pillar of the bourgeoisie, launched with particular vehemence by the LIVING THEATRE, he made a classic statement of the plight of the liberal radical in an elitist culture: 'The Festival has never been revolutionary. How can one deny that it is the prisoner of the bourgeois capitalist society with which we are all fed up? But it is precisely its ambition to find within this framework a slightly less bourgeois, slightly less capitalistic ground.'

Wakefield Master. This title denotes and conceals from us the identity of the highly individual dramatist who wrote and adapted a portion of the Towneley Cycle of mystery plays in the early part of the fifteenth century. Among his hallmarks are a lively colloquialism, a penchant for social satire and frequent use of local (Wakefield) allusions. Five complete plays out of the thirty-two in the cycle can be assigned to the Wakefield Master. These are *Noah*, the two *Shepherd Plays*, *Herod* and *The Buffeting*. He also probably had a hand in at least eight other plays, including *The Killing of Abel*. The best-known work by him, still frequently performed, is also one of his best, *The Second Shepherds' Play*.

Rosemary Woolf, *The English Mystery Plays*, 1972.

Wallack. An acting family of English origins whose important work was done in New York. The most notable members were:

(1) *James William Wallack* (1794–1864). An indefatigable transatlantic traveller (he is said to have made the crossing thirty-five times), James Wallack bought the New York Lyceum in 1852, renaming it Wallack's, and remained its manager until 1861. He was a man of some dignity, whose stock company was rehearsed with unusual care.

(2) *John Johnstone Wallack* (1819–88). Nephew of James and the active inheritor of his role as manager of Wallack's. He performed under the stage name of Lester Wallack and was a notable Aguecheek and Charles Surface. Under his guidance, Wallack's Theatre became identified during the 1860s with the comedies of T. W. ROBERTSON and he maintained a primarily English repertoire when other New York theatres were looking increasingly for American plays. The first Wallack's Theatre closed in 1881 and Lester opened a second the following year with one of his frequent revivals of *The School for Scandal*. His *Memoirs* were published the year after his death.

Webster, John (*c.* 1580–1634). Very little is known of the life of this remarkable English playwright. He may have been a member of the Merchant Taylors' Company and the John Webster who was clerk of the parish of St Andrews, Holborn. What is clear is that he was, from about 1602, one of the writers who worked plots into plays for PHILIP HENSLOWE. Webster was more systematic than most of the writers who worked in this collaborative style. As R. W. Dent has made plain in *Webster's Borrowings* (1960), he kept a detailed commonplace-book in which he noted striking poetic passages from other writers. Almost all

Webster's finest lines, and there are many of them, had been used before. Such studious plagiarism was not uncommon in Elizabethan England, but Webster is the master of the craft. The extraordinary fact is that his two finest plays, *The White Devil* (*c.* 1612) and *The Duchess of Malfi* (*c.* 1613), are among the most original products of the richest period in English drama. They are tragedies in which affairs of state are treated with a domestic intensity. The new philosophy has put all in doubt and Webster's characters strive unavailingly to fashion for themselves a meaningful life in a disintegrating world. The one other extant play which may be by Webster alone is the uncharacteristically careless tragicomedy, *The Devil's Law Case* (*c.* 1610). He wrote an interesting Induction to MARSTON's *The Malcontent* for its performance by SHAKESPEARE's company in 1604, and several of *The Overburian Characters*, including that of 'An Excellent Actor', are believed to be by him.

Peter B. Murray, *A Study of Webster*, 1969.
Brian Morris (ed.), *John Webster*, 1970.

Wedekind, Benjamin Franklin (1864–1918). When Wedekind was born, in Germany, his father had just returned from fifteen years in the land of the free, and his son's forenames (Wedekind came to call himself simply Frank) show that the fervour that took him there survived. The adventurousness was inherited. Wedekind left home after a row with his father, which he never forgave HAUPTMANN for drawing on in his play *Das Friedensfest*, worked as an advertising manager and then a journalist in Zurich, and when his father died suddenly in 1888, took off on a tour of the European capitals. His interest in the circus was sparked off by that tour. Circus images abound in his plays, and the atmosphere is often there when the image is not. The grotesque combination of the tawdry and the precise, the uncertainty in the audience as to who is playing what confidence trick on whom, the need to be in control, and the threat to that control of private emotion; all these recur. It may even be that Wedekind's structural preference for the *montage* method that would be further exploited by the German EXPRESSIONIST playwrights owed something to the sequence of 'acts' in the circus programme.

   The first of Wedekind's plays to attract attention was *Spring Awakening* (1891). No one dared perform it. As recently as 1965, the Lord Chamberlain banned it in England. The main characters are all children, but the subject is the crime of adult secretiveness about sex. Together with the two 'Lulu' plays, *Earth Spirit* and *Pandora's Box* (1895), it has earned Wedekind the half-truth of a reputation as a writer about sex. He certainly challenged European hypocrisy, and his own affairs were notorious. But it was the social mechanism rather than the sexual impulse it pretended to repress that was his real target. His involvement with the satirical magazine *Simplicissimus* led to his imprisonment in 1899 for *lèse majesté*. This is the crime for which the deposed hero of *King Nicolo* (1901) is imprisoned. It is a bitter play, in which autobiography is only partly submerged by historical distancing. *The Marquis of Keith* (1900), despite the virulence of its attacks on bourgeois acquisitiveness, is lighter. Wedekind, though frightened by the bourgeois urge in himself, fulfilled it in his hysterical marriage, which was contracted in 1906 and lashed on until his death.

Max Spalter, *Brecht's Tradition*, 1967.
S. Gittleman, *Frank Wedekind*, 1969.
Alan Best, *Frank Wedekind*, 1975.

Weigel, Helene (1900–72). Married BRECHT in 1929, shared his exile with him from 1933 to 1948, returned with him to Berlin in 1948, and led the Berliner Ensemble after his death in 1956. Weigel was Austrian and a fairly successful actress when Brecht met her in 1923. She played Widow Begbick in the 1928 production of *Man Equals Man*, and the title role in *The Mother* in 1932. It was almost certainly because he wanted a part for her in a Swedish production in 1939 that Brecht wrote Kattrin as a mute in *Mother Courage and Her Children* (Weigel spoke no Swedish). In the event, the play was not performed in Sweden. It had its premiere in Zurich in 1941, with Therese Giehse as Mother Courage, the role which Weigel made her own after 1949. Looking like a survivor of the concentration camps, she acted with the energy of an athlete. In repose she looked as plain and beaten as one of the women Käthe Kollwitz drew, but she was indomitable.

Weiss, Peter (1916–82). Playwright, painter, film-maker and journalist, Weiss was born in Berlin, the son of a Czech Jew and his Swiss wife. The rise of Hitler sent the family into frantic exile – 'I belonged to a group of wanderers who had gone into the land of horror' – and it was not until 1939 that they finally settled in Sweden, where Weiss continued to live. An early interest in surrealism and the grotesque is retained in the play that made Weiss famous, *The Persecution and Assassination of Marat as performed by the Inmates of the Asylum of Charenton under the direction of the Marquis de Sade* (1964). This can be performed coolly, after BRECHT, or hotly, after ARTAUD, as it was memorably in PETER BROOK's London production in 1964. Its various versions mark the progress of its author from political doubt to the certainties of Marxism. *The Investigation* (1965) is a documentary account of German guilt told through transcripts of the Auschwitz trials. Weiss probably intended it as an attack on capitalism, but it is not as clearly so as *The Song of the Lusitanian Bogey* (1967), *Discourse on Vietnam* (1968), *Trotsky in Exile* (1970) and *Hölderlin* (1971).

Ian Hilton, *Peter Weiss*, 1970.

Wekwerth, Manfred (1929–   ). East German director whose pursuit of a dialectical theatre marks him out as an inheritor of the theatrical philosophy of the mature BRECHT. Wekwerth joined the BERLINER ENSEMBLE in 1951 and became one of the team of dramaturg-directors who worked with Brecht in the last years of his life. With Bruno Besson, Wekwerth completed the rehearsal of Brecht's last play, *The Days of the Commune* (1956). Much of his directorial work has been collaborative after the fashion of the Berliner Ensemble. He worked with Peter Palitzsch on a sparkling new production of *Arturo Ui* (1959) and on Baierl's *Frau Flinz* (1961), with Joachim Tenschert on Brecht's version of *Coriolanus* (1964) and with Erich Engel and Karl von Appen on WEISS's *The Investigation* (1965). His resignation from the Berliner Ensemble in 1971 was a protest against a fossilization that he considered disloyal to the memory of Brecht. The company was greatly strengthened by his return in 1978.

Welles, Orson (1915–85). To call this American actor, director and media-wizard flamboyant is to ask the adjective to do a lot of work. He made his acting debut in Dublin in 1931 and his reputation in America in the thirties. Having toured with KATHARINE CORNELL in 1933 and 1934, he organized a Theatre Festival in Woodstock, Illinois. It was early evidence of an extraordinary flair which was confirmed by his work in Harlem with the Negro People's Theatre of which he was made director in 1936. In 1937 he became a director of the FEDERAL THEATRE PROJECT. At the Mercury Theatre, during that year, he presented a mercilessly anti-fascist production of *Julius Caesar* in modern dress (the negro *Macbeth* in Harlem had had a nineteenth-century Martinique setting), as well as DEKKER's *The Shoemaker's Holiday* and SHAW's *Heartbreak House*. Welles's interest in SHAKESPEARE has trapped him into all kinds of excesses. He played Othello in 1951 in London, and Lear in New York in 1956 (he was in a wheelchair throughout the run, having damaged one ankle in rehearsal and the other on the first night. 'If Mr Welles had had three legs, he would have tripped three times,' wrote Eric Bentley). His film versions of *Othello* and *Macbeth* are execrable –with magic moments – and *Chimes at Midnight*, in which he plays Falstaff, is the only major contribution he has made to Shakespeare on film. His place among film-makers is assured by *Citizen Kane* and *The Magnificent Ambersons*, and among film-actors by his Harry Lime in *The Third Man*. His sensational radio version of *The War of the Worlds* threw many Americans into panic in 1938. It was an epitome of the extraordinary charisma of the young Welles. That he declined into mountainous decadence is probably true, however sad. As early as 1955, KENNETH TYNAN wrote of his decision to stage a version of *Moby Dick*, 'At this stage of his career it is absurd to expect Orson Welles to attempt anything less than the impossible. It is all that is left to him.'

Richard France, *The Theatre of Orson Welles*, 1977.
Barbara Leaming, *Orson Welles*, 1985.

Wesker, Arnold (1932–   ). English playwright, born in the East End of London, and brought up among idealistic Jewish communists. The trilogy of plays that made his reputation – *Chicken Soup with Barley* (1958), *Roots* (1959) and *I'm Talking about Jerusalem* (1960) – calls directly on his youthful experience. Wesker's determination not to follow his hero Ronnie Kahn's decline into ineptitude was figured in his founding of Centre 42, committed to the provision of culture to the working class, which he directed from 1961 to 1970. That the experience was disillusioning is implicit in *Their Very Own and Golden City* (1965) and, particularly, in *The Friends* (1970). Wesker's reputation has been in undeserved decline, and the quality of his later work has not been fully recognized. *The Old Ones* (1972), *The Wedding Feast* (1974) and *The Merchant* (1977) are accomplished and energetic. Wesker's war against drama critics has been vigorously conducted. It is not easy to know how far it has contributed to his recent neglect. *Caritas* (1981) at the NATIONAL THEATRE did nothing to help him recover an audience, but the interesting one-woman show *Annie Wobbler* (1984) has done better.

Glenda Leeming and Simon Trussler, *The Plays of Wesker*, 1971.

Whiting, John (1917–63). English playwright who stood curiously aloof from the much-publicized renaissance of English drama after 1956. Whiting was trained as an actor and worked sporadically in British theatres both before and after World War II. He cared for plays much more than he cared for the theatre. *A Penny for a Song*, directed by PETER BROOK in London, was the first of his plays to be professionally staged. It is a whimsical study of English eccentricity, written in a prose that borrows some of its lucidity from poetry. *Saint's Day*, staged later in the same year, is a darker play. Whiting's concern with spiritual upheaval is here, as often, overlaid with the symbolism of religious conversion. His plays occupy some of the same ground as those of T. S. ELIOT. *Marching Song* (1954) is perhaps the best and *The Devils* (1961) the most compelling. It was staged by the ROYAL SHAKESPEARE COMPANY during their first full London season. Whiting's insight and seriousness were demonstrated by the criticism he wrote for the *London Magazine*, usefully collected under the title *Whiting on Theatre* (1966).

Eric Salmon, *The Dark Journey*, 1979.

Wilde, Oscar Fingal O'Flahertie Wills (1854–1900). Irish-born writer and talker, whose best work has been aptly called 'heightened conversation'. His first two plays, *Vera: or The Nihilists* (1880) and *The Duchess of Padua* (1883), have been largely forgotten, but he wrote them in search of financial success. The second is an Elizabethan pastiche, complete with prose and blank verse, and written with an eye to SARAH BERNHARDT. The radical tendency in both plays is only partly disguised by the occasional flippancy and the cursory plotting. Since HUGO and SHAKESPEARE have exhausted every subject, Wilde told a friend, there is no chance of originality or real emotions, 'only extraordinary adjectives'. His third play, *Salome* (1891–2), certainly has plenty of those. It was written in French, as a bait for Bernhardt, and she bit. The play was scheduled for her London season in 1892, but the Lord Chamberlain banned it. Its first staging was in Paris in 1896, when Wilde was in Reading Gaol. The play has its admirers, but the melodies of the prose are, in reality, a parody of the quavering style made popular by MAETERLINCK. Wilde's theatrical success began with the production of *Lady Windermere's Fan* in 1892. He called it 'one of those modern drawing-room plays with pink lampshades'. It is distinguished from other plays of its kind because it is wittier, and because Wilde invented in it one in his line of aristocratic dandies, mouthpieces for his scathing commentary on English culture which was partly his own pose, partly his conviction, and partly an aggressive but dreadfully necessary self-protection. *A Woman of No Importance* (1893) and *An Ideal Husband* (1895) are blood brothers to this play. It is in *The Importance of Being Earnest* (1895) that Wilde displays his originality as a dramatist. Auden has called it 'the only pure verbal opera in English'. The first months of 1895 found Wilde with two successes running simultaneously in London. The second half saw him through to disgrace and imprisonment for homosexual practices. In prison and in subsequent exile in Paris, he thought up plots for plays, but completed none.

H. Montgomery Hyde, *Oscar Wilde: A Biography*, 1976.
Alan Bird, *The Plays of Oscar Wilde*, 1977.
Katherine Worth, *Oscar Wilde*, 1983.

Wilder, Thornton (1897–1975). American playwright and novelist, who combines a subtle and intelligent delight in formal experiment under the influence of PIRANDELLO with an optimism about human motives that runs counter to post-war confrontational gloom. His best-known play is *Our Town* (1938), which demands simple staging for its chronicling of daily life in a New England village. *The Merchant of Yonkers* (1938), in its revised form as *The Matchmaker* (1954), was the basis for the enormously popular musical *Hello Dolly!* (1964). Wilders had adapted his original script from the Austrian dramatist NESTROY, which is fair evidence of the thoroughness of his knowledge of German literature (he is the author of a book in German on GOETHE). *The Skin of Our Teeth* (1942) is an idiosyncratic fantasy on human survival, admired in its time, but now out of it. Wilder is a master of the neglected art of the one-act play. Among his best are *The Long Christmas Dinner* (1931), *The Happy Journey to Trenton and Camden* (1931), *Pullman Car Hiawatha* (1931) and the *Plays for Bleecker Street* (1960–61), the last-named written for performance in Greenwich Village.

Donald Haberman, *The Plays of Wilder*, 1967.

Wilkinson, Tate (1739–1803). This English actor and theatre manager was celebrated by a contemporary as 'the greatest dramatic general of England's provinces'. Certainly it was his ingenious control of the York circuit of theatres from 1770 until his death that constituted his greatest contribution to the British theatre. His own acting was blighted by an irrepressible urge to mimicry. As Othello at Bath in 1759 he was mistaken by some for SPRANGER BARRY, so slavish was the imitation. In later life his own eccentricities were marked enough to encourage CHARLES MATHEWS to include an imitation of him in his *At Homes*. His *Memoirs* (1790) and *The Wandering Patentee* (1795) are invaluable and lively accounts of provincial theatre life in the late eighteenth century.

George Hauger, 'Ten Years of a Provincial Theatre', in *Theatre – General and Particular*, 1966.
Charles Beecher Hogan, 'One of God's Almighty Unaccountables', in *The Theatrical Manager in England and America*, ed. Joseph Donohue, 1971.

Wilks, Robert (1665–1732). When assassins hired by a jealous rival in love murdered William Mountfort in 1692, Wilks returned from a season in Ireland to take his place. He was an actor of some note, especially in comedy, at his best in gentlemanly roles like that of Sir Harry Wildair in FARQUHAR's *The Constant Couple*. With COLLEY CIBBER and BARTON BOOTH, Wilks formed an effective management of Drury Lane from 1710 until his death. Where there were problems, they were as often as not caused by Wilks's hot temper.

Williams, Tennessee (Thomas Lanier) (1911–83). American playwright, born in Mississippi, of an absentee father, who called him 'Nancy', and a genteel mother, who preserved dreams of antebellum Southern days of wine and roses. From 1944, when *The Glass Menagerie* opened, to 1961, when *The Night of the Iguana* was produced on BROADWAY, Williams experienced an extraordinary share of both popular and critical acclaim. He deserved it. *A Streetcar Named Desire* (1947) is superbly told, *The Rose Tattoo* (1951) would be better appreciated if people would laugh with instead of at its excesses, *Cat on a Hot Tin Roof* (1955) is a durable classic, and the screenplay of *Baby Doll* (1956) a playful variation on the theme of false frigidity. To be sure, Williams's version of Southern Gothic is peculiarly decadent. He has felt free to admit his homosexuality only in the permissive seventies (in *Memoirs*, 1975, and the highly personal novel *Moise and the World of Reason*, also 1975, for example), but homosexuality, though rarely stressed in his plays, is equally rarely absent from them. The homes, hotels and townships of Williams's plays are a paradise for beautiful studs, though they may find themselves castrated (*Sweet Bird of Youth*) or even eaten (*Suddenly Last Summer*) for their pleasurable pains. These are the sexual phantasies that have fuelled pornography, and Williams's tall tales are an acting out of the battle in him between the pornographer and the shame-laden Puritan. Because he is one of them, Williams has always had great sympathy for people whose lives have been untidy. His own reputation took a battering with the 1962 production of the comparatively plotless symbolic work *The Milk Train Doesn't Stop Here Anymore*, and the succession of disasters that followed it contributed to his mental breakdown in 1969. Subsequent plays concerned themselves often with the plight of the failing artist, for example with Scott and Zelda Fitzgerald as the ostensible subject in *Clothes for a Summer Hotel* (1980). The most interviewed playwright in the history of drama, Williams was the beneficiary and the victim of the American cult of psychoanalysis.

Foster Hirsch, *A Portrait of the Artist: The Plays of Tennessee Williams*, 1979.

Wilson, Robert (d. 1600). Wilson joined the Earl of Leicester's Company of players when it was formed in 1574 and gained a reputation as a comic actor. In 1583, together with eleven other actors, he formed Queen Elizabeth's company and five years later joined Lord Strange's Men, later to become the Lord Chamberlain's Men, the company to which SHAKESPEARE belonged. His three surviving plays, *The Three Ladies of London* (?1581), *The Three Lords and Three Ladies of London* (?1589) and *The Cobbler's Prophecy* (1594), show the framework of the Morality play being stretched by vivid social observation (though elements of the latter are present even in the earliest Moralities).

Wilton, Marie (1839–1921). After making a sex symbol of herself in burlesques at the Strand, Marie Wilton astonished the theatrical world by turning to straight drama in 1865. Not only that. She even took the risk of buying a major share in the management of the disreputable Queen's Theatre in Tottenham Street which she renamed the Prince of Wales's, cleaning it up (she put antimacassars over the stalls and carpeted the aisles), and commissioning plays. It became the home of the plays of T. W. ROBERTSON, and the centre of theatrical reform. In 1867 she married SQUIRE BANCROFT, and her subsequent career ran in strict parallel to his. She had been loved for her legs at the Strand, and for the cheeky joy of her acting in the early years at the Prince of Wales's. The dwindling into Victorian marriage was probably regrettable – but at least she had heard the chimes at midnight. She proved herself a shrewd manager in the competitive world of the London theatre and boosted the gathering claims of women to govern their own careers in the theatre.

Witkiewicz, Stanislaw (1885–1939). Polish dramatist, painter, novelist and occasional explorer, Witkiewicz was born in a part of Poland then under Russian rule. His father was a famous artist and, under his influence, the precocious boy began to paint and to write. A later influence was the anthropologist, Malinowski, with whom Witkiewicz visited the South Seas and Australia. He served in the Russian Imperial Guard during World War I and was in St Petersburg during the Russian Revolution of 1917. Returning to Poland, he changed his name to Witkacy and, often under the influence of drugs, with which he experimented, wrote over forty plays. His pursuit of what he called 'pure form' was an attempt to associate the drama with modern movements in art and music. Always conscious of the 'monsters' in his mind, Witkacy translated his grotesque visions into a set of visual images unreliably linked by allusive plots. His first play, *Maciej Korbowa and Bellatrix* (1918), is a nightmare prophecy of the horrors of totalitarianism. *They* (1920) is another catastrophist piece which proposes that 'they', who run our lives, may be lunatics. *The Independence of Triangles* (1921) is a Kafkaesque fantasy about the reduction of people to the mindless efficiency of insects. *The Water Hen* (1921) is a dream play in which the collapse of civilization is presented in disconnected images. Witkacy's bizarre humour is dominant in *Dainty Shapes and Hairy Apes* (1922), mixed in with violence and apocalyptic images. Coherence and hope are victims in all Witkacy's plays, including the best known, *The Madman and the Nun* (1923), *The Mother* (1924) and *The Shoemakers* (1927). Had he written in a language better known than Polish, he might have shared with ARTAUD an honoured place as an innovator. His own attempts to stage his plays were sporadically successful, but the plays themselves were badly received. Rediscovery of this tormented writer's work began with a performance of *The Cuttlefish* (1922) in Cracow in 1955. Sixteen years earlier, unable to face the advance of the Nazis into Poland, Witkacy had slit his own throat.

Woffington, Peg (*c.* 1717–1760). Irish-born actress, the daughter of a Dublin bricklayer who died when she was six, leaving the widow and two daughters in hardship. Peg was persuaded, for financial reasons, to join a juvenile acting troupe and made her adult debut in Dublin in 1734, but her triumph came when she dared to challenge the memory of ROBERT WILKS as Sir Harry Wildair in FARQUHAR's *The Constant Couple*. She played the part at Covent Garden in 1740 and endlessly thereafter. COLLEY CIBBER snatched her into the Drury Lane company, where she acted with CHARLES MACKLIN and with DAVID GARRICK, who became her lover. Woffington was quick-tempered and fun-loving. There were stories of GREEN ROOM fights with KITTY CLIVE and rumours of associations with high-ranking gentlemen, rakes and actors. Garrick had hoped to marry her, but was deterred by her unwillingness to limit her friendships with other men. Her acting career was busy. In addition to Sir Harry Wildair, she was an admired Rosalind in *As You Like It* and a lively Mistress Ford in *The Merry Wives of Windsor*. Above all, though, it was her playing of BREECHES PARTS that attracted audiences. Her robust health failed suddenly in 1757 during a performance of *As You Like It* at Covent Garden and she had to be helped from the stage. Loved by men and envied by many women, Peg Woffington gathered legends around her while she lived and the legends increased after her death. *Masks and Faces* (1852), a successful play by TOM TAYLOR and Charles Reade, takes her as its heroine.

Janet Dunbar, *Peg Woffington and Her World*, 1968.

Wolfit, Donald (1902–68). English actor whose anachronistic sustaining of the Bensonian touring tradition was evidence of his stupendous appetite for performance. He made his debut in York in 1920 but was not much noticed by critics until his appearances at the OLD VIC in 1929–1930. Usually at his best when he could be larger than life, he was a surprisingly controlled Hamlet at STRATFORD in 1936. In 1937 he formed his own Shakespearean company and toured the provinces with it. For the rest of his life, his solution to any lack of employment with existing theatres was to assemble a group of his own, usually in conjunction with his wife, Rosalind Iden. There is no doubt that Wolfit indulged in ham-acting on occasions, but it must equally be admitted that his Volpone (1938), King Lear (1943) and Tamburlaine (1951) are among the greatest stage events of the twentieth-century British theatre. He was a survivor from the days of greasepaint and glory. In 1957, the year in which he was knighted, he was making magnificent melodrama out of Montherlant's gloomy *The Master of Santiago* at the Lyric, Hammersmith.

Ronald Harwood, *Sir Donald Wolfit*, 1971.

Woollcott, Alexander (1887–1943). American dramatic critic whose exuberance was constant, but whose discrimination was unreliable. He was with the *New York Times* from 1914 to 1922, with the exception of two years with the American army, and from then until 1928 successively with the *New York Herald*, the *Sun* and the *New York World*. He abandoned daily journalism in 1928 after a damning review of O'NEILL's *Strange Interlude* appeared before the play had opened, though his 'Shouts and Murmurs' column in the *New Yorker* continued to entertain the American public for many years after that. Something of a performer himself – Brooks Atkinson has called him 'a virtuoso fat man' – Woollcott writes best about actors. His biographical accounts of MINNIE MADDERN FISKE, Charlie Chaplin and the Marx Brothers are lively. His dramatic criticism has been conveniently selected in *The Portable Woollcott* (1946).

Wycherley, William (1640–1716). Wycherley's father was a Shropshire lawyer whose passion for litigation led to his calling for the imprisonment of his own son, the playwright's brother, for debt. Wycherley pursued his education in France, returning to England when the restoration of the monarchy was imminent. He attended Oxford University, but left without taking a degree, studied law without enthusiasm at the Inner Temple in London and took advantage of the pleasures of the city, which furnished raw material for his comedies. The first of these, *Love in a Wood* (1671), was dedicated to the Duchess of Cleveland, one of Charles II's mistresses who later became Wycherley's. His second play, *The Gentleman Dancing Master* (1672), was adapted from the Spanish of CALDERON, but his third, *The Country Wife* (1675), is one of the most original and lively comedies in English. Here Wycherley mercilessly exposes the lubricity and hypocrisy of a society where sex and money are endlessly interchangeable and reputation is the almighty god. His last play, *The Plain Dealer* (1677), is almost disconcertingly savage, though its wit and deft plotting brought it a deserved popularity. In 1679 Wycherley made a mercenary marriage to the Countess of Drogheda, offending Charles II who had other plans for him and doing himself no good at all. When the Countess died in 1681 she left him nothing but debts, and he spent the years from 1682 to 1686 in a debtors' prison. Released and given a pension by James II in 1686, he spent the last thirty years of his life trying to preserve his money and bolster up his literary reputation by publishing verse. The verse was unimpressive, and it is as a dramatic satirist with a dazzling gift for dialogue and a mastery of the *double entendre* that Wycherley is remembered.

W. Connely, *Brawny Wycherley*, 1930.
Rose Zimbardo, *Wycherley's Drama*, 1965.

Yeats, William Butler (1865–1939). Irish poet and playwright. With LADY GREGORY and Edward Martyn, he founded the Irish Literary Theatre in 1899, presided over its transformation into the ABBEY THEATRE, and remained, often controversially, its director until his death. Yeats is a major poet, but probably not quite a major playwright, though there are few writers who have searched as fascinatedly for the idea of a theatre. His theatrical views and essays appear variously among his critical works, in *Plays and Controversies* (1923), *Autobiographies* (1926) and *Dramatis Personae* (1935), for instance. Many of his plays turn to Irish legend, enjoying both the enigma and the simplicity of folk-tales. The self-questioning hero Cuchulain interested him particularly, from *On Baile's Strand* (1904) and *The Golden Helmet* (1908, revised as *The Green Helmet* in 1910) to the very late *The Death of Cuchulain* (1939). *The Pot of Broth* (1902) is an experiment in rough-and-tumble folk farce, but Yeats is more at home with twilight and mystery. His 'Plays for Dancers' (1916–21) followed an encounter with Japanese NOH plays, reflecting also an increasing involvement in occult symbolism. Masks, colours and patterns of staging were aspects of a pursuit of strange truth. Formalism meets pagan wildness in *The Player Queen* (1919) and in the three plays of 1938, *The Herne's Egg*, *A Full Moon in March* and *The King of the Great Clock Tower*. Notable among the other plays, *The King's Threshold* (1903) is an eloquent fable on the power of poetry, and *Purgatory* (1938) is a masterpiece of mysterious precision. It is for making people doubt the immanence of mystery that the Wise Man of *The Hour-Glass* (1903) is condemned to death. Yeats did not make the same mistake. As he wrote to Lady Gregory in 1919, 'I desire a mysterious art, always reminding and half-reminding those who understand it of dearly loved things, doing its work by suggestion, not by direct statement, a complexity of rhythm, colour, gesture, not space-pervading like the intellect but a memory and a prophecy.'

Peter Ure, *Yeats the Playwright*, 1963.
Karen Dorn, *Players and Painted Stage*, 1983.

Zadek, Peter (1926–   ). German director whose Jewish parents fled to England in 1933. Zadek worked in English theatres from 1949 to 1960, acquiring a fondness for improvisational freedom that is not common in Germany. On his return to his native country he directed BEHAN's *The Hostage* at Ulm, testing his audience with a play that had emerged through the hit-and-miss of JOAN LITTLEWOOD's experimental rehearsals. At Wuppertal in 1967, Zadek staged an imaginative production of O'CASEY's anti-war play, THE SILVER TASSIE, delighting in controversy. He was appointed director of the Bochum theatre in 1972 and collaborated with Tankred Dorst on a political piece called *Little Man – What Now?* He is a flamboyant entertainer who enjoys provoking his audience and collaborating with his actors. In his production of *King Lear* at Bochum (1974) he combined VAUDEVILLE with GRAND GUIGNOL, contriving nonetheless to make the death of Cordelia outstandingly moving. PETER STEIN has referred to Zadek's work on *King Lear* and *The Winter's Tale*, performed on two tons of green slime, as 'Shakespeare in underpants'.

Zola, Émile (1840–1902). This French novelist, who was forced into overproduction by the need to earn money, is of theatrical importance largely because of the essays collected in *Naturalism in the Theatre* (1881). It should not be forgotten that NATURALISM, of which Zola was a major spokesman, was intimately connected with developments in science, particularly medical science. It followed in the wake of Darwinism. Of his own novel *Thérèse Raquin* (1867), which he dramatized in 1873, Zola wrote: 'I simply applied to two living bodies the analytical method that surgeons apply to corpses.' This was the kind of ruthless accuracy that he called for in the theatre. It is the call for plays that will show 'a fragment of existence' ('slice of life' was the alternative phrase coined by Jean Jullien) that is most commonly remembered; but Zola's use of physiology to modify the idea of character is, in many ways, a more important feature of his naturalism.

L. A. Carter, *Zola and the Theatre*, 1963.
F. W. J. Hemmings, *Émile Zola*, 1966.

IV   Theatrical Miscellany

Theatrical Miscellany

Afterpiece. When, in the eighteenth century, the custom of granting free admission to patrons who arrived at the theatre after the third act of the play was replaced by the HALF–PRICE system, managers had to pad out the programme. It became common practice to follow the main item, whether tragedy or comedy, with a one-act farce or comedy. Many of the best of these – GARRICK, FOOTE and MURPHY were masters of the art of the afterpiece – proved more popular with audiences than the main 'attraction'. Resourceful dramatists gave their comedies a double life, by presenting them first as full-length plays and then by cutting them down to a single act.

Benefit. There had been writers' benefits in the Elizabethan theatre, but the benefit system for actors began in about 1686 as a compliment to ELIZABETH BARRY and quickly became customary, lasting in London until the mid-nineteenth century and a little longer in America. The British provincial theatre retained the system into the twentieth century – the manager of the Exeter Theatre Royal, for instance, was still taking a benefit during the pantomime season in 1928. The normal benefit was accorded each season to a single leading actor of the resident company at a theatre, allowing him or her to take all the profits once the charges had been met on a particular night. Exceptionally, and often for charitable reasons, an actor might be awarded a 'clear' benefit, with the management meeting the charges. Lesser performers might have hoped to share in a joint benefit. The system, however well intended, was liable to abuse, not only by unscrupulous actors, but also by managers who used the promise of a benefit to fix salaries unnecessarily low. It was the introduction of the long run rather than any solid urge towards reform that accelerated the end of the benefit system.

St Vincent Troubridge, *The Benefit System in the British Theatre*, 1967.

Bettymania. A journalistic description of the extraordinary cult following that greeted the first London performances of William Henry West Betty (1791–1874). Having made his debut in Belfast at the age of eleven, Betty was the sensation of London for two seasons from 1804 to 1806. Billed as 'the young ROSCIUS' – a conscious challenge to the memory of the English Roscius, GARRICK – he played Hamlet at Drury Lane in 1805, and the town flocked to see him. It was even rumoured that a sitting of the House of Commons was suspended to enable the members to witness the infant prodigy at work. The *Morning Post* noted that 'the war and Bonaparte were for a time unheeded and forgotten'. DOROTHEA JORDAN on the other hand, speaking for the many actors whose noses were put out of joint by the furore, sighed for the days of King Herod. Poor Betty, who was certainly beautiful and probably talented, was the victim of his grasping father's ambition. After an abortive undergraduate career at Cambridge, he attempted a theatrical comeback in 1812, but the magic was no longer there. He abandoned the struggle in 1824, three years after trying to kill himself, and lived in comfortable retirement for a further fifty years.

Giles Playfair, *The Prodigy*, 1967.

Bodley, Sir Thomas (1545-1613). The great bibliophile who founded the Bodleian Library in Oxford held plays in low esteem. He wrote to Thomas James, keeper of his library, in 1612:

> Sir, I would you had forborne to catalogue our London books, until I had been privy to your purpose. There are many idle books, and riff-raffs among them, which shall never come to the library, and I fear me that little, which you have done already, will raise a scandal upon it, when it shall be given out by such as would disgrace it, that I have made up a number with almanacs, plays, and proclamations: of which I will have none, but such as are singular . . . . Haply some plays may be worth the keeping: but hardly one in forty.

Bodley's attitude was not unusual. Plays were considered ephemeral, and it was not established practice to turn them into books. It says much for the ambition and boldness of BEN JONSON that he should have issued his own plays, in the proud luxury of a folio edition, in 1616. Without Jonson's example, it is unlikely that SHAKESPEARE's friends would have collected his published and unpublished work into the First Folio of 1623. A note, dated 8 June 1642, in the hand of the then Master of the Revels, Sir Henry Herbert, shows that Bodley's strictures could be taken further: 'Received of Mr Kirke for a new play which I burnt for the ribaldry and offense that was in it – £2.' Whatever the play was, we can be fairly certain that Herbert destroyed the only complete copy.

Brayne, John (d. 1586). Not much is known about Brayne, beyond the fact that he was James Burbage's brother-in-law, and that it was to him that Burbage turned to help raise money to build the THEATRE in 1576. Despite the excellent return Brayne must have got on his investment, he had run into difficulty at the time of his death, perhaps because his soap-making business in the George Inn at Whitechapel was experiencing a slump. What we do know, from the details of a court case, is that Brayne's widow was dissatisfied with James Burbage's business dealings. In 1590, she took Robert (and probably Ralph) Myles and Nicholas Bishop with her to the Theatre to demand her rights. They were met there by James Burbage and his not-yet-famous son, Richard. It was RICHARD BURBAGE who belaboured Robert Myles with a broomstick, then, as Nicholas Bishop complained to the court, turned on him, threatening him with the same broomstick while 'scornfully and disdainfully playing with this deponent's nose'.

Breeches part. This term was first used in the eighteenth century to describe male roles which were customarily considered appropriate for actresses. PEG WOFFINGTON's popularity as FARQUHAR's Sir Harry Wildair, which she played from 1740 until her retirement in 1757, established a vogue which lasted well into the nineteenth century. Having seen Ellen Tree in a part that he had made famous, that of Ion in a tragedy by Talfourd, MACREADY commented, 'a very creditable woman's effort, but it is no more like a young man than a coat and waistcoat are'. But by then, the breeches part had been assimilated into the attractive world of the fairy extravaganza, whence it passed into pantomime. The principal boy is a twentieth-century descendant of Peg Woffington.

Bristow, James. There is a famous entry in HENSLOWE's Diary that has shocked and intrigued many readers: 'Bought my boy James Bristow of William Augustin player the 18 of December 1597 for £8.' This heartless-seeming purchase of a boy-actor by a theatre manager may not have been exceptional. Augustin was certainly pleased by the deal, since it brought him more than he was likely to earn in a year on the stage. As for James Bristow, we know nothing more about him, except that Henslowe was paying him three shillings per week in 1600.

Bunn versus Macready. The career of the outrageous Alfred Bunn (1798–1860) did nothing to advance theatrical taste in England. Indeed, if 'Poet' Bunn is remembered at all, it is for his efforts on behalf of English opera and for his quarrel with MACREADY. The occasion of the quarrel is known in detail from Macready's Diaries. Since 1833, Bunn had been in the unique position of lessee of *both* the PATENT THEATRES, Drury Lane and Covent Garden. His abuse of power was a constant thorn in the side of Macready, leading tragedian at Drury Lane; but the final blow came in 1836, when Macready read on a playbill the information that he was to play 'the first three acts of *Richard III*' on 29 April. To the conscientious Macready, such mutilation of SHAKESPEARE was intolerable; to the vain Macready, the compulsion to perform a part in which he knew he was considered unsuccessful was unnerving. Nonetheless, he went through with it, but when, on leaving the stage, he saw Bunn sitting at the table in his office, Macready could contain himself no longer:

> I struck him as he rose a backhanded slap across the face. I did not hear what he said, but I dug my fist into him as effectively as I could; he caught hold of me, and got at one time the little finger of my left hand in his mouth, and bit it. I exclaimed: 'You rascal! Would you bite?' He shouted out: 'Murder! Murder!' and, after some little time, several persons came into the room. I was then upon the sofa, the struggle having brought us right round the table.

Bunn's account in *The Stage both Before and Behind the Curtain* (1840) differs in emphasis:

> I was examining bills and documents previous to their payment on the following morning, when without the slightest note of preparation my door was opened, and after an ejaculation of, 'There, you villain, take that – and that,' I was knocked down, one of my eyes completely closed up, the ankle of my left leg which I am in the habit of passing round the leg of the chair when writing violently sprained, my person plentifully soiled with blood, lamp-oil and ink, the table upset and Richard III holding me down. On my naturally inquiring if he meant to murder me, and he replying in the affirmative, I made a struggle for it, threw him off and got up on my one leg, holding him fast by the collar, and finally succeeded in getting him down on the sofa, where, mutilated as I was, I would have made him remember *me*, but for the interposition of the people who had soon filled the room.

Macready was mortified by the undignified scuffle and by the subsequent scandal, but his career benefited from it. Popular sympathy, as well as that of his fellow-sufferers under Bunn, was all on his side, and offers of starring engagements flooded in as never before.

Camp. In the Addenda to the *Shorter Oxford English Dictionary* (1973 edition), the year 1909 is proposed as the first in which the adjectival use of this word to mean 'ostentatious, affected, theatrical' became current. The origin is unknown, though one possibility is indicated by a comment of Cecil Beaton's: 'Hearty naval commanders or jolly colonels acquired the "camp" manners of calling everything from Joan of Arc to Merlin "lots of fun".' Readers of Evelyn Waugh's society novels or, more particularly, the work of Ronald Firbank are brought into contact with the 'camp' world, but a quicker way is to attend first-night parties in almost any English or American theatre. The dictionary goes on to define the word as 'effeminate or homosexual'. That is too restrictive. You can be camp without being homosexual, though only if some of your best friends are. At its best, in the style of NOEL COWARD, camp behaviour is wittily pertinent. At its worst, it is a tiresomely predictable way of preserving actors from any serious contact with their audience.

Capsule criticism. ALEXANDER WOOLLCOTT used this term as the title of an essay on curtly definitive dramatic criticism. Many of the best examples are American: Stanley Kaufmann on Gertrude Lawrence's BROADWAY appearance in *Skylark,* 'A bad play saved by a bad performance'; Robert Benchley on a long-running comedy, 'People laugh at this every night, which explains why a democracy can never be a success'; Walter Kerr on *I Am a Camera,* 'Me no Leica'; Tallulah Bankhead from the stalls during a revival of MAETERLINCK's *Aglavaine and Selysette,* 'There's less in this than meets the eye'; Kaufmann again, 'Business was so bad they were shooting deer in the balcony'. Among English critics, Bernard Levin often tried, but generally failed, to emulate American capsule criticism. JAMES AGATE and KENNETH TYNAN had the wit but lacked the brevity.

Censorship. Censorship of one kind or another has been a part of theatre since its origins. It is the highest compliment that can be paid by authority to the potency of live drama – except, perhaps, that of relishing it. In England, the first statute of regulation was pronounced in 1543 under the pious title of 'An act for the advancement of true religion and for the abolishment of the contrary', and the shifting of responsibility on to the Master of the Revels, a Court officer in the service of the Lord Chamberlain, began in 1545. The power of the Master of the Revels was more strictly defined in the wake of the furious MARPRELATE CONTROVERSY of 1589, and the history of English drama from then until the closing of the theatres in 1642 is pitted with encounters between offending playwrights and offensive Masters.

Edmund Tilney, Master of the Revels from 1578 to 1610, for instance, instructed the authors of *Sir Thomas More* to 'leave out ye insurrection wholly, and the cause of it'. The aim of censorship was to protect God, the Church, the State and living persons from abuse. Since 'abuse' is only effective in the eye of the observer, the potential restriction of the right of the drama to say anything serious about anything serious is obvious.

Although Charles II permitted the reopening of theatres to the public, he did so under controls stricter than ever before. The Letters Patent stipulated that London was to have only two playhouses, and KILLIGREW and DAVENANT were made responsible for censoring all the plays performed there. They interpreted their task idiosyncratically, however, and for the high-minded protectors of the nation's virtue, Restoration drama was a cesspit. JEREMY COLLIER's was only the most vigorous of many voices raised against its 'immorality and profaneness'. His famous *Short View* (1698) was written two years after the censorship of books had been abolished. In published form, then, plays were subject only to the laws of the land, but live performance was more carefully monitored. Instructions from William III himself cautioned against plays 'containing expressions contrary to religion and good manners'. In dutiful response, the eighteenth-century stage provided mealy-mouthed comedies and noble tragedies presenting life and language as they should be.

The satirical urge, though, could not be so easily contained. *The Beggar's Opera* (1728) concealed an attack on Robert Walpole but audiences were not fooled. FIELDING went so far as to lampoon the royal family in *The Welsh Opera* (1731). The outburst of theatrical satires alarmed Walpole sufficiently to make him scheme for sharper control over the live drama. Using as his pretext a scurrilous play called THE GOLDEN RUMP (he may have had it specially written), he carried through Parliament in 1737 a Licensing Act which greatly strengthened the authority of the Lord Chamberlain in all matters theatrical. For over two centuries the Chamberlain's powers remained much as defined in that Act. The work of censorship devolved on to full-time 'Examiners of Plays', many of them manifestly ill-qualified for the job. DAVID MERCER recalled visiting polite ex-Guards officers in the Chamberlain's Office in about 1960 to bargain about swear-words over cups of tea. Once he was given the instruction to replace the expletive 'Christ!' with 'Old John with his head on a plate!' At much the same time, Henry Livings was allowed to retain a scene of frustrated seduction provided that 'it takes place behind the sofa out of view of the audience'.

Various attempts were made to abolish the Chamberlain's powers of censorship, most effectively in 1909. In that year, spurred on by the brilliant rhetoric of GEORGE BERNARD SHAW, a Joint Select Committee reviewed the position. A letter sent to that Committee by Arnold Bennett spells out the main argument against the separate censorship of the drama: 'the existence of the censorship makes it impossible for me even to think of writing plays on the same plane of realism and *thoroughness* as my novels'. The power of the Lord Chamberlain survived the deliberations of the 1909 Committee, and official censorship of the drama was not abolished until the Theatres Act of 1968.

Richard Findlater, *Banned!*, 1967.

Change of heart. During the eighteenth-century heyday of sentimental comedy, it was not considered sufficient to have the young lovers brought together by some DEUS EX MACHINA because the villain (or ill-tempered father) might then remain unreformed. A change of heart in the final act was preferred, however psychologically improbable. The plays of RICHARD CUMBERLAND and Hugh Kelly are by no means the silliest of the kind, though they are the best known. GEORGE COLMAN the Younger recalls a play that was sent to him by an aspiring dramatist during Colman's management of the Haymarket. The love-knots in this text were untangled in a single stage direction: 'Here the Miser leans against the wall and grows generous.'

Clap-trap. As a political expedient, clap-trap is a kind of compulsory reassurance, demanded from an audience after the vehement expression of safe sentiment. Praise of the English policeman at a Conservative Party Conference is a clap-trap, as is praise of Lenin in the Soviet praesidium. SHAKESPEARE's Henry V may not be innocent of clap-trap, but it flourished most in the theatre with the birth and development of stout-hearted British MELODRAMA, particularly of the nautical and military kind. The prolific dramatist Frederick Reynolds recommended in his 1827 *Reminiscences* 'the praise of Laws, Jack Tars, Innocence, an Englishman's *castellum*, or Liberty' as reliable clap-traps, and the recommendation held good for the rest of the nineteenth century. The cruel and extraordinary vogue for Walter Reynolds's old-fashioned melodrama *Young England*, produced in London in 1934, showed the scant respect for clap-trap among the sophisticated spectators who hooted and jeered the play to 'success'. There was a brief revival of the style during World War II, but Churchill's clap-trap was better than the playwrights'. The contemporary theatre is a perilous place for patriots.

Clark, Creston. This American actor's performance as King Lear drew from Eugene Field one of the wittiest of all dismissive criticisms: 'All through the five acts of that Shakespearean tragedy he played the King as though under the momentary apprehension that someone else was about to play the ace.'

Coates, Robert ('Romeo') (1772–1848). Even in a profession where colourful characters have never been thin on the ground, 'Romeo' Coates stands out. His sobriquet records a memorable occasion in 1810 when he rented the Theatre Royal, Bath to appear in SHAKESPEARE's tragedy with himself in the title role. Appearing in London in the same role he favoured a bright blue cloak, scarlet pantaloons, a full wig and tall hat and several hundred pounds' worth of jewellery. Prior to committing suicide he carefully spread a handkerchief on the stage floor. His performance brought him immediate if short-lived notoriety and for a time he was a fashionable figure in London, driving around barnacled with jewels in a carriage surmounted by the shining figure of a peacock. But his Shakespearean interpretations did not catch on.

Collier, Jeremy (1656–1726). English pamphleteer, who would be forgotten but for his *Short View of the Immorality and Profaneness of the English Stage* (1698). This was the most notable among the many attacks on Restoration comedy, and was instrumental in persuading CONGREVE to abandon the theatre. Collier would probably rather have been remembered for his *Ecclesiastical History of Great Britain* (1708–14), or as a ferocious non-juror, whose support of the Stuarts continued to get him into trouble almost until his death.

J. W. Krutch, *Comedy and Conscience after the Restoration*, 1924.
Sister Rose Anthony, *The Jeremy Collier Controversy*, 1937.

Coocher. This American term for a solo dancer in burlesque probably originated from the sensational appearance of Catherine Devine at the 1893 Chicago World Fair. Billed as 'Little Egypt', she took the unprecedented step of exposing her stomach in order to imitate 'the ancient harem dance of bondage'. Disguised under the name of hootchee cootchee, the undulations of this simple belly dance developed into the sophisticated art of striptease, a term invented by two press agents of the promoting Minsky Brothers in about 1922. According to Harold Minsky, the first modern striptease was performed by 'Curls' Mason in 1921. It was not long before striptease had established itself as an essential part of the American burlesque show, reaching new heights of acceptability with the greatest coocher of them all, Gypsy Rose Lee (1914–70).

Irving Zeidman, *The American Burlesque Show,* 1967.

Corpse. Theatrical slang meaning 'to laugh uncontrollably'. An actor who experiences corpsing at its worst – that is, when the audience remains entirely straightfaced – will understand the strange association of laughter and death. The word originated to describe, more precisely, the intention of one actor to force another into 'killing' himself with laughter by doing or saying something unexpected. RALPH RICHARDSON corpsed his fellow-actors on one occasion, when on a pre-London tour with a new, and not very popular, play. Having first alarmed them by collapsing on stage, he staggered to the front and gasped, 'Is there a doctor in the house?' One member of the audience stood up. 'Bloody awful play, don't you think?' asked Richardson and went back to carry on acting.

Cut and run. This metaphor, deriving from a nautical emergency (cut the cable and get out to sea without weighing anchor) was interestingly applied, at the end of the eighteenth century, to the malpractice of cutting lines and leaving the stage. A heartless cut and run could leave other actors with some terrible problems. Towards the end of his long career, A. E. Matthews once forgot his lines when he was supposed to be answering the telephone. 'It's for you,' he said to the only other actor on stage at the time – and left.

Deus ex machina. The classical Greek theatre developed a crane mechanism which enabled the raising and lowering of 'flying' actors. The descent of a god in this machine for the purpose of unravelling the plot became an accepted convention. What was beyond human resources could be solved when the god got out of his machine. A similar device was common in the Jacobean MASQUE and there is probably some parody in SHAKESPEARE's exploitation of it for the Jupiter episode in *Cymbeline*. Later the term came to be used to describe anyone who dropped in at the end of a play to set everything to rights.

Diorama. The Diorama was invented by Louis Daguerre, who opened a Diorama in Paris in 1822 and a second in Regent's Park, London in 1823. It was a spectacular development from transparency painting. The viewers sat in darkness in front of a huge painting (45 feet by 70 feet was an average). Lighting effects (the introduction of daylight through artfully placed shutters) gave the picture an illusion of three dimensions, achieved by painting on both sides of a translucent calico cloth. Light reflected from in front would show a sunlit ruin, for example, and this would be slowly transformed by back-lighting into a moodily moonlit version of the same building. Exploitation of the Diorama in the theatre was largely the province of CLARKSON STANFIELD, who painted several for Drury Lane and Covent Garden between 1823 and 1839. The last consisted of 'illustrations' for the Chorus in MACREADY's *Henry V*, but the most spectacular were entertainments in their own right. The Christmas audiences at Drury Lane, for example, were feasted with travelogues, lasting about twenty minutes, of a sea-voyage from England to Gibraltar and Constantinople (1828), a tour of Windsor (1829), a journey over the Alps (1830), a boat-ride along the Grand Canal in Venice (1831), a trip to Niagara Falls (1832) and a voyage up the Nile (1833). To provide this spectacle, Stanfield covered calico twenty feet high and several hundred feet long with transparency painting which was then wound round rollers to produce a moving picture elaborated by lighting effects. 'From its commencement to its close,' wrote a contemporary admirer, 'nothing is presented to the spectator but an unbroken series of magnificent and finished pictures.' (See also PANORAMA.)

Doggett, Thomas (*c.* 1670–1721) When George I came to the throne, Doggett marked the occasion by inaugurating the Doggett Coat and Badge race for Thames watermen, still run annually on 1 August. He was also a good comic actor, for whom CONGREVE wrote some parts, and, for a brief period, joint manager of Drury Lane with CIBBER and WILKS.

Dry. The word is used in the theatre to describe what actors do when they forget their lines and fall into a paralysed silence. A famous example is that of the bit-part actor who was playing Ratcliff to CHARLES KEAN's Richard III. He was so alarmed by the ferocity with which Kean, working himself into a lather before the Battle of Bosworth, turned on him to ask, 'Who's there?' that he forgot the second of the two lines allowed him in COLLEY CIBBER's version of the text:

> Ratcliff, my lord. 'Tis I. The early village cock
> Hath twice done salutation to the morn.

After he had taken a second run at it, and still got no further than ''Tis I. The early village cock . . .', Kean inquired in a powerful stage-whisper, 'Then for God's sake, why don't you crow?' A more resourceful actor would have known how to FRIBBLE. SQUIRE BANCROFT recalls one old

stager who regularly forgot his lines, particularly after his Saturday
drink, and substituted for them a stock speech, 'which he delivered with
great solemnity to whoever might be on the stage with him at the time,
no matter what the circumstances, the period or the costume of the play.
Whether prince or peasant, virtuous or vicious, whether clad in
sumptuous raiment or shivering in rags, it was all the same to him, and
at the end of his harangue he stalked off the stage, leaving his unhappy
comrades to get out of the difficulty as best they could. These were the
never-changing words: "Go to; thou weariest me. Take this well filled
purse, furnish thyself with richer habiliments, and join me at my
mansion straight!"'

Dumb show. The curious history of the dumb show in the English
theatre might, with subtle arguments to help, be continued right up to
the era of the silent movie. A popular feature of Tudor pageantry, the
dumb show was already a little old-fashioned by the time SHAKESPEARE
used it in *Hamlet*. It had found a spectacular place in the Court MASQUE,
favoured by James I, by the time Shakespeare used it in *Macbeth*. But
that play was consciously aimed to flatter the King, and we should not
be surprised at the use of an old form recently assimilated into a new
one. After the Restoration of Charles II, dumb shows emerged in a
different form, through the speechless character of Harlequin, and
through Harlequin (see HARLEQUINADE) they took their place in the
English pantomime. They had also a place in the popular mode of
MELODRAMA. There is a dumb character at the centre of *A Tale of
Mystery*, the first English play to be officially styled a melodrama; and
writers of melodrama were fond of the trick which allowed a mute to
convey vital information in dumb show. The translation from KOTZE-
BUE's *Deaf and Dumb* by Benjamin Thompson (1800) may have set the
fashion, but a glance at Allardyce Nicoll's list of plays by unknown
nineteenth-century authors (taking no account of those by known
authors) gives us *The Dumb Boy* (1821), *The Dumb Brigand* (1832), *The
Dumb Recruit* (1840), *The Dumb Driver* (1849) and *The Dumb Sailor*
(1854). Nicoll's list omits the splendid provincial piece, *The Dumb Man
of Manchester*, and the many plays written for Madame Celeste (1811–
1882) have never been separately listed. Celeste was French and famous
in the English theatre for her expressive dance and mime long before she
first ventured to speak a word of English on the stage, in 1838. At the
Adelphi, where she was a star, house playwrights wrote dumb shows for
her for almost a decade after 1830. It was above all in the melodramatic
figure of Frankenstein's monster that the dumb show made its
transition from the stage to the silent screen.

Easter Rising. The best known of the many plays about the short-lived uprising in Dublin in 1916 is SEAN O'CASEY's *The Plough and the Stars*. Others include DENIS JOHNSTON's *The Scythe and the Sunset,* Paul Vincent Carroll's *Coggerers,* G. P. Gallivan's *Decision at Easter* and Micheál MacLiammóir's *Easter, 1916.* Less well known even than some of these plays is the fact that Padraig Pearse, the scholarly leader of the Easter Rising, wrote a play called *The Singer,* in which his role of sacrificial victim to the English authorities was prefigured.

Eidophusikon. See LOUTHERBOURG, PHILIP DE.

Elizabethan actors. Most Elizabethan actors are known, if known at all by name, only because of sparse references. Job Bacon is mentioned in a stage direction as 'ready to shoot off a pistol'; Black Dick was an extra with the Admiral's Men; Robert Daborne 'died amphibious by the ministry'; Hugh Davis had his tawny coat 'eaten with the rattes'; John Garret had a drink problem; Robert Reynolds performed in Germany under the name of 'Pickleherring'; and Gabriel Spencer was 'slayen in Hogesdon fylldes by the hands of Bengemen Jonson bricklayer'.

Equity. The idea of creating a trade union for actors was publicly voiced in England in 1906, but not until nine years after the actors' strike of 1920 did Equity come into being. It is an unruly union whose resolutions usually come from the extreme left and are opposed from the middle to the extreme right. Nonetheless, it has overseen a vast improvement in the working conditions of actors. English Equity is a strange mixture of the restrictive and the embarrassingly inclusive. You can earn a card by working in strip-joints or seaside variety shows, but only with difficulty by acting in plays. American Actors' Equity has been more exclusive. Founded in 1912, it deals only with performers in the LEGITIMATE theatre.

Fiasco d'estime. Peter Ustinov coined this phrase to describe the response to Stravinsky's *The Rite of Spring* at its first performance in 1913. It might be attached to many plays. BEN JONSON's *Sejanus,* CORNEILLE's *Le Cid,* CHEKHOV's *The Seagull* (at its St Petersburg premiere), HUGO's *Hernani,* SYNGE's *The Playboy of the Western World,* JARRY's *Ubu Roi,* Henry James's *Guy Domville* and PINTER's *The Birthday Party* would be among the candidates.

Fires. Theatre fires have become mercifully rarer since the introduction of electricity and the (sometimes obstructive) tightening of fire regulations. The burning of the GLOBE in 1613 was without casualties. At the opposite extreme is the destruction by fire of a Chinese theatre in 1845, when 1,670 people died. Seventy-five serious disasters occurred in American theatres between 1798 and 1876, when the Brooklyn Theatre fire killed three hundred. The position in England was no different. In Exeter, for example, the theatre in Bedford Circus was burnt to the ground in 1820, less than a year after the installation of improved gas lighting. Its replacement was gutted in 1885, at the cost of one pig belonging to a pantomime clown. Before the end of 1886, a new theatre had been built and opened. There, on 5 September 1887 at a performance of *Romany Rye*, at least 186 people were burned or asphyxiated. It remains the worst disaster in English theatre history. Those on stage were at risk too. Clara Webster, a Drury Lane ballerina, burned to death in full view of the audience in 1844 when her dress was set alight by a gas jet. At the Pavilion in 1864, Mary Ann Thorne as Columbine performed an unscheduled pirouette in order to disguise a loss of balance, and was burned to death when her dress came into contact with a ground row of gas lights. At the Princess's the year before, Ann Hunt, a ballerina, caught fire in the wings. Her friend Sarah Smith was burned to death when she tried to beat out the flames.

Fribble. This was the word used in the seventeenth-century English theatre to describe the technique of ad-libbing to cover lapses of memory. In RICHARD BROME's *The Antipodes*, Lord Letoy refers fondly to one of the actors he employs to perform his plays as 'one that never will be perfect in a thing he studies', but adds, with a generosity unusual in a playwright:

> If he can fribble through, and move delight
> In others, I am pleas'd.

Genesius. A persistent legend tells of the actor Genesius, who was required to perform a mockery of Christian baptism before the Emperor Diocletian. To his deep discomfort, he experienced a conversion to Christianity during the performance, confessed as much to Diocletian, was tortured and, after refusing to recant, beheaded. The story has been dramatized by LOPE DE VEGA, ROTROU and Henri Ghéon.

Golden Rump, The. In 1737, Robert Walpole was under more vigorous attack in the London theatre than any public figure had ever been. FIELDING was filling the Haymarket with satirical pieces and the success of GAY's *The Beggar's Opera* (1728) was still vivid. Then a very convenient thing happened. Henry Giffard, manager of the theatre in Goodman's Fields, reported to Walpole that he had received an anonymous manuscript full of scurrilous abuse of the King and of his ministers. Walpole quoted from the play in the House of Commons in support of his claim that there was a need for stricter theatrical control. The scenic feature was a huge pair of golden buttocks, into and out of which the pilloried politicians could climb, and the appropriate name of the play was *The Golden Rump*. Walpole won his point, and 1737 saw the introduction of a Licensing Act of unparalleled restrictiveness. Minor theatres were closed, and the office of the Lord Chamberlain given new powers to demand the cutting of offensive passages. As a reward for his vigilance, Henry Giffard was given £1,000; but his theatre lost its licence. The manuscript of *The Golden Rump* has disappeared. Whether or not it ever existed, it proved useful to Walpole.

Green baize. Well into the nineteenth century, it was the custom in many theatres in England to lay a green carpet on the stage when a tragedy was to be performed. The practical intention was to protect the costumes of those characters destined to die during the course of the play, but the green baize soon came to symbolize the very spirit of tragedy. By the nineteenth century, the decorum that had dictated its use in the Restoration had been replaced by a cruder sensationalism. The laying of the baize during an interval between scenes was used to excite an audience's nervous expectation.

Green room. The reason why the sitting-room in which post-Restoration actors gathered to entertain friends came to be called the 'Green' room is not known. Perhaps the best-known one – at Drury Lane – was originally painted or curtained in green. Or perhaps the GREEN BAIZE was stored in it.

Grundy, Mrs. This lady, who has come to represent English disapproval of everything from pre-marital sex to Sunday newspapers, was invented by the playwright THOMAS MORTON (1764–1838). The curious fact is that she never appears on stage in *Speed the Plough* (1800), though she exerts a constant pressure on Farmer Ashfield's worthy wife, for whom the crucial questions are, 'What will Mrs Grundy say?' and 'What will Mrs Grundy think?'

Half-price. The custom of admitting privileged patrons free of charge after the third act of a play was a feature of certain Restoration theatres.

In the eighteenth century, managers contrived to impose a half-price entrance-fee for latecomers, but had to extend the entertainment to justify the charge. (See AFTERPIECE.) Having dined and drunk well, the half-price audience was often unruly, and an attempt was made to withdraw the reduction in the London theatres in 1763. The consequent rioting was so serious that half-price was immediately restored, and it survived in London until the 1870s, and for even longer in some provincial cities.

Handkerchief. The most famous handkerchief in the history of drama is Desdemona's. When Alfred de Vigny's translation of *Othello* was presented at the Théâtre Français in October 1829, the mention of the word 'mouchoir' caused an outcry in the audience. No object so vulgar had ever been referred to on that stage. MEYERHOLD, on the other hand, planned a whole production of the play round a design idea which would have a bare, green-carpeted stage, and just off-centre, brilliantly lit, a white handkerchief with an embroidered strawberry motif. A handkerchief was also the cause of one of the most infamous quarrels in stage history. Playing Hamlet in Edinburgh on 2 March 1846, MACREADY, as was his wont, waved a handkerchief ('I must be idle,' was the accompanying line) before the play-within-the-play, and the American actor FORREST hissed from the audience.

He-man. One of the least interesting roles for actors, and one which was often demanded by playwrights in the declining days of MELO-DRAMA and the rising vogue of gangsterism, is that of the muscular male, whether hero or villain. Successive Tarzans worked at it in Hollywood. On the stage, according to Heywood Broun, Montague Love found an answer: 'Mr Love's idea of playing a he-man was to extend his chest three inches and then follow it slowly across the stage.'

House UnAmerican Activities Committee. The attempts of this 'patriotic' committee to root out communism in Hollywood created havoc in the lives of many American actors and writers between 1938 and 1968. Among those summoned to appear were BRECHT, his musical collaborator Hanns Eisler, JOHN HOWARD LAWSON, ELIA KAZAN, CLIF-FORD ODETS, LILLIAN HELLMAN, LEE J. COBB, PAUL ROBESON and ARTHUR MILLER. A comic high-spot came during the cross-questioning of HALLIE FLANAGAN, who mentioned the work of CHRISTOPHER MARLOWE and was asked whether Marlowe was a communist. Brecht's masterly deception of the rather stupid investigators is also a good one-act comedy; but the proceedings were not at all funny, and the brutal treatment of Larry Parks was a third-degree tragedy.

Eric Bentley, *Thirty Years of Treason*, 1972.

Ireland, William Henry (1777–1835). When the engraver, Samuel Ireland, became interested in the pickings to be made on Shakespearean 'relics', his son, always eager to impress, began to forge some. A property deed, a will (giving SHAKESPEARE a bastard son), and two 'original' plays appeared. On 2 April 1796, at SHERIDAN's Drury Lane, Shakespeare's newly discovered tragedy of *Vortigern* was presented before a packed house, with a cast including a decidedly unhappy JOHN PHILIP KEMBLE. The real author, William Henry Ireland, was nineteen, and had written the piece in two months.

Bernard Grebanier, *The Great Shakespeare Forgery*, 1966.

Irish acting. In the early years of the ABBEY THEATRE, the company went on regular tours abroad in order to make enough money to survive. It was their lack of gesture and their confident speaking of colourful dialogue that particularly impressed English critics, still familiar with the broader style of nineteenth-century MELODRAMA. Asked by a reviewer how they had achieved such stillness, Sara Allgood (1883–1950), one of the original Abbey company, replied: 'Sure, when we started we didn't know enough to move, so we stood still; now we know better than to move unless we must.'

Kemble versus Caine. The most famous put-down in the history of the Garrick Club was delivered by the actor Henry Kemble to the novelist and playwright Hall Caine. Caine had amassed a fortune by writing unctuously for the unctuous, and considered himself the greatest living writer. A few days before the 1906 confrontation with Kemble, he had announced in the Garrick Club that 'there are no writers of genius except myself and a few friends, and I am not certain about my friends'. When Kemble found himself sitting opposite Caine at lunch, he stopped eating, walked round the table to Caine, and said, 'Sir, I think you are the most unpleasant person I have ever met.' Caine took no notice, and Kemble started to walk out, but paused at the door and returned to add, 'I have come back to tell you that I once met a more unpleasant man than you – it was in a little public house in Oldham.'

Kirby, J. H. (*fl.* 1840). Kirby was, for years, the leading actor of the Bowery Theatre in New York. So powerful was he in the final scene of *Richard III* that the saying, 'Wake me up when Kirby dies', became proverbial on the East Side of the city.

Kynaston, Edward (*c.* 1640–1706). 'He made the loveliest lady that ever I saw,' enthused Pepys after seeing Edward Kynaston on stage.

Kynaston was one of the last boy-actors to play women's roles, and the ladies in the audience found it amusing to be seen driving in the park with him, still in his female attire. Later in his career he was a fine actor of heroic roles.

Lamb, Charles and Fanny Kelly. Chance has preserved the bachelor CHARLES LAMB's letter of proposal – the only proposal he ever made – to the actress Fanny Kelly. The correspondence is a touchingly decorous one:

20 July, 1819

Dear Miss Kelly,

We had the pleasure, *pain* I might better call it, of seeing you last night in the new Play. It was a most consummate piece of Acting, but what a task for you to undergo! at a time when your heart is sore from real sorrow! it has given rise to a train of thinking, which I cannot suppress.

Would to God you were released from this way of life; that you could bring your mind to consent to take your lot with us, and throw off for ever the whole burden of your Profession. I neither expect or wish you to take notice of this which I am writing, in your present over occupied & hurried state. – But to think of it at your leisure. I have quite income enough, if that were all, to justify for me making such a proposal, with what I may call even a handsome provision for my survivor. What you possess of your own would naturally be appropriated to those, for whose sakes chiefly you have made so many hard sacrifices. I am not so foolish as not to know that I am a most unworthy match for such a one as you, but you have for years been a principal object in my mind. In many a sweet assumed character I have learned to love you, but simply as F. M. Kelly I love you better than them all. Can you quit these shadows of existence, & come & be a reality to us? can you leave off harassing yourself to please a thankless multitude, who know nothing of you, & begin at last to live to yourself & your friends?

As plainly & frankly as I have seen you give or refuse assent in some feigned scene, so frankly do me the justice to answer me. It is impossible I should feel injured or aggrieved by your telling me at once, that the proposal does not suit you. It is impossible that I should ever think of molesting you with idle importunity and persecution after your mind [was] once firmly spoken – but happier, far happier, could I have leave to hope a time might come, when our friends might be your friends; our interests yours; our book-knowledge, if in that inconsiderable particular we have any little advantage, might impart something to you, which you would every day have it in your power ten thousand fold to repay by the added cheerfulness and joy which you could not fail to bring as a dowry into whatever family should have the honor and happiness of receiving *you*, the most welcome accession that could be made to it.

In haste, but with entire respect & deepest affection, I subscribe myself.   C. LAMB.

This was Miss Kelly's reply:

Henrietta Street, *20th July, 1819*

An early & deeply rooted attachment has fixed my heart on one from whom no worldly prospect can well induce me to withdraw it, but while I thus *frankly* & decidedly decline your proposal, believe me, I am not insensible to the high honour which the preference of such a mind as yours confers upon me – let me, however, hope that all thought upon this subject will end with this letter, & that you will henceforth encourage no other sentiment towards me than esteem in my private character and a continuance of that approbation of my humble talents which you have already expressed so much & so often to my advantage and gratification.

Believe me I feel proud to acknowledge myself
Your obliged friend
F. M. KELLY.

Charles Lamb wrote once more:

20th July, 1819

Dear Miss Kelly,

Your injunctions shall be obeyed to a tittle. I feel myself in a lackadaisacal no-how-ish kind of a humour. I believe it is the rain, or something. I had thought to have written seriously, but I fancy I succeed best in epistles of mere fun; puns & *that* nonsense. You will be good friends with us, will you not? let what has past 'break no bones' between us. You will not refuse us them next time we send for them?

Yours very truly,   C.L.

Do you observe the delicacy of not signing my full name?
N.B. Do not paste that last letter of mine into your Book.

Langtry, Lillie (1853–1929). The daughter of the Dean of Jersey belongs more properly with LOLA MONTEZ, Cora Pearl and Hortense Schneider as one of the great theatrical courtesans than with major actors and actresses. She made her debut, respectably enough, with the BANCROFTS at the Haymarket in 1881, but the debut was unusual. It had long been acceptable for actresses to marry into 'society': Lillie Langtry reversed the order, becoming an actress *after* she had been accepted into the best drawing rooms. JAMES AGATE, after watching a 1940 embroidery on her life called *The Jersey Lily*, noted in his diary: 'In her early days she had that beatific expression characteristic of Victorian prettiness – like a sheep painted by Raphael.' The Prince of Wales was the most prominent victim of her charms, though the play records a period when he was in competition with Prince Louis of Battenberg. It is not easy to distinguish fiction from fact in any account of Lillie Langtry. She seems to have worked quite hard to maintain her own theatre company and a large racing stable.

James Brough, *The Prince and the Lily*, 1975.

Layfield, Thomas (*fl.* 1750). This popular Dublin actor was playing Iago to Thomas Sheridan's Othello when he brought the performance to a sudden shocked halt by saying:

> Oh my Lord! beware of jealousy,
> It is a green-eyed lobster.

It was either the cause or the first sign of madness. Layfield spent the few years that remained to him in a Dublin asylum. (This story is told by both Thomas Sheridan and JOHN O'KEEFE.)

Legitimate drama. The words 'legitimate' and 'illegitimate', when applied to drama or theatre, have a simple origin in the Letters Patent, issued by Charles II to THOMAS KILLIGREW and WILLIAM DAVENANT in 1662. By giving to these two loyal servants of his exile a monopoly over the performance of all plays in the City of Westminster, he established their legal right to challenge any rival theatres or anyone who had the effrontery to present a play within their territory. The 'legitimate' drama, that is to say, was confined to the PATENT THEATRES. But opportunistic promoters exploited a loophole in the Letters Patent. When, after all, is a play not a play? The answer, in the eighteenth and early nineteenth centuries, seemed to be 'when it has a lot of music or songs in it', and the 'illegitimate' drama, presented in 'illegitimate' theatres, was originally, and of legal necessity, musical. As the eighteenth century progressed, and as more and more enterprising opponents of the Patent monopoly flouted its authority, the distinction between legitimate and illegitimate became increasingly blurred. By the time the Theatres Act of 1843 abolished the unique claim of Drury Lane and Covent Garden on the performance of the legitimate drama during the London theatrical season, that claim was already so generally ignored that it was virtually worthless – except perhaps for its nuisance value. The distinction, though, has lingered into the twentieth century, and actors will still sometimes talk of 'legit' work (the abbreviation is much more common than the full word) as a contrast to 'illegit' employment in, for example, television advertisements.

Limelight. The credit for discovering that calcium oxide, or quicklime as it is popularly known, gives out a dazzling light when heated to incandescence, probably belongs to Lieutenant Thomas Drummond, a Royal Engineer engaged in the 1824 survey of Ireland. Its first theatrical use was most likely at Drury Lane in 1838 (not at MACREADY's Covent Garden as has been normally supposed). By directing a stream of oxygen, later a mixed stream of oxygen and hydrogen, onto a cylinder of quicklime, limelight men, perched in the flies, produced an impressively powerful floodlight effect, as well as risking their lives and those of most people in the theatre. The first recorded use of focused limelight was at CHARLES KEAN's production of *Henry VIII* at the Princess's Theatre. Its great exponent was HENRY IRVING. Limelight was still being used in theatres until well into the twentieth century.

Terence Rees, *Theatre Lighting in the Age of Gas*, 1978.

Malaprop, Mrs. A provincial gentlewoman, aunt to the romantically inclined Lydia Languish in SHERIDAN's *The Rivals*, Mrs Malaprop has donated to the English language the word 'malapropism'. In inventing her name, Sheridan distorted the French phrase *mal à propos*. In inventing her defect – a love of long words in severe disproportion to her ability to pronounce them – he exploited a long line of beloved stage-characters going back to SHAKESPEARE's Dogberry and beyond. As so often, Sheridan is content to do better what has been well done before. Certainly Mrs Malaprop is a splendid creation. She is not a social snob, like Lady Bracknell, but an intellectual one – 'few gentlemen nowadays', she bemoans, 'know how to value the ineffectual qualities in a woman' – whose ludicrous humour it is to pride herself on her gift with words, her 'nice derangement of epitaphs'.

Marprelate controversy. In 1588–9 several pamphlets were issued from an underground press in London. Signed by 'Martin Marprelate', they were wittily abusive of the established Church in general and of bishops in particular. Their author, still unidentified, was a Puritan, an extremely humorous one. It was partly as a result of the scandal caused by the pamphlets that humour was knocked out of Puritanism. The pamphlets attracted enough attention to require a response from the leaders of the Church of England, and a vigorous pamphlet war was waged. Among the writers engaged on the Church's behalf was JOHN LYLY, whose association with the boy actors of St Paul's was well known. Through their association with Lyly, the Children of Paul's became embroiled in the controversy, as did the adult Queen's Men. As victims of Martin Marprelate's Puritan disapproval, actors and play-wrights took the side of the Church. They might have expected to be rewarded. But once the Martinist press had been captured (in August 1589), the authorities were determined to kill the controversy as quickly as possible. Probably because they would not let it die, the boys of St Paul's were banned from performing (the ban lasted from 1590 to 1599), and the Queen's Men lost favour. It was an ironic victory for the elusive 'Martin Marprelate'. More significantly, it demonstrated the risks involved for any theatre company which dared to declare itself in matters involving Church and State.

Meggs, Mrs Mary (d. 1691). Better known as 'Orange Moll', Mrs Meggs was a widow in 1663, when she was granted a thirty-nine year licence to sell oranges and other food in the newly established theatre under the management of THOMAS KILLIGREW. She held the licence for nearly twenty years. Pepys recalls a performance of *Henry IV* when 'a gentleman of good habit, sitting just before us, eating of some fruit in the midst of the play, did drop down as dead, being choked; but with much ado Orange Moll did thrust her finger down his throat and brought him to life again'. That was in 1667. By 1682, Orange Moll was queening it too much, and the newly amalgamated companies of Drury Lane and Dorset Garden sold the licence to someone else. There was more at stake than oranges. It seems certain that Mary Meggs ran a lucrative sideline in procuring. NELL GWYN was one of her victims (or beneficiaries).

Menken, Adah Isaacs (1835–68). American actress, probably born in New Orleans where she was brought up. Her real name is uncertain, since her father is unknown. At a fairly early stage in her colourful career she invented him in the person of a Spaniard called Ricardo Fuertos, and round about 1861 began to call herself Dolores. She made the first of several marriages – to a Jewish musician called Alexander

Isaacs Menken – in the name of Adah Bertha Theodore. By that time she had been a dancer, a small-town actress, a circus-rider and a sculptor's model. At each she may have been competent, but was certainly not outstanding. In 1859, after failing to make any impact in the New York theatre, she made a much-publicized and probably bigamous marriage to a well known boxer called J. C. Heenan. It was a short-lived and ugly relationship, but it helped to bring the ambitious Menken into the public eye. The masterstroke was delayed until 1861, when, at a theatre in Albany, she appeared as Mazeppa in a familiar dramatization of Byron's poem. With cropped hair and pink tights, she looked naked but not masculine. It was as Mazeppa that she became known in Britain (she played the part at Astley's Amphitheatre in 1864) and Europe. Her physical daring was genuine, but she had a terrifying craving to be loved and to be admired by men. To satisfy it she was prepared to play the vamp with writers. Dickens, to whom she dedicated her volume of poems, *Infelicia* (1868), was one who almost succumbed, and Swinburne certainly wanted to, but it was DUMAS *père* who did. Their affair was Menken's last sensational triumph. By the time she died in Paris, her fame was declining.

Paul Lewis, *Queen of the Plaza*, 1964.

Montez, Lola (*c.* 1818–1863). Of all the theatrical rags-to-riches stories, that of Lola Montez is the most improbable. Her real name was Marie Dolores Elize Rosanna Gilbert. Her father was a soldier and her mother, of Spanish descent, had ideas above her station. It was to escape an arranged marriage to a sixty-year-old judge that Marie Dolores eloped with a British officer. He took her to India and left her. She returned to London and made an inglorious attempt to earn a living as a dancer under the assumed name of Lola Montez. From London she went to Brussels, where she warded off starvation by singing and begging in the streets. With a wealthy German protector, she next moved to Warsaw, where she sang and danced on the opera stage. It was in 1842 that she met Franz Liszt and made him her lover. In Paris in 1844 she was courted by DUMAS *père* and admired by Balzac, HUGO and de Musset, but her main lover was a journalist called Dujarier. Dujarier was killed in a duel, despite her much-publicized and possibly heroic attempts to take his place, and his legacy enabled Lola to establish herself in Munich. There she utterly beguiled Louis I, King of Bavaria, was created Comtesse de Lansfeld and became a power in the land. Hostility towards her contributed to the Revolution of 1848. Before himself abdicating, Louis was forced to sign a decree banishing Lola from Bavaria. In London in 1851 she made a probably bigamous marriage and was forced, once again, to take flight. She went to America in 1852 and returned to the stage as actress and dancer. Her first tour included a sensational performance of a play called *Lola Montez in Bavaria* and solo performances of her Spider Dance. She died in poverty in New York.

William Bolitho, *Twelve against the Gods*, 1929.

Murdered actors. The list includes:

Anonymous. The following announcement appeared in the *Guardian* of 20 September 1974 under the heading 'Hammer Death' in the News in Brief column:

> An aspiring actress who auditioned for the lead role in a play called 'Hammer' was bludgeoned to death by the playwright with a sledgehammer, according to a detective.

Nothing more. No place was mentioned, and no names. The implication seems to be that any actress who auditions for a part in a play with a name like that should expect to be bludgeoned to death. *The Mousetrap* would be safer.

Booth, John Wilkes (1838–65). After he had shot Abraham Lincoln, Booth leapt from the President's box on to the stage. In the landing, he broke a bone just above the ankle of his left leg. Even so, he escaped to his waiting horse and rode off. Twelve days later, on 26 April 1865, he was hiding out in a barn near Port Royal, Virginia. The leg was gangrenous and he was unable to get away when he was discovered. The searchers set fire to the barn to force him into the open and Sergeant Boston Corbett felled him with a single, unnecessary shot. Several years later, Corbett coolly asked EDWIN BOOTH for free admission to a performance on the strength of having killed his brother.

Bowen, William. On 17 April 1718, William Bowen, a senior member of the Drury Lane company, was drinking with JAMES QUIN in the Fleece Tavern in Cornhill. Bowen took offence during a dispute that began jocularly, demanded satisfaction and was mortally wounded during the ensuing duel. Quin was found guilty of manslaughter, and the verdict was probably just. One witness pointed out that, 'Mr Bowen and Mr Quin had often had disputes, and always used to be jangling.'

Chung Ling Soo (1861–1918). American illusionist whose real name was William Ellsworth Robinson. He was one of the great exploiters of

Eastern mystery. In 1904 he introduced into his act the notoriously risky bullet-catching routine. At the Wood Green Empire on 23 March 1918, the bullet-retaining mechanism in the rifle fired by his assistant failed – or so it was assumed. Why, then, was the right lung accurately pierced? Robinson's assistant, though, was a marksman.

Clun, Walter. On 2 August 1664, Clun was 'killed and laid in a ditch' near Kentish Town. The motive may have been no more than robbery. Clun was a member of the King's Company and one of Samuel Pepys's favourite actors. The gossip John Aubrey, noting that Clun, like BEN JONSON, had one eye lower and bigger than the other, speculates that 'perhaps Jonson begott Clun'.

Copland, H. B. This American actor was literally killed by a dramatic critic. He was playing juvenile leads at the Varieties Theatre in New Orleans in 1860 when he took exception to observations made about one of the actresses in the company by John Overall in the *True Delta*. Having tracked Overall down in Sam's saloon on St Charles Street, Copland demanded that he withdraw the comments. In the ensuing quarrel, Copland was shot in the leg by Overall. The leg was amputated, but tetanus developed and he died within a few days. Overall was tried but acquitted on a plea of self-defence.

Duffy, William. Duffy was one of the leading American actors from 1820 until his death. This occurred in 1836, when he was manager of a theatre in Albany, New York. One of his company was an actor called Hamilton in whom Duffy took an interest. No one ever satisfactorily explained why, in February 1836, Hamilton suddenly stabbed him to death. There was a trial and Hamilton was acquitted on grounds of self-defence. It is possible that Hamilton doubted the verdict. 'Overcome with remorse, he wandered away from his accustomed haunts, and perished miserably in a remote corner of Tennessee.'

Fragson, Harry (1869–1913). Born in Surrey and christened Leon Potts, Fragson made his name in Paris as a singing and piano-playing comedian. He was booked to replace Dan Leno in the Drury Lane pantomimes from 1905 to 1907, and made famous the song 'Hullo, Hullo, Who's Your Lady Friend?' His father, formerly a brewer, lived in retirement in Fragson's Paris flat, where he became irrationally jealous of his son's friends. His mind may have been finally unhinged by the relationship between Fragson and the wife of the operetta composer, Henri Christiné. Whatever the explanation, the facts are clear. Having finished an engagement at the Brighton Hippodrome, Fragson returned to Paris on 27 December 1913, walked into his flat and was shot in the head by his father. Nearly 20,000 people attended his funeral in Paris. Victor Potts, declared unfit to plead, was sent to a lunatic asylum.

Hallam, Thomas. On 10 May 1735, CHARLES MACKLIN stabbed Hallam in the left eye with the point of his stick. They were in the Drury Lane GREEN ROOM, and the quarrel was about Macklin's wig, which he had found Hallam wearing. Macklin was hot-tempered at the best of times, and 1735 was not one of those for him. He did his best to help the wounded Hallam, according to medical belief at the time, by urinating in the injured eye. Hallam died the following day. Accused of murder, Macklin defended himself skilfully enough to get the charge reduced to manslaughter. He was sentenced to be branded on the hand.

Knell, William. On 13 June 1587, during the visit of the Queen's Company to Thame in Oxfordshire, Knell drew his sword on a fellow-actor called Towne. In what the coroner's inquest concluded was self-defence, Towne plunged his sword through Knell's neck. This squalid event was given rise to some speculation about the 'lost years' of SHAKESPEARE. Since the Queen's Company went on to perform at STRATFORD, did they look to compensate for the loss of an actor by recruiting Shakespeare?

Letine (1853–89). George Gorin, known as Letine, was the leader of a popular bicycle act in the music-halls. In 1889 he was taken to court by Nathaniel Curragh, who considered him the causer of his daughter's death the year before. (She had, in fact, died of consumption a few months after leaving Letine's act.) The case was dismissed. On 21 June 1889, Letine was about to go through the stage door of the Canterbury Music Hall in Lambeth when Curragh rushed out of the shadow of a railway arch and stabbed him with a dagger. He then crossed the road and shot himself in the mouth. Curragh recovered and was declared insane. Letine died in St Thomas's Hospital.

Mountfort, William (1664–92). Considered by many to be the outstanding heroic actor of his age, Mountfort was also an author of comedies and a witty performer in foppish parts. He was married to a minor actress, Susanna Percival, and popular as a stage-lover of the notorious ANNE BRACEGIRDLE. It was Mountfort's ill-fortune that a loutish young officer, Captain Hill, lusted after Bracegirdle. With the equally disreputable Lord Mohun, Hill plotted to kidnap the actress during the winter of 1692. Fortified with drink, he and Mohun grabbed her and tried to make off with her in a coach, running away when the attempt was foiled. In the kind of mood that turns modern 'football hooligans' into killers, they decided to punish the unknowing Mountfort for their frustration. In Norfolk Street, just off the Strand, close to midnight, Mohun accosted Mountfort whilst Hill first hit him from behind and then ran his sword through him. Mohun was tried before the House of Lords, which accepted his plea that he had no idea that Hill intended to murder the actor. Hill, meanwhile, had escaped into obscurity.

Novarro, Ramon (1899–1968). On 30 October 1968, two brothers, Robert (aged twenty-two) and Thomas (aged seventeen) Ferguson, were admitted to the Laurel Canyon home of this famous star of the silent screen (Ben Hur among many other roles). During the course of the evening Novarro fed them, showed them photographs, told their fortunes with cards, read their palms . . . and was killed by them. The murder was unplanned. Novarro and the Fergusons were total strangers.

Oddo. This was the sole name of the Negro doorkeeper and bit-part player at the Camp Theatre in New Orleans in 1823. At the time, the theatre was shared by an English-speaking and a French-speaking company. An actor called Beebe, who was a member of the English company, demanded admission backstage on a night in February 1823 when the French company was in possession. Oddo refused to let him in and Beebe stabbed him with a swordstick. Oddo died a few days later. At his trial, at which he was vehemently supported by a group of New Orleans Freemasons, Beebe was acquitted on grounds of self-defence.

Otto, Hans. The communist leader of the Berlin Actors' Union was arrested and interned by the Nazis. On 24 October 1933 he was murdered in the Internment Camp.

Porter, Benjamin C. On 19 March 1879, Porter was waiting with MAURICE BARRYMORE and Ellen Cummings in the station bar at Marshall, Texas. The train to their next venue on the tour of SARDOU's *Diplomacy* was late. James Currie, a roughneck deputy sheriff and railroad employee, made some comments on the morals of actresses and Barrymore, who had been a prizefighter, took off his coat. Currie shot him in the shoulder and then shot Porter in the abdomen. He was acquitted in two bent trials.

Raikh, Zinaida. Russian actress, who married MEYERHOLD after a disastrous first marriage to the poet Esenin. When Meyerhold was arrested in June 1939, he left a frightened Raikh alone in their flat off Gorky Street in Moscow. It was there that her mutilated body was found a few days later. Stalin's thugs were very like Hitler's.

Ray, Martha (1742–79). Martha Ray's career as a singer/actress never got started. She became, instead, the mistress of the unpopular First Lord of the Admiralty, Lord Sandwich, when she was eighteen and he forty-two. She bore him three children, was kindly treated (though never admitted to Sandwich's social circle) and lived tolerably if not happily, even after her noble lover had got wind of the passion felt for her by an army officer thirteen years her junior. By the time he killed her, this young officer, James Hackman, had resigned his commission and become a clergyman. On 7 April 1779 he followed her to Covent Garden, where she watched BICKERSTAFFE's *Love in a Village*. Hackman's wild intention was to shoot himself in front of her, but on the spur of the moment, when she came out of the theatre to climb into Lord Sandwich's carriage he shot her instead, botching his immediate attempt at suicide. He was hanged on 19 April, having written a note to a friend in the coach that took him to the gallows: 'Of her fame I charge you to be careful.'

Spencer, Gabriel. This minor actor was killed in a duel on Hoxton Fields by BEN JONSON. The date was 22 September 1598 and the weapon a 'three-shilling rapier'.

Tate, Sharon. The best known of the victims of Charles Manson and his polluted 'family'. On the evening of 8 August 1969, in a dementedly inspired search for kicks, the 'family' chose at random a house where Sharon Tate, over eight months pregnant, was entertaining three house-guests. They killed all of them (Tate's husband, the film-director Roman Polanski, was working in London), not knowing who they were. They discovered the identity of their victims on breakfast television.'It really blew my mind,' observed Susan Atkins, one of the killers.

Old Complaint, the. This is the theatrically favoured euphemism for habitual drunkenness among actors. Notorious sufferers included EDMUND KEAN and GEORGE FREDERICK COOKE. It is recorded of the latter that when hissed for being drunk at Liverpool he turned on his audience, saying, 'What! do you hiss me! – hiss George Frederick Cooke! you contemptible money-getters! You shall never again have the honour of hissing me! Farewell! *I* banish *you*,' and adding after a pause, 'There is not a brick in your dirty town but what is cemented by the blood of a negro!' (Liverpool was a harbour for slaving ships at the end of the eighteenth century.)

Old Price Riots. After the burning of Covent Garden Theatre in 1808, public subscriptions combined with insurance money to bring in

£121,000 for rebuilding. A lavish new Theatre Royal was ready for opening 373 days later. The playbill for this momentous occasion included a small ruled-off portion:

The Proprietors, having completed the New Theatre within the time originally promised, beg leave respectfully to state to the Publick the absolute necessity that compels them to make the following advances on the prices of admission:

FIRST PRICE	HALF PRICE
Boxes, *Seven Shillings*	*Three Shillings and Sixpence*
Pit, *Four Shillings*	*Two Shillings as usual*

The Lower and Upper Galleries will remain at the old prices.

The raising of prices in the Pit hurt the pockets of the most committed theatregoers. What was even worse was the placing of the public boxes. They had been pushed up to the fourth tier of the building by the proprietors' determination to tempt wealthy patrons into paying a year's subscription for the splendid third-tier private boxes. When JOHN PHILIP KEMBLE came out to speak the prologue on the night of 18 September 1809, he was drowned out by catcalls. The noise continued throughout the performance of *Macbeth* and on through the AFTERPIECE, *The Quaker*. And it continued, augmented by horns and rattles, for sixty-seven nights. Public anger centred on the unfortunate Kemble. Abusive songs were written, Cruikshank and many others drew cartoons and caricatures, derisive medals were struck (John Bull riding on Kemble, who was portrayed as a donkey) – everyone took sides. The proprietors made the mistake of engaging Daniel Mendoza and several other prize-fighters as bouncers, and the rioters responded by hiring bruisers of their own. The Bow Street runners were brought in and individual rioters were arrested and tried, having been identified by the box-office keeper, Brandon. Eventually a compromise was reached – the boxes stayed at seven shillings but the pit was returned to its old price. What most hurt Kemble was the surrender to the demand that Brandon be dismissed. (He was re-employed in 1812.)

One-play actors. Many actors, particularly in the television age, dread the prospect of being associated with a single part. The theatre has many precedents. Lavinia Fenton (1708–60), who created the role of Polly Peachum in *The Beggar's Opera* in January 1728, retired on it six months later. Her earlier performances are forgotten. ADAH ISAACS MENKEN (1835–68), once she had played Mazeppa, never succeeded as anything else. James O'Neill (1847–1920), father of the playwright

EUGENE O'NEILL, was forced by popular pressure into repeating his role as the Count of Monte Cristo until it became a burden. Frank Mayo (*fl.* 1870), having acted all over the United States for sixteen years, achieved sudden fame as Davy Crockett, the uneducated frontiersman with a grip of iron and a heart of gold, in a play by Frank H. Murdoch, and was never allowed to play anything else. Even the great TOMMASO SALVINI (1829–1916) might have played nothing but Othello for all the difference it has made to his reputation. For thirty years after 1899, WILLIAM GILLETTE became so identified with Sherlock Holmes that no one could remember which one looked like the other. Doyle's illustrator, Frederic Dorr Steele, explained much later that, 'Everyone agreed that Mr Gillette was the ideal Sherlock Holmes, and it was inevitable that I should copy him.'

One-play authors. The list would vary from compiler to compiler, but most would include Leopold Lewis (1828–90), whose play 'from the French', *The Bells*, rocketed HENRY IRVING to fame in 1871, Solomon Ansky (1863–1920) whose drama of demoniac possession, *The Dybbuk*, was superbly staged by the HABIMA company in Moscow in 1922, Brandon Thomas (1857–1914), forgotten as an actor and as the composer and singer of coon songs in the London music halls, but remembered for *Charley's Aunt* (1892), and James Elroy Flecker (1884–1915), whose flamboyant verse-play *Hassan* was opulently produced at His Majesty's Theatre in 1923. The brilliant Russian, Griboyedov (1795–1829), is the author of one supremely original play, *Woe from Wit*, first performed in 1831. Edmond Rostand (1868–1918), a belated Romantic, is generally known only for *Cyrano de Bergerac* (1898). Another French poet and playwright, Roger Vitrac (1899–1952), had his first two plays directed by ARTAUD. *Victor* (1928), an iconoclastic farce, has survived into a more permissive age. R. C. Sherriff (1896–1975) deserves to be remembered for more than *Journey's End* (1928), his World War I drama. It may be that a list of one-play authors compiled in the year 2000 will include the name of JOHN OSBORNE.

Panorama. In 1786–7, Robert Barker invented the Panorama and, in 1794, opened 'The Panorama' in Leicester Square, London. It consisted of two large circular paintings, the upper 50 feet in diameter and the lower 90 feet. Both pictures were lit by daylight from the roof of the rotunda, and the illusion of reality was achieved both by the cunning perspective and by the absolute exclusion of all extraneous reference points for the observer's eye. The observer stood or sat on a central platform, thirty feet from the paintings, the larger of which was about 30 feet high and 283 feet in circumference. The theatre, though it could not copy the circular form nor replicate the optical illusion, did what it could. A moving panorama by Thomas Greenwood (a picture several hundred feet long turned on rollers) enhanced the Drury Lane pantomime in 1800 and such exhibitions remained a feature of theatrical spectacle until they were displaced by the more advanced DIORAMA.

Part. In the Elizabethan theatre, an actor's 'part' in the whole play was a physical reality. The playhouse scribe would write out the play from the author's copy – but only once. That copy would then be chopped into 'parts', and each part pasted together in sequence. Only the briefest of cues were written in, since time and labour permitted no more. ALLEYN's part in *Orlando Furioso* has survived. It forms a roll about seventeen feet long (Alleyn, of course, had the biggest part), marks no scene divisions, has two-word or three-word cues (sometimes only one), short stage-directions in Latin (longer ones in English), and carries numerous alterations in Alleyn's own handwriting. To 'possess' a part in an unpublished play, an actor had to possess the roll that carried it. If the roll was lost, if an unscrupulous actor left with it to join another company, a new one would have to be written out. It was part of the theatre book-keeper's job to keep an eye on the 'parts'. Even more vital was that he should guard the prompt-copy, the only complete version of the play, other than the author's own 'foul papers'. If the prompt-copy were to fall into the hands of a rival company, there were no copyright laws to prevent them from staging the play. All that was required was the payment of another playhouse scribe to write it out for chopping into 'parts'. Jerome K. Jerome records a curious survival of the quantitative approach to 'parts' in the late nineteenth-century stock companies, where parts were rated in terms of 'lengths' on the basis of one length equalling forty-two lines.

Payroll. Even the great PATENT THEATRES of the nineteenth century had to employ actors on terms not unlike those of the tiny stock companies in small provincial theatres. The difference was in the variety of kinds of play that might be performed and in the size of the payroll. MADAME VESTRIS, for example, had to pay a weekly wage to almost 700 people when she took over the management of Covent Garden in 1840. The list read as follows:

Company – Gentlemen	38
Chorus Singers	8
Ladies	34

Band	32
Officers	9
Box-keepers	2
Check and Money takers	15
Bradwell's Department – Workers	60
Supers	22
Scenery Department (Painting-room)	10
Sloman's Department – Carpenters	26
For Working Pantomime	80
Cassidy	1
Gentlemen's Wardrobe – Workers	24
Dressers	14
Extras	18
Ladies' Wardrobe – Workers	42
Dressers	14
Attendants	2
Mrs Thomas and Mrs Lewis	2
Supers – *Midsummer Night's Dream*	52
Pantomime	37
Extra Chorus and Band	13
Property Department	4
Printers, Billstickers, Upholsterers, Housekeeper etc.	57
Watch and Fire men	5
Police	4
Attendants at Bar – Boxes	16
Pit	18
Gallery	8
Place-keepers	7
Box-keepers (Deputies)	10
Total	684

Pepper's Ghost. One of the most popular of nineteenth-century trick effects was developed by J. H. Pepper, a director of the Royal Polytechnic Institution. Using the principle that glass is both transparent and reflective, he contrived to place a reflected 'ghost' on stage with a flesh-and-blood actor. The Ghost Illusion was first displayed in 1862, and in the following year reached the Britannia Theatre, Hoxton, where several plays were written specifically to exploit it. It was, of course, ineffective if the Ghost had words to say.

Plinge, Walter. This English actor was invented by the BENSON company at the end of the nineteenth century. He may initially have been the actor's euphemistic way of announcing his intention to get himself a beer ('I'm just dropping in to see Mr Plinge'), but he became the accepted name to be placed against a character's name in the programme to disguise the doubling of roles. Walter Plinge has often played a comparatively insignificant Duke of York, or a visiting tradesman. Unlike his American counterpart, George Spelvin, who made his debut in New York in 1886, Walter Plinge is not known to have played the part of an animal.

Pong. Theatrical slang meaning 'to continue to speak in blank verse when you have entirely forgotten your words'. It was well known that F. R. BENSON was an expert ponger and it was a skill he encouraged in other members of his company. (cf. FRIBBLE.)

Prompter. The English-speaking theatre has never adopted the Continental custom of placing the prompter in a roofed enclosure downstage centre, from which vantage-point he would sometimes accompany the actors by reading aloud the whole play as it proceeded. It is to this custom that Guido Noccioli alludes in his diary of ELEONORA DUSE'S 1907 tour of the Americas. On the day before the opening in Buenos Aires of a new play by Enrico Butti, Noccioli records: 'I wouldn't say that the Signora has mastered her part, but she is now following the prompter with greater ease.'

Pujol, Joseph (1857–1945). A French baker, who turned entertainer when he discovered that his extraordinary talent for farting was marketable. Under the unconcealing stage name of 'Le Pétomane', he had a long and successful career. He even farted before Queen Victoria.

Rosciad, The. The best known, and possibly the most vigorous of the many eighteenth-century verse satires on the theatre, Charles Churchill's *The Rosciad* (1761) was published at the author's own expense, and turned him into a celebrity. Churchill is highly selective in his praise and generous in his abuse. GARRICK was much gratified by Churchill's accolade:

> Hence to thy praises, Garrick, I agree,
> And, pleased with Nature, must be pleased with Thee.

But the majority of the theatrical profession smarted under Churchill's lash. Horne Tooke records an occasion when a number of actors had assembled in the Bedford Coffee House planning to take their revenge on the poet. Informed of the budding conspiracy, Churchill went to the Bedford, 'boldly marched up, and drawing off his gloves with great composure, called for a dish of coffee and the Rosciad, in a tone of voice that by no means indicated the least spark of apprehension'.

Sandford, Samuel (*c.* 1638–*c.* 1704). All that we know about Sandford is that he was type-cast as a villain in the Restoration theatre. COLLEY CIBBER called him 'an excellent actor in disagreeable characters'. This is not surprising, if Aston is right in describing him as 'diminutive and mean, (being Round-shoulder'd, Meager-fac'd, Spindle-shank'd, Splay-footed, with a sour countenance and long lean arms)'.

Silver Tassie, The. By 1928, when O'CASEY sent the manuscript of *The Silver Tassie* to the ABBEY THEATRE directors, he was established as the leading Irish dramatist. YEATS's letter of rejection is a classic example of fatal misjudgment. It severed relationships between the two men, and led to O'Casey's resolution not to return to Dublin. It was left to the master-showman Charles Cochran to promote the play. SHAW's letter of congratulation, published in *The Times* in November 1929, is an Irish counterblast to Yeats's dogmatism.

> *Sean O'Casey, Esq.*   82 Merrion Square
>   20 April 1928
> My dear Casey ... I had looked forward with great hope and excitement to reading your play, and not merely because of my admiration for your work, for I bore in mind that the Abbey owed its recent prosperity to you. If you had not brought us your plays just at that moment I doubt if it would now exist. I read the first act with admiration, I thought it was the best first act you had written, and told a friend that you had surpassed yourself. The next night I read the second and third acts, and tonight I have read the fourth. I am sad and discouraged; you have no subject. You were interested in the Irish Civil War, and at every moment of those plays wrote out of your own amusement with life or your sense of its tragedy; you were excited, and we all caught your excitement; you were exasperated almost beyond endurance by what you had seen or heard, as a man is by what happens under his window, and you moved us as Swift moved his contemporaries.
> But you are not interested in the great war; you never stood on its battlefields or walked its hospitals, and so write out of your opinions. You illustrate those opinions by a series of almost

unrelated scenes, as you might in a leading article; there is no dominating character, no dominating action, neither psychological unity nor unity of action; and your great power of the past has been the creation of some unique character who dominated all about him and was himself a main impulse in some action that filled the play from beginning to end.

The mere greatness of the world war has thwarted you; it has refused to become mere background, and obtrudes itself upon the stage as so much dead wood that will not burn with the dramatic fire. Dramatic action is a fire that must burn up everything but itself; there should be no room in a play for anything that does not belong to it; the whole history of the world must be reduced to wallpaper in front of which the characters must pose and speak.

Among the things that dramatic action must burn up are the author's opinions; while he is writing he has no business to know anything that is not a portion of that action. Do you suppose for one moment that Shakespeare educated Hamlet and King Lear by telling them what he thought and believed? As I see it, Hamlet and Lear educated Shakespeare, and I have no doubt that in the process of that education he found out that he was an altogether different man to what he thought himself, and had altogether different beliefs. A dramatist can help his characters to educate him by thinking and studying everything that gives them the language they are groping for through his hands and eyes, but the control must be theirs, and that is why the ancient philosophers thought a poet or dramatist Daimon-possessed.

This is a hateful letter to write, or rather to dictate – I am dictating to my wife – and all the more so, because I cannot advise you to amend the play. It is all too abstract, after the first act; the second act is an interesting technical experiment, but it is too long for the material; and after that there is nothing. I can imagine how you have toiled over this play. A good scenario writes itself, it puts words into the mouths of all its characters while we sleep, but a bad scenario exacts the most miserable toil. I see nothing for it but a new theme, something you have found and no newspaper writer has ever found. What business have we with anything but the unique?

Put the dogmatism of this letter down to splenetic age and forgive it.

W. B. Y.

Whitehall Court
London

Charles B. Cochran
Apollo Theatre
London.

My dear Cochran,

I really must congratulate you on *The Silver Tassie* before it passes into the classical repertory. It is a magnificent play; and it was a magnificent gesture of yours to produce it. The highbrows should have produced it; you, the unpretentious showman, did, as you have done so many other noble and rash things on your Sundays. This, I think, will rank as the best of them. I hope you have not lost too much by it, especially as I am quite sure you have done your best in that direction by doing the thing as extravagantly as possible. That is the worst of operating on your colossal scale; you haven't time to economize; and you lose the habit of thinking it worth while.

No matter! a famous achievement. There is a new drama rising from unplumbed depths to sweep the nice little bourgeois efforts of myself and my contemporaries into the dustbin; and your name will live as that of the man who didn't run away. If only someone would build you a huge Woolworth Theatre (all seats 6*d*) to start with O'Casey and O'Neill, and no plays by men who had ever seen a £5 note before they were 30 or been inside a school after they were 13, you would be buried in Westminster Abbey. Bravo!

G. B. S.

Skid-talk. This American version of the mixed metaphor was developed in New York by the journalist Bunny McLeod. It involves the narrow failure to match the second half of a sentence with the first half. McLeod's skid-talk featured sentences like, 'For your information, let me ask you a question' and, 'Norman tells me a thing one day and out the other'. Sol Hurok (d. 1974), the theatrical impresario, borrowed the techniques of skid-talk to summarize the problems of a commercial theatre: 'If people don't want to come, nothing will stop them.'

Stock characters. The following descriptions are selected from Jerome K. Jerome's *Stage-Land* (1890):

The Hero. 'His chief aim in life is to be accused of crimes he has never committed . . . . Moral speeches are, undoubtedly, his leading article, and of these, it must be owned, he has an inexhaustible stock. He is as

chock-full of noble sentiments as a bladder is of wind .... The Stage
hero always wears patent leather boots, and they are always spotlessly
clean. Sometimes he is rich, and lives in a room with seven doors to it,
and at other times he is starving in a garret; but in either event, he still
wears brand-new patent leather boots.'

The Villain. 'He wears a clean collar, and smokes a cigarette; that is how
we know he is a villain. In real life it is often difficult to tell a villain from
an honest man, and this gives rise to mistakes .... If a man dies,
without leaving a will, then all his property goes to the nearest
villain .... Our advice to Stage Villains generally is as follows – Don't
have too many accomplices; and if you *have* got them, don't keep
sneering at them and bullying them. A word from them can hang you,
and yet you do all you can to rile them. Beware of the comic man. When
you are committing a murder, or robbing a safe, you never look to see
where the comic man is. You are so careless in that way. On the whole, it
might be as well if you murdered the comic man early in the play. Don't
make love to the hero's wife. She doesn't like you; how can you expect
her to? Why don't you get a girl of your own? Lastly, don't go down to
the scenes of your crimes in the last act.'

The Heroine. 'We all have our troubles, but the Stage-heroine never has
anything else .... It is over the child that she does most of her weeping.
The child has a damp time of it altogether .... The Stage-heroine's
only pleasure in life is to go out in a snowstorm without an umbrella, and
with no bonnet on. She always brings her child out with her on these
excursions. She seems to think that it will freshen it up. The child does
not appreciate the snow as much as she does. He says it's cold. . . . Life is
bad enough, as it is; if there were many women, in real life, as good as the
Stage-heroine, it would be unbearable.'

The Comic Man. 'He follows the hero all over the world. This is rough
on the hero .... He is a man of humble station – the comic man. The
village blacksmith or a pedlar. Sometimes he keeps a shop, and, in the
way he manages business, it must be an expensive thing to keep, for he
never charges anybody for anything, he is so generous. All his
customers seem to be people more or less in trouble, and he can't find it
in his heart to ask them to pay for their goods, under such distressing
circumstances. He stuffs their basket full with twice as much as they
came to buy, pushes their money back into their hands, and wipes away
a tear. Why doesn't a comic man come and set up a grocery store in *our*
neighbourhood? He is very good, is the comic man. He can't 'abear'
villainy. To thwart villainy is his life's ambition, and in this noble object
fortune backs him up grandly. Bad people come and commit their

murders and thefts right under his nose . . . . The comic man always rows with his wife, if he is married, or with his sweetheart, if he is not married. They quarrel all day long. It must be a trying life, you would think, but they appear to like it.'

The Lawyer. 'The Stage lawyer never has any office of his own. He transacts all his business at his clients' houses. He will travel hundreds of miles to tell them the most trivial piece of legal information. It never occurs to him how much simpler it would be to write a letter.'

The Adventuress. 'She sits on a table and smokes a cigarette . . . . The adventuress is generally of foreign extraction . . . . It is repentance that kills off the bad people in plays. They always repent, and the moment they repent they die . . . . No Stage adventuress can be good while the heroine is about. The sight of the heroine rouses every bad feeling in her breast. We can sympathize with her in this respect. She is not oppressively good. She never wants to be "unhanded", or "let to pass". She is not always being shocked or insulted by people telling her that they love her; she does not seem to mind it if they do.'

The Servant Girl. 'They quarrel a great deal over their love-making, do the Stage servant girl and her young man, and they always come into the drawing-room to do it . . . . All the male visitors are expected to kiss the Stage servant girl when they come into the house, and to dig her in the ribs, and to say, "Do you know, Jane, I think you're an uncommonly nice girl – click." They always say this, and she likes it.'

The Child. 'It is clean and tidy. You can touch it anywhere and nothing comes off . . . . The Stage child's department in the scheme of life is to harrow up its mother's feelings by ill-timed and uncalled for questions about its father.'

The Peasants. 'They are so happy. They don't look it, but we know they are, because they say so. If you don't believe them, they dance three steps to the right and three steps to the left back again. They can't help it. It is because they are so happy.'

The Good Old Man. 'He has lost his wife. But he knows where she is – among the angels! She isn't all gone, because the heroine has her hair.'

Stock plots. In *Theatre Guyed* (1935), A. E. Wilson offers guidance to would-be writers of FARCE. Among reliable themes:

The harassed male who finds it necessary in the interests of the plot to impersonate a woman.

The sap-headed person who finds himself in the clutches of a designing 'vamp'.

The unoffending nit-wit who discovers that he is wrongfully suspected of being a crook.

The mild-mannered fathead who has someone else's baby planted on him.

The weak-kneed innocent who is called upon to perform prodigies of valour on behalf of some distressed damsel who never appears to be worth half the trouble and fuss.

Among characters whose very presence causes laughter:

Colonels	Uncles
Mothers-in-law	Mayors
Kitchenmaids	Charladies
Solicitors	All foreigners
Curates	Poets
Policemen	Drunkards
Tradesmen of any kind	Old maids
Country folk generally	

Necessary accessories include:

Any number of doors	Some cupboards
Grandfather clocks	Trunks to hide in
A quantity of telegrams	A generous allowance of telephones
A bed or beds	
Cocktails and whisky decanters	Pyjamas

Among articles whose exhibition or mere mention provokes laughter:

Babies in arms	Nightdresses
A battered top hat	Ladies' underwear
A black eye	Garters
A man deprived of his trousers	A decrepit umbrella
Brokers' men	A smashed egg

Anyone who has been dragged out of the water
An explosion in which someone has been grievously injured.

The situation comedies on contemporary television might provide additions to the list, but would demand surprisingly few excisions.

Stock scenery. In *The Case of the Stage in Ireland* (1758), the unnamed author asserts with great clarity: 'The stage should be furnished with a competent number of painted scenes sufficient to answer the purposes of all the plays in the stock, in which there is no great variety, being easily reduced to the following classes. 1st, Temples. 2dly, Tombs. 3dly, City walls and gates. 4thly, Outsides of palaces. 5thly, Insides of Palaces. 6thly, Streets. 7thly, Chambers. 8thly, Prisons. 9thly, Gardens. And 10thly, Rural prospects of groves, forests, desarts &c. All these should be done by a master, if such can be procured; otherwise, they should be as simple and unaffected as possible, to avoid offending a judicious eye. If, for some particular purpose, any other scene is necessary, it can be got up occasionally.'

Suicides. Among actors' suicides, two are particularly bizarre. The Russian actress, E. P. Kadmina, killed herself in 1881 by taking poison on stage during a performance. (TURGENEV's story, 'Clara Milich', is based on this event.) And in Boston in 1888, an American actor called George R. Parkes donned a suit of stage armour before drowning himself.

Tableau. This word, frequently used in stage directions of nineteenth-century plays, describes a practice which was a logical outcome of the vogue for pictorial staging. Actors, having taken up significant positions, would hold them, often until the curtain descended or until applause died away. Sometimes, when the curtain rose again, it would reveal a new and equally significant tableau. The copying of an actual picture was a refinement. In Act II of T. W. ROBERTSON's *Ours* (1866), for example, Blanche and Angus are called upon to 'form Millais' picture of the "Black Brunswicker".' Such a tableau would be carefully rehearsed, with a copy of the actual picture on display for the guidance of the actors.

Tableaux vivants. The first audiences of GILBERT and Sullivan's *Ruddigore* (1887) would have related the scene in which the Portrait Gallery in the Castle becomes suddenly animated to the *tableaux vivants* of the earlier half of the nineteenth century. There is a similar scene in J. R. PLANCHÉ's *The Court Beauties* (1835). The frozen pictorialism of the stage TABLEAU had been a popular feature of MELODRAMA throughout the century, and the *tableau vivant* was a logical development from it. It became, during the Regency period, an elegant social entertainment in its own right. The intention was to present subject matter from myth, famous works of art or notable historical events, and to present them in the elite setting of a well appointed drawing-room. Authentic costume and the adopting of highly theatrical 'attitudes' were expected. Nelson's mistress, Lady Hamilton, was a celebrated exponent, and there was clearly an element of sexual display and voyeurism, more readily accepted in private than in public. In *The Mother's Manual* (1842), Frances Trollope recommends the *tableau vivant* as a way of attracting suitors to a nubile daughter. But the theatre did not relinquish the *tableau vivant* to the drawing-room. The famous horseman Andrew Ducrow presented 'living statues' behind a specially erected frame at Astley's Amphitheatre during the 1820s, and by the 1830s *tableaux vivants* had found their way into the early music halls under the title of *poses plastiques*. It is a short step from the *poses plastiques* of the 1830s to the Windmill Girls of the 1930s.

R. D. Altick, *The Shows of London*, 1978.

Theatre haters, baiters and regulators. Opposition to the theatre and attempts to control it have a history as long as that of the theatre itself. It is appropriately ironical therefore that one of the earliest and most formidable opponents of the drama in Western culture should also be the author of some of the finest dramatic writing in Western literature. No looseness of language is involved in referring to Plato's *Symposium* and the *Trial and Death of Socrates* as intensely dramatic. Both have been successfully dramatized on stage and television with very little alteration. Many of the other dialogues would be almost as successful in performance. But in two of them especially, the *Republic* and the *Laws*, Plato is fiercely critical of the drama, dramatists, actors and audience. His arguments against drama are part of a wider attack on poetry and representation. In the first place the tales and legends of the epic poets, from which the dramatists took their plots, are denounced as both false in themselves and improper examples of conduct for citizens to follow. Though Plato had a high regard for AESCHYLUS and SOPHOCLES, he clearly felt something like contempt for the dramatists of his own time, and refers in the *Laws* to a theatrocracy having replaced a true intellectual aristocracy in Athens. EURIPIDES was to him little better than a mouthpiece for tyrants, the dramatic equivalent of the smooth-talking and dangerous Sophists. As for ARISTOPHANES, Plato could hardly have had any high regard for the man who held up to ridicule his revered mentor Socrates.

But it was not merely the lamentable productions of contemporary dramatists and the general objection to falsehood and impropriety that Plato held against the drama. Believing as he did that true reality lay in the world of Universal Forms, of which the phenomenal world was only an imperfect imitation, he believed the (dramatic) poet to be only an imitator of an imitation, and one which was subject to no rule or measure. What was worse, dramatic writing, working through the senses, appealed to the emotions, whereas the perfection of the soul – man's true end – depended on its purification through abstract intellect. When it came to dramatic performance, the appeal to the senses was even more direct and dangerous. Finally, the business of acting was bad not only for the audience who watched it (pandering to emotions which should be strictly controlled) but for the actors themselves, since it was a kind of degradation of their nature as human beings. The 'negative capability' which enables an actor to play any kind of character leaves his own character a negative quantity, and Plato notes that dramatic talent often goes with a certain weakness of character. No wonder he would have expelled dramatic poets and banned dramatic performances in his ideal republic, or at least tolerated them only under strict control, for, as he writes in the *Laws*: 'Legislator and poet are rivals and the latter can only be tolerated if his words are in harmony with the laws of the state.'

Plato's arguments have been rehearsed, rebutted and repeated with variations throughout the centuries. The fathers of the early Christian church added an argument against plays that was to be heard as late as the eighteenth century, namely that plays were a form of pagan idolatry and therefore unfit for a Christian polity. Tertullian, Chrysostom, Jerome and Augustine are only the most distinguished of a long line of Church fathers who condemned plays, players and playhouses in the roundest of terms. The Third Council of Carthage (AD 397), on which Augustine served, forbade not only clergymen but the laity too from permitting or being present at any kind of public entertainment, 'it being always unlawful for all Christians to come amongst unbelievers'. Tertullian, who composed his *De Spectaculis* especially to wean Christians away from heathenish shows, tells of a woman who came back from the playhouse with an evil spirit within her. When the spirit was exorcised and charged with attacking a Christian it replied, 'I have done nothing but what I can justify, for I seized her on her own ground.' Lactantius makes a point which was to become depressingly familiar, namely 'the better the rhetoric, the greater the mischief'. Chrysostom rails at his flock for encouraging bawdy actors – 'you laugh when you should frown and commend what you ought to abhor' – and, with unimpeachable logic concludes, 'for were there no audience, we should have no acting. And therefore those who join in the crime will ne'er be parted in the punishment.' Jerome sees in Isaiah's words, 'Woe to them that put bitter for sweet and sweet for bitter', a warning to stay away from the theatre, while Augustine sums up a long and sustained attack on the theatre with the words, 'When the playhouses go up [and] religion goes down.'

These and other patristic authorities were quoted at length and with
relish by JEREMY COLLIER several centuries later in his celebrated *Short
View of the Immorality and Profaneness of the English Stage* (1698), a
work which was both a symptom and a cause of the reaction from the
forthrightness of Restoration drama in the early eighteenth century.
Long before Collier's attack appeared the Christian church had at first
taken over the drama and then disowned it. Opposition to the drama had
for a long time centred not only on the harmful effects of plays but on the
dissolute life which the actors were alleged to lead. In Europe, as late as
the time of MOLIÈRE, actors were denied the sacraments and burial in
consecrated ground. In England until 1572 no distinction was made
between actors and vagrants, and with the passing in that year of an act
which safeguarded the status of accredited players, and the construction
four years later of the first public playhouse, the attack on theatre and
theatregoing grew more vociferous than ever. Not only the divines of
'Puritan' persuasion but the city fathers themselves attacked the
playhouses on every conceivable ground and some quite inconceivable
ones, ranging from the playhouse as a place where evil characters
gathered to watch evil goings-on to the plague as God's punishment for
the wickedness of playgoing. 'The cause of plagues is sin', preached
Thomas White from Paul's Cross in 1578, 'and the cause of sin are
plays: therefore the cause of plagues are plays.'

With the establishment of the secular theatre came the need for its
regulation and control. The subsequent history of theatre-hating in
Britain is closely related to the history of CENSORSHIP. Independent
outbursts of Puritan indignation did not, however, cease merely
because they could be channelled through the Lord Chamberlain's
Office. The Christian church has not found it easy to accept state control
of an institution which can challenge virtue without breaking the law. In
1875 the American preacher T. de Witt Talmage included the theatre
among the 'Sports that kill' in a book addressed to the English as well as
to his countrymen, and F. C. Vernon-Harcourt published an autobiography outlining his conversion *From Stage to Cross*. 'The theatre,
under judicious control, may be made a medium of pleasure,' he
admitted, 'but as a spring and source of soul-saving influences it has
been hermetically sealed for all time by the hand of Satan himself.'
Certainly the high peals that can be heard when MRS GRUNDY rings the
bell in Fleet Street sound still. After the ROYAL SHAKESPEARE COMPANY
had begun its THEATRE OF CRUELTY season in 1964, Emil Littler
protested to the *Daily Telegraph*:

As a governor of the Royal Shakespeare Company and a member of the executive I have dissociated myself from this programme of dirt plays at the Aldwych. These plays do not belong, or should not, to the Royal Shakespeare. They are entirely out of keeping with our public image, and with having the Queen as our Patron.

And Michael Bogdanov, director of HOWARD BRENTON's *The Romans in Britain* (1980), was taken to court for procuring actors to commit an act of simulated sodomy by rape. Mrs Mary Whitehouse, always in the forefront like a decently covered figurehead on the galleon of Good Behaviour, explained to the *Guardian*: 'One is concerned about protecting the citizen, and in particular young people. I am talking about men being so stimulated by the play that they will commit attacks on young boys.'

Political theatre-hating is more dangerous and much less easily mocked than its religio-moral counterpart. The Stalinist imposition of socialist realism on a wildly inventive post-revolutionary theatre was an act of vandalism. So were the activities of the HOUSE UNAMERICAN ACTIVITIES COMMITTEE under McCarthy. America had had a foretaste of these in the witch-hunts of the twenties, instigated by Attorney General A. Mitchell Palmer. France experienced an outbreak of convulsive conservatism in the government's reaction to the theatre's involvement in the 'revolution' of 1968, as did Greece under the Colonels. It is probably true that a theatre that gives no offence is dead, but it will always be difficult to avoid doing the right thing for the wrong reasons.

Type-casting. There is nothing wrong with recognizing that certain actors, whether by virtue of appearance, manner or voice, are better suited to certain roles than others. But the system of type-casting is open to abuse. It is one thing for SHAKESPEARE to write parts particularly suited to the talents of WILL KEMPE or ROBERT ARMIN; but it is quite another for a nineteenth-century playwright to find himself forced to write whole plays with particular character-types in mind. Those who wrote for established stock companies had to provide parts to suit the available actors, each of whom would have an unalterable 'line of business'. An acting edition of Colin Hazlewood's *Waiting for the Verdict* (1859) spells out the division of labour according to lines of business:

Lord Viscount Elmore	Second walking gentleman
Lieutenant Florville	Juvenile [lead]
Humphrey Higson	Second low comedy
Blinkey Brown	First low comedy

Sir Henry Harrington	Responsible
Jonas Hundle	First heavy man
Jonathan Roseblade	First old man
Jasper Roseblade	Leading man
Rev. Owen Hylton	Second old man
Grange	Utility
Thorpe	Utility
Lord Chief Justice	Very responsible
Serjeant Stanley	Second heavy man
Grafston	First walking gentleman
The Sherriff	Responsible
Martha Roseblade	Leading lady
Sarah Sawyer	Chambermaid [or soubrette]
Mrs Burnly	Utility

Such rigidity has an inevitable effect on the writing of plays for a professional theatre constrained by its own limitations. But twentieth-century complacence would be ill-advised in the light of the methods used for casting films and television series. (See also STOCK CHARACTERS.)

Up-stage. To 'up-stage' a fellow-actor is to draw the audience's attention away from him or her and focus it on yourself. The word derives from the post-Restoration English stage, when the performers stood down-stage (i.e. at the front) of the proscenium arch to deliver their lines. By standing a little up-stage of his colleagues, a wily actor could keep his full face towards the audience whilst forcing those in dialogue with him to turn a little into profile. As JOHN O'KEEFE notes in his *Recollections* (1826), 'when two knowing ones are on together, each plays the trick upon the other. I was much diverted with seeing MACKLIN and Sheridan, in Othello and Iago, at this work: both endeavouring to keep back, they at last got together up against the back scene'.

Whittlebot, Hernia. This was the pen-name under which NOEL COWARD published his first volumes of verse, *Poems* (1923) and *Chelsea Buns* (1925).

Yankee criticism. When the MOSCOW ART THEATRE visited the United States of America in 1923, critical response was inevitably mixed. This verse response to *The Cherry Orchard* was published in the *New York Times* on 11 February 1923. Gaev, referred to as 'that great big goof', was played by STANISLAVSKY himself. The author of the poem was John V. A. Weaver.

A 100 Per Cent American Speaks

The wife says 'What you want to see them for?
It's only a bunch of dirty Bolshevicky
That's tryin' to turn the country upside down
The way they done their own. Why don't they stay
In Russia, where they belong?' And so I says,
'Well, I'll go there and give the stuff the razz.'

I stands in line for a couple of hours or so
And finely gets a seat in the gallery
In with the foreigners and all the garlic.
The name of the show was called 'The Cherry Orchard',
And the first two acts was sure the bunk to me –
A lot of people runnin' up and down
In a great big room, carryin' suitcases and trunks,
And whisperin' in the corners. After that
They sat around in a silly-lookin' field,
With hay, and done a whole lot more talkin',
And it sounded like they was talkin' English
But makin' up words just while they went along.
I couldn't make out nothing from the program,
And so I ast one of them Bolshevicky
Behind me if he wouldn't put me wise
And so he says it was a real rich family
That didn't know how to manage property
Because they couldn't keep their minds on it
And when they tried to talk, got makin' jokes.
And one of the birds that useta be a slave,
Or I guess his old man was, well, anyway,
This bird was tryin' to tell 'em what to do.
He says that they should take the Cherry orchard
And cut it up in little lots – you know,
Like Pleasant Heighths – suburban subdivision –
That sort of thing, and sell 'em. And that way
They could save half the old farm. See? But they
Just wouldn't listen. They was nice enough,
But nit-wits, see? And in the third act, then,
They're havin' a dance, and waitin' for the news
From the auction sale. The brother went to the auction
With money that they borrowed from a aunt,
And just when they're havin' the swellest kind of a time

The brother comes back. And he says the money
Wasn't enough. And so they lost the place.
And what do you think? The guy that was a slave
He went and bought it! And he comes in soused,
And yells around about how proud he is.
So then the last act's where they got to move,
~~And packin' up the stuff, and sayin' good-bye,~~
And – listen, I can't make out yet how it happened
But when that great big goof looked at the orchard,
And I could hear the axes cuttin' the trees,
And all of a sudden this six-foot bird breaks down,
And stuffed his handkerchief right in his mouth,
And real tears in his eyes – can y' imagine?
I just set there and blubbered like a baby.
I sure do hope nobody didn't see me.
Just think of a bunch of low-down Bolshevicky
That can't talk even a word of English, makin'
A hard-boiled egg like me cry like a kid!
And me not understandin' what they said!
I tell you what. It's just like I was watchin'
A movie where somebody told me what
Was goin' on, and not a wild movie, either,
Hardly anything happenin' at all,
But with the best actors that ever was.
Why did it get me? I ain't goin' again.
I don't like things that I can't understand,
And yet can get me like them foreigners did.

Index of Entries

Theatres, Companies and Dramatic Genres

Theatre People

Theatrical Miscellany

Index to the Essays

List of References to Plays

Love's Last Shift	Colley Cibber
Love's Sacrifice	John Ford
Lovesick Court, The	Richard Brome
Lower Depths, The	Maxim Gorky
Lucky Sam McCarver	Sidney Howard
Lucretia Borgia	Victor Hugo
Luther	John Osborne
Lying Lover, The	Richard Steele
Lying Valet, The	David Garrick
Macbeth	William Shakespeare
Machine Wreckers, The	Ernst Toller
Maciej Korbowa and Bellatrix	Stanislaw Witkiewicz
Mad Dog Blues	Sam Shepard
Mad World, My Masters, A	Thomas Middleton
Madame Sans-Gêne	Victorien Sardou
Mademoiselle Jaire	Michel de Ghelderode
Madheart	Amiri Baraka
Madman and the Nun, The	Stanislaw Witkiewicz
Madmen and Specialists	Wole Soyinka
Madras House, The	Harley Granville Barker
Madwoman of Chaillot, The	Jean Giraudoux
Magda (Die Heimat)	Hermann Sudermann*
Magic Glasses, The	George Fitzmaurice
Magistrate, The	Arthur Wing Pinero
Magnificence	Howard Brenton
Magnyfycence	John Skelton*
Maid of Orleans, The	Friedrich von Schiller
Maid of the Mill, The	Isaac Bickerstaffe
Maids, The	Jean Genet
Maid's Tragedy, The	Francis Beaumont and John Fletcher
Major Barbara	George Bernard Shaw
Makropoulos Affair, The	Karel Čapek
Malavikagnimitra	Kalidasa
Malcontent, The	John Marston
Man and Boy	Terence Rattigan
Man and Superman	George Bernard Shaw
Man Equals Man	Bertolt Brecht
Man of Mode, The	George Etherege
Man of the World, The	Charles Macklin
Man Who Came to Dinner, The	George S. Kaufman and Moss Hart
Man Who Married a Dumb Wife, The	Anatole France*
Map of the World, A	David Hare
Marat/Sade	Peter Weiss
Marching Song	John Whiting
Margaret Fleming	James A. Herne*
Maria Stuart	Friedrich von Schiller
Mariana Pineda	Federico Garcia Lorca
Marie Tudor	Victor Hugo
Marion de Lorme	Victor Hugo
Marquis of Keith, The	Frank Wedekind
Marriage	Nikolai Gogol

Marriage à la Mode	John Dryden
Marriage of Figaro, The	Beaumarchais
Marriage of Mr Mississippi, The	Friedrich Dürrenmatt
Marrying of Ann Leete, The	Harley Granville Barker
Mary Barnes	David Edgar
Mary of Scotland	Maxwell Anderson
Masks and Faces	Charles Reade and Tom Taylor
Masque of Judgement, The	William Vaughn Moody
Masque of Kings, The	Maxwell Anderson
Masquerade	Mikhail Lermontov*
Massacre at Paris, The	Christopher Marlowe
Masses and Men	Ernst Toller
Master Builder, The	Henrik Ibsen
Master Harold and the Boys	Athol Fugard
Master of Santiago, The	Henri de Montherlant*
Master Olof	August Strindberg
Match at Midnight, A	William Rowley
Matchgirls, The	Robert Mitchell*
Matchmaker, The	Thornton Wilder
Maternity	Eugène Brieux
Maydays	David Edgar
Mayor of Garrett, The	Samuel Foote
Mayor of Zalamea, The	Calderon de la Barca
Measure for Measure	William Shakespeare
Medea	Euripides
Médée	Pierre Corneille
Melodrama Play	Sam Shepard
Men without Shadows	Jean-Paul Sartre
Menaechmi	Plautus
Menteur, Le	Pierre Corneille
Merchant, The	Arnold Wesker
Merchant of Venice, The	William Shakespeare
Merry Wives of Windsor, The	William Shakespeare
Merton of the Movies	Marc Connelly and George S. Kaufman
Metamora	John Augustus Stone*
Meteor, The	Friedrich Dürrenmatt
Michael and His Lost Angel	Henry Arthur Jones
Mid-Channel	Arthur Wing Pinero
Midsummer Night's Dream, A	William Shakespeare
Mikado, The	W. S. Gilbert and Arthur Sullivan
Milk Train Doesn't Stop Here Anymore, The	Tennessee Williams
Minna von Barnhelm	Gotthold Lessing
Minor, The	Samuel Foote
Miracle, The	Karl Vollmoeller*
Misanthrope, The	Molière
Miser, The	Molière
Mithridate	Jean Racine
Mogul Tale, A	Elizabeth Inchbald
Money	Edward Bulwer
Monica's Blue Boy	Arthur Wing Pinero
Monna Vanna	Maurice Maeterlinck

Monsieur Perrichon's Voyage	Eugène Labiche
Month in the Country, A	Ivan Turgenev
Moon for the Misbegotten, A	Eugene O'Neill
Moon in the Yellow River, The	Denis Johnston
Moonlighter, The	George Fitzmaurice
Mother	Karel Čapek
Mother, The	Bertolt Brecht
Mother, The	Stanislaw Witkiewicz
Mother Courage and Her Children	Bertolt Brecht
Mother's Day	David Storey
Motion of History, The	Amiri Baraka
Mourning Becomes Electra	Eugene O'Neill
Mourning Bride, The	William Congreve
M.P.	T. W. Robertson
Mr Gillie	James Bridie
Mr H.	Charles Lamb
Mr Puntila and His Hired Man Matti	Bertolt Brecht
Mrs Daintree's Daughter	Janet Achurch
Mrs Dane's Defence	Henry Arthur Jones
Mrs Warren's Profession	George Bernard Shaw
Much Ado about Nothing	William Shakespeare
Murder	Anthony Shaffer*
Murder in the Cathedral	T. S. Eliot
My Fair Lady	Frederick Loewe and Alan Jay Lerner*
My Foot My Tutor	Peter Handke
My Heart's in the Highlands	William Saroyan
Mystery-Bouffe	Vladimir Mayakovsky
Nathan the Wise	Gotthold Lessing
Ned McCobb's Daughter	Sidney Howard
Nekrassov	Jean-Paul Sartre
New Gossoon, The	George Shiels
New Way to Pay Old Debts, A	Philip Massinger
Newly Married, The	Bjørnstjerne Bjørnson
Nicomède	Pierre Corneille
Night and Day	Tom Stoppard
Night Music	Clifford Odets
Night of the Iguana, The	Tennessee Williams
Night over Taos	Maxwell Anderson
No End of Blame	Howard Barker
No Exit (Huis Clos)	Jean-Paul Sartre
No-Good Friday	Athol Fugard
No Man's Land	Harold Pinter
Non-Stop Connolly Show, The	John Arden and Margaretta D'Arcy
Noonday Demons	Peter Barnes
Norman Conquests, The	Alan Ayckbourn
Northern Lass, The	Richard Brome
Not for Children	Elmer Rice
Not I	Samuel Beckett
Notorious Mrs Ebbsmith, The	Arthur Wing Pinero
Now They Are Singing Again	Max Frisch
Nuts in May	Mike Leigh

Passing Day, The	George Shiels
Passion in Six Days, A	Howard Barker
Patience	W. S. Gilbert and Arthur Sullivan
Patriot for Me, A	John Osborne
Patriots	Lennox Robinson
Patron, The	Samuel Foote
Paul Pry	John Poole*
Paul Twyning	George Shiels
Peace	Aristophanes
Peace in Our Time	Noel Coward
Pearl	John Arden
Peer Gynt	Henrik Ibsen
Peg o' My Heart	J. Hartley Manners*
Pelican, The	August Strindberg
Pelléas and Mélisande	Maurice Maeterlinck
Penny for a Song, A	John Whiting
Penthesilea	Heinrich von Kleist
Peribanez	Lope de Vega
Pericles, Prince of Tyre	William Shakespeare and George Wilkins (?)
Perkin Warbeck	John Ford
Persians	Aeschylus
Peter Pan	J. M. Barrie
Petrified Forest, The	Robert Sherwood
Phèdre	Jean Racine
Philadelphia Here I Come	Brian Friel
Philaster	Francis Beaumont and John Fletcher
Philistines, The	Maxim Gorky
Philoctetes	Sophocles
Phoenix Too Frequent, A	Christopher Fry
Physicists, The	Friedrich Dürrenmatt
Pie-Dish, The	George Fitzmaurice
Piggy Bank, The (La Cagnotte)	Eugène Labiche
Pillars of Society	Henrik Ibsen
Pique	Augustin Daly
Pirates of Penzance, The	W. S. Gilbert and Arthur Sullivan
Pizarro	Richard Brinsley Sheridan
Plaideurs, Les	Jean Racine
Plain Dealer, The	William Wycherley
Play	Samuel Beckett
Play	T. W. Robertson
Play of the Weather, The	John Heywood
Play Strindberg	Friedrich Dürrenmatt
Playboy of the Western World, The	J. M. Synge
Player Queen, The	W. B. Yeats
Playgoers	Arthur Wing Pinero
Playing with Fire	August Strindberg
Plaza Suite	Neil Simon
Plenty	David Hare
Plough and the Stars, The	Sean O'Casey
Plunder	Ben Travers
Political Tinker, The	Ludwig Holberg

Ralph Roister Doister	Nicholas Udall
Rape upon Rape	Henry Fielding
Rats, The	Gerhart Hauptmann
Real Inspector Hound, The	Tom Stoppard
Real Thing, The	Tom Stoppard
Reckoning, The	Ann Jellicoe
Recruiting Officer, The	George Farquhar
Red Noses	Peter Barnes
Red Oleanders	Rabindranath Tagore
Red Roses for Me	Sean O'Casey
Red Scarf, The	Augustin Daly
Rehearsal, The	George Villiers, Duke of Buckingham
Relapse, The	John Vanbrugh
Relative Values	Noel Coward
Relatively Speaking	Alan Ayckbourn
Renegado, The	Philip Massinger
Representative, The	Rolf Hochhuth
Resistible Rise of Arturo Ui, The	Bertolt Brecht
Restoration	Edward Bond
Restoration of Arnold Middleton, The	David Storey
Return, The	Roger Planchon
Return of Peter Grimm, The	David Belasco
Reunion in Vienna	Robert Sherwood
Revenge	Howard Brenton
Revenger's Tragedy, The	Cyril Tourneur (?)
Rhinoceros	Eugène Ionesco
Richard II	William Shakespeare
Richard III	William Shakespeare
Richard of Bordeaux	Gordon Daviot*
Richard's Cork Leg	Brendan Behan
Richelieu	Edward Bulwer
Ride over Lake Constance, The	Peter Handke
Riders to the Sea	J. M. Synge
Right You Are, If You Think So	Luigi Pirandello
Ring round the Moon	Jean Anouilh (translated by Christopher Fry)
Rip Van Winkle	Dion Boucicault and others
Rise and Fall of the City of Mahagonny, The	Bertolt Brecht and Kurt Weill
Rising of the Moon, The	Lady Gregory
Rival Queens, The	Nathaniel Lee
Rivals, The	Richard Brinsley Sheridan
Road to Mecca, The	Athol Fugard
Road to Rome, The	Robert Sherwood
Road to Ruin, The	Thomas Holcroft
Robbers, The	Friedrich von Schiller
Robert Macaire	Frédérick Lemaître and others
Rodogune	Pierre Corneille
Roi s'amuse, Le	Victor Hugo
Romans in Britain, The	Howard Brenton
Romeo and Juliet	William Shakespeare
Romulus the Great	Friedrich Dürrenmatt
Ronde, La	Arthur Schnitzler

Sejanus	Ben Jonson
Senora Carrar's Rifles	Bertolt Brecht
Separate Tables	Terence Rattigan
Serjeant Musgrave's Dance	John Arden
Serpent, The	Jean-Claude van Itallie*
Servant of Two Masters, The	Carlo Goldoni
Seven against Thebes	Aeschylus
Shadow of a Gunman, The	Sean O'Casey
Shall We Join the Ladies?	J. M. Barrie
Shaughraun, The	Dion Boucicault
She Stoops to Conquer	Oliver Goldsmith
She Would If She Could	George Etherege
Shenandoah	Bronson Howard
Sherlock Holmes	William Gillette
Shoemakers, The	Stanislaw Witkiewicz
Shoemaker's Holiday, The	Thomas Dekker
Shoemaker's Prodigious Wife, The	Federico Garcia Lorca
Show Boat	Jerome Kern and Oscar Hammerstein*
Siege of Rhodes, The	William Davenant
Sign in Sidney Brustein's Window, The	Lorraine Hansberry
Silence	Harold Pinter
Silent Woman, The	Ben Jonson
Silver Box, The	John Galsworthy
Silver Cord, The	Sidney Howard
Silver King, The	Henry Arthur Jones and Henry Herman
Silver Tassie, The	Sean O'Casey
Simon the Cyrenean	Ridgeley Torrence*
Simplicissimus	Frank Wedekind
Singer, The	Padraig Pearse*
Sir Bengt's Wife	August Strindberg
Sir Patient Fancy	Aphra Behn
Sir Thomas More	William Shakespeare and others
Sister Beatrice	Maurice Maeterlinck
Sisterly Feelings	Alan Ayckbourn
Sisters	David Storey
Six Characters in Search of an Author	Luigi Pirandello
Sizwe Banzi Is Dead	Athol Fugard
Skin Game, The	John Galsworthy
Skin of Our Teeth, The	Thornton Wilder
Slave, The	Amiri Baraka (as Leroi Jones)
Slave Ship	Amiri Baraka
Sleep of Prisoners, A	Christopher Fry
Sleeping Clergyman, A	James Bridie
Sleeping Prince, The	Terence Rattigan
Sleuth	Anthony Shaffer*
Slight Ache, A	Harold Pinter
S-1	Amiri Baraka
Social Success, A	Max Beerbohm
Society	T. W. Robertson
Soft or a Girl?	John McGrath
Soldiers	Rolf Hochhuth
Soldier's Fortune, The	Thomas Otway
Some Kind of a Love Story	Arthur Miller

Tartuffe	Molière
Taste of Honey, A	Shelagh Delaney*
Tearing to Pieces of Le Cid, The	Roger Planchon
Teeth 'n' Smiles	David Hare
Tékéli	Guilbert de Pixerécourt
Tempest, The	William Shakespeare
Tender Husband, The	Richard Steele
Test, The	Pierre Marivaux
Thark	Ben Travers
That Good Between Us	Howard Barker
Thébaide, La	Jean Racine
Their Very Own and Golden City	Arnold Wesker
Théodore	Pierre Corneille
There Shall Be No Night	Robert Sherwood
Thérèse Raquin	Émile Zola
Thespis	W. S. Gilbert and Arthur Sullivan
They	Stanislaw Witkiewicz
They Knew What They Wanted	Sidney Howard
Thieves' Carnival	Jean Anouilh
This Doubtful Paradise	Brian Friel
This Happy Breed	Noel Coward
Thomas and Sally	Isaac Bickerstaffe
Thor, with Angels	Christopher Fry
Three Daughters of M. Dupont, The	Eugène Brieux
Three Sisters, The	Anton Chekhov
Three Weeks after Marriage	Arthur Murphy
Threepenny Opera, The	Bertolt Brecht and Kurt Weill
Thunder Rock	Robert Ardrey*
Thyestes	Seneca
Ticket-of-Leave Man, The	Tom Taylor
Tide, The	Ann Jellicoe
Tidings Brought to Mary, The	Paul Claudel
Tiger at the Gates	Jean Giraudoux
Time and the Conways	J. B. Priestley
Time of Your Life, The	William Saroyan
Timon of Athens	William Shakespeare
Tinker's Wedding, The	J. M. Synge
'Tis Pity She's a Whore	John Ford
Titus Andronicus	William Shakespeare
To Damascus	August Strindberg
To Marry, or Not to Marry	Elizabeth Inchbald
To Oblige Benson	Tom Taylor
Tobias and the Angel	James Bridie
Toilet, The	Amiri Baraka (as Leroi Jones)
Tooth of Crime, The	Sam Shepard
Top Girls	Caryl Churchill
Torquato Tasso	Goethe
Tosca, La	Victorien Sardou
Touch of the Poet, A	Eugene O'Neill
Tower, The	Hugo von Hofmannsthal
Tower of Nesle, The	Alexandre Dumas, *père*
Toys in the Attic	Lillian Hellman
Trachiniae	Sophocles

Traitor, The	James Shirley
Transfiguration	Ernst Toller
Translations	Brian Friel
Traveller without Luggage	Jean Anouilh
Travels of the Three English Brothers, The	John Day
Travesties	Tom Stoppard
Tread the Green Grass	Paul Green
Trees in the Wind	John McGrath
Trelawny of the 'Wells'	Arthur Wing Pinero
Trial by Jury	W. S. Gilbert and Arthur Sullivan
Trick to Catch the Old One, A	Thomas Middleton
Trifles	Susan Glaspell
Trilby	Paul M. Potter*
Trip to Calais, A	Samuel Foote
Triptychon	Max Frisch
Troilus and Cressida	William Shakespeare
Trojan War Will Not Take Place, The	Jean Giraudoux
Trojan Women	Euripides
Trotsky in Exile	Peter Weiss
True-Born Irishman, The	Charles Macklin
True West	Sam Shepard
Trumpets and Raspberries	Dario Fo
Truth, The	Clyde Fitch
Turandot	Carlo Gozzi
Turkey Cock, The	Slawomir Mrozek
Tutor, The	Reinhold Lenz*
Twelfth Night	William Shakespeare
Twelve-Pound Look, The	J. M. Barrie
Two Executioners, The	Fernando Arrabal
Two Gentlemen of Verona, The	William Shakespeare
Two Noble Kinsmen, The	William Shakespeare and John Fletcher
Two Roses	James Albery*
Ubu Roi	Alfred Jarry
Uncle Vanya	Anton Chekhov
Under Milk Wood	Dylan Thomas*
Under the Gaslight	Augustin Daly
Underpants, The	Carl Sternheim
Undiscovered Country	Arthur Schnitzler (translated by Tom Stoppard)
Upholsterer, The	Arthur Murphy
Utopia (Limited)	W. S. Gilbert and Arthur Sullivan
Vagabond King, The	Rudolph Friml*
Vampire, The	Dion Boucicault
Vampyre, The	J. R. Planché
Vandaleur's Folly	John Arden and Margaretta D'Arcy
Venceslas	Jean de Rotrou
Venetian Twins, The	Carlo Goldoni
Venice Preserved	Thomas Otway
Venus Observed	Christopher Fry
Vera; or, The Nihilists	Oscar Wilde

White Cockade, The	Lady Gregory
White Devil, The	John Webster
White Dresses	Paul Green
White-Headed Boy, The	Lennox Robinson
Whitewashing Julia	Henry Arthur Jones
Wholesome Glory	Mike Leigh
Who's Afraid of Virginia Woolf?	Edward Albee
Who's the Dupe?	Hannah Cowley
Widow's Vow, The	Elizabeth Inchbald
Wild Duck, The	Henrik Ibsen
Wild Goose Chase, The	John Fletcher
Wild Oats	John O'Keefe
William Tell	James Sheridan Knowles
William Tell	Friedrich von Schiller
Winslow Boy, The	Terence Rattigan
Winter's Tale, The	William Shakespeare
Winterset	Maxwell Anderson
Witch of Edmonton, The	Thomas Dekker, John Ford and William Rowley
Witching Hour, The	Augustus Thomas
Wits, The	William Davenant
Wives as They Were and Maids as They Are	Elizabeth Inchbald
Wives' Excuse, The	Thomas Southerne
Woe from Wit	Alexander Griboyedov*
Woman, The	Edward Bond
Woman Hater, The	Francis Beaumont
Woman Is a Weathercock, A	Nathan Field
Woman Killed with Kindness, A	Thomas Heywood
Woman Never Vexed, A	William Rowley
Woman of No Importance, A	Oscar Wilde
Women Beware Women	Thomas Middleton
Wonder: A Woman Keeps a Secret, The	Susanna Centlivre
Workhouse Donkey, The	John Arden
Workhouse Ward, The	Lady Gregory
Woyzeck	Georg Büchner
Wreckers	David Edgar
Yard of Sun, A	Christopher Fry
Yellow Jack	Sidney Howard
Yeoman of the Guard, The	W. S. Gilbert and Arthur Sullivan
Yerma	Federico Garcia Lorca
You Can't Take It With You	Moss Hart and George S. Kaufman
You Never Can Tell	George Bernard Shaw
Young England	Walter Reynolds*
Young Man in a Hurry, A	Eugène Labiche
Young Mrs Winthrop	Bronson Howard
Younger Generation, The	Stanley Houghton
Zack	Harold Brighouse
Zoo Story, The	Edward Albee

THE HISTORY OF VINTAGE

The famous American publisher Alfred A. Knopf (1892–1984) founded Vintage Books in the United States in 1954 as a paperback home for the authors published by his company. Vintage was launched in the United Kingdom in 1990 and works independently from the American imprint although both are part of the international publishing group, Random House.

Vintage in the United Kingdom was initially created to publish paperback editions of books acquired by the prestigious hardback imprints in the Random House Group such as Jonathan Cape, Chatto & Windus, Hutchinson and later William Heinemann, Secker & Warburg and The Harvill Press. There are many Booker and Nobel Prize-winning authors on the Vintage list and the imprint publishes a huge variety of fiction and non-fiction. Over the years Vintage has expanded and the list now includes great authors of the past – who are published under the Vintage Classics imprint – as well as many of the most influential authors of the present.

For a full list of the books Vintage publishes, please visit our website
www.vintage-books.co.uk

For book details and other information about the classic authors we publish, please visit the Vintage Classics website
www.vintage-classics.info

Imogen,
Obviously

"Um. What?"

Edith looks delighted. "Do we know him?"

"Absolutely not."

"Not *yet*—but we will! Let's call him Bruce. Or Bryce?" Gretchen tilts her head. "Bruce. I'm thinking . . . sophomore. And he's from somewhere cool."

Otávio looks up from his phone. "Who's Bruce?"

"MAINE. He's from Maine."

I blink. "Is Maine cool?"

"And he likes lobsters. Because he's from Maine." Gretchen shrugs. "Sorry, that's all I know about Maine."

"Mmm. Are we done?"

"WAIT. No. No. Hold up." Gretchen presses both hands to her cheeks. "New target. Okay. Okay, just stepped out of the second door. Not the facial hair guy. Green hoodie, next to the girl—"

"Even better. Guy with a girlfriend."

"A girlfriend wearing a carabiner and a thumb ring?"

I bite my lip. "Maybe?"

"Hey—sorry! Hi! I'm here!" Lili skids to a stop on the sidewalk, sneakers only halfway on her feet. She hugs me, hugs Edith, ruffles Otávio's hair, and then hugs him, too. Then she turns stiffly to Gretchen. "Hi."

"Hi." Gretchen nods.

Lili claps. "Okay! Should we . . ."

"Yes! Okay, um. See you guys at home?" I say. "Gretch, really, thank you for driving."

9

"No prob. Hey." Gretchen meets my gaze. "You good?"

"Yeah. Yup! Of course."

Lili rolls her eyes faintly and reaches for my suitcase.

Gretchen hugs me. "Tell Bruce we say hi, okay?"

"And no flossing," Edith adds, her dimple flashing with even the quickest of smiles. Just like mine does.

Texts with Gretchen

GP: Okay we're off!! Have FUN!!!

GP: And take lots of pictures with your man!!!! 👯 👯 👯

GP: Ok but seriously, let me know if you need a rescue

GP: I can swing back and pick you up, for real

GP: I don't leave til tomorrow morning

GP: anyway, I love you, have fun at COLLEGE

2

"Rescue?" Lili's eyes narrow. "From *me*?"

"Oh, no—I think she just means, like. College." I gesture vaguely toward campus.

Lili stops short. "Hey. Are you worried?"

"No! I'm fine. I'm good! Just Gretchen being Gretchen."

"Yeah. She's extremely Gretchen." Lili veers us down a winding concrete path. "Anyway. Hi! This is Blackwell!"

"Hi, Blackwell!"

It's my first real glimpse of campus. My future home.

I mean, I've passed it hundreds of times. Dad even drove me up and down the side streets once. But that was more like peeking into someone's house through a ground floor window. This is like stepping into the foyer.

Lili's already playing tour guide. "That's the central quad, and that brick building is the new performing arts center."

"Wow. It's so . . ." I trail off, gaze landing on a gray stone building, wrapped in vines. "It's like a fairy-tale cottage."

She laughs. "That's the registrar's office."

"It's too pretty!"

"Now you know why I've been on your ass to visit!"

"I know. I know—"

"But, hey—at least you've visited me the exact same number of times as Gretchen!"

My cheeks go warm. "No, I know. Lili, I'm sorry—"

"I'm kidding." Lili shoots me a wry glance. "It's fine, okay?"

"Yeah. No, I'm just." I swallow. "Everything got so crazy, with applications and homework, and the car stuff. And then Nana's wrist—"

"Right. No, Immy, I get it. Seriously."

"I just don't want you to think I didn't—"

"I don't! Really. I'm just glad you're here." She smiles. "It's going to be perfect."

And maybe it will be. Maybe it'll be one big extended sleepover, just like when we were kids. We used to spend entire weekends together—building fairy houses, playing Mario Kart, getting ice cream at Seneca Farms. In the summer, we'd basically just go back and forth between my house and hers, like it was some kind of joint custody arrangement.

I had entire rituals at Lili's house. I was such an early bird when I was little—up and wide awake before six in the morning, even though Lili and Otávio slept until at least nine or ten in the summers and on weekends. But those mornings were some of the best times of all. I'd tiptoe downstairs in my pajama shorts, Lili's beagle mix, Mel, trailing behind me. Lili's parents were almost always up by then, and Lili's dad would say, "Bom dia, querida!" He'd make me milky coffee with lots of sugar before disappearing with a book. Then I'd settle in on the couch with Mel and Lili's mom, and usually we'd get through an entire movie before Lili came down. It's how I found most of my favorites—*But I'm a Cheerleader, Clueless, Reality Bites*. Basically every nineties rom-com ever made. Lili's mom used to watch them on VHS after she moved to New York, when she was trying to master colloquial English.

The point is, Lili and I are really more like cousins than friends, which is why visiting her at college should feel like picking up where we left off. Like unpausing a movie. But now that I'm here, I'm wondering if the pause even happened. Maybe I stopped and everything else just kept going.

"Oh, this is kind of cool," Lili says. "There's, like, this whole network of underground tunnels connecting the buildings on this side of campus."

"Like a storm shelter?"

"You could probably use them for that." She stops at a bench, propping her foot up. "I don't know why they were built. You're not even really supposed to go down there—you have to find someone who knows which specific doors are unlocked."

"So it's like a secret society?"

Lili laughs, tugging the back of her shoe up over her heel. "Totally not. Do you remember my friend Tessa?"

My mind conjures the image of a ponytailed girl in boyish plaid—present in so many of Lili's photos, it's pretty clear they're best friends. I guess she's kind of the new and improved me.

"Her brother's a junior here, and he brought us down there last semester. It's so cool. And creepy. But cool-creepy. The walls are covered in graffiti, but it's all from the eighties and nineties. It's like a time capsule."

Lili smiles back at me so easily, it makes my chest tug. I don't think I've ever seen her this wide-open. I mean, maybe at home, when it's just the four of us—her, me, Edith, and Otávio. But never at school. Even though she had a whole group of friends from her grade, she never seemed to fully relax around them.

Here, though—she's smiling and waving at acquaintances as we pass them, saying, "That's Clara from my philosophy class," or, "Okay, so Mika actually did a TikTok collab with that guy—forgot his name, but it was the one with the little candy house. Did you see that one?"

I did. Three times, and I texted it to Gretchen, too.

Lili's friend Mika is sort of TikTok famous—mostly for creating these really detailed dioramas and using a green screen video app to make it look like they're dancing inside them. I can barely wrap my head around the fact that Lili's friends with an actual celebrity. Though all of Lili's friends are basically celebrities to me, from her stories and pictures alone.

Lili veers off the quad, leading me down one of the residential streets near campus—mostly frat houses with giant Greek letters on display, populated by shirtless guys on lawn chairs.

All of whom seem to have missed the memo that it's March in upstate New York.

She stops in front of a slatted wood house with colorful flags draped from most of the windows. "So . . . this is Rainbow Manor. It's kind of the queer frat house? People live here, but they also do events and community outreach work. Stuff like that." She shoots me the quickest half smile. "And they throw the best parties."

It's like stepping into an alternate universe—sorry, but I've known Lili Cardoso since she was three years old, and parties are her personal hell. This is a girl who carried thick, dog-eared Tamora Pierce books all around camp every summer, just in case there was unexpected free time and someone tried to talk to her.

It must be different with her college friends. Her so-called pack of queers. They found each other at an orientation-week mixer, and they've been a ride-or-die squad ever since. Lili's first real queer friendships.

I'm really happy for her. Obviously.

Even if I feel a little far away from her sometimes.

It's hard to explain, because it's not like she's trying to phase me out. I've lost track of how many times she's invited me to crash in her dorm for a weekend. And when her roommate moved off campus after winter break, it was basically a standing invitation.

I really meant to take her up on it.

But sometimes I get in my head about things like this. I

16

think it's the way Lili talks about this place—not a trace of snark or cynicism. Pure marshmallow. I know it's a good thing, but it's a little unnerving. It's like her whole life clicked into place as soon as she left.

Which makes me the backstory. A relic of Lili's heteronormative small-town childhood. I even look the part—a cardigan that's almost as long as my skirt, my sandy-brown ponytail bobby-pinned on the sides. Even my purse looks a little too hometown preppy—a miniature crossbody satchel in brown fake leather.

Maybe this would be easier if I looked like Gretchen— cotton-candy pink hair and a wardrobe ripped straight from the set of *Euphoria*.

"For real, are you okay?" Lili asks. "You're eerily quiet."

I blink. "Oh! Sor—"

"Don't apologize—I'm just saying. Also, we're home!" Lili gestures at a trio of brick buildings arranged around a cozy grass courtyard. "The middle one's Rosewood—that's us. But all three are mostly freshmen."

I pause to take it all in. The three structures—mismatched but complementary, connected by a network of intersecting paths. Everywhere I look, there are students on benches, on blankets, roaming in packs of two or three or six, with messenger bags and backpacks. Absolutely none of them look like freshmen. They look years and years older than me.

"Let's drop off your bag," Lili says. "Are you hungry? When do you want to eat?"

"Whenever—"

"Immy, no. Don't do the people-pleasing thing."

"I'm not!"

"You are!"

"Well, I don't mean to!"

"Yeah, I know." She laughs a little, then exhales. "Sorry."

"No, *I'm* sorry—"

"Or not! Let's just not. We're not sorry. We're remorseless. Got it?" She hugs me sideways.

I grin. "Got it."

We've barely taken two steps toward the dorm when a guy sneaks up behind Lili, covering her eyes with his hands. "Guess who!"

Lili doesn't even pause. "Declan, meet—"

"Imogen!" He kisses my cheek. "Finally."

He breaks into a smile, revealing a tiny gap between his front teeth, and for a moment, I'm speechless. I know him from Lili's pictures, of course—this runway model of a boy. He's white, with icy-blond hair and an angular face. Meeting him in person really does feel like a celebrity encounter.

Except for the part where he recognized me, too. I don't know why it didn't occur to me that I might exist to Lili's new friends the same way they exist to me.

Declan grabs my suitcase, brushing off my startled thanks. "Babe, we've been *waiting*. We've heard quite a lot about you."

I glance sideways at Lili. "Oh yeah?"

"I talked some serious shit," she says. "They hate your guts now."

"Not even close." He turns to me, lowering his voice to a stage whisper. "Don't worry, I tune out every time she starts talking—"

Lili shoves him. "Hey, what's the plan for dinner?"

"Funny you should ask! We were just about to head to Winterfield. Hoping to 'beat the rush,' as the young folk say."

"Oh, those young folk. Always beating the rush. What a smoking-hot new slang expression."

Declan laughs, opening his mouth to respond, but he's interrupted by a pair of new arrivals—Mika and Kayla. And it's that same unnerving déjà vu.

I recognize Mika from TikTok, of course. They're Japanese American and nonbinary, styled with their own blend of masculine and feminine aesthetics—soft-glam makeup and hair barrettes, boy-cut jeans, and a bird-printed button-down. I think Lili told me they're from the Minneapolis suburbs. It's still so strange to me that someone in Minnesota would even have upstate New York on their radar. Kayla being from Albany makes a little more sense. She's tall and lanky, with deep brown skin, angular cheekbones, and Sisterlocks pulled into a bun. I know she's an anime geek—Lili said she used to do cosplay. She does a jokey fake gasp when she sees me. "Is this *the* Imogen?"

"Yes. Hi! Kayla, right?" My hand twitches at my side—I don't know if I'm supposed to put it out for a handshake, or what. Is this a hugging situation? Should I go in for the cheek kiss like Declan?

Mika tucks a lock of hair behind their ear and smiles. "Feels like we already know each other."

"You're coming here in the fall, right?" Kayla asks. "Like, officially?"

"Yup! Yeah, I'm excited," I say, nodding really fast—mostly to distract from what Edith calls my Resting Bunny Face: wide-eyed, soft, forever on high alert. I don't think it's as bad as it used to be—now I only really slip into bunny mode when I'm meeting someone new. I can always feel when it's happening, because it's like my mouth unhooks from my brain for a minute. Even if I'm in the middle of talking. It's fun.

I come by it honestly, though, because my dad does it too. He's always been shy, the way I am. My mom loves telling the story of how she thought Dad was a huge film buff for years, since he took her to so many movies when they first started dating. Really, it was just so he wouldn't have to talk. But then Mom got him a vintage popcorn bucket for Christmas, so he had to spend the next few years *pretending* to be into movies, because he didn't want to hurt her feelings. Pure Imogen energy, basically.

But Dad hides it better than I do—either that, or he's better at disappearing to the basement when he needs to. Still, I can always tell when his brain goes offline. It's sort of tucked into the pauses when he talks.

"I think it's going to be amazing," my mouth adds. "I know how much Lili loves it here."

I play it back in my head—okay, good. I sound mostly normal. *Amazing. Lili loves it.* Just some basic Imogenericisms.

"Okay, I love that?" says Kayla. "The *maturity*. Love to see it."

Lili rubs her forehead. "Ha. Okay, so. I don't want to hold you guys up. We still need to drop this bag off, but we can meet you at dinner. Is Tessa coming?"

"Haven't heard from her yet. Probably still with the himbos," says Declan.

"I'll poke my head in just in case." Lili turns to me. "Her room's right next to ours. Actually, you share a wall with her."

The way Lili talks about it, you'd think I was moving in permanently.

What's weird is realizing she's not entirely wrong.

Texts with Gretchen

IS: Awwww, thanks

IS: I'm good though, seriously

IS: Everyone's really nice!!

IS: Gretch it's so beautiful here

GP: Good!!!! Just got back

GP: Wait

GP: Did you meet Mika 🤩

IS: Yes 😊

GP: gsfdgjhsjfj;lk;k';

GP: Tell them I say hiiiiiiiii

GP: WAIT

GP: don't do that

GP: Play it cool

IS: I'll try haha

IS: I think we're meeting them for dinner later

GP: SHUT UP

GP: IMOGEN YOU'RE HANGING OUT WITH MIKA
        HIYASHI

GP: okay okay we're cool, we're chill

GP: I mean, what are they like in person?!!!! Tell me
        EVERYTHING

3

The halls of Lili's dorm are narrow, with white cinder-block walls, tightly looped gray carpets, and the same rectangular flourescent light fixtures we have at school. But there are homey touches, too—the word *hello* spelled out in washi-tape block letters, taped event flyers, and a giant white sheet of paper tacked up near the bathroom, half-covered with doodles and handwritten quotes. Right away, I spot one attributed to Lili, written with purple marker in someone else's handwriting: *To be or not to be; that is the chest hair.*

I wouldn't call it a gut punch—more like a tiny, sharp poke beneath my rib cage. Other people's inside jokes always hit me like that, but I can never quite pin down the feeling. A variation on loneliness, maybe.

"Okay, brace yourself," Lili says, pulling out her room key. "My room is basically a closet."

There's a dry-erase white board stuck to Lili's door, featuring a chibi-style drawing of two cats with their tails looped into a heart. Taped above it are a pair of cloud-shaped construction-paper signs, just like the ones I've seen on most of the doors we passed.

WELCOME, EMILIA
WELCOME, SYDNEY

I let out a laugh as soon as Lili opens the door. "So when you said it's the size of a closet, you meant Kylie Jenner's closet."

"Okay, it's small for a double!"

"How often does Sydney stay here again?"

She makes a face at me, parking my suitcase next to one of the beds. There are two of them, flush against perpendicular walls, both made with quilts and sheets I recognize from home—Lili's home. Her favorite rainbow-haired unicorn, Puppy, is tucked under the covers of one of them.

I guess it's a *little* on the cozy side—less because the room itself is small, and more because the furniture comes in pairs. Two desks, two dressers, two wardrobes, two short wooden bookshelves. But it's all so covered in Lili's familiar clutter, I feel instantly at home. There's an assortment of Pop-Tarts and granola bar boxes on top of one of the dressers, intermingling with ceramic horse figurines and month-old birthday cards. Her bookshelves are pure chaos—Homer, Virgil, Euripides, and Aristophanes, alongside Madeline Miller, Roxane Gay, and a memoir by someone who used to be on *The Bachelor*. And of course, Lili's postcard collection is on full display, sticky-blobbed to the walls in random clusters. Niagara Falls next to the printed cover of Issue 1 of *Check, Please!* "Tracy Mitrano for

Congress" next to "Bem-vindo a São Paulo."

But above both beds, it's just photos—rows of prints, sloping subtly downward because Lili's never met a straight line in her life. The ones above my bed are mostly from this year—group selfies and sunny snapshots of her friends in various combinations. But the ones above Lili's bed are from home.

I cross her room for a closer look, smiling at the lineup: my family's barn at sunset, Penn Yan's Main Street, a double rainbow over Keuka Lake. Small-town New York state in tiny four-by-six glimpses. And mixed throughout: family portraits, childhood pictures. Naturally, there are at least a dozen pictures of Mel, plus the one from my tenth birthday where Lili's *dressed* as Mel. I'm standing beside her in that one, dressed as my cat Quincy, and we're both wearing glow necklaces and holding up our overstuffed trick-or-treat pillowcases. There's one of Lili and Otávio, ages seven and five, beaming, in matching white Corinthians soccer jerseys—and beside it, taken almost a decade later, Lili literally crying while getting a book signed by Casey McQuiston. She's even got the photo her mom insisted on snapping two summers ago, the year we scooped ice cream at Seneca Farms. Lili was at the height of her moody black eyeliner phase, glaring over the counter. I'm posed dutifully beside her with a metal scoop and a how-can-I-help-you smile.

But my favorite picture of us is the one from last summer's Pride, a week after Lili came out. She's wrapped in a pink, yellow, and turquoise flag, and I'm leaning against her, elbow propped on her shoulder. Edith took the picture, and she must have said something funny right beforehand, because we're clearly both howling with laughter.

"I love everything about this," I say, settling onto Lili's bed.

"Ha—thanks." Lili plops down beside me. Then she stares straight ahead for a moment without speaking. "Okay, we gotta talk," she says finally.

My heart flips. "Oh—"

"Nothing bad! I mean, not, like, catastrophic? I don't know." I nod slowly, and she looks at me. "So. My friends—"

"Seem great! Seriously. They're so nice."

"Yeah, no, definitely, but that's . . ." She trails off, scooping her dark hair off her neck—twisting it up, letting it fall. "I know that was a little weird out there—not because of you," she adds. "Imogen, no. If you apologize right now, I will actually kill you."

I press a muffling hand over my mouth, and she laughs.

But then she sighs. "So here's the thing. My friends here are so *queer*."

"So are you." I pause, furrowing my brow. "Oh, God—do they think—I don't want anyone to feel unsafe, or—"

"Immy, come on—no one thinks you're a queerphobe." She shakes her head at me, smiling. "And yes, I know I'm queer. I'm valid. All of that. I guess it's just me seeing the way—I don't know. They have their shit together, you know?"

"Okay—"

"Like Kayla?" she adds. "She came out in middle school. She took a girl to the eighth-grade dance and kissed her on the

26

dance floor. Right in the school gym."

"Whoa, nice!" I say, cringing before the words have even left my lips. My voice always pitches higher when people talk about girls kissing—which makes literally no sense, seeing as I'm surrounded by queer people 24/7. I know Gretchen finds it annoying sometimes. Though other times, she says it's adorable, and that I'm an innocent bean with Mommy's-first-day-at-PFLAG energy. But that just makes me even more self-conscious.

Maybe the awkwardness is just one of those small-town things you have to shake off and unlearn. Apart from Pride Alliance meetings, it's not like Penn Yan is some sort of queer haven. I can't even fathom two girls kissing on the dance floor of my middle-school gym. The image doesn't compute. I know there were one or two gay couples in my grade back then, but it was kind of a quieter thing. Not a secret, but definitely not front and center.

And everyone in Pride Alliance talks about how hard it is to date people from our school. Gretchen says it's because everyone knows everyone in Penn Yan. And you can't exactly hold hands with a girl in the cafeteria when your teachers are friends with your homophobic parents. Hypothetically speaking, that is, since Mama Patterson isn't homophobic, and neither are my parents or Lili's. But I guess homophobia managed to leak into the atmosphere somehow. Even Edith, who's basically never *not* been out, hadn't dated anyone before Zora.

I really wish I could be more casual about this stuff.

"So that's Kayla," says Lili. "Tessa and Mika both had girlfriends in high school. Actually, middle school too, for Mika—they were with their ex for, like, five years. And Dec's from Manhattan, so who even knows? He's on a whole other level. It's hard not to feel inadequate, you know?"

"Because you haven't dated anyone?"

Lili and I used to joke about that a lot. We were the Forever Alone Club. No boyfriends. No random hookups. Just a pair of perpetually single besties who spent way more time hanging around animals than boys.

It's not that I didn't want a boyfriend. I did. I *do*. I fall in and out of crushes all the time. It's just not something I talk about much—I don't even get into the specifics with Gretchen and Lili. Crushes have always felt viscerally private to me. I know that's weird. It's definitely sort of lonely. But I don't think being single ever made me feel inadequate.

"It's not that." Lili frowns. "Not exactly? I just feel like such a baby queer sometimes. I'd only been out for three months when I got here."

"They shouldn't judge you for that."

"They didn't." Lili pauses. "I kind of told them I came out in high school."

I feel so out of my depth. "Do people really care when you came out?"

"I mean, my friends don't." Lili covers her face with both hands. "I don't know, I was being a dumbass, and—okay." She gives a short, muffled moan before pulling her hands away. "I have to tell you something."

Suddenly, it's summer again—that Sunday evening in June. Lili had been roped into stopping by this girl Brianna's graduation party, which was exactly as boring and awkward as we'd expected. So we left early. She drove me home. I remember it was raining, just barely, and I was a little hypnotized by the droplets streaking down the passenger window. And then Lili stopped at a red light on Main Street and said my name out of nowhere.

"So I think—I'm probably pan. Like pansexual?"

She was staring straight ahead when she said it, didn't even miss a beat when the light turned green. But she was biting her lip just like she is now, and I almost wonder—

"Um." She laughs nervously, and I'm jolted straight back. Lili's dorm room. Something she needs to tell me. "Promise you won't hate me," she says.

I laugh. "I promise I won't hate you."

"Uh. You might." She blinks, presses her lips together, then starts talking really quickly. "Okay, it was orientation week. Everyone's hanging out in my room, and I guess somehow the topic of dating came up. So I was sitting there, just—not saying anything, feeling like such an imposter—"

"You're not—"

"I know! I know it's ridiculous. Not even sure what was in my head at that point, but I just wanted to be more—legit, I guess? So I was like, 'Yeah, totally, I totally had a girlfriend,' except—Immy, I was *not* selling it. Like, at all."

"You don't need to sell anything! You're already completely legit."

"I was being a dumbass, remember? So, at the same time, I'm just panicking, because clearly, they were going to see right through me, and it's like, *cool, cool.* Everyone's gonna think I'm a straight girl faking the whole thing, right?"

"You're—did they?"

"Not at all! Like, they didn't even question it! They were just like, 'Oh, nice, how did you two meet?' So of course now I'm scrambling a little—like, well fucking done, Emilia, have fun making up a fake ex-girlfriend on the spot." She shuts her eyes briefly. "But then Tessa—she was sitting right where you are, and all of a sudden, she's like, 'Oh, is this her?' And she points to this picture." Lili scoots sideways, tapping the edge of one photo.

It's the one where we're laughing, from Pride.

"Oh!" I blush. "She thought—"

"Yeah."

"I mean, it's funny," I say.

"I told her you were," she says softly.

I laugh a little. "That I'm . . . your girlfriend?"

The word feels weird on my tongue, almost alien.

"Ex-girlfriend. We amicably broke up last summer. I'm so sorry. Ugh. It's so shitty and creepy, I know."

I blink. "No! No, it's—"

"It just—it seemed like such an easy answer at the time. Which is no excuse. I just didn't think it through. Any of it." She lets out a panicked laugh. "Like the fact that my quote-unquote 'ex-girlfriend Imogen' is a real person they'd be meeting one day."

I try to wrap my head around it. "So they know I'm me. They just think we dated?"

Lili presses both hands to her cheeks. "We got together on

31

New Year's, broke up in July, but that's it. You're you, we're best friends, we grew up together, all of it. Everything else is true. Oh—but you're queer. They think you're bi." She winces a little. "Sorry."

"No, it makes sense. Of course I am. Would be. If we dated. Obviously." I nod, really fast.

"Okay, you're being *too* cool about this. Immy, I lied! I erased your identity."

"My straight identity? I don't think that's a thing."

"Stop saying what you think I want to hear! You're allowed to feel a certain way about this."

"But it's not a big deal."

"The fact that all my friends think you're queer? And that we dated? You're cool with that?"

"I mean, why wouldn't I be?"

Lili shakes her head. "How are you not freaked out? Like, you have to be wondering if I'm secretly in love with you, right?"

"What? No—Lili—I didn't—"

"I promise I'm not. I'm just saying, you have a right to be kind of unsettled by this. I don't even mind if you blow my cover. I mean, I *mind*. But if you want to set the record straight, we totally can. I get it."

I open my mouth and shut it, head still spinning. I'm a little stuck on the part where Lili thinks *I* think she's in love with me.

Which she's not. And I don't.

But the fact that she thinks I'm wondering that? Like I'm that special kind of straight person who assumes all queer people can barely keep their pants on around her?

I mean, admittedly, I do wonder sometimes what queer girls think of me. But it's just the occasional fleeting thought. Definitely not a you-love-me kind of thing.

Not that I'd mind if a queer girl was into me. I'd honestly find it super flattering.

I hug Puppy the unicorn close to my chest. "So it's just . . . I'm bisexual? And we used to date, but we're friends now. And other than that—"

"Just that. Everything else is real, I promise. No fake dates or memories or anything. Just stuff we actually did. Like the ice-cream crawl and all the barn stuff and when we took Mel and Eloise to Watkins Glen. I didn't change any of that. They just probably think we went home and made out afterward. But we don't have to talk about that part," she adds quickly. "I really don't want to make you uncomfortable—"

There's a knock. Lili looks at me.

"I'm not uncomfortable. Seriously."

"Okay, well. I fucking owe you one," she murmurs, before calling out, "Come in!"

The door opens, and a girl in a bathrobe walks in—white, with short, shower-damp, dark hair, holding a plastic toiletry bucket. Obviously Tessa—though her hair was longer in most of Lili's pictures. There's something unforgettably open about her face—her big brown Winona Ryder eyes, her Clea DuVall freckles.

"Hey, are we meeting everyone at Winterfield? I can be

33

ready in five. I just—" She stops short. "Oh my God—Imogen, hi! I'm Tessa. Sorry—I usually wear clothes."

"Hi! Yup. Imogen," I say. "I wear clothes, too."

She does this quick, bubbling laugh—like a low-pitched giggle, really—and her smile reminds me of getting your braces off. Not that I've ever seen Tessa with braces. No idea if she even had them. I just mean there's an element of surprise to her smile. A little flash of *oh wait*.

Then she runs a hand through her hair, and there's something so boyish about the gesture, it leaves me a little off-balance.

"I feel so underdressed next to you," Lili says, stepping into the stairwell.

I peek down at my skirt. "Do you think I should—"

"No, you look perfect. I'm the one who looks like a zombie camp counselor." She pauses mid-staircase to pull the backs of her sneakers over her heels. "Hey. You sure you're okay with everything?"

"You mean the ex-girlfriend thing?"

"I just don't want you to feel like you can't be yourself, you know?" She glances back over her shoulder. "Almost there—one more floor."

We reach the bottom, and Lili leads me into a hallway that looks just like hers—cinder-block walls and wooden doors, some propped open, bursting with laughter or music or video game noises. Everything smells like a movie theater.

"Popcorn dinner. What a lifestyle," says Lili.

Tessa steps out of the elevator as soon as we pass it. "Fancy meeting you here."

Lili arches her brows. "Too good for the stairs?"

"The himbos wore me out." Tessa's gaze flicks to me, cheeks going red. "Not. You know. Sexually. I'm not—I'm a lesbian. Who can't stop talking. Apparently." She swipes at her bangs, nudging them sideways. Now that her hair's a little drier, it's settled into the sort of perfectly disheveled tomboy bob I could never pull off in a million years. Not quite chin-length. I've always loved hair like that, though, especially when it wings out at the ends a bit, like Tessa's does. I mean, if I were really bi, I bet I'd fall for her based on hair alone.

"Okay, Declan says he's now a—direct quote—'gaping wound of hunger.'" Lili looks up from her phone. "Bro, you are *literally* in a dining hall surrounded by food. Does he think he's not allowed to eat until we get there?"

"We better go save him." Tessa bumps her own fisted hands together. "Imogen, are you ready to experience culinary perfection?"

"Oh," Lili says. "This is not that."

5

We set off down one of the paths that loops behind the dorms, and Tessa fills us in on her game of capture the flag. With the so-called himbos, who wore her out, but not sexually. "So the flag's supposed to be visible," she says, "but since Callum literally can't go five seconds without cheating—"

"Callum's her brother's friend," Lili explains.

"Yeah, Cal's, like, the king of the himbos. Or he thinks he is. He's an asshole, though. Like, his entire personality is just . . . anus."

"I didn't even know himbos had a monarchy," I say.

Lili and Tessa both burst out laughing, and I have to bow my head so I don't look too blatantly pleased with myself.

My stomach feels like the first day of school. Butterflies and panic. Tessa's pivoted to talking about how someone named Dan may or may not have a secret girlfriend, but I keep losing the plot. Because secrets and girlfriends are pretty much my whole entire problem right now—a problem that's looming

36

larger and larger the closer we get to the dining hall.

It just feels like such a minefield all of a sudden. One wrong detail, and the whole story crumbles. I don't think Lili even gets how precarious this is. Sure, I can trot out a few greatest hits from our friendship, but what if someone asks about our first date? Our first kiss? There's no truth there for me to lean on. What if my version of the story doesn't line up with whatever she's already told them?

Also, what if I'm not believable as a queer girl?

Because that's the thing. I'm not just straight—I'm hopelessly, blindingly, *obviously* straight. Gretchen says queer people have a sense for this kind of thing, a sort of unspoken recognition. It's just something you know in your gut.

"Like gaydar?" I'd asked, which made her laugh.

"Kind of? It's like—you can just tell. I think it's evolutionary. It's a safety mechanism, right? You're like, okay, this person's probably not going to hate-crime me."

I got this twinge in my chest when she said that. Queerness recognizing queerness. It's kind of beautiful when you think about it.

I really do wish it was mine sometimes.

I remember the first Tuesday of ninth grade, my first ever Pride Alliance meeting. Gretchen made us get there ten minutes before the meeting even started—which meant ten minutes spent hovering near the door of Ms. Dugan's classroom like we were on a stakeout mission. Gretchen was so excited, she was practically slaphappy, but I was getting more and more nervous by the minute.

I couldn't shake the feeling that the group would kick me out on sight. I kept picturing the conversation grinding to a halt the minute I stepped into the room. There'd be a few moments of chilly silence. "Can we . . . help you?" someone would finally ask.

Of course, that first meeting ended up being so totally chill, I couldn't believe I was worried in the first place. The group was smaller than I'd expected—not sure why I'd basically pictured the NYC Pride march in the middle of Penn Yan High School, but there were just about a dozen people there that day. Gretchen and I were the only freshmen, but even that was kind of a cool dynamic. Like being the beloved youngest cousins at a family reunion. Everyone seemed sincerely happy to have us there. And when I got tongue-tied in the welcome circle, no one rushed me—which made it easier to push through the shyness.

"I'm Imogen. She/her," I'd said. "And I have a queer sister."

6

The dining hall's so much bigger than I expected. Definitely bigger than my school's cafeteria and probably twice as loud, even though only about half the tables are full. With its domed, windowed ceiling, it looks like a giant circular greenhouse.

Lili and Tessa lead me to a partitioned-off serving area near the back windows, with all these little counters and food stations to pick from. There's a grill called the Burger Joint, in between a sandwich counter and a vegetarian stir-fry station. There's a pizza corner with gluten-free *and* vegan options, and I haven't even looked at the salad and pasta bars yet. I can hardly wrap my mind around the array of choices.

Tessa takes one look at my face and laughs. "Yeah, it's a lot. But I've got you." She grips her tray with one hand, patting my arm with the other. "Let's narrow it down. What's your stance on pizza?"

"Deeply pro."

"Hey." Lili nudges me with the edge of her tray. "Buttery

grilled cheese at two o'clock."

"Ooh, paintbrush?" asks Tessa.

"Paintbrush."

Which turns out to be a grilled-cheese technique involving a pastry brush and a giant bowl of melted butter. "It's joy in food form," Lili says. "Better than chocolate. Better than puppies."

"You shouldn't eat puppies," I say.

We finish loading our trays and head to the registers, where Lili pays for everything with a swipe of her student ID card. Tessa's right behind us—we pause at the edge of the dining space to wait for her.

"You ready?" Lili's voice is perfectly casual. But there's something sewn into the folds of the question. *It's showtime, Imogen. Lights, camera, action.*

By the time we settle in at the table, Declan, Kayla, and Mika are almost entirely done eating. But no one seems to be in any hurry to leave. Lili slides in next to Declan. "All good on the gaping-wound front?"

Kayla raises her eyebrows. "Do I want to know?"

"Fully healed, thank you," Declan says, patting his stomach and yawning. "Also, you literally just missed security escorting two Chi Phi bros out the back."

"Um, you're really going to bury the lede like that? Tell them why they were escorted out." Kayla shakes her head. "These dudes were *on a table* performing a striptease—"

40

"Half a striptease," says Declan.

Mika leans in. "They're both missing the point. The striptease was just misdirection. They're up there baiting the security officers, and meanwhile, their accomplices are strolling out of here with a vat of ice cream. And you know who it was?" They turn to Lili. "The sex carnival guy."

Lili gasps. "It was *not*."

"No joke."

"Who's the sex carnival guy?" I ask, and everyone laughs. Which makes my cheeks go warm, even though I know—I *know* they're not laughing at me. But I feel so out of the loop. Two steps behind. Like I'm visiting another country and I only know half the language.

"Yeahhhhhh," Lili says, pressing the heel of her hand to her forehead. She turns to me. "Did I ever tell you about Sydney's party?"

"Sydney, your roommate?"

She nods. "Yup. So this was, like, October, I think? Sometime in the fall—Sydney was still there, obviously. And I was out somewhere that night—"

"It was the Halloween party!" Kayla interjects.

The Halloween party. My heart tugs sharply at the memory. Waking up to pictures of Lili and her friends grinning in their coordinated costumes, piled onto someone's extra-long twin bed. I'd gone to a house party with Gretchen, but it was boring and weird, and no one understood our costumes. We were home and in pajamas by ten.

"Right, right," Lili says. "So it's—I don't know—two in the morning. I'm just getting home—Tess is there, too. And it turns out, in our absence, Sydney's decided to have an orgy."

I feel my eyes go wide. "Oh—"

Lili pats my shoulder. "Not a literal orgy. But yeah, my room looks like a bomb went off. The whole place reeks of beer. Sydney's *nowhere*. Meanwhile, you could hear people throwing up in the bathroom. The retching noises." She shudders. "And I'm here totally sober, totally speechless. Tess is standing there with her jaw on the floor—"

"It's true." Tessa nods solemnly.

"And then I realize"—Lili claps her hands together—"there's a pair of total strangers hooking up in my bed."

"Oh no . . ."

Lili hangs her head. "Right in front of Puppy."

"Okay, tell her the next part," says Kayla, eyes dancing.

Lili mutters something under her breath.

"What was that, babe?"

Lili sighs. "I said, 'The sex carnival is over.'"

"Said?" Tessa bites back a smile. "I think it was more of a bellow."

"And then I washed my sheets eight times."

"And the world gained an iconic new concept," Kayla concludes. "Sex carnival."

Lili grimaces. "What a legacy."

"Well, that and Jean-Claude," I point out.

Lili buries her face, but I can tell that she's smiling.

Kayla waggles her eyebrows. "Uh-oh. Who's Jean-Claude?"

"Her fake Twitter persona. Jean-Claude LePoisson, age twenty-four, he/him. Spoke only Google-Translated French."

"A certified sexy bichon," Lili adds.

"*Was* he sexy?" I ask, "or was he just holding five baguettes?"

Declan props his phone between two trays. "We have a bio. I repeat, we have a bio." He clears his throat. "Je suis Jean-Claude et j'habite en France. Very convincing. Especially with the geotag underneath for Rochester, New York."

"Also fake! Just less fake. Jean-Claude forgot to change the location when he stole the account."

"So, to be clear—your French catfish persona is an account thief," says Mika.

"Yup! He stole the handle from a twenty-nine-year-old lesbian in Rochester named Melissa. Who was also me." Lili taps her chest. "Age eleven. No idea I was queer."

"A repressed queen!" Kayla grins. "See, this is incredible. Now we know who to call for dirt on Lili."

"I have dirt," I confirm.

Lili holds up her middle finger and kisses its tip. Tessa turns to me, grinning. "Yeah, we're keeping you."

I grin back, feeling almost heady with my own lack of restraint. I'm never this unlocked around new people. But maybe college is really that different from everything that came before it. Maybe I'll make this place mine.

I can actually picture it. Me, a year from now, fully absorbed into this group. By then, we'd have our own language—layers of inside jokes and references, incomprehensible to everyone but us. Entire conversations tucked into the quickest exchanged glances.

I think about Lili, and how her face lights up every time she talks about Blackwell. It's like she's fallen in love with this whole entire place.

So maybe I'll fall in love with it, too.

The sun's just starting to set as we make our way back to the dorms—the group's disbanding, but only temporarily. We're meeting in about an hour for a trivia night in the student center.

"It's super chill," Lili assures me.

"The most chill," Tessa adds. "And you can win money."

"Except we don't, because we're really bad," Lili says.

"Okay, but hear me out." Tessa points at her. "I think tonight's our night."

Lili smiles a little. "Oh yeah?"

"I'm just saying. We've got Imogen now."

I let out a startled laugh. "What?"

"True." Lili grins.

"*And* Jean-Claude," Tessa adds. "He'll definitely come through on all the French questions."

"There has never, ever been a French question."

"We just have to be strategic! Play to our strengths." Tessa pokes my arm, and my heart does the quickest half flip. "What's your area of expertise?"

We reach the dorm, and Lili swipes her keycard to open the door.

"Um." I pause. "Overthinking?"

"Ooh, nice. Yup. Always need one of those on the team," Tessa says.

"She's being modest," Lili says, glancing back at me. "Immy, you're a literal award-winning chef. You're just not going to mention that?"

Tessa stops short. "You're an *award-winning chef*?"

"Yeah . . . I don't want to brag, but"—I bite back a smile—"I kind of swept the ten-and-under category in the Li'l Cookies Library Fundraiser Bake-Off."

"Yeah you did." Tessa high-fives me.

"Best Rice Krispie Treat of my life," Lili says.

"Thanks! It's the recipe from the back of the Rice Krispies box."

"Still counts!" Lili presses the elevator call button. "And— let's see. She makes the absolute best vision boards."

"Like at the eye doctor?" Tessa tilts her head. "Read this line of letters and numbers? Which way is the E pointing?"

I laugh. "No. It's like a visual aesthetic collage, kind of?"

"Wait, let me pull up my Notes app and write these down," Tessa says, tugging her phone from her pocket. "Okay, Imogen's . . . areas . . . of expertise. Rice Krispie Treat making, vision boards—"

"And typing with a cat in her lap," Lili adds as we step inside the elevator. "She's great at that. Oh, and emoji precision."

"What?" I smile.

"Like, you're really good at finding the exact right emoji."

"Thank you?"

"Most people get lazy about it. But not you." Lili presses the third-floor button, turning back to Tessa. "Ooh, put down that she's good at looking like she's not paying attention when she's actually paying *perfect* attention. Like, it's actually kind of creepy."

I nod. "These all sound like very normal trivia categories."

"Yeah, we've got it in the bag," Tessa says, tapping her toe against mine with a grin.

7

Lili shuts the door, plopping beside me on the edge of my bed. "How are you holding up? This is a lot, I know—"

"No, it's great! I'm good."

She stares me down.

I laugh. "Really!"

"You're not overwhelmed?"

"Why would I be overwhelmed?"

"Um. I don't know." Lili leans back on her palms. "Being here? Meeting everyone? Having to play along with my big dumbass lie—"

"But it was fine! It wasn't even a thing."

I mean, it's just backstory, right? The past is *always* just backstory.

I think about that sometimes—how the only way to let someone into your reality is to retell it. Even true things come out filtered, imperfect, and muddled. So what's the harm in Lili taking it a step or two further?

"Okay, but it's stressful! And Immy, I know you! I know your little hamster-wheel brain was already freaking out about whether my friends were going to like you—which, for the record, Kayla's already texted me to say you're awesome, and Mika said you're—and I quote—'transcendently sweet.'"

My cheeks go warm. "That's so nice—"

"And don't even get me started on little miss flirty-pants Tessa—"

"She's—what?" I look up with a start.

"Oh, don't worry! It's Tessa. She does that."

"No! Yeah, no—I wasn't worried." I pause. "Did I seem worried?"

"Not at all. I'm just saying—"

"Because it wouldn't bother me. You know? Like, I'm not freaked out by it."

"By Tessa being a flirt?" Lili looks slightly bewildered.

I blush. "By, you know. Girls in general. Sorry." I cover my face with both hands. "I'm acting really straight right now, huh?"

Lili laughs. "What?"

"I just don't want to make anyone uncomfortable. And I don't want to blow your cover." I peek through my fingers. "I know I'm not the most believable queer girl."

"That's—sorry, but *what*? Immy, I don't even know what that means. 'Believable queer girl?'" Lili blinks. "What makes a queer girl believable?"

"I don't know," I say softly.

The truth is, I've never quite been able to pin it down. The way queerness announces itself. And how it seems so intuitive for people. How people just seem to *know*.

I mean, there's Gretchen's whole unspoken-recognition gaydar thing. But it's more than that. There's a certain aesthetic to queer girlhood. Or maybe it's several aesthetics, but I don't fit any of them. I don't have Tessa's tomboy energy or Gretchen's pink hair, or a jean jacket like the one Edith wears every day. Even Lili, in her ringer T-shirt and gym shorts, looks potentially queer. Like she *could* be queer.

I wouldn't even know where to begin. Bulk order of enamel pins? Some kind of hair transformation? I've never dyed my hair, and it's never been shorter than shoulder-length. And I probably wear dresses and skirts more than pants. I'm pretty sure there were a few years in elementary school where I *only* wore dresses. All my socks had to have either lace or ruffles.

I'm not explaining this well.

I try to put it into words, and it just sounds like a list of surface details and stereotypes. I bet I'd be laughed off campus if I said any of this out loud. Or canceled. Probably both. But there's got to be some kernel of truth buried in there, right? There have to be some sort of visible markers of queerness. Otherwise, how could so many people know at a glance that I'm straight?

Maybe it comes down to vibes. Or that particular sort of awkwardness straight girls sometimes get around queer girls. Gretchen called me out for that over the summer.

The entire conversation is burned into my brain, beat by beat.

We were cross-legged on the floor of her bedroom, analyzing a bunch of DMs and texts she'd gotten from this girl named Ella. They'd met a few weeks earlier at one of those summer STEM enrichment programs. Gretchen couldn't decide if the texts were flirtatious, and she kept talking herself in circles about it. And since I don't have a clue what flirting looks like, I was basically just nodding along.

Until Gretchen stopped mid-sentence. "Hey, can you try not to do that?"

When I looked up from her phone, she was blinking back tears. She wiped her eyes with the heels of her hands.

"I—I'm not sure what I should stop doing," I'd stammered.

"You seriously don't see it."

I shook my head.

"Well, just so you know, it's been pretty hard to talk with you about girls I like. And I've been feeling that way for a while now."

I remember it felt like my lungs had stopped working. "About—girls?"

"You're, like, palpably uncomfortable! You don't even make eye contact when I talk about Ella. And it's *every time*. Whereas with Caden—anytime it's a guy, you're all in." She lets out a breath. "And I get it. I get that you can relate more when it's a guy. But my crushes on girls are real too! And they're important to me! And yeah, it's funny that you get so flustered about it, but it also kind of makes me not want to share them."

Her voice cracked a little when she said that, and I sat there, half-frozen, half-frantic. I cast my thoughts back to all the other times Gretchen had talked about Ella, about Caden, about anyone. *Had* I felt uncomfortable?

I didn't think so—but then again, would I even have realized it if I was? Unconscious queerphobia does exist, after all.

I was so flooded with guilt and shame, I could barely wrangle the words. "Gretch, I'm so sorry. I don't even know what to say."

"It's fine. You didn't know," she'd said. "I appreciate you apologizing, though."

"I can't believe I made you feel like that."

"Yeah . . . it's kind of one of those things. Like, we live in a queerphobic society, you know? It's almost impossible not to internalize at least some of that. But it's good, because once you're aware of your biases, you can actually start to work on them," she'd said. "And I'm always happy to help with that stuff. Always."

Texts with Gretchen

IS: Okay so

IS: Just got back from dinner, heading to trivia in a sec

IS: But M is totally cool; and down-to-earth, zero influencer vibes

GP: AHHHH that's so great

IS: They're pretty quiet in person! Like waaaay more introverted than they are online

IS: You know how there's always that one person in the group who doesn't talk a lot, but they're always super engaged

IS: Like they're clearly taking EVERYTHING in?

GP: Uh, Immybean, that's you 😂

GP: you're the Mika of pride alliance!!!

IS: HAHAHAHA

IS: Wow

IS: That is extremely flattering

IS: So like the thing about Mika is they're completely not awkward

IS: Quiet but not awkward

GP: The rarest combination!!!!

GP: Ahhh this makes me so happy

GP: Look at you, all grown up

GP: Your first night out on campus!!!

8

My first night out on campus.

I know it's just trivia, not an orgy. Not even orgy-adjacent. But there's no stopping the rush of butterflies in my stomach as I follow Lili and Tessa up the central staircase of the student center. There's a lounge area tucked into one of the back corners of the space—bland and functional, like a waiting room, or one of those seating areas at the mall. Other than a few square tables in the center, it's mostly just chairs and couches arranged into clusters.

"So, there are usually, like, five teams," Lili says. "Three or four people per. We're always the biggest group."

I spot Declan and Kayla in a pair of blue-gray armchairs on either end of a short, rectangular table. In between them, Mika's perched on the edge of a couch, leaning forward to write on a white board. Just enough room for Lili, me, and Tessa to scoot in beside them.

A moment later, a Black girl in a beanie steps into the center of the space, trailed by a white girl holding a miniature dry-erase board. "Hello, hello! Where are my trivia fiends?"

A loud *woooooo* erupts from a trio of girls in bodycon dresses and heels.

"All right! Let's do this. For those who don't know me, I'm Sasha, and this is Erin." Sasha pauses, peering around the space. "Okay, cool, lots of familiar faces, a couple new people. Let's run through the rules really quickly. So, we've got twelve questions. Erin's going to read each one out loud, and then we'll start the clocks. You've got three minutes to confer with your group and write your answer on the white board."

Erin holds up her white board, beaming like a TV presenter.

"When time's up, drop your markers, and we'll see what you've got. One point for every right answer—wrong or incomplete answers get nada. No partial credit. Um. And then there's the wild card round at the end, where you can wager your points. The team with the highest point total at the end gets the jackpot."

Erin rubs her thumb and forefinger together and mouths the word *ooh*.

Sasha continues. "And I know you wouldn't dream of it, but just a reminder! No googling, no texting your space-engineer auntie or whatever. Honor system, okay?" She gives an exaggerated thumbs-up. "Okay! Let's lock in those team names."

Mika holds up the dry-erase board, displaying the words *l'equipe: Jean-Claude LePoisson* in elegant cursive.

Lili does finger guns. "Funny."

Minutes later, Sasha claps a few times to get everyone's attention. "Okay! Diving in. Erin, take it away!"

Erin glances down at her paper. "All right! Question number one! What is the body's largest organ?"

Skin. I think?

Mika's already uncapping the dry-erase marker.

"Skin. Definitely," says Lili.

"Definitely," agrees Kayla.

"Markers down, boards up!" Sasha declares. "And the answer we're looking for is . . . skin!"

I shoot Lili a grin. "Aren't we supposed to be bad at this?"

"Oh, they'll get harder."

"Okay, let's see . . ." Erin scans her page of questions. "The 1999 film *10 Things I Hate About You* was inspired by which Shakespeare play?"

The Taming of the Shrew, I think.

"*Much Ado About Nothing*?" says Kayla.

I stop short, all my certainty gone in an instant.

Could it be *Much Ado*? Did *Taming* just burrow its way into my head somehow?

Maybe I've been wrong about this for *years*.

Although.

It kind of has to be *Taming*, right? The plot tracks pretty closely—even the character names line up. Does that mean Kayla's wrong?

I rub my cheek, feeling weirdly unsettled.

Gretchen told me about this experiment once, where a psychologist asked groups of people to compare the lengths of different lines. Solomon Asch—that was the psychologist's name. I love when the syllables of someone's name match with mine.

Asch was studying conformity, but he was sneaky about it. He'd always put one clueless subject in a group of people who were secretly in on the plan. Then, sometimes the undercover people would all say the same wrong answer on purpose—just to see if the real test subject would go along with it.

"Most of the time, they did," Gretchen had told me. "Even when the right answer was completely obvious. But these people actually convinced themselves they were wrong. They overruled their own visual perception."

Gretchen had been dumbfounded by this, but to me, it made sense.

Perfect sense. Too much sense.

It's definitely *The Taming of the Shrew*, right? One hundred percent. So.

I draw in a deep breath and say it.

Kayla smacks her forehead. "Yes! Thank you. No, you're totally right."

"Two for two!" Tessa high-fives me. "What did I tell you? Tonight's our night."

And by the time we hit the halfway point, I'm starting to think she may be right. We haven't missed a single question yet.

Erin clears her throat. "Next up! What animal is featured on California's state flag?"

"Oh, come on. State flags?" Declan says.

"Not California!" Tessa shakes her head. "Look at us. A Philadelphian, a Minnesotan, a New York City kid, and three upstate New Yorkers."

"I literally don't know what my own state flag looks like," says Mika.

I pause. "Is it a bear?"

"Oh?" Declan asks.

"I don't know! It might not be—"

But I'm right. And then the next question's practically made for me. "What actress starred alongside Noah Centineo and Madelaine Petsch in the 2020 Netflix romantic comedy *Shop Talk*?"

"Kara Clapstone," I say.

Lili grins. "Your sister would actually disown both of us if we missed this one."

She's not even joking—*Shop Talk* has basically been Edith's religion since the trailer dropped. Even though Gretchen says it's assimilative, unrealistic garbage made for straight people. Not just Gretchen, I guess—lots of people online seem to feel the same way about it, especially because Kara Clapstone is straight in real life. But Edith doesn't care about the *Shop Talk* discourse—I'm not sure she even knows about it. She doesn't seek that stuff out the way I do.

Like the first time I watched *But I'm a Cheerleader*. Before I'd even left Lili's house, I was already scouring the internet for other people's reactions. But that just made me more confused.

Every think piece felt like the definitive final word—and then I'd be fully convinced by the exact opposite points in the next one. I was a human sailboat, blown in every direction by a storm of decades-old media discourse.

Am I allowed to love this? That was always the question.

When Sasha confirms our answer, the whole group lets out a cheer and high-fives me.

"Killing it!" Lili says.

"Wait." Kayla's hands fly to her mouth. "Lex Appeal missed that one. Are we actually—"

"Next question," says Erin. "What singer was born with the name Robert Allen Zimmerman?"

"Uh," Kayla says.

Declan shakes his head.

Mika and Lili both tilt their palms up.

"Don't know, but he sounds Jewish!" says Tessa.

Five pairs of hopeful eyes turn to me.

I wince. "I'm sorry. No idea."

Lili elbows me. "Stop feeling bad."

"I know, but—"

"Nope. Not on you. This is an act of collective dumbassery."

We end up guessing Robbie Williams. It's our first wrong answer of the night.

Then Erin asks what breed of cat has no tail, and we miss that one, too. Every single one of us thought the word was *minx*. But it's *manx*.

"No sad faces," says Kayla, tucking an errant loc behind her ear. "Let's rally. We've got this, okay?" She coaxes us in for a big group fist bump—and I get this happy jolt in my chest when our hands come together.

"Okay, folks!" says Sasha, once we've scored the last question. "The current standings are . . . tied for fourth place, each with nine points—Lex Appeal and the Meaty Ogres! In third, with ten points—Team Jean-Claude LePoisson!"

"We're not last?" Kayla's jaw drops. "We're not last!"

"In second place, with eleven points—Team Panda! And in the lead, with a perfect twelve points, Team Down Low Too Slow!" Sasha concludes, and the three girls in bodycon dresses let out the world's loudest *WOOOOOOO*.

Tessa shakes her head. "Every week. They're totally drunk, too, but man. They know their shit."

"All right! Now it's time to decide how many points you want to wager for the wild card," says Sasha, while Erin fishes a messenger bag out from under a table.

Kayla exhales. "We've got to do this, yeah? We've gotta go all in."

Mika, nodding solemnly, draws a giant stylized *10* on the white board.

"So for tonight's wild card," Sasha says, "we present: *Where's Waldo?*—speed edition."

Lili turns to me with huge eyes, both hands over her mouth.

"We'll set the clock, give you a page number, and then

you've got thirty seconds to find Waldo. You find him, you get your points!"

When Erin hands Mika our team's Waldo book, Lili doesn't miss a beat. "Give it to Imogen."

Mika looks from Lili to me, eyebrows raised. "Have you memorized it?"

I laugh a little. "No."

"So you're just really good at this?" asks Tessa.

"A little bit." My chest floods with warmth.

Sasha opens her phone timer. "And . . . go!"

It takes me all of twelve seconds to find him. "There." I tap the corner of the page.

"Holy shit," Tessa says.

The timer goes off before anyone else finds Waldo, and Team Jean-Claude LePoisson just *erupts*.

"WE WON! WE FUCKING WON!" Kayla's jumping up and down. Suddenly, we're all out of our seats, a tangle of hugs and high fives.

"Immy! You did THAT!" declares Lili.

"*We* did—"

"Uh-uh. You're the MVP," Kayla says. "Own it."

It takes a full five minutes to calm down enough to take a picture with our "trophy"—a wrinkled ten-dollar bill. It's the most beautiful ten-dollar bill I've ever seen in my life.

"New favorite picture. Texting it to all of you!" Tessa turns to me. "Imogen, let me add you to the group chat."

The group chat. I'm joining the group chat.

It's so thrillingly official.

And a moment later, there it is: the six of us in full color, beneath the fluorescent lights of the student center lounge. Lili and me, and her four best friends from college.

Maybe they're my friends now, too.

9

The walk back to the dorms feels otherworldly. Like a movie montage—nothing but vibes and soft edges.

Kayla smiles up at the stars. "We really beat the Down Lows."

"A miracle," says Mika. "They were very graceful losers, though."

"Yeah, they're super nice." Kayla turns to me. "They just show up with their thermoses of booze every month and completely annihilate us. It's like their pregame. They're probably at a frat party now."

"Literal hottest girls on earth," Declan says.

Even in the darkness, Kayla's eye roll is unmissable. "You have the most basic goddamn taste, I swear to God."

"Babe! Are you jealous?"

She shakes her head. "His ego after getting one question right. Incredible."

"Okay, Albany—you take the New York City questions next time."

"Anyone else have no idea Tribeca was an abbreviation?" Lili says, glancing up from her phone.

Tessa points to her. "Me! I just thought it was a name. Like Rebecca."

"Three Rebeccas," I say. "Tribeca."

There's a sudden chorus of beeps and vibrations—my phone buzzes against my leg through the side of my bag. When I tap the screen, a notification informs me I've been tagged in one of Lili's pictures—our victory photo, of course.

Kayla smiles down at her phone. "Cuuuuute."

"Our little family," says Mika.

I study the photo—the group of us in a staggered line, Lili and Mika holding either end of the ten-dollar bill like it's the world's smallest banner. The lighting's atrocious, but every single one of our expressions is pure, unfiltered joy. It's the kind of picture you have to smile back at.

My phone buzzes again. *Tessa Minsky started following you.*

I shoot her a quick smile—she's walking right beside me, sipping on some kind of snack pouch. When I follow her back, she grins and starts typing.

A DM pops up a moment later. Noticing your bio says nothing about Waldo skills??

I don't even pause to glance at her. Instead, I exit my DMs, tap the Edit Profile button, and type "Skills: Waldo" right after my pronouns.

A few seconds later, Tessa laughs under her breath. Then: *touché, Scott, touché*

I get this flutter in my chest when I read that. *Scott.*

No one's ever called me by my last name so casually before, and I think—

I really like it.

She takes another sip of her snack pouch, eyes glinting.

I lean in for a closer look. "Is that—baby food?"

"No. Kind of? It's just applesauce. But the pouch is its most delicious form. Like, you can taste the difference." She holds it up for me to study. "How come no one ever talks about how much better it tastes from the pouch?"

"Because babies can't talk?"

"I'm just saying." She pats the side of it fondly. "It's an objectively superior applesauce distribution system."

"Objectively! Wow."

"Think about it—it's portable, easy to eat, doesn't require a spoon."

By now, the group has drifted a few yards ahead of us, even Lili. But it feels so cozy somehow. Is this what my life looks like in a year? Walking alongside new friends through a grassy courtyard under the stars? When I see the sign for Rosewood Hall, will I think: *home*?

"Okay, but sometimes you just want applesauce with a spoon." I shrug. "The world needs both."

Tessa grins. "The bisexuals have spoken."

I smile nervously back.

She really, truly thinks I'm bi. Didn't even question it for a minute. No one did.

I was so sure Lili's friends would see through me. They'd feel the heterosexuality radiating off me in waves.

"But I feel like it's slightly more fluid," Tessa adds, and I almost lose my footing for a second.

Applesauce. Right.

People always say sexuality is fluid. Or it can be.

But I've never quite been able to figure out what that means.

Like, what changes, exactly? Is it just a shift in terminology? Does attraction really, truly change over time? Is it different for every person?

Can you just . . . become queer?

I'm not even talking about dating. Obviously. Seeing as I've never dated anyone. Or kissed anyone.

I've had crushes. On boys. That's always been pretty straight-forward.

But when I try to imagine dating girls, the concept's so unwieldy. Even the idea of having dated one makes my head spin. *My ex-girlfriend, Lili.*

I picture her face—her long-lashed brown eyes, full lips, expressive dark brows. There's no question Lili's pretty, but the idea of kissing her is as weird as the thought of kissing my sister. My brain can't take it seriously.

But with girls in general?

I mean, it would depend on the situation. Let's say a

hypothetical girl needed me to kiss her to make her crush jealous. Or to discourage some guy from hitting on her. Or if we were at a party on campus and her ex walked in with another girl. If the hypothetical girl in question asked me to, I'd *definitely* ~~hypothetically kiss her.~~ It wouldn't be a big deal at all.

Except—it would be my first kiss. So maybe it's a slightly big deal in that sense. I'm not necessarily dying for my first kiss to be a favor for an acquaintance.

It just wouldn't be the absolute end of the world, is all. Favor or no favor.

Of course, it would have to be a favor—otherwise it would be problematic, for sure. I don't want to be that straight girl who kisses queer girls and discards them like it's not even real. Or it doesn't count. Or they should be grateful I bothered.

Gretchen had to school me on the issue once when we were freshmen. I'll never forget the flatness of her voice when she said, "Hey. Uh. Imogen, can I talk to you about something?"

It was the last full day of school before fall break, so we were all extra goofy in Pride Alliance. I remember a bunch of people were confessing their queer celebrity crushes, and I guess I thought I was supposed to weigh in. So I said I'd kiss Clea DuVall as Graham in *But I'm a Cheerleader*.

If Clea wanted to. Obviously.

It was such a stupid thing to say, in retrospect. Maybe I thought I sounded open-minded.

"I know you weren't trying to be problematic," Gretchen had said, and at first, I'd thought she meant the movie itself.

Or maybe the issue was me—loving a movie that wasn't mine to love.

She settled into a chair across the circle from me, even though everyone else had gone home at that point. It freaked me out a little bit—the small stretch of extra distance between us. I remember straining to read her expression.

"It's just that there's this whole history with the way straight women treat queer women," Gretchen said. "Straight women will joke about being queer, or how they wish they were lesbians—that kind of thing. I guess they think we'll be flattered? But the reality is, no, we'd literally rather you just understand and acknowledge your own privilege as a cishet woman. You don't have to appropriate our attraction. And I know you were kidding with the whole Clea DuVall thing, but like . . . queer women are real? It's not a joke for us. It just really hurt to hear that."

"I'm so sorry." The air spilled from my lungs like they were untied balloons. "I totally get it. I'm just. I'm so sorry."

"No, it's fine! Now you know," Gretchen had said, softening like she always does. Apologies disarm her so quickly. She always seems to expect people to put up a fight. But I'd never shout down an actual queer person about queer stuff. How could I?

Sometimes I think about what that moment must have felt like for Gretchen—how it must feel every time a straight girl casually tries on queer attraction for clout.

Or for fun.

Or because everyone else in the room is discussing it.

I know the bi thing hasn't always been super easy for Gretchen. Her mom's amazing, but the town they moved from is even smaller than Penn Yan. And Gretchen doesn't really pass as straight most of the time in the way Lili does. Or even Edith, who usually only gets clocked as queer on sight by fellow queer people. But with Gretchen, even before the pink hair, it was the cut of her jeans, or her bangs, or her eye makeup.

I remember once we were in the bathroom at the little movie theater in town. A girl—white skin, dark hair, at least twenty pounds of eyelashes—stepped out of a stall with her skirt tucked into her very sheer tights. Underwear fully visible. Definitely a see something, say something situation. Even though I hate talking to strangers, I was rehearsing an intervention in my head.

But luckily Gretchen swept in before I had to—so I stood at one of the sinks, watching the whole thing play out in the mirror.

"Hey," Gretchen had said, but the eyelash girl was fully absorbed in her phone. So she tapped the girl's arm, and the girl looked up with a glare that made the air feel ten degrees colder. Gretchen seemed taken aback. "Um, I just wanted—"

"I'm not interested."

"Wait, what?"

"I *said*." The girl set her phone down on the ledge of a sink, leaning in to study her reflection while she washed her hands. "I'm. Not. Interested."

Gretchen laughed shortly. "In what?"

Eyelash girl shut off the sink. "I don't know how to make this any clearer." She turned to face Gretchen, enunciating every single word. "I date men."

My mouth fell open. "She wasn't—"

Gretchen cut in. "Cool! Want to know what I'm not interested in? Your ass. You know how I know that? Because I can see the whole fucking thing."

Then Gretchen turned on her heel and walked straight out of the bathroom. Not a single glance back. Orpheus, take notes. It was—and I mean this completely sincerely—absolute legend behavior.

Of course, I followed her—stopping for just a second in the doorway, because my dumbass bunny brain needed to make sure the mean homophobic girl had sorted out her skirt situation. She had.

Gretchen, for her part, seemed almost chillingly calm about the whole interaction. We left the theater, found her car, and buckled in.

She didn't say a word.

But instead of leaving the shopping center, she just drove across the strip and reparked in front of CVS. For a moment, she gripped the steering wheel, practically frozen.

Then her whole body deflated.

She turned to me, stupefied. "Did she really fucking say that? Seriously? Do straight girls even hear themselves? Do they have, like, any self-awareness at all?"

"Self-awareness from the girl with her skirt in her tights?" Gretchen let out a choked laugh. "Immy, I'm *tired*."

"I know."

"Like, it's so pervasive. This girl doesn't know shit about me. ~~Oh, I have dyed hair? I'm wearing overalls? Hey, I must want to~~ fuck you in a movie theater bathroom." Gretchen exhales. "The sheer *arrogance*."

"You might say . . . she showed her ass." I glanced slyly at Gretchen, who laughed and shoved a hand over my face.

"You fucking nerd. I love you so goddamn much."

And I felt the way I always feel when I manage to cheer someone up. Like I just made the rain stop with a wave of my hand.

DAY TWO
SATURDAY
MARCH 19

Texts with Gretchen

GP: Good morning, sunshine!!!!! How was your first night of college?

GP: Did you sleep?

GP: Did you floss??

IS: Good, yes, yes

IS: (of course)

IS: What about you? Are you on the road yet??

GP: Not yet

GP: Soon though

GP: Waiting for SOMEONE to get off the phone

GP: She's talking to Grandma

GP: I keep giving her puppy eyes

GP: She's not budging

IS: Aww, okay

IS: Tell Mama AND Grandma P I say hi though

GP: Will do!

GP: So what's the college life agenda for today

IS: Haha I don't know

IS: Lili's still sleeping

GP: Oh no wait

GP: That's so awkward??

GP: What do you do if you get hungry

IS: No, it's fine!

IS: She has pop tarts and stuff

IS: And she left me her swipe card in case I want to go
        to the dining hall

IS: I may text the group chat in a bit to see if anyone's
        up

GP: The group chat huh

GP: Look at youuuu

IS: ☺

10

One quick text to the group chat. Easy breezy, no pressure—right?

But I can't seem to bring myself to type the words. Or even open the text thread. What's the texting equivalent of tongue-tied?

It just feels too—I don't know. Presumptuous? A little too uh-hi-why-is-this-townie-high-school-child-texting-us-at-eight-a.m.-on-a-Saturday?

If I were home right now, I'd have been up for at least an hour already, spring break notwithstanding. All three dogs would be walked, the cats would be fed, and I'd be on the couch, attempting to read *Evelyn Hugo* amid a steady stream of Mom questions. *Now, is that the one Edie loves, about the actress? How is it? Oh, sweetie, what was the name of that singer you like? Not Lorde. The one whose relatives were on the* Titanic. *Immy, what does* sus *mean?*

I squeeze my eyes shut, breathing past the lump in my throat.

I just feel so far from home right now.

And so far from last night, from that glittering walk back to the dorms. How do I find my way back to that feeling?

I check my phone again.

They're probably all still sleeping, anyway. Even Tessa, who claims to be an early bird. She told me to text her if I get hungry before Lili wakes up—which seemed like such a sensible plan in the haze of last night. Now I can't imagine following through with it. In a way, it's even more intimidating than the thought of texting the whole group.

I keep thinking about what Lili said. How she thought Tessa was flirting with me. If I invite Tessa to breakfast, does that count as flirting back? Would I be leading her on? Would I be queerbaiting?

What if I already am, just by going along with Lili's whole story? Pretending to be bisexual. Even if it's not technically queerbaiting, it's definitely appropriation.

I set my phone facedown on my chest, right over my skittering heart.

I should just forget about breakfast. May as well get my shower out of the way while the bathroom's still quiet.

I've been dreading that—my first dorm shower. But I think I've finally figured out a nudity avoidance system. It's a whole tedious production involving the bathroom cubbies, a full extra outfit, and a hanging waterproof bag. I can't imagine walking down the hall in just a towel—even though no one else seems to mind it. One guy sauntered out last night with just a strategically placed washcloth. I was brushing my teeth at the time, and I almost choked on toothpaste.

Am I too big of a prude for college?

I tiptoe past Lili, slipping into the wide, empty hallway—so quiet, it's almost unnerving. Even waking at three in the morning to pee, I could still hear chatter and music spilling from a couple of rooms.

The bathroom's overhead lights are still off, but the glow from a night-light is enough to see the shower knobs. I pull the curtain closed, and for a moment, I just stand there. Eyes squeezed shut. Still in my pajamas.

It's the first time I've really been alone since I got here.

Maybe that's what scares me most about college. It all feels so public. How do people live so casually with strangers? With roommates? When do you ever get the chance to wind your heart back to normal?

The moment I step into the hallway, there's Tessa—in sweatpants, a T-shirt, and a tiny Star of David necklace. She stops short. "Scott! I was just about to text you. Any interest in breakfast? Have you eaten?"

"Oh—yes! I mean, I haven't."

"Okay, awesome. My treat."

I shake my head. "You don't have to do that! I can grab Lili's card—"

"Nope. I've got meal points to burn." Tessa pats her back pocket.

Lili's still passed out, so I dump my toiletries and pajamas on the end of my bed. Then I swipe my phone off the nightstand, popping off a quick text so she knows where I am.

Tessa looks up from her phone. "You ready?"

"Ready." I smooth the sides of my cardigan down over my shorts. Knowing I got dressed in a shower stall this morning makes me slightly paranoid that I've missed some critical buttons or zippers. Just a fun little stress cherry on top of this morning's anxiety sundae.

I'm getting breakfast with Tessa.

Which means I'll have to carry on a breakfast-length conversation with Tessa.

Tessa, who isn't a stranger—but I don't know if I'm allowed to call her a friend yet either. That's what makes it so hard, though. No one expects you to go beyond surface level when it's an actual stranger, so you can step outside your own brain if you need to. Flip the switch into bunny mode. It gets tricky with the in-between people.

I wish Gretchen were here. She'd know just how to play it. She has this way of turning small talk inside out, finding all the real parts underneath.

I follow Tessa out through a side door, and the morning chill prickles my legs with goose bumps. "Okay," she says, "what are we in the mood for? Dining hall? Student center?"

"Oh! Um. Whichever one has the best spoon applesauce,"
I say.

"Wow, who raised you?"

"Cory and Kelly Scott."

Tessa stops short. "Your mom's name is Kelly? *My* mom's
name is Kelly!"

"Are you saying . . . there's more than one Kelly?"

"Okay, Scott—you know what?" She shakes her head at me
smiling, and my heart does this stumble.

"What?"

She bites her lip, but it still tugs up at the corners. "Nothing."

"What?" I smile back.

"Nothing!" She laughs and turns to face me, walking backward like a tour guide. "I just have you figured out—that's all."

"Oh, really?"

"Yup. You're a closeted goofball."

I laugh, startled. "What?"

"And a troll. But in a subtle way. And you're very sweet
about it. Here, I'm taking you through the quad," she says,
veering us down a short, tree-lined path.

Suddenly I'm staring at the view from every campus bro-
chure, every postcard, even the website's landing page—the
stone clock tower, flanked by old lecture halls and columned
administrative buildings. My gaze lands on the vine-draped
registrar's office, and I realize with a start that it's the same

quad Lili showed me yesterday—just a different vantage point. I can barely take it all in, it's so beautiful.

The part that really gets me, though, is the lawn that surrounds it. It's intersected by sun-dappled paths, lined with quaint wooden benches, and a few of the trees have started to sprout tiny red blossoms. It's not even ten in the morning, but students are already everywhere—jogging or talking or sprawled out, reading, on blankets. Movement and stillness. The whole space feels alive.

"Pretty, huh?" says Tessa.

Before I can even respond, a puppy stumble-runs toward us, almost tripping over her ears. "Oh God. *Hi.*" I kneel to pet her, my ponytail slipping over my shoulder. "Hi, cutie. Where'd you come from? Are you a basset hound?"

"New friend?" Tessa crouches beside me.

I check the bone-shaped tag on her collar. "Aww. Hi, Daisy. That was my goat's name."

"A goat, like, a *goat*?"

"Mmm. Yeah, she was the goat kind of goat." I scratch Daisy's ears, sighing happily. "Is this what college is like? Puppies materializing out of nowhere?"

I press my nose to Daisy's snout, and it's like pressing pause on the entire world.

I read somewhere that animals have some kind of hormonal calming power, and I really do think it must be true. At the very least, it's true for me. Like when I was too shy to talk for my whole first week of kindergarten, until my mom talked my teacher into letting me hold the class guinea pig during circle time. I still remember the twitch of his heartbeat under his fur, the way it seemed to put me under a spell.

Daisy's owner jogs over to reclaim her, and I watch her wagging tail recede into the distance. A moment later, Tessa hugs me. "You good?"

I look up, startled. "Yeah, why?"

"That just looked like a tough goodbye." She presses her heart. "No judgment, Scott. Breakups are hard."

I elbow her, and she laughs—and I try not to grin at the sound of it.

Texts with Gretchen

GP: Imogen, can you explain to me

GP: Why twenty billion people all just decided to take I-86

GP: Right now

GP: At 11 am on a Saturday

IS: Twenty billion people 🫠

GP: AT LEAST

GP: We're not even past Binghamton yet!!!!!!!

GP: Coming up on 3 hours dfghjklkjhg

GP: Vassar you better be worth it

IS: I mean if 20 billion people are heading there, that's probably a good sign?

GP: Hahahaha I love you

GP: Okay I have approached Mama Patterson for comment

GP: She says "sweetie, please, let me just" and then a horn honk and then "oh come the fuck on"

GP: Fourth f-bomb in 20 minutes 😸

GP: College tours are FUN

IS: I'm sorry!!

GP: Ehhhh

GP: It's fine

GP: It'll be fine

GP: Anyway, how are you???

GP: Still liking your future?

11

My future.

Gretchen's not wrong, but it hasn't sunk in yet. My brain's so zoomed in on this visit, I keep forgetting it's just a preview.

But maybe that's how it should be. No pressure to build this weekend into something it's not. No need to shove each moment under a microscope, just to pin down how I feel.

"I'm taking you back the long way," Tessa says, as we leave the dining hall. "Have you seen the scissors yet?"

"The sculpture?" I shake my head. "Just in pictures."

I remember Lili's sheer delight when she first saw it on the website—giant metal scissors made to look like they're plunged into the ground. At the time, she was still deciding between Blackwell and Ithaca College, but the scissors sealed the deal.

"It's a *sign*." She turned to me, wide-eyed. "From the town with the world's largest griddle to the school with the world's largest scissors."

I wasn't entirely sure they *were* the world's largest. And I definitely didn't see the point of basing huge decisions on the presence or absence of large metal objects.

What I did know was that Blackwell College was much closer to Penn Yan than Ithaca was.

"Definitely a sign," I said, nodding.

Tessa cuts sharply left, leading me past one building and behind another—and there it is. We're practically in its shadow.

"Hi, scissors." I peer up at the wide-open V of its handles.

"What do you think?" Tessa asks. "Everything you dreamed of?"

"Eleven out of ten." I pull my phone out—and even though I've got a pile of unread texts, I tap straight into my photo app.

"Want to be in it? I can—wait, actually—" Tessa cups her hands around her mouth, jogging toward a guy in a baseball cap. "Andrew!" He stops, circling back to give her a fist bump. Tessa points vaguely at the scissors before handing him her phone.

The next thing I know, I'm crouched beside her, beaming side by side in the triangular space between the scissor blades. "It's all about the vibes," Tessa says.

"Is the vibe decapitation?"

She laughs. "Pre-decapitation."

Andrew snaps a few more pictures and returns Tessa's phone, giving her hair a quick ruffle before he leaves.

"So, how do you know Andrew?"

"Oh, he's one of the himbos. Friends with my brother." Tessa smiles down at the screen for a minute, swiping and tapping. "Okay, texting these now!"

"Right! I forgot your brother goes here."

"Yup!" We set off down one of the paths. "Dan—he's a junior. He's the best."

"So he's a himbo?"

"He wishes." Tessa laughs. "No. His friends are himbos—he's how I *know* the himbos. But he's kind of, like, you know. Scrawny Jewish guy. Loves sports. Knows all the stats. Emphatically not a jock."

"Do you have to be a jock to qualify as a himbo?"

"You know, it's actually been a while since I've reviewed the himbo qualifications."

I grin, and she grins back, and it's almost unnerving how easy this is. We've spent the whole morning together, but I don't think there's been a single awkward silence. It's unprecedented.

I mean, it's unprecedented for *me*.

We're almost at the edge of the courtyard. "So, Dan's twenty," she says, "I'm eighteen, and our sister, Rachael, is sixteen. All June birthdays, almost exactly two years apart. But they're both Geminis, and I'm a Cancer." She nods significantly. "What about you?"

"Siblings or zodiac?"

"Mmm. Both."

"Okay, well." I smile a little. "I turned eighteen on Halloween."

"A Scorpio. In-te-rest-ing." She tilts her head.

I pause, raising my eyebrows for a moment. "And I have a sixteen-year-old sister. Edith."

"She's queer, too, right? Lili told me you have a little baby gay sister."

"Definitely. Super queer, really funny. Kind of chaotic?" I nod. "You guys would get along."

Tessa bursts out laughing. "Because she's queer and chaotic?"

"And funny!"

"Well, I *am* a middle-child Jewish lesbian with ADHD." She waves her hands in a flourish, and I laugh. "Okay, but I'm actually so jealous you have a queer sister. Like. What a win."

"Aww. So Dan and Rachael aren't queer?"

"Nope. I'm the token gay. I mean, as far as I know." She tilts her palms up. "They were pretty cute when I came out, though. They kidnapped me and brought me to the Big Gay Ice Cream shop in the Gayborhood."

"The what in the what?"

"In Philly! That's where I'm from. Well, I'm from the Main Line. The Big Gay Ice Cream shop closed, though. I actually cried. I think it still exists in New York? The city, I mean."

My brain sprints to catch up. "I had no idea ice cream could be gay."

"It can," Tessa says. "It even tasted gay. I actually think Dan and Rachael got gayer from eating it."

"Is that how it works?"

"Yup," she says, as we pass a bank of benches at the edge of the quad. "Dan especially—instantly fifty percent gayer. He literally drives a Subaru Outback now."

I laugh. "That's what my parents drive."

"Of course they do. They created two queer kids."

My chest goes tight. It's so easy to forget I've been lying through my teeth this whole time. I wonder what Tessa thinks I was like as a kid.

Probably like Edith, I guess.

Edith, who announced on the first day of preschool that she was going to marry a girl. When she played house, there were always two mommies. Sometimes she'd get distracted in the grocery store, staring at pretty women—once she even plucked a sunflower out of a cut flower display and gave it to one of them in the checkout line. She couldn't have been older than five at the time. I don't even think she'd met an out lesbian in real life at that point.

Queerness was just something Edith implicitly understood—like how babies pick up languages without even trying.

"Oop," Tessa says, glancing up from her phone. "Lili needs confirmation that you're alive. She says you're not answering your texts."

"Oh! God. Sorry. I haven't checked in a minute."

"Your texts or your pulse?"

I smile a little. "Neither."

She presses two fingers to my wrist. And there's a tiny, soft thump in my chest.

"Okay," she declares after a moment. "Pulse is good. You're definitely alive."

I blink. "I should text her, huh?"

Tessa's already typing. "Nah—I'm on it. Anyway, we're home."

I text Lili a quick apology anyway, with some extra emojis to drive the point home. Then Tessa lets us into the dorm with her keycard.

I swipe through our scissor photos while we wait for the elevator, and Tessa grins down at my screen. "Look how totally unfazed we are by our impending decapitation."

"Honestly, we seem pretty fine with it."

"Good for us!"

I zoom in a bit to do a closer crop on my favorite of the bunch. It really is cuter than it has any right to be—nothing but easy smiles and sunlit faces.

I post it to Instagram with a scissor emoji for the caption, right as the elevator doors slide open.

Texts with Gretchen

GP: IMOGEN

GP: WHO ARE YOU SCISSORING

GP: WHAT'S HAPPENING

IS: Wait

IS: What?????

GP: 📎

GP: Don't get me wrong, I'm happy for you 😂

IS: OMG

IS: I would NEVER

IS: Post that online I mean!!!!

GP: 👀

IS: GRETCHEN NO

IS: Hahaha omg

IS: I just meant like

IS: I don't want you to think I'm saying OMG I WOULD NEVER, like I'm grossed out or scandalized

IS: By a very natural and beautiful expression of intimacy

GP: This

GP: Wow

GP: This is my favorite conversation

IS: Should I edit the caption

IS: Like would other people read it like that? 🙊

GP: Haha depends

GP: Are they gay

GP: You know, this could actually be the test

GP: What do u think of when you see ✂️

GP: Gay Rorschach!!!!!

IS: Please say you're joking

IS: I tagged Tessa in this

GP: Aww is Tessa gay??

GP: Then I guess it's a grand gesture!!!!!!

GP: Promposal walked so public scissoring invitation
        could run

IS: GRETCHEN PLEASE

GP: 💀 💀 💀

GP: Immybean it's fine

GP: You're YOU

GP: No one thinks you're dropping sexmojis on the main

IS: 😑

GP: Okay also can we just acknowledge TESSA
GP: She's actually so hot??
GP: She used to have longer hair, right?
GP: I recognize her
GP: From Lili's page
GP: Kind of a soft butch vibe now, huh. I like it

IS: I don't know what soft butch means, but she did
       have longer hair

GP: Sweet heteropotamus
GP: ✂️

12

When we reach Lili's room, Kayla's leaning in the doorway like a catalog model—legs crossed, hand grazing the doorframe, locs swept into a ponytail. But she steps into the room when she sees us, leaving space for us to follow.

"Oh, hey!" Lili looks up from her desk chair. "How was the scissor?"

My cheeks flood with heat. "Good. Yes! It was great."

I sneak a quick glance at Tessa, who seems completely unfazed. Then again, Tessa's not the one dropping coded sex solicitations into her Instagram captions.

God, I don't even one hundred percent know what scissoring *is*. All I can picture are naked Barbies with interlocked legs mashing up against each other. Which, clearly—

It occurs to me, suddenly, that Kayla just asked me a question.

"Oh! Sorry—I zoned out."

"You're good!" Kayla says. "Just gauging your opinion on

the issue of small German sausages."

I stare at her. Has it always been like this? Has everyone been constantly talking about sex this whole time, and I've just never picked up on the code?

I clear my throat. "You mean—as a euphemism?"

"Oh, she means a literal sausage," Lili assures me.

"Well, technically, it's liverwurst pate in a sausage casing. But it's smaller than you're thinking." Tessa raises both pointer fingers, inching them closer together to demonstrate. Which turns out to be unnecessary because, a moment later, Kayla whips out the actual sausage. Right here in Lili's dorm room, with only a single clear sandwich bag for protection.

She holds it up by the ziplock, eyeing it with begrudging respect. "The beast itself."

It's about the size of my thumb, sealed in orange plastic— the label reads *BRAUNSCHWEIGER Liverwurst* in Oktoberfest font.

I almost drop my phone. "Oh, I hate it."

"It's an abomination. Literal violence wrapped in plastic." Kayla nudges aside my clothes and toiletries from this morning, sinking onto the edge of my bed. "Apparently, it was in a company gift basket Declan's mom got for Christmas? And for some demonic reason, Dec decided to bring it back with him after break."

"Scott, you should definitely touch it," says Tessa. "I don't think you can really *understand* the sausage until you feel how

96

warm and squishy it is—"

"I'm fine!"

Lili laughs. "You'd probably die if you opened it at this point. Like, I actually think just cracking the seal would release toxic death fumes into the air. Mika won't go near it."

"And he just brought it here?" I ask. "Like . . . as a souvenir from home?"

"God only knows what goes through that white boy's head."

I pause. "And how do you have it?"

"Because," Tessa says, "they've turned it into a diabolical back-and-forth revenge game."

"Like hot potato," chimes Lili.

Tessa beams. "Exactly. Like a fucked-up game of hot potato."

Kayla nods. "So I'm in class yesterday, digging around my bag for my minty Life Savers—"

"They keep her from falling asleep in class," Lili explains.

"That, and they're delicious," says Kayla. "Anyway, I find the roll and eat one, but I'm still really tired, so I grab a second one. Then, right before class ends, I go for a third—and what do I find?" Kayla holds up the sandwich bag. "This fucker, rolled into the Life Savers wrapping with a couple of mints on either end. I actually threw up in my mouth when I saw it."

"Which completely defeats the purpose of the breath mint!" adds Tessa.

Kayla dangles the corner of the bag between two fingers.

"So now? Payback. I know my girl Tess is in." She looks from Lili to me, her face deadly serious. "The only question is: Are you?"

Lili translates. "Imogen, would you like to hide a tiny sausage in Declan's room?"

Suddenly, Kayla launches off the bed, drops to one knee, and holds the sausage aloft like a diamond ring.

What could I possibly say but yes?

Texts with Gretchen

GP: Detour!!! Getting lunch in Woodstock

GP: Have you been here? It's cute!

IS: I have not, but that's where my grandparents met!

GP: WHAT

GP: Like the actual festival??

IS: Yup!

GP: NO WAY

GP: WHY HAVE YOU NEVER MENTIONED THIS

GP: WHY HAVE I HEARD THE PANCAKE STORY
        NINETY MILLION TIMES

GP: BUT NOT THIS

IS: Haha idk!

GP: I can't even process this info!!!!!!

GP: Wow

GP: Like what other secrets are you hiding??

GP: Other than ✂️

IS: See, now I don't even want to tell you what I'm
        about to do with a tiny German sausage

GP: IMOGEN

GP: What are you about to do

GP: With a tiny German sausage

GP: ????

13

Kayla lays out the mission in urgent, hushed tones. "He just left for the painting studios," she says, "and Lili's friend Clara lives on his hall—she's gonna let us in, so we don't have to try to figure out the tunnels. Which is great, because I don't fuck around underground."

"That's actually my favorite Dr. Seuss book," says Tessa. "*I Don't Fuck Around Underground.*"

"*I Don't Fuck Around Underground, Said the Hound,*" I add.

Lili looks up from her phone and blinks, shaking her head.

"Page one," Tessa says. "'I know this might astound, but I'm kind of tightly wound, and thus I don't fuck around in the depths of underground,' said the hound."

"'Because fucking around underground,' the hound expounded, 'is bound to make a sound,'" I say, without hesitation.

"So . . . whenever y'all are done with whatever the fuck that was," Kayla says.

Lili taps her phone screen. "Okay! Clara just confirmed that Dec's room is unlocked and open for business."

"She picked the lock?" I ask. I don't know if I should be scandalized or impressed.

Lili shrugs. "He probably left it open."

"Can I just say that our timing is *perfect*? It's supposed to rain tomorrow and then get chilly, and"—Kayla smiles fondly down at the sausage—"that's right, little man. Guess who's going straight into Declan's winter gloves."

"Right down into one of the fingers," adds Tessa, "for a squishy surprise."

I press my palm to my cheek. "This is a whole other level of gross."

We step outside and barely make it ten feet into the courtyard before Kayla stops short, tugging Lili back by her sleeve. They both stand, frozen, for a moment, staring at one of the dorms—presumably Declan's. A moment later, Lili raises her phone up to her mouth like it's a walkie-talkie.

"Two professional spies in the making," Tessa murmurs. "Such finesse."

I laugh. "So how did you decide to align with Kayla over Declan?"

Tessa pauses, glancing briefly at Kayla and Lili, before leaning in closer. "I'm not aligned with Kayla," she says quietly. "I'm aligned with chaos."

I raise my eyebrows.

"I'm playing both sides. Neither of them has any idea. I'm actually the one who thought of the Life Savers thing."

I shake my head, awestruck. "You are—"

"Absolutely!" Tessa interjects suddenly. Her eyes flick sideways as Kayla and Lili sidle back up. "Of course I can take a picture of you with the sausage!"

"You want a picture with the sausage?" Kayla looks at me strangely. "This sausage?"

"She does!" Tessa pats my shoulder, grins, and steps back a few feet, phone aloft.

"She *definitely* does," Lili adds.

"If you say so." Kayla shakes her head, takes the sausage bag out of her purse, and then peels the sides back, letting the sausage poke out like a banana.

I shoot Tessa a quick grimace—she smiles innocently back. Then, I carefully pluck the sausage out of the bag, pinching its plastic wrapping between my fingers like a claw machine.

I have never, ever seen Lili open her camera app this quickly.

"This is incredible," says Tessa, voice threaded with laughter. She grins down at Lili's phone screen while I pass the sausage back to Kayla. "Scott, oh man. Your expression in these."

Lili holds her phone up. "I'm framing this."

The photo's zoomed close on my face, which I'm sure would make me self-conscious under any other circumstance. But everything about the expression is just so undeniably, hilariously *me*. Cheerful smile and panicked eyes, in brazen contradiction. I laugh. "Oh God."

"A masterpiece," says Tessa, meeting my gaze with a grin.

In the sunlight, her eyes are the exact color of acorns.

14

Clara ushers us in through the dorm's front door with the subtlety of a Disney villain, before creeping back down the hall on her tiptoes. Kayla turns to face us. "We ready?"

Lili and I nod.

Tessa flashes a thumbs-up.

It's eerily quiet for a Saturday—I guess everyone's either grabbing lunch or still sleeping. Declan's room is on the first floor, around the corner from the front entrance.

Kayla points at the 114 above his door. "Here we go."

I nod without speaking—my heart's beating so fast. The door creaks a little when Kayla opens it, and I almost jump out of my skin. She freezes in the doorway, peering around the dark space. "Coast is clear."

Once we're all inside, Kayla pulls the door shut behind us and flicks on the lights. "So here's what we're looking for." She pulls her phone out, taps the screen a few times, and tilts it up to show us a photo.

Lili smiles. "I know her."

In the picture, Lili and Declan are posed on either side of a snowman, and Declan's waving at the camera. Kayla zooms in on his gloved hand. "Dark gray, kind of a thick material, and it bunches in at the wrist."

"It'll be the one that looks . . . like a glove," Tessa adds.

"I mean, yeah." Kayla lets out a quick laugh. "Okay! I'm gonna start checking coat pockets."

I scan the room, suddenly struck by a pang of déjà vu—which makes no sense. Maybe it's just that this whole room looks like a movie set. It's a single, so it's a little smaller than Lili's, but there's something so bright and open about the space. There's a fake brick accent wall and an actual closet in back. All the art above his desk is framed and perfectly centered. And the books on his shelf are stripped down to their spines—all white hardcovers. Even the clutter on top of his dresser feels intentional: a pink paper peony, a short stack of moleskine notebooks, and—

A shoebox-sized, made-to-scale, painstakingly detailed replica of this bedroom.

"Wait—oh! I've seen this on TikTok." I press a hand to my cheek. "This is, like—wow. *Unbelievable* in person."

"Right? Dec and Mika did this one together. They're both so sickeningly talented." Lili settles onto the floor near his dresser, while Kayla repositions Declan's peacoat over the back of his desk chair.

"Should we check the closet? I kind of just want to see

Declan's closet." Tessa opens it slowly, glancing back over her shoulder at me. "Okay, Waldo queen. Work your magic."

I nod slowly, taking in the space—small, but crisply organized with a bunch of stacked plastic drawer units. "Oh my God, it's so neat," Tessa says, shaking her head. "Okay, sorry, this level of cleanliness, but he's holding on to that nasty rotten sausage? I don't know, man. It's giving serial killer."

Kayla and Lili both laugh from across the room.

"I mean, if he's palming it off on Kayla," I point out, "he's not *technically* holding on to it. Oh!"

Tessa's eyes widen. "Did you find something?"

I crouch next to the drawers. "Look—tassels. Could be the end of a scarf?" I reach for my phone, snapping a quick picture.

"Ooh, good call. Never forget this moment," says Tessa.

I laugh. "No, I mean, I want to be able to put it back exactly the same as we left it, right? With the drawer cracked a little like this, tassel hanging out . . ."

"Oh. Shit. You're good—"

"FUCK," Lili hisses, scrambling to her feet. "Clara just texted. He's coming back. I don't know why—fuck."

"Get the light!" Kayla whispers.

"No time. Just hide!"

Tessa yanks the closet door shut, sinking to the floor beside me. For a moment, all I hear is frantic rustling and a few muttered curse words. But then, sure enough—

The door creaks open.

I quickly silence my phone—and Tessa mouths *oh* and does

the same. She's sitting so close, the act of slipping her phone back into her jeans makes our arms brush together.

My heart's going a little bit haywire.

Outside: A few short footsteps. Then a pause. Then the creak of Declan's bedframe.

Tessa turns to me incredulously. *Is he gonna nap?* she mouths, pantomiming sleep with prayer hands pressed to her cheek.

I shrug, palms tipped up.

Another low creak.

She shoots me a panic face, but it quickly breaks into a smile. I can barely catch my breath for a moment.

This closet

Is just

So small. She pokes my knee, and I let out a fake, noiseless gasp.

I poke her back.

She scrunches her nose at me.

A bubble of laughter rises up from my chest for no reason. But then Tessa clamps a hand over my mouth, and it makes something twist inside me.

The skin of her palm on my lips.

I keep hearing Gretchen's voice in my head.

She's actually so hot??

Is Tessa hot? I never know how hotness gets decided. Or where it stands in relation to cuteness. Or sexiness. Or beauty in general.

A door opens and shuts, and Tessa pulls her hand back with a start. For a few interminable moments, we sit frozen in silence, ears cocked toward the door.

Then, at last, there's more rustling and a single dull thud. "Hey," Kayla says under her breath. "All clear."

Tessa opens the door a crack—then opens it all the way to find Kayla, shaking her head and looking vaguely shell-shocked. Lili army-crawls out from under the bed, settling in beside her.

"Were you both under there?" Tessa asks.

"Oh yes. And our boy's hand?" Kayla exhales. "Two inches from my face."

"Needed his phone charger, apparently," adds Lili. She shoots me a wry smile. "Exciting first mission?"

Declan's gloves are, in fact, in the scarf drawer, which makes Kayla sigh in relief. Lili shoves the sausage into the glove's middle finger, and we try to match my photo when we put everything back. But once the sausage is in, we don't linger—I think we're all still a little flustered.

Kayla splits off, heading to her own dorm, and I end up sort of drifting behind Tessa and Lili. They're talking about some party they went to at Rainbow Manor. Or a future party they're planning to go to. I can't focus long enough to figure out which.

I guess my brain's still in Declan's closet.

How do I explain the part where Tessa's smile made my chest hurt?

Or when she covered my mouth with her hand and I sort of wanted to kiss it.

It's like scrolling through someone else's pictures, catching a glimpse of yourself in the background. That sudden jolt of *hold on, wait, go back!*

Was that me?

Texts with Gretchen

GP: Hello hi I would like an update on the 🌭 situation

GP: Was it fun

GP: Was it wrapped

IS: Definitely wrapped

IS: 📎

GP: Oh my god, your face

GP: 💀

GP: This is my new favorite Imogen picture

GP: You and your tiny German sausage

IS: Thank you, it was very tiny

IS: Have you guys made it to Vassar yet?!

GP: Pulling in now!!!

GP: Slightly freaking out bc they just emailed me that the girl who was supposed to host me had to leave campus suddenly for a family emergency

GP: (Per her tiktok, the "emergency" appears to be the Wallows performing in Albany)

IS: Oh no! Wait—what are you going to do?

GP: I mean tonight I have to stay in the hotel with Mama P 👻

GP: They're going to try to find someone else for tomorrow though

GP: It just sucks because I can't really go out if I'm staying with my mom, and then there probably won't even be any parties tomorrow because Sunday

IS: I'm sorry ☹

GP: Tbh I'm concerned about the integrity of my pros/ cons lists when I'm not even getting the full dorm experience

IS: Yeah but what if you went to a party and it was the worst, and then you just assumed parties at Vassar suck in general

GP: True true good point

GP: Haha imagine the Worst Party

GP: We have to plan it

IS: Oh definitely

IS: Okay

IS: The menu: fish and only fish

IS: The guest list: literally only those guys from men's rights forums who talk about getting cucked

GP: YES!!!!

GP: Just a bunch of incels from the manosphere, hangin'
         around the fish table, rating hott girlz on a scale
         from one to ten

IS: The music: Kid Rock deep cuts

IS: Dental office lighting

GP: And creepy baby dolls on display

GP: With human teeth

IS: I hate this party so much

GP: I could check no on a billion RSVP cards

GP: and it wouldn't be enough

15

By sunset, we've all claimed prime spots on Lili's floor—Declan, Mika, and Kayla with their backs against one bed; Lili, me, and Tessa against the other. Lili turned the overhead lights off, leaving only the hazy glow from a trio of lamps. In the background, we've got Mitski's new album streaming faintly through Declan's fancy mini Bluetooth speakers. It's as cozy as a slumber party, down to the not-quite-empty pizza box in the center of the room. Turns out, you can buy whole pizzas downstairs—Lili's dorm has a late-night snack bar.

I'm working my way through the pair of crusts I've saved for last, while Tessa leans closer, holding her phone out in front of me. "Full-paragraph comment. Every single TikTok." She pauses to grin up at Mika. "I love your parents so much."

Mika smiles a little. "I went home for break, and they'd printed a bunch of screen grabs to display on the fridge. Right next to the Christmas cards. *And* they printed out Jade's top nine Instagram collage post. How do they even find this stuff?"

"Is Jade your sister?" I ask.

"Ex-girlfriend. My parents are slightly obsessed with her."

I press a fist to my mouth. "Oh no . . ."

"No, it's fine! We're best friends. We grew up together— like, we still talk literally every day. And she's at Cornell, so we get to visit a lot. I'm pretty sure my parents think we're still secretly dating?"

Kayla laughs. "Mika, *everyone* thinks you're secretly dating."

"And you all have beautiful imaginations." Mika scoots forward to grab another pizza slice.

"Okay, for real," Tessa says, "it's pretty amazing that you and Jade still get along that well. Same with you two." She looks from Lili to me. "Just the fact that an overnight trip with your ex was even on the table."

"I have sleepovers with my exes," says Declan.

Kayla rolls her eyes. "Not that kind of sleepover, Don Juan."

I hug my knees to my chest, feeling the tips of my cheeks go warm. "Yeah, it's—you know. It's been totally fine."

Lili shoots me a quick, awkward smile. "Right. Definitely."

"Oh man," says Tessa. "I tried the friendship thing with Jillian, and it worked for a little while. But it got weird when she started dating someone."

"I get that," I say.

"Not because I was jealous," Tessa adds quickly. "It was just awkward. Like, she'd mention her new girlfriend all the time, but she did it in this back-off-Tess kind of way. Like I'm about to make a move? Come on."

Lili laughs. "Didn't she slide into your DMs, too, the first time she saw another girl on your Instagram?"

"Oh, *immediately*. And I'm like, 'Um, so that's my cousin Annie.'"

I hug my legs tighter, trying to ignore the nervous kick in my chest. "She must have freaked out the next time you started dating someone."

"Every time. Every girl. All zero of them." Tessa shoots me a quick, sideways smile.

I smile back, not entirely sure if she's kidding. She has to be, right? There must be thousands of girls with crushes on Tessa. I mean, I'd be losing my mind over Tessa if I were queer.

I keep thinking about Declan's closet—and how we sat so close, our knees overlapped.

"Oh!" Mika yawns and stretches. "Did we figure out the deal for tomorrow yet?"

"What's tomorrow?" asks Lili.

"Costumes! For Friday. The dark academia party."

Kayla claps. "Yes! I want to do a thrift store run. Remember that store in Waterloo I went to with Audra and that guy Dilf? Audra's my roommate," she adds, glancing at me.

"His name was Dilf?" Tessa laughs, short and incredulous. "Like . . . a DILF?"

"*Is* he a DILF?" Lili asks.

"No idea. I think it's just a nickname?" Kayla shrugs. "I *hope* it's a nickname. He's that white guy with the eyebrow ring and the really light blue eyes, who kind of looks like a cult leader? And he has a bong named Creature?"

"Of course he does." Tessa looks sincerely delighted.

"Anyway, the point is, it was a very cheap store, and I want to go back," Kayla says. "Anyone interested?"

Lili shoots me a querying glance, and I nod and shrug.

"I'm in if these two are," Tessa says, bopping my head, and then Lili's. And I'm pretty sure I've slipped into someone else's life.

DAY THREE
SUNDAY
MARCH 20

Texts with Gretchen

GP: I'm supposed to have my tour today and it's raining 😭 😭 😭

GP: Are you guys getting this hell weather too?

GP: It's not even the romantic kind of rain, I wouldn't even want to kiss in it

GP: Maaaaaaybe if it was hot Tessa ✂️ 😏

16

Either my phone's gotten brighter or the room's gotten darker. I squint at Gretchen's texts, rub my eyes, and flip it over, screen down.

It's barely past seven, and Lili's still sleeping. I'm so tired, even yawning feels like too much effort. But every time I try to close my eyes, they spring open, so I just peer through the inky black until I can make out where the walls end. It takes a full minute for me to realize the drumroll of pounding raindrops isn't just Lili's white-noise app.

I tug my phone off the charger, staring again at Gretchen's short stream of texts.

I could write back to the part about hell weather, right? Add a couple of emojis and press send. It doesn't have to be that deep.

I can't explain why that scissor emoji makes me so jumpy. I know that Gretchen's just teasing. Obviously. But I feel so weird about it.

Why do I feel so weird about it?

It couldn't be lesbophobia, right? That wouldn't even make sense. My two best friends are queer women. I have a gay little sister. Other than Otávio, I literally don't have any close friends who *aren't* queer.

Though that's what every bigot says, right? *Queerphobic??? Me??? BUT I HAVE A QUEER FRIEND!!*

I reread Gretchen's texts, feeling strangely out of orbit. The thought of her and Tessa kissing makes my brain short-circuit.

And in the rain? Sorry, but what kind of rain *would* be romantic to kiss in? I get that it looks cool in movies. But in real life, you'd be clammy and cold and your socks would soak through, and you'd probably just be worried the whole time about your phone getting wet. Unless you're so desperate to kiss this particular person, you don't even notice the discomfort. Or you do, but it's worth it.

I guess that's the whole point.

"Hey! You're dressed." Lili sits up in bed, yawning. "Morning."

"Morning! Guess what I made."

She rubs her eyes, blinking. "You . . . what?"

"A dark academia vision board!" I hold my phone up.

"Ohhhh. Nice." She nods dazedly.

"For the thrift store. Just to use as a reference. If people want to, I mean."

"That's amazing," she says, another yawn breaking through. "They're gonna love it."

123

"You haven't even seen—"

"I know, but Immy, your boards are always perfect." She clasps her hands and stretches them up, then back, then side to side. "Because you're very, very intense about them."

"Rude but accurate." I smile into my own fisted hand.

I know I can get a little overly invested in this stuff, but a proper vision board is serious business. Because it has to work as a cohesive whole—which means being intentional about color palette and positioning. But, of course, the real magic is in the details. And it's not just about matching plaids with tweeds.

A good vision board knows its audience. Which, in this case, means masculine, feminine, *and* androgynous aesthetics, sized to fit everything from Kayla's height to Lili's curves to my own pear-shaped, corn-fed squishiness. At the end of the day, an outfit only works if you can imagine a real person wearing it.

For example, Tessa. Dressed like Timothée Chalamet in *Little Women*.

Specifically, the vest and the little necktie bow he wears in that scene with Florence Pugh, when Amy explains to Laurie how marriage is an economic proposition.

That, but on Tessa. I can picture it perfectly.

Hours later, I'm huddled next to Lili under the awning behind her dorm, holding her umbrella while she texts. "Okay! They're pulling up in a sec."

I glance back over my shoulder. "Should we wait for Tessa?"

"No, she's not coming. The himbos are dragging her to Wegmans."

It hits me like a punch for some reason.

"Oh," I say.

Lili opens her umbrella, positioning it over our heads. "Ready to make a run for it?"

We barrel toward Kayla's parked minivan—a big, clunky Honda Odyssey that looks like it came straight from the carpool line, covered in animal-rescue bumper stickers, with a few little dents in the back. I'm shivering and half-soaked by the time we reach it, and I scramble in behind Lili when the back doors slide open. It's one of those minivans with three rows—Mika's riding shotgun and Declan's in the back, so we take the middle. "It's like a school bus, I know," Kayla says. "Tell me you come from a big family without telling me you come from a big family."

I buckle my seat belt, trying to smile normally. "How big's your family?" I ask.

Kayla starts backing out of the space. "Well, I'm the youngest of four. So when I graduated, my parents went out, bought a Mustang, and gave me this beaut." She pats the steering wheel. "How do you like those ass dimples? Courtesy of my brother, who dents the car every time he backs out of the driveway."

"As an only child New Yorker, this is highly unrelatable content," Declan chimes from the back.

"I'm sorry—were you not the center of attention for five seconds?"

I make myself laugh along with the group, but I feel a little droopy inside. Almost wistful.

Tessa's not coming. And I don't know why I care.

Texts with Gretchen

IS: Hell weather has landed in Geneva as well 🙂

IS: We're going shopping though

IS: ~~Getting costumes~~ for the dark academic party

IS: *academia

GP: DARK ACADEMIA YES

GP: So fucking jealous

IS: No don't be!!!

IS: It's next weekend, I won't even be there 👻

IS: I'm just the fashion consultant

GP: Uh oh, I see ellipses!!

GP: Vision board landing in 3 . . . 2 . . . 1 . . .

IS: 📎

GP: atta girl

17

Hand-Me-Down Closet is about fifteen minutes from campus, in a dreary shopping center tucked behind the outlet mall. "We're really here," Lili says, one hand pressed to her heart. "Dilf's favorite thrift store."

"The one and only," says Kayla.

The parking lot's practically empty—probably par for the course on a rainy Sunday. Lili nudges me as Kayla pulls into a spot. "Immy, text them your vision board!"

"You made a vision board?" asks Kayla.

"It's just a thing I threw together—"

"She woke up at the crack of dawn. Scoured the internet for *hours*—"

"One hour! Not even." I press send, my cheeks going warm.

"Heyyyy," Declan says. "Nice."

"Yeah, you nailed it," Kayla murmurs, zooming in on her screen while she unbuckles. "Look at all those brooding white people."

She laughs, and I smile. "Yeah, no. They are."

We dash inside, wiping our feet on the mat in a damp huddle. I peer around the space—this definitely isn't one of those curated vintage boutiques on Linden Street. It's fluorescently lit chaos: bar mitzvah T-shirts and shoulder-padded suit jackets, interspersed with stretchy short dresses and every possible iteration of denim. But I can already spot a few intriguing tartans and blazers, half-hidden among the racks. I love treasure hunting in stores like this. It's the ultimate hidden-object game.

Almost makes me wish I could stay for the party.

I think I'd want to wear a dress or a skirt. Something vaguely Victorian, but not too on-the-nose. Jo March vibes, but not like I raided her closet. Old-timey collegiate.

"What the fuck even is this?" asks Lili, holding up what appears to be the skeleton of a lace-up bodice. "Are you just supposed to put the stringy part over your nipple and hope for the best?"

"Maybe you wear it over a real shirt?"

Mika drifts over. "Have you seen any suspenders?"

Lili points out a display of accessories in the back corner, before circling back to a rack of dresses. "Okay, some of these dresses are actually cute. Immy, you should try stuff on!" She runs her fingertip down one of the zippers. "What's the optimal skirt length? Are we talking Christian mommy blogger? Spicy Christian mommy blogger?"

"Emilia Cardoso. Ma'am. What kind of porn are you watching?" asks Kayla.

"Wouldn't you like to know—ooh!" Lili hands me a deep green shirtdress. "Here—this is very you!"

"Really cute," I admit, though I can already tell it's going to be tight over my hips.

Of course, having one dress to try on makes me want to round up a few more—and by the time I reach the fitting rooms, I've managed to gather an armload. The rooms turn out to be surprisingly luxurious. Maybe not Anthropologie level, but they're well-lit, with plenty of space for the half dozen or so pieces of clothing I've gathered. I spread everything out as much as possible—dresses on hooks, pinafore over the back of a chair, skirt hanging from the doorknob. I don't love trying on clothes, but I love the part that comes right before it, when every dress seems like it just might change the whole game. Must be the Halloween baby in me. I've always loved a good low-stakes transformation.

Unless it's not a transformation at all. Maybe it's recognition. It's that little click of *hi, me, nice to meet you!*

As expected, the bottom half of the shirtdress is tight enough to make even the spiciest Christian mommy blogger blush. Definitely not wearable if I plan on bending or sitting. Or even breathing, really. But just as I'm about to peel it off, my phone buzzes—Tessa responding to the inspiration board in the group chat.

This is so extra, I love it

And then: Also guys wtf is this rain

There's a grumpy-faced selfie attached—wet bangs and rain-spattered cheeks, the entrance to Wegmans visible in the background.

I smile down at my phone.

It occurs to me that the top half of this dress fits perfectly. And half of a perfectly fitting dress is all you really need for a selfie. Now I just have to rein in the bunny eyes, tuck those weird hanks of hair behind my ears, and—

"Hi, hello! Reporting for outfit feedback duty."

Lili's voice, just outside the fitting room. I shove my phone into my bag so forcefully, I half expect it to split a hole through the bottom. "Almost done—sorry!"

"Immy, if you make me quote a Rachel Hollis book title at you, I swear to God."

I nod quickly, even though she can't see me. I'm pretty sure only half the lights are on in my brain.

But I manage to pull on a gray plaid pinafore over my *Upstate of Mind* T-shirt, and it's actually pretty perfect. Super cheap, for one thing—probably because there's a fairly big hole in the waistband. But it's in the back, and it's right at the seam, so I bet I could sew it closed. I could even duct-tape it. Anyway, I really like it, even paired with my random fake-retro T-shirt. Honestly, the longer I stare at the mirror, the more I love the whole weird combination. It makes me look . . . kind of queer? Like the kind of girl you'd meet at a gay coffeeshop or something?

Or, you know. Literally every straight, white girl after two days on an American college campus.

I step out, and my heart's in my throat. I don't know why this feels like a test.

"Um, okay, I *love* the pleats." Lili taps her chin. "Let's see a spin."

"So, there's kind of a hole in the butt—"

"The spiciest Christian mommy blogger! I love it!"

"Let me see!" Kayla slips out of the stall next door, wearing what appears to be an ivory lace wedding dress.

Declan glances over. "Miss Havisham. Nice."

Kayla flips him off without missing a beat.

Then she grins at me. "Look who's serving up the biggest bi energy."

"Me?" I blink.

"Bi vibes? Through the roof," Declan says.

Lili's eyes meet mine for the barest split second, and she bites back a smile.

"As much as I hate to agree with this asshole," says Kayla.

Declan side-hugs her. "Look at this girl pretending she didn't stop the clocks when I left her at the altar."

Kayla wrinkles her nose, and Lili laughs—I'm pretty sure I'm laughing too. But my brain's on another planet entirely. It's in a completely different solar system.

Biggest bi energy. Bi vibes through the roof.

It's clearly a compliment—or a solidarity thing, since Kayla and Declan themselves are both bi. So it's not that I mind it. Of course not. It just doesn't entirely compute.

I'm straight. So how are my bi vibes through the roof?

Is it really just the aesthetic? Am I two lemon squares and a haircut away from making out with girls at a Clairo show?

Or does it all come down to confirmation bias?

Kayla and Declan think I give off bi vibes. Because Kayla and Declan think I'm bi.

Kayla pulls around to the back side of Rosewood and twists in her seat to face me, brown eyes gleaming. "Imogen, we gotta talk."

I look up, startled. "Oh! Okay—"

"Did you or did you not just purchase a plaid pinafore?"

"I . . . did?"

"Mm-hmm. And would you say said pinafore would fall under the aesthetic umbrella of what we might refer to as 'dark academia'?"

I smile a little. "Probably."

"Probably?" Kayla taps her phone and hands it back to Lili. "Ms. Cardoso, will you please direct the defendant's attention to exhibit A?"

"My vision board?"

"And will the defendant please describe the attire of the brooding white person in the bottom left corner?"

"It's . . . a gray plaid pinafore."

"Precisely." Kayla bangs her fist on her palm like a gavel. "You have a costume. Therefore, the court of Kayla Richardson hereby summons you to return to campus this Friday and attend one party at Rainbow Manor."

"Hereby seconded," says Declan.

"Thirded," says Mika.

"It's not a vote," Kayla says. "It's a decree."

"You guys." I'm smiling so hard it makes my cheeks ache. I glance at Lili. "I probably shouldn't . . ."

"Right. I forgot you're on the avoid-campus-for-another-six-months visitation schedule," Lili says, and I know—I *know* she's just teasing.

But the sharp edge to her tone wipes the grin clean off my face. And judging by the ripple of awkward forced laughter, I'm not the only one who hears it.

Texts with Gretchen

IS: Okay that looks like a castle!!

IS: BEAUTIFUL

GP: RIGHT?

GP: You should have seen it last night

GP: Vassar at sunset 💯

GP: Remember when the sun existed 🏚️ 🏚️

IS: I kind of like it with the gray sky background though

IS: Like, it's spooky

IS: But cozy

GP: If you say so lol

GP: BUT HEY GUESS WHAT

GP: I think they found someone to host me tonight ✌️

IS: Oh! Wait

IS: That's awesome

IS: So you'll get to stay in the dorms?

GP: I mean I'm lowkey scared to get my hopes up

GP: And then end up back in the hotel with my mom lol

IS: Okay, but Mama P is in fact amazing

GP: That is true

GP: Oh, she says hiiiiiii

GP: And she hopes you're having so much fun!!!!

GP: So much!!!!!

IS: Thanks 🖤

IS: Driving back from thrift store now

IS: But I think we're all meeting back up for dinner at
       Lili's favorite diner?

IS: Which is apparently called Diner

IS: It's off campus, I hear the pancakes are the BIGGEST

IS: Well

IS: Second biggest 😊

18

But by the time dinner rolls around, no one seems to care much about pancakes.

Or the fact that I'm leaving tomorrow.

Declan's the first to reply. So . . . you might want to take a quick peek out the window lol

"Has it gotten really bad out there?"

Lili reaches back to tug the blinds up, peering through the glass for a moment. "Wimp. It was way worse this morning."

"You think he's trying to bail?"

Our phones both buzz again—Mika. Ooh, yeah. I don't know if it's a diner night. May just heat up soup and make some tiny furniture.

Declan writes back with a full array of chair and couch emojis.

I stare at my screen, feeling strangely out of breath for a second.

"Really?" Lili scowls. "On your last night?"

"It's fine. I totally get it."

"It's not even raining that hard!"

I peek out the window again. "I mean, it's not great."

Another buzz—this time it's Kayla. haha i guess we should take a literal rain check

"Okay, I guarantee these losers forgot it's your last night," Lili says, tapping into the text box. "Watch, they're gonna—"

"Don't!" My heart jumps. "Please."

Lili shoots me a perplexed smile. "I wasn't going to, like, *bully* them. I was just going to remind them you're leaving—"

"I know. Yeah. I just—that just feels so weird. I don't want to pressure them into hanging out with me."

"Immy, they just forgot. It's not personal."

"I know." I stare at my knees, feeling so weird in my skin all of a sudden. Like I'm being pinpricked from the inside.

I guess it's just a little embarrassing, right? The way I thought it was real. My college friends. The group chat. Just one of the pack, right? Like I wasn't just some random high school kid they met literally two days ago.

Like I'd carved out some kind of home with these people.

By now, it's almost seven, and Tessa still hasn't replied to the group chat. Lili stands and stretches. "All right, I'm giving up on her. Do you want to just grab stuff from the snack bar? We can bring it up here and watch a movie if you want."

"Sure."

"Okay . . ." Lili grips the doorframe. "What do you *want* to do?"

"I'm fine with whatever! Really."

She sighs. "Immy, come on. Don't do this."

"Don't do what?"

"Your people-pleasing schtick! I'm tired of it. Save that shit for strangers, and just be real with me!"

And with that, she takes off down the empty dorm hallway. I chase after her, stung. "I am real with you!"

She stabs the elevator call button with her finger. For a moment, neither of us speaks.

"I'm not trying to people-please," I say, finally. "I'm just—"

"No, I know. Immy, I know—"

"I just honestly don't care if we watch a movie, okay? That's all."

"I *know*." She bites her lip. "Sorry. It just sucks that it's raining, and now everyone's bailing on the diner, and I really wanted your last dinner to be special."

"It is special!"

"The snack bar is the actual antithesis of special. It's like the food version of a white sock."

The elevator chimes, doors sliding open to reveal a soaking wet Tessa carrying a soggy paper grocery bag. "Hi! Wait— are you guys heading to the diner? Let me just drop this stuff off and change into something a little less, uh"—she glances

139

down—"wet T-shirt contest."

"Diner's off—everyone bailed. Have you been getting our texts?"

Tessa shakes her head. "Phone died. Not, like, water damage. Just forgot to charge it. They really bailed?"

Lili nods and I shrug.

"Okay, well. Their loss." She shifts the grocery bag in her arms. "I got those vanilla scones—Scott, you would *love* them. Okay, wait, this bag is definitely about to disintegrate. Give me a sec to get situated."

"And plug your phone in," Lili adds, already halfway to her room.

"Yes! That. Also, hold up—I have the *best* dinner idea."

"Oh yeah?" Lili's back in her room by now, with the door left wide-open. But I hang back with Tessa, while she fumbles for her keys. "I can take the bag—"

"Nooo, ma'am. That is my gross bag, thank you very much. You're too dry and too pure."

"Like toilet paper."

"Exactly." Tessa grins. "Okay, here. Can you grab my keys, maybe?" She lifts the grocery bag higher, revealing a carabiner attached to one of her belt loops.

"Oh. Yeah! Should I . . . like. Just take the key off?" My cheeks go warm.

"Or just take the whole thing off the loop—probably easier, right?" Tessa watches me, beaming. "I love how hard you're concentrating right now. You should probably be a surgeon."

"Or a locksmith."

"Why not both?" Tessa says.

I unlock the door and push it open, and Tessa bumps it with her hip to hold it for me. But I linger in the doorway. "I like your room," I say, suddenly shy.

It's smaller than Lili's, and there's only one bed—hastily made with white sheets, patterned with tiny gnomes. There's a shaggy gray rug on the floor, currently covered with short stacks of books and scattered index cards. Just like Lili's room, the walls are one big gallery of photos and posters—a Bowie lightning bolt, a vintage map of Hershey Park, and the words *this must be the place* in stylized yellow and green.

"Talking Heads," I say. "I love that song."

"It's my favorite." She shoots me a quick smile, setting her bag down on top of her desk.

"Well, if it isn't the on-call surgeon." Lili smiles up at me from her laptop when I enter the room. "Who's gonna tell Tess you fainted watching that birth video in Girl Scouts?"

"That video was a nightmare. I stand by it."

"Oh, you definitely weren't standing."

I laugh, cheeks going warm. "Irrelevant. That birth was extremely vaginal—"

"Are you guys talking about extreme vaginas without me again?" Tessa asks. She leans against Lili's doorframe, already

141

fully transformed—fresh gray hoodie, dry pair of gym shorts, and a very cute attempt at a ponytail. Slung over one shoulder is a lumpy Blackwell College duffel bag. "Who's ready for a picnic?"

19

It's like being in *Willy Wonka*—like I'm about to step out into the candy garden. But instead of chocolate and sunshine, it's just a dimly lit, graffiti-covered hallway. And, of course, we aren't outside at all.

We're beneath.

"So these are the tunnels," Tessa says, gesturing loosely. "It's mostly just hallways like this, but there are a few bigger rooms as you walk through."

I peer around. "It's so empty."

"I think Sunday night's pretty quiet. People come down here on the weekends, though."

"Thus the decor," Lili adds, stepping around a few flattened beer cans and a tired-looking disposable vape.

The tunnel widens into what's clearly an abandoned laundry room, judging by the dilapidated washers and dryers. The only other furniture in sight is a single tattered green sofa. Tessa tugs on a string hanging from the ceiling, flooding the space with sharp, fluorescent light. "This," she declares, "is the spot."

"This is where we're eating?" Lili squints down at the sofa.

"Ooh, don't sit there. That's a sex couch." Tessa unzips her duffel and takes out an actual red gingham picnic blanket.

"You know this is, like, a *really* creepy place for a picnic, right?" Lili nods slowly.

I settle in cross-legged on the blanket. "I like it. It kind of reminds me of the barn."

"Immy, it is absolutely zero percent like your barn."

"You have *a barn*?"

Lili laughs. "She has two!"

"I do not!" I turn to Tessa. "The second one's just a shed."

She scoots in beside me. "So do you just straight-up live on a farm?"

"Kind of? It's not a farm farm. But—I don't know—it's a little farmier than a big backyard? Like, my parents grow their own vegetables and we have eleven pets—that kind of thing."

"Eleven?"

I count them off on my fingers. "Three dogs, six cats—seven, if you count the feral one we leave food out for. And then my sister has a rabbit—"

"Flossie Bunny!" says Lili.

"And I have a hamster named Elizabeth."

Tessa raises her eyebrows. "That is a *very* pretty name for a hamster."

"Thank you! I got her during my *Pride and Prejudice* era."

Tessa laughs, and my chest goes taut. Shifting to face me,

she asks, "Where did Daisy live?"

I just look at her.

"Daisy the goat?" Lili asks.

"I can't believe you remember my childhood goat's name."

"Your childhood goat." Tessa smiles. "How many goat names do you think I'm keeping track of?"

"God, I don't even know. Millions, probably." I bite back a grin. "And she lived in the barn."

"Of course she did."

"But we really just use it for storage at this point."

"Well, it's also a performance venue," adds Lili.

"Right!" I nod. "There's a whole stage area in the back for concerts."

"There were *concerts*?"

Lili nods. "Sold-out shows every weekend. We had an extremely devoted fandom of stuffed animals."

"This is downright majestic," says Tessa.

"It was a golden age," confirms Lili. "We used to have sleepovers out there in the summer."

"And we turned it into a haunted house one year for my birthday," I say.

"I officially want your life. Hamster named Elizabeth, barn sleepovers, Halloween birthday." Tessa shakes her head at me. "How does that even work?"

"The barn sleepovers?" asks Lili.

"The Halloween birthday! Do you get double candy?"

"Oh, I wish!"

"Great wardrobe options, though," Lili says.

Tessa looks at me. "I bet I can guess all your costumes."

"All eighteen?"

"Well, the first one's easy," she says. "It's that little pink-and-blue-striped hat from the hospital."

"Nope! Home birth."

"*Wow.* Bet that was interesting for the trick-or-treaters."

"We love a good vaginal birth," Lili says.

Tessa laughs. "Okay, wait, I'm not done guessing! Mmm. I'm getting strong cat vibes. Headband ears, face paint . . ." She streaks her fingers over her cheeks, like she's giving herself whiskers.

"Just figured that out from the vibes, huh?" asks Lili. "Nothing to do with my wall collage?"

"As a matter of fact, that's where the vibes came from."

"As a matter of fact." I shoot Tessa a quick smile. "Let me guess—you were one of those cardboard-box-costume kids."

"That's really what you think of me, Scott?"

"Do I think you've worn a cardboard box in public? Yes."

"Absolutely," says Lili.

Tessa raises a finger. "Okay, you're not wrong—"

"Knew it!"

"—but it wasn't, like, an intact box by the time I was wearing it. Not usually," she adds.

"So it was multiple Halloweens."

"Purim too sometimes." Her eyes crinkle. "Once, my siblings and I won the costume contest at temple, because everyone else was Esther or Mordecai. We were a Nintendo Switch."

"You were not," Lili says.

"For real! Dan was the screen, and he drew this pixelated Purim scene on the chest part. And then me and Rachael were the blue and red controllers. It was pretty cute, since we used to be basically identical. My hair was longer then," she adds, turning to me.

My heart flips. "You cut it pretty recently, right?"

"Over break. My mom was a little weird about it at first. I think she saw it as this big declaration of lesbianism."

"But she's not . . ." I pause. "Would she see that as a bad thing?"

"Oh, no—I mean, I was already out. And they're fine. My parents, I mean. Like, they're liberal Jews, donate to the Human Rights Campaign, love *Schitt's Creek*, all of that. They just get a little weird sometimes about the fact that it's *me*."

"I don't like that," says Lili.

"Yeah . . . I think they just needed time to get used to the fact that, no, I will not in fact be marrying a nice Jewish boy. I mean, you'd think my elementary school tie collection might have clued them in, but." She shrugs. "Like, there's literally a video of me at age *three* singing along to 'Fast Car.' Tracy Chapman. Come on, Mom."

"Baby gay Tessa," says Lili. "What a legend."

Tessa turns to me. "What about you? Are your parents cool?"

"Like objectively cool?" I start to ask, but then my cheeks

go warm. "You mean are they cool with me being—queer? Yeah, absolutely."

"Elizabeth took it well?"

"She was actually pretty quiet about it. Though to be fair, she had, like, an entire corncob in her cheeks at the time."

"Blaming her biphobia on the corn," Lili says. "Tale as old as time."

I laugh, feeling slightly light-headed. "But my parents are cool. Yeah. I, um. Technically came out when I was Lesbian Elsa for Halloween. I was seven."

I can feel Lili looking at me.

I look pointedly away. "But they totally already knew," I say quickly. "They were just waiting for me to say it. I remember all these books started showing up on our shelves, though, about parenting queer kids. And they'd always make this big show of not implying the genders of our future partners."

I feel sick. Like, actually sick.

I just stole my sister's entire coming-out story.

And for what? To add fake texture to the other fake things Tessa already believes about me? Did *Frozen* even exist when I was seven?

But Tessa just smiles. "Hey—three down!"

"Three down?"

"Gory home-birth baby, cat, and Lesbian Elsa!" she says, counting them off on three fingers. Two truths and a lie.

Texts with Gretchen

GP: Leaving art center now, am about to meet my hostess with the mostess!! WISH ME LUCK

GP: But first, here's a selfie where I look translucent 📎

GP: Art center lighting confirming Mom and I are indeed both very white

GP: Hope you're having fun at the diner!

20

I can't sleep. Maybe I've forgotten how. Every time I close my eyes, my foot starts itching, or my pillow feels lumpy, or there's a random burst of laughter in the hallway. Even Lili's white-noise app feels unsettlingly loud.

Almost as loud as my brain.

I can't seem to keep my thoughts from going off-leash.

Like right now. I'm in bed.

But I'm also on a balcony wearing my prom dress. Not my actual prom dress, though. It's the prom dress I *almost* bought, before deciding it was too ruffled and girly and born to hand jive. But when I lean back against the stone balustrades, that's what I'm wearing. Then Tessa steps out in a half-buttoned black shirt, like Graham wears in *But I'm a Cheerleader* when they sneak out to the bar. *Hey, can I ask you something?* she says, eyes as bright as the moon. So I panic a little, scrambling for the perfect words to diffuse the awkwardness. But then she leans in—

No—wait.

She doesn't lean in. She bites her lip nervously and clears her throat. *Do you want to go out sometime? Like—a date?*

Oh! I say. *Tessa. I'm—so sorry.* My voice cracks. *I'm actually straight.* And she laughs sadly. *Yeah, I know. Just had to try. You'll let me know if you're ever . . . not straight, though, right?* And then we exchange wistful smiles, and I say, *Definitely,* and I bury my head in her shoulder—

Actually, no. There's no balcony, no formalwear. We're back in the tunnels, like earlier, only this time we're alone. *So I need you to be my fake girlfriend,* she says, and I laugh and ask why. *Because my ex is in town. She thinks I'm still in love with her, and I've got to show her I've moved on.*

Oh! Okay—

I promise I'm not secretly in love with you, she adds.

No, I wasn't. Ha—

Unless you want me to be.

Want you to be what?

Secretly in love with you. Her gaze meets mine, wide and nervous.

I stare back, and then—

Maybe my eyes spill over with tears.

Hey. Oh. I didn't mean to upset you.

I let out a choked little laugh. *You're not. No. I just. I'm—I thought I was straight.*

Imogen. She wipes away one of my tears, cupping my cheek in her hand.

And I think. *Oh. Maybe—*

DAY FOUR
MONDAY
MARCH 21

Texts with Gretchen

GP: Yeahhh I have to tell you about this girl I'm staying with

GP: ~~Immylou Immybean~~

GP: Are you still sleeping??

GP: Who are you and what have you done with Imogen???!!

21

My eyes jolt open, heart skittering in my chest.

I'm in a sea of white noise. Completely untethered. Across the room, Lili's chest rises and falls, slow as water.

Unless you want me to be. Secretly in love. With you.

Unless.

I think I might be a horrible person.

Because this Tessa thing? This is worse than normal lying. It's queerbaiting.

Or at the very least, I'm appropriating queerness. Not even just the aesthetics, either. Apparently, my brain thinks *queerness itself* is some kind of thought exercise.

Me: a certified asshole straight girl who sees a lesbian existing and thinks it's a love declaration. Tuck my skirt into my tights, and I'm literally the eyelash girl from the movie theater.

But the worst part is, this isn't the first time it's happened.

I used to get a little hung up on certain girls when I was

younger. Not always. Just sometimes. Especially if I found out they were queer.

It's hard to explain, and it definitely wasn't something I talked about. I guess I could never find a way to describe the feeling without it sounding like a crush. But it wasn't anything like my actual crushes. On boys. It wasn't that thunderstorm of feeling—electric, all-consuming, blaringly loud in my head.

With girls, it was more like that feeling you get when you finish a book and your brain can't quite shake it.

Like when this girl Nisha Khatoon from the track team started coming to Pride Alliance meetings. She sat next to me in the welcome circle her first day, and I remember how weirdly suspenseful it was, wondering if she'd say her labels when she introduced herself.

But that was it. It's not that I wanted to *date* her. She just had the sort of tomboyish confidence and easy laugh that made me want to be her friend. And—

I guess I kind of understood that if I *were* queer, I'd probably be attracted to her.

Just like with Tessa.

There was this one girl who used to come into Seneca Farms when Lili and I worked there. She was white with a curly bleached pixie cut, and I never learned her name, but she always ordered a butterscotch waffle cone. I knew she liked girls, too, because she showed up once wearing a shirt that said *le dollar bean*. I used to count the number of people ahead of her in line, trying to figure out if I'd end up scooping her order. Sometimes I even wondered if butterscotch girl was secretly making the same calculations. Not that she had any reason to like me. Or even notice me.

It was just a thought I liked to carry around sometimes.

But it always felt like someone else's daydream—something I walked out of the store with and forgot to pay for.

Texts with Gretchen

IS: I'm up I'm up, sorry!

IS: Tell me about this girl!! 👀

IS: I take it that means you got to stay in the dorms

GP: Oh I most certainly did

GP: Immy this girl

GP: Piper

GP: I want you to imagine

GP: The straightest girl of all time

GP: A straight girl! At Vassar!!!!

GP: And not a cool straight like you

IS: How can you tell she's straight??

GP: hahahahahahahahhhha

IS: No, for real!

GP: How do I know thee girl is straight? Let me count the ways

GP: She has mass produced canvas wall art

GP: On her dorm room wall

GP: "Live Laugh Love"

GP: Put on 3 inch heels for brunch

GP: Also woke up two hours early to make beach waves

in her hair and then PONYTAILED IT

GP: PIPER, WHY

IS: So it's just that she's girly?

GP: I mean yeah, but it's also a certain vibe

GP: You kinda know it when you see it

GP: Oh god, okay so

GP: All her photos are like ten girls in bikinis posing as a group on the beach

IS: Photos of girls in bikinis

IS: But in a straight way

GP: Exactly, you get it

GP: Anyway I have officially reunited with Mama P, and we are heading to Sarah Lawrence!!!

GP: In Bronxville

GP: I believe you're familiar with it 😏

IS: Yeahhhh hahaha

IS: Well, safe travels to Bronxville, which I now know is not a nickname for the Bronx!!

IS: Much like Prussia was not, in fact, an alternate name for Russia

IS: The more you know 🤗

22

I don't say goodbye to Tessa.

I mean, her door's closed, so she's probably sleeping. Or in class. Either way, it's for the best, since I don't really trust my face right now. *Hey, Tessa, guess who just had some extremely normal lucid dreams about you being in love with me! Bet you love hearing that from straight girls.*

"You've got your charger, right?" Lili presses the elevator button, still gripping my suitcase. "Toiletries?"

"Think so?" I rub my eyes.

"Aww—looks like someone's ready to get a good night's sleep in her own bed."

I yawn through a laugh. "Do I look awful?"

"No, you just look like those sleepy angel figurines from the Windmill."

I look at her. "You mean the dead angels?"

"Whoa! They're not *dead*—"

"Lili. The bases literally say, 'In Loving Memory.'"

161

"Well, maybe it's just a souvenir?" She presses her forehead, stifling a laugh. "From a fun memory with an angelic person? An angelic *alive* person!"

"Oh, okay—"

"Like—for example—you." She pokes me with her car keys.

I try to smile, but it falters. "Yeah. I'm not an angel."

I'm a culturally appropriating piece of trash, in fact. Just your run-of-the-mill hetero egomaniac, dabbling in some good old-fashioned telepathic queerbaiting.

It's like I'm incapable of being normal around queer women.

"I'm problematic," I say, hardly louder than a whisper.

She laughs. "Why are you problematic?"

"I don't know." I pause, hand stalling on the door handle of Lili's Toyota Camry. She presses the button to open it, and I take the passenger seat. "I just feel like I maybe overstepped a little this weekend."

She tilts her head toward me. "How so?"

"Maybe *overstepped* isn't the word. I just . . . feel like I was centering myself in queer spaces. Under false pretenses. I don't know if that makes sense."

"Imogen." Lili grips the steering wheel, staring for a second at the dashboard. Then she blinks, buckles her seat belt, and turns the car on. "That's—okay, so I know—I *know* you're being sincere. Not trying to invalidate your feelings. But."

I smile a little. "But . . ."

"Centering yourself in queer spaces? Like, what, my room?"

I shake my head. "*Metaphorical* spaces—"

"Also! In what universe are you responsible for the false pretenses here? I literally roped you into this! Except not actually literally, because there were no literal ropes involved!" She glances up at the rearview and out the back windshield, pulling out of the parking space at a snail's pace.

"It's complicated, though."

"But it's really not. I have a dorm room, and I invited you to stay there." She shrugs, shifting out of reverse. "And guess what! I'd do it again!"

"Okay then." I laugh.

Lili's quiet for a moment. But just as we're about to exit the student lot, she shoots me a quick sideways glance. "Hey. You know you're always welcome here, right? Anytime. Open invitation. I don't give a single shit how problematic you think you are."

My throat goes tight. "Thanks."

"And you should seriously come back Friday for the party."

"You guys and this party." I smile.

"I'm just saying! It's going to be *amazing*."

"Evidently!"

I sneak a glance at Lili's profile, still a little stunned by her enthusiasm. Back home, every party we ever went to was my idea—and even that was just because I felt like I had to. Usually because I'd promised Gretchen. Or because I'd panicked and told someone random that I'd be there. And since my brain likes to turn every off-the-cuff verbal commitment into a blood vow, it was really just a matter of talking Lili into coming with me.

So we'd end up shuffling awkwardly around the edges of some house party for an hour. But we'd always leave early, giddy with the relief of our recovered freedom. Then we'd spend the whole night talking about how much parties suck, even the Pride Alliance ones.

So, when did parties stop sucking for Lili? Was it when I stopped being the person she went with?

"So . . . that's a yes?"

"Lili, no. You should get to experience that with your actual queer friends—"

"—all of whom want you there, too."

"Because they think I'm queer."

"Okay." She shoots me a look I can't quite decipher. "But they also just like you."

Through the window, I watch a Mennonite wagon pull up a dirt driveway, into one of the farms—such a common sight here, my eyes would normally skim right over it. But now I can't stop thinking about that used disposable vape in the Blackwell tunnels. A whole different planet, twenty minutes and a staircase away. It's like stepping out of a noir film into the afternoon sunshine.

Lili turns left onto my street, and I take in all the houses and yards as we pass. Pebbled paths leading up to wooden front doors. The Johnsons' giant fenced-in garden. Metal patio chairs and covered firepits. Everything's just the same as I left it.

Which makes sense, given that I've only been gone for three days. Why does it feel like so much longer?

My parents' car is in the carport, so Lili veers right to park near the barn, turning to face me. "I can't tell if you just don't want to come to this party—or if you *do* want to come but feel like you shouldn't."

"It's not that," I say quickly. "I just think I should probably stick around Penn Yan. I still need to finish some stuff up before next Monday."

"Ah, yes." Lili cuts her eyes upward. "Stuff."

"Just like—homework. And my dad wants us to go through some of the boxes in the shed. Stupid stuff."

Lili lets out a short laugh. "You can just say you don't want to come. It's fine! I don't need a list of excuses."

"They're not excuses!"

"Fine." She exhales. "It's just—it seemed like you had a good time this weekend. You know?"

"I did!" I turn in my seat, my throat suddenly thick. "Lili, I *did*. It was perfect. It was *everything*."

Her expression softens. "Okay. Good. I just—really wanted you to feel at home there. Since it *is* your home. Will be, anyway."

"Five months." I exhale.

"Fastest five months of your life," she says, smiling. "You'll see."

Texts with Gretchen

GP: OMFG I'm at a meet and greet thing and guess who's here

GP: 📎

IS: No way!!!!!

IS: At Sarah Lawrence?

GP: Yes!! She's a student ambassador now

GP: She's even CUTER how is that possible???

GP: That's it, I'm turning in my deposit

IS: Olivia . . . why am I blanking on her last name

GP: Olivia Fields!!!!

GP: Wait no, Olivia FIELD

GP: Singular

IS: Oh no . . . bad news

IS: Not singular

IS: (I'm looking at her Instagram)

IS: I think she has a boyfriend

GP: Yes! She's bi!

IS: Oh, I mean she's taken

GP: Oh right

GP: Maybe she's poly?

~~GP: Okay nvm I just walked up~~ and she said hi and she
absolutely didn't recognize me, like not even a
glimmer of recognition

GP: Ripping up the SL deposit now

GP: Submitting a late application to Blackwell, saving
myself for hot Tessa, lol

23

Home really has its own soundscape. Rustling leaves and bird-songs and Mom's wind chimes on the side of the house, near the garden. All these beats and ticks and clanks I've never noticed until now. My feline welcoming committee swoops in before I even reach the front door—Adrian and Demi, weaving in and out of my legs, meowing like the world's ending. I keep letting go of my suitcase to scratch their heads and pet their tails down. As I get closer to the door, I can hear faint TV noises. Edith, in full spring break mode.

It's all so completely mundane. I could cry with relief.

I let myself in through the front, and all three dogs rocket toward me. "Hi, babies. Oh, hi!" Eloise leaps up, setting her paws on my shoulders, and I press my nose to her snout.

"Do I hear an Imogen?" my mom calls up from the base-ment. The school she works at is on spring break this week, too, which means she's probably already elbow-deep in home projects. I leave my suitcase by the door, plopping beside Edith on the couch. She pauses *The Owl House* and stretches. "Hey! How was it?"

"Really fun. Hi, Flossie-bun." Flossie looks up from Edith's lap, twitching her nose at me.

"That's it? Really fun? That's all you've got?"

"It was fun!"

"Yeah, duh. It's college." Edith shakes her head. "But was it life-altering? Transformational? Are you forever changed?"

"Hi, hi, hi! I'm here!" Mom says, coming up the short basement stairs in her overalls. "Oh, I want to hug your little face, but I'm covered in primer. Just finished the base coat inside the shed." She holds both arms up, showing off several big streaks of white paint.

The shed is my parents' current obsession. It looks like a little wooden house, for the most part—smaller than the barn, but closer to the house. We've always just used it for storage— off-season clothes, garden tools, extra rolls of toilet paper, that sort of thing. But my mom got this idea to clear it out and turn it into an extra room off the back of our house. Apparently, my dad's even going to build a little covered walkway to connect them.

"What'd you do with the boxes?"

Edith bites back a smile. "You should see the basement."

"We'll get it all put away by the end of break," Mom says. "I was thinking we could move the futon in there and get some Christmas lights up. Nice and cozy. We'll get good Wi-Fi out there, too." She leans down to pet Smokey and Eloise, who both have just burst in from somewhere behind me. "Anyway, I'm hopping in the shower, and then I'll run to town and grab groceries for tonight. Wish it would warm up a little! Saturday was so nice, wasn't it? Oh, but I'm so glad you're home, Immy. We missed you!"

I smile up at her. "Me too."

Texts with Tessa

TM: Scott you are NOT going to believe who I just saw

TM: You're going to be so jealous!!!

IS: Who??

IS: Is it someone famous 🙀

TM: Better 📎

IS: Daisy!!!!!!!!!!!!!!

IS: Oh my god

IS: Her EARS

IS: And her little tongue

IS: Was she licking your eye??

TM: SHE WAS AND I LOVED IT

TM: I literally can't believe I just ran into her again

TM: I think she misses you though

IS: Aww, I miss her too!

IS: Tell her me and Eloise say hi 📎

TM: Eloise!!!

TM: Haha I love when their ears flip back like that, she
        looks like George Washington

TM: What a distinguished lady!!!!

TM: Eloise, you look nice too 😊

24

Edith cranes her neck toward my phone. "Ooh. Who's that?"

"Oh! Just—some of Lili's people."

"Hold UP. College people?" She scoops Flossie off her lap, leaning closer. "Oh my God—are you texting Dylan?"

"Who's Dylan?"

"Lili's friend! The guy who looks like an ice prince?"

"You mean Declan?"

Her hands fly to her mouth. "Did you hook up with him?"

"What?" I shake my head, smiling bewilderedly. "No!"

"Then why are you sitting here smiling at your phone like a smitten kitten?"

"I'm not!" I lean back into the couch cushions, rolling my eyes to the ceiling. "Oh my God. No! I didn't hook up with Declan. Or anyone."

"You're just texting him."

"No!" I swipe Mom's dragonfly throw pillow off the couch and throw it at Edith. "I've literally never texted Declan, ever.

Other than the group chat."

Edith grips her head with both hands. "You're in the *group chat*?"

"I'm in *a* group chat." I laugh a little, heartbeat finally inching back to normal. The group chat is definitely safer territory than certain other topics. Like Edith's clown car of a theory that I hooked up with Declan, for example. At least my college group chat is a thing that exists.

And by that, I mean it *existed*. Seeing as there hasn't been a single new message since Kayla requested a rain check last night.

They've probably reverted to their original group chat, without me.

Of course they've reverted to their original group chat without me. I'm Lili's friend from home who visited for three days. That doesn't exactly confer lifelong best friend privileges. And yeah, they talked a good game about wanting me to come back this weekend—but when push came to shove, no one even seemed to care that I was leaving.

Except Tessa, I guess.

Does that make us real friends?

It sort of feels like it. Or at least we're getting there. That would explain the weird dreams from yesterday, right? Maybe that was just my mind trying to pin down our friendship status. Better that than the mortifyingly problematic alternative: I met a lesbian and immediately assumed she was in love with me. *Oh ur a lesbian?? Do u like have a crush on me or something??? Sorry, sweaty, I date guyssss.*

Edith flops backward and sighs. "I can't believe you're just sitting here texting your little queer college group chat. Are you guys just bouncing around hilarious inside jokes? Are you spilling all your secrets, Immy?"

"Secrets?" Heat floods my cheeks. I guess I've always kept certain thoughts private, but I've never really thought of it like that.

Tessa sort of feels like a secret, though. Probably because I just straight-up lied when Edith asked me who I was texting. Well—technically, Edith assumed I was talking to the group chat, and I just went along with it.

Kind of like how I went along with Lili's fabricated relationship backstory. And how I let everyone believe I'm bisexual.

It really begs the question: When, exactly, did I get so comfortable with lying?

Texts with Gretchen

GP: IMOGEN GUESS WHAT

GP: 🕸️

GP: ~~SOMETHING LGBT JUST HAPPENED~~

IS: What?!!

IS: Omg did you make out with someone??? Gretchen, it's the middle of the afternoon

IS: How?!

GP: lol cool your jets Immylou

GP: No 🤫

GP: YET

GP: But the vibes are full force

GP: And I'm in her room right now 😊

IS: WHAT

IS: !!!!!!

GP: To be fair, she's my host 😄

GP: BUT LOOK AT HER 📎

GP: She's so cute, her name is Brielle

GP: Don't you think she looks like Barbie Ferreira??

IS: I see it!!!

GP: AND WE FOLLOW EACH OTHER NOW

GP: What's my move, do I post a thirst trap??

IS: Maybe just talk to her?

GP: Lol she's in class

GP: Just trying to keep things moving in the right direction

IS: Ohhh okay

GP: WHAT DO I DO

GP: I don't want to look too eager!!!

IS: Hmmm

IS: Would she know the thirst trap is for her specifically?

IS: Can it be a general thirst trap?

IS: Sorry, I'm a little out of my depth here

IS: I don't know how any of this works, I'm sorry 🏛️

GP: My sweet virgin queen

GP: All thirst traps are targeted

GP: And general

GP: They are both

IS: Can you clarify in the caption

IS: "This thirst trap is intended for all audiences"

GP: Hahaha ilu

GP: Okay new plan

GP: Doing a throwback to Silk Chiffon

GP: A SUBTLE thirst trap

IS: I love that picture!

GP: I'll tag you ☺

GP: Oop wait

GP: I hear footsteps

GP: NEVER MIND, THIRST TRAP CAN WAIT

GP: It's ONNNN

Texts with Tessa

TM: No, for real!!!

TM: This is like

TM: Actual tradition at this point

TM: On Rosh Hashanah it is decided, and on Yom Kippur it is revealed 😎

IS: I mean that does sound very official

IS: So how do you pick

IS: Can it be any famous person?

TM: Yup!

TM: But it can't be anyone we've done before

TM: And we all have to agree

TM: Full consensus

TM: Which btw is not easy with Dan and Rachael!!!

TM: And I guess you kind of have to pick someone with a lot of iconic fashion moments

IS: Ah okay that makes sense

TM: Also parental assistance is strictly forbidden!!!!

TM: And you CAN'T show anyone your costume until Yom Kippur

IS: So you wear the costumes to temple?

TM: Omg I wish!!!

TM: No, we do the reveal right after

TM: It's a good distraction from fasting though

TM: Like yeah, okay, we're starving, but at least we look like Harry Styles

TM: I mean 📎

TM: Literally the only time I've worn pearls 😂

IS: The green pants!!!!!

TM: I KNOW

TM: They're actually sweatpants, I still sleep in them sometimes and dream about Harry

TM: (Platonically!!!)

IS: This is

IS: Sheer chaos

TM: Why thank you 😊

25

Naturally, dinner's a huge production. Cornell chicken, carrots, and salt potatoes, because my parents felt the need to welcome me home with the most comically upstate New York meal imaginable.

"You guys get that I was, like, twenty-five minutes up Route 14, right?"

"Well, it felt far," Mom says.

"They were kind of pining for you, Immy," says Edith. "These two are definitely not ready for you to graduate."

"Oh, come on, now. We're totally cool! Back me up, Cor."

"Cool as Keuka," Dad says.

The funny thing is, a few hours ago, college seemed entirely sealed off from real life. A universe inside a universe, like a snow globe. Or like one of those dreams you forget as soon as you open your eyes.

But it all feels jumbled together right now. The buttery grilled cheese, the tunnels, the walk home from trivia night.

All these brand-new moments, slipping into every corner and crevice of home. The piles of clutter on the counter. The horrific framed tableau of middle-school pictures. The painting of cherries I made in first grade that came out looking like a giant, bright red penis. Future and past, sharing space.

And then there's Tessa.

We've been texting pretty much continuously all day.

"When are you two getting together?" my mom asks, and I almost jump out of my chair.

"What—do you mean?"

"You said she's coming back tomorrow, right? Just Vassar and Sarah Lawrence this time?"

Gretchen. Right.

"Oh—yeah. We haven't made any definite plans yet." I nod quickly. "We'll just play it by ear, I guess."

Mom picks up her fork. "I'm excited to see where she ends up. I'll tell you, that kid is a trip. Smart cookie, though. Always has been. Oh my goodness—remember her little business cards?"

Edith looks amused. "Gretchen had business cards?"

"You don't remember that, sweetie? It was right when she moved here. I don't even think she was advertising anything. Just, you know. Letting us know she was here."

"Oh, she lets us know," my dad says, and Edith startles all the cats just from laughing.

Texts with Gretchen

IS: Sure is quiet in this text thread

IS: 👀 ???

IS: Patiently awaiting updates 👀

Texts with Tessa

IS: Oh I mean

IS: It's party central here

IS: Got my main dude here with me

IS: 📎

IS: This is Quincy 🖤

TM: Shut up

TM: Is that a cat

TM: Like a regular cat

IS: Kind of 😂

IS: He's a ragdoll

TM: Quincy, you are the biggest cat I've ever seen

TM: Hands down

IS: He's thirty pounds 🐱

IS: You should hear him talk! He has a really low voice

IS: And kind of a vocal fry

IS: It's like MOAWWWWWW

IS: And he's almost 15, I think he might be immortal

TM: I'm obsessed with him

TM: Fuck parties

TM: Wait okay not like Fuck Parties as in parties where
        you fuck
TM: Fuck parties as in
TM: "Parties can fuck off now, I'm hanging out with my
        immortal cat"
TM: *Your immortal cat 😅

IS: We can share him
IS: Fifteen pounds each

TM: Oh thank god
TM: Brb, canceling karaoke night to devote myself to half
        a Quincy

IS: Karaoke night!! Omg
IS: That actually sounds really fun 🔊

TM: I've never done it!

IS: Me either 👻
IS: 95 percent chance I'd wimp out at the last second

TM: No way!!

IS: No like

IS: I'd probably go kind of mute

IS: Happens to me sometimes when I'm nervous

TM: Aww Scott

TM: Really?

IS: Yeahhhh 😬

IS: It's fun

TM: Okay but you're actually so brave though??

IS: 😂 😂 😂

TM: YOU ARE

TM: Look at last weekend!

TM: Like you just showed up to this whole new
        environment

TM: Won the fuck out of trivia, engaged in criminal
        sausage behavior, made puppies appear

TM: Like that's brave!! Idk man

TM: College visits are so intimidating

TM: The first time I visited, I basically stayed in Dan's
        room the whole time

IS: That's so sweet though?? 😳

IS: Oh my god speaking of college trips

IS: So my friend is at Sarah Lawrence tonight

IS: And I think she might be hooking up with her
        student host?

IS: Like right now??

TM: Whoa!! Nicely done

IS: A very informative college visit haha

TM: Oh definitely

TM: Listen, Scott, if you need an info session of that
        nature, let me know

TM: Could probably be arranged 😉

IS: Haha, noted 😂

26

I can't find my off switch tonight. Every time I try to close my eyes, they spring right back open.

Which makes no sense. Nothing's incomplete or out of place. I'm in my bed, in my room, in the house I was literally born in. Same posters, same books, same grayish-blue walls. Same white sock flopping out of the laundry basket, same toilet paper roll in the corner of Elizabeth's tank, same empty water glass on my nightstand.

But I feel so unzipped for some reason. Like someone left me wide-open.

I sit up in bed, staring at the seams of my quilt.

Then I sigh and pull my phone from its charger.

It's like pressing a bruise. That stupidly predictable jolt of pain.

People always talk about FOMO, but this doesn't feel like fear at all. It's an ache. Staring at a tiny handheld screen, watching someone else's memories coalesce in real time.

Blackwell College is less than thirty minutes away, and it might as well be the moon.

It's a story told in snippets. A group selfie, tongues out. Declan rolling his eyes so hard, only the whites show. A dimly lit TikTok of four people walking, filmed from behind. Lime-green text superimposed over a photo of Mika holding a microphone. *Adele is QUAKING*

A random Monday night out. It's the most ridiculous thing to care about.

As if the group was supposed to cancel all joy when I left. As if I was ever a part of the group to begin with. I'm a high school kid who got to try on college for a weekend, but that's not my real life. Not yet.

But will this tight-knit group of queer kids even want to hang out with me once they find out I'm straight? The truth has to come out eventually, right? It's not like I can fake being bi forever.

A text from Tessa pops through, and I'm so startled, my phone almost slips from my hands. There's a video attached, plus the caption: *Our girl can SING!!??*

I turn the sound on and press play—and it's really just a ten-second clip of the back of some guy's head. But Lili's easy vibrato is unmistakable—even the high notes always sound so effortless.

I know just which decade-old picture to send in reply.

I swipe back in time through my "throwbacks" album until I find it—a quick shot taken from the side of the barn. Lili onstage, with two short rows of stuffed animals, propped up against hay bales. Can confirm, I write.

~~Tessa writes back immediately.~~ Omg YES

And then: Wait is that Puppy?? 🐴

Of course, I reply. He's her biggest fan!

Tessa starts typing, and the world shrinks to fit into three tiny dots.

In my stomach: a shooting-star feeling, out of nowhere.

Something's glitching.

The way my heart's pounding straight through my chest.

The way my brain's completely stuck on Tessa. If I didn't know better, I'd almost think this was an actual crush.

But how do I know if it's real?

How do I know I'm not just being a pick-me? Or a people pleaser. What, Lili needs me to pretend I'm bi? I'll be so bi, I'll forget I'm pretending.

Unless.

I don't know, maybe I'm overthinking this.

Do I just . . . have a crush on her?

It seems so far-fetched, though. It would be one thing if I'd never met a queer person before. But my sister's queer. My best friends are queer. If it weren't spring break, I'd be spending tomorrow afternoon at a Pride Alliance meeting.

My mind spools back again to that first day, my first welcome circle. "I have a queer sister," I'd said.

It didn't even occur to me to say I was straight. I guess Edith

189

being queer felt like a complete story already. Her queerness implied my straightness. Because one queer kid made sense, but two in one family? Overkill.

And I know that's ridiculous. Factually inaccurate. Disproven in an instant by the Wachowski sisters, by Tegan and Sara. There was literally a pair of nonbinary siblings at the meeting that day. But I think the idea got lodged in my brain somehow anyway.

Maybe it's just that I know what being a queer kid looks like, and it looks nothing like me. I've never stolen a sunflower for a woman in the supermarket. I've never trick-or-treated with a lesbian flag sewn into my dress. Queerness isn't some distant hypothetical concept to me. It's right there. It always has been.

It's funny, because if you say the word *queer*, my mental image is Gretchen.

But I measure queerness against Edith. I've always measured it against Edith.

And Edith has always known she's queer. It's just never been a question. Even in preschool, Edith was into lesbians the way some kids were into unicorns.

If I were queer, wouldn't I at least sort of know?

It's my own brain. I have open access to it. No one's redacting parts of the story. *Especially* not something as fundamental as who I'm attracted to. And I know denial exists. But this *isn't* denial. Denial's a curtain with a clear truth behind it.

There's no curtain to pull back here. I'm staring straight at this question, shining every light on it, and still—

Scott, help, they're trying to make me sing!!!

I stare at my phone, at a total loss. Every possible response feels too flirtatious, too thirsty, too wistful. Too unbearably earnest.

And it *really* doesn't help that Tessa thinks I'm bi.

Because that's the thing about being straight. It's like having a built-in force field. It doesn't matter if you're laughing too loud or blinking a lot, or if that text was Too Much. When you're straight, cute girls literally don't have to worry about you catching weird, awkward feelings. Because you like boys, and she's not one, and that's the whole story.

I think I miss it.

Being straight.

I mean, I miss people thinking I'm straight. And by that, I mean I miss people *knowing* I'm straight.

Because I am. Straight.

One girl can't topple your entire sexuality, right?

DAY FIVE
TUESDAY
MARCH 22

Texts with Tessa

TM: Hello yes it's two in the morning

TM: And I'm writing to inquire about the 15 pounds of cat I ordered

TM: Upon careful consideration, I would like to request the front half please

TM: ie the soul, not the hole

TM: The tongue, not the dung

TM: The mouth, not the south

TM: ➡️🐕✔️

TM: 🐕⬅️🚫

TM: Okay I'm done I'm done I promise 😬

27

Unless it's not just one girl.

The thought lands in my brain with an echoing thud.

My eyes snap open, and I yawn my way into a sitting position, rubbing my eyes.

Unless—

I stare up at my poster wall until the images swim out of focus.

Unless it's not just one girl.

The words settle into my head, putting down roots.

Unless it's not just one—

But.

I don't get crushes on girls.

That's how I know Tessa is a fluke, not an actual crush. It's my brain trying to fit in with Lili's cool queer friends. Kind of like how Gretchen spent two weeks in Edinburgh last summer and came back with an accent and a whole new vocabulary.

If anything, it's some strange kind of role-play. Like method acting.

I mean, let's just call it what it is, right? I'm appropriating queer attraction. Like I did with Clea DuVall. And Nisha. And the le dollar bean girl. And all the others. *Not just one.*

But they weren't crushes. They *couldn't* have been crushes, because crushes aren't a thing you can hide from yourself.

Why am I even getting so stuck on this? I know what attraction feels like. I know what it feels like to want to kiss someone, and this isn't about kissing.

Though. It's not *not* about kissing.

But it's different, somehow, in a way I can't quite explain.

I guess you could call it a preoccupation. Or like a tiny pull I felt when I was near them. Not quite the same as a regular friendship.

Like taking the word *friendship* and underlining it.

Getting dressed feels like I'm sleepwalking. My weather app says it's chilly out. Sweater weather. As in, the actual weather outside. Not "Sweater Weather" the song, which TikTok says is yet another code for being bisexual. Kind of like lemon squares and cuffed jeans and not being able to sit in chairs normally.

I wish any of this made sense to me.

I settle in at my desk, pretzeling my legs in the chair. Which is how I always sit in chairs. I guess that's slightly weird?

How weirdly does a person have to sit to count as bisexual?

I keep turning the memories over in my head. The rustle of track pants against plastic chairs. The smell of butterscotch ice cream. The flat softness of felt rainbows. I remember all the details, but I can't quite conjure the feelings.

Maybe it would help if I was a little more methodical about it. I'm five months away from being in college, after all. Why not treat it like academic research? I could take one quick trip down the online rabbit hole, in the interest of triage.

Poke around for a second, rule it out, and be done with it.

Texts with Tessa

IS: Thank you so much for reaching out!

IS: The full contents of your shipment can be found in the attached inventory label

IS: For your reference, it states

IS: "The anus, not the brainus"

IS: We thank you for shopping with us

28

I can't believe how fast my heart's beating. I keep scanning the room, as if some stranger might pop out from under the bed to catch me in the act.

Of typing on my phone. That's the act.

This has to be a whole new level of unglued.

I open a private browser—which makes this feel like a bigger deal than it is.

It's not any kind of deal, really. Just three words and a question mark. No jumping to conclusions. I won't even jump to hypotheses—

My phone vibrates, and my heart leaps into my throat.

Text from Gretchen. **Heyyyy are you going to be home in like 2 hours??**

I catch my breath. **I think so, yeah**

Okay, noted! she writes, adding a winky emoji.

I feel so blurrily out of body. Like I'm my own reflection in water. I tap back into my browser, type three words, and press enter.

Pages and pages of results. Thousands of them. So many, it's hard to know where to start. I can't believe there are actually quizzes for this. It's like a television montage.

The definitive sexual orientation quiz

Are you bisexual or straight? Take this test!

Am I seriously doing this? Am I the biggest cliché on earth?

Though the fact that it's a cliché is wild to begin with, because you really shouldn't need a test to tell you your own sexuality. Maybe if you know you're queer and are just trying to home in on the exact label—I can see how that would be helpful. But the existence of queerness itself?

I pull back, staring at my posters for a minute before clicking the link. Don't want to seem too eager, I guess. True and utter clownery, given that I'm literally alone in a room. Also, why is my brain turning this into a capital-*E* Event? *Please rise for the momentous occasion of Imogen Scott confirming her heterosexuality via online quiz.*

I tap one of the links—an ad pops up for meeting singles in my area.

Then: a rainbow-flag stock photo that hasn't been formatted for mobile, followed by a paragraph of intro text. I keep scrolling until I reach the first question—though it's really more of a fill-in-the-blank statement.

I'm _____ attracted to people of my own gender.
only
sometimes
never

Only. Sometimes. Never. Only sometimes never.

I read it again.
I'm _____ attracted to people of my own gender.

It's a trick question, right? If I knew the answer to that, why would I be taking this test? I don't need the definition of bisexual. I want to know what it *feels* like. How do you know what counts as attraction?

Second question:
I have romantic daydreams about _____.
Only one gender (not my gender).
Only one gender (my gender).
Multiple genders.
No one.

Okay, got it, but . . . how literal am I supposed to be here? Do I round up to the choice that's most generally applicable? Or do I count every tiny little exception?
And what counts as an exception?
Also, how many exceptions until it's not really an exception?

I think about Clea DuVall and Kristen Stewart and Nisha and le dollar bean. And maybe the felt rainbow girl from Girl Scouts. And that girl Ilana, probably. And—

Tessa.

What if I'd stayed on campus. What if I'd gone to karaoke night.

What if we'd left early. Ended up in her room, with the door shut. What if we'd let the hallway chatter fade.

Maybe Tessa would have looked up at me with questioning eyes, smiling faintly.

Maybe I'd have smiled nervously back.

Tucked my hair behind my ears.

And maybe I'd have settled in softly beside her, my hands pressed flat on her gnome bedsheets. A millimeter from hers.

I can see it.

She'd draw a quick, shaky breath. "Hey."

"Hey," I'd say back. But—

My phone buzzes.

Texts with Tessa

TM: Oh you think you're so funny, don't you

TM: Psh I know your type

TM: Sitting right there with your giant kitty cat and your spoon applesauce and your little dimple

IS: What do you have against dimples???? 🙃

TM: Oh I am emphatically pro-dimple, Scott

TM: I just think

TM: Certain people should be a little more mindful of how their dimples might affect the general public

TM: That's all 😶

IS: I see

IS: Hmm

IS: 📎

TM: Okay that's just unfair

TM: 🙃 🙃 🙃 😍

29

I stare at the photo on my screen, a little bit stunned by my own boldness.

I just sent that. To *Tessa*. And it's so—

Fully clothed. Nana-approved. Nothing but face and neck and shoulders. Let's be totally clear.

Just a random little selfie of me smiling. With my very visible dimple.

I feel fizzy with nerves. Or guilt. Both, really. I guess it feels like I'm trespassing. Like I've slipped backstage without a pass. I've crept out of bounds.

I mean, I can't even deny it at this point. I'm definitely flirting. With Tessa.

Tessa, who is definitely a girl.

I reread our last few texts, and my heart's not even a pinball machine. It's the entire arcade.

She's flirting back.

It's not a question. There just isn't any other way to read it.

Except—

It's Tessa. She does that.

Isn't that what Lili said? That Tessa's a flirty-pants who flirts with everyone?

So then, how do you tell in that case? How do you know if someone's flirting with you, or if they just have a flirty personality? And is it ever both?

How do you know—how do you *really* know if someone likes you?

Especially with girls. It gets so blurry sometimes. Two girls will hug each other right in front of you, and you'll have no idea if they're girlfriends or besties or what. Unless they're actively making out, you need floating heart emojis and a movie score to interpret it.

Is that where the queer aesthetic stuff comes in? Gretchen and her thumb rings? Edith's jean jacket?

But how could this be about *clothes*? Is the le dollar bean girl straight until she puts on the shirt? Is *every* straight girl just an out-of-uniform bisexual?

Maybe Tessa wasn't even flirting. She could have just been humoring me.

The mortification hits like lightning—a bright bolt of shame in my chest.

What if she's *not* flirting—but she thinks *I* am. Does she cringe every time she sees my name pop up in her texts? *Ohhhh, does this child have a crush on me? Yikes!*

It's the summer after fourth grade all over again. I remember how enthralled I was by Dad's new apprentice. Who, to be clear, was a literal grown man with facial hair. When he and Dad worked from home, I'd plant myself in the basement with a book or a cat, ~~sneaking glances at his face when I thought he wasn't looking.~~ We even had a real conversation once. He asked me if I wanted to be a contractor when I grew up. I said no. And then I walked around for the rest of the day with neon-red cheeks and a fluttering stomach. Me, a child, openly thirsting over a twenty-two-year-old man. In front of my dad. Undeniable clown behavior.

But this is at least a little different, right? For one thing, I'm eighteen, which makes me very decidedly not a child. In fact, it's the exact same age as Tessa. Unless my math is wrong, we're literally just four months apart.

Though I know it's not that simple.

She's in college. I'm in high school. It's a whole different universe, really. I'm pretty sure Tessa's not asking teachers for permission to pee these days. Nor is she holding the unlockable bathroom door shut with her foot while she does it. I'd even go so far as to guess that Tessa rarely has to pass through gauntlets of fifteen-year-olds dry-humping each other against banks of lockers every time she wants to grab a textbook.

And that's not even opening the whole living-with-your-parents can of worms. Imagine being used to the privacy of dorm rooms, only to be stuck frantically buttoning your shirt back up because your girlfriend's mom knocked on the door.

"Imogen?" My mom knocks on my door.

Honest to God, I practically jump out of my skin.

30

Mom cracks the door open, smiling. "You've got a visitor, sweetie."

I shove my phone away and spring out of my chair, stomach fizzing like a volcano.

There's no way. None. That's not how reality works. And it's definitely not—

"Helloooo!"

The door creaks open.

There's a tiny, sharp twist in my chest. "Hi! Oh my God, you're back! How'd you guys get here so fast?"

"By waking up way too fucking early." Gretchen sets a plastic bag down on top of my dresser and flops onto my bed. "Mama P was like, 'No, ma'am, I don't want to be anywhere *near* Manhattan at rush hour.'"

"Probably a good call." I scoot in beside her.

"Definitely. I'm just tired. Had a late night." She shoots me a sly, sidelong smile.

I raise my eyebrows. "Wait. Did you—"

"Mayyyy-be."

"With Brielle?" I shake my head. "You actually hooked up with your student host?"

Gretchen grabs one of my pillows and buries her face in it.

"That's, like, a God-tier college visit achievement."

"I knowwww." She lets out a muffled giggle.

"So . . . does this mean Sarah Lawrence is the one?"

Her eyes peep up from over the pillow's edge. "Well . . ."

I look at her. "Wait—did you hear back?"

"Um. So . . . I actually have some news." She dumps the pillow, slides off the bed, and swipes her plastic bag off the dresser. She hands it to me, eyes gleaming. "Open it!"

I reach inside, pulling out a fluffy pink teddy bear, the exact same shade as Gretchen's hair. He's wearing a red shirt that says simply: *Vassar.*

"So you'll have something to remember me by," she says.

My mouth falls open. "It's official? You're going to Vassar?"

"I'm going to Vassar!" Gretchen's eyes well up with tears—which makes me tear up, too.

I jump up to hug her. "Gretch! Oh my God!"

"I can't believe I got in!"

I bite back a smile, and she grins at me. "What?"

"Nothing!"

"Imogen Louise Scott. *What?*"

I laugh. "I just love your reaction. You're brilliant. You're the valedictorian. Teachers are obsessed with you, you crushed the SAT, you could probably publish your essay in the *New York Times* if you wanted—"

"Um, *what?*"

"Or at least the *Chronicle-Express!*" She rolls her eyes, but I keep talking. "I'm just saying, it's sweet! You don't even see how incredible you are."

"I just can't believe we're both in college." She exhales. "It's so *weird*. It doesn't feel like real life."

Turns out, Mama P's been in the kitchen this whole time—Mom appears to have talked her into some kind of weird floral tea. "Look at these college girls," she says, smiling in that same conspiratorial way that Gretchen sometimes does. It always makes me feel like I'm in on some unspoken joke.

"Congratulations, sweetie! Your mama just told me the big news." Mom squeezes Gretchen's shoulders. "You should be so proud. Are you excited?"

"Hasn't really sunk in yet." She laughs.

"Oh, well, that's because we haven't properly celebrated yet!" Mama P sets her mug down and stands. "I don't know about you all, but I think this calls for a Seneca Farms trip. Kelly, what do you think?"

Mom presses a palm to her forehead. "I wish I could! But we've got Curt coming to install the air-conditioning in the shed. And then I want to get the tape down so it's all prepped to paint tomorrow." She exhales. "Wow, this is turning out to be quite the production, huh?"

"Sure sounds like it! Kelly, why don't you take the morning off tomorrow? The girls can handle painting."

"Oh, that's too big of a job. I couldn't ask them to do that—"

"Nonsense. I'll send Gretchen over in the morning. Is eight o'clock too late?"

"Too *late*?" Gretchen blinks.

"Are you sure?" my mom asks.

"Our absolute pleasure." Mama P presses her palms together. "And we'll get out of your hair now, too. Is Edith around? Does she want ice cream?"

It's like shaking the cat treat container—Edith's in the doorway within moments, shoes tied and ready.

Texts with Tessa

TM: But it's not an actual farm?

IS: Haha no

IS: Totally not, it's just an ice cream shop

IS: But also fried chicken

IS: Though that's in kind of a separate building

IS: It's literally the best ice cream on the planet btw

TM: That's what Lili says!!!

TM: But idk man

TM: Can't forget the big gay ice cream shop!!

TM: Hmm maybe this calls for a taste test

IS: DO IT!!

IS: It's such a quick drive from Geneva!!

IS: Right in Penn Yan

TM: Just like 20-30 min, right?

TM: From Geneva to Pennsylvania Yan

TM: Omg shut up autocorrect

IS: Haha autocorrect is right though

IS: That's what it's short for!!

IS: Pennsylvania Yankee

TM: NO WAY

TM: Oh man, I dig it

TM: I mean, kind of a weird choice of name for a town in NY, not gonna lie

IS: Haha PY is weird choice central

IS: Has Lili told you about the griddle

IS: And the pancake

TM: Nooooo

TM: 👀

IS: Oh we're heading out!!!

IS: Hold that thought 🥞

31

It's too cold for ice cream under the pavilion, and there's a bit of a spring break crowd indoors. But we manage to snag the corner booth just as someone's leaving. "Gretch, slide in next to the girls for a second! I need a picture with those pretty cones." Mama P snaps a few horizontal pictures, popping them straight into her message app.

My phone buzzes a moment later with the notification. I have a whole text thread with Mama P, just for pictures. I bet there'd even be some from eighth grade if I scrolled back far enough.

Gretchen scoots back in next to her mom, tapping her screen. "Cute! I'm posting this."

I smile, watching her type one-handed, stopping every so often to lick away the drippy parts of her cone. "You know you don't actually have to post in real time, right?"

"Phone and cone, Immy," says Edith. "Do it for your fans."

"My fans. So, like . . . Mom?"

"Don't count her out! She's building her platform."

"Her profile picture is a bunny," I say. "From Google Images."

But of course I'm already tapping into Instagram, ice cream firmly in hand.

Gretchen's right—it really is a cute picture. With Edith in the middle, our side-by-side hair looks like Neopolitan ice cream. We're all smiling, cheek-to-cheek, behind double-scoop Oreo sugar cones that cover half of our faces. But you can still kind of see my dimple poking out if you look closely enough.

I wonder if Tessa will look closely enough.

By the time I press post, Edith's already halfway down to her cone. She swallows, licking her lips. "So, Vassar, huh?"

Gretchen smiles. "Are you guys surprised?"

"A little bit!"

Edith scoffs. "Come on. It's *Gretchen*—"

"Not surprised that you got in," I rush to add. "I just didn't know it was the frontrunner! I really thought you were suffering through it with that Live, Laugh, Love girl."

"I was playing it cool! Didn't want to jinx myself." Gretchen smiles. "Anyway, Piper's not the worst. We've been texting—"

"Wait—"

"Not like that!"

"Imogen, I want to hear about Blackwell! Your mama said that was your first real visit to campus, right? What an adventure!"

I shrug, feeling my cheeks go warm. "I mean . . . it's just Geneva."

"It's still exciting! Oh, you girls are just going to thrive in college. I'm telling you—Gretchen thinks I'm a broken record, but it's so true. These are such transformative years—"

"And you're going to learn *so much* about yourselves," Gretchen concludes, perfectly nailing her mom's intonation.

"Okay, smartass. You'll see." Mama P tugs Gretchen's ponytail, turning back to me. "Did you feel like you got a sense of what it's like there?"

"Oh!" Gretchen yelps. "Oh my God. Hot Tessa commented on my picture!"

I blink. "She—"

"Oh—wait. Ha. Okay, she commented on a picture I was tagged in. *Your* picture. But still! She said, and I quote, 'Is it gay, though?' With the little thinker emoji!" Gretchen laughs. "I want to reply! Is that weird?"

"Saying what?" Edith asks.

"Saying, 'Fuck yeah, it's gay!'" She turns to me. "Should I follow her? What do I do?"

My heart thuds so hard, I can practically hear it. "I—"

"Who is this, now?" asks Mama P.

"Lili's friend. And apparently Imogen's friend, too, even though she's *wasted* on you. Freaking heterosexuals." She shakes her head at me, smiling.

I swallow back a wave of annoyance.

And then I feel guilty for being annoyed in the first place. Gretchen can like Tessa. She can like whoever she wants.

I just wish she'd stop talking about Tessa like she's some kind of celebrity crush.

God, Lili would roll her eyes to the moon if she knew.

32

I used to think Lili was just being territorial. We both hung out with other people sometimes, of course, especially at school. But it was different with Gretchen. For one thing, she moved to our school in eighth grade—the year Lili started high school.

I remember the end of summer that year felt like counting down to my own execution. I had this recurring daydream where I was sitting alone at a lunch table, lit by a spotlight for some reason. Everyone in the cafeteria was staring at me, and all you could hear were amplified chewing sounds. I just couldn't get it out of my head.

And then this new girl showed up, with purple streaks in her hair and enamel pins all over her backpack. Gretchen wasn't even five feet tall back then, but her presence could fill entire rooms somehow. The last new kid I'd semi-befriended had moved here from New York City, and for the entire first month of our friendship, I legitimately thought that's where Gretchen was from, too. She just seemed to know so much about *everything*—gerrymandering, chaos theory, and what people meant when they used the eggplant emoji. And she especially loved to talk about things like compulsory heterosexuality and gender performance. She'd even post graphics sometimes to educate people online.

Of course, Edith followed her around like a little queer puppy. And my mom seemed charmed by her—adults always love Gretchen, because she isn't weird or shy around them. The only person she couldn't win over was Lili. There's just always been this undercurrent of tension between them.

I remember one particular Tuesday—May of last year, not long before Lili came out. Gretchen and I had stopped in for ice cream at Seneca Farms after our Pride meeting, and Lili had walked the four blocks from her house to meet us.

It's all right there in my brain, every detail. I'd grabbed a cup of ice cream for Lili and set it on the shadiest patch of table. But it was practically soup by the time Lili arrived, and I was already down to the last few bites of my cone. Gretchen's progress was slower—probably because she was doing most of the talking.

I guess you could call it debriefing. There'd been a new Pride member that day—a junior named Dallas who had declined to give labels or pronouns. Gretchen found the whole thing discomforting. "Like, I'm torn," she'd said. "Because on the one hand, no one should have to share that. But on the other hand, I felt a little unsafe, and I think that's worth acknowledging."

"Unsafe?" Lili had asked, sliding onto the bench beside me.

Gretchen nodded. "I feel like even having one cishet person there really changes the vibe. There's just this extra potential for judgment and scrutiny—not you, Immylou, you know that."

"But how do you know they're cishet?" asked Lili.

"Well, that's what's tricky about it! They could totally be closeted. Which is why I would never, like, kick anyone out or question their right to be there."

Lili's eyes narrowed. "But you . . . are questioning their right to be there."

"No . . . I'm literally discussing my lived experience as a queer person in a queer space."

Lili didn't respond, but the air felt so thick all of a sudden. I remember watching ice cream drip from Gretchen's cone onto the table—she seemed to have forgotten about it entirely.

Gretchen kept talking. "I guess I just find it kind of unfair that the onus is on queer people to come out and share our labels. Allocishet people don't have to because they're the default. So it just becomes this whole self-perpetuating dynamic that protects allocishets from having to declare their positionality—which makes queer people even more vulnerable."

"Right, but how do you know who's allocishet? You don't," Lili said, gripping the edge of the bench between us.

"I get that—"

"Okay, but do you? Because it sounds like you're talking about a specific person who showed up to a Pride meeting and—very pointedly—didn't label themselves? You're really reading that as allocishet?"

"I mean, Dallas clearly doesn't want to be called queer," Gretchen said.

"So don't call them queer! But don't act like they don't belong there."

"I didn't! I offered them doughnuts—Imogen, didn't I?"

I looked up with a start. "Um. You did. Yes—"

"Like, this is literally just me talking about my own safety in a *designated queer space*."

"But why would you assume bad faith?" Lili insisted. "Why would someone show up to a Pride meeting to be shitty to queer people?"

I remember how Gretchen's eyes flashed when Lili said that. I could practically hear the thud of my heart hitting the ground beneath me.

"You really think that doesn't happen?" Gretchen's voice cracked. "Lili, that's why the club at my middle school disbanded! Because every goddamn week, the same group of assholes from the basketball team would show up claiming a bunch of labels and pronouns they learned from some fucking cringe compilation. And they were blatantly doing it to mock us, but you couldn't say anything, because then you're invalidating them. Until eventually it was just too exhausting to deal with, and the group stopped meeting."

Lili exhaled then. "I mean, yeah, that's fucked up. I'm really sorry, Gretchen." Then she turned abruptly back to her cup of melted ice cream, fishing an Oreo out with her spoon. And she didn't say anything else about it all night.

But when she drove me to school the next morning, she ranted about Gretchen the whole way there. "I *hate* that she went through that. I hate it! But does she really think that's what's going on here? With this random unlabeled kid? Come on."

I hugged my backpack to my chest, flustered. "I mean, I don't think it's anything about that person in particular. It's more that the situation brings up trauma for her. It makes sense that she'd be a little hypervigilant."

"No, I get that." Lili was quiet for a moment. "But what's the solution? Not let anyone in the door until Gretchen decides they're queer enough?"

"No. I don't know." I turned to stare out the window. "I just feel like it's not really our place to decide one way or another, you know? Since Gretchen's queer . . ."

Lili didn't speak then, but her face in that moment is still pinned to the wall of my brain, like a photograph. Her lips, pressed so tightly together they were practically white; nostrils flared; dark eyes flashing. I didn't really know what to make of it. I never understood why Lili got so prickly about Gretchen's discourse.

Until she drove me back from Brianna Lewis's graduation party a month or so later. Then I got it.

Texts with Gretchen

GP: IMMY

GP: SHE FOLLOWED ME BACK

GP: AND LIKED MY COMMENT

GP: Okay okay it's ON

GP: And I never posted my thirst trap!!!!

IS: I thought that was for Brielle 🤔

GP: 2 birds, 1 stone lol

GP: Anyway thirst traps are for general audiences, remember 🤗

GP: How soon is too soon tho, hmm

GP: Also I need you to find out if she's single and what her type is and if she's open to long distance lol

GP: Signed, a uhaul bisexual

33

I feel like an overfilled balloon. The slightest touch, and I'll pop.

I set my phone down on my bed without responding.

I don't get where this is coming from—why Gretchen's suddenly so fixated on Tessa. They've never met, never talked, never even interacted online until now. The only thing Gretchen knows about her is that she's cute. Pretty. Beautiful.

Hot. Whatever that means.

She's never even heard Tessa's laugh.

I sink back onto my pillows, both hands pressed to my chest. It's still light out. Still at least an hour before dinner. It's just me staring at the blankness of my own bedroom ceiling.

I don't know how to shake this feeling loose.

I rub my eyes and sit up, reaching for my phone. But it isn't Gretchen I'm texting.

Okay I know this is probably super random, I write, **but I was kind of thinking about stuff**

Ellipses—Lili's already typing.

Stuff?

I don't know. I was talking to Gretchen at Seneca Farms today, and it reminded me of last year

With Dallas

Ah, that was a fun one, writes Lili.

I know. I stare down at my screen, eyes prickling. I was just thinking about what I said to you that day. Like how it wasn't our place to disagree with Gretchen's take, because she was actually queer.

I don't even remember you saying that, writes Lili.

I do. I pause. And I shouldn't have said it. I'm so sorry.

Immy, it's fine!! I wasn't even out yet. 😄

I start to reply—but suddenly, she's FaceTiming me. I tap accept, and she pops into frame with a smile that's halfway between baffled and amused. "So what's this about?"

"I don't know." I shake my head. "It was just weighing on me. Like, you were telling me something so important, and I wasn't even listening."

Lili opens her mouth and then shuts it. "Immy, no. You can't do that. You're really gonna beat yourself up for not magically knowing I was queer?"

"I guess." I swallow. "It's more the fact that I didn't even consider it. Like I just had Gretchen in one box and you in another. She was queer and you were straight."

"But that's how being in the closet works! I'm not saying it's fun, but . . ."

"Yeah." I scrunch my nose. "I'm just sorry I made it even harder."

"Okay, that's very sweet and totally unnecessary," she says, laughing. "Here, one sec, I'm taking you onto my bed." Lili's background jerks around for a second, while she crosses the room and resettles. "Okay! So, like—where did this come from?"

"The Seneca Farms stuff?"

"Yeah. Just looking for new stuff to feel guilty about, or what?"

"Nooooo—"

"So, yes. Immy, seriously. You're good. Can we just blame Gretchen? I love blaming Gretchen."

"I know." I smile a little. "She was being kind of weird today, I guess."

"Uh-oh. Was somebody discoursing again? Wait—let me guess." Lili pitches her voice higher. "Excuse me, I'm a real-life certified Actual Queer Person. Are you literally talking over me right now?"

"No!" A laugh tries to break through, but I choke it back. "She wasn't."

"Not this time."

"Okay, she's not *that* bad."

"Then why do you look so pissed off?" Lili asks.

"Me?"

"Mm-hmm." Lili peers into the screen, tapping her lip.

226

"Yes, I'd say you are . . . cloudy . . . with an eighty percent chance of precipitation."

"Is this a weather report for my face?"

"Ooh. Possible thunderstorms. Flooding, tornadoes. We suggest you take cover immediately."

I crack a smile. "I'm just being grumpy about stupid stuff."

"What kind of stupid stuff?"

"Just random stuff." I bite my lip. "Like—I don't know. She's buddying up to Tessa on Instagram. I don't know why I'm annoyed by that, but—"

"Tessa, like *our* Tessa?"

"I—yeah." I blush.

"Sorry, but—how do they even know each other?"

"They don't. Tessa just commented on one of my pictures, and then Gretchen followed her, and Tessa followed her back."

Lili's eyes narrow. "That's weird."

I shrug. "I think I'm overreacting, though. It's—"

"Hey, speaking of Tess." Lili sits up, her tone suddenly shifting. "I meant to check in earlier. Um."

I freeze. "About what?"

"I know you guys have been texting a lot."

"Is that—okay?"

"Oh, totally! Of course. I just . . ." She pauses, studying my face. "I didn't know if you wanted to, like, come clean about stuff. The backstory."

"Like—the ex-girlfriend stuff?"

Lili nods. "And the sexuality stuff. If you want! Up to you. Just wanted you to know I'd be fine with it. Either way."

"Oh. Okay." My heart flips. "I'm—"

"Or I could tell her," she adds. "I don't know. Just if you feel like—if it starts to seem relevant. You being straight."

I feel my cheeks go red-hot. "Like—I'm leading her on?"

"No! Oh—Immy, not like that. I don't know." She laughs nervously. "I'm reading way too much into this, huh? Okay, you know what? Pretend I didn't say anything."

"No, you're fine," I say slowly. "It's just—"

The sexuality stuff.

Speaking of Tess.

The words tiptoe to the edge of my tongue, then hastily retreat. Like a kid working up the nerve to dive off the high board.

It's not that I'm scared. Not exactly. It just feels so official to even broach the topic out loud. Especially when I can't quite decide if these feelings are real.

Because if I actually liked girls, wouldn't I be more like Edith? Or like Gretchen, who's basically an encyclopedia of bisexual memes. Or even Lili, who knew she was pan for years before coming out. *That's* what queerness looks like. Not me pulling muscles in my brain trying to figure out what even counts as attraction.

The whole thing just seems a little too convenient, you know? *Oh, Imogen? That girl who suddenly thinks she might be bi after spending a few days with the cool queer kids? Imogen, a known people pleaser? Couldn't be faking it!*

I just can't glue down the thought. The question sounds less real in my head every time I ask it.

Texts with Tessa

TM: FOUR!!!!

IS: Four? 👀

TM: Ahem
TM: Gory homebirth baby, lesbian elsa, cat
TM: Cheerleader!!!

IS: Ohhhh
IS: Gretchen posted her throwback, haha
IS: That was my eighteenth birthday 😊

TM: Pretty dang cute, Scotty
TM: I'd say it's your best since Lesbian Elsa

IS: It's actually a lesbian cheerleader!
IS: Like Natasha Lyonne in BIAC

TM: BIAC 🫠

IS: But I'm a Cheerleader!
IS: It's my favorite movie 🖤

TM: RIGHT! Duh
TM: Wow

TM: My lesbian credibility in tatters

IS: Nah
IS: Credibility fully intact

TM: Okay but what if I told you
TM: I've never seen it 😅😅😅

IS: Lol you're fine!!
IS: Neither has Gretchen
IS: Technically, they're not even BIAC costumes
IS: We're MUNA and Phoebe Bridgers from the Silk
        Chiffon music video!

TM: I LOVE THAT SONG
TM: Have never seen the video!!
TM: Is there a BIAC reference?

IS: Uh yes 😆
IS: Just a bit

TM: Okay, I'm finding it
TM: And I'm literally going to stream the movie tonight

IS: Omg, you don't have to!

TM: Imogen please, my reputation is on the line

IS: No seriously

IS: Idk, you may not even like it

IS: Gretchen has some kind of issue with it

IS: I think she thinks it's for straight people

TM: But I'm a Cheerleader?

TM: Doesn't Natasha Lyonne hook up with a girl?

IS: Yup Clea DuVall

IS: And yeah, Gretchen has a lot of opinions 👻

IS: I just mean don't feel pressured to watch it!

TM: But it's your favorite movie!!!

IS: Well what's your favorite movie? I'll watch that

TM: My favorite movie! Huh

TM: Hmm

TM: Can it be a tie?

IS: Totally

TM: Okay! Then I think . . . the princess bride and booksmart

TM: Oh! And mean girls

TM: And ET

TM: Back to the future

TM: WAIT ALSO

TM: DEBS!!!!!!

TM: And before sunrise/before sunset

TM: And inside out!!

TM: Joy is my girl 😊

TM: And Priscilla 👑🖼️

TM: Omg and Ferris Bueller!!

IS: Wow 😆

IS: You know what you're like?

TM: Uh oh 😄

IS: You know how sometimes you go to Wegmans for
        one thing

IS: Like a loaf of bread

IS: And you end up leaving with half the bakery section
        and a cart full of produce??

IS: You're that

IS: In human form

TM: Scott.

IS: 🫣

TM: Brutal

IS: I know

TM: Yet so accurate

TM: Wait

TM: Also Bend it like Beckham!!!

TM: That movie is SO GAY

TM: I mean it's not

TM: Like it actually hurts

TM: But I still love it

IS: Me too!! ⚽

IS: You have excellent taste btw

TM: 😊

DAY SIX

WEDNESDAY
MARCH 23

Texts with Tessa

IS: WOW okay 😂

IS: So you liked it, huh?

TM: Like

TM: I'm obsessed

TM: I need a rewatch ASAP!!

TM: You'll watch it with me, right?

TM: You don't have to wear your cheerleader costume

TM: You *can*

TM: But you don't have to

IS: Noted 😂

IS: Omg I'm so happy you liked it!!!

IS: My comfort film ♥

IS: And Tessa, the princess bride 🎞️

IS: Loved it

IS: How did I go so long without watching it??

TM: I need to rewatch that, too!!

TM: I haven't seen it in years, I feel like a fake fan

TM: Though to be fair I did frame a picture of princess buttercup for my bookshelf

TM: When I was like 10

TM: Nbd, just pretending she was my girlfriend

IS: Ohhh that's so cute 😆

TM: Definitely still on display in my room 😬

TM: I told my ex it was a picture of my cousin Annie from Westchester

IS: Ooh good call

IS: Wouldn't want her to think anything was going on between you and a fictional princess

IS: From a movie that came out in 1987

TM: Right!! Could have been catastrophic 🙈

TM: Though Jillian might actually have been pissed, who knows

IS: She was really weird about stuff, huh?

TM: Sometimes

TM: I mean we were really young too, so that was definitely part of it

TM: Dated sophomore year mostly and the beginning of junior

TM: Though we were friends first

TM: Like best friends

TM: For YEARS

TM: Kind of like you and Lili I guess?

TM: But waaaaay messier

IS: You mean the breakup?

TM: Honestly, all of it

TM: Like it was this really intense friendship

TM: But we were also kind of frenemies I guess??

IS: Omg, I can't imagine you having a frenemy!!

TM: Right?? I'm allergic to conflict

TM: I guess it was more like she was mad at me a lot and
        I didn't always know why

TM: I was just sad and confused mostly

TM: And then sometimes it was totally fine

IS: Oh, that must have been so hard

TM: Kind of? I don't know

TM: I think we were just so incompatible

TM: She's kind of serious about things

TM: Like she doesn't really joke around much

TM: Or maybe it's more that our senses of humor didn't
        really click

IS: Ahhh okay

IS: That's actually kind of a huge deal imo

IS: The humor thing

TM: Oh, 100%

TM: Honestly, that may be the most important thing

TM: For me, at least

IS: And you haven't really dated anyone since then, yeah?

TM: Nope 😅

IS: Can I ask why not?

IS: Seriously fine if you don't want to answer that btw

TM: I don't mind at all!

TM: Though I don't know if there's like a clear answer for that

TM: I think it's probably a combination of things

TM: Like I had a really stupid crush on a straight girl most of senior year

TM: Also I'm just a wimp about that stuff in general

TM: I don't know haha

TM: What about you?

IS: You mean with Lili?

TM: Yeah, or even just in general

IS: Haha well I'm definitely a wimp

IS: Idk, I haven't actually dated anyone

IS: Besides Lili

IS: Which barely even counts lol

TM: Wait, why wouldn't it count? 😂

IS: Oh I guess

IS: It was such a short period of time

IS: And the energy wasn't even really that romantic

TM: Huh

TM: Maybe that's why you guys were able to bounce back to being friends again so easily

IS: I guess so!

TM: Do you think it would get awkward though if one of you started dating someone

IS: Totally not

IS: I'd honestly just be happy for her

IS: Or vice versa

IS: I know that's probably weird!!

TM: Not at all!

TM: I think it's really cool

IS: Me too

TM: Hmm

IS: Oh my god
IS: Tessa it's almost 2:30

TM: Whoa!
TM: Look at us
TM: Hey maybe we're night owls AND early birds!!

IS: That sounds healthy

TM: 😛

IS: Seriously, don't you have class tomorrow????
IS: Today I mean
IS: Yikes

TM: Eh, not til 10
TM: I'll live
TM: I'll steal Kayla's Life Savers 😊

34

You'd think I'd be a total zombie this morning. Tessa and I didn't stop texting until almost three a.m., and even then, I was too amped to keep my eyes shut. It was probably close to four by the time I drifted off—but here I am, not even four hours later, in sweats and an old academic bowl T-shirt. Hair pulled back, heart still fluttering.

The doorbell rings right at eight, and I rush to answer it. "Wait." I pull open the door. "You're not Gretchen."

It's Otávio, looking only marginally awake in sweatpants and an already paint-spattered T-shirt. "I think your mom wanted the top half of the walls painted, too," he says, shrugging serenely.

"Rude." I grin, stepping back to let him inside. I kind of love that five-foot-nine Otávio is our token giant, but he definitely has some kind of point. Edith is five-five, I'm barely five-four, and Gretchen's *maybe* five-one. If you're being generous.

We step out the back door and straight back into the shed,

where Mom is crouched, stirring paint. There's blue tape along all the trim, and the entire floor is covered with a plastic drop cloth. It's so strange seeing the shed without its metal storage shelves or stacks of boxes. Between that and the white coat of primer, it actually looks weirdly spacious. A little smaller than Lili's dorm room, maybe, but not much. And I bet it's at least as big as Tessa's.

Mom coats one of the rollers in light mint green, running it along a plastic paint tray to squeeze off the excess. "Thank you so much again," she says, handing the roller to me. "You guys go ahead and get started. I'll send Gretchen back when she gets here. And then I think I'm going to just lock myself downstairs for a few hours and knock out my conference prep. Dad's home today, though. Is Edith still sleeping?"

"No idea."

"I'll investigate." Mom stands, pressing her palms to her thighs.

Otávio cues up some sort of instrumental guitar playlist on his phone—he can be very dreamy and timeless like that. He turns the volume up and sets it down on the drop cloth, as far from the rollers and buckets as possible. I used to help my parents with paint projects sometimes, and I forgot how much it calms my brain down. Even better is the fact that Otávio's sort of shy and quiet like I am, so we're perfectly happy working in silence. Slow and peaceful, like the first summer day on the lake.

Until Edith appears in the doorway, looking like her birthday came early. "Guess what guess what guess what!" She bounces into the shed, Gretchen trailing behind her. "Kara Clapstone came out!"

I laugh. "Gretchen, why are you wearing a trash bag?"

"It's a paint poncho!"

"Who's Kara Clapstone?" Otávio asks.

"An actress! She played the nerdy girl in *Shop Talk*, and she's about to be in that coven show. Here, you'll recognize her." Edith hands him her phone.

"Cool. So she's queer?"

"Yup—bisexual!" Edith grabs a roller, glancing back over her shoulder at Gretchen. "Still think *Shop Talk*'s for straight people?"

"Oh, one hundred percent," Gretchen says. "It's not about Kara. It's about the straight gaze."

"There are . . . straight gays?" Otávio looks bewildered.

Gretchen laughs, tapping just below her eyes. "Gaze like *gaze*. It's made for straight audiences."

"Right, of course," Edith says. "This movie about queer girls, written and directed by two queer women, starring a queer woman . . . is for straight audiences."

Gretchen smiles. "Don't get me wrong—I'm thrilled for Kara! And, like, it definitely helps."

"Helps what?"

"I don't know—the general optics, I guess? Obviously,

having a straight lead actress was kind of an iffy choice—"

"But she wasn't straight," Edith says.

"Sure, but she said she was. And sapphic representation is already so rare in Hollywood." Gretchen settles in cross-legged on the drop cloth. "So I can see why people would want those roles to go to actual queer people. It's about equity. And authenticity—"

"How is Kara not an actual queer person?" Edith's voice comes out sharp.

"She *is*! Of course she is. I'm just saying, I get where the Kara discourse is coming from."

I press my thumb to my lips. "There's Kara discourse?"

"I guess it's more like people rehashing some of the earlier discourse?" says Gretchen. "Like there were queer people who critiqued Kara's casting when they first announced it. Now everyone's turning on them and saying they pressured her out of the closet."

"I mean. They kind of did," Edith says.

"Well, I think they expressed valid frustration. It was a mainstream gay movie! Obviously, there's going to be backlash when people see *yet another* queer role go to a straight woman. What did she think would happen?" Gretchen tugs at the edge of her paint poncho. "It just sucks, because now people are using it as this gotcha moment. Like people should have some-how known not to criticize her work, because she'd eventually turn out to be bi?"

"But it's not about criticism of her work." Edith sets her roller on the paint tray. "They're mad that she said she was straight—"

"Right, because—"

"And now they're tripping over themselves to find reasons to still be pissed about it! We've already got Twitter randos questioning her motivations for coming out. 'Oh, she's just saying she's bi to get out of valid criticism!' 'Oh, she's doing it to get more press for the coven show!'"

Otávio wrinkles his nose. "That's kind of gross."

"Can we just be happy for her?" Edith shakes her head. "Plus, the shit she's getting from other actors. You know the girl who played the gay trombone player in that battle of the bands movie?"

"Jeanette Jaymes?"

"Yeah. So, like, five seconds after Kara's announcement goes live, Jeanette drops this shady Instagram post about how straight-passing bisexuals love to tweet about how queer they are from their boyfriends' beds." Edith scowls. "And then she dirty deleted, but seriously? Let the woman live!"

And just like that, I'm blinking back tears. Which is ridiculous. This is a ridiculous thing to cry about.

I mean, it's a ridiculous thing for *me* to cry about.

Because I'm not Kara Clapstone. I don't even know Kara Clapstone.

Gretchen exhales. "I mean . . . biphobes are gonna biphobe.

It sucks." She leans in to paint along the edge of the trim. "But at the same time, Kara's pretty straight-passing, so there's privilege there, right? She's not going to be harassed by bigots and homophobes. She's a wealthy white actress with a boyfriend! In LA!"

I pause. "Isn't she from rural Alabama, though?"

"She sure is." Edith does jazz hands. "And now she's got five thousand college sophomores explaining to her that if she's actually bi, she should have come out before the movie released. Because it would have meant so much to her fans."

Something twists in my chest.

I wonder if Kara Clapstone's town in Alabama is anything like Penn Yan. It's probably worse—at least Penn Yan gets to be in New York state. But we're not exactly Manhattan. I remember the summer Edith and I made a game out of counting all the aggressively right-wing T-shirt slogans at the Yates County Fair. We had to stop after an hour because it was too depressing. *Don't tread on me. God, guns, and glory. I oil my gun with liberal tears.* And at school, you basically can't even pee without having to read whatever fresh slur just popped up on the walls. Otávio and I started bringing Sharpies into the bathroom to black them out, but it's like Whac-A-Mole.

I think people forget how different things can be in different places.

"It's clown behavior," says Edith. "I'm sorry, no. Kara Clapstone doesn't need to set her coming-out timeline according to your weird parasocial entitlement."

"Totally agree! I'm glad she waited until she was ready!" Gretchen says.

"So stop discoursing," Edith snaps, "and leave her alone!"

Then she storms out of the shed, letting the door clang shut behind her.

Texts with Tessa

IS: Hello I just painted a shed

IS: And there was discourse

IS: And now I need a shower

IS: 😭 😭 😭

TM: Okay wow I have questions

TM: What was the shed discourse???

TM: And can it be fixed by a shower? 🤔

IS: Haha I wish it was shed discourse

IS: I love shed discourse

IS: This was

IS: I don't even know where to begin

IS: 😵

IS: OKAY NEW TOPIC

IS: How was your morning

IS: Did you make it through stats

TM: Hahahahaha oh man

TM: Soooo

TM: Want to see what falling asleep while taking notes looks like?

TM: 📎

TM: womp womp womp 🏁

IS: Omg are those your notes??

IS: AHHH I'm so sorry

IS: Can you get a copy of someone else's?

IS: I feel so bad

TM: Scott, omg no!!! Don't feel bad

TM: It's fine! I can get the TA's notes

TM: It's legit one of my accommodations, I just always forget it's an option 😂

TM: Please don't feel bad!!!!

TM: Honestly stats is basically math, I promise I don't get it any better when I'm awake 👻

IS: I don't get tit either

IS: *IT

TM: OH 👀

IS: Oh my god

TM: I mean, you definitely could 😆

TM: Lots of tit

TM: All the tit

IS: TESSA NO 😄

IS: NO MORE TIT DISCOURSE

TM: *titcourse

TM: 😌

35

Otávio's on the track team, but I've never seen him move like he does when we finish the shed. He's probably halfway home before Gretchen and I have a chance to wash the paint off our hands.

Dad's in the kitchen, assembling a makeshift lunch buffet—bread, jelly, SunButter, fruit, and tortilla chips. "How's the shed looking?"

"Amazing," says Gretchen, smiling so brightly it makes my head spin. If it weren't for the angry nineties music blasting from Edith's room at top volume, I'd almost think the tension in the shed never happened. It's like when you're reading a book and you accidentally skip a whole page. That same little tug of, *wait, what*?

Did I just misread the entire mood of that interaction?

I mean, Otávio looked like he wanted to jump out the window, and Edith was practically boiling over. But here's Gretchen, casually pulling the crusts off her sandwich and chatting with my dad about where she thinks the futon should go.

What did she think would happen?

I always feel so out of my league when it comes to queer discourse. It's like I'm surrounded by people doing synchronized dances on tightropes, and I'm just trying to keep my feet planted.

Like the whole gay-media-for-straight-people meme. The straight gaze. Or when the topic of queerbaiting comes up sometimes in Pride Alliance. Not just about scripted TV shows and movies—I guess queerbaiting happens with certain celebrities, too. Like when allocishet influencers hint at being queer, just for clout. Or when they make money from media with overtly queer themes. Sometimes cis straight musicians will even make their lyrics ambiguously queer on purpose.

I'm always a little unnerved when the subject of queerbaiting comes up, though. Maybe because I'm not good at spotting it in the wild. The problem is, I can't always tell if someone's allocishet in the first place.

I guess it goes back to what Gretchen always says, about how queer people are hardwired to recognize each other. That would explain why no one else in the group seems to have trouble seeing it.

Though.

Sometimes they almost seem to see it *too* well.

That's the thing that keeps throwing me. Obviously, it's not my place to speak over queer people on this. But I can't shake the thought.

It isn't only Kara Clapstone. Just a few weeks ago, a Broadway actor got dragged for taking a role that should have gone to a queer guy.

Turns out, he was one. He ended up coming out on Instagram, just so people would stop hassling him about it. I remember reading his caption over and over, feeling sick to my stomach. I'd never even heard this actor's name until that day, but I was on the verge of tears for a week. Something about that discourse sliced straight through me.

Something about this discourse does too.

"So I joined the admitted students Discord server," Gretchen says, dumping her crusts into the compost. "But it's not super active yet. The Reddit admissions megathread is popping off, though. People have been sharing their stats—like scores and grades and stuff. I'm kind of intimidated!"

"Sounds really intense," I say vaguely.

"*So* intense! You haven't joined the Blackwell Discord, right? Do they have a Discord? I don't know how it works. Does someone in the incoming class have to make one?"

"I don't know." I yawn, tucking my ankles around the legs of the barstool. Now Gretchen's talking about some kind of summer orientation meetup, but my mind's still swirling with questions about Kara Clapstone.

Like whether she just came out to her family, too.

Maybe they already knew. Or maybe they'd wondered. Or not.

The first time she said it out loud, was she scared?

Was she sure it was real?

"You should see if Blackwell has one," says Gretchen.

I nod fuzzily, watching my dad put all the lunch stuff away. Lids on jars, loaves sealed off. "Okay."

"I'll poke around Reddit and see what comes up," Gretchen says. "Also, I kind of feel like watching a movie. Is that weird? Why do I feel like that's such a nighttime activity?"

Dad looks up at me. "Peanut, where's Edith?"

"Oh. Um. Probably in her room?"

"Talking to Zora." Gretchen shakes her head affectionately. "Wait, you know what we should watch? What was the documentary Nicole was talking about last week?"

I stare at her, more than a little bit gobsmacked. Does she really think Edith's just chilling in her room right now, Face-Timing her girlfriend? She has to know Edith's pissed at her, right?

"The one about that wellness influencer cult guy. Here, I'll look it up—"

"Oh, you know what?" Dad's eyes meet mine, for just a moment. "Immy, I actually need you to go through the boxes today. Your sister, too."

"Oh!" I open my mouth and then close it. The relief I feel is so unexpected, I'm practically speechless. "Okay. Um. Gretch, maybe tomorrow?"

"No. Ugh. We're going to the outlet mall. She shakes her head, looking glum. "Friday?"

I give her a thumbs-up. "That works."

The moment the door shuts behind her, it's like my brain comes off mute. I'm wide awake for the first time all day.

Texts with Tessa

TM: Feeling any better?

TM: Did you get to shower off all that discourse?

IS: Haha yes!

IS: Shower actually did help I think

IS: I was in such a bizarro mood, I don't even know

TM: What was the discourse??

TM: Only if you want to talk about it of course

TM: I don't want to rehash stuff!!!

IS: Oh no, it's fine! You're not rehashing

IS: Idk if you've seen that Kara Clapstone came out

IS: From shop talk

TM: I saw!!!!

TM: Ohhhh man, was there discourse?

IS: I guess? I haven't really gone down the rabbit hole yet, but Edith and Gretchen were arguing about it

IS: Long story

IS: Anyway, better now!! All showered with an elderly kitty in my lap

TM: Is it Quincy??????

IS: Of course

IS: He's the only one who gets to stay in my room

IS: Bc he's the only one who can be trusted not to eat his little hamster sister

TM: We love an uneaten hamster!!!

TM: Wait hold on one sec

IS: Okay!

TM: I'm back!! Sorry

TM: The himbos are being insufferable

TM: I swear to god it's like having ten older brothers who adore you

TM: But give you shit literally all the time

TM: Thus I am now in the hallway outside Dan's suite

IS: Omg, go hang out with your ten brothers! Sorry!!

TM: No thank you 😊

IS: No for real, I'll let you go!

IS: I should go anyway

IS: Edith and I are supposed to go through some boxes from the shed apparently?

IS: Like old storage stuff, should be interesting

IS: Definite potential for embarrassing Lili content

TM: Oh well in that case 😄

TM: Counting on you to send me everything

IS: I will!

TM: I know 😊

Texts with Gretchen

GP: On Privacy, Privilege, and Positionality: Is Kara Clapstone's Announcement Too Little, Too Late? 🔗

GP: Okay I actually really like this take

GP: Kind of unpacks some of the issues I had with how everything's being framed

GP: Curious to know what you think!!

36

I don't click Gretchen's link. Even the headline puts a pit in my stomach.

I never know how to navigate this stuff. Of course I want to listen to queer perspectives. But what do you do when there's no consensus? How do I know which queer perspective to defer to?

Either way, I'm just a straight girl talking over queer people. Unless I'm not.

Okay, but what are the odds of that? Occam's razor says the simplest explanation is probably true. So what's actually more likely? That I magically turned queer over the course of a weekend?

Or that I'm doing what I do in every situation—trying to be exactly what everyone wants me to be.

Something thuds near the bottom of my bedroom door—Edith, knocking with her feet. "Hey, help me with these," she says, peeking out over a pair of stacked cardboard boxes. But when I make a grab for the top one, she clarifies, "No, I mean, there are like six more in the basement. Dad actually does want us to go through them, apparently?"

I laugh. "Yeah, why else would he have asked us to?"

"To rescue you from Gretchen. You know that was the whole point, right?" Edith sets the boxes down on my bed, herding me out the door for another load.

"You don't think you might be projecting?" I side-eye her as we step into the hall. "Just a little?"

"I mean, that's what he literally told me."

"Wait, really?"

"He said, and I quote, 'I think your sister needed a little bit of a Gretchen detox today.'"

"Dad said *detox*?"

"He's a king! What can I say?" She taps a short stack of boxes with her toe. "Here, these three are ours, plus the two big plastic ones by the couch."

It takes us three more trips downstairs to get them all, plus a quick stop in the kitchen to fuel up on Mom's fancy Lindt chocolate.

"Okay, what does he want us to do with this stuff?" I ask, settling onto the rug with one of the big plastic tubs. "Just, like . . . go through it?"

"And consolidate it. We're supposed to decide what to keep, donate, throw away . . . I don't really remember what's in them, though."

I nudge the lid off the first tub. "Looks like clothes." I pull out a tiny white hoodie covered in hand-painted black spots, with a pair of black socks sewn on as ears. "This is from *101 Dalmatians*, right?"

"My theatrical debut!" Edith tugs it out of my hands, hugging it close. "Okay, I'm starting a pile. Definitely keeping the sentimental stuff."

Of course, the entire tub turns out to be sentimental stuff—tie-dyed camp T-shirts and costumes and my favorite cat-patterned dress from preschool. I stop short at the sight of Edith's perfectly preserved Lesbian Elsa dress, stomach twisting with guilt. There's no soft way to spin it. I'm literally holding a lie in my hands.

By the time we reach the bottom of the tub, every single piece is in the keep pile. "Marie Kondo is shaking and crying right now," says Edith.

Luckily, the next few boxes are a little easier to trim down. Old school assignments go straight to the recycling bin—other than the obvious gems, like first-grade Edith's drawing of "The Horniest Unicorn." Then there's a full box of plastic figurines and favor-bag prizes for the donate pile, and a few tattered squishies for the trash. Edith casually sets aside a small collection of stray Barbie limbs for unspecified purposes. "This is fun. It's like going through a tiny serial killer's trash." She pulls out a small plastic treasure chest. "Hello, are you full of baby teeth?"

"Why are we saving this?" I hold up a hardened blob of

air-dry clay covered in sequins.

"Because it's a beautiful, timeless work of art?"

I stick it in the trash pile, alongside a collection of pipe cleaner bracelets and dried-up slime. I legitimately think I could scrawl a smiley face on an orange peel, and my parents would save it for decades. There's an entire box of original Imogen and Edith drawings, too, plus a few of Lili's old horse pictures. We used to hide out in the barn with our sketch pads, tucked up next to the hay bales for hours. Lili knew how to add dimension and shading, and she could blur her pencil lines with two fingertips. Sometimes she'd let me color them in, too, because I was good at keeping things inside the lines.

It's strange, seeing all these relics lined up like that, side by side. Santa letters and movie tickets and the dress I wore to freshman year's homecoming dance. All strung together like beads on a necklace.

I break into a box of old photos, while Edith settles in with her own fifth-grade diary.

"Listen to this masterpiece. 'Hi, Diary. Here are all the reasons today was bad. Number one, Mr. Dye is a buttwhole'—" She looks up. "With a *w*. Butt. Whole."

"I mean, it kind of works."

"'Number two, we had kickball in PE but Patrick bunted and that is cheating but he didn't get in trouble. In conclusion, number three is there were no middle seats left on the bus, only the back which is bullies and the front which is buttkissers and now I always have to sit alone because Imogen doesn't go to my school because she is in sixth grade. Love, Edith. P.S. What starts with F and ends in u-c-k? A firetruck! LOL. Otávio heard it from Lili!'"

"Oh." I look at her. "Edie."

"Right? Fuck Patrick!"

I press my cheek. "I made you ride alone with the butt-kissers."

"No way. I picked the bullies." She pokes me with a Barbie leg. "Please tell me you're not blaming yourself for graduating elementary school."

"I'm not. I'm blaming that buttwhole Mr. Dye."

"Why did I talk so much about butts and men?" Edith makes a face, flipping to the next entry.

I turn back to the photo box, lifting out a short stack of prints. Me, perched on Dad's shoulders, hands pressed flat on his head. Baby Edith staring into a mirror. The two of us dangling our feet off the dock at Nana's house. Me at the library, proudly holding up my plate of award-winning Rice Krispies Treats. Edith in her heart-shaped glasses. There are so many with Lili and Otávio, too—lined up beside hay bales or sprawled on the couch. Lili and me manning a table stacked high with boxes of Girl Scout Cookies.

I look up at Edith. "You know, I felt the same way you did in fifth grade—when Lili moved up to middle school. Eighth grade, too."

"And now," Edith adds.

I pause. "College is different, though. You kind of expect that to change things."

Edith looks at me. "Do you think it has?"

"What do you mean?"

"Changed things." She sets her journal on the rug, stretching. "What about this weekend? Did it feel different with Lili?"

"No! I mean, not really? Not in a bad way." My heart twists. "I don't know. It's probably easier, because Geneva is so nearby."

"Yeah, but nearby isn't here," Edith says.

"Yeah."

For a moment, neither of us speaks. But then—

"I'm kind of dreading it," says Edith.

"Dreading college?"

"Dreading you leaving for college!"

"Wait." I stare at her. "Really?"

"I mean, I'm taking your room," she says quickly, "so that's good. It's gonna be my greenhouse. I think I'm going to try being a plant mom."

I nod slowly. "Huh."

"All I'm saying is it's going to be a little weird when you're gone." She shrugs. "And I'll probably miss you."

I press a fist to my mouth. "Edie—"

"Like a little bit! Enough to passive-aggressively remark upon it in my diary sometimes. That's all." She shakes her head, laughing. "Stop looking at me like that!"

It's just funny, I guess. We've always been so attached at the hip, but I've never really thought of it as Edith needing me. Or missing me.

I would have sworn it was the other way around.

Texts with Tessa

IS: Oh hello 🐐

IS: 📎

TM: Omg IS THAT DAISY?!????

TM: The most beautiful goat!!!

TM: Oh my heart

IS: She was the best 🐐

TM: So that's clearly you on the left

TM: Edith on the right

TM: You guys look so much alike, it's wild

IS: I know 😂

IS: Her hair is blonder

IS: And she's like an inch taller than me now

IS: But otherwise 👻

TM: I love it

TM: We're like that too!! Let me find a pic

TM: 📎

IS: TRIPLETS!!! Wow, even Dan

IS: Is this from your bat mitzvah?

IS: Wait no

IS: Must be Rachael's bat mitzvah, right??

TM: Actually I think it's my cousin Walter's bar mitzvah?

TM: That's Annie aka Buttercup's little bro haha

TM: But he's Rachael's age, so same era!!

TM: Don't worry, I would never spring a pic of 12 year old me without warning

TM: Your body isn't prepared for that level of titcourse

TM: Or lack thereof 😬

IS: 😂

IS: I think I can handle it

IS: I mean 📎

TM: Oh

TM: WHAT

TM: Is that 12 year old Imogen 🫨

IS: Eleven 🫠

IS: First day of sixth grade

TM: Scott

TM: Your shirt

TM: Cattitude 💀

IS: As you can see

IS: I was very cool in middle school

TM: You were 😄

TM: Okay hold on, let me find my bat mitzvah pics

TM: Just know

TM: You won't be able to unsee this

IS: I'm ready 💪

TM: Ok wait

TM: I'm going to show you two

TM: A case study

TM: All right, the backstory is that my parents made me
        wear a dress to the ceremony, but I got to pick my
        own clothes for the party

TM: So here's me being awkward as fuck outside the
        temple 📎

TM: And then

TM: Taken literally the same day . . .

TM: A twelve year old tomboy icon 🕶️ 📎

IS: OMG

IS: These are both incredible!!!

IS: Aww were you really tiny or was that just a big Torah
        😄

TM: Both 😄

TM: Idk, I think they're all kind of big

IS: Also, you are legitimately so cool???

IS: Your little pinstriped pants and suspenders 🏩

IS: And all the socks!!!!

IS: You look so happy

TM: Those were our favors!!

TM: The bottoms say "shut up and dance at Tessa's bat mitzvah"

TM: I was OBSESSED with that song

TM: Actually they say "Shut ⬆️ and dance" because my mom thought it would be more polite? Idk

TM: and they have like those traction dots on bottom so you can wear them on the dance floor

TM: I still wear the extras sometimes 😊

IS: I would literally only wear those socks if I had them

IS: I'd do laundry every day

TM: I'll get some for you!!!

TM: Next time I'm home!

IS: Omg I promise I wasn't hinting!!

TM: No I know!! Haha

IS: I seriously can't get over these pictures

IS: The contrast 😆

IS: You're like that lesbian tiktok trend

TM: Wait what 👀

IS: Where they're like 'oh, you're into masc girls? no problem!'
IS: And they whoosh their hand in front of their face and BOOM 😌

TM: I literally have no idea what you're talking about 😂 😂 😂

IS: Really???
IS: That was like my entire FYP for two weeks!!!

TM: Ma'am, that is between you and your algorithm 🙊

IS: 🙊
IS: Wait hold on, Edith just busted in
IS: Oh I think we're gonna watch Shop Talk 🖤

TM: Okay, but no discourse allowed 🖤

DAY SEVEN
THURSDAY
MARCH 24

37

Edith spends the night in my bed, which is how I know she's still upset about Gretchen.

It's what we've both done since we were tiny, anytime we feel sad or stressed or adrift. Like the time we couldn't find Adrian for two entire days, or the night before Edith got her tonsils out. Even really trivial stuff, like when Edith's kindergarten teacher said she couldn't wear her Jason mask in the Halloween parade. There's just something about the rhythm of her breathing that reels me back to shore. I think it must be the same for Edith, too.

We watched all of *Shop Talk*, even the bonus footage. But we don't even mention Kara's announcement. Or Gretchen. Or the discourse.

And I don't click Gretchen's link.

I haven't texted her back since she sent it. I know that's pretty spineless of me.

It's just—when I pick up my phone, all I want to do is talk to Tessa. I may be getting slightly addicted.

I'm trying not to overthink it.

Tessa FaceTimes me just before ten in the morning, and I can barely catch my breath in time to press accept.

"Hi!" Her face pops into frame—wide brown eyes, pink cheeks, hair tucked behind her ears, the dull green of campus behind her. The image is just a little too blurry to make out her freckles, but my brain fills them in. "I was just—" She stops short, breaking into a smile. "Okay, wow, it's you! It's your face!"

It's my face. I touch my cheek as if to confirm it.

I think my heart's trying to kick down my rib cage. "That's kind of FaceTime's whole thing."

I settle in cross-legged on my bed.

"I *know*. But I've gotten so used to texting you now! It's like—wait, sorry, is this okay? FaceTiming?"

I laugh, slightly breathless. "Of course."

"Okay! Sorry. Yeah—I was trying to text and walk, but it was taking too long, and then I almost tripped off the curb. So I was like, 'Okay, you know what, Scott, I'm just gonna'—anyway, hi! This is my walk to class."

"Ooh, what class? Stats again?"

"No, thank God. Social psych today. Stats is tomorrow. Hey." She looks suddenly flustered. "So. Speaking of tomorrow—I've got an idea."

I scoot back toward the headboard. "An idea?"

"Mm-hmm." Tessa grins, and I grin back, and I can't quite pinpoint why this moment feels so surreal. "So, I think—"

Someone screams, just out of frame, and Tessa's eyes dart sideways.

"Oy. Okay. Frat bro swiped some girl's hat, and now they're both laughing. All good. Anyway! I think you should come tomorrow."

"Oh!" My heartbeat quickens. "You mean—"

"To the party. Just think about it, okay? Rumor has it you already have an outfit."

"That's true."

"And I checked with Quincy. He said he's totally chill holding down the fort."

"Well, in that case . . ."

"Wait, is that a yes?" Her tentative smile makes my heart catch.

I smile back. "It's yes-adjacent." I pause. "Let me talk to Lili."

Texts with Lili

IS: Okay, question for you

IS: If I wanted to attend a certain party tomorrow night

IS: On a certain college campus

IS: Would that still be an option, maybe? 😅

LC: Wait, seriously??

IS: Only if it wouldn't be any trouble!!!

IS: I know this is so last minute

IS: Totally totally understand if it's a bad time

LC: No, it's good!

LC: I'm just surprised 😄

LC: You seemed totally not into it on Monday

IS: No no I promise I was into it 🙈

IS: I'm sorry

IS: I was just overthinking some stuff

IS: And then Tessa mentioned it again today

IS: Idk, I figured it was worth checking?

LC: Ohhhhhh so you just needed the invitation to come from Tessa

LC: I see how it is 😄

IS: What? No!!!

IS: I didn't mean it like that!!

IS: I'm sorry 🙈 🙈 🙈

LC: Immy omg I'm kidding

LC: I'm so glad you're coming!!!

LC: Like I'm fucking hyped

LC: Actually, why don't I come down and pick you up
        tomorrow

IS: No!! I think I can get the car

LC: Seriously, I need to grab some costume stuff at
        home anyway

LC: It's perfect

LC: And I'll just drive you home in the morning, or
        whenever you want

IS: You sure? 🥺

LC: Look he's already waiting for you 📎

IS: Aww, hi Puppy

IS: See you soon 🦄

Texts with Gretchen

IS: Hey! Okay so

IS: I think I'm actually going back to Blackwell tomorrow
        night

IS: For the dark academia party

IS: I'm so sorry, G!! I know we were talking about
        hanging out then

IS: Maybe Saturday??

IS: Anyway, sorry, go have fun at the outlet mall!!!

IS: Get those deals 💪

Texts with Tessa

IS: So

IS: Looks like I'll see you tomorrow 😊

38

I press send.

And then I spend a full minute of my life staring at my phone screen, before remembering Tessa's in class.

Class. Not avoiding me. Not scrambling for a way to explain she was actually kidding about the party. Literally no reason to think that. Because she's in class. Which I know for a fact, since I walked her there.

Therefore, I'm chill now.

Until a text comes through, and I grab my phone so forcefully, the entire charger unplugs and comes with it.

It's just Mom. **Sweetie, are you busy? Building a bookcase for the shed, could use a hand!**

I plug the charger back in, feeling almost light-headed. It's unsettling, if you think about it—the way your whole mood can be hijacked by nothing but words on a screen. Tiny black lines on a glass rectangle.

When did everything but Tessa start feeling like background noise? At what point, exactly, did my brain decide we were doing this?

Doesn't even feel like I'm in the driver's seat at this point.

I leave my phone plugged in on my nightstand. I don't want to be weird in front of Mom.

I find her on the floor of the shed, surrounded by wooden planks and little plastic bags of bolts and screws. "Oh, hey." She looks up from some kind of instructional diagram. "Does this make any sense to you? I can't figure out how it's supposed to line up. It's the one with the three holes, but I think they're on the wrong side."

She hands me the sheet, and I stare at it for a moment. "Are you sure you're not holding the board upside down?"

"But shouldn't the white part be faceup?" Her brow furrows.

"Eventually, but I think the whole thing's upside down when you're building it. You just flip it over at the end. Here, I just need the little wrench thingy."

Mom hands it to me. "Huh."

And for a minute, my brain seems to settle. I'm just tightening screws and lining up corners, while Rufus Wainwright's voice ripples through Mom's phone speakers.

But then—

"So tell me about this costume party," she says, tucking

her elbow over her head for a stretch.

"Oh! Um. It's not really a costume party? Just kind of a theme party, I think . . ."

My mind veers off course without warning.

Tomorrow. The party. *Tessa.*

If her class started at ten, it's probably over around eleven, right?

Though maybe that's just Monday-Wednesday-Friday classes. Maybe Tuesday-Thursday classes have to run longer to make up for that missing third day. Ninety minutes, maybe? Eleven thirty?

Also, what time is it right now? I don't wear a watch. Normally, I just check on my phone, but I left it upstairs so I wouldn't be weird and obsessed. Clearly, that's going great.

"I think that's as tight as they go, right?"

I look down to find I've locked my screw in so tightly, it's almost level with the wood.

"Oop," I say, blushing.

The problem is, the more I worry about weirdness, the weirder I get. And the harder I try not to act like I have a crush, the more it's starting to feel like one.

By the time we screw the last shelf in, I've turned into a line of ellipses. Nothing but stuttering anticipation. I should be in my room by now. My phone's gravitational pull should have reeled me in straightaway.

But I linger in the shed for some reason, long after my mom heads in for lunch. Even though there's nothing out here but an empty bookcase.

Nothing but space.

It feels bigger than my bedroom somehow, even though it's not.

There's just something appealingly half-baked about it. Unfinished, in progress, suspended in time. I try to imagine its final form, but every time I picture it, it's different.

"Immy?" The shed door creaks open, revealing Gretchen. "Your mom said you were out here. You okay?"

"Oh—yeah! Hi! I thought you were shopping today."

"I was." She laughs. "I texted when we left, but then I just figured I'd drop my mom off and swing by. Had to make sure I saw you before you headed back to Blackwell."

I flush. "I'm so sorry about tomorrow."

"What? Immybean, no—you're good! God, I mean. At least one of us should get to experience a college party this week. Here, wait, let's head back in." She reaches both hands out, and I let her tug me up.

"You're not pissed that I ditched you?" I dust off my jeans, following her back out of the shed and in through the kitchen. Of course, Adrian and Binx are immediately on the scene, double-teaming us with a whole repertoire of meowing and ankle weaving.

"Do I look pissed?" Gretchen bends down, petting them both. "Aww, hi, kitties. Anyway, I bought you something today!

Just wanted to drop it off."

"What? No, you already—"

"Had to. It was screaming your name." She swipes a tiny brown shopping bag off the counter and hugs it to her chest. "Don't worry, it's small. Super cheap. Here, let's go to your room."

"Cheap?" I fall into step beside her, peering at the bag. "Does that say J.Crew?"

"J.Crew Factory! Plus, it was on sale."

When we reach my door, Gretchen opens it without the slightest hesitation. She's forever at home, wherever she goes. I've always been a little in awe of that. She pulls out my desk chair and turns it toward me. "You sit here."

I laugh. "What is this?"

"You'll see! Close your eyes," she commands. A moment later, there's a soft tug on my ponytail. "Wait, where's your little circle mirror?"

"Dresser, maybe? Or the bookcase?"

"Yes! Aww—Vassar Bear looks so cute with your books! Got to take a picture of that for the 'gram."

There's a pause, a quick patter of footsteps, and then—

"Okay! Open your eyes, but you're going to need both mirrors, so . . ."

She grips my shoulders, nudging me toward the full-length mirror on the back of my door. "You ready?"

She hands me the smaller mirror, and I line up my reflections so I can see the back of my head. "Oh!" I say.

"How cute is that?"

It's my regular ponytail, but now there's a perfect black bow tied around it.

"You don't actually have to tie it," Gretchen says, like she's reading my mind. "It's like a little rubber band. You just slip the bow on top, and the ribbons kind of hang down the sides. And it's velvet!"

I reach back to touch it—it's soft and stiff all at once. "Oh, I love it."

"It's for the party! Isn't it so dark academia?"

"Ohhhh." I nod. "Definitely. Wow. It's perfect."

"Couldn't resist." Gretchen leans her head in closer, smiling into the mirror like we're posing for a picture.

Texts with Tessa

TM: OH MY GOD

TM: Are you for real??????????????

TM: Scott!!!!!!!!!

TM: I'M SEEING YOU TOMORROW

TM: I mean

TM: Obviously I'm really chill about this 🙈 🙈 🙈

IS: Me too, yup, totally nonchalant 🤫

TM: 🙀 🙀 🙀

TM: Also btw I'm obsessed with this 📎

IS: Haha I didn't even know she posted that

TM: Scott, how are your bookshelves so gay????

TM: They make mine look like a church library

TM: And I'm not even Christian!!

IS: 😅

TM: Can you explain to me

TM: Why you have three identical copies of One Last
Stop 🥴

IS: Oh I mean

IS: One's signed, one's my reading copy, and one's for
       emergencies

TM: Emergencies 💀

39

Gretchen perches on the end of my bed, eyeing me curiously. "Who are you talking to?"

"Oh! Um, Tessa. Lili's friend."

"I know who Um Tessa is." She waggles her eyebrows. "Do you always smile like that when cute girls text you?"

I look back at her, speechless.

"Oh my God, your face right now." Gretchen nudges her foot against mine. "Come on! You can admit Tessa's hot, right? Please tell me you see it. I don't care if you're the straightest girl on earth."

"No, she is. Yeah. She's—cute." I press a hand to my cheek. "I don't know if I'm the straightest girl on earth, though."

I stop short, feeling like my heart's trying to break free from my chest.

"Oh?" Gretchen tilts her head toward me, eyes gleaming.

"I don't know," I say again, quickly. "Maybe. I'm just sort of thinking about it. Am I really . . . fully straight? You know?"

"Oh, sweetie! Did Tessa turn you gay?"

"I—"

"Kidding! I'm kidding. Oh, you're so cute. Okay, don't panic. You're not gay."

"Right—I know. It's just, like. Crush feelings, I guess?"

She laughs. "About Tessa?"

I shrug, hugging my knees to my chest.

"Ah yes. Okay, so Tessa's got what I like to call the Ruby Rose effect, right? Like, the specific vibes are different from Ruby, of course, and I think Ruby's genderfluid. But it's still that straight-girl-magnetism thing."

"Oh, no. Tessa's not straight—"

"I knowwww. I mean she *attracts* straight girls. Like you."

I pause. "Oh."

"I'm just saying, it's normal! Seriously—Tessa's super cute."

"No, I know." I tuck my chin between my knees, a lump starting to catch in my throat. "Yeah. I just feel . . . like it's different. Maybe? I don't know. It might just be in my head. Nothing's, like, happened," I add quickly. "And she's not—interested. I think. It's just a crush. Maybe."

Gretchen smiles a little. "Okay. So. You don't think she's into you. And you . . . don't know if you're into her?"

"I know it's weird."

"Have you tried passing yourself a note? 'Do we like her? Check yes or no!'" She giggles. "You could try reading your own diary."

"This is so embarrassing—"

"Oh, honey! No, no, no—sorry!" She scoots closer, her arm encircling my shoulders. "I don't mean to embarrass you! I'm just not sure what you mean."

"What I mean?"

"When you say you're not sure if it's a crush. What would keep you from knowing that?" She pokes my cheek. "Like, how do you know when you have a crush on a guy?"

"I mean. I just know? But this is different." I shake my head. "I don't know how to explain it."

"Well," Gretchen says slowly. "If you had a crush on her, it would feel like a crush."

"I think it does, though? Just a different kind of crush."

Gretchen draws back, eyeing me appraisingly. "Okay, how about this?" she says finally. "Do you want to fuck her? No? Then you're safe."

I open my mouth and then shut it, head spinning in a million directions at once. *Safe?* Like being queer is some kind of dreaded outcome?

And is "wanting to fuck" the only indicator of attraction? That can't be true, right?

I try to imagine what sex with Tessa would feel like, but my brain won't even go there. Kissing? Yeah, maybe. But *sex*?

There's no way she'd want that. And even if she did, I'm pretty sure I'd be awful at it.

"I don't know," I say finally, voice barely louder than a whisper. "I haven't really thought about it."

Gretchen smiles, squeezing my shoulder. "Then I think you

have your answer."

Suddenly, I'm blinking back tears.

"Oh, sweetie!" Gretchen's expression softens. "Aww. Hey. You know it's okay to be straight, right?"

I swallow thickly. "I know—"

"You're already enough, Immy. Okay? Don't forget that."

"Thanks." I scoot forward, feet on the ground. "Um. I should probably—"

"Wait—oh, I didn't mean to upset you! Are you mad?"

"No! Yeah, no, I'm fine." I stand, turning to shoot her a quick, forced smile. "Just realized I was supposed to help Edith with, um—"

"Immy."

"I'm fine!"

Texts with Gretchen

GP: Hope you're not upset!

GP: I just think it's important to understand the nuance here, yk?

IS: I'm not upset

GP: Ok good lol

GP: Oh!! Can you let Edie know there's a little surprise waiting for her on your porch

GP: It's a 🌱

GP;   Apparently she's planning to become a plant mom?? 🙀

DAY EIGHT
FRIDAY
MARCH 25

Texts with Tessa

TM: OMG SO

TM: I just talked to Declan

TM: Not only did he find 👞

TM: He found it on Tuesday!!!! And didn't tell us 🏛

TM: Wait til you hear what he's planning

TM: It's diabolical 🙈

TM: ANYWAY, MORE IMPORTANTLY, HI

TM: I'M SEEING YOU TODAY 😱

40

"Whoa." Edith appears in my doorway. "Hi. What are you doing?"

I tuck another sweater into my suitcase. "Packing?"

"That giant-ass suitcase? For one night?" She shuts the door, strides across the room. "Why are you bringing fifty cardigans?"

"You mean four?"

"It's one night!" Edith swipes my argyle green sweater out of my hands, peering into my suitcase. "All right, intervention time. What do you actually need? Pajamas, toiletries, clothes for tomorrow morning, party clothes. That's it! You're done!"

"No, I'm not. My pinafore still has a hole in the butt." I exhale, pressing my hands to my cheeks.

"Okay? That's literally gonna take five minutes. When's Lili coming?"

"Around eleven?"

"Immy, that's in two hours. You're fine. Ooh, I like this."

She holds up the black velvet bow. "Very on-theme."

"It's from Gretchen. Oh, I'm supposed to tell you she got you a plant? In the kitchen, on the windowsill."

"Of course she did." Edith shakes her head, smiling wryly.

I tilt my head. "Is this a thing? Gretchen buying you plants?"

"No . . ." Edith pauses, removing another cardigan from my suitcase. "But Gretchen stirring shit up with people and then making up for it with gifts is a thing."

I look at her. "I—didn't know you guys had ever really argued. Until the Kara Clapstone thing, I mean."

"We haven't. I'm talking about you."

I freeze. "What do you mean?"

"Come on. It's *Gretchen*. She lives for drama. Remember when Otávio gave money to the Salvation Army guy?"

"I mean, I wouldn't call that drama. She was just trying to explain the issues with that organization."

"I know. And I'm not saying she's wrong. She's just a little intense about it sometimes."

"I think she's just challenging us to be better allies."

I mean, I *like* that Gretchen's good about checking me on stuff. Sometimes I really need it. Like when I used to think bisexual meant someone could only like two genders. Or when Quinn Santiago asked for ideas about where to buy a binder in person, and I—with mortifying sincerity—suggested Staples or OfficeMax.

Do you want to fuck her? No? Then you're safe.

I keep thinking about the way Gretchen's eyes glinted when

she asked it. She didn't even pause to let me answer.

Not that I have an answer.

Should I have an answer?

Edith's still looking at me. "Look, I love that girl to pieces. You know that. I'm just saying, it's not always so black and white."

"I know, I know."

"Good." She flips my suitcase closed. "Okay, you go sew up your pinafore's butthole—"

"Butt-*whole*. With a *w*."

She splays her hand over my face. "Goodbye. And don't even think of sneaking any cardigans back in."

The second I slide into the passenger seat, Lili turns to me, beaming. "Big news!"

"Ooh—what?"

"Declan found the sausage!" she says, and I open my mouth to reply. But then her expression shifts. "Wow. I got scooped by Tessa, huh?"

"Er." I blush. "Yeah."

We buckle up, and Lili turns the car on.

"You guys have gotten pretty close this week, huh?"

"Me and Tessa?" My voice jumps. "Did she say that?"

"I mean, she hasn't put her phone down in days." Lili glances at me. "You trading me in for a new bestie?"

"Lili, no—oh my God—"

"I'm kidding!" Her smile flickers. "Look, as long as you

don't replace me with Gretchen, we're good."

I try to laugh, but it comes out like a sigh. "Yeah . . ."

"Wait." Lili stops at a red light, twisting to look me straight on. "What did she do?"

"Gretchen?"

"Mm-hmm. Definitely getting Gretchen-was-discoursing-again vibes."

"No!" I laugh. "I mean, yeah, but that's not . . ."

I trail off, suddenly not sure where my brain's even heading.

The thing is, Gretchen's not even doing anything wrong. It's just this dynamic that's always kind of been there with us. Basically, there's a version of me who lives in Gretchen's head, and as long as I stay within a certain radius of that, we're fine. But when I veer too far off course—I start to feel kind of hazy sometimes.

Maybe I'm more liquid than most people are. I always seem to take the shape of my container.

Usually, it's a sort of relief, letting Gretchen remold me.

41

Everything at Blackwell is just how I left it: the same white paths and stone arches and vine-covered fairy-tale buildings. The weather's cooled down again—jackets and scarves are out in full force, even this close to noon. But the courtyard's still bustling with laughter and footsteps and faint strains of music. You can almost taste that it's Friday.

My stomach hasn't stopped fluttering since we got here.

I hoist my suitcase up the front stairs, loving that I know which dorm is Rosewood. I call the elevator while Lili signs me back in at the front desk, and once we're in it, I know exactly which button to press. It's as automatic as home.

Third floor. Same cinder-block walls, same posters, same paper mural of quotes. I don't even think anyone's wiped a single doodle from their white board.

My eyes go straight to Tessa's closed door.

"She's in class," Lili says flatly, unlocking her door. "Don't worry—she'll be back for the party."

My cheeks go warm. "Oh—"

"Guess you'll have to hang out with me in the meantime!" Lili steps inside, leaving the door open for me—but she doesn't glance back. She just crosses to her desk chair and opens her laptop, like she's settling in to write a thesis.

I pause in the entryway, watching her.

"Are you coming in?"

"Yeah. No, definitely." I nod quickly, dragging my suitcase and pulling the door shut behind me. "Hey—um. Are you—"

"Not mad at you." She exhales.

I press my lips together. "It kind of seems like you are, though?"

"Okay, well, I'm not."

I sink onto the edge of Lili's spare bed, scooping Puppy into my lap. We're both quiet, but the air itself feels taut and charged. Telephone-wire silence, my dad calls it.

But then Lili tucks her legs up into her chair, circling her arms around them. "Ugh. I'm sorry."

"For—what?"

"For being a grumpy little bitch?"

I laugh. "You are *not*—"

"It's just." She stares at the floor for a second. "I don't know. I feel like I'm missing something? You've been avoiding me for months—"

"Avoiding—"

"Immy, you *have* been. How many times have I invited

304

you here? A dozen? I didn't know if you were mad at me, or if I'd hurt you somehow without realizing it. I couldn't believe it when you told me you applied here. I couldn't even talk you into visiting for a weekend."

I stare at her, almost speechless. "I—I promise it wasn't like that. At *all*. I'm so sorry. You didn't do anything wrong. Oh my God." I blink back tears. "Lili, I'm sorry."

"I don't need an apology! I just—I don't get it, you know? You refuse to come visit for literal months, but now you're back a week later? Because *Tessa* invited you?" Her voice catches. "And I'm glad you get along with my friends! Seriously. I'm just, like—what's the deal? What am I not understanding?"

"You're not—" I cover my face with both hands. "I'm sorry. I wasn't—I didn't mean for it to seem like I was avoiding you."

"Okay?" A tear breaks through, but she wipes it roughly away. "So—"

"Lili, I was so—" I try to push down the lump in my throat, but it's hopeless. "Intimidated," I say.

"By my friends?"

"By them. Or, like—the idea of them. And by how happy they made you." I sniff. "I didn't know if they'd like me—"

"Okay, well, they're obsessed with you, so."

"I don't know." I exhale shakily. "You're so happy here—and God, Lili, I love that. I love that you get to just live, and be queer, and you've got this whole little family of queer people. It's amazing."

She wipes her eyes without speaking.

"I just wasn't sure how I fit into the picture, you know?" I shake my head. "It felt like you'd found this really sacred space, and I didn't want to invade it."

Lili looks at me incredulously. "Immy, I *cried* when you told me you were coming here. I was so fucking thrilled. You're my best friend."

"You're mine, too!" I say, eyes watering all over again.

"Ha! Suck it, Gretchen." She wipes another tear with the heel of her hand, smiling triumphantly.

I laugh, but it comes out flat.

Lili raises her eyebrows. "You're still not going to tell me what Gretchen did to you?"

I pause. "I mean, I'll tell you if you want. It's just not much of a story, I guess? Basically . . . we were talking about crushes, and she was kind of weird about it. That's it."

"Weird like—making fun of you? Making fun of the guy?"

"No, no. Not like that. Not . . ." I trail off, rubbing my still-damp cheek. "It was subtle. Kind of hard to explain. Like, she wasn't being mean? She just wasn't, like, taking it seriously."

"Okay." Lili rolls her chair closer. "So you have a serious crush."

"No! I don't know. I don't even know if it *is* a crush." Lili stares me down until the tops of my cheeks go warm. "I guess that's what I was trying to . . . decide. But it kind of felt like Gretchen decided for me."

Lili taps her lower lip with her thumb—neither of us speak for a moment.

"Okay, so." She pauses, shooting me a look I can't quite decipher. "You were like, 'Hey, I think I have a crush on this person,' and Gretchen's like, 'Ha ha, no you don't'—is that kind of what happened?"

I open my mouth and then shut it.

On this person. That's—

Neutral.

Person. *Person.* Not guy.

I tuck my chin into Puppy's rainbow mane, making his horn flop sideways. "Yup. Basically."

We're quiet again.

Until Lili suddenly leans forward. "Remember Brianna Lewis's graduation party?"

"The party or the car ride?"

"What do you think?" She laughs a little. "You know I was scared shitless, right? You were the first person I came out to."

"Other than your family."

"Nope," she says. "You."

I look up at her, finally. "I thought you said—"

"I know. I was just—I don't know—trying to take the pressure off, because I knew you'd feel this huge responsibility to make it into some big perfect moment."

My hand goes still on the edge of the bed. "I had no idea."

"I know."

"I'm so sorry. God. I should have—"

"Made it into some big perfect moment?"

"I mean . . ."

Lili meets my gaze. "But you did! You made space. You took it seriously. You know there's not a script for this, right?"

I nod.

She pauses. "You know. If you ever had something you wanted to tell me, I could make space for that, too."

42

Something you wanted to tell me.

It's not like the code's hard to crack here. Lili clearly knows something's up, and she's just waiting for me to say it. She's practically holding up cue cards.

I'm sort of dying to know what kind of vibe she picked up.

Right now, she's staring into the mirror with laser focus, a bobby pin clenched between her teeth. "See, this is why I never wear my hair up."

"You sound like an amateur ventriloquist," I say.

She slides the last bobby pin into place. "Not sure being a ventriloquy expert is the flex you think it is."

I laugh, hugging Puppy to my chest. As if that's going to tamp down my drumrolling heartbeat.

It's impossible to explain what I'm feeling. Joy plus wistfulness plus early spring sunset. Faint laughter from the courtyard seeps through Lili's open window, intermingling with the "getting ready" playlist streaming from her phone.

It occurs to me that we've never done this, in all the years we've known each other. I don't think we've been to a party that was worth changing shirts for.

I sing along under my breath to the music, smiling at Lili.

She shakes her head, smiling back. "I can't get over you knowing every word of every gay song ever."

"I'm the one who introduced you to 'Silk Chiffon'!"

The first time I saw the music video, I seriously thought I was dreaming. My favorite movie, in song form. One verse in, and I'd already texted it to half a dozen people.

"You know that's why Gretchen dyed her hair pink, right?" I add. "Phoebe Bridgers in that music video is, like, her entire aesthetic."

"I hate agreeing with Gretchen." Lili plops down beside me on the bed. "Man, your *face* right now. You look like someone offered you a million kittens."

My cheeks go warm. "I'm just happy to be here."

"Okay, Pollyanna Banana. Let's fix your cute bow."

I gather my hair back and release it, shifting sideways so she can adjust the bow around my half ponytail. You could say I'm slightly obsessed with how my dark academia outfit came together. It's pretty simple—gray plaid pinafore from the thrift store, buttwhole-free at last. I'm borrowing Lili's black button-up boots, but everything else is just stuff from home—my white Peter Pan–collar shirt, black tights, black cardigan.

When Lili's done with the bow, she tugs some of my hair

forward, arranging it over my shoulders. "Love it. You look like a Samantha doll."

I laugh. "You look like someone who writes letters with a quill and uses sealing wax."

"Mission accomplished." She taps open the selfie camera on her phone, scooting in beside me, and I'm pretty sure this is the most I've ever liked my own face. My cheeks are flushed, my hair's the right amount of wavy, and the light from Lili's window makes my eyes look navy blue. Lili holds her arm out and smiles, and the scent of her hair makes me think of Goldfish crackers and YouTube and Snoopy sheets and the time she got stuck in the baby swing at my house and my dad had to chainsaw her out of it.

The quintessential Lili smells. She really is my whole childhood.

"O . . . kay. Posting now, tagging you. Caption is"—she stands and paces while typing—"'Dark academia party aesthetic on point.'"

Gretchen texts me a screenshot literally five seconds later. *INCREDIBLE, LIFE AFFIRMING, 12/10!!!*

I set my phone down on the bed without responding.

"Uh-oh. That's not a million-kitten face." Lili shuts one eye. "Who are we ghosting?"

I shake my head. "No one. I mean—Gretchen. But I'll write back later. I'm just not in a Gretchen mood right now."

"Not being in a Gretchen mood is a mood," Lili confirms.

311

Texts with Gretchen

GP: STILL NOT OVER THAT PIC!!! 🔥

GP: Okay fine fine don't text me

GP: SIGH

GP: No jk you're living your college life and I love that for you

GP: You look gorgeous Immybean, go have FUN

43

"The troops are assembling in Kayla's room," Lili says, shutting her window and sneaking one last glance in the mirror. By the time we step out into the hallway, my heart's firmly lodged in my throat.

Tessa's door is closed. And Lili doesn't even knock when we pass it. Which is—

Fine.

I mean, I'm sure she's coming. She's the one who talked *me* into coming.

But as far as I know, she hasn't been back to her room all afternoon.

I spend the whole walk to Kayla's trying to figure out how to casually ask Lili about it, but every version of the question feels about as subtle as screaming into a microphone. Not that I've been particularly subtle up until now, I guess.

If you ever had something you wanted to tell me.

Normally, we'd need a keycard to get into Kayla's dorm, or

we'd have to call her to come down and open the door. But a guy Lili knows from orientation group lets us slip through the entrance behind him. Already, there's this palpable buzz in the air. The entire first floor feels like a block party—people drifting from room to room in one messy jumble of laughter and music, liquor, and weed.

Kayla's in a double room on the third floor—apparently her stoner roommate is out of town all weekend. There's no question that the side plastered with anime art prints is Kayla's. Above her desk, there's a little gallery of family photos, arranged around a framed vinyl collector's version of Janelle Monáe's *Dirty Computer* album. Whereas Audra's decor pretty much boils down to one giant cloth tapestry and a bunch of string lights. But somehow a few flickering candles pull the whole thing together, softening the chaos to something cozy and intentional. Kayla, Declan, and Mika are piled onto Kayla's bed, drinking out of teacups, while music streams from someone's phone.

Not a Tessa in sight.

"The triumphant return of Imogen!" Kayla half sings. "You two both look amazing." But my chest feels so hollow and sharp, I can barely muster a proper response. Ten minutes ago, I was so in love with this outfit. Now I just feel vaguely overdressed.

"Those are some classy cups," says Lili, sinking into Kayla's giant beanbag chair. She scoots to make room, and I plop down beside her.

"Beverages, ladies?" asks Declan. He stretches his legs out, hooks his feet around the base of Kayla's desk chair, and slowly reels it back toward the bed. There's a dining hall tray perched on top of the seat, holding two large bottles and a few empty teacups. "Rolling bar," he says, winking.

"He's wearing his actual prep school uniform blazer right now," Kayla says, sipping her drink. "Just putting that out there in case you thought this boy was even a little bit dope."

"Babe, it's fine. No one cares that you weren't cool in high school." Declan grins back at her. "Speaking of corrupting the youth! Imogen, what can I get you?"

"Um. What are the options?"

"Literally only raspberry vodka and orange juice."

"And water." Mika holds up their cup. "Goes down better with Zoloft."

"Exactly. Water if you're on anxiety meds," says Declan, "and vodka if you *should be* on anxiety meds."

"Raspberry sounds good! Thanks," I say, which makes Lili full-on gape at me. But I'm not in the mood for a big Baby's First Drink announcement, so I just pretend I'm absorbed in Declan's bartending skills. And I guess Lili gets the message, because she doesn't say a word about it, even when I almost choke on the first sip because it tastes like a Starburst soaked in rubbing alcohol. She just watches me warily until I shoot her a forced grimace-smile.

The second sip's a little better, though.

By the fifth, I'm hardly shuddering at all.

Then, before I know it, I'm past the halfway point of my

315

teacup, and there's this happy fuzzy feeling curling around the edges of my brain. Because tonight's going to be top tier, Tessa or no Tessa. How could it not be? It's my first college party, I'm dressed like an old-timey schoolgirl, and I don't know who made this playlist, but it's A+, the most perfect vibes—Hayley Kiyoko, Lil Nas X, King Princess. It's actively hard to keep from singing along.

"You good?" Lili murmurs.

"Magnifique, Monsieur LePoisson," I say. The song switches to Clairo's "Sofia," and I gasp, which makes Lili laugh. I could go on for hours about how Clairo is an actual genius. But I feel a little boxed into my own head right now. Almost like bunny mode. The words are *there*, but they keep dying on my tongue.

I really thought alcohol was supposed to make the talking part easier. So far, it's just making my brain louder.

I try to focus on the song, because I don't want to miss the line about Clairo loving Sofia with her hair down. It makes my throat catch every time—there's just something so earnest about it. Imagine being loved with your hair down. Loved without an agenda, without an audience. Never having to earn and re-earn it. Love without modulation.

The door creaks open.

And Tessa walks through it. Wearing a brown tweed suit. With a vest.

She fingers the collar of her shirt, flushed and breathless. "Sorry! Laundry catastrophe. Some dude took my clothes out of the dryer—*dumped* my clothing on the floor, soaking wet, and put his gross boxers in there. Like, BRO, I PAID FOR THAT CYCLE. And there were no other free dryers, so now I've got clothes hanging all over my room. And *then* I had to borrow a shirt from my brother. But! I'm here!"

I don't know how to stop staring. Tessa in an old-fashioned suit, hair already starting to break out of her ponytail. Her frantic energy, her sweet flash of a smile. She looks like a hot young professor on the first day of class.

Our eyes meet, and in my brain, it's like daybreak.

44

Tessa asks if anyone wants a refill, and she's looking right at me, so I hand her my teacup. Then she settles in on the floor, half-turned toward Lili and me, one leg bent at the knee in a triangle. Like a menswear catalog.

I'm feeling warm and kind of spinny, and second drinks really do go down easier than first drinks. And the talking part's easier too. Normally there's a whole security system in my brain, checking and rechecking every single thought before it's allowed to leave my mouth. But now the guard's gone off duty.

"Wait." I set my cup down. "Is *this* the party?"

Kayla laughs. "Imogen, no! We're just trying not to show up too early."

"Right. Totally. Definitely." I nod. "It's totally early. It's only . . . nine."

If Gretchen were here, she'd be calling me a sweet baby nerd. An innocent bean. I don't mind it for the most part. But I guess I'm kind of glad to be out of her orbit for a second. It

318

makes tonight feel a little more mine.

Tessa nudges my foot with her shoe and shoots me an early-bird-solidarity yawn. The song switches to Conan Gray's "Heather," and the opening chords make me feel so wistful, I almost can't catch my breath for a second. But Tessa's still smiling at me, so I smile back, except now I'm blushing, and I'm pretty sure the eye contact should have ended by now. Only I can't look away, because Tessa's so cute, and her smile is like sunshine on water.

I think I've slipped inside a daydream. Something about the flickering candles and the music and the pinballing conversation. Kayla starts talking about Sailor Moon, and somehow it turns into a whole confessional story hour about our first crushes. Our first *queer* crushes.

Am I still problematic if I say Clea DuVall?

I mean, I can't say Tessa. You can't just *say* that.

"Robin Wright in *The Princess Bride*," Tessa says, shooting me a split-second glance.

"Truly the Starbucks of white-girl lesbian awakenings," Declan says, and Tessa does that low Tessa giggle. Which is pretty much a declaration of war against my heart.

"Mine was Jade," Mika says. "I just didn't know that it was a queer crush until later."

"Excuse me—you and Jade? That's not a crush. That's *love*." Kayla presses her hand to her heart. Mika just bites back a smile.

Then Lili starts talking about this regional Girl Scout

convention we went to when she was in fifth grade—I was in fourth. "We had to make these little pin crafts to trade with troops from other counties, like as an icebreaker—Immy, do you remember this?"

"SWAPs? Of course I remember."

"Yes! SWAPs. So the idea is that you end up with a whole collection of different ones. They were pretty cute. I think ours were pompom horses?"

"No, *yours* were pompom horses, because you're a horse girl," I say. "Mine were bunnies."

"So what happened?" asks Mika.

Lili clasps her hands. "So there's this one girl from, you know, some other town in central New York. Curly hair, and she was wearing overalls. And her pins were—"

"Felt rainbows," I say.

Lili blinks, shooting me a surprised half smile. "How do you remember that?"

"Um." My cheeks go warm.

"Hold up," Kayla says. "You're telling me this girl literally shows up at Girl Scouts to turn girls gay?"

I sip from my teacup and shrug.

Kayla shakes her head. "Goddess behavior."

"Patron saint of queer awakenings," adds Mika.

"Well, it wasn't my awakening." I pause. "I mean, it wasn't my *first* awakening."

"Ooh, spill it, babe," says Declan.

I can practically hear Lili's jaw slamming to the ground, but

320

I keep my eyes fixed straight ahead. "So. Um. This new girl had just moved here—not *here*. I mean home. Penn Yan. Anyway, she moved from New York City, and she had double-pierced ears, so third-grade me was like, holy crap, I have to be friends with her. Also, I was pretty sure we were *meant* to be friends, because she was Ilana with an I, and I'm Imogen with an I, and we hung out on the playground the whole first week. And I had this daydream where me, her, and Lili were a group of three best friends. It was so vivid. Like, to the point where I used to get stressed out about hypothetical future friend rivalries."

Lili looks both stunned and amused. "How did I not know about this?"

"Because she got absorbed into this group of popular girls who used to coordinate their outfit colors, and she never talked to me again."

"*Mean Girls* is real." Kayla nods gravely, and I laugh.

"I mean, she wasn't Regina George or anything. She was just in that group. And she moved back to the city a few years later anyway."

When I look up, everyone's still watching me expectantly, like they're waiting for some kind of punchy reveal.

"Oh! That's it," I say, flustered. "Sorry. That was—wow, I just told you guys a really pointless story."

"Not pointless," Lili says faintly.

Here's what I don't say: I looked Ilana up on Instagram last year. Out of nowhere—she just popped into my head for some reason. It was strange—she looked completely different than

I remembered. Less makeup than she used to wear in middle school, for sure. And her nose was pierced. But I think it was mostly the way she was smiling in every photo. A lot of her pictures were with this one particular girl, though I never figured out if she was Ilana's girlfriend. I don't even know if Ilana's queer. But I spent hours investigating the issue. And in retrospect, maybe that means something.

All these moments, scattered and separate. All these disconnected dots.

45

It's close to ten by the time we set off for Rainbow Manor, and the air's so cold it makes my cheeks prickle. Lili waits until the others are a few feet ahead before linking her elbow through mine. She looks at me hesitantly. "So, Ilana and the overalls girl. That's not fake backstory."

I shake my head, heart tugging sharply.

"We don't have to talk about it," she says. "Unless you want to. Immy. God. We don't have to go to this party."

I laugh. "But I want to go to the party. That's literally why I'm here!"

"Okay, but—" She stops short, and I realize Tessa's circled back to meet us.

Lili releases my elbow, side-hugs me, and jogs to catch up with the others. "Scotty Scott," Tessa says, falling into step beside me. "I liked your queer-awakening stories."

Which gives me this quick spike of panic. It suddenly occurs to me just how far I've strayed from my stolen Lesbian

Elsa narrative. Though Tessa's smile is so wide and sincere, I'm pretty sure she doesn't think anything's off.

"I like yours too, but"—I lean closer—"do they know she's your cousin?"

"Okay, you know what? That's enough of your cattitude." She tilts her head, smiling.

"Keep it moving, slowpokes!" Declan hollers, gloved hands cupped to his mouth. "Less flirting, more walk—"

Kayla slaps a hand over his mouth, herding him forward. "Carry on," she calls out over her shoulder. "Take your time. All is well."

"*He's* a slowpoke," Tessa mutters, but my brain's still stuck on the part where we're *flirting*. Is this flirting? Just . . . this? Joking and talking?

Do I want it to be flirting? Because I'm—

My foot slips off the curb, just enough to make me lose my balance—but Tessa hooks her arm around my waist to catch me. "Whoops!"

I turn toward her, burying my face in the wool of her blazer. "Did you steal this jacket from an old-timey professor, or what?"

"Yes, actually! From my dad."

"You're the real deal, Minsky," I say, and her last name feels thrillingly strange on my tongue.

Tessa looks down and then back up at me, her smile almost shy.

Okay, I'm pretty sure this is flirting.

"You guys ready?" Lili asks, stopping in the middle of the sidewalk. The house looks bigger, somehow, than it was last weekend, with even more Pride flags on display. The walkway's lined with tiny LED tea lights, and muffled music seeps through the walls.

Stepping closer, I see there's a sign on the door.

Welcome to Rainbow Manor: If you're out, come on in!

46

The entryway funnels us straight into Rainbow Manor's living room. It's crowded—not as bad as a movie frat party, but denser than any house party I've been to. The furniture's been pushed to the perimeter to make space for a makeshift dance floor, girl in red streaming from a speaker on one of the side tables. The decor's pretty simple, but some of the details are cool—fake candles, beige globes, stacks of books, dark velvet cushions. Overall, kind of a moody vintage library vibe.

Either Mika, Declan, and Kayla have already moved to another room, or they've been absorbed into the throng of people on the dance floor. "Here, link up," Lili says, grabbing my hand. So I grab Tessa's, and we move through the crowd like a chain.

"Lili!" calls out a brunette in a suit and a newsboy cap. They hug Lili, wave to Tessa, and smile at me. "Hi! Vitoria. They/she," they say, glancing over their shoulder. "Sorry, I've lost Nora *and* Alix."

"Nora's right behind you." Lili laughs, pointing to a pony-tailed blond girl with a bunch of piercings. She's wearing a turtleneck sweater and trousers, and I catch a flash of a woven striped bracelet when she waves—black, white, gray, and purple. Lili leans closer to me. "Okay, Vitoria's from Brooklyn, and they're a classics major, and, um, I don't know Nora's major, but I'm pretty sure—you're from the South, right?"

"Yup! Georgia." Nora nods.

"Right! So—okay, you know Tessa. And this is Imogen—she'll be a freshman here next year."

"Very cool! Are you visiting from Philly?" Nora asks.

"Oh, no, just Penn Yan. It's like thirty minutes away."

"She's my BFF from home," Lili adds.

I release Tessa's hand, cheeks burning.

"Go dance! We have to find Alix," Vitoria says as the song switches to Lorde.

We end up on the edge of the dance floor, where people are dancing in clusters or grinding or making out. I don't know if I'm dreaming or if my mind's just gone blank. It's beyond bunny mode. This is just . . . a totally different league from trivia or the tunnels, or even drinking in Kayla's room.

Lili spots Mika on the dance floor and waves. Then she turns back to Tessa and me. "You don't see Kayla or Declan, do you?"

Tessa shakes her head. "If they're making out—"

"I will ascend," Lili says. Then she pauses. "Oop—okay, no, Dec's dancing with some guy."

Mika's already a little flushed and sweaty by the time they reach us. "Hi!"

Lili tugs one of Mika's suspenders back onto their shoulder, raising her eyebrows. "You look like you've been having fun."

Mika laughs. "I'm dancing—come on!"

There's nothing delineating the dance floor from the rest of the space, but it feels like stepping onto the moon. Even dancing as an awkward quartet is the coolest moment of my life, by a mile. Except then the song switches to Doja Cat, and people rush to the dance floor, filling every pocket of space. Now I'm pressed so close to Tessa, I can feel the quiet curve of her breasts.

She meets my eyes, and her face is bewilderingly close. I've never been this aware of my body before. Every inch I move feels like a decision.

Suddenly Lili's hand is on my upper arm, but I can't quite hear what she's saying.

"What?" I lean closer.

"Bathroom! Come on." She grabs my hand—and the next thing I know, she's leading me past the kitchen and down a short hallway. But the bathroom's occupied, so we just lean against the wall, side by side.

"I don't actually have to pee," Lili says, and then she stops short. "Okay, now I do, but more importantly." She stares me down, and I guess she's still a little drunk, because she pokes me in the forehead. "You."

"Me?"

328

"So like." She pauses. "I don't know how to ask this. I don't know. I just—"

The bathroom door swings open, and someone in a full-on raven costume lurches toward us, wings raised. "NEVER-MORE."

We stand in stunned silence for a second.

Then Lili yanks me into the bathroom, shuts the door, and locks it. "Okay, you stay there," she says, stepping back into this sort of toilet nook, separated by a sliding partition door. "Immy, you're gonna hear me pee!"

"I've literally wet your bed."

"Ha ha, true." She starts peeing. "Okay, listen, I'm not trying to do the overbearing big sister thing, but I just want to make sure you're good. Like. You're happy?"

Staring at myself in the mirror is a little like watching myself in a movie. I'm so flushed, but in a good way. Almost like I'm glowing.

I wonder what Tessa thinks when she sees me.

"You okay?"

"Oh! Yeah, of course!"

"Immy." The peeing sound stops. A moment later, Lili flushes the toilet and slides the partition back open, studying me in the mirror while she washes her hands. "You're not—you know you don't have to prove anything to anyone, right?"

My cheeks flood with heat. "I know."

"Okay." She pauses. "'Cause you know—like, you *know* I'm in favor. As long as it's for you. Not, you know, 'the backstory.'"

She does air quotes, still studying me intently in the mirror. "It's real, right?"

I nod quickly, throat feeling thick all of a sudden.

"Oh no. No no no. No crying." Lili shoves me softly. "Immy."

I laugh, a little breathlessly.

She hugs me, quickly and tightly. "Okay! You gonna pee or what?"

On the toilet, I cover my face with both hands. I—

I think I just came out?

Sort of? Or did the coming out part happen back in Kayla's room, when I talked about Ilana and the SWAP girl?

Or maybe none of it counted, because I didn't say the words.

Bi. Bisexual. *Lili, I'm bi.*

It feels bigger than I want it to be. Do I really have to announce this? Can't I just feel something and live inside it while it's happening and not analyze it to death?

47

By the time we're back, Mika and Tessa have retreated to the edge of the dance floor again, joined by Declan, who's apparently ditched the random guy. I don't think they see us yet, though. Tessa's nodding along to something Mika's saying, laughing a little, and I'm just so fascinated by every detail of her. The way her sleeves are a little too long. Her fidgetiness—the way she's always bouncing on her feet, pushing her bangs out of her eyes. The way her smile never needs a warm-up. Then she catches me staring, and her whole face lights up. My heart jumps into my throat.

We make our way toward them. Declan's clearly drunker than he was when we got here. He grabs both of our hands, tugging us closer. "Where's Kayla? She's not answering her texts!"

Lili shrugs. "Maybe she's hooking uppppp."

"That's what I said!" says Mika. Declan glowers at both of them.

Tessa steps closer. "Hey, you're back."

"Back," I say faintly. I'm so nervous, I'm practically shaking. I think talking about this with Lili might have made it real.

The song slows down, but my heartbeat doesn't.

Tessa bites her lip. "Want to dance?"

"Dance, like . . . dance?" I nod. "Okay, yeah."

She puts her hands on my waist, and I lean in closer, letting my fingertips graze the ends of her ponytail, the wings of hair at the nape of her neck. My heart's beating so hard, it feels like my ribs might crack open. I've slow danced before—at homecoming, junior prom, even the eighth-grade dance.

But this already feels different. Not because Tessa's a girl. The difference is quieter, tucked away in my chest. It's a shift from a spiraling *I hope I'm doing this right* to the ache of *I hope*.

Tessa's eyes catch mine, and her lips tug up at the corners, just barely. And the noise in my brain falls away.

All the times I said I'm straight. All the times everyone's said I'm straight.

There it was, underlined and written in bold. How could I miss it?

Like finding Waldo and realizing he was never really hiding.

48

By now, the music's louder, the dance floor's fuller, and the air smells like candles and sweat. People keep stripping off layers, flinging them on the couches and chairs that line the room's perimeter, and there's a pair of broody-looking schoolgirls making out right in front of me. But I feel a little removed from it all. Lili and I are leaning against a stretch of wall near the entryway, basically taking turns yawning.

"Where are they?" Lili groans. "I'm starving."

She's been trying to round everyone up for at least twenty minutes, but Kayla and Declan have disappeared again, and Mika's gone off to find them. Plus, Tessa's been in the bathroom line for approximately a century, and I'm not trying to be dramatic about this, but it feels like someone turned off the sun.

My gaze drifts back to the schoolgirls. I've never been more painfully aware of the fact that I've never kissed a girl before. Or anyone, of any gender. It's funny how I lived without kissing for eighteen years, and now I think I might die if it doesn't happen tonight.

But how on earth do I get there? How does anyone get there? Kissing isn't something you can be measured and gradual about. Once you start doing the tilty-head thing, I mean—your cards are pretty much on the table, right?

Maybe the schoolgirls will make it easier to broach the topic. *Looks fun—should we try it?*

I can't picture those words coming out of my mouth. I'd need a million more raspberry vodkas and a lobotomy and at least two hours to practice my lines in front of a mirror. But Tessa's already crossing the dance floor, so I guess the lobotomy's off the table. I don't even have time to catch my breath.

She's taken her ponytail out. And what am I even supposed to say about that? What is there to say that Clairo hasn't already said?

She reaches us just in time to hear Lili let out an emphatic "Holy *shit*."

"You okay?" Tessa asks. Then she scoots in beside me and smiles. "Hi."

Lili's staring at a photo on her phone. "Mika took this." She shoves the screen in front of us. "Am I losing my mind, or . . ."

I study the photo—it's clearly taken outside, on what looks like a deck. Other than a few blurry light spots—Christmas lights, maybe—the image is dark and grainy. But there's just enough contrast to make out two figures leaning against a railing in the background of the picture, and it's really unmistakable.

On the left, Declan's bright blond hair. Right beside him, Kayla's Sisterlocks and choirgirl posture.

Tessa frowns. "I don't get it."

"That's Kayla and Dec," Lili says, tapping the screen.

"I know, but—"

"The hands," I say.

"Thank you!" Lili pinches and zooms until the screen basically looks like a blurry screenshot from an ultrasound, but still.

Those are clearly hands. And they're clearly twined together.

"Oh shit," Tessa says.

Lili exhales. "I KNOW."

"Are they . . . secretly together?" I ask.

"I don't know!" Lili looks at Tessa.

"I mean—like, it would be one thing if they were making out, right? Like, okay, whatever, it happens. But hand-holding?" Tessa leans closer and gasps. "Is Kayla wearing the sausage gloves?"

I stare at the screen, mostly so I won't stare at Tessa.

Is kissing really that small of a deal to her?

Another text from Mika pops up. **So I'm just gonna back away slowly 🙈 meet you out front?**

49

The air hits like a slap the second we step through the door.

"Scott, you're shivering." Tessa starts to shrug off her blazer. "Here—"

"No, I'm fine! I promise."

Mika rushes toward us, bouncing on their feet. "Wow, this weather. Let's move."

"How are Kayla and Dec sitting out there in this?" Lili asks, falling into step beside Mika.

Tessa hangs back, next to me. "I know you think you're Elsa," she says, and I let out a shivery laugh. "Come *on*. It's a cool jacket. At least do it for the outfit."

"I don't want to ruin *your* outfit. And it's really more my face and hands anyway. I need gloves and one of those robber masks."

"Hmm." Tessa turns to face me, grabbing both my hands, and my stomach does a quick-drop roller coaster swoop. I can't take my eyes off her face—the curve of her freckled cheeks, her short hair falling loosely into place around her ears. She presses my hands together in prayer position and cups her own hands around them, rubbing them a little on the sides with her thumbs.

Lili glances back, shooting me a questioning eyebrow raise over her shoulder.

I flash a quick smile, and she and Mika keep moving.

"How's that? Warmer?" asks Tessa.

My chest flutters. "Yeah."

"Good. Let me get the palms."

I try to twist my hands around, back-to-back, and the awkwardness makes Tessa giggle. "No, no. Here. This one"—she takes my right hand, crosses it over my chest, and tucks it into my armpit—"goes here, and *this* one . . ." She presses my left hand between both of hers, and suddenly we're standing so close, the tips of our shoes are touching.

Then she switches my hands out to warm the right one. "There," she says, finally.

I drop my hand but don't step back. I may or may not still be breathing.

She's just the tiniest bit taller than me—two inches, maybe. If I stood on my tiptoes—

"Is that what Kayla and Declan were doing back there?" I blurt. "Warming each other's hands?"

Tessa laughs. "Yup. And now they're probably warming each other's lips."

I swear to God, I'm like a pointillist painting of myself. I'm just colors and dots.

"Okay, but it's *whatever*, right? It happens?"

"What?" She studies me, grinning.

"You said that!"

Her quick, shaky laugh makes me melt. "But I don't actually think that. Kissing's not *whatever*."

"I've never done it."

"Never done what?"

"Kissed anyone."

Tessa's eyes flare wide. "You and Lili never—"

"Oh, yeah. Obviously. I meant other than Lili." Fuck. Fuck. "Lili and I kissed . . . so much. We were always kissing. Wow, I'm talking a lot about kissing, aren't I?" I laugh sharply. "Sorry—I'm not, like, obsessively thinking about kissing."

"Me neither. Totally not."

Suddenly, I'm on the tips of my toes, kissing her lips so quickly, it barely feels real.

She stares back at me, wide-eyed. But if she's surprised, I'm downright dumbfounded. I just—

Kissed Tessa. I *kissed* her.

I mean, it's not that I haven't pictured the kissing. But I've always imagined it as a thing that happens to me. Something I get swept up in. In my mind, I'm *never* the one who initiates it.

I can't be. Because that would mean this is something I'm certain about.

Tessa lets out a soft breath. "I'm—"

"Immy?"

Lili's voice.

Tessa and I spring apart, even though I know Lili's too far up the path to see us—not that she'd be weird about it either way. But the whole thing's inherently weird, given that I have no idea how Tessa feels about what just happened.

Or how badly I want it to happen again.

By the time Lili reaches us, she's breathless. "Sorry! I was gonna let you catch up, but, uh. Gretchen's here? And my brother, and your sister—"

"Wait—what?"

"Yeah . . . they're outside my dorm. I mean, they're inside now—I let them in. But I didn't want you to be surprised—"

"But." I shake my head slowly. "It's almost midnight."

"I know. I know. Are you—I don't know if you want to, like, talk to them, or . . ."

My heart feels like it's bouncing off the walls of my chest.

I can't—

I mean, I barely feel up to the task of existing as Gretchen's cishet best friend. Or Edith's straight big sister. And I'm *definitely* not up to being straight in front of the girl I just kissed.

Lili pats my arm. "Hey. I've got your back."

"You okay?" Tessa asks softly.

I'm pretty sure my lungs have shut down.

DAY NINE
SATURDAY
MARCH 26

50

Gretchen, Otávio, and Edith have taken over a cluster of chairs in the lobby, overnight bags piled at their feet. I breathe in, trying to steady myself. I feel completely unstrung.

"Surprise!" Gretchen's the first to jump up and greet me with a hug. "Couldn't miss the chance to see Dark Academia Imogen in person."

I barely register any of it. So many questions are jostling for space in my brain, I don't even know where to start. Did Gretchen plan this? *When* did Gretchen plan this? Also, how did they find Lili's dorm, and does Gretchen need a visitor parking permit, and are they staying overnight, and where are they sleeping, and, most importantly, what on earth is happening? Why—literally *why*—are they here?

"What's up," Otávio says, fist-bumping Tessa.

Right. Otávio would know the dorm. One mystery down.

Tessa turns to smile at my sister. "Hi! You're definitely Edith."

"I definitely am!"

"Oh man, even the dimple." Tessa looks from Edith to me.

"Tessa, right?" Edith says. There's this tiny lilt in her voice that makes me wonder what Gretchen's told her.

"So you guys just . . . decided to come up here?" asks Tessa.

"Oh, we were in the neighborhood." Gretchen says, with this little hand wave she does when she's trying to show off her thumb ring. She turns to Tessa. "It is . . . very cool to meet you in real life."

Tessa looks slightly bewildered. "You too."

"You've been taking good care of my bestie, right? You haven't been throwing her into any parties with no training wheels?" Gretchen hooks an arm around my shoulder.

"Everything's—great," I croak.

"Good." Gretchen squeezes my shoulder, reclaims her hand, and turns right back to Tessa. "Okay, wow—your suit is perfect, by the way."

I need a pause button. I need to sort through my thoughts, but everything's moving so fast. The party feels like it happened a century ago. And that lightning-fast kiss feels like it never happened at all.

I always forget that Gretchen has game in ways I can barely imagine.

It probably helps that she's actually queer. Like, I'm pretty sure she wouldn't have thrown down one chaste kiss and called it a night. How do I even compete with someone like Gretchen? And why would I? How could I stake any sort of claim here when I'm not even sure I'm really bi?

That word again. How could two letters wreak so much emotional havoc? *Bi*.

Why do I feel like I'm stealing?

"Okay," Lili says. "So, I'm gonna take these guys upstairs to drop their stuff off, and then we'll all head out to the diner. I can fill them in on . . . everything we've been up to this week."

I shoot her a quick, grateful smile—even though I'm not sure how she's planning to spin things. I guess she'll make sure everyone's on the same page about the backstory, for one thing.

Maybe she's just trying to buy me time for a talk with Tessa.

The talk, I mean. Because at this point, it's inevitable. I've been careening straight toward it since the moment I kissed her.

I wait until they're in the elevator before turning to face her. But the words get stuck in my throat.

How am I supposed to talk about this here, with drunk strangers stumbling in and out of the front door every second? How do I lay out the full messy truth under the fluorescent lights of Lili's dorm lobby?

Deep breath. "Can we go outside?"

"Only if you take the jacket," Tessa says with a flash of a smile.

"Fiiiiiiine."

She helps me into it, giving the collar a quick tug, and then we step back out to the courtyard. It's not particularly private out here, given the big lobby windows. So.

No kissing, I guess.

Not that Tessa's going to want to kiss me again once she finds out I'm straight. Or that I *was* straight? But was I?

How does this work? Am I stepping into a room or turning on a light?

I aim for a smile, but it doesn't quite stick. "I have to tell you something," I say in a rush.

The ground feels like it's tilting beneath me. The thought of dropping this bomb here and now makes me dizzy. But I kind of have to come clean, right? There are too many ways this could fall apart. This can't be a thing Tessa hears from anyone but me.

I shut my eyes for a moment. "You know the whole thing about Lili and me? How we used to date? That's . . . not quite true."

Tessa's eyes widen. "Oh—"

But then the door to the lobby swings open. "We're back!" Edith says.

Gretchen looks me up and down. "Cute blazer," she says slowly.

Her voice is as sharp as the edge of a knife.

51

It's sheer panic all the way to the diner. I feel like I'm on an airplane—strapped in tight with no legroom, tens of thousands of feet above my own life.

Gretchen sidles up to Tessa, who keeps glancing back at me with an expression I can't quite decipher. Tessa, who probably feels completely betrayed. Or at the very least, I'm sure she thinks I'm a total liar. That's basically where we left off, right? I lied my face off about dating Lili, and now she knows. Really, the only question is whether she's pieced together yet that I'm straight.

Was straight? Thought I was straight?

The diner's surprisingly crowded for one in the morning. All college kids, of course—flushed and tipsy, sharing plates of cheese sticks and French fries. "They do soft pretzels on weekends," Lili says, scanning the space for an empty table. She points to a booth near the back. "Okay, tight squeeze, but I think that's the best we're gonna do."

Now I'm picturing myself pressed up close beside Tessa, not a single molecule of air between us. I'd blow my own cover to bits before we even put in a drink order. I mean, Otávio could probably be talked into thinking I was just playing a part for the sake of the backstory—and God only knows what Gretchen's thinking right now.

But Edith? She'd know.

Of course, the problem solves itself when Gretchen scoots into the booth right behind Tessa. Which means the only seat left is on the other side of Gretchen.

It's the one spot where I can't see Tessa's face. Which is—

Probably for the best. Looking at Tessa is almost as dangerous as touching her. At least I won't accidentally stare my way out of the closet.

But the funny thing is, the more I think about coming out, the more I kind of want to do it. I want to hear what the words sound like out loud, in my voice.

But not here. Not right now.

If I do it here, I'll have to come out in two directions at once. There's just no way to spin it without admitting to Tessa that I wasn't out to begin with. That I thought I was straight.

Even though I'm not. And I wasn't.

I don't *think* I was.

But then again, do I *really* know that? Does anyone really, truly, one hundred percent know? Like, there has to be a chance

347

I talked myself into this, right?

This is what internalized biphobia sounds like. I know that. I know.

And I swear it's not something I'd ever think about bi people in general. It's just—me.

I've always had such a pliable center. I *like* being who people expect me to be. It's not that I'm trying to change who I am. I just want who I am to make sense. In every context. Without any uncertainty or contradiction. Which means pinning down who I'm supposed to be in any given situation and adjusting my feelings accordingly.

Here's a fun riddle: a people pleaser walks into a diner with five other people, and every single one of them wants her to be someone different.

Is that what's happening? People saw me as queer for a week, and it stuck?

A waitress stops by for our order—soft pretzels, pancakes, and coffee. Every core food group represented. Then Lili dives in with a full slate of meandering party anecdotes, clearly an attempt to steer the conversation toward neutral ground. But I only really start to relax when Otávio admits he's never heard of dark academia—which basically guarantees a good thirty minutes of collaborative explanation, complete with YouTube clips and probably a detailed analysis of my vision board.

Maybe we can stretch that until the part where we pay and leave. If I can just get through this meal, I'll find a way to pull Tessa aside on the walk home. I'll tell her everything.

And then I'll come out to everyone else. Separately. In orderly succession.

But then our food arrives, and Gretchen turns to Tessa in the pause that follows. "So, you're a lesbian, right?"

"Yup! Or gay. Or queer. Whichever."

"Cool. Okay, question." Gretchen grips the edge of the table. "Would you ever date a bi girl?"

I stare at my plate. The outline of my pretzel starts to blur.

"Uh. Yeah. Of course," Tessa says, sounding puzzled.

I can hear the smile in Gretchen's voice. "Really? Isn't that kind of unusual? I think it's amazing, don't get me wrong."

"I . . . don't know what you mean."

It's the softest I've heard Tessa speak, the whole time I've been here.

I really wish I could see her face.

"No, for real," Gretchen says. "It's a thing. I mean, I honestly get the hesitation. You get a lot of straight girls pretending to be bi, which makes a lot of lesbians think we're *all* faking it."

Edith shakes her head. "Gretchen, what are you talking about?"

"I mean, I definitely don't think that," says Tessa.

"Okay, but let's say you like a girl, and then it turns out that she's faking it. What would you do?"

Tessa laughs uncomfortably. "I *really* don't think that's a thing."

"You'd be surprised," Gretchen says, so cheerfully, she's practically singing.

Lili's fork lands on the table with a clang. "Well, that's biphobic as fuck."

"Uh, I'm literally bi," Gretchen says. "And I'm sorry, but this actually affects me? Straight girls who do this are why everyone thinks bi girls are undateable."

"I don't think bi girls are undateable," Otávio chimes in.

"I don't either!" Tessa says.

Lili slams her hands down. "Great! New topic."

"I don't think we're done with this one," says Gretchen.

Edith is looking straight at me, brow furrowed and tense. Lili, on the other hand, looks like she wants to commit murder.

Otávio appears to be enjoying his pancake.

Gretchen shrugs. "I'm just saying—"

"Okay, you want to talk about it?" I cut her off, anger coursing through me so suddenly, it feels like it could split me in two. "Fine. Lili and I aren't exes. I lied."

"No." Lili shakes her head. "Nope. *I* lied. Months ago. And then I roped you into it! This is so completely not your fault—"

"Yeah, but I still went along with it!"

"So you guys . . . are still together?" Tessa asks.

"What? Oh, no," I say quickly. "We never dated."

"Fuck." Lili covers her face. "Okay—"

"I've never dated a girl," I add. "Or a boy. Or anyone. And I wasn't Lesbian Elsa. I was Straight Anna."

Lili cuts in. "Okay, here's how it went. I was an insecure little fuckhead who made up a whole backstory that Imogen didn't even know about until this week. And the only reason she went along with it is because she's the best friend on earth."

"Oh." Tessa's voice is barely audible. "So you're—you're straight?"

"A hetero queen," declares Gretchen.

I turn to her, dumbfounded.

"This isn't Imogen's fault," Lili says, looking distressed. She turns to Tessa. "You can't be mad at her."

"I'm not mad."

"I'm not straight," I say, eyes prickling with tears. "Gretchen, I told you that."

"Did you? Because what it sounds like is a pick-me straight girl appropriating queerness because she thinks it will make everyone happy."

Lili shakes her head, looking like she's about to explode. But before she can even open her mouth, Edith swoops in. "Uh, why the fuck do you think you get any say in Imogen's identity?"

"Because it's my label!" Gretchen says, eyes pooling with tears. She wipes them angrily away with her palm. "And it's not some fun fucking afterthought. This—being queer, being *bi*—I don't get to turn it off when I'm not in the mood. You know when people started clocking me as queer? Elementary school. Ever been called a slur in front of your mom at Walmart, Imogen? Have you ever been told, 'Oh yeah, my dad's not really comfortable with you spending the night'? I used to get off the bus crying my eyes out because some sixth grader kept saying I was going to hell. And then, when I finally, finally have *one* safe place, the fucking basketball team burns it to the ground." She lets out an angry, choked laugh. "How about the girl from the movie theater with her fucking skirt up her ass. 'I'm not interested. I date boys.' Uh, cool story. You're not even cute. And I'm exhausted. It's exhausting. And now you—do you even like girls, Imogen? Like, are you actually attracted to girls?"

I try to speak, or even breathe, but it feels like my throat's caving in. I just—

Don't know what to think. Maybe she's right. It's not real. I don't want to kiss Tessa. Not that it would matter if I did. There's no way in a million years she'd want to kiss me at this point.

I can't stop blinking. "I'm gonna go."

It came from my mouth, but it doesn't sound like my voice. It doesn't even feel like I'm speaking.

"Alone? Immy, it's one in the morning—"

"I can walk you back," says Otávio.

"I'll wait outside. Just let me—" I jump out of the booth, feeling like the whole world's watching me stumble. Tables and tables of blurry faces. I push through the door, barely even noticing the cold anymore. There's a shadowy spot a few feet from the door, where I can settle in beneath an overhang. It's not private. I guess nothing ever is.

I cover my face with both hands.

A bell chimes faintly a moment later, and the door to the diner swings open. "Imogen?"

My sister.

"Hey." She scoots in beside me. "Guess who's getting a brand-new, freshly ripped, Lili-shaped asshole right now."

I let out a tearful laugh. "Oh, I bet."

"God. Immy. I'm so happy for you." She hugs me. "So you're—I'm guessing you're not gay. Are you bi?"

"I think so?" My heart skips a beat. "I'm not faking."

"Okay, first of all, fuck Gretchen—"

"She's right, though! It makes no sense." I shake my head. "Like it just suddenly pops up? That's not normal. You've always known you were queer. Lili's known for years—"

"Doesn't matter! Immy, you can't let her get into your head about this. Everything she said, all of that"—Edith gestures vaguely at the diner—"that's Gretchen's baggage. It has nothing to do with you, okay? She's being awful, and she knows it!"

I smile a little. "I don't think—"

"Look, on some level, she knows it. She has to. She's just—you know, she's scrambling right now. You sort of flipped her world upside down with this one. You being queer means she's been wrong this whole time. Which is why she's telling herself you're faking, or you don't *deserve* to be queer, or whatever the fuck she's implying. Because otherwise, she has to sit with the fact that she just treated a fellow queer person like absolute shit."

For a moment, we're both silent. I swallow back a lump in my throat. "But what if I'm the one who's wrong?" I say, finally.

"About who you like?"

I press my cheeks. "How do I know it's not a fluke? What if I only ever fall for one girl?"

353

"Then you're bi." She pats my arm.

"What if I'm talking myself into it?"

"Not a thing—"

"Okay, but what if the girl I like is kind of—I don't know—boyish?"

"Is she a boy?" Edith asks.

"No."

"Sounds pretty bi." I laugh, wiping my eyes, and Edith hugs me again. "She likes you, too. You know that, right?"

"She—"

"Come on. You're not subtle—"

"I'm not?"

"Immy, you're literally wearing her jacket. And let me tell you, she's not even *trying* to hide it. I was sitting right across from her. That girl is—" She stops short, glancing through the window behind me. "Uh, coming out here." Edith kisses my cheek. "I love you. I'll see you back at the dorm. Or not! Live your life."

52

Tessa steps out of the diner, and I forget how to breathe.

This girl, in her vest with no blazer, cheeks flushed from the cold. She looks around, smiling a little when she spots me leaning against the brick facade. "Hi. So. Um. The others are going to hang for a minute, but"—she swallows—"maybe you and I could walk back?"

As soon as she says it, I know. Category five *letting you down gently* vibes. My first big bisexual heartbreak, coming in strong on day one.

No way out but through, though, so I nod quickly. And then I pretty much keep my eyes glued to the sidewalk.

She hesitates. "So that was—"

"A shitshow. I'm so sorry."

"No! You didn't do anything wrong!"

"I mean, I lied to you about Lili," I say, as we veer down the side street, toward campus. "And about being bi."

"But you are bi."

I shoot her a faltering smile. "Okay, but I'd get it if you were skeptical."

"What?"

"Under the circumstances."

"No. God. Imogen." She stops, turning to face me. "I'm not skeptical. I would never be."

I finally look up at her.

And instantly burst into tears.

"Oh! Oh no. Scott—Scotty. Hey." She hugs me, and I bury my face in the spot where her chest meets her shoulder. "Don't listen to the pink-haired girl, okay?"

I laugh tearfully. "I'm getting your vest wet. And I stole your blazer."

"I love it on you," says Tessa.

The air rushes out of my lungs.

She studies my face, wide-eyed, and it's like the entire universe shifts. She touches her fingertips to mine for a moment.

Then she takes my whole hand in hers. "This okay?" she asks softly.

"Yeah." I nod, wiping away a tear with my other hand. I smile back at her. "Sorry."

"Hey. Are you—God, you just *came out*. Oh man. That's really big. And at the diner!"

"I know!"

"Did you ever think you'd come out at a diner called Diner?"

I laugh. "I didn't think I'd come out. I didn't think I was

queer. Which—God, it's so obvious, too. How did I miss it?"

"Too busy looking for Waldo?"

I face-palm. "Not me spending my whole life bragging about how observant I am."

"Comphet's a bitch." Tessa squeezes my hand. "And it probably didn't help to have Little Miss One True Queer Gretchen screaming in your face all the time about how straight you are."

I laugh, but it comes out half as a sigh. "I promise she's not usually that aggressively wrong."

"You mean the girl who just informed me I don't date bi girls?" Tessa stops walking, turning to face me again. "Because I'm pretty sure all I've been able to think about this entire night is dating a bi girl. And kissing a bi girl. And—"

I kiss her. And this time, there's no hesitation, no second-guessing, not a single beat of *Wait did that just happen, did I just do that, and why and how and what does it mean?*

None of that. Just a full-force, hands-in-hair, forget-where-I-am, holy-shit kind of kiss. She cups my cheeks in her hands and our foreheads bump together, which makes both of us giggle for a second.

But then she presses even closer somehow, moving her mouth against mine, and it cracks my heart wide-open.

"Sorry. Uh. Excuse me," someone mutters, stepping around us on the path.

Tessa draws back a bit, flustered but smiling. "Okay, new plan. Do you want to go back to—"

"No. Nope. Absolutely not," I say—but the look on her face

stops me short. "Wait, you mean go back to the diner, right?"

"Oh my God, Scott." She leans in to kiss me again. "I meant my room."

"Ohhhhhhh. Yeah. Yes." I laugh.

Somehow our hands find each other's, fingers fitting together like notes in a song.

53

The five-minute trip back to the dorms is somehow the slowest walk of my life.

"Minsky!" a guy calls out as soon as we enter the courtyard. "Tess!"

"We didn't hear it. Keep walking," she mutters.

Waiting for the elevator is agony.

But when it arrives empty, Tessa smashes the button for the third floor, and then we kiss the whole way up. Kiss in the hallway. She's got one hand in my hair as she fumbles with her carabiner in the other, and then we kiss again as soon as the door shuts. Aching and frantic, like a movie. Every surface of the room is draped in the laundry she set out to air-dry. We kick our shoes off. I drop the blazer.

"So you've never kissed a girl," Tessa says, smiling and breathless.

"No, I have."

"Wait—"

"Tonight," I say. "Right after we left the party. Really cute freckle-faced girl from Philly." I touch her cheek.

Tessa touches my mouth. "How are you real?"

The way she's looking at me gives me this liquid-gold feeling. I sink back until I'm sitting on the edge of her bed, pulling her down with me. She tucks a lock of hair behind my ear and kisses me again, until I can barely sit upright. She kisses my forehead, my cheeks, the crook of my neck, and I don't know if I'm falling or blooming. The way our ankles overlap. The ache below my navel. I kiss her again, and my mind's as quiet as snowfall.

A week ago, Tessa was just a face in Lili's college pictures. A week ago, I'd never been kissed. A week ago, I thought I was straight.

It's like learning to read—the way the letters and phonemes click into place. That sudden burst of meaning.

I smile up at her. "I always thought I'd have my first kiss in front of the pancake griddle."

"Okay, what is this mysterious pancake griddle?"

"The world's biggest pancake griddle! It's in Penn Yan."

"And people just, like, kiss in front of it?"

"No, they made a pancake on it! 1987. The world's biggest pancake ever—well, at the time. My parents actually got to eat part of it."

She sits up suddenly. "You're descended from pancake royalty?"

"I mean, yeah," I say, "but deep down, I'm just a normal

girl. You don't have to treat me differently in pancake situations."

"Pancake situations," agrees Tessa. "Breakfast, for example."

"Exactly."

"Okay, so"—she flops back down, rolling onto her side—"*do* they let people make out on the griddle?"

"In front of the griddle! It's mounted to the outside of a building. So . . . I mean, as long as the clothes stay on, I guess so?"

She taps her finger to my lip. "Interesting."

I pause. "Speaking of whether or not clothes stay on—"

"Also interesting," she says, eyes going wide.

"I don't mean—" I blush. "I'm not saying, like—get *naked*—"

"You sure?"

"Oh—"

"I'm joking!" she says. "Sorry. I mean—I'm not joking. I want to—like, I definitely want to, but not until you want to. Or *unless* you want to. You know what I mean. Now I'm shutting up."

I giggle. "I know."

She studies my face like she's memorizing a poem. "Hey, let me know if *any* of this is too fast. I know it's been, like, an emotional night. And your sister's here—"

"Let's not talk about my sister."

"Oh man. I was always so scared I'd randomly butt-dial

Dan or Rachael or, like, my parents in the middle of hooking up."

"Oooh. Don't do that."

"I won't." She reaches back and pulls her phone out of her pocket. "See? No butt-dials."

"Love that for us!"

She taps my nose. "Wait."

I smile up at her, taking in the soft lines of her profile while she opens her music app. Her eyes crinkle at the corners—I know she knows I'm watching.

"Okay!" She stretches over me, setting her phone on the nightstand. The audio's a little quiet—just a regular phone speaker—but even the first few instrumental notes make my heart flip. I trace her freckles with my fingertip from one cheek to the other and sing the first word along with David Byrne.

Home.

"It's my—"

"Favorite." I kiss her. "I know."

"You're my favorite," she says, and I laugh. Then I sit up just enough to peel my tights off. And my cardigan. "Not trying to get overheated," I explain.

"Oh, yeah. Good point. Very dangerous." Tessa pauses— then taps her belt buckle. "Should I, um—"

"Yes. I mean. Belt. Pants. Whatever. If you want—"

"Okay. Yeah." She nods quickly, and I could swear it's my heart that's unzipping.

I shut my eyes for a moment, letting the music fill every crack in my surface.

This must
be the place.

My phone buzzes under my thigh, almost startling me off the bed. Turns out, I've missed a whole stack of texts from Lili.

Okay Gretchen went home

Followed by a GIF of Harry Styles waving goodbye and blowing a kiss, and then:

The kiddos are still here tho

They're gonna crash tonight in my room

Which means we're a little short on beds in here, you should probably find alternate lodgings for the night 😏

And then a frantic addendum:

OKAY BUT JUST TO CLARIFY you are welcome to come back to my room anytime, we're in here, we love you, door's open!!!!!

"Are they like, 'where are you'?" asks Tessa.

I set my phone next to hers on her nightstand, turning to face her. "No, they're—"

My words melt away when I see her. Tessa in an undershirt, white with short sleeves, the straps of her sports bra faintly visible underneath.

Nothing on bottom but boy shorts.

My heart's spinning cartwheels. I don't think I realized

363

until this moment just how much clothing she usually wears. Hoodies and jeans and shorts. Even her dark academia clothes had extra layers. I guess she was *technically* naked under a bathrobe when we met, but if I think about that too long, my heart might combust. She's so pretty, it's actually kind of unbearable. Boyish and girlish, all at once. She's a little huskier than I realized. Narrower than I am, but with an unexpected softness.

What would it feel like to touch her bare skin with mine?

I fidget with the hem of my skirt, unsure if I should take off my pinafore, too. I wonder what she thinks I look like underneath. If she's thought about it at all. To be honest, it's weird that *I'm* thinking about it. I don't typically get too wrapped up in body stuff. I'm kind of in that in-between space where I'm bigger than most actresses but small enough that people aren't shitty to me, and it just hasn't really been an issue for the most part.

But maybe that's because no one's actually *seen* my body before. I don't even really wear bathing suits, other than summer trips to Nana's house on Cayuga Lake. And this is very much not Nana's house on Cayuga Lake.

The song restarts itself. *Home.*

I imagine Tessa unzipping my pinafore, unbuttoning the shirt underneath it. Maybe she'll think my stomach's too soft. Maybe she'll find the twin scars on my back where a doctor scooped off two birthmarks. Or she'll feel the little connect-the-dot zits running along my spine. Or she'll—

"Hey." She reaches up with both hands, tugging me down beside her. When she leans onto her side, our faces aren't even an inch apart. Her hand falls to my waist. "I can't tell if you're thinking or panicking or—"

"Both. But in a good way?"

"Oh, right, the *good* kind of panic." She cups my cheek with her hand. "Let's not rush this, okay? It's so new. You should take the time to figure out what you want."

"I want this, though."

"Yeah, me too! But—"

"And I promise this isn't just, you know. Me figuring stuff out. Or experimenting—"

"Oh! No—Imogen. I know you're not. I just mean, like—I don't want you to think you have to be some cool, sophisticated queer seductress girl, you know? You don't have to try stuff because you think that's what I want."

I sit up. "You don't think I'm a cool, sophisticated queer seductress girl?"

"Totally not." She sits up beside me.

I scoff, tugging her backward onto the pillows, tangling our bare legs together. She touches my lips with hers, just for a second, and I smile back up at her.

She lets out a quick, breathless laugh. "Oh my God, this is—you know that part of *The Lion King* where they're having sex in the forest—"

"People had sex in *The Lion King*?"

"No, lions had sex in *The Lion King*—"

"*What?* Sorry—when?"

"'Can You Feel the Love Tonight'! Imogen, they were rolling around the whole jungle—"

"I thought . . . I thought they were just, like—being in love?"

"Yeah, but then Nala gives him that look—remember? Like. *Heyyyyyy.*" Tessa leans in and kisses me. "And that's us! We're lions having sex! Except we're *not* having sex, because we're not gonna rush!"

"To be clear, we're also not lions," I say, shooting her a smile that turns into a yawn halfway through. "Sorry—"

"No—geez—what time is it?"

I crane my neck toward the pair of phones on Tessa's nightstand. "Almost three in the morning. Yikes—sorry! I can give you your bed back—"

"I don't want my bed back. Sleep here."

I look up at her. "Really?"

"Imogen." She rolls back down beside me, scoops my hair back, and kisses me. "Do you need me to spell it out? I've been"—she kisses me—"losing my goddamn mind"—she kisses me again—"ever since that dog wandered over, and you just—boom"—another kiss—"dropped down and hugged her. The look on your face. And then you're like, 'My goat was named Daisy.'"

"She was!"

"I know!" Tessa laughs, tucking a lock of hair behind my ear.

Then she buries her face in the crook of my neck, and every breath she breathes feels like a love letter.

54

My eyes don't want to stay closed. It's been like this for at least an hour—me, staring dazedly into the dark, memorizing every inch of Tessa's blank white ceiling.

My head's a shaken snow globe, glitter suspended in liquid. When I touch my lips, they feel tender. I don't know how to make any of this feel real.

I kissed a girl.

She kissed me back.

And now I'm in her room, in her bed, close enough to feel her chest rise and fall as she breathes. I don't know how people do this. How do you turn your brain off after kissing? How do you stop cataloging every point of contact between your over-lapping bare legs?

Also, how do you unremember the fact that you didn't wash your face before bed? Not to mention brushing or floss-ing, which is why your breath now tastes like the apocalypse, and also your bladder keeps chiming in to say, *What's up, hey,*

Imogen, hey, about that alcohol last night, about those liquids—

I just have this feeling that getting out of bed will break the whole spell. What if Tessa wakes up regretting everything? What if she sits up in bed, hugging the edge of her blanket in horrified silence? *I was in my underwear*, she'll realize, *and Imogen didn't even try to breach the waistband.*

Does she even like girls?

Does she want to fuck me, or not?

Except—no. Nope. Tessa wouldn't think that. This is my warped little bunny brain freaking out for no reason. Last night was perfect. I mean, other than the part where Gretchen called me a pick-me straight girl. But the rest of it was dreamy perfection wrapped in starlight, and now I'm lying here with bee-stung lips and a hundred new doors unlocked in my brain. Miles of uncharted territory.

Here I was, so sure I'd mapped out every inch of myself.

How do you get your own sexuality wrong? How is that even possible?

I feel on the verge of tears all of a sudden. But I can't tell if it's exhaustion or panic or just the fact that every part of this is light-years away from my normal.

And there's Tessa, sound asleep on her side, hand curved sweetly around the edge of the pillow. A stripe of dark hair falls over her cheek, tickling the corner of her mouth.

I want to tuck it behind her ear and kiss her. I want to click my heels and teleport home.

Close my brain for renovations. Imogen Scott, currently

under construction.

If I could call a time-out. Just for a second.

I slide out of Tessa's bed as carefully as possible, scanning the room for Lili's boots from last night. But since they've apparently vanished, I grab a pair of Tessa's flip-flops instead, strangely thrilled to find they fit me perfectly. Queer girl Cinderella.

The hallway's totally empty. Good. No one here to witness me wandering out of Tessa's room like I'm coming out of sex hibernation.

Which I'm *not*. Because we didn't. Have sex, that is.

The bathroom's lit only by a night-light, but by the time I'm done peeing, I can make the cubbies out well enough that I'm eighty percent sure it's Lili's toothpaste I'm borrowing. I attempt to finger-brush, studying my face in the mirror.

I look like the end of an action movie—flushed cheeks and dark circles, hair haphazard. Stripped totally raw.

55

"But what if Gretchen's right?" I blurt.

"Uhhhh." Edith stares at me, blue eyes glassy with sleep. "Have you . . . been here this whole time?"

"I mean, think about it! If I was wrong about it before, how do I know I've gotten it right this time? Like, how am I supposed to trust myself? And now I've dragged Tessa into it, and—"

"You didn't"—Edith yawns—"drag Tessa into anything. What time is it?"

"Nine seventeen."

Edith pulls herself up, gaze flicking from Lili's empty bed to Otávio's nest of blankets on the floor. "Where'd they go?"

"Bathroom, I think? I don't know."

She nods slowly.

"Do you think I was using her?"

"Lili?"

"Tessa!"

Edith blinks. "For what?"

"For attention? Or to make people like me, or to seem more interesting—"

"Oh, are we just listing out biphobic stereotypes?"

"What if I *am* the biphobic stereotype?" I cover my face.

Edith lets out a startled laugh. "This is wild. I don't think I've ever seen you just, like, completely lose your shit like this."

"No, I always lose my shit like this. Just not out loud."

She looks at me. "So this is what your brain sounds like?"

"I mean. Pretty much?"

"Huh. All the time, or just after sex?"

"You think I had *sex*—"

"You had SEX?" I look up to find Lili wide-eyed in her bathrobe, Otávio a half step behind her. I didn't even hear the door open.

"Noooooo!" I cover my face with both hands. "I didn't have sex! We just—you know."

"What did I miss?" asks Otávio.

Lili pats his shoulder, turning back to me. "I didn't even hear you come in last night."

"Yeah, no—it was late."

"And now she's freaking the fuck out," Edith chimes in.

Lili pauses—but then she stabs her finger in my general direction. "Oh, hell no. I know what this is."

"Er . . . what?"

"This is that thing where you're like, 'Oh no! I'm freaking out! She totes doesn't like me!' and she's in there like, 'Oh man oh man—"

I laugh. "She does say *oh man*."

"Yeah, but this is like a sad *oh man*. Like, 'Ohhhhhh maaaaaan, that girl is SO not into me.'"

"Right!" Edith punches my arm. "And meanwhile, we're all like, 'YOU ABSOLUTE DUMBASSES, OPEN YOUR GOD-DAMN EYES—,'"

"THANK YOU!" Lili clasps her hands. "But nooooo. Rather than talk it out like normal people, you're gonna avoid each other and then—I don't know—maybe throw in a grand gesture later, but that's not going to happen until you're both *completely* miserable, and for what? WHY?"

I open my mouth and then shut it. "So . . . you think I should go talk to her?"

"Immy, I mean this in the nicest way possible, but I will physically drag you next door to make this happen," says Lili. "There will be rugburn. On your ass, probably."

Edith grins down at her phone.

"Um. Okay." I slide off the bed, and it's like I've lost the reins of my own body for a second.

I put Tessa's flip-flops back on. Cross the room. Pass Lili's desk.

But I stop short before opening the door. "Wait!" I whirl around. "What's the etiquette, though? Do I knock?" I pause. "Okay, yeah, I should knock. Obviously. Sorry. Never mind."

I take a deep breath and step into the hall.

* * *

Thirty seconds later, I'm back in Lili's room. "She's not there," I say.

"Uh, what?"

"I mean, I knocked, but . . ."

"Nope. Absolutely the fuck not." Lili hooks an arm around my shoulders, marching me back to Tessa's door. "Tess?"

She knocks. Then knocks again.

No answer.

Lili pulls her phone out of her back pocket, opens her texts, and starts typing. Her phone vibrates in her hand a moment later, and she makes a noise that's half exhale, half scoff.

"What—what happened?"

"Nothing. She's in her brother's room." Lili presses a hand to her forehead.

"Oh! When did she—"

"I don't know. I assume sometime after you left and dove into bed with your sister. The two of you. I swear to God. Same exact kind of weird." She taps her screen again, biting her lip. "Okay, you know what? I'm gonna get some laundry to do at home when I drop you guys off. And while it's running, maybe you fill in some of the gaps for me here? Like . . . she knew you were leaving this morning, right?"

I nod, a lump rising in my throat. "Yeah."

"Okay." Lili's brow furrows. "Hmm."

"I mean . . . she disappeared right when she knew I'd be leaving. Seems pretty straightforward, I guess."

"You think she's avoiding you?"

I shrug.

"But . . . you haven't texted her."

"No." I shake my head. "Yeah, I don't know. I don't want to pressure her or make it a big deal—"

"Yeah, but." Lili pauses. "I mean, you sort of left in the middle of the night, yeah? Which is fine! But, you know. You might want to text her so she doesn't think you ghosted?"

"Oh." I nod slowly. "You think I should—"

"If you want! Sorry—I'm—yeah. I'm not trying to give you unsolicited advice—"

"No, you're fine! I'm just—I don't want her to think I was ghosting. I wasn't!" My brain feels a little swirly. "Not on purpose. I should text her, huh?"

Lili tips her palms up. "I mean—I think so."

"Okay. Yeah. I'll just, um." I look down at my phone and back up at Lili. "What should I say?"

"That's all you, Immylou. You've got this." She pokes the tip of my nose. "Okay! Grabbing my laundry!"

She disappears into her room, but I'm still frozen in place. Alone in a dormitory hallway, staring at Tessa's shut door.

56

I keep sneaking glances over my shoulder, little quick scans of the courtyard. When we step off the curb into the parking lot, I legitimately almost trip over my suitcase.

"Hey." Lili slows her pace to wait up. "Everything's going to be fine. This isn't, like, your last chance to talk to her. We're talking about a thirty-minute drive. Not even that."

"I know—"

"Seriously, drive back up next weekend. Drive up tomorrow if you want!"

"Yeah." I nod. "Maybe."

Lili grabs my suitcase, rolling it around to her trunk, and I take one more glance back. Just in case of—I don't even know what.

Something.

But there's nothing. Only murky gray skies and Edith and Otávio trailing behind us like sleepy ducklings.

I take my phone out again, staring down at my text chain

with Tessa until it's just a blur of blue and gray bubbles. The problem is, no combination of words seems right. Or even in the vicinity of right. I keep deleting every message I start.

Just wanted to say how much I loved last night—

How much I liked last night—

Just wanted to say last night was really fun—

Hi, we made out last night and then I disappeared and then you disappeared and now I'm going home, and I know you don't want to be official girlfriends or anything, obviously, lol, but I just want you to know I really liked it—more than liked it. Unless you disagree, in which case I liked it just enough that you should feel good about your kissing abilities, but not enough that you should feel ANY pressure, okay?? And maybe you can respond with an emoji or something? Just to give me a clue where you stand??

I think about how the delete button looks like a house knocked on its side.

I tap it and watch the words unravel backward, letter by letter.

Edith dives into Lili's passenger seat before I even think to call shotgun, and her first order of business is hooking her phone up to Lili's Bluetooth. For a minute, everything's silent, apart from the low hum of the engine.

Until the soft instrumental notes start to rise like a church hymn.

"Oh? Oh? What's that?" Edith twists around the passenger

seat, holding her fist up like a microphone. "Could it be the iconic 1987 hit song 'Faith' by the late and great George Michael?"

Otávio rubs his temples. "Oh boy."

Edith ignores him. "Presenting . . . live in concert for the first time since Christmas break . . . the Scodoso siblings!" She revs up her air guitar.

Lili laughs. "Fuck yes. After this, 'Dancing Queen,' okay?"

"Nope," Otávio says. "No ABBA before noon."

"The way you say that like you're not the lead singer on 'Waterloo.'"

"Immy!" Edith cuts in. "Pay attention! Your part's coming—"

"Maaaaaay-be," I chime in, right on cue.

Lili shoots me a grin in the rearview mirror. "Still got it."

I don't miss a single lyric. It always amazes me how music can do that—the way it puts down roots in your brain. Close your eyes, and you're time-traveling. I could be eight years old, singing into Lili's unplugged karaoke microphone for an audience of stuffed bears. *Downright majestic*, Tessa had called it.

With my eyes shut, it's almost too easy to slot her into the picture, too—smiling and sleepy, squished into the back seat between Otávio and me. Eyes rimmed with dark circles, hair winging out in a thousand directions. Honestly, this girl could revolutionize the whole aesthetic of sleep deprivation.

I really, really need to text her.

"So what's the plan for telling your parents?" Lili asks. "*Are you gonna tell them?*"

I look up with a start. "About Tessa?"

She laughs. "About you!"

"I can help you write your coming-out speech!" chimes Edith.

For a moment, it doesn't quite compute—the idea that coming out exists outside the context of Tessa.

The fact that me being queer is just—mine.

"I don't want to do a speech—"

"Yeah, no, totally. Speeches are overrated. Ooh, you know what you should do?" By now, Edith's fully twisted in her seat, eyes gleaming. "Invite Tessa over, but sneak her out into the shed. And then I'll be like, 'Hey, Mom and Dad, can you guys drop this totally irrelevant item off in the shed for me?' And we'll time it so they show up and find you guys just making out—"

"That's—"

"And they'll be like, 'Edie, stop making out with girls in the shed,' but then you'll turn around and say, 'Guess what, bitches—it's IMOGEN.'"

I stare at her. "Wow."

"Okay, first of all," says Lili, "Imogen's never said the word *bitch* in her life. Second of all, what's the point of having a shed if you're not going to use it to make out with girls?"

"How often *do* you make out with girls in the shed?" Otávio asks.

"Never. My girlfriend lives five hours away. We've literally never met in person. Guys, this is all hypothetical. Just trying to inject a little creativity here."

"Oh. Yeah, no, I'm okay," I say, nodding politely. "I think

I'll just do it the regular basic-bitch way."

Lili's jaw drops. "I stand corrected!"

I shoot her a smile, before turning to peer out the window. The sky looks even more foreboding than it did when we left. It's definitely about to start pouring. Any minute now.

We're almost home at this point—though it looks like Lili's taking the long way to my house, right through the middle of downtown Penn Yan. Maybe she misses it.

I try to imagine myself a year from now, turning at all the same stoplights. Driving through the town I've always lived in, down streets I know so well, they're practically a part of me—Clinton Street, past Hamilton, and a left on Main. Coming back home. I know moving thirty minutes up the road to Geneva isn't some big, earth-shattering transition, but it's still going to be different, right? I don't think I've ever left Penn Yan for longer than a week or two.

I catalog the stores as we pass them. Long's Cards and Books, where Edith and Gretchen sometimes rearrange the YA section so all the queer books face out on the shelves. And the candy emporium, where Otávio once cried for ten minutes after trying a chocolate bar with pop rocks. There are a couple of artisan shops, where you can buy hand-painted wineglasses or cutting boards engraved with the outlines of all the Finger Lakes. And the Pinwheel Market. Milly's Pantry.

"Tessa would like Main Street," I say.

In the rearview mirror, I catch Edith and Lili exchanging quick glances.

"She would!"

"Want me to go get her?" asks Lili. "I'll do it. I will turn this motherfucking car around so fast, so help me, God—"

"Wait! Pull over!" I lean forward, far enough to see out Otávio's window.

Edith twists around, raising her eyebrows. "At the griddle?"

My cheeks flood with heat.

"I want to post a picture," I say.

Texts with Gretchen

GP: Wait are you home??

GP: Can I come over

GP: Please

GP: I want to talk about what happened

GP: You were hurt and I feel bad

57

"Yeah, that's not an apology." Lili hands my phone back, rolling her eyes.

It's just us now—other than Mel, who's snuggled between us, sleeping. We've already dropped Edith off at our house, and Otávio's inside. Even Lili's parents are MIA. So now we're just hanging out on Lili's metal patio glider while her laundry runs, waiting for the rain to start. Lili's always loved that moody, thick air that comes just before the sky breaks.

"So is Gretchen, like, tracking your location or something?" she asks, yawning.

I laugh. "I mean . . . it could be the iconic, highly visible Penn Yan landmark I posted."

With a kiss emoji for the caption.

Tessa hasn't liked the post, though.

"Still a shitty apology." She scowls. "She really sat there and typed, 'You were hurt.'"

"I know, I know."

"Can't you just see her waving a bloody knife around? 'Oh, you were stabbed? I feel bad!'" She scrunches her nose. "Are you gonna talk to her?"

"I mean . . . probably not today."

"I vote never," says Lili—but then she shakes her head. "Sorry, I'm trying to be less of a piece of shit about this."

"Lili, you're not—"

"I'm just, like, *incandescently* angry. This is primal rage. *Reptilian* rage."

"At Gretchen?"

"Yeah, at Gretchen! And, you know what, I knew she was going to pull something like this. I fucking knew it. She can't handle anyone sticking one goddamn toe outside of whatever little box she's shoved you into."

I ruffle Mel's fur, tilting my head toward the trees. "So you kind of . . . knew?" I ask, after a moment.

"About Gretchen being a nightmare? Or about you being bi?"

I smile faintly. "About me."

"I mean—before this week? Not particularly." She tilts her head. "I guess I always saw it as a possibility? Like, you wouldn't be the first *very* committed ally to . . . level it up a little."

I let out a sheepish laugh. "Yeah . . ."

"You know, you and Tess were off-the-charts funny this week."

I look up at her. "Really? Was it totally obvious?"

"Totally. Well, at least on Tessa's end." Lili pauses to tuck her legs up. "It was very cute. Tessa, on, like, Tuesday, developed this sudden sociological interest in the ethics of dating your friends' exes. Totally hypothetical, of course. Just taking a casual poll, you know—seeing where I stood on the issue in general. I'm sitting there, like, oh, honey, you are *not* as subtle as you think you are."

I giggle. "What did you say?"

Lili leans her chin on Mel's head. "I mean—I said I didn't have an issue with it, because I obviously don't, but—Immy, that was a tough one! Because at that point, I assumed it was one-sided. You know, like, I didn't think you were gonna be interested in dating a girl. And since I'm the one who planted the seed in the first place by telling everyone you were bi—I just didn't want to put either of you in a weird spot."

"Oh. Right—"

"So then I tried to put out feelers with you, but of course you gave me absolutely nothing. Nada."

"I'm sorry." I press a hand to my cheek, grinning.

"Oh my God, please don't be. That's literally not—yeah, no. I'm the dumbass who lied in the first place—" Mel lifts her head with a start, and Lili lowers her voice. "Desculpa, anjinha—you're okay. Back to bed."

"Hi, cutie." I stroke her head.

"But then I started getting the feeling it *might* not be one-sided? Like when you suddenly wanted to come back for the party—I was like, *huh*. And then yesterday, when you were telling me how Gretchen was such a dick about your crush."

I nod slowly.

"Right, so. By the end of that conversation, I was like—I don't know—maybe sixty percent sure the crush was Tessa? Sixty-five percent? Just a hunch. It was the way you were talking about it . . . the fact that Gretchen didn't believe you. Which, by the way, is *profoundly* fucked up."

"Yeah, definitely." I pause. "Though it wasn't so much that she didn't believe me about Tessa. She basically just said Tessa's some kind of magic lesbian who attracts straight girls."

"Wow. Yeah. That's not a thing." Lili lets out a short laugh. "I mean—okay, fine, if you're out there crushing on girls and you want to call yourself straight, you do you. But Gretchen Patterson of Penn Yan, New York, is not the final fucking word on other people's queerness."

I laugh, a little sadly. "I know."

Lili's quiet for a moment. "It's like the Kara Clapstone thing. People saying she should have come out sooner because it would have meant so much to her fans or whatever. Even Gretchen talking about that unlabeled kid in Pride Alliance. I'm like—how did we get here? When did we decide this stuff needed our input?"

"But I get where she's coming from." I bite my lip. "You want to know your safe space is actually safe."

"Safe for who?" Lili counters.

"Yeah. That's—hard. It's complicated."

"Right." Lili pauses. "You know, I feel guilty sometimes for not coming out in high school."

"Guilty?"

"I don't know. I was talking to Mika last week about the DMs they get from baby queer kids. Trans kids. Some of them are like twelve years old. Mika's account means so much to them. And it's literally just the fact that Mika's this cool Japanese American nonbinary college kid out there existing and thriving and making art. Because some of them don't know *any* openly trans people in real life." Lili shrugs. "Maybe I could have been that for some little Brazilian pansexual kid in Penn Yan."

"Are there other Brazilians in Penn Yan?"

She laughs, scratching Mel's head. "Totally not. But you know what I mean."

"Well, yeah, but"—I glance at her—"isn't that just like what people were saying to Kara? That she should have come out sooner for her fans? But she didn't owe that to anyone. And neither do you."

"I know, I know."

"Also, you're my Mika. You know that, right?"

She snorts. "I am not."

"Lili, the whole backstory thing? That was actually really helpful."

"You mean when I lied to all my friends and made you go along with it?" She eyes me skeptically.

"It did! I think it helped just having people take it as a fact. Like. I'm Imogen, I'm bi." My breath seems to catch for a second. "I was so entrenched in thinking of myself as the token straight, world's best ally. You know? Like, that was my autofill. And the idea that I might not actually be straight seemed . . . a little too convenient, I guess? Or unrealistic. You can just picture someone rolling their eyes about it, right? Like it's some kind of peer pressure thing. All my friends are queer—"

"Maybe because you're drawn to fellow queer people?"

"I guess." I scrunch my nose. "Why do I feel like I'm just making all of this up?"

"Probably because of toxic-ass Gretchen. Or the five million other Gretchens out there on the internet. Some queer people just really seem to love shitting on other queer people. Every day, someone's out there weighing in about whether bi and pan girls even count as queer to begin with. Or we're only queer under certain circumstances. They'll say it with their whole chest. Absolutely zero awareness that their very specific queer experience isn't one hundred percent universal. And it's almost always this very white, very Western framework—completely rooted in colonization. No acknowledgment of regional differences, generational differences—just the same people relitigating the same semantic fuckery. But it still gets in your head! I feel like half of us are just drowning in imposter syndrome all the time. More than half, probably. I know I've been there."

I look at her. "Really?"

"Why do you think I made up the whole thing about us dating?"

"Yeah, but that was pretty much right after you came out. You seem so confident now."

"Sometimes I am," she says, "and then ten minutes later, I'm convinced I'm somehow faking it in my own head."

"That's how I feel!" Suddenly my eyes brim with tears.

"It's the worst. And it's such bullshit." She shakes her head. "And like, there's this whole other part of it where I'm pretty sure I'm panromantic asexual, actually. Or demisexual. I don't even know. And I haven't dated anyone. Which isn't *because* I'm asexual." She shrugs. "Sometimes I feel like, oh my God, why am I giving this so much mental energy? I'm literally home watching Netflix. Like. Who the fuck even cares? But I care! It matters."

"Of course it matters. It's a whole big piece of who you are."

Lili's phone alarm rings. "Oop—laundry's done! Hold that thought."

She scoops up Mel and stands.

"Hey," I say, peering up at her. "I love you."

She makes a face.

"I do!"

"I knowwww. And now I have to say it back, or else I'm an asshole." She rolls her eyes, smiling faintly. "You earnest little bisexual. I love you, too."

Texts with Gretchen

GP: Hey, I'm sorry

GP: Just wanted to say that

GP: I'll stop now, you don't have to reply

GP: But I'm sorry

58

Gretchen's texts pop up all at once just as Lili starts the car. "Tell me that's not who I think it is," says Lili, turning in her seat to back out of the driveway.

"Okay, but to her credit, she said sorry this time. Twice!"

"Baby learned a new word?"

I smile wryly. "I guess so."

I set my phone in Lili's cupholder, and neither of us speaks the whole way down Lili's street. But at the first red light, she shoots me a glance. "I keep thinking about everything Gretchen said at the diner. All the bullying—the basketball team. The guy at Walmart."

"She's had a pretty rough time." I nod.

"Yeah, she has." Lili pauses. "And obviously, it hasn't been like that for me. I know I'm not signaling queerness when I walk down the street. I'm not trying to hide it. I just—I just wear what I like. So am I less oppressed than Gretchen? I don't know! No one's called me the d-slur. But am I gonna tell the truth, the whole truth, and nothing but the truth to my Catholic grandmother in São Paulo? Uh. Maybe one day? Like, you know what I mean, right? I'm pretty sure Gretchen's not navigating that. So which one of us is more queer?"

"Well." I pause. "I'd have to see the two of you trying to sit in chairs."

"Yeah, what even is that? I'm *great* at sitting in chairs."

I look pointedly at her left leg, currently propped in an awkward triangle on the driver's seat.

"Shut up." She bites back a smile.

"But you're right," I say. "It's like there's this idea that you have to earn your label through suffering. And then you have to prove it with who you date, how you dress, how other people perceive you."

Lili nods. "Yup. Or else you don't count. Fuck that shit, though. We don't have to prove anything to anyone."

"Fuck that shit," I say.

Lili lets out a startled laugh. "Okay, new plan. Reply to Gretchen now. Like, right now. When you're in this exact mood."

I turn to the window, smiling. It's finally started drizzling, but there's no way this is all the rain we're getting. Lili bypasses Main Street—Route 14 is always faster. "Maybe you should hang at my house until it passes?"

"The rain, or my reptilian rage toward Gretchen?"

"Both?" I laugh and reach for my phone, sneaking another quick peek at the likes on my griddle post.

None from Tessa.

Which makes it all feel like a dream. The whole week, even. The tunnels and Declan's closet and texting until three in the morning. Coming out at a diner called Diner. Kissing a girl on the way back to her dorm. Now that I'm home, it feels almost preposterous.

I touch my lips again. Top and bottom.

"Edie grabbed your suitcase, right?" She glances back at the trunk. "Okay! I should probably try to beat this rain, huh?"

"Lili, I don't know—"

"If it gets bad, I'll swing back home." She leans over to hug me. "Hey, let me know when she comments, okay?"

"If," I say, and Lili makes the weirdest face ever. Like a smile trying to sew itself shut.

Texts with Gretchen

GP: IMMYYYYYYYY

GP: Can you just let me know you're seeing these??

IS: Hey, I'm here

GP: YES!!!! HI!!

GP: Okay, hi! Don't be mad

IS: . . .

GP: . . .

GP: ?

GP: What do the ellipses mean

IS: I mean

IS: I guess I'm just wondering what that was about

IS: At the diner

GP: Um, jealousy?

IS: Of me and Tessa?

GP: Kind of

GP: Idk, more like the idea of Tessa

GP: Or I guess

GP: The idea that you could bumble along as straight
      and then fall into a relationship with a girl because
      why not

IS: Okay first of all, closeted and straight aren't
      interchangeable
IS: You get that, right?

GP: Yeah but
GP: Idk Imogen
GP: Can you really call it closeted? You literally thought
      you were straight

IS: Then call it questioning

GP: But you weren't!
GP: I'm sorry, but were you really actively interrogating
      your straightness
GP: Sorry, it's just like
GP: Labels have meanings, you know? It's how we're
      able to talk about shared experiences
GP: That's like the whole foundation of the queer
      community
GP: I know you probably think I'm trying to nitpick here,
      but I'm not
GP: Just trying to understand I guess
GP: Obviously I'm happy for you

GP: And Tessa

GP: You know that, right?

GP: Anyway, hope you guys are having fun 🖤

GP: You should take her to the candy emporium next!

59

I sink onto my bed, trying to scoop Quincy into my lap. But he shoots me a withering look, standing and stretching in defiant silence.

I puff my cheeks out and sigh, leaning all the way back on my pillows. It barely even looks like daytime in here—not a single wink of sunlight spilling through the gaps in the blinds. And of course I didn't bother flipping on the light switch.

Bumble along as straight.

Could you really call it closeted?

Maybe I just need to explain it more clearly. I could walk Gretchen all the way back to the beginning. To the girl with felt rainbows, to Ilana, to the le dollar bean girl. That tiny pull—so easy to miss in the moment, so painfully obvious in retrospect. I could take her through my entire unabridged history of attraction.

I could show her the quizzes in my private browser history. Shut her down, point by point.

I could ask her why she gets to decide what counts as questioning. And who counts as queer. And when she talks about the queer community, who does she mean? Who gets let in? Who gets shoved out? And what do you do with the fact that no two people seem to do queerness in quite the same way?

Maybe shared experiences shouldn't be the foundation at all.

Maybe it should be a promise to hold space for variation.

I could ask her why I wasn't allowed to have the crush I absolutely, one hundred percent had on Clea DuVall.

I could ask.

But then I might have to ask myself some things too.

Like why I thought I needed her permission in the first place.

Or why I tied myself in knots wondering whether I was allowed to love my favorite movie. Especially when the real question was tucked behind it all along.

Why? Why do I love it?

Why am I completely enthralled by this movie about a girl who doesn't know she's queer?

Who thinks she can't be queer, because she's a cheerleader.

Because she doesn't look queer. Or seem queer.

I tap out of my messages and into my camera, flipping to selfie mode. But I don't take a picture. I just stare at my face.

Sleepy blue eyes, ponytail coming undone. I smile at myself, and my dimple breaks through.

Hi, Imogen, I think.

I stand and cross the room to my bookcase. To my absurdly gay bookcase. Past my absurdly gay poster wall. My childhood bedroom, screaming at the top of its lungs this whole time.

There are still a few storage boxes stacked near my wall.

I pluck the pink teddy bear from my bookshelf, drop him into a box, and press the lid down. And then—

I freeze.

You should take her to the candy emporium next!

My heart flips upside down.

Tessa's not—

I pull my phone from its charger, checking my post again.

Nothing. No Tessa. But then.

I pull up her pictures.

Suddenly, the clouds rip wide-open.

60

I don't bother with socks. No boots. No raincoat. I don't care.

I leap for the door, while Quincy stares at me, gobsmacked.

But just as my hand hits the knob, it bursts open. "Immy!" Edith holds her phone up, bouncing on her heels. "Look—"

"I know. I'm—I need the car. Where's Mom?"

"No way. She's not going to want you going out in this. Here." She thrusts the car keys into my hand. "I'll deal with them."

"Um. Okay." I inhale. "Don't tell them—"

"Imogen. I would literally never."

"I know, I know. I'm just—I'm definitely going to. Tonight. Maybe. But—"

She hugs me. "Go!"

The windshield's getting pummeled—my wipers can barely keep up. But I take the roads at a turtle's pace. Thank God I'm not going far.

Main Street's a ghost town in the rain. Empty intersections at every light. But I see it as soon as I pass Cam's Pizzeria. The rain blurs out the words painted on its flat metal surface, but I know them by heart. *Birkett Mills. The Annual Buckwheat Harvest Festival. Penn Yan, New York. This is the original griddle used to make the . . .* WORLD RECORD PANCAKE. *September 27, 1987, 28' 1".*

There's a Subaru Outback parked in front. I pull my twin Outback beside it, opening the door the second the car stops. Then, squinting through the rain, I see Tessa break away from the narrow overhang by the mill's entrance. Soaked within seconds. Then again, so am I.

I swipe a lock of hair out of my eyes, but it clings slickly to my cheeks. Totally pointless. I can't stop smiling. I reach for her hand. "Hop in!"

"No way." She tugs me closer, laughing. "We're already wet! You hop out."

So I do. Slam the door shut. I run straight into her arms. "You're here!"

She lets out a breathless laugh. "I saw your picture! I should have just texted, but—" Her eyes meet mine. And my heart does a whole ballerina leap in my chest. "Oh man. I don't know. It wouldn't have been dramatic enough. Anyway, I suck."

"Wait—what?"

"I should have texted you first thing in the morning. I shouldn't have made you put out a bat signal." She bites her lip. "I shouldn't have left."

"But I left first! I'm the one who should have texted you! You must have thought I was ghosting—"

"No. No way. I just—thought you might have had second thoughts, and I didn't want to make it weird for you. At least that's what I told myself." She wipes her cheek, uselessly. "Really, I was just scared."

"Of me?"

"I really like you." She blurts. "And this doesn't usually happen. Not, like, this much, and this fast, and—this is *so* not fair to you. You've barely even had a chance to work it all out in your head. I know last night was a lot. Like, it was so much, and I completely understand being freaked out. I think I overstepped—"

"You didn't! You didn't overstep. I'm not freaked out. I shouldn't have made you feel like I was."

"No! No, it's just—Scott, I'm kind of the veteran here, you know? Like I know how huge this is. It's kind of seismic, right? And I think I should have let you settle into it more. Or checked in more about how you felt."

How I felt.

Dizzy, off-balance, unsteady. Like my bones were too big for my body. Like I couldn't zip myself closed. Like I'd colored outside my own outline, stepped out of frame, made myself three-dimensional.

"I couldn't sleep," I say softly. My lips are so close to her ear, I don't know whose raindrops are whose. "I was so aware of you."

Tessa nods.

"I've never existed in the same space as someone like that. It's so different from what I expected. Kissing's so different from the inside. And I don't think I really thought about what happens after—"

"Like—"

"Not sex," I say quickly. "I mean, not just sex. It's the whole afterward part. Like brushing your teeth, washing your face. Looking in the mirror. That stuff. And everything's the same, but you're different. Like you've unlocked this whole new part of yourself, and now you're moving things around to make room for it. Recalibrating." I bury my face in the soaked shoulder of her hoodie for a moment. "Does that make sense?"

"Yup. Yeah." She draws in a breath.

"And I just kept thinking—*Am I doing this right? Do I kiss like a straight girl?* I thought I *was* a straight girl until this week—"

"You don't kiss like a straight girl. Also, that's not a thing. But even if it was a thing—listen, I believe I speak for every person you've ever kissed, and you. Do not. Kiss like a straight girl. Case closed."

I laugh. "Okay."

Tessa leans closer, just barely.

She's looking at me like I'm something to pin a wish on. A shooting star, a line of birthday candles, 11:11.

I almost lose my breath for a second. I can read every freckle on her nose. "Hi."

She pushes a wet strand of hair aside to kiss my forehead. And then she kisses my lips.

So I cup my hands around her face and kiss her back. In the middle of the day. In the middle of Penn Yan's beautifully deserted rain-battered Main Street.

Tessa's so close, but I press in closer, and she lets out the softest-edged sigh. Her hands trail the hem of my waterlogged shirt, and I swear it feels like taking off sunglasses. Clarity and brightness.

I want to laugh until I sob. I want to memorize this feeling—every shade, every shadow, from every angle. I slide my fingertips along her cheekbones, catching raindrops.

The way she's watching me makes me feel boundless. Doors flung open, no fences. Earnestness, all the way down.

I still can't believe this moment is real, that I get to live inside it. Everything's clammy and cold, and we're both completely soaked through. But it's worth it.

Obviously.

I feel like sunlight through lace.

61

But kissing in dry cars is nice, too. Tessa digs two towels out of the back seat, both covered in Labrador hair from some himbo-related dog-park adventure. They barely dry us off, and they make us both smell like wet dog. It's so gross. I'm so happy.

"Perfect," Tessa says, kissing the crown of my head.

It's the kind of kiss that screams *girlfriend*. I think? As opposed to friend-of-a-friend you made out with a few times?

I twist in my seat to face her. Suddenly the word's in the center of my brain, lit in neon.

Girlfriend.

I don't know what's more surreal—the thought of having a girlfriend or being one.

But how do you broach the question? *Do* you even broach the question? Am I a clingy high school girl just for thinking it? A naive baby queer who imprints on every cute tomboy who glances in her direction?

Then again, she's *here*. In my town.

That has to mean something. Right?

Tessa takes my hand over the gearstick, threading our fingers together. "What do you think, Scott—should I just set up a tent by the mill for five months?"

"I mean, I do have a house." The tips of my cheeks go warm. "It's just that my house comes with parents."

My voice sounds like a baby cartoon mouse. Perfect.

She taps the heel of her hand to my nose like she's honking it. "Look, I'm happy to hang with parents. Parents love me. Well, not the homophobic ones, probably, but in general? I'm a parental love machine." She stops short, pointing at me. "Not, like, in an I-want-to-hook-up-with-your-parents way, though. God. Yeah, no. First of all, you know I'm not into dads."

I blink. "Hey, I'm kind of obsessed with your brain."

"Oh, you know. Just a little move I have called ADHD. Chick magnet. Works like a charm."

I grin. "Really?"

"Absolutely not. I mean. Yes ADHD. No magnetism."

"None? You sure?" I scoot closer, leaning over the gearstick to kiss her.

She grins and exhales. "Okay."

"I don't want you to go."

"Me either." She presses her forehead against mine. "Though . . . we should probably think the parent stuff through."

"I mean, I know they'll be cool about it. They didn't bat an eye with Edith."

"I know, but it's still a pretty big moment, right? Coming out to your parents." Her eyes go soft. "I don't know. I just want you to be able to be in control of this one. You didn't get that last time."

"Yeah." My heart flips.

I think about Gretchen asking Tessa if she'd ever date a bi girl. Her voice was so casual, almost cheerful, but I could sense the storm brewing just beneath its surface. It's that shift in pressure you feel before the thunder's even audible.

But I actually think the worst part came before that.

When I stumbled over myself, trying to explain how I felt about Tessa.

The way Gretchen treated the whole conversation like a movie she'd seen before. She was so amused by it all. So certain my feelings weren't real. She didn't leave even an inch of space to entertain the idea they could be.

"You know it's okay to be straight, right?" she'd said.

Gretchen was the first person I came out to.

Gretchen will *always* be the first person I came out to.

Maybe one day we'll talk about it. Maybe I'll find the words, and she'll find a way to hear them. Then we'll cry and hug and years will pass, and we'll move past it. It'll be just a little bump in our backstory.

Or maybe for us, it ends here.

Maybe Gretchen's my backstory.

Group Chat with Kayla and Tessa

KR: omg the wurst thing happened, and your expertise is needed

KR: and I do mean wurst 😉

KR: y'all around?

Kayla changed the subject to sausage party 🌭

IS: Noooo 🏠 back home

IS: Like Penn Yan home

TM: I am also currently in Penn Yan 😳

TM: Heading out in a few min though, what's up

KR: imogen!! ngl, I legitimately forgot you don't already go here

KR: come back sooooon

IS: I will 🖤

IS: So what's the wurst news??

KR: ah yes

KR: a tale of treachery

KR: starring everyone's favorite token white boy

KR: so dec ends up in my room last night

KR: to be clear, this was after the party

KR: and he did not stop at home first

KR: straight back to my room

KR: anyway, i wake up, reach for my phone, and guess what's on my nightstand

---

IS: 🌭 🤢 ??

KR: yeppp. so, like

KR: kind of shady

KR: keeping in mind that the circumstances of him being in my room were not sausage related

TM: OR WERE THEY wink wink 😉

KR: cool, thanks for including the wink emoji, that really clarified what you meant by wink wink

TM: No prob

KR: anyway, i go to brush my teeth, open my toothbrush holder

KR: guess what's jammed in there

KR: ANOTHER FUCKING SAUSAGE

KR: so i go back to my room and

KR: sausages EVERYWHERE. all the same goddamn brand

KR: did he buy them in bulk????

KR: and i cannot emphasize enough that this motherfucker came straight over after the party

KR: like either this man had 15 sausages on his person all night or he stashed them earlier while we were pregaming

KR: clearly premeditated!! AND HOW DID HE KNOW HE'D BE COMING BACK HERE

IS: 15 sausages?? 🫨

KR: MAYBE MORE!! I DON'T KNOW! I KEEP FINDING THEM

KR: guys we gotta go BIG

KR: i want a long con

TM: YES, draw it out

TM: One a day

KR: right, that was my initial thought

KR: but then i realized i'm the one who'd have to sneak around in there 15 times

IS: Could you mail them?

KR: 🤔

KR: tell me more

IS: Like, sending them anonymously

IS: In envelopes

IS: One by one

IS: I guess that would be kind of expensive though

IS: Maybe illegal

TM: Hahahahahahaha

TM: Imagine being the FBI dude assigned to this case

KR: okay, so we've got some possible felony charges in the mix

KR: and yet

KR: possibly worth it 😼

TM: I mean if you're not willing to risk an FBI investigation, is it even really revenge??

TM: At some point, the sausage casing's gotta come off

TM: Okay not literally, though!!!!!! 😫

TM: Please continue practicing safe sausaging

IS: Okay wait

IS: What if you didn't go big

IS: What if you went . . . small 😏

KR: 👀

IS: I just wonder

IS: How long it would take him to notice an itty bitty
sausage

IS: In his itty bitty diorama

KR: WHAT

KR: YES

TM: Holy shit

TM: Like a teeny tiny one right??? Made to scale

KR: FIFTEEN TINY SAUSAGES IN HIS TINY LIL
BEDROOM

TM: Someone loop in Mika!!!!!!!!!

KR: am literally walking to their room right now lol

KR: OH

KR: WAIT nvm

KR: they left this morning

KR: last-minute trip to Cornell

KR: to see jaaaaaaaaaade 😚

TM: Is it finally happening????? 💀

KR: UMMMM HOLD UP

KR: SPEAKING OF GRAND GESTURES

KR: TESSA WHY TF ARE YOU IN PENN YAN

KR: WHAT DID I MISS

KR: ARE YOU TWO GIRLFRIENDS?????

62

I almost drop my phone. "I—um."

Tessa lets out a nervous laugh. "Right."

The rain's finally stopped, but we're still in her car. Which is still parked by the griddle. Because, it turns out, alternating between kissing and texting is a wholesome and well-balanced way to spend thirty minutes. In fact, I'm pretty sure I could have rounded out the whole hour like this, if it weren't for a particular text from Kayla. Asking a particular question.

In all caps.

Which, incidentally, is exactly how the question appears in my brain.

WELL, TESSA, ARE WE?? ARE WE TWO GIRL-FRIENDS??????

"Like, we don't have to decide that. Obviously." I nod, staring straight through the windshield.

"Right! Totally not. Maybe we just . . . let it play out?"

"Yeah! That sounds—that's great!"

"Okay, great," she concludes, pressing her hand to my cheek. Then she kisses me with such tender focus, it makes my brain go blurry.

It's another ten minutes before I talk myself out of Tessa's car and into my own. But before I even turn the ignition on—

"Imogen, wait!" Tessa calls through her lowered passenger window. She gestures for me to lower my window too. "Hey. I want to see you again."

"Me too." I break into a smile.

She shoots me a thumbs-up. "Okay! cool. See you soon, then."

"Definitely."

I reach for the keys.

"Okay, just clarifying, though—I don't mean it in a cool-yeah-I'll-be-in-touch way," she adds. "More like in a what-are-you-up-to-next-weekend kind of way. Or midweek. Anytime." She laughs, a little breathlessly. "Is that too much? We don't have to say midweek. I'm shutting up."

"Midweek's good."

"Or tomorrow."

"Even better." I laugh.

"Okay, wait, one more thing! Just putting it out there that I do enjoy a good prom, if that were to arise."

"Noted."

"I'd be a really good date. Wouldn't blink in the pictures. Highly doubt I'd forget the corsage. Very devoted in general."

She nods solemnly. "In related news, I'm known to be an excellent girlfriend."

"Is that so?"

"Big-time. Just as a general FYI, of course. Anyway! Like we said. No need to decide right now. Let's just see what we want—"

"I want to be your girlfriend." It leaps off my tongue before I can stop it. "Okay?"

"Wait—" Her mouth slips open. "Really?"

"If you—"

"Are you kidding?" She springs out of the driver's seat and around the front of her car, closing the distance between us with one last bounce of a step. "Underlined, bold, giant-font yes."

I laugh through my open window. "Wow, you sound pretty sure about that."

"Tattoo it on my face."

"I can't wait for the part where you kiss me," I say.

And it's true: I can't wait.

I can't wait, so I don't.

ACKNOWLEDGMENTS

I've been thinking a lot about the idea of community. Or *communities*, plural. For me, the word holds a good deal of messy complexity—its nuances are hard to pin down. What does it mean to belong to a community, or several? Who sets the boundaries? Is a community always a tangible group? Can it be a feeling, a vibe?

No idea. I just know I could never have written this book without mine.

Here are a few of the people I mean:

My editor, Donna Bray, and my agent, Holly Root—who both immediately understood why this book mattered to me, carved out the space for me to write it, and helped me find all the sweet parts.

My beautiful/brilliant/iconic/amazing teams at Balzer + Bray, HarperCollins, Root Literary, UTA, and my international publishers, including: Paige Pagan, Taylan Salvati, Katie Boni, Patty Rosati, Sabrina Abballe, Shannon Cox, Shona McCarthy, Maya Myers, Almeda Beynon, Lisa Lester Kelly, Lana Barnes, Alessandra Balzer, Alyssa Maltese, Heather Baror-Shapiro, Mary Pender-Coplan, Laura Pawlak, Tom Bonnick, Rachel Horowitz, Sam White, Sarah Lough, Sarah Alice Rabbit, and Leonel Teti.

Kelly Quindlen, Ashley Woodfolk, Emery Lee, and Carlos Silva, for being the world's smartest, most thoughtful early readers.

Julie Waters for helping me crack this story open.

Jennifer Dugan, for Shop Talk and lots of beautiful adventures upstate.

Jeri Green, who's seen me through all of it.

Sophie Gonzales, who kind of saved me.

Gillian Morshedi, whose essay changed the whole game.

The absurdly talented Caitlin Kinnunen, for giving Imogen her voice.

Jewell Parker-Rhodes, Lilliam Rivera, Joe Bruchac, and Meghan Goel, who are the best thing to ever happen to my Mondays.

Alex Andrasik, Katie Smith, and the rest of my upstate New York literary family.

Gabe Dunn, who showed up with courage, compassion, and sincerity for one of the hardest, most important conversations I've ever had.

The friends who helped me keep my head above the discourse: Jasmine Warga, Mackenzi Lee, Aisha Saeed, David Arnold, Adam Silvera, Angie Thomas, Jacob Demlow, Rod Pulido, Rose Brock, Jaime Semensohn, Matthew Eppard, Katy-Lynn Cook, Kate Goud, Brandie Rendon, Anderson Rothwell, Amy Austin, Dahlia Adler, Lauren Starks, Louise Willingham, Heidi Schulz, Jaime Hensel, Tom-Erik Fure, Sam Rowntree, Diane Blumenfeld, Steven Salvatore, Rachael Allen, Julie Mottl, Mason Deaver, Emily Townsend, Julian Winters, Lindsay Keiller, Adib Khorram, Emily Carpenter, Manda Turetsky, Chris Negron, George Weinstein, Sarah Beth Brown, Becky Kilimnik, Adante Watts, Nic DiPrima, Jason June, Mark O'Brien, Nic Stone, JC Lillis, Cale Dietrich, Zabé Ellor, Cindy Otis, Leah Johnson, Kimberly Ito, Kat Ramsburg, Jamie Pacton, Casey McQuiston, Savy Leiser, RK Gold, Eline Berkhout. And SO MANY OTHERS. I'm so lucky to know you.

The many, many incredible librarians, booksellers, influencers, and all the rest of you bookworms. You make this job so much brighter.

My family: Eileen Thomas, Jim and Candy Goldstein, Caroline, Mike, and Max Reitzes, Sam Goldstein, Leigh Shapiro, Gini, Curt, Jim, Cyris, and Lulu Albertalli, Brittany Girardi, Gail McLaurin, Lois and Don Reitzes, Linda Albertalli, and all my Thomases, Bells, Wechslers, Levines, and Bermans.

Quincy—you are so loved and so missed.

Teddy and Willow, who were as persistently and noisily helpful as always.

And Brian, Owen, and Henry. Obviously, obviously, obviously.